# The Global Manager

# The Global Manager

## Contemporary Issues and Corporate Responses

Otto Lerbinger
*Professor Emeritus, Boston University, USA*

palgrave
macmillan

First published 2014 by
PALGRAVE MACMILLAN

Palgrave Macmillan in the UK is an imprint of Macmillan Publishers Limited, registered in England, company number 785998, of Houndmills, Basingstoke, Hampshire RG21 6XS.

Palgrave Macmillan in the US is a division of St Martin's Press LLC, 175 Fifth Avenue, New York, NY 10010.

Palgrave Macmillan is the global academic imprint of the above companies and has companies and representatives throughout the world.

Palgrave® and Macmillan® are registered trademarks in the United States, the United Kingdom, Europe and other countries

ISBN: 978–1–137–31054–5

This book is printed on paper suitable for recycling and made from fully managed and sustained forest sources. Logging, pulping and manufacturing processes are expected to conform to the environmental regulations of the country of origin.

A catalogue record for this book is available from the British Library.

A catalog record for this book is available from the Library of Congress.

# Contents

# Foreword

When we choose to work in other countries, we expand our geographical scope. The same must be done with our minds: we must remove the blinders that have kept us focused on familiar things and consider new visions and ideas. The geography of our minds must extend to new regions. This fact is recognized in all international relationships as we become sensitive to a wider range of social, economic, political, and cultural factors. In the international sphere we are faced with a wider range of players and issues that add to the complexity of resolving problems, making decisions, and communicating. The intent of this book is to explore these intricate challenges faced by managers who operate across borders in this widening world.

Three waves of books have addressed the internationalization of business. The first wave began after World War II, when multinational enterprises (MNEs) began spreading throughout the world with the accelerated pace of globalization. Books such as John Fayerweather's *Management of International Operations: Text and Cases* (New York: McGraw-Hill, 1960) and Raymond Vernon's *Sovereignty at Bay: The Multinational Spread of U.S. Enterprises* (New York: Basic Books, 1971) discussed this development. The presence of MNEs became a reality and they challenged nation-states, which were torn between welcoming their capital and technology and fearing their power.

The second wave focused on the tensions and conflicts that arose in relations between business and government, which is illustrated by Robert Grosse's *International Business and Government Relations in the 21st Century* (Cambridge: Cambridge University Press, 2005). As civil society also grew, business realized that it must also relate to NGOs and other groups that increasingly challenged it to change its policies and behavior. A third wave of books accordingly recognized the enormous growth and influence of civil society and urged business to relate not only to government but also to the third sector, as illustrated by Rob Van Tulden and Alex van Zwart's *International Business-Society Management* (London and New York: Routledge, 2006). It recognizes that a multinational corporation's (MNC's) concern for its reputation makes it a vulnerable target for confrontations with nongovernmental organizations (NGOs) and government. It also recognizes that dialogue and bargaining between a MNC and its stakeholders are the most important ways to alleviate tensions and, more importantly, to find ways of working together for the common good.

These three waves of books focused mainly on the institutional aspects of international business and were accompanied by books describing differences in economic and political systems. Believing that culture was the central feature of international dealings, several authors concentrated on it. They were concerned with cultural differences in language, values, beliefs, and social habits of people in an organization, group, or society that reflect how they think, communicate, and behave. Two illustrative books are Richard D. Lewis's *When Cultures Collide: Managing Successfully Across Cultures* (London: Nicholas Brealey Publishing, 1996) and David C. Thomas's *Readings and Cases in International Management: A Cross-Cultural Perspective* (Thousand Oaks, CA: Sage Publications, 2003).

This book extends the third wave, now representing the triangle of business, government, and civil society, along with a recognition of cultural differences among nations and regions. When managers try to recruit people who "fit into the organization," they are talking about organizational culture. When managers try to adjust to differences in the attitudes and behavior of people they encounter in various parts of the world, they are talking about managing across cultures.

The focus of this book is twofold. First, to recognize the extended number and kinds of international players in the institutional settings of business, the state, and civil society, and, second, to analyze the formidable issues that arise from interactions among them. Although the various economic, political, social, and cultural systems that define the international arena are important structural features, they need expression through the issues that are connected with them. Contemporary issues are seen as reflecting the stresses and conflicts that arise from the organizations and institutions that make up society; they also reflect the constraints of the physical world within which they operate. Issues represent the most dynamic and controversial aspects of relationships. They include support or opposition by others to what we do or want, statements and actions that propose changes to established understandings, and significant events that augur problems and possibly crises that must be confronted.

This book condenses the major issues of concern to international managers into three major issue areas: (1) economic, (2) socio-political and cultural, and (3) the physical and technological. As detailed in Part II of the table of contents, the first area includes resistance to globalization, economic development, and replenishing and upgrading human resources. The second area includes religious friction with Islam, threats to nation brands such as China and the United States, and corporate responsibility for human rights violations. The third area includes sustainability, climate change, and technology. These issues were selected from newspapers, magazines, broadcasts, academic and trade journals, various reports of major developments concerning players, and discussions with communicators in public relations, public affairs, marketing and communications.

The guiding method for this selection was to identify the topics of discussions and negotiations among the international players. These topics often reflect the international agendas of organizations, changes to be desired or resisted, and strains in relationships. Problems and tensions that might evolve into crises were given particular attention.

Corporate responses to issues are an integral part of this book and hopefully contribute concepts and skills that are often neglected in the curricula of schools of business or management. The responses are discussed in the last two parts of the book. Part III covers the necessary strategies and skills of public affairs and communication, often called "soft power." Specific topics include diplomatic communication, public relations, marketing, government affairs, lobbying and negotiations. Part IV discusses the internal aspects of management responses. They are subsumed under the increasingly prominent and vital subject of corporate governance, which provides direction and guiding values to an organization. Global corporate citizenship, based on corporate social responsibility, is one base of corporate governance. The other is a growing public expectation that business balance its pursuit of profit with greater attention to acting in the public interest.

The construct of the *global manager* is used in this book. A global manager embodies the values, outlooks, and attitudes that go beyond his or her specific title or specialization. It is he or she who is sensitive to the cultures of people and institutions in different countries and knows how to interact with them. A global manager deplores rigid boundaries, which includes the manner of thinking. Thus readers will recognize that modern management requires an interdisciplinary approach. Just as the traditional Principles of Organization and Management course evolved into the Organizational Behavior (OB) course by applying the insights of psychology and sociology, the modern international business or management course draws on all the social sciences and the field of international relations. Our minds are thereby opened to new ways of looking at an international situation and finding inventive solutions.

# Acknowledgments

Many people and experiences have provided the inspiration and knowledge for this book. James A. Morakis was a major contributor. His areas of expertise include media relations, issues management, crisis management, investor relations, constituency building, community relations, opinion research, advertising, publication, and video production. He headed up the international public affairs activities of Exxon Corporation, which spanned operations in Europe, Africa, South America, Central America, the Middle East, and the Asia-Pacific region. I was able to meet with many of his colleagues to discuss the issues they faced and their strategies for optimal corporate responses. To me he played the role of a diplomat, but he preferred not to usurp that traditional title of foreign service officers.

Flora Hung-Baeseake, associate professor at HongKong Baptist University, introduced me to China and its complexities. She arranged for me to lecture to student bodies and faculty in Hong Kong, Macau, and Beijing. I had the opportunity to present the subject of crisis management to the board of directors of Guangdong Daya Bay Nuclear Power Station. Yi-Ru Regina Chen, an assistant professor at Hong Kong Baptist University, shared her research on the strategic management of government affairs in China, on which she wrote a book, *The Business of Corporate Government Affairs in China*. MinJung Sung, chairman of the Department of Advertising and Public Relations at Chung-Ang University in Seoul, South Korea, has continually discussed with me many thoughts about communication and management practices in her country and elsewhere. Yvonne Lo, an entrepreneur in Shanghai and the author of a book on nonprofit organizations, welcomed me to Beijing and introduced me to the subtleties of Chinese society.

My continuing involvement with Boston University's London Programme, especially with Professor Tobe Berkovitz, has kept me in touch with developments in British business, government, and education. Another professor, Roy McLarty, generously shared his experience in teaching a course, International Management Environment. In Europe, three former students have been a great help: Jasper Fessmann, who understands German political institutions; Rosanna Cirigliano, who is familiar with the publishing and other businesses in Italy; and Leda Karabella, from Athens, Greece, whose knowledge of law, management, and conflict resolution helps guide business executives in "Getting to Yes."

I owe special thanks to Janice Barrett, chairman of the Department of Communication at Lasell College and a former colleague at Boston University, for many thoughtful exchanges of ideas and for giving me the opportunity to test run this book in a classroom attended by management and communication students.

Lectures and seminars which I gave in many parts of the world have exposed me to important business, political, social, and cultural ideas and values. The cities and countries include Medellin and Bogota in Colombia; Santiago in Chile; Brisbane, Melborne, and Sidney in Australia; Manama in Bahrain; and Karachi in Pakistan. In Karachi, Anwar Rammal and his son, Karim, enlightened me on restrictions placed on business and the special problems faced by expatriates who work for foreign subsidiaries.

I also want to acknowledge my former professors at the University of Chicago, the Massachusetts Institute of Technology, and Harvard University for the knowledge and insights that provided the intellectual background for this book. They include economists Milton Friedman, who taught me the principles of the free market system; Charles Kindleberger, who introduced me to the world of international trade; and Walt Rostow, who explored the stages in economic development. Other professors were Karl Deutsch, who examined the impact of economic history, and Talcott Parsons who ably integrated the fields of anthropology, sociology and social, psychology in his conceptualization of the social system.

Finally, I want to thank the international students in my classes who over the years strengthened my resolve to learn from them and relate my teaching to them. I also want to thank Kenneth Holmes for expediting communications regarding the manuscript.

# part 1

# multinationals engage players in the global arena

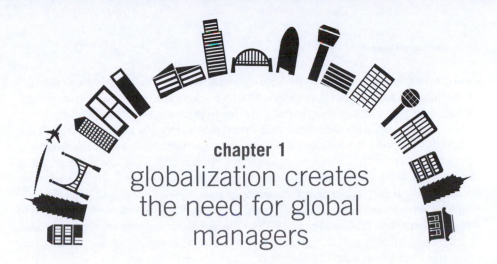

# chapter 1
# globalization creates the need for global managers

**Objectives**

1. *Understand why globalization has created the need for global managers.*
2. *Recognize the differences between the domains of international business and international business.*
3. *Appreciate the importance of why multinational corporations must learn to establish sound relationships in the international arena.*
4. *Understand the stakeholder relations and triangle approaches taken to identify the constituents and "players" with which it must deal.*
5. *Learn how issues are identified and chosen and how the issues management process helps.*
6. *Understand the key attributes of a global manager.*
7. *Recognize the rise of corporate diplomacy and its similarity with traditional diplomacy.*

The irreversible reality facing business is the long-term shift from a local to a global marketplace. People, goods, and ideas easily travel across geographic boundaries, increasing the wealth of nations and improving living conditions of people. The meshing of economies into integrated global markets, called globalization, has elevated many businesses to the status of multinational enterprises (MNEs) that face magnified challenges.[1] Their markets are widespread, their network of relationships is wide and their sociopolitical environments are complex.

The globalization movement has been the most powerful and pervasive force in the modern world. It continues to expand as fast as optic fibers are stretched around the world and aircraft and ships travel across the seas. People, goods, and ideas easily move across geographic boundaries, increasing the wealth of nations and improving living conditions. This meshing of economies into integrated global markets is the joint result of national economic policies, overseas expansion of business organizations, and development of international institutions.

## The forces that created globalization

In his influential book, *The World Is Flat*, Thomas L. Friedman, a *New York Times* columnist, explains globalization and describes the ten forces that created globalization and the "multiple new forms and tools for collaboration that this flattening has created."[2] These forces explain how a shift in ideologies, technological advances, and management innovations penetrated existing barriers and led to greater international trade.[3]

Friedman starts with the momentous event of November 9, 1989, when the Berlin Wall fell. "It tipped the balance of power across the world toward those advocating democratic, consensual, free-market-oriented governance, and away from those advocating authoritarian rule with centrally planned economies."[4] He characterizes communism as "a great system for making people equally poor" and capitalism, in contrast, as making " people unequally rich."[5] He linked this first force with the coming together in the late 1980s and early 1990s of the global information revolution, created by diffusion of personal computers, fax machines, Windows, and dial-up modems connected to a global telephone network.

In explaining his second force, he continues with the theme of technological advances by referring to August 9, 1995, when Netscape went public. Friedman considers Netscape's browser one of the most important inventions in modern history because of two developments: the PC-based computing platform went to an Internet-based platform and Netscape developed proprietary-free protocols like HTTP. This innovation enabled hordes of people to get connected with one another and led the way for the subsequent digitization revolution.

The power of information technology was advanced by a third and fourth force as work flow software enabled all internal departments – sales, marketing, manufacturing, billing, and inventory – to become interoperable no matter what machines or software each of them was running – and as open-sourcing led to such modern manifestations as blogs.

Outsourcing and offshoring are Friedman's fifth and sixth forces. Outsourcing – which was stimulated by the Y2K problem at the turn of the 21st century of requiring existing computers to accommodate the year 2000 as well as the 1900s – enabled an organization to transfer activities like call centers elsewhere. India became a major destination of outsourcing by taking advantage of the world's abundance of fiber optic cables. Offshoring meant sending labor-intensive work to low-wage countries like China, which also had the advantage of having acquired new technologies and modern business practices.

Supply chaining, the seventh force, was a similar development. It enabled Wal-Mart to move 2.3 billion general merchandise cartons a year down its supply chain to its stores. Its sophisticated information systems enabled it to know "exactly what its customers were buying and could feed that information to all the manufacturers, so the shelves would always be stocked with the right items at the right time."[6] An eight force, insourcing, enabled companies like UPS to design and synchronize global supply chains for both large and small companies.

The ninth force, in-forming, represented by Google, Yahoo!, and MSN Web search, became a total equalizer by giving everyone the same basic access to overall research information that anyone has. The final force, which Friedman calls The Steroids (Digital, Mobile, Personal, and Virtual), amplified and further empowered all other forms of collaboration from more places than ever.

Friedman's review of the ideological, technological, and managerial innovation forces convincingly demonstrates that globalization is more than simply removing trade barriers among nations. It forced companies to fundamentally change the way they conducted business. He believes globalization has presented us with new opportunities, new challenges, and new partners. He fears that new threats accompany these benefits, the greatest ones being an excess of protectionism and excessive fears of another 9/11 "that prompt us to wall ourselves in, in search of economic security."[7] Both, he says, would be a disaster for us and for the world. The scope of international business and management has accordingly expanded and includes an extended role for multinational corporations (MNCs) and other private and public sector entities. Under the banner of the free market system, corporations have spread sales and operations throughout the world and thereby become MNCs. Globalization has created the need for the internationalization of business.

In his following book, *Hot, Flat, and Crowded*, Friedman moves to a new phase of globalization that addresses two enormously powerful forces that are impacting our planet in fundamental ways: global warming and the soaring global population growth.[8] Just as globalization forced companies to fundamentally change the way they conducted business by presenting them with new opportunities, new challenges, and new partners, they must now reinvent themselves by adopting what he calls a "Code Green." It refers to a plan to "tackle some of the biggest challenges facing our business and our world," which he describes as combating climate change, reducing waste, safeguarding natural resources, trading ethically and building a healthier nation."[9] Friedman quotes an apt Chinese proverb that says, "When the wind changes direction, there are those who build walls and those who build windmills."[10] Global managers must be among the windmill-building leaders who are willing and able to find answers to the challenges of the new hot, flat, and crowded world.

# Management approaches to globalization

## The international business and international management domains

Two approaches have dominated the internationalization of business: international business (IB) and international management (IM), which are accorded separate domains by the Academy of Management. IB, as Charles W. Hills points out in his *International Business* text, focuses on functional policy areas.[11] They include the strategy and structure of the IB; business operations of exporting, importing, and countertrade; global manufacturing and materials management; global marketing and R&D; global human resource management; accounting in the IB; and financial management in the IB. These specialized functional areas are represented by books such as *Human Resource Management in a Global Context*, *Sustainable Global Outsourcing*, and *Strategic International Marketing* in the international setting.[12]

This international setting is described by IB with reference to: (1) national differences in political economy and culture; (2) global trade and investment environment, including international trade theory, political economy of international trade, foreign direct investment, and regional economic integration; (3) global monetary system, including foreign exchange market, foreign exchange and international monetary system, and global capital market. Furthermore, Alan M. Rugman and Thoms L. Brewer's *The Oxford Handbook of International Business* includes several chapters on the history and theory of the MNE, on the political and policy environment, strategy for MNEs, managing the MNE, and regional studies.[13]

Instead of focusing on the functions of business, the IM approach is more broadly concerned with management processes. As reviewed by Jean J. Boddewyn, the IM division of the Academy of Management describes its domain as "Content pertaining to management theory, research, and practices with an international or cross-cultural dimension."[14] Some general subjects typically included are internationalization, decision making, and negotiation. A major topic mentioned is "investigations of the cross-border differential impact of cultural, social, economic, technological, and political forces on organizational forms and management practices." Boddewyn sees two central issues as defining the IM domain: (1) why, when and how a business firm decides to "go international," and (2) why, when, and how its organizational behavior is altered by internationalization. She concludes that even "defining 'international management' remains a tricky issue."[15]

Nevertheless, in his textbook, *International Management,* Rajib N. Sanyal offers this definition: "International management involves planning, organizing, leading, and controlling the people working in an organization on a worldwide basis in order to achieve the organization's goals."[16] A distinguishing feature of the international aspect is that these management tasks are performed in multiplace political, cultural, and economic environments. Managers must devise competitive strategies on a much larger geographical scale and potentially deal with 185 sovereign countries each of which can create rules and regulations within their borders.

To complement the IB and IM approaches, a third one is represented by this book – a focus on international relations (IRs) as practiced by global managers – managers who operate in several locations, across borders and time zones, and know how to deal with different cultures. IR centers on associations with the large number and variety of players in the international arena and the contemporary issues with which they must deal. The title of this book, *The Global Manager,* was chosen to emphasize the importance in management of the international realm and the ability of management to build enduring relationships.

## Central importance of relationships

Relations with a new set of international players in host societies are a distinctive aspect of an IB as distinguished from a domestic one. Sincere and sustainable relationships must be established with those whose cooperation is needed to achieve organizational goals. These relationships go beyond the typical establishment of business operations and the marketing of products and services. A wider range of contacts must be cultivated and new networks formed. Narrow economic transactions are expanded by getting to know one's customers, business partners and other stakeholders, and to recognize and promote connections with government and civil society bodies on all levels. The forging of new international relationships might also include investing in the construction of physical and social infrastructure that supports business relationships, such as subsidiary offices and communication facilities. Global managers must be aware that in the process of building sound relationships with other players they are also constructing a global social system.[17]

Among the first writers on the special importance of relationships in an international context were George Lodge and Richard Walton.[18] They recognized that to compete globally American corporations had to change their relationships both inside and out. They must move away from the adversarial, arm's length, short-term, contractual, and rigid ways of the past toward cooperation, intimacy, long-term planning, consensuality, and flexibility. Global managers were advised not only to improve their interpersonal communication skills but also to alter their attitudes, values, and concept of a business.

Corporations that build relationships are more likely to succeed. Samuel B. Graves and Sandra A. Waddock call them "visionary companies" and "built-to-last companies" and say that they focus on more than profits by treating their multiple stakeholders generously. They refer to a study that shows that these companies outperform others both financially and in the ways they treat other primary stakeholders as well as showing a concern for the environment.[19] Visionary companies have a core ideology that consists of "end values," such as integrity, service, helping humanity, meritocracy, valuing people, improving the quality of life, making contributions, and alleviating pain and disease. These values are increasingly important in the international sphere.

## Relationships constitute social capital

The expanded social ties and networks constitute a firm's social capital. In his book *Bowling Alone: The Collapse and Revival of American Community*, Robert D. Putnam defines social capital as "connections among individuals – social networks and the norms of reciprocity and trustworthiness that arise from them."[20] An article in *BusinessWeek* further describes it as "the sum of complex, dense networks of connections, values, norms, and reciprocal relationships in a community."[21] Social capital is part of an organization's intangible asset of goodwill, which can add considerable value to its net worth.

Canadian researchers at Simon Fraser University's Centre for Innovation in Management (CIM) and York University's Schulich School of Business believe social capital has important applications in business and international affairs. CIM Executive Director Ann Svendsen said, "We are really only just beginning to see how social capital might be applied to business." Paul S. Adler and Seok-Woo Kwon suggest a threefold benefit: (1) to provide access to broader sources of information; (2) to increase a manager's influence, control, and power by accumulating stored-up obligations from others and by bridging disconnected groups; and (3) encouraging compliance with local rules and customs and thus reducing the need for formal controls.[22] Especially in the international arena, social capital is a critical resource that must constantly be replenished and strengthened.

The global manager appreciates the value of social capital because it constitutes the foundation of trust which makes relationships possible. The enterprise becomes a corporate citizen by seeking to reduce social costs, such as harm to the environment, and to increase social benefits by helping to solve social problems and stimulate economic growth. Many students entering MBA programs recognize the value of this social perspective and choose schools that offer programs in green business, social enterprise, and sustainability.[23] These same values support the constant endeavor of global managers to explore opportunities for mutual benefit that help strengthen social capital.

## Influence of national culture

The field of IM recognizes that the study of different cultures is important for an understanding of diverse, globalized business environments. MNCs recognized this when they outgrew their cultural boundaries and engaged in cross-border corporate mergers and acquisitions. Awareness of cultural differences helps global mangers understand what works and what does not in activities ranging from negotiations to marketing. A decade ago American executives working abroad were known for their lack of preparedness in understanding the cultures of countries to which they were assigned. As stated by one retired senior vice president from a major corporation: "We have the technology and we know the business but we are not prepared as a country to deal with cultural differences...."[24] Since then culture has become the most common approach by business in understanding different regions and countries.

A definition of culture is "that complex whole which includes knowledge, belief, art, morals, law, custom, and any other capabilities and habits acquire by man as a member of society."[25] Geert Hofstede, who established the most widely used system of studying cultural variables, defines culture as "the collective programming of the mind which distinguishes the members of one category of people from another."[26] Other major contributors to an understanding of cultural differences among a wide range of nations are Fons Trompenaars and Charles Hampden-Turner.[27] They recognize that "Every culture distinguishes itself from others by the specific solutions it chooses to certain problems which reveal themselves as dilemmas."[28] For example, some cultures such as the Swiss and German, will be guided by universalistic rules and others such as the Italian by consideration of particular persons and circumstances. (This dilemma is called universalism versus particularism.) Players in the global social system must reconcile these different cultural solutions and be assuaged by Trompenaars's experience that there is no "one-best way of managing."[29] Yet, they must agree on a workable basis for moral reasoning if a global social system is to be constructed.

Cultures play a major role in the industrialization of nations, says Tom Friedman who in narrower economic terms describes a nation's cultural endowments as the "internalized values of hard work, thrift, honesty, patience, and tenacity, as well as the degree to which it is open to change, new technology, and equality for women."[30] He further states that the more a culture absorbs foreign ideas and best practices and meld those with its own traditions, the greater advantage it will have in a globalized world. Supporting Friedman's view is David Landes who in his book *The Wealth and Poverty of Nations* argues that certain cultural attitudes in the Arab-Muslim world "have in many ways become a barrier to development, particularly the tendency to still treat women as a source of danger or pollution to be cut off from the public space and denies entry into economic activities."[31] He says Islam thrived when it fostered a culture of tolerance, as in Moorish Spain.[32]

# The enlarged field of players and issues

When the business arena embraces the entire world, the field of players is naturally enlarged – not only in numbers but also in variety. Beyond an organization's stakeholders lie a host of groups, organizations, nation-states, and international organizations that must be reckoned with. Similarly, issues of increasing variety and complexity occur more frequently.

## Global players

### The stakeholder model

The idea of stakeholders was first associated with public relations, although it referred to them as "publics." These are defined as any group affected by the actions of an organization or, in turn, which could affect it. A major contribution of public relations professionals has been to identify and differentiate the audiences related to an organization. Public relations texts typically use a "wheel" chart that depicts an organization at the hub and extends its spokes to its several publics. In his book, *Strategic Management: A Stakeholder Approach*, R. Edward Freeman replaced the term "publics" with "stakeholders" and introduced the concept of stakeholder management.[33]

The stakeholder model divides stakeholders into primary and secondary ones. The primary ones represent the factors of production of capital, labor, and land – a subject discussed by economists. The resulting stakeholders are investors who contribute capital, employees who contribute labor, and the community which contributes not only land but also the infrastructure of roads, ports, electric, and gas utilities. Economists match these "inputs" with "outputs," namely, the goods and service produced. The consumers who purchase them are also considered stakeholders.

Recognizing that organizations are also affected by laws, regulations, and various "rules of the game," the stakeholder model includes secondary stakeholders. They consist of governments on all levels, community and citizen groups, nonprofit organizations (NPOs) and professional societies. Broadly speaking, these constitute an organization's socio-political environment, so that term is increasingly preferred to secondary stakeholders. The environment is sometimes included as a stakeholder. It is represented by environmental groups that champion the issue and are treated as secondary stakeholders.[34] In addition to environmental groups, other "uninvited guests" such as advocacy groups might consider themselves stakeholders, warned Freeman and James R. Emshoff in "Who's Butting Into Your Business?"[35]

The maps of primary and secondary stakeholders have been extended to include additional components. In his *Organization Theory and Design*, Richard L. Daft devotes a chapter to "an organization's environment," which describes the multiple sectors of financial resources, human resources, raw materials, industry, socio-cultural, government, economic, technology, and international. Similarly, the concept of the "extended enterprise" was conceptualized by James E. Post, Lee E. Preston, and Sybil Sachs who listed three categories of stakeholder groups: (1) resources, (2) industry structure, and (3) social-political setting.[36]

Managers are advised to keep lists of their stakeholders and for public affairs purposes indicate at least the following: (1) the basis of the relationship, (2) attitudes toward the company – whether cooperative, antagonistic, or neutral, (3) issues important to a stakeholder group, (4) its stand on each issue, (5) kind and amount of power possessed by it. Supplementary lists can be created for specific situations or campaigns that might, for example, include relevant public officials.

## The triangle model

To reflect the growth in the number and variety of players in the global arena, writers in international management refer to the triangle of the major institutions in society: business, state (government), and civil society. Business includes internal business alliances and partners and firms in the supply chain; it also includes other MNCs as potential allies and competitors. The state includes nation-states, comprising the host countries in which firms operate, and supranational organizations such as the United Nations, the European Union, and several important international organizations such as the World Trade Organization. Civil society includes the myriad of health and social welfare services, educational and recreational institutions, cultural and religious organizations, and business and professional associations.

The categories in the triangle approach are not rigid, as illustrated by the development of state-owned enterprises (SOES), which meld the powers of business and state. State capitalists do not just run companies; they also manage huge pools of capital in the form of sovereign-wealth funds (SWFS) Among the largest are Abu Dhabi Investment Authority which controls $627 billion; Saudi Arabia's SAMA Foreign-Holdings Co. which in December 2011 controlled $473 billion; China's SAFE Investment Company with $568 billion and China Investment Corporation with $410 billion. Overall, they control about $4.8 trillion in assets, which is expected to rise to $10 trillion by the end of this decade.[37] SWFS are of two types: (1) savings, by making productive investments, and (2) economic development, mostly to secure reliable sources of resources. SOES create serious issues for MNCs as discussed in later chapters. The most important concern control over world natural resources and the handing over of intellectual property rights in establishing business.

Another part of the triangle, civil society, focuses on the increasing importance of nongovernmental organizations (NGOs). They are more than the kind of NPO described by Theodore Levitt as the "third sector," whose traditional role was to care for the "casualties" of society that were neglected by the government and business sectors.[38] The role of NGOs increasingly is to monitor the activities of MNCs and, when found deficient or irresponsible, to pressure them to change their policies and behavior. In this capacity, they fulfill the function associated with the state. However, they also monitor the performance of government action and inaction. In both ways, NGOs help maintain social order and balance of power.

A third feature of the triangle approach is the increased role of public opinion and cultural forces as a foundation for the three institutions. Public opinion has been a major concern of public relations because it serves as a barometer of a company's standing with the general public or specific publics of consumers and others. Public attitudes and behavior are influenced by the culture of a particular region, country or other group of people. Familiarity with different cultures therefore helps a company understand the thinking patterns of diverse people and what works and does not work.

## Global issues

Issues are of central important to international relationships because they reflect the understandings and misunderstandings that arise from organizations and institutions that comprise society. Problems must be recognized that cause stress and conflict among the various players in the international arena. These problems are the raw material of the issues that define the dynamic and controversial aspects of relationships. They include support or opposition by others to what we do or want, statements and actions that propose changes to established understandings, and significant events that auger problems and possibly crises that must be confronted. Disruptive events, such as protests, demonstrations and boycotts, are discussed, as well as verbal attacks and lawsuits by competitors, NGOs, and supranational organizations.

A major purpose of this book is to familiarize global managers with international issues. Part II lists this book's selection of critical contemporary issues. They meet one or more of three criteria: (1) they are championed by influential and powerful entities, often international organizations and NGOs; (2) they may lead to serious tensions among players; and (3) they have the potential of escalating into crises.

### Selection of issues

How does a global manager choose issues that require attention? Some will be obvious because they arise out of the interactions with other players. Some issues will arise from crises that erupt and the challenge is to recognize issues underlying so-called simmering crises. The constant challenge is to identify issues that may affect an organization and thus require attention. Global managers should engage in the process of issues management that starts with continuous scanning and monitoring of the socio-political environment. They must cover the publications and websites of international organizations and NGOs. For example, a human rights issue might be raised by the United Nations or an NGO, or it might be the focus of media coverage, as happened to Nike.

Special international events and publication of surveys on international matters sometimes indicate issues. For example, at the 2012 annual World Economic Forum, a survey identified 50 global risks, which were divided into five categories: (1) economic, (2) environmental, (3) geopolitical, (4) societal, and (5) technological. The experts and industry leaders who were consulted named the following most urgent risk in each category: chronic fiscal imbalances, rising greenhouse gas emissions, terrorism, water-supply crises, and cyber attacks. Respondents also ranked the likelihood and potential impact of each threat. The top five global risks in terms of likelihood were (1) severe income disparity, (2) chronic fiscal imbalances, (3) rising greenhouse gas emissions, (4) cyber attacks, and (5) water-supply crises.[39] At some annual meetings, a special issue is highlighted, as Klaus Schwab did in 2002 when he invited about 40 religious leaders to talk about whether Islam is on an endless collision course with the West.[40]

Surveys conducted by individuals are another way to identify issues. For example, Jeffrey E. Garten, former dean of Yale School of Management, interviewed 40 CEOs and identified these issues of concern to society and business, many of which apply internationally:

- taxation of the Internet,
- the 'digital divide' at home and abroad,
- international rules to prevent global monopolies,
- protection of intellectual property rights around the world,
- a framework to balance science and morality in the biotech revolution,
- the delivery of affordable health care,
- the security of pensions for aging populations,
- the growth of global crime syndicates, and
- the spread or infectious diseases in areas where people are too poor to buy medicine.[41]

International issues can also be identified by talking with managers at other companies, trade association officials, leaders of NGOs, and the heads of international bodies such as the World Trade Organization or World Bank. Issues can also be gleaned from newspapers, magazines, broadcasts, academic and trade journals, various reports of major developments concerning players, and discussions with communicators in public relations, public affairs, marketing and communications. Publications such as *The Economist* and the *Wall Street Journal* are excellent sources, often however, after an issue becomes a problem or crisis for a company or industry.

The issues selected for this book are condensed into three major issue areas: (1) economic, which includes resistance to globalization, economic development, and replenishing and upgrading human resources; (2) social and cultural which includes religious conflict, stresses on nation brands, and corporate responsibility for human rights violations; and (3) the physical and technological, which includes sustainability, climate change, and technology.

## Issues management process

Within the context of the public affairs function the important management process of issues management has been developed. Of the five steps, the first is variously called scanning, monitoring, or surveillance of an organization's socio-political environment. In step 2, the issues are prioritized – based on the criteria of imminence of action, impact on the organization, and actionability – so that concentrated attention can be given to the most important ones. In step 3, the selected issues are analyzed, using such criteria as the nature of an issue, its life cycle stage, identification of political participants, importance of public opinion, amount and kind of media coverage, and its legal, regulatory, and constitutional context. In step 4 strategy options are formulated, which concern whether to be reactive, proactive or interactive, whether to undertake voluntary policy changes, and whether to act alone or as a member of a coalition. In step 5 the chosen strategy is implemented.[42,43]

One purpose of issues management is to help a company anticipate an emerging issue so it can seek either to contain or resolve it. Another purpose is to influence public opinion before others do, because once opinions are crystallized they are difficult to change. Thus, if an emerging issue gains momentum and the public is likely to become aware of it, a company acts quickly to shape opinions. Should legislators in a country or international bodies such as the European Union become interested in an issue, it can escalate to legislative action or a crisis. Corporate responses are replete with interest group strategies, media strategies, and governmental strategies that can be initiated to influence the outcome.[44]

# The global manager

The term *global manager* is adopted from Christopher S. Bartlett and S. Ghoshal's *Harvard Business Review* article "What Is a Global Manager?"[45] They caution against the idea of a "universal global manager." Instead, they explain that a global manager may be (1) global business or product division managers who must build worldwide efficiency and competitiveness, (2) country managers whose unit is the building block for worldwide operations, or (3) worldwide functional specialists. The reference to a global manager in this book is any manager who has a significant role in relating to players in the international arena. Besides heads of international operations of a parent company and its foreign subsidiaries, it includes managers in organizational "boundary spanners" positions: public affairs, public relations, marketing, purchasing, and human resources. Their roles are reflected in this book in chapters dealing with issues as well as corporate responses to them.

The global manager's focus on IR is associated with the field of diplomacy. Traditionally diplomacy has concentrated on relationships with nation-states. For that reason, the tradition of top ranking international-relations programs, such as the London School of Economics and Political Science, Tufts University's Fletcher School of Law and Diplomacy, and Johns Hopkins School of Advanced International Studies has been to concentrate on a study of the history and characteristics of different nations and their interactions with one another. It is likely, however, that global managers deal with a wider range of players than nation-states, which are the focus of diplomats, and must deal with a more complex global environment that includes the issues discussed in this book.

As explained by Janice Stein, founder and director of the new Munk School of Global Affairs at the University of Toronto, the word international implies a collection of static land masses, whereas "global" "encompasses a more 21st-century vision: one in which power is diffusing; in which economies are increasingly interconnected; in which groups of people live within countries but are not necessarily defined by them; and where polar ice, fresh water, and fibre optics are as strategically important as land."[46] Stein's description of global affairs suggests the challenges faced by global managers and the need for a wide repertoire of knowledge and skills.

Global managers have an understanding of global affairs. They know how to deal with the growing number and variety of players in the global arena as globalization and democracy spread. Accompanying the players is the profusion of issues. As suggested by this book's subtitle, *Contemporary Issues* are a major concern of global managers. They must find the international equivalent of what has been done in their home countries under the banner of public affairs – learning to deal with the issues arising from increased government regulation and confrontations with advocacy groups. The great challenge to global managers is that their companies must cope with a broad range of issues that arise from their relationships with global players.

## Key attributes of a global manager

### Familiarity with other cultures

Familiarity with other cultures is a basic requirement of a global manager. Knowing what tendencies in thinking and preferred values people in other geographical regions have is a tremendous asset in communicating and dealing with them. It helps a manager understand what issues are likely to be salient and how different groups of people will respond to them. For example, a country with a preference for particularism on the cultural dimension of "universalism versus particularism" is unlikely to respond to the issue of human rights. And knowing that people in Spain, Italy, and France will behave more emotionally than those in Germany or the United Kingdom helps a manager in the United States. or United Kingdom. not to recoil from seemingly "affective" language and to recognize that cool, rational approaches are not always befitting. As Trompenaars and Hampden-Turner state, in southern regions and in many other cultures, "business is a human affair and the whole gamut of emotions are deemed appropriate. Loud laughter, banging your fist on the table or leaving a conference room in anger during a negotiation is all part of business."[47]

A common belief is that living in several cultures sensitizes a manager to a wide range of communications behavior variety and that being able to converse in at least two languages is the way to acquire familiarity. Talking about his own company, Stephen Green, CEO of HSBC notes that all of the executives running the company's largest businesses have worked in more than one, and nearly all in more than two, major country markets. Fred Hassan, CEO of Schering-Plough, however, downplays the importance of overseas assignments saying, "Putting people in foreign settings doesn't automatically imbue new attitudes, and it is attitudes rather than experiences that make a culture global."[48]

Nevertheless, schools of management are encouraging its graduates to explore new places in the world – literally. The University of Pennsylvania's Wharton School started offering short-term classes in countries that include China, Israel, and South Africa. It also offers concentrations in global finance and management. The school's dean, Thomas S. Robertson, states that 25% of its MBAs are now taking international positions and that MNCs want students to be more and more international and able to operate in different cultures. At Toronto's Munk School, students in the Master of Global Affairs graduate program are required to work abroad for the summer between their two years of study.[49]

The approach taken in many international management programs is to discuss the subject of culture directly and to address some important "fundamental dimensions of culture." Drawing on experience with over 30,000 participants all over the world, Trompenaars and Hampden-Turner list seven dimensions: (1) universalism versus particularism, (2) individualism versus communitarianism, (3) neutral versus emotional, (4) specific versus diffuse, (5) achievement versus ascription, (6) attitudes to time, and (7) attitudes to the environment.[50] These are also called "cultural bifurcations," cultural dilemmas, and pattern variables on which cultures disagree.[51]

Much knowledge about foreign countries and cultures can also be acquired through the available media of films and TV documentaries, news reports from local as well as international sources, websites, blogs, and books. For those attending universities, daily contact with classmates from virtually every country has become routine. Classroom discussions, especially of case materials, allow a lively interchange that enlarges the understanding of all. Educational experiences are a surrogate for actual experience, although not in the depth and variety of presence in another country. Many cases described in this book at least familiarize the reader to a variety of situations faced by global managers and the tools they use to construct solutions.

## Appreciates diversity of views and people

A global manager not only recognizes national differences in backgrounds and cultures of players but also sees these differences as opportunities. He or she embodies the world-oriented geocentric view of MNCs (see Chapter 2) that superiority is not equated with nationality. Instead collaboration is sought between subsidiaries and headquarters to establish universal standards and permissible local variations.

Agreeing with Bartlett, a global manager believes global management is all about legitimizing diversity and diverse views in an organization, including those based in cultural differences.[52] People from other cultures can be a source of "scarce information, knowledge, and expertise – the key resources required in the development and diffusion of innovation worldwide."[53] People from other cultures, he says, think, argue, and perceive things very differently. They recognize particulars as diverse as consumer tastes and government requirements. A manager who recognizes this potential stands a much better chance of succeeding in a global context. Diversity includes the capability to promote worldwide innovation and learning, which has become increasingly important.[54] This results in greater creativity and innovation, just as groups perform better than individuals in solving complex problems.

## Possesses relational skills

Bartlett states that global managers are individuals who possess special relational skills. They must be sensitive and responsive to national differences and be open-minded, not arrogant or ethnocentric.[55] He says, "the great challenge for multinational companies in the next decade will be to establish the confidence of society at large, governments in particular, and even of individual consumers, to assure them that they are worthy of their trust."[56]

Relationship-building is enhanced when managers possess what Daniel Goleman calls emotional intelligence, which is the title of his book.[57] A key aspect is the ability to understand others and "act wisely in human relations."[58] Goleman lists five needed abilities: (1) knowing one's emotion (self-awareness), (2) managing emotions, (3) motivating oneself, (4) recognizing emotions in others, and (5) handling relationships.[59] Emotional intelligence embraces some aspects associated with diplomatic skills, which enables a global manager to improve relationships with a wide variety of players in the international sphere.

## Practices stakeholder management

Management policies and strategies must mirror the kinds of mindsets and ideologies required of a global manager. Host countries and their citizens expect MNCs to demonstrate how they too will benefit from their presence. The classical ideology that business is run for the sole benefit of its owners increasingly becomes obsolete. It may still be a necessity for primitive enterprises facing desperate economic situations but should be shed by enterprises as they become larger and global. The contrasting managerial ideology, which underlies a stakeholder relations management approach, recognizes the need for organizations also to satisfy the expectations of other stakeholders besides investors, such as customers, employees, and the community. This shift in ideology is so great that some companies, such as Shell, speak of corporate transformation. Others explore the options inherent in the concept of global corporate citizenship.

## Believes in "Soft Power"

The global manager must modify existing strategies as well as apply new ones to deal with relationships in the international arena. The term *soft power* introduced by Joseph S. Nye, Jr. expresses the main thrust of these strategies. He defines soft power as "the ability to get what you want through attraction rather than coercion or payments. It arises from the attractiveness of a country's culture, political ideals, and policies."[60]

Soft power shares some attributes of power stemming from social relationships, as suggested by author Boris Holzer. He refers to the observation of the German sociologist Max Weber that the essence of power lies in the opportunity to assert and carry out one's will in a social relationship even against resistance.[61] Holzer further explains, "In addition to being subject to national regulation, corporations have to take into account the more informal normative expectations of advocacy groups, social movements and other sectors of civil society."[62] In short, an MNC must consider how they are impacted by the forces in the socio-political environment.

Global managers must become familiar with three communication strategies and skills discussed in Part III: (1) diplomatic communication, (2) public relations and marketing, and (3) public affairs. In exercising soft power, global managers must exercise a two-way symmetrical communications approach. They must be willing to listen and change their own policies and behavior as well as attempt to influence others.

## Serves as chief communicator

Of necessity, the modern business executive spends much time in communicating with others. As stated by public relations counsel or Nathaniel Sperber in his *Manager's Public Relations Handbook*, "The chief executive – the communicator – is the one person who speaks the one language common to all differing corporate specialists as well as to the various publics. This language is not a specialized jargon, compartmentalized by a single vertical discipline. The CEO … is the focal point at which all the beams meet to provide overall enlightenment. And because he make things coherent, his statements have a laserlike impact."[63]

The modern executive must unquestionably possess communication and relation-building skills because more than anyone else, he or she represents the organization to the outside world.[64] This description particularly applies to global managers. More candor would be a good way for CEOs to restore their role as a company's communicator-in-chief. As stated by Garten, "For their own sake, it's time to break radio silence and declare their positions on what practices are proper and how the improper ones should be fixed.... It would take only a dozen major CEOs to give the business community a good chance of rebuilding its reputation."[65]

Agreeing with this prescription, Robert L. Dillenschneider says that the CEO is still recognized as "the ultimate spokesperson for the organization, the embodiment of the brand and the official storyteller who knits together the company's past, present and future."[66] CEOs are the guardians of their company's reputation. They account for 50% of a company's reputation, according to Burson-Marsteller research.[67] This research identifies three key drivers of a CEO's reputation: (1) high ethical conduct, (2) believability, and (3) communication of a clear vision inside company. Other drivers are: attracts/retains quality management team, motivates and inspires employees, cares about customers, manages crises/downturns effectively, communicates clear vision outside company, increases shareholder wealth, and executes well on strategic vision.[68] This is why Warren Buffet tells his staff, "If you lose dollars for the firm by bad decisions, I will be understanding. If you lose reputation for the firm, I will be ruthless."[69] On average, the business influencers surveyed believe it takes nearly four years (3.65 years) for a company to rebuild a blemished reputation.[70]

## Ascendency of corporate diplomacy

Today's CEOs who serve as global managers must be much more than a communicator-in-chief. He or she must have the sensitivities of a diplomat in the everyday running of a company abroad – to make sure that various publics are not offended and, even more, that public expectations are recognized. The reality that a firm's environment consists of more than markets is painfully clear. Depending on the industry, the pressures of the socio-political environment in various locations throughout the world are mounting, and thereby create a need for a response. The top executives in the parent and subsidiary companies need to be statesmen who command diplomatic skills.

### Private sector diplomats join traditional diplomats

Diplomacy is no longer the exclusive province of traditional diplomats who served as country ambassadors. Private sector diplomats are playing an increasing role in IR, representing MNCs, NGOs, and civil society representative. In dealing with players from the three types of institutions, global managers serve as the private sector's diplomats. The number of meetings, negotiations, and purposeful conversations in which MNCs, NGOs, and other entities in civil society participate with the various players in the aggregate outstrip those of traditional diplomacy by nations. This reality has been recognized by several writers in the field of diplomacy.

In his *Modern Diplomacy*, R.P. Barston notes that the catalogue of nonstate actors ranges "from traditional economic interest groups through to resource, environmental, humanitarian, criminal and global governance interests."[71] He also recognizes "the greater fusion of public and private interests," saying, "In this way the state is assuming or incorporating into its public diplomacy an increasing number of private interests." The results of this fusion are "internationally negotiated joint ventures, financial support, trade promotion and conclusion particularly of bilateral agreements to facilitate and protect foreign investment and other economic interests."[72]

Christer Jonsson and Martin Hall, the authors of *The Essence of Diplomacy*, also see an enlarged role by private sector diplomats. They state that "today's notions of a globalized world envisage an international society with a diminished role, if not obsolescence, of the state and enhanced roles of other actors, such as MNCs, NGOs and transnational networks."[73] Another supporter of this view is Raymond Cohen, author of *Negotiating Across Cultures: International Communication in an Interdependent World*, who states that "Private business and nongovernmental organizations are other major actors [in addition to nation-states] on the contemporary international stage."[74]

Yet these new diplomats build on the knowledge and skills of traditional diplomacy. Sir Ernest Satow's *A Guide to Diplomatic Practice*, defined diplomacy as "the application of intelligence and tact to the conduct of official relations between the governments of independent states."[75] The *Encyclopedia Britannica* gave a similar definition, "Generically, diplomacy is the act of intercourse between independent and free national entities with a view to the establishment or enhancement of some predetermined end agreed upon between them."[76]

An ambassador requires the ability to "gauge the temperament and intelligence of those with whom he had to deal and to use this knowledge profitably in negotiation."[77] Another writer, Abraham de Wicquefort, a Dutch subject, said that the most important qualities of an ambassador are prudence and moderation. Prudence was equated with the gifts of silence and indirection, "the art of 'making it appear that one is not interested in the things one desires the most....'" Moderation was defined as the ability to "curb one's temper and to remain cool and phlegmatic in moments of tension."[78] These gifts were particularly important in the conduct of negotiations and the drafting of treaties, important activities of a diplomat. In a statement congruent with modern books on negotiation such as *Getting to Yes*, another writer, Francois de Callieres urged governments not to seek victory in negotiation, for this could only defeat one's best interests. Instead, a negotiator should seek to harmonize the interests of the parties concerned.[79]

## Corporate diplomacy – an emerging trend

Because of the prominence of MNCs in the international arena, it was inevitable that the term *corporate diplomacy* would be invented. It recognizes the importance of a corporation's sociopolitical environment and applies public affairs and public relations knowledge and skills to deal with it. It appeared in 1995 as the title of a 51-page report called *Corporate Diplomacy: Principled Leadership for the Global Community*.[80] The report examines ways in which corporations can play a proactive role in community building; more specifically, what role corporations can assume in filling the leadership gap – at the local, national, and international levels – given cross-border economic, cultural, technological, and information transactions that have made the task of governing more difficult.

The boundary between corporate affairs and government diplomacy has already been crossed. When China's President, Hu Jintao was on his way to meet President Bush in his first presidential visit to the White House in April 2006, he first stopped in Seattle to visit Boeing and Microsoft. Bill Gates hosted a dinner at his home for Hu Jintao.[81] And just as the private sector assists government in its public diplomacy objectives, the government assists business through what is called commercial diplomacy. This refers to "activities by foreign ministries and embassies in support of their country's business and finance sectors … in particular the effort put into looking after the well-being of a country's own nationals abroad."[82] During her tenure as Secretary of State, Hillary Clinton gave a high priority to representing American business interests and helped companies like Westinghouse Electric, and Boeing win business contracts. She ordered U.S. embassies to make such help a priority.[83] As the next chapter describes, Microsoft enlisted such help in its antitrust problem with the European Union.

The term corporate diplomacy was again used in 2003 by Ulrich Steger in *Corporate Diplomacy: The Strategy for a Volatile, Fragmented Business Environment*.[84] Applying a broad framework, Steger explains what managers can do to manage the business environment when facing such challenging situations as confrontations with activist groups, government regulations, and environmental and human rights issues. His solutions embrace the activities of issues management and crisis management and employ the framework of business–society relations. These subjects have been standard content in the literature of corporate public affairs and business–society relations, and addressed by the Public Affairs Council.[85] Although Steger applied corporate diplomacy mainly to domestic relationships in a country, it can also account for differences in political and social systems among nations and regions as well as peculiarities in their customs, values, and other cultural preferences. Relationships with NGOs, supranational organizations, and nation-states become especially important when corporate diplomacy is exercised abroad.

Using numerous cases and empirical studies, Steger describes the nonmarket forces that require a growing share of corporate attention. He notes that companies are increasingly intertwined with the surrounding society, even though markets are their dominant concern and they are not charged with the goal of "care for the common good." Thus they must deal with interests, institutions, ideas and rules that lie outside the market domain, which is the role of corporate diplomacy. Accordingly, after quoting the *Oxford English Dictionary's* definition of diplomacy as the "art of, skill in dealing with people so that business is done smoothly," he describes corporate diplomacy as "an attempt to manage systematically and professionally the business environment in such a way as to ensure that 'business is done smoothly'."[86] These explanations of corporate diplomacy reinforce its meaning as the application of public affairs, marketing, public relations, and communication to the larger business environment. Steger, however, rarely extends this model to the international arena, although it is of even greater importance.

Steger recognizes corporate social responsibility and stakeholder relations as important parts of corporate diplomacy. This view is supported by Antony Burgmans, Unilever's former CEO, who in the foreword to Steger's book, states that in the modern turbulent world, "there is more to business than just profitable growth." He believes that corporate social responsibility must be seen as integral to the operating tradition of companies, saying, "Running a business that meets the needs of stakeholders (consumers, customers, suppliers, shareholders, etc.) can also release social value."[87] Stakeholder management recognizes that managers must run an enterprise not just to maximize stockholder wealth but also to attend to the needs, values and objectives of other stakeholders. These stakeholders can be invited to participate in a variety of public affairs activities.

## Corporate "Secretaries of State"

Corporate diplomacy is also recognized by Clyde Prestowitz, a former U.S. Trade Negotiator, who believes that CEOs should at least have "real secretaries of state" in their organizations. Furthermore, "Instead of just lawyers, CEOs should be looking for global affairs executives with language and regional knowledge along with personal contacts.… And such executives should regularly be discussing key U.S. strategic issues with the grand strategy players here and abroad."[88] A similar remedy is proposed by public relations Counselor John Budd, who suggests creating an Office of Diplomacy or expanding the purview of public affairs and public relations departments to include the international arena. Public affairs and public relations practitioners, along with lawyers, are considered boundary-spanners because as insiders they relate to people on the outside. Some managers, such as those in marketing, dealer relations, purchasing, and supplier relations, also engage in frequent outside contact.

Some corporations are literally embracing the concept of diplomacy by opening in-house "state departments" and hiring persons with diplomatic backgrounds. Boeing hired career diplomat Thomas R. Pickering as senior vice president of IR for its Washington headquarters in 2001, after he had served as U.S. undersecretary of state for political affairs. He had taken the graduate program of Tufts University's Fletcher School of Law and Diplomacy.[89] The job at Boeing was specially created for him and led to such headlines in *The Moscow Times* as "Boeing's Ambassador Sees Supersonic Future."[90]

His job was to make Boeing, the largest U.S. exporter, a global company. The need for this shift was stated by a former employee, "Boeing is incredibly mono-cultural.… It has an international presence in the customer fleet, but very little (overseas) manufacturing."[91] Around 1998, it had more than 250 communicators inside the United States. but just two outside the United States. One of Pickering's first messages was to highlight the company's links with foreign suppliers. He said that on the commercial side, 60% of Boeing's aircraft is made outside the company and that it has more than 200 suppliers in the United Kingdom, with 35,000 to 40,000 employees.

Besides new organizational designations, Pickering's second globalization target was the internal culture. "We are now seeking to change some of the ways in which we do business to become more … overtly global." The company hired about 20 foreign heads, including about a dozen former diplomats, for its in-house "state department" to preside overall Boeing's business in particular countries.[92] The main qualification of these individuals was that they are foreign nationals who bring specialized knowledge of their own country to the company and yet operate as if they are ambassadors from Boeing, Pickering explained. Although acknowledging that the role of diplomats may be less helpful where the decision maker about an aircraft sale is not a government, he says they can still be useful in providing help on government regulations, such as air traffic control.[93]

In Japan, Boeing used the approach of hiring an American with 16 years experience in the country, with excellent language skills and good contacts with the Japanese defense establishment and with the Diet. "For the first time in a recent visit we had an opportunity for our president to sit down with their defence minister and talk about future defence relationships," said Pickering.[94]

## The future

In time, more MNCs may be incorporating *diplomacy* in their name for international public relations and public affairs activities. They recognize that their economic activities abroad are hugely affected by nonmarket forces that are more numerous and complex than those faced within the home country. In the meanwhile, some consulting services are referring to corporate diplomacy. For example, China Concept Consulting, which was formed to help global companies capture China business opportunities, divides its services into five business groups: (1) industry intelligence, (2) business strategy, (3) corporate diplomacy, (4) risk management, and (5) private equity. It described corporate diplomacy as "Our in-depth knowledge of the unique dynamics of Chinese and Western business practices and perceptions allow us to communicate properly between international clients and their Chinese counterparts."[95] Among the firm's services are licensing, public relations, crisis management, JV negotiation, tax negotiation, and delegation management. In addition to such new firms, affiliated branches of well-established public relations firms provide similar services in China and India. Government relations, says Harold Burson, founder and chairman of Burson-Marsteller, is the major concern of affiliates in China and India.

# Conclusions

This book about contemporary issues and corporate responses draws on the domains of IB and IM, but adds a third approach, which is IR. Establishing sound relationships is not only important in basic business relationships but also in dealing with an organization's stakeholders and the myriad of players in the international arena. In mapping a MNC's socio-political environment, both the model of stakeholder relations and the triangle of business, the state and civil society are used.

It is the global manager who must respond to issues and mediate relationships. The construct of a global manager is used to represent all managers who have significant responsibility in dealing with players in the international arena. Global managers possess special attributes that combine a wide range of personality traits, attitudes, perspectives, values, and skills. These qualities are similar to those associated with diplomats. Not surprisingly, therefore, the term "corporate diplomacy" has entered the business lexicon and more references are made to the role of the private sector in diplomacy.

## Revision Questions

1. Globalization focuses on the international arena where it has produced more players and more issues. What are useful ways of categorizing global players? Name the categories and give some examples.
2. Name the different types of issues associated with the international arena and give an example of each.
3. The approach of this book is to focus on international relation. How does this differ from the traditional domains of international business and international management?
4. What are the attributes of a global manager? Is the concept of a global manager useful?
5. What is the evidence that a field of corporate diplomacy exists? What are the similarities with traditional diplomacy?

## Discussion Questions

I. At this stage is globalization causing more problems than producing benefits. Should globalization be slowed down or modified? If so, what should be done?
II. Argue whether the distinction between the domains of international business and international management is meaningful. What special approaches to international issues might you expect from each one?
III. Argue whether there's really a difference between a global manager and a typical graduate of a business school. Would the attributes ascribed to a global manager also apply?
IV. Diplomacy is a special art best left to people in the various foreign affairs positions. Do you believe that business should avoid identification with diplomacy?

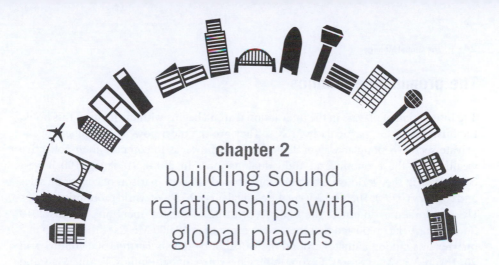

# chapter 2
# building sound relationships with global players

**Objectives**

1. Recognize the power of multinational corporations (MNCs) and the importance of supranational organizations, nation-states, and civil society organizations.
2. Know the ways the United Nations can exert influence over MNCs and a particular proclamation that is relevant to them.
3. Know some of the actions the European Union has taken against MNCs.
4. Understand some of the political and cultural differences among nation-states.
5. Know some of the major types of civil society organizations and what actions that have, or might, take against MNCs.
6. Recognize the crucial importance of establishing sound, long-term relationships with other players in the international arena.

Multinational corporations (MNCs) play an increasingly prominent role in the global arena and engage in relationships with players of all types and on all levels. They deal with supranational organizations such as the United Nations (UN) and European Union (EU); international organizations such as the World Trade Organization (WTO); individual nation-states; and civil society entities, especially nongovernmental organizations (NGOs). Some of the dealings reflect routine exchanges of information and opinions while other interactions may lead to understandings, disagreements, confrontations, and conflicts. Some entities will explore possibilities of collaborative relationships to address major issues. The goal of communications by MNCs with international players is to build sound long-term relationships with other global players so that organizational goals can be achieved.

This chapter elaborates on the variety of players in the international arena and ways in which MNCs interact with them. Several illustrative cases, such as Microsoft's dispute with the EU, are discussed. Many other situations are described in Part II in connection with major issues facing global managers. The handling of these relationships with international players requires special finesse, modeled after the field of diplomacy. Questions arise of mutual recognition, appropriate manner, and innovative discussion of opportunities and problems. The hope is that all players can learn to "get along globally" to achieve both individual and mutual goals and aspirations.

# The prominence of mncs

The interaction of players in the international arena begins with the focus of this book, the business sector, particularly MNCs. They are the most powerful members of the private sector. A popular way of depicting their power is to compare their collective wealth with the economies of individual nations. In 2011, 51 of the 100 largest economies in the world were corporations (based on a comparison of corporate sales and country GDPs). Their sales were the equivalent of 27.5% of world economic activity. U.S. corporations dominate the top 200, with 82 of the top mentions.[1] In his 2010 book, Stuart Hart reported that there were more than 60,000 MNCs with more than a quarter of a million affiliates around the world.[2] The top six *Fortune* 500 countries in 2011 were Wal-Mart Stores, ExxonMobil, Chevron, ConocoPhillips, Fannie Mae, and General Electric.[3] According to *Forbes* magazine, 75 of the 200 largest corporations in 2005 were U.S. based – more than the nets of the three nations of Japan, France, and Germany.[4]

Not surprisingly, the view that "In many ways corporations have supplanted governments as the dominant economic force in the world" is increasingly voiced.[5] Because of their high visibility, large size, and identifiable foreignness, MNCs are often singled out for special attention by governments and other powerful players, such as NGOs. They are vulnerable because they are perceived as neither belonging to nor pledging any patriotic allegiance to any home nation-state. Some host foreign governments doubt whether MNCs recognize their national interests. They are fearful that such enterprises will escape a country's control mechanisms and that the foreign enterprises will introduce elements into the national economy that will weaken the control by their national leaders.

The orientation of an MNC can be discerned by whether it describes itself as ethnocentric, polycentric, or geocentric.[6] An ethnocentric management believes in the superiority of its own ethnic group – that they are more trustworthy and reliable than foreigners in subsidiaries. Advice, counsel and directives would flow from headquarters to subsidiaries in a steady stream, and home-country managers would be recruited and trained for key positions everywhere in the world. Complex products would be manufactured in the home country and secrets kept among trusted home-country nationals. Another culture would be judged solely by the values and standards of one's own culture.

In contrast, a polycentric MNC has many centers, especially of authority or control that allows subsidiary companies to be managed by local citizens. A geocentric MNC takes a world view where headquarters consists of managers representing multiple nationalities. Rather than orienting themselves toward either the home country or the host country, top managers consider the organization's goals, plans, and performance from a broader, worldwide perspective. Communication is encouraged among subsidiaries. The best managers, regardless of their nationality or location, are selected for the assignments that fit their skills and abilities.

The trend is toward the geocentric model which reflects the maximum degree of multinationality of an enterprise and is positively related to its long-term viability. As Howard J. Perlmutter states, "The payoffs are a more powerful total company throughout, a better quality of products and services, worldwide utilization of best resources, improvement of local company management, a greater sense of commitment to worldwide objectives, and last but not least, more profit."[7] The globalization movement has fostered and accelerated the geocentric view.

# Supranational organizations

## United Nations

The UN is the most prominent world institution. The UN interacts mainly with nation-states in fulfilling its primary goal of preserving world peace. It is located in an 18-acre New York City compound which is international territory, not part of the United States or any other country. It was created at the 1945 San Francisco Conference to replace the League of Nations. Its initial 51 country members grew to 192 in 2007 and now consists of 193. Its stated aims are to facilitate cooperation in international law, international security, economic development, social progress, and human rights issues.[8]

Organizationally, the UN is divided into administrative bodies – including the General Assembly, Security Council, Economic and Social Council, Secretariat, and the International Court of Justice (ICJ) – and a collection of autonomous specialized and affiliated agencies, such as World Bank, International Monetary Fund (IMF), World Health Organization (WHO), and United Nations Educational, Scientific, and Cultural Organization (UNESCO), and United Nations Children's Fund (UNICEF).

MNC interactions with the UN are largely symbolic but sometimes involve substantive issues that call for action by them. An example of largely symbolic support by MNCs is support for the UNICEF report of sexual exploitation of children and adolescents. This is a major global issue recognized at a worldwide UNICEF conference. It was stated that children living on the margins of society were especially vulnerable to sexual abuse, including those who are poor, those who work as domestic servants or live on the street, and those caught in conflicts and natural disasters. [9]

## Millennium development goals

MNCs and other private sector players have become involved in the fulfillment of the UN's goal of freeing humankind from extreme poverty, which is of special concern to developing nations. This concern was embodied in the UN's Millennium Development Goals statement signed in September 2000. All 192 UN member states agreed to try to achieve the following eight Millennium eight goals by the year 2015:

- Halve the proportion of people living on less than $1.25 a dollar (at purchasing power parity).
- Ensure all children complete primary school.
- Educate boys and girls equally.
- Reduce the mortality rate among children under five by two-thirds.
- Reduce the maternal mortality rate by three-quarters.
- Halt and begin to reverse the spread of HIV/AIDS, malaria and other major diseases.
- Halve the proportion of people without access to safe water and sanitation.
- Increase aid and improve governance.[10]

To measure progress on these Millennium Goals, the UN annually publishes the Human Development Index (HDI), a comparative measure ranking countries by poverty, literacy, education, life expectancy, and other factors. Sadly, the UN is better at proclaiming goals than meeting them, for their pledges typically become "debased currency."[11] Major country problems in meeting Millennium Goals are lack of infrastructure, such as roads and hospitals, and high population growth. The UN reports that in 1990 there were 237 million Africans under age 15; in 2007 that figure grew to 348 million, and by 2015 it is expected to top 400 million.[12] To achieve some goals with the aid of NGOs, such as persuading villagers in India to cooperate with a government construction program for toilets, NGOs have had to learn the art of marketing, for example, offering people a commission for persuading their neighbors to buy a toilet.[13]

Combating malaria – one of the world's worst scourges – is a major goal and has attracted support by corporate philanthropies. The pledges include $168.7 million from the Bill & Melinda Gates Foundation, $2 million from Ted Turner's United Nations Foundation, and $218 million from a coalition of corporations led by Marathon Oil Corporation.[14] WHO reported 247 million malaria cases in 2006 and 881,000 deaths, most of them children younger than five in sub-Saharan Africa.

## World economic institutions

### World Bank

The World Bank is a vital source of financial and technical assistance to developing countries around the world. It was established on July 1, 1994, during a conference of 44 countries in Bretton Woods, New Hampshire. Headquartered in Washington, DC, it has offices in 100 countries around the world with 10,000 employees. It is made up of two unique development institutions owned by 185 member countries: International Bank for Reconstruction and Development (IBRD) and the International Development Association (IDA). The Bank's mission is global poverty reduction and the improvement of living standards. The IBRD focuses on middle income and credit-worthy poor countries, while IDA focuses on the poorest countries in the world.

Together they provide low-interest loans, interest-free credit and grants to developing countries for education, health, infrastructure, communications, and many other purposes. Examples of projects approved in 2007 are the promotion of innovation to enhance competitiveness in Uruguay; water sector development in Morocco; the Third National HIV/AIDS Control Project in India; and Road Maintenance and Rehabilitation Project in Papua New Guinea.[15] Unfortunately, some of the health projects in India, involving $569 million in loans, have been found rife with fraud and corruption, as uncovered by a "Detailed Implementation Review," by the World Bank.[16]

### International Monetary Fund

The International Monetary Fund (IMF) is the central institution of the international monetary system – a system of international payments and exchange rates among national currencies that enables business to take place between countries. It was established by treaty in 1945 to help Western governments manage their currencies and to promote the health of the world economy by being a lender of last resort to distressed emerging-market countries. Headquartered in Washington, DC, it is governed by a global membership of 184 countries. Many important decisions by the Fund require 85% approval by shareholder nations, with votes apportioned to each country based on its general position in the world economy. The United States has effective veto power because its share accounts for about 17% of the total vote. [17]

The IMF encourages countries to adopt sound economic policies. In exchange for providing temporary financing for members running low on hard currency, it demands tough and sometimes harsh market-minded reforms. These have included cuts in government spending, interest-rate increases, and privatization of state-owned companies. The IMF believes that reforms will eventually lower poverty, but knows that they do not always sit well with the public. The IMF's insensitivity to the impact of their conditions on working people have caused deeply ingrained ill-will.

## World Trade Organization

The World Trade Organization (WTO) is the only global international organization dealing with the rules of trade between nations, replacing the General Agreement on Tariffs and Trade (GATT). The goal is to help producers of goods and services, exporters, and importers conduct their business. *The Economist* described it as "a fractious club of 144 member countries that acts by consensus. Any single country, however small, can block proceedings." Critics view the WTO as "an unbridled, secretive outfit that skews trade rules for the benefit of big business."[18]

Nonetheless, the WTO serves as a referee for many trade disputes. A persistent one is by American news and entertainment industries against China for the way in which it regulates the import and distribution of foreign publications, films, and music.[19] A central problem is that the government runs or supervises virtually all print and broadcast media and subjects them to Communist Party propaganda official oversight. Import restrictions serve the double purpose of controlling objectionable content and protecting local industry. The import of foreign films is restricted to no more than 20 each year. A WTO ruling upheld American complaints, but China may choose to appeal and insists that its channels for publications and audiovisual products are extremely open.

## The European Union

Among supranational organizations, the best known after the UN is the regional institution of the EU. This economic and political entity celebrated its 50th birthday in March 2007. Starting with six countries – Belgium, France, Germany, Italy, Luxembourg, and the Netherlands – it grew to 27.[20] They are united in their commitment to peace, democracy, the rule of law, and respect for human rights. In specified areas, they work together in their collective interest through EU institutions to administer sovereign powers jointly. The EU has the power to enact laws that are directly binding on citizens from its Member states.[21] The EU accounts for between a third and a fifth of the world economy, depending on how exchange rates are set.[22] The EU's post-expansion population was 503 million in 2012, three-fifths larger than the United States's 312 million in 2011.

Other measures of its importance are that four of the rich-country members of the G8 group are European, as are two-thirds of the members of the Organization for Economic Cooperation and Development (OECD), another mostly rich-country club.

The EU has experienced both successes and failures. The most notable success is that its 50 years of existence have brought peace and prosperity, including the reunification of a continent formerly divided by the iron curtain of communism. This achievement is symbolized by the conversion of national currencies to the euro, which serves as "a powerful symbol of European co-operation." The conversion required major campaigns in the EU as a whole as well as by individual countries to win public acceptance. (England, Denmark, and Sweden did not agree to convert their currencies). With the cooperation of banks, it became an example of cooperation between public and private sectors. In 2012, however, that cooperation was facing the test of failing economies, budget deficits and bank indebtedness of Ireland, Italy, Greece, Spain, and Portugal.

Nation-states sometimes resist EU efforts to create European markets when the EU applies the principles of the free market system to break up national monopolies. One such effort has been to break open the bloc's energy market, such as Electricite de France SA, by pushing the idea of "ownership unbundling" – forcing companies that own both transit networks and the utilities that sell energy to consumers to split off one of those businesses. In the natural gas industry, French President Nicolas Sarkozy arranged the merger of Gaz de France SA and Suez SA, creating a French natural gas giant.[23] The EU is also applying pressure on labor markets which *The Economist* says requires a trimming of overly generous welfare states and the injection of new competition into products markets, especially for services, which account for two-thirds of EU-wide GDP.[24]

### EU takes antitrust action – Case of Microsoft

The EU has regulatory authority in Europe that can affect the activities of MNCs. General Electric (GE) was one of the first companies to run into a roadblock when it tried to acquire Honeywell International in 2001. After winning approval from antitrust authorities in the United States to acquire the company, GE sought similar approval from the EU but was turned down.[25] The appeals of the then GE President Jack Welch failed to reverse the decision. The climate has since improved, as shown by GE's success in getting approval for its $2.3 billion acquisition of Instrumentartum.[26]

More than GE, Microsoft stands out as a company that has most experienced the power of the EU and its executive arm, the European Commission (EC). In the United States, Microsoft had faced a suit by the Justice Department on the grounds that it was behaving in a monopolistic manner that was detrimental to competition. It narrowly avoided antitrust action by becoming a fast political learner and quickly amassing the whole panoply of political resources to influence government. These resources included political campaign contributions, hiring of legal talent, use of think tanks, direct and grassroots lobbying, public relations and TV advocacy advertising, funding and distribution of opinion polls, and charitable giving.[27]

Having won the battle in the United States, Microsoft now faced the same charges in Europe but with more determined and stubborn antitrust authorities. It had yet to develop the public relations, public affairs, and legal acumen to fight the likes of Europe's tough antitrust chief Neelie Kroes. In March 2004, the EU ordered Microsoft to pay EUR497 million, which at the time was the largest fine ever handed out by the EU. In July 2006, Microsoft was fined an additional EUR280.5 million for not complying with a 2004 decision to stop the practice of packing a variety of software with its Windows operating system. Kroes threatened further fines of up to EUR2 million and in July 2006 added EUR280.5 million more in fines for noncompliance with the EC order to make its Windows protocols available to rival software makers.[28] In fall 2007, a EU court upheld Kroes's position, a ruling that at the time established her as the most influential antitrust regulator in the world.[29]

After Microsoft appealed to the Court of First Instance, it was again rejected and the court upheld a record fine of EUR497 million.[30] The occasion was a major event as lawyers on all sides of the case flocked to Luxembourg to hear the decision read from the bench. Such attention, said *The Wall Street Journal,* is "normally paid to the travails of royals or the fate of national soccer teams."[31] In February 2008, the EU fined Microsoft EUR899 million ($1.35 billion) for failing to comply with the 2004 antitrust order. Although Microsoft repeatedly pledged to resolve the issue and disclose more technical information, Kroes did not sound convinced. "Talk, as you know, is cheap," she said.[32]

In July 2009, Microsoft yielded to the EU on the browser issue by agreeing to give European users of its Windows software a choice of Web browsers. Users could opt to turn Microsoft's Internet Explorer off and install such browsers as Google's Chrome and Mozilla's Firefox. The company said its proposal was contingent on the EU settling the case without a fine.[33]

In Europe, Microsoft apparently lacked the clout it had in the United States, but it stood ready to adopt new tools. It took advantage of a new U.S. government practice of using commercial diplomacy to assist individual MNCs. In a bold diplomatic maneuver, Microsoft enlisted the help of the U.S. government to pressure the EU to accept the Vista program. The U.S. ambassador to the EU sent an official two-paragraph email to EU regulators and officials of 27 EU member countries noting that relations between Brussels and Microsoft "hit a new low."

Reflecting Microsoft's view, the email also complained that EU regulatory procedures "have lacked transparency and fairness and, if accurate, would be of substantial concern to the U.S." U.S. embassies across Europe also sent emails expressing U.S.'s concerns. The day after the emails were sent there was talk of a breakthrough.[34] Interestingly, C. Boyden Gray, the new U.S. ambassador to the EU was a former White House counsel who had previously worked as a lobbyist representing Microsoft in the company's antitrust battles with U.S. authorities. These efforts, however, did not prevent EU authorities from charging Microsoft with new antitrust violations in January 2009.[35]

## EU restricts genetically modified crops and foods

The efforts of biotechnology firms Monsanto, DuPont and Novartis to gain acceptance of their bio-engineered seeds and foods have been facing public and governmental resistance in Europe. The case illustrates the power of the EU and the need for MNCs to deal with it. The firms argued that economic models showed that global malnutrition would increase if biotech was stopped. The case also shows the role of public opinion and groups in civil society.

The interactions of MNCs with the EU demonstrates the importance of knowing how to deal with this additional layer of government beyond the nation-state. Besides the Microsoft case, EU's antitrust regulators accused Intel Corp, the world's biggest computer-chip maker, of monopoly abuse. A competitor, Advanced Micro Devices (AMD) had complained that Intel was blocking its access to the market by paying computer makers rebates to keep their usage of AMD chips down and by selling chips below cost to thwart AMD from winning key accounts.[36] In May 2009, Intel was fined it EUR1 billion ($1.44 billion).[37] As these cases indicate, government relations activities by MNCs are highly important.

In 1998, the EU declared a moratorium on approving new biotech products. Frustrated in dealing with the EU and its "curious decision-making procedures," Argentina, Canada, and the United States in 2003 decided to challenge the EU at a higher level, the WTO.[38] Their case claimed that the moratorium amounted to protectionism, which was prohibited by the WTO. The following year the EC, the EU's executive body, approved a strain of sweet corn for human consumption, with the restriction that it must clearly be labeled as "genetically modified."[39] The WTO is investigating whether the EU's GM labeling law is legal.

In 2006, the WTO made an interim ruling that the EU and six member states broke trade rules by barring entry to GM products between June 1999 and August 2003. The EU consequently ended its moratorium, but Green Party members of the European Parliament were still defending national bans on GM crops in certain EU member states.[40] In another action, the EU approved the first GM food since 1998 when BASF applied for cultivation of a GM potato, called Amflora, for use in industrial processes, such as paper production.[41] Despite some EU approvals, the United States vows to fight for GM products in the WTO until complete approval is secured.

# Nation-states

Nation-states comprise the "host countries" inhabited by MNCs. Their governments determine how welcoming their countries are to companies that wish to start operations in them and what terms to impose. For this reason, some approaches to international management emphasize the importance of understanding various economic and political structures and different cultures.

## Differences in economic and political systems

Few controlled economies – where economic power is almost totally concentrated in the hands of government officials and political authorities – exist in the world. Such economies exhibit state ownership of property, price and wage controls, minimum worker safety, and little environmental regulation. Most countries of the world follow the norms of the free market system, but some countries, such as Venezuela and Bolivia, are reverting to "new socialism." Other variations are that countries such as France and Sweden have more social welfare legislation and labor unions in European countries are generally more powerful.

Other patterns appear in various countries. South Korea is known as the home of the Chaebol, which are large conglomerate groups, often family-owned, such as Samsung and Hyundai.[42] Elements of corporatism exist in Slovenia and the Netherlands. Corporatism is defined as "a living being that organizes all the main concepts of the body politic and determines political behavior." It says that the state, politics and society are not and cannot be separated and that "the fundamental objective of the corporative culture is the survival of the nation...."[43] NGOs and activist groups, as well as employer organizations, are encouraged to participate in the political system. In the Netherlands, which is a constitutional monarchy, corporatism is reflected in its many political parties and organized interest groups.

**State-Owned Enterprises (SOES):** A development of major importance in recent years is the growth of SOES, which combine a business with the state. The extent of government ownership varies. The United Nations Conference on Trade and Development defines a SOES "as one in which the state owns more than 10% of the shares."[44] No longer reporting to state ministries, state-owned companies are listed on the stock market and embrace globalization.

*The Economist* describes two types of SOES. One is the "party state" in which the state exercises a degree of control over the economy that is unparalleled in the rest of the state-capitalist world. A second type are "national champions" wherein the firms are formally privately owned but enjoy a huge amount of either overt or covert support from their respective governments."[45] Even in the most successful Chinese SOES, top executives are "cadres first and company men second. They care more about pleasing their party bosses than about the global market."[46] All of the world's 13 biggest oil firms are state-backed, controlling more than three-quarters of the world's oil supplies. The world's biggest natural gas company is Russia's Gazprom.

State enterprise is spreading, making up most of market capitalization. Governments are striking deals across the world. Some former socialist economies continue to operate under authoritarian governments and various degrees of centralized control. In 2005, about one-third of China's economy was still directly controlled by government SOES, mainly in key sectors such as defense and utilities. China early decided to deregulate telecoms by breaking them into four competing firms, but competition among them was discouraged.[47] Private companies are often beholden to state banks for capital and to local officials for favors and contracts. Struggles between central government and local officials, who want to protect jobs in their own backyards, continue. Both levels of government have encouraged foreign investments, but local governments can more easily approve small investments with a minimum of paper work.[48]

## Civil society

The powerful spread of globalization has stimulated growth of civil society. MNCs face thousands of civil society organizations, especially NGOs, that work and advocate at the global level. They largely account for the rise of the anticapitalist and antiglobal-ization movements concerned about inequities and harms. They object to MNCs' often singular pursuit of business goals at the expense of the environment, human rights, and other values – values represented by civil society. It is important to become familiar with these organizations and to learn when to expect confrontations and when to welcome collaboration.

Nonprofit organizations (NPOs) are a major component of civil society, covering an amazingly large number and wide range of organizations. They use their surplus revenues to achieve their goals rather than distribute them as dividends. Like NGOs, they are independent of any form of government and are part of civil society. Not surprisingly, the terms NPO and NGO are sometimes confused and used interchangeably. After the formation of the UN, NGOs became popular and were associated with international issues. NPOs are often seen in the context of corporate social responsibility programs. Companies such as Panasonic have learned that because they are tied to issues of public interest, NPOs often can contribute to solving social problems. They also often have a better grasp of market needs and distribution networks than private companies and can therefore help in developing new products and services.[49]

In 2006 there were over 1.9 million NPOs in the United States, embracing groups in the arts, culture, and humanities, hospitals and healthcare organizations, schools on all levels, religious organizations, social agencies and charities, environmental groups, labor unions, international and foreign affairs, and some NGOs. They accounted for 5.2% of the gross domestic product (GDP) and 7.2% of the labor force in 2004.[50] Collectively, they attend to the needs of the whole person, the community and society.

Although many civil society organizations still restrict themselves to providing client services, they have become best known for actively, and sometimes very aggressively, advocating and pursuing social reforms. Activists among these groups see themselves as a "countervailing power" to the state or MNCs and as a source of resistance to unwanted social consequences of globalization. As stated by Leonora Angeles and Penny Gurstein, editors of *Learning Civil Societies*, "Civil society is a re-emerging critical force in the construction of a new citizenship, mediating between the public and the private spheres in a pluralistic democracy."[51]

These organizations often serve as de facto regulatory agencies. Harvard University's John Ruggie found that civil society organizations (mainly NGOs) act upon the global corporate sector as one of the major drivers of direct expression and the pursuit of human interests beyond those mandated by the state.[52]

Families are given much attention in economics in that they supply the factors of production of labor, capital, and land. One academic, Nancy Folbre, chose the term *invisible heart* to describe the contributions made by families, especially women, in providing motivated human beings by being loving and caring.[53]

## Prominent role of NGOs

Among civil society organizations, NGOs have become especially important because of their inordinate influence and impact on nation-states and MNCs. Beyond contributing to the general welfare, civil society actually promotes the interest of MNCs themselves. "They help stabilize socio-economic conditions and thus ensure the long-term viability of the business environment, especially in developing nations."[54] There they contribute to "society-building." They help formulate and enforce the ground rules with which both public- and private sector actors have to abide. NGOs typically confront MNCs on such issues as environmental degradation and human rights. The growth of NGOs has been rapid. Christopher Gunn, author of *Third Sector Development*, reported in 2004 that there were more than 50,000 international NGOs, compared to fewer than 20,000 only a decade ago.[55]

Some NGOs, such as Amnesty International, Transparency International, and Greenpeace, have become "superbrands" in that like MNCs they too have increasingly become multinational. Many NGOs have attached themselves to the globalization issue as a way to promote their interests and gain public support. As *The Economist* suggests, "The campaigners need big business as a tic-bird needs a wildebeest. By alighting on big companies, they can often force through changes that would be hard to achieve through the political process alone."[56] They can change things in Nigeria, for example, more easily by boycotting Shell than by lobbying the Nigerian government.

NGOs can become adversaries when they monitor business practices and pressure MNCs to act in more socially responsible ways. They are known as attackers, watchdogs and monitors of the policies, and actions of governments and MNCs.[57] They are very effective, say public relations counselors Michael McDermott and Jonathan Wootliff, because they: (1) play the offensive all the time, (2) simplify complex issues, (3) form unusual coalitions, (4) have a clear agenda, (5) move at Internet speed, and (6) know how to feed on the media. They hit where it works: a company's customers, legislators and regulators, the media and, now becoming more important, financial markets.[58]

Occasionally, a NGO confronts a country. Greenpeace did this when it challenged the Soviets in July 1983 on the issue of whaling by deliberately violated Soviet territorial waters in the Bering Sea. Ostensibly Greenpeace was there to photograph the whaling operation but it is suspected that their real aim was to be captured by the Soviets and thereby create an international news event. Similarly, in January 1989 Greenpeace hindered whaling in the Antarctic by the Japanese.

### Shell's Brent Spar boarded by greenpeace

NGOs frequently confront MNCs. In early 1994, Shell and Exxon faced the problem of disposing the Brent Spar, an oil storage buoy in the North Sea. Originally commissioned in 1976, it was now redundant and had been nonoperational for five years. Shell commissioned no less than 30 separate studies to consider the technical, safety, and environmental implications of its disposal. It decided on deep sea dumping within U.K. waters as the low cost option with little environmental impact. It received permission to dump from the U.K. Department of Trade and Industry and, following the guidelines of the new convention on the marine environment, the U.K. government notified other European nations of the plan. Receiving no response within the 60-day deadline for objections, the U.K. government issued the disposal license to Shell effective in the first week of May. Shell's decision making was based on the use of experts and dealing with regulatory requirements. NGOs, however, were not consulted because it was not the norm at the time.

Greenpeace, one of the super-environmental groups, was aware of the disposal date and occupied the Brent Spar on April 30, 1995. It argued that Brent Spar was a "toxic time bomb" containing 5,500 tons of oil and that "no justifiable grounds" existed for sinking it. Were it to happen, Greenpeace argued, 500 other obsolete oil platforms might similarly be "dumped."[59] Known for its clever tactics and publicity generation, Greenpeace members boarded the rig and chained four of themselves on it so that sinking it would be tantamount to murder. Greenpeace produced pictures of its members braving the water cannons of Shell's tugboats. The impression was that of a bully (Shell) beating up on a small kid (Greenpeace activists). This violated anthropologist Margaret Mead's warning that Americans (and, presumably many other people) do not like bullies. Greenpeace also mobilized politicians against deep sea sinking.

Facing boycotts, Shell in Germany and the Netherlands pressured headquarters to cancel the dumping plan. Shell's petrol sales in Europe fell by 20–30%, particularly in Germany where protesters launched violent attacks on Shell petrol stations.[60] In the first three weeks of June, after the number of media reports increased drastically, the Royal/Dutch share lost 3% of its value, which amounted to EUR2.3 billion loss.[61] On June 20, Shell announced that it had called off plans to sink the Brent Spar, only hours before it was due to be sunk. It had painfully learned the power of Greenpeace. In retrospect, Shell realized that it would have been better to consult with Greenpeace as well as with the government.[62]

A week later Shell engaged in damage control. In Germany, it took out a one-page advertisement in 100 national and local newspapers with the title "We will change." While admitting its mistakes, it maintained that the decision to dump at sea was correct on technical and environmental grounds. In Denmark, Shell targeted its message by sending letters to 250,000 credit card holders explaining its policy.[63]

The Brent Spar experience contributed to Shell's transformation into a more socially responsive corporation. It revised its code of conduct, published an annual *Shell Report*, which includes environmental issues, and instituted a Sustainable Development Management Framework in order to integrate sustainable development in decision making. The framework contains three core themes: performance with a long-term view, dynamic and caring innovator, and acting on strong business principles.[64]

Interestingly, Greenpeace later admitted that it had made a mistake about the quantity of the remaining pollutants on the Brent Spar, basically confirming the figures provided by Shell. It offered Shell an apology, but its credibility suffered. Greenpeace nonetheless maintained that the sinking of Brent Spar would have been wrong. Greenpeace is not often so interested in pursuing the truth. When Exxon sought to continue using an oil tanker that inspection showed to be in seaworthy condition and invited Greenpeace, along with the media, to board the ship and see for themselves, Greenpeace rejected the invitation.[65]

### Collaborative and antagonistic relationships

When NGOs confront an MNC, a nation-state or other entities, both parties must ponder the impact on the ensuing relationship. A welcome trend is that some MNCs and NGOs are now collaborating to resolve societal problems. MNCs also form alliances with one another to achieve political purposes, such as lobbying to curb corrupt practices by foreign companies, even though they typically compete with one another in the economic marketplace.

Some NGOs have established contacts with specific individuals in corporations so that conflicts could be resolved. For example, when People for the Ethical Treatment of Animals (PETA) learned that LL Bean and Eddie Bauer inadvertently used certain kinds of imported leather which they agreed not to use, the member of PETA who had contacts with individuals in those companies called them and the problem was solved. As the PETA representative said, "These are human relationships ... you have somebody to call in the event they are doing something objectionable."[66] Linda Hon, who cited this example, says it is an example that explains "how organizations can ethically and effectively communicate and build quality relationships with activist publics."[67]

MNCs may also collaborate with nation-states. In the United States, MNCs have assisted U.S. State Department public diplomacy efforts to counter anti-Americanism. Many NGOs recognize the advantages of creating partnerships and strategic alliances with governments and MNCs, both as a source of funding and a way of exerting influence on practical affairs. From an MNC's viewpoint, a major advantage in partnering with an NGO is that the latter's credibility is high. Edelman's 2012 TrustBarometer showed that for the fifth year in a row, NGOs were the most trusted institution in the world, and in 16 of the 25 countries surveyed, more trusted than business.[68] Studies have shown that they are more trusted than governments.

NGOs face the danger, however, that their credibility will be exploited by being coopted by partnering corporations or government. This is illustrated in TNX's inclusion of two environmental groups in seeking government approval for further acquisitions. In another example, when the Nature Conservancy, one of the biggest U.S. environmental groups, discussed signing an agreement with the state-owned company that owns and manages the Three Gorges Dam in China, it was both praised and criticized for its cooperation.[69] When an NGO becomes too identified with the organizations it monitors, the public begins to doubt its independent status. Excessive dependence on government grants can also undermine the independence of an NGO.

Although MNCs sometimes see marketing advantages of partnering with NGOs, they do so mainly for nonmarketing reasons. For example, Ford's reputation was likely enhanced by dealing with HIV/AIDS in South Africa and the Bank of America's reputation by its partnership with the Swedish environmental organization The Natural Step. In determining whether there is value in partnering with an NGO, an MNC is advised to consider four potential advantages: (1) an NGO's local knowledge stemming from their close work with grassroots movements; (2) an NGO's local network and partnership within a local community; (3) the social capital of an NGO and the credibility that it has developed over time in a country; and (4) an NGO's past partnerships with government.[70]

MNCs must face the likelihood that they will be dealing with NGOs, so they must be careful in how they view them. "Business cannot afford to fall into the trap of automatically seeing NGOs as enemies," said Sir John Brown, BP's CEO. He added, "don't accept the myths that they're all communists intent on destroying capitalism, that they want to stop progress, and are not interested in solutions."

Recognizing that some NGOs use terrorist tactics and hold such extreme views that negotiations are impossible, another observer, Jonathan Wootliff, the former Communications Director for Greenpeace International who currently works with global corporations to build effective corporate accountability strategies, advises:

- Do not underestimate or ignore NGOs,
- Do not rely on threats and litigation in dealing with them,
- Do not create confrontation,
- Do not think of them as all the same,
- Know who is watching you (often on Internet sites),
- Use the Internet as an advocacy tool and be prepared to move fast,
- Develop opportunities for dialogue, and
- Do talk their language.[71]

The United States could learn much from other countries about forming productive nonprofit–government relations, according to research published in *Nonprofits and Government: Collaboration and Conflict*.[72] NPOs in most countries have strong partnerships with government rather than the antagonistic relationships that dominate U.S. thinking. Government is a major source of funds and in some countries such as Germany and the Netherlands, where public authorities are under a legal obligation to support NPOs, give them a distinct bargaining advantage. Autonomy and independence are far less sacrificed than it is often assumed.[73]

## Some criticisms of NGOs

NGOs are sometimes criticized for acting like elitist organizations completely divorced from the masses. An article discussing this divides NGOs into three categories, according to the function they perform: (1) those that provide immediate relief to the victims of war, natural calamities, accidents, etc.; (2) those that concentrate on long-term social and economic development; and (3) those that concentrate on social action and negotiate with the World Bank, IMF, WTO, and other UN agencies. These categories are related to historical periods: early colonialism, helped by religious missionaries; the Cold War's threat of communism; and the spread of Western ideology in countries of Asia, Africa, and Latin America. When compared with their European counterparts, American NGOs are described as sub-contractors for the government projects in the Third World, serving as tools of American policy. As evidence, the fact is cited that more than 80% of the total spending of these NGOs is provided by funds from the government.[74]

## Labor unions acting globally

Labor unions are an important part of civil society. Although they have been losing power in the United States, where union membership comprises only about 7% of the civilian labor force, they are still a powerful force in most European countries, where they have achieved wide acceptance. A trend that MNCs must watch is that labor unions, concerned about multinationals and business-friendly trade agreements, have begun to act globally.[75]

Unions work alongside the International Labor Organization (ILO) to remove underage children from garment factories and coffee fields. Unions leaders are also demanding reforms in the World Bank and IMF, as their participation in the Seattle protests indicated.[76] The AFL-CIO has taken up the worldwide fight against AIDS, joining those demanding debt relief for developing countries and looked for ways to help workers in developing countries connect to the Internet. Labor unions seek ways to confront global capitalism on a more level playing field. Although progress is slow, today more labor leaders and workers around the world recognize the need for global unionism, and are looking for ways to give the old idea of worldwide worker solidarity a viable form for a new era.

The idea of global unions goes back to 1848 when Karl Marx and Friedrich Engels exhorted the workers of the world to unite. Confederations of unions in similar industries, such as metalworking, began to form across borders in the late 19th century, during an earlier wave of globalization. But in the United States and elsewhere, the idea remains new and alien to many labor leaders, even as those same international union groupings – now called Global Union Federations (GUFs) – confront a seemingly borderless economy dominated by MNCs. Examples of GUFs are the International Transport Workers' Federation, which consists of 650 transport unions, the International Textile Garment and Leather Workers Federation which brings together 217 affiliated organization in 110 countries, and Public Services International representing some 650 affiliated trade unions in 150 countries. [77]

# How mncs can build sound relationships

Principles of sound relationship management have been developed from the fields of organizational communication and development and both public relations and marketing. They apply to MNCs operating in the international arena.

## Basic components of a sound relationship :

1   **Mutually beneficial social contract:** A social contract is an understanding between an MNC and host countries or other stakeholders about the benefits each is to receive from a relationship. Both parties have confidence that each will do what is expected of them to satisfy the needs of the other and to treat each other fairly and justly. This requires an MNC to reach out and make an effort to understand the expectations, needs, interests, and concerns of a stakeholder or other player.

    A social contract may refer to explicit contractual terms, such as between an oil company and an oil-producing country. An example is the renegotiated contract between Petrobras, the Brazilian state-owned company, and Bolivia. [78] However, a social contract goes beyond formal economic contracts and includes general understandings between an MNC and its stakeholders. In its employee relations, for example, a company may expect high productivity and effort to improve product quality; in return, employees expect competitive wages and salaries and a healthy work environment.

2   **Disclosure of information:** An MNC must be open and recognize the right to know of its stakeholders. Investors have the right to "full and timely disclosure," which in the United States is backed up by Securities and Exchange Commission regulations. Employees and customers are entitled to safety and health information. Customers in China, for example, have a right to know that the chemical melamine is not in their babies' milk. Communities must be given information about dangerous products produced in their neighborhoods. The amount and quality of information

must be appropriate, accurate and truthful.

3 **Receptivity to information and feedback**: An MNC should seek information from others and be attentive to their attitudes. Global managers practice the "art of listening" and constantly set up systems for receiving information, for example, surveys, advisory boards, task forces, focus groups, and town-hall meetings. They are also interested in feedback – responses to what they do – by setting up grievance systems with employees, complaint systems and hotlines with customers, and readership surveys with audiences.

4 **Respect privacy and confidentiality:** Violations of the privacy rights of others are avoided, just as others are expected to recognize the confidentiality of company proprietary information. An early dispute in the EU was the transfer of medical information about patients from one country to another. Where the line is drawn is always subject to discussion and mutual agreement. One of the issues facing banks in countries such as Liechtenstein and Switzerland is the extent to which depositor information can be kept secret from the home governments of their clients.

5 **Power-sharing and collaboration:** The information and ideas received from others influence decision making and, in advanced relationships, decision making is shared through collaboration, for example, by meeting with consumers or consumer groups directly, exchanging information and views in advisory boards, and establishing public/private partnerships. Dialogue and negotiations are encouraged and win-win, reflecting mutual benefit, is the goal.

6 **Countervailing power:** Conflicts with other stakeholders are expected when the above power-sharing processes are inadequate or break down. Groups – such as consumer organizations, labor unions, and environmental groups or other NGOs – are recognized, and dialogue and negotiations considered.[79]

7 **Social responsibility to others is recognized.** Beyond the parties with whom one normally deals, there is a mutual commitment to be socially responsive to other interests, especially when social costs are created. This is the subject of corporate social responsibility, including philanthropy and cause-related marketing, and is the subject of Chapter 15 which discusses global corporate citizenship.

## Relationship outcomes

The outcomes of organization–public relationships have been summarized by James Grunig and Hi-Hui Huang as follows: (1) control mutuality: "the degree to which partners agree about which of them should decide relationship goals and behavioral routines," (2) trust, (3) relational satisfaction: "degree to which both organization and public are satisfied with their relationship," and (4) relational commitment: "an enduring desire to maintain a valued relationship."[80]

### Trust

Trust is the basic outcome of sounds relationships. The dictionary defines trust as "assured reliance on the character, ability, strength, or truth of someone or something."[81] It is also defined as "a willingness to risk oneself because the relational partner is perceived as benevolent and honest."[82] Trust is particularly important in the international arena because social capital, which produces trust in well-established communities, may not exist. When both the organization and a stakeholder group fulfill each other's expectations and produce mutual satisfaction, trust is advanced. This happens, for example, employees feel they are paid fair wages and benefits and that other personal needs are cared for; investors feel that the dividends or interest received are satisfactory; the community is happy with the jobs provided, taxes paid, and other benefits received from a company; customers are pleased with the variety, quality and price of products and services purchased.

Trust among all participants in common endeavors is the fundamental requirement for successful enterprises. As the relationship literature states: Organization–public relationships are likely to be considered successful to "the degree that the organization and publics trust one another, agree on who has rightful power to influence, experience satisfaction with each other, and commit oneself to one another."[83] Trustworthiness is also one of the foundations of credibility (the others being expertise and popularity). Communications are severely impaired when the credibility of someone is doubted, resulting in a lack of belief.

## Mutual satisfaction

Although trust is the most important outcome of sound relationships, other related outcomes are also achieved. One is "relational satisfaction," which engenders loyalty to one another. It is defined as the "degree to which both organization and public are satisfied with their relationship"; each is committed to the other and they want the relationship to continue. As Hon and Grunig state, "the extent to which each party believes and feels that the relationship is worth spending energy to maintain and promote" measures commitment.[84] They therefore have a long-term time perspective. An organization does not just keep employees for short-term needs but looks to future workforce requirements. And responsibility to customers goes beyond satisfaction with a current transaction to promise for long-term product stewardship.

## Harmony and social stability

Another outcome of good relationships is harmony and social stability, which in various nations is problematical. It is the norm, however, in the Confucian cultures of many Asian countries. The literature on relationship outcomes treats this subject in terms of control mutuality – "the degree to which partners agree about which of them should decide relationship goals and behavioral routines... an enduring desire to maintain a valued relationship."[85]

Social stability must be earned through improved policies and by engaging in participatory decision making with NGOs and others. It is evidenced when various parties are willing to face problems and conflicts in their relationship and seek to find agreement. In the words of Roger Fisher and Scott Brown in *Getting Together: Building Relationships as We Negotiate*, a tolerance is built for conflict.[86] The authors remind us that the party with whom we negotiate is also entitled to have interests, and these may differ from ours. Perhaps that is why the American Management Association definition of management is getting things done through other people for mutual benefit. The ultimate benefit of establishing good business–society relationships for an MNC is the acceptance of it and the free market system.

# Conclusions

Global managers interact with many international public sector and private sector players, making a knowledge of them important. Among public sector institutions, the UN is best known, but MNCs are likely to be more affected by the WTO and the IMF. On a regional level, MNCs have had several significant skirmishes with the EU on such major issues as antitrust and acceptance of genetically modified crops and foods.

Among private sector players, the role of civil society organizations has grown. NGOs have been the most active among them. They have been demanding a greater voice in the affairs of MNCs, nation-states, the EU, and the UN. Although associated mainly with environmental issues, such as Shell's disposal of the Brent Spar oil rig, NGOs have also had many confrontations with the pharmaceutical industry over the HIV/AIDs issue in South Africa and with Nike over human rights issues. A positive trend is the willingness of some NGOs to form collaborative relationships with MNCs.

The building of sound, enduring relationships with other international players must be the goal of MNCs that expect to operate profitably in the long run. An examination of the ingredients of a healthy relationship should therefore be examined and efforts made to achieve the criteria.

## Revision Questions

1. Discuss and illustrate the roles and power of the three major institutions in the international arena: MNCs, supranational organizations, and civil society.
2. Describe some confrontations faced by MNCs in dealing with the EU and NGOs.
3. Describe some of the political and cultural differences among nation-states.
4. What kind of multinational company is the following: "We distribute our products in about 100 countries. We manufacture in over 17 countries and do research and development in three countries. We look at all new investment projects – both domestic and overseas – using exactly the same criteria"?[87]
5. Why is the establishment of sound and durable long-term relationships a major concern of global managers? How can such relationships be maintained with NGOs?

## Discussion Questions

I. Discuss how MNCs must think and do things differently when they are seen as having supplanted governments as the dominant economic force in the world?
II. In the classification of MNCs as ethnocentric, polycentric or geocentric companies, what are the advantages and disadvantages of being a geocentric company?
III. Who was right in the Brent Spar incident: Shell or Greenpeace? Why? What lessons can be learned from this confrontation?
IV. Why should MNCs care about trying to establish harmony and social stability in its relationship with other players? Don't these concerns interfere with the operation of the free market system?

part 2

contemporary
issues

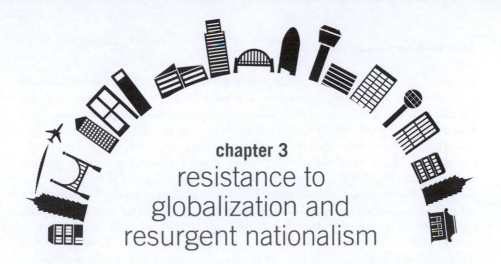

## chapter 3
# resistance to globalization and resurgent nationalism

**Objectives**

1. Appreciate the benefits of globalization, including noneconomic benefits, and also to understand some major arguments against globalization based on its impact on income and wealth disparities.
2. Recognize that public opinion surveys reflect growing antipathy toward globalization.
3. Understand the sentiments underlying protests and know what groups have organized major protests throughout the world and the degree to which they were successful.
4. Recognize the indicators that nationalistic sentiments and actions are on the rise and what countries establish and exploit nationalistic policies.
5. Recognize and understand at least five remedies that have been proposed to preserve the globalization movement.

Under the banner of the free market system, corporations have greatly expanded sales and operations throughout the world since the end of World War II. After the abandonment of mercantilism over two centuries ago, support of free trade among nations has grown steadfastly. The voices favoring globalization were so strong and seemingly unanimous that MNCs were unaware that resistance was developing. Occasional articles appeared about job loss in the United States and huge trade deficits, but the need to reexamine globalization remained unrecognized.

The "Battle of Seattle" in 1999 served as a wake-up call for MNCs and the world institutions of the World Bank and International Monetary Fund (IMF). Organized protests by students, trade unions, and a variety of civil society organizations changed the landscape of globalization. Annual protests became commonplace and more critical articles about globalization appeared in publications. Their flavor is reflected in Jane Sasseen's *BusinessWeek* article, "Economists Rethink Free Trade." She wrote: "something momentous is happening inside the church of free trade":

> Doubts are creeping in. We're not talking wholesale, dramatic repudiation of the theory. Economist are, however, noting that their ideas can't explain the disturbing stagnation in income that much of the middle class is experiencing. They also fear a protectionist backlash unless more is done to help those who are losing out.[1]

The impact of globalization was being reevaluated by economists ranging from Alan S. Blinder, former vice-chairman of the Federal Reserve and member of the Council of

43

Economic Advisers in the Clinton Administration, to Dartmouth University's Matthew J. Slaughter, an international economist who served on President George W. Bush's Council of Economic Advisers. Slaughter pointed out that income growth had all but disappeared in recent years and that inflation-adjusted earnings had fallen in every educational category other than the 4% who held doctorates or professional degrees.[2]

Faith in globalization, along with the free market system, received its greatest challenge with the global recession of 2008. When the economic stimulus plan was discussed in Congress, the ultra-protectionist slogan "Buy America" was heard. A surge of protectionism appeared worldwide. According to a World Trade Organization (WTO) survey, 16 countries launched 85 new antidumping cases during the first six months of 2008, compared with 61 investigations the year earlier.[3] Trade barriers of other kinds also loomed. The United States announced that it would increase tariffs on French cheese and Italian water; Egypt increased tariffs on sugar imports, and Brazil and Argentina asked Mercosur, the Latin American free trade area, for tariff increases.[4] Nationalism reappeared as nations sought to safeguard their key industries.

Because of doubts about globalization, managers turned to risk management to identify global risks, analyze them, and figure out how to deal with them. The broader perspective of "enterprise risk management defined enterprise risk management" (ERM) became especially appropriate.[5] The Conference Board defines ERM as "an in-depth, proactive approach to preventing, mitigating, and otherwise dealing with all the relevant risks to an organization – strategic, operational, financial, legal, and so on."[6] As stated by Richard Apostolik, CEO for the Global Association of Risk Professionals, "We're a global society now, and we need to review risk on a global basis."[7] The highest priority objective is to ensure that risk issues are considered in decision making and avoid surprise and "predictable" failures. Too often "known unknowns" remain buried within "silos" because of poor risk management processes. Douglas W. Hubbard, the author of *The Failure of Risk Management*, calls it a comprehensive approach to risk for the firm.[8]

## Assessment of globalization

A rethinking about the benefits and costs of globalization has been occurring. Economic textbook writers such as Nobel Laureate Paul Samuelson and Princeton University Alan S. Blinder who strongly supported globalization later raised warning flags.[9] The time is right for an assessment of the benefits and costs or globalization and the extent to which it is sustainable.

### Benefits of globalization

The chief benefits of globalization are the generation of higher living standards for people and the stimulation of economic growth in countries engaged in free trade. According to research by the Organization for Economic Cooperation and Development (OECD), foreign firms in a country pay better than domestic ones and create new jobs faster, which is even more true in poorer countries than rich ones. Wages paid by foreign firms in Turkey, for example, were 124% above average and their workforces expanded by 11.5% a year, compared with 0.6% in local firms.

Productivity gains are achieved through greater competition and technology transfer. Big firms are the principal conduit for new technologies, as evidenced by the fact that 70% of all international royalties on technology involve payments between parent firms and their foreign affiliates.[10] Other studies show that the income of people in countries that have adopted the free market system are substantially higher than those in other countries. The annual income of the poorest tenth of the population in the least free countries was around $728 whereas the poorest tenth of those in the freest countries did nearly ten times as well, with an average income of $7,017.[11] Furthermore, as consumers people benefit through cheaper goods and more choice.

The theory of comparative advantage is usually invoked to explain why productivity increases in countries engaged in trade. David Ricardo, the English economist who argued against England's protectionist corn laws, stated that "all countries can raise their living standards through specialisation and trade. Even if one country can make every-thing more cheaply than every other it still gains from focusing on the goods in which its relative advantage is greatest ...."[12] In the modern world, however, Ricardo's theory is replaced or supplemented by other ideas. Paul Krugman of Princeton University, who received the 2008 Nobel Prize in Economics, observed that a handful of countries dominate trade and in many cases both import and export similar goods.[13] His theory incorporates such factors as consumers' desire for diversity in their purchases, for example, Americans buying European-made BMW motorcycles while some Europeans want American-made Harley-Davidsons.

## Noneconomic benefits

A neglected aspect of globalization is that it benefits society as a whole and not only the economic system. Harvard Economics Professor Benjamin M. Friedman focuses on this aspect in his *The Moral Consequences of Economic Growth*.[14] Drawing on Enlightenment thinkers whose ideas were central to the creation of America as an independent nation, he lists the crucial elements of a moral society: openness, tolerance, economic and social mobility, fairness, and democracy. These qualities are promoted when a society experiences economic growth. People have to feel that they are better off, however, not only that they may have a satisfactory standard of living.

He fears that the moral character of American society may be at risk if it does not again achieve increasing prosperity as it did in the decades following World War II. Such prosperity must be achieved by a sufficiently broad cross section of a country's population, he says, if it is to foster social and political progress. But in the last three decades of economic growth in the United States, except for a brief period in the late 1990s, only a small slice of the American population has benefitted.[15] Despite the increased prevalence of two-earner families and two-job workers, most Americans were not getting ahead economically. The Census Bureau reported in September 2011 that the income of the typical American family had dropped for the third year in a row and was roughly where it was in 1996 when adjusted for inflation.[16]

The consequence is that the social fabric of America is being frayed. One indication is the antipathy to immigrants not known in the United States since before World War II and in some respects since the 1880s. But with the temporary return of economic advance for the majority of Americans in the mid-1990s, neither anti-immigrant rhetoric nor resistance to affirmative action played a role in the elections in 1992 and 1994.[17] In the national discourse on immigration in 2007, however, sentiments against immigration and giving amnesty to some 12 million "illegals" reached a high pitch.

Benjamin Friedman traces similar consequences to periodic slow growth in some European countries. In reviewing Britain's experience, he concludes that moral progress was more likely achieved when its citizens' standard of living was rising, and to move in the opposite direction when living standards stagnated.[18] In France, the average real wages of workers was blunted during economic downturns because of its more highly unionized labor force, but at the expense of continuing high unemployment. In early 2005, unemployment was nearly 10%, lower than the 12% in 1997 but higher than 8.5% in 2001.

As discussed in Chapter 6, the violence in the French suburbs can be attributed to the high unemployment of Muslim youths. The antiracist remarks made by Jean-Marie Le Pen, founder of the National Front in 1972, reinforced his image of a man known as a nationalist, xenophobic, anti-Semitic, and openly racist.[19] In reviewing Germany's history, Friedman attributes the Nazis' rise to power and subsequent attacks on human rights to the economic and political chaos of the Weimar years and especially its decline into the Great Depression.[20]

Benjamin Friedman sees the greatest need in the United States "to restore the reality, and thereby over time the confident perception, that our people are moving ahead."[21] He is amenable to public policy changes if that is needed to attain economic growth that can advance the standards of living of most of its citizens. Included in all the discussions about globalization, the connection between economic growth and the values of openness, tolerance, mobility, fairness, and democracy that Friedman documented must not be ignored.

## Costs of globalization

Opponents of globalization see its dark side in job losses in developed countries, increasing disparities in income and wealth, and the disturbing fact that the standard of living of the world's poor has not been rising.

### Job losses

The main fear of globalization in developed countries is loss of jobs, with much of the blame placed on unfair competition from overseas low-cost sweatshops. In the United States, between 1997 and 2003, about 2.9 million jobs were lost overseas to trade, according to the Federal Reserve Bank of New York.[22] In import-competing industries alone, 6.4 million manufacturing jobs were lost in electrical machinery, radio and television, apparel, motor vehicles, footwear, blast furnaces, knitting mills, toys, and sporting goods. Giant U.S. companies such as General Electric, International Business Machines and United Technologies had taken many of their operations overseas and become global enterprises with international workforces. Their expansion has mainly been overseas as U.S. multinationals were "decoupling from the U.S. economy," leading Michael Mandel of *BusinessWeek* understandably to ask "Multinationals: Are They Good for America?"[23] That is the question MNCs must answer.

The loss of jobs to foreign competition in the United States depressed wages and cut worker benefits as companies facing foreign competition sought to keep wages as low as possible. Of reemployed workers, two-thirds earned less on their new job than they did on their old jobs, and one quarter experienced earnings losses in excess of 30%. A consequence of globalization is that labor unions have suffered a decline in membership and bargaining power.

The loss of jobs that factory workers experienced for a generation was now experienced by educated, middle-class people as service jobs were outsourced or offshored to developing countries.[24] The new industrial revolution, said Blinder, was characterized by communication technology which allows services to be delivered electronically from afar, putting as many as 40 million American jobs at risk. His list of "highly offshorable" occupations and the number of jobs affected includes:

|  | Number of Jobs |
| --- | --- |
| Bookkeeping, accounting | 1,815,340 |
| Computer programmers | 389,090 |
| Data entry keyers | 296,700 |
| Financial analysts | 180,910 |
| Graphic designers | 178,530 |
| Medical transcriptionists | 90,380[25] |

Blinder told an audience at a Council on Foreign Relations forum that "offshoring" – the exporting of U.S. jobs – would be "the big issue for the next generation of Americans."[26]

The good news for American workers is that some jobs are beginning to return to the U.S. Indian call centers, considered a symbol of globalization, have lost their luster as customer relations became a major concern. Delta Air Lines said that backlash from customers convinced them to stop using India-based call centers to handle sales and reservations.[27] Chrysler made the same decision to improve customer relationships. Other companies also became aware of the disadvantages of offshore production Caterpillar Inc. returned some heavy-equipment production to a new U.S. plant as it became aware of such disadvantages of offshore production as shipping costs, complicated logistics and quality issues.[28]

The effect of Japan's Fukushima nuclear disaster reinforced awareness of the dangers of relying on vulnerable supply chains. Further reasons for the return of jobs to the United States is that increasing labor costs in China are narrowing the gap with American labor, and the lower value of the dollar makes U.S. products more price competitive. This return is heralded by Charles Fishman in his article, "The Insourcing Boom," in which he explores "the startling, sustainable, just-getting-started return of industry to the United States."[29]

## Income and wealth disparities

Job losses and changing composition of the labor force have resulted in rising wage inequality and increased income and wealth disparities. Over the past decade most

OECD countries have experienced rising wage inequality, as reflected in such headlines as "Gap Between Rich and Poor Widens."[30]

In the United States, an outcome of jobs losses has been a reduction of American incomes. The Census Bureau reports that from 2000 to 2010, median income in the United States declined 7% after adjusting for inflation.[31] The median income in 2010 was an inflation-adjusted $49,445.[32] In his article, "Can the Middle Class Be Saved," Don Peck reports that in 2005, three Citigroup analysts found that the richest 1% of households earned as much each year as the bottom 60% put together. According to census data, the 1% – a label that became common after a much-cited 2003 study of American income inequality – have an annual household income of about $380,000 a year. [33] They also possessed as much wealth as the bottom 90%.[34] The number of ultra-high-net-worth individuals in the United States – those with at least $30 million in investable assets – was 94,970 in 2006.[35] The rich last had this high a share of total income in the 1920s.

In the United Kingdom, the annual average income of the top 10% of earners in 2008 was nearly 12 times higher than that of the bottom 10% – almost L55,000 versus L4,700. In 1985 the ratio was 8:1. This pay gap grew more rapidly since 1975 than in any other high-income country, according to an OECD's study.[36] Furthermore, the money earned by the country's top 1% doubled from 7.1% of the total U.K. income in 1970 to 14.3% in 2005. And just prior to the global recession, the top 0.1% of the top earners accounted for 5% of total pre-tax income. Wealth disparities in the United Kingdom have similarly widened over the past 30 years. A report, "An Anatomy of Economic Inequality in the UK" shows that the richest 10% are now 100 times better off than the poorest. [37] The household wealth of the top 10% of the population stands at L853,000 and more – over 100 times higher than the wealth of the poorest 10%, which is L8,800 or below.

### Poor of the world not helped

Beyond the United States, the main criticism of globalization is that globalization is not helping many poor countries. Inequality of income around the world, often seen as the antithesis of justice and fairness, is growing, with the result that poverty remains entrenched in the Third World. The World Bank reported that the number of poor in the developing world was almost 1.4 billion in 2005.[38] The promised "convergence" – reducing the disparity in incomes and wealth between rich and poor countries – has not been achieved, asserts Joseph E. Stiglitz in his *Globalization and its Discontents*.[39] He acknowledges that although globalization has brought enormous benefits to some countries, notably China, in other cases convergence was not achieved. For example, the North American Foreign Trade Act (NAFTA) has not reduced the disparity in income and wealth between Mexico and the United States; too often wealth goes to a few people at the top who do not compensate the losers.

According to economists Pinelopi Koujianou Goldberg of Yale University and Nina Pavcnik of Dartmouth, "While globalization was expected to help the less skilled … in developing countries, there is overwhelming evidence that these are generally not better off, at least not relative to workers with higher skill or education levels."[40] Many economists also say that those with the education and skills to take advantage of new opportunities are the winners. Technological change favors those with more skills, and advances in communications have favored those working on Wall Street.

The IMF is often called the main villain in keeping poor countries poor. Stiglitz found deep underlying flaws in IMF economics, mainly its belief in market fundamentalism – the belief that markets by themselves lead to economic efficiency. He believes that the IMF has failed in its mission, pointing out that many of its policies have led to global instability, as evidenced in the Asian financial crisis of 1997 and the consequent Russian crisis in 1998. He says, IMF policies of fiscal austerity, privatization, and market liberalization show little evidence of being an effective road for growth. It appeared, says Stiglitz, that the IMF's objectives have changed from serving global economic interests to serving the interests of global finance. The IMF has since agreed with him, says Stiglitz, that "allowing unfettered flows of speculative capital is extremely risky."[41]

In sum, John F. Kennedy's famous aphorism that a rising tide lifts all boats is no longer true. "They know the economy is white hot," says political analyst Charlie Cook, "but they also know they aren't in it . ... There's a feeling that some people are getting theirs, but we aren't getting ours."[42] *Newsweek* columnist Robert Samuelson concludes, "No one should be happy with today's growing inequality. It threatens our social compact, which relies on a shared sense of well-being." While not fully understanding why workers feel this way, he believes "globalization, weaker unions, increasingly skilled jobs, the frozen minimum wage and the 'winner-take-all society' are factors. Another voice, *BusinessWeek* writer Michael Mandel, observes, "Incomes are not rising in much of the world, and adoption of market-based policies such as open capital markets, free trade, and privatization are making developing economies less stable, not more."[43]

Stiglitz concludes that the asymmetries of globalization actually wreck some boats and drag them to the bottom. He says globalization can help the developing world to take advantage of the discoveries and innovations made in developed countries, but they raise several concerns: (a) the rules of the game that govern globalization are unfair; (b) globalization advances material values over other values, such as concern for the environment or life itself; (c) globalization has taken away much of the developing countries' sovereignty and has undermined democracy in the sense that they are unable to make decisions in key areas that affect their citizens' well-being; (d) there are many losers in both developing and developed countries; and (e) the economic system that has been pressed upon developing countries is inappropriate and often grossly damaging.[44]

Even the OECD, which is a staunch believer in free trade, warned of a popular backlash. In its annual labor study, reported in 2007, it warned, "Millions are benefitting from globalization, but at the same time there's a feeling something's wrong with the process," said OECD Secretary General Jose Angel Gurria. He concedes that globalization has probably contributed to slow wage growth in the United States and Europe in recent years and is also partly to blame for rising income inequality The report said that politicians in the United States and Europe will find it increasingly difficult to sell voters on the benefits of free trade and open markets.[45] Globalization's benefits and social costs, therefore, must be reassessed and corrective policies and actions considered.

The danger of not addressing antiglobalization sentiments is that powerful sentiments by protesters may lead to protectionism. Global managers must be willing to examine and adjust wage and benefit contracts. Collective bargaining, more common in Europe than the United States, is still a good practice.

To help promote the globalization movement, business, government, and other proponents of globalization must vigorously engage in communication programs with employees and the public to demonstrate the benefits of globalization. The challenge is reminiscent of post-World War II when business feared that its system of free enterprise was threatened by socialistic sentiments in Europe and launched so-called economic education programs. More recently, many companies have published social reports or posted them on their websites. They can be used to address globalization concerns.

## Public attitudes toward globalization

The views of Stiglitz and others who voice discontent with globalization are reflected in public opinion surveys. A March 2008 poll, commissioned by *The Economist* and conducted by YouGov in Britain and Polimetrix in the United States, found that while slightly over 50% in Britain thought free trade was "generally a good thing" only a little over 30% of Americans thought so. Only about 25% of Americans said "globalization's impact on the domestic economy" was good and over 50% thought it was bad. Again, the British had slightly more positive opinions and are more internationally minded.

A GlobeScan poll released in April 2011 shows a sharp drop in American enthusiasm for the free market, the ideology that underpins globalization. Asking whether the free market economy is the best system, only 59% of Americans agreed. In 2002, when GlobeScan began tracking views, four in five Americans saw it as the best system for the future. Since 2009 support fell 15 points in a year. In contrast, the Chinese and Brazilians are now more positive than Americans.[46] The undesirable consequences of globalization have had an impact on public opinion.

The semantics of globalization influences opinions. People are not opposed to globalization when described as "global interconnectedness." A 2003 Pew Global Attitudes Project defined interconnectedness as "the experience people have in four of its aspects: growing trade and business ties, faster communication and travel, the growing availability of foreign culture, and the wide variety of products available from different parts of the world."[47] Although recognizing some of globalization's discontents, people were for the most part not inclined to blame such troubles on growing interconnectedness. People generally even took a favorable view of the institutions associated with globalization – MNCs, the IMF, and World Bank.

Exploring some discontents, however, the survey reported that "people in every region are deeply concerned about a range of worsening financial and social problems in their lives – a lack of good paying jobs, deteriorating working conditions, and the growing gap between rich and poor.[48] People everywhere also strongly believed that their "traditional way of life is getting lost." In many countries, the percent of respondents saying the gap between the rich and poor was getting worse included 67% of Americans, 68% in Great Britain, 77% of Canadians, 82% in France, and 90% of Germans. The percentages were even higher in Argentina (94%), Russia (92%), and the Slovak Republic (91%). The survey also reported concerns about the pace of life, fast food, too much commercialism, and genetically modified foods.

People's attitudes toward globalization are shaped by their personal circumstances and experiences with it. In developed nations, consumers have been the major beneficiaries of lower prices, and in developing nations more people have found jobs and were able to improve their standard of living. In the United States, employment has been polarizing into high-wage and low-wage jobs. Globalization and technology favor the most-educated workers but are eroding demand for workers who do routine tasks in factories and offices.[49] These differences among people influence their attitude toward globalization and must be considered in policy making and communication programs discussing the subject.

# Opposition to globalization grows

Resistance to globalization throughout the world is evidenced by three developments: (1) organized protests, (2) the resurgence of nationalism as reflected in the Dubai Ports controversy, and (3) a rebellion against free trade in several Latin American countries.

## Organized protests

The globalization issue has sparked protests in the United States and many countries of the world. The protests show how civil society groups successfully exerted pressure on the international organizations of the World Bank and IMF. A study of these protests is helpful in understanding how to management crises of confrontation.[50]

### Seattle – The turning point

The November 1999 "Battle of Seattle" is recognized as the turning point in opposition to globalization. The success of an ad hoc coalition of environmental, labor, human rights, consumer, and other activist groups that demonstrated against the WTO meeting was a dramatic reminder of the resurgent power of nonbusiness interest groups. In contrast, business appeared uninformed or complacent about the potential impact of the coalition.[51]

The media reported that some 60,000 demonstrators participated, including 200 radicals who broke windows and typically got most of media attention. Long before the WTO meeting, 2,500 campaigners attended a teach-in on the evils of globalization. E-mail was a potent tool that helped activists coordinate their activities. Lori Wallach, a Harvard-trained lawyer, and head of the Public Citizen's Global Trade Watch, a U.S.-based NGO that studies trade issues, was recognized as the leading planner of the Seattle demonstration. She was the glue that held together such diverse groups as environmentalists, human and civil rights groups, consumer groups, labor unions, farmers, religious groups, and think tanks. Wallach had rejected the notion that globalization holds the key to alleviating poverty and underdevelopment.[52]

Most of the demonstrators were united by one thing: "their opposition to the expansion of a system that promoted corporate-led globalization at the expense of social goals like justice, community, national sovereignty, cultural diversity, and ecological sustainability."[53] Some of the irritants were export subsidies, especially to farmers; America's tax breaks worth some $2 billion a year, with Microsoft and Boeing being big beneficiaries; and the abrasive style of Charlene Barshefsky, the America's top negotiator. "Many developing countries bridled at her clumsy attempts to impose an American-drafted deal that ignored their concerns." *The Economist* feared that the debacle in Seattle was a setback for freer trade and that it dealt a huge blow to the WTO.[54]

The Seattle protests highlighted two developments. The most important was the increasing role of NGOs in domestic and international affairs. The second was recognition of the strategic use of the Internet, which has no "central leadership or command structure; it is multi-headed, impossible to decapitate." It can sting a victim to death, says a RAND study by David Ronfeldt and John Arquilla. Negotiators and diplomats could no longer ignore this potent form of communications.[55] In recognition of the changing climate, business embarked on plans to win more advocates for free trade and globalization.[56]

## Other protests

Subsequent meetings of world bodies on the subject of trade – mainly the World Bank, the IMF, G-8 meetings, the World Economic Forum – were also marred by protests. The April 16–17, 2000 meeting of the IMF and World Bank in Washington, DC, drew 10,000 protestors; they were prevented from reaching the meeting site by some 10,000 policemen. A meeting of the Asia-Pacific Summit of the World Economic Forum in Melborne, Australia, in September 2000 drew 5,000 protesters, and the meeting of the World Bank and IMF in Prague in September 2000 attracted 10,000 activists (with the Friends of the Earth deciding to sit that one out).[57]

At the Prague meeting, protestors were repeating some of their arguments voiced in Seattle and making some progress. They proclaimed that "IMF-backed market reforms and World Bank-financed infrastructure projects – dams, roads, mines and the like – end up damaging both the poor and the environment in the developing world."[58] Patrick Toomey, an activist from Washington, DC, said, "Globalization has come to mean a certain way the process can happen, where the sine qua non is open markets for multinational corporations. We're for a globalization that benefits people."[59] According to one World Bank official, activists "effectively seized" the agenda of the meeting.

World Bank President James Wolfensohn and IMF Managing Director Horst Hoehler listened to NGOs. Even though they were unwilling to make concessions, Wolfensohn invited NGOs to sit on panels during the weekend's seminars and Koehler proposed that IMF officials meet regularly with the NGOs.

Among those who noted that protesters were scoring some points was U.S. Treasury Secretary Lawrence Summers. He commented, "I think the protests are a manifestation of a broad concern that needs to be reflected, because it captures important aspects of reality and it's a political imperative in terms of making sure that global integration proceeds in a way that works for people."[61] But he acknowledged the benefits of globalization, saying, "Far more people are poorer in the world because they live in countries that are insufficiently integrated in the global economy than are poor because they live in countries that are too integrated into the global economy."[62]

Politicians are seen as being more sensitive to public opinion than are business leaders. When business leaders were asked, in a survey conducted before the 2006 World Economic Forum began, whether politicians and CEOs paid too much attention to public opinion, 208 corporate leaders who responded thought that 63% thought so of politicians but only 13% thought so of business executives.[63]

## World Economic Forum

The World Economic Forum was founded in 1971 by Klaus Schwab and serves as a "lofty pulpit for those who preach that the best way to promote prosperity world-wide is through globalization of business, free trade and a reduced role for government."

Meetings are typically held in Davos, Switzerland, the town immortalized by Thomas Mann's *The Magic Mountain*, NGOs and other nonbusiness groups have been included. At the January 2001 meeting, the forum invited 59 NGO representatives, philanthropic organizations, labor groups, and other independent bodies, up from 46 the previous year. Among them were officials of Amnesty International, the U.S.-based AFL-CIO, and Jeremy Rifkin, an American author and globalization critic known for campaigning against genetically modified food. Also attending were six U.S. senators, a few state governors, UN Secretary General Kofi Annan, and presidents of South Africa, Nigeria, Colombia and Mexico, and big-name corporate executives, for example, Microsoft's Bill Gates and AOL Time Warner chairman Steve Case.[64] Because it is also attended by about 300 influential journalists, Davos has become a media event.[65]

In the January 2002 meeting, the Economic Forum discussed global economic integration. Considering broader issues, Klaus Schwab made a special effort to invite about 40 religious leaders to talk about whether Islam is on an endless collision course with the West.[66] In the 2008 meeting – attended by some 2,500 business, political, religious, and cultural leaders – attention was drawn to growing strains on the world's basic resources, food and water.[67]

## Opposition by the Group of 22

When delegates from 148 countries met at a WTO meeting in Cancun in September 2003, a new bloc of larger developing countries, dubbed the Group of 22, was formed under the leadership of Brazil.[68] They held firm in their opposition to wealthier country aims, which included approval of trade-enhancing measures such as investment rules and antitrust policies. In agriculture, the Group of 21 stuck with demands that the United States and Europe eliminate their $300 billion a year in farm subsidies."[69] The focus was on cotton, because "farm subsidies in developing countries can wreak havoc in villages thousands of miles away. The United States spends around 2.5 billion a year and the EU another $700 million helping their cotton farmers," which has had the effect of depressing cotton prices to historic lows.[70] Brazil and China, however, wanted to maintain high protections for their own farmers and manufacturers while insisting that rich countries drop nearly all subsidies and tariffs."[71] Robert Zoellick, Bush's top trade man, cast Brazil as leader of the "won't do countries." After the failure of multilateralism at Cancun, the United States declared that it would promote globalization by moving toward bilateral agreements, a move Stiglitz believes should be strongly discouraged.[72]

# Resurgence of nationalism

A major sign of opposition to globalization is expressed by resurgent nationalism and opposition to the free market system. In his *International Business Management*, John Fayerweather defines nationalism and national interests as "a condition of mind, feeling, or sentiment of a group of people living in a well defined geographic area, speaking a common language, possessing a literature in which the aspirations of the nation have been expressed, being attached to common traditions, and, in some cases, having a common religion."[73]

The underlying problem of resurgent nationalism, according to Raymond Vernon – called the "oracle of globalization" by *The Economist* [74] – is an uneasiness by national leaders in the countries in which MNCs operate that such enterprises will escape the control mechanisms that the leaders have devised, and fearful that the foreign enterprises will introduce elements into the national economy that will weaken the control of those national leaders.[75] Often an MNC is seen as an outsider to be distrusted and repelled.

## Nationalist sentiment flares in Brazil

On November 7, 2011, an oil spill caused by a Chevron deep-sea oil well, called Frade, 230 miles northeast of Rio de Janeiro flared into fierce nationalist sentiment in Brazil. Although Chevron quickly brought the situation under control within four days, Brazilian politicians and journalists were infuriated. The Brazilian federal prosecutor, Eduaro Santos de Oliveira, sued Chevron for the equivalent of $11 billion for alleged environmental damage. He filed charges against George Buck, president of Chevron's Brazil subsidiary and 16 other employees of Chevron and its main drilling contractor, Transocean. They were accused of "crimes against the environment" – that they knew they were drilling in a high-pressure reservoir, recklessly proceeded anyway, and caused severe ecological damage. They were prohibited from leaving Brazil. In early April, Oliveira escalated his total damage claim to $22 billion. Chevron had voluntarily shut down the entire Frade field after a second, but minor, seepage occurred.[76]

Bungled public relations accounts for part of the Brazilian reaction. Chevron had almost nothing to say in public in Brazil for the initial four days after discovering the accident. Buck had been instructed by Chevron's company headquarters in San Ramon, California, to remain silent until he and his colleagues had a sense of what had happened. He waited until two weeks after the accident (November 21) before he publicly stated, "Chevron takes full responsibility for this incident." At a congressional hearing in Brasilia two days later, he added, "Sincere apologies to the Brazilian people and the Brazilian government." In his subsequent series of public appearances, Buck delivered lengthy engineering and geology lectures in English to reporters who do not speak English. Recognizing his ineptness as a public spokesman, he admitted to his colleagues, "I'm just a driller."[77] He was deficient in crisis communication.

## "Economic Patriotism" in Europe and the United States

In several European countries, particularly France and Germany, and in the United States, nationalism has been expressed as economic patriotism. A major public controversy arose in the United States when on February 13, 2006, Dubai Ports World (DP World) announced that it agreed to buy Peninsular & Oriental Steam Navigation Co. of London, which owned and operated the Port of New York and other U.S. facilities.[78] The United States, the world's chief proponent of the free market system, demonstrated that it has not been immune to nationalistic sentiments. DP World, the third-largest port operator in the world, with 51 terminals in 30 countries across five continent, is a state-owned entity of the Emirate of Dubai, which is one of seven tribally based Persian Gulf sheikdoms that united in 1971 to form the United Arab Emirates. When the announcement of the purchase was made, Democrats and Republicans in Congress protested sharply, with some members viewing Dubai as a security risk. Americans were reminded that it was an Arab country that served as a jump-off point for 9/11 hijackers.[79]

Because of national security concerns, investments like Dubai's in the United States must be approved by a 12-member interagency panel, the Committee on Foreign investment (CFIUS), which is headed by the Treasury. This government panel was set up in 1975 to review the national security implications of potentially sensitive foreign-investment deals, particularly those involving military equipment manufacturers. The deliberations of CFIUS are secret, but administration officials provide periodic briefings and written summaries of all actions taken. In 2007, the Senate and House passed measures to strengthen congressional oversight of the vetting of foreign acquisitions and making the process more transparent.[80]

In Europe, France feared that Europe was becoming a liberal, open, free market zone. "France will never let Europe become a mere free-trade area," vowed former President Chirac.[81] Referring to resistance by the agricultural sector, he pointed out, "Farming is seen as tied up with France's regional gastronomy, its healthy food industry plus a charming rural world that foreigners love too."

Economic patriotism has also been applied to mergers and acquisitions by MNCs. Protection from takeovers is seen as a matter of national identity and well-being. France's Ex-Prime Minister Laurent Fabius wants measures to protect firms from hostile takeovers and to penalize attempts by firms to relocate in their search of lower costs. France has identified ten "strategic" industries, including casinos, that must be sheltered from foreign predators. Fueling the concern about foreign takeovers is the global orientation of MNCs.

## Sovereign wealth funds

The Dubai Ports controversy heightened awareness of the increasing investments made by sovereign wealth funds – funds owned by governments and invested abroad for income. But these funds can also be used to promote national interests. Countries amass such funds through oil sales or trade surpluses. Several governments understandably want to earn a higher return than provided by their previous purchases of U.S. Treasury bonds. Sovereign wealth funds are huge, although they hold a bare 2% of the assets traded throughout the world.[82] They are expected to grow, however, and reach $10 trillion by 2012. Morgan Stanley estimated in early 2008 that the UAE's Abu Dhabi Investment Authority owned $875 billion in assets, Norway's Government Pension Fund–Global owned $380 billion, and Singapore's GIC owned $330 billion.[83]

Keeping national interests in mind, Germany recently focused on protecting its businesses from foreign-government investors out of concern over potential acquisitions by newly cash-rich state corporate giants in Russia and China. German Chancellor Angela Merkel proposed legislation to protect German companies from unsolicited takeover attempts by foreign government-operated funds.[84] The United States has also raised barriers to the acquisition by foreign companies and nations of vital U.S. resources and facilities.

Russia's new National Wealth Fund, which began operations in February 2008 starting out with $32.7 billion, is reactivating fears in Europe and the United States that investments might be used to pursue political goals. Russia has a track record of mixing politics and business. The most publicized case occurred in January 2006 when the state-controlled gas giant OAO Gazprom briefly cut supplies to Ukraine in a dispute over prices, a move that disrupted exports to Europe in the middle of winter. A more recent case is the accumulation by Russian state-controlled OAO Bank VTB in a 5% stake in aerospace giant European Aeronautic Defence & Space Co. (EADS).

Contradictory statements by Russian officials raised doubts about Russia's announced motive of seeking only financial benefits, not control over corporations or political gain. Russian presidential aide Igor Shuvalov said that Russia might dump its stake if EADS was not more forthcoming about cooperation projects with Russia's aerospace industry. France and Germany see EADS as a sensitive strategic company in that it supplies military technology, including the ballistic missiles for France's nuclear submarines. Furthermore, Vladir Putin's top foreign-policy adviser, Sergei Prikhodko, said Russia might raise its take in EAD to over 25%, which would give it power to block major decisions.[85]

Responding to the fear that foreign governments are less interested in money than in power, sovereign investors have not sought board seats and avoid having any ongoing say in company operations.[86] As long as their objectives are purely commercial, fears of political manipulation are muted. To minimize the risk of future conflicts, the IMF has agreed to work on a code of conduct for sovereign wealth funds. The main scheme is to make them more transparent.[87]

Funds run by foreign governments held $3 trillion in assets at the beginning of 2008.[88] They are expected to be worth $10 trillion by 2012, and more will be heard about fears that governments are less interested in money than in power. *The Economist* states that countries could turn to financial protectionism.[89]

## Rebellion against free trade in Venezuela and Bolivia

In Venezuela and Bolivia, globalization has been challenged in a nationalistic rebellion against free trade and the principles of the free market system. Early in January 2007, after he became president of Venezuela in 1999, Hugo Chavez raised the banner of "21st century socialism," following the model of Cuba's Fidel Castro. He vowed to nationalize the country's biggest telecommunications and electricity companies – which were controlled by U.S. firms.[90] Later in the month he carried out his threat when he ordered his telecommunications minister to seize control of a Verizon-controlled telecommunications company before paying compensation to its U.S. owners.[91]

As a further part of his nationalization drive, Chavez asked oil companies to accept state control of their operations. When ExxonMobil and ConocoPhillips refused, he simply nationalized their holdings. Faced with less control of their investments and smaller returns, the two companies decided to quit Venezuela.[92] To replace their source of capital and technological knowhow, the country's state-run oil company, Petroleos de Venzuela SA (PdVSA), is expected to seek international partners.

Following Venezuela's example, Bolivia also targeted foreign companies by turning the heat on energy companies. Bolivia is rich in natural gas, having the second largest reserves in Latin America. Following the model of the free market system, Bolivia's former president, Sanchez de Lozada, a multimillionaire and son of a diplomat and owner of mines, announced his plan to export natural gas to the United States. This news was greeted by demonstrations in December 2003 that continued for several weeks and led to several deaths in clashes with police. Protesters erected barricades and blocked roads. *The Lehrer News Hour* carried the story of "Bolivia: Backlash Against U.S. Style Free Market System."[93]

"People have had it," said Kathryn Ledebur, a U.S. analysts based in Bolivia with the Andean Information Network, a left-leaning think tank. The gas, she says, is "a symbol of globalization, frustration, and the feeling that the government is not interested in the welfare of the people."[94] Lozada resigned, blaming antibusiness groups, which he described as radicals. He said the gas issue was distorted and that sale of surplus gas would have helped Bolivia get out of its economic crisis. But many feared that only the elite interests would have benefitted, leaving the masses, that earn only about $2 a day, not better off.

The antiglobalization sentiments reflected in Venezuela and Bolivia are the result of asymmetrical economic relationships between foreign MNCs and their host countries. Their national economies were not receiving adequate benefits – some would say they were being exploited – and a new "social contract" had to be negotiated. Most of Latin America's new or newish presidents have leftist leaning, including Chile's Michelle Bachelet, Brazil's Luiz Inacio Lula da Silva, and Nestor Kirchner of Argentina. Although they want to keep the liberalizing reforms of the 1990s, they want to combine them with better social policies.[95]

What Latin Americans mainly want, rather than socialism, is a fairer distribution of income and a state that gives greater social protection, according to the latest Latinobarometro poll taken in 18 countries across the region.[96] On the other hand, Latin Americans are becoming more equivocal towards the market economy. Compared to 2006, lower percentages of people in Latin America as a whole "strongly agree" or "agree" that a market economy is the best for your country."[97] That means that slightly over half of respondents across the region still favor the market economy.

# Making globalization work better

Stiglitz's *Making Globalization Work* presents a widely accepted viewpoint that "Globalization does not have to be bad for the environment, increase inequality, weaken cultural diversity, and advance corporate interests at the expense of the well-being of ordinary citizens."[98] His basic assessment of globalization is that it has not been managed well and needs more and smarter government intervention. Instead of providing a bigger dose of free markets, his remedy is to make the free market forces that underlie globalization work better. Rubin thinks likewise; he asks, if so many Americans are actually losing ground, should not government do something about that?[99] On the level of MNCs, one might ask, should not something be done about stakeholder management practices to create greater symmetrical benefits for their stakeholders.

Several remedies address dissatisfaction with globalization. Discussed below, these are: (1) more equitable trade agreements, including the curbing of special trade interests, (2) democratizing world economic institutions, (3) providing trade safeguards for workers and the environment, (4) spreading the rewards of globalization, for example, addressing income and other inequalities.

## More equitable trade agreements

As the nationalism of countries such as Venezuela and Bolivia and the Doha round of trade talks have demonstrated, poorer and usually less developed countries are dissatisfied with the deal they get from the richer, developed countries. Franz Fischler, EU's agriculture commissioner outlines the ways the United States and other rich countries violate free trade principles: "the $3.2 billion the U.S. used in 2003 for export credits to give their exporters an unfair advantage on the world market; the billions spent every year on export dumping under guise of 'food aid'...."[100]

The Doha Round, launched in 2001 shortly after 9/11, was intended to correct the grievance that previous rounds of trade negotiations had treated poor nations unfairly by failing to open the very sectors, notably agriculture, that would most likely help the world's poor.[101] But subsequent meetings, starting with Cancun and the rise of the Group of 22 described earlier, stalled almost immediately as European countries and the United States were unwilling to make sufficient concessions, especially in agriculture.[102] The United States and European Union have moved closer to agreeing on new limits for agricultural subsidies and tariffs, but concessions, called "purely statistic gimmickry" by Brazil Foreign Minister Celso Amorium, have not gone far enough.[103] A new issue has been introduced, namely, asking developing nations to open their markets to foreign law firms, banks, and other services.[104]

Stiglitz concludes, "In part, free trade has not worked because we have not tried it: trade agreements of the past have been neither free nor fair. They have been asymmetric, opening up markets in the developing countries to goods from the advanced industrial countries without full reciprocation."[105] He believes that social contracts should be drafted between developed and less developed countries. He wants to help the poorest countries of the world by having all countries open their borders to them. Europe already has open trade with poor nations, but the United States has moved more slowly. Labor flows should also be liberalized to become more symmetrical with free capital flows. Countries should open their doors to unskilled labor and then gradually to higher skilled levels. The wages at each level would thereby tend to become more equal worldwide.

### Curb special trade interests

Trade agreements, which should be only a few pages long, run into over a thousand pages because so many special interests violate free trade principles by seeking to advance their own interests, states Stiglitz.[106] Among the many examples of what many call corporate welfare is the four billion dollars of subsidies received by cotton farmers, most of which goes to benefit about 3,000–4,000 people. If the subsidy were cut, about ten million of the world's subsistence farmers would benefit. Brazil has already won a fight in the connection with the 1994 New Trade Agreement (an update of the General Agreement on Tariffs and Trade) when it challenged U.S. cotton subsidies. Referring to Europe, Stiglitz says that if the subsidy of about $2 dollars per cow were removed, many people who fall below the World Bank's poverty line of $2 dollars would benefit.[107]

## Democratize world economic institutions

The world institutions that have promoted globalization – WTO, IMF, and World Bank – have been too narrowly wedded to the interests of financial institutions, even to the point of being viewed "as a conspiracy to enrich bankers."[108] These institutions reflected what became known as the "Washington consensus," a set of policies supporting global-ization beyond the promotion of trade and foreign direct investment. It also included fiscal discipline, fewer subsidies, tax reform, liberalized financial systems, competitive exchange rates, privatization, deregulation and measures to secure property rights.[109] Stiglitz offers the example that besides reflecting the interests of the advanced industrial countries, or more precisely, special interests such as agriculture, oil, and finance, the IMF at one point demanded that it be allowed to force developing counties to open up their markets to speculative capital flows and "hot money rushed in and out of these countries, leading to increased global instability."[110]

Capital in the form of direct foreign investment is usually beneficial because it enables countries with limited capital to undertake productive investments. But capital in the form of "hot money," money that is temporarily invested in order to make a quick profit, is highly unstable and, as Stiglitz noted, can cause financial crises. Paul Bluestein's *The Chastening* describes the East Asian crisis which swept through global financial markets from mid-1997 to mid-1999.[111] Book reviewers Vijay Joshi and Robert Skidelsky say that what comes through clearly in Bluestein's study is that the "High Command" – the IMF, the U.S. Treasury, and the central banks of the main creditor countries – "did not have much understanding about what to do to stop the flight of capital, default on loans, and the contagion of collapsing currencies, which spread rapidly from Thailand to much of East Asia and then to both Russia and Brazil."[112] IMF bailouts only exacerbated the situation. As tens of billion of dollars exited these countries, currencies and stock markets plunged and brought millions of middle-class people into poverty overnight.[113]

Such examples convince Stiglitz that institutions such as the World Bank and IMF must be democratized to remove the dominance of MNCs and special interests. Robert Rubin, former Treasury Secretary and former executive co-chair of Citigroup, specifi-cally suggests that a way to keep market-based capitalism stable, broadly prosperous and equitable is to have its excesses checked through the countervailing power of government, labor unions and other institutions.[114]

## Provide trade safeguards for workers and the environment

The arrangement worked out in the United States with trade agreements is that if workers lose jobs because of trade liberalization they receive unemployment insurance and retraining to carry them over to the next job. The Trade Adjustment Assistance (TAA) program was established in 1962 to help workers adversely affected by increased imports and shifts in international investment and production. TAA provides workers with income support, training, and job-search and relocation assistance. More than 25 million workers and their families have been helped.[115] A Health Coverage Tax Credit was added in 2002, but it has not performing well. According to a survey by the Government Accountability Office, no more than 12% of workers at any site were taking the credit. They must follow an arduous ten-step process to qualify for a government healthcare subsidy. Besides the hassle, the program is expensive and many of the workers the program is supposed to help don't have the education level to understand.[116]

Federal Reserve Chairman Ben Bernanke makes the further recommendation of making health and pension benefits more portable. He offers three principles broadly accepted in our society that can help guide public policy: economic opportunity should be as widely distributed and equal as possible, economic outcomes need not be equal but should be linked to a persons' contributions, and people should get some insurance against very painful outcomes.[117]

Expansion of worker protection is one of the policy options proposed in a paper commissioned by the Financial Services Forum to address criticisms of globalization. The study was commissioned by CEOs of top financial services firms to address "sudden economic dislocation" caused by a plant shutdown or other factors.[118] Congressional Democrats are also seeking additional safeguards. One is a higher threshold for labor rights by using protections outlined by the United Nation's International Labor Organization, including tougher enforcement of conventions on collective bargaining, discrimination, child labor and forced labor. A second is paying greater attention to the environment, particularly illegal logging in the Peruvian rain forest. A third is the creation of a new position of U.S. "Trade Enforcer" who would bring trade disputes before the WTO.[119]

## Spreading the rewards of globalization

The fundamental opposition to freer trade and investments is that many countries and people are being hurt. Instead of interfering with trade, Lawrence Summers, the former U.S. Treasury secretary and Harvard University president, argues that other means must be found to address the salient concerns about inequality.[120] Among the most important are the measures discussed below.

### Tax globalization's big winners[121]

The taxation system is a powerful tool to redistribute the benefits of globalization taxing the winners more and the losers less. At present some features of the tax system further help the winners. Top executives of private equity funds, for example, can keep as much as 20% of the profits of their funds which are then paid out to them and taxed at the low capital-gains rate of 15%, rather than top personal income-tax rate of 35%.[122] The classical solution is to make the federal income tax more progressive.

Matthew Slaughter and Kenneth Scheve, a Yale political scientist, have proposed a better solution in *Foreign Affairs* magazine.[123] They start by saying that the commonly proposed responses of investing more in education and trade adjustment assistance for dislocated workers are no near adequate. TAA, they say, "incorrectly presumes that the key issue is transitions across jobs for workers in trade-exposed industries."[124] This overlooks the pressures of globalization and the spreading economy-wide effects via domestic labor-market competition.

They focus on the Federal Insurance Contribution Act (FICA) – the payroll tax – which currently taxes 15.3% on the first $94,200 of gross income, with an ongoing 2.9% flat tax for the medicare portion beyond that. In what they call "a new deal for globalization," they would combine further trade and investment liberalization with eliminating the full payroll tax for all workers earning below the national medium, which in 2005 was $32,150 and included 67 million workers at or below this level.[125] To compensate for the lost revenue from the bottom half of workers, they would raise the payroll tax on others.

## Better education and other remedies

More and better education has been a favorite remedy because America's economic future depends on the development of innovative technologies and products. But it is a long-term affair that does not help in the short run. Moreover, the United States is falling behind other nations. Foreign K-12 students consistently outperform American students on math and science. The College Board reported in September 2011 that scores in the Scholastic Aptitude Test (SAT) for the high-school graduating class of 2011 fell in the three subject areas of reading, writing and math.[126] Fewer students are entering degree programs in science, math, and engineering. Only about a third of U.S. bachelor's degrees have been in science and engineering while in contrast 59% in China did in 2001, 56% in South Korea in 2000, and 66% in Japan in 2001.[127]

# Conclusions

Globalization has unquestionably led to vast improvements in economic growth throughout the world and should be promoted. But its benefits are disproportionately distributed. "The anti-globalization forces are now in the ascendancy," states C. Fred Bergsten, a prominent advocate of globalization, who is the former U.S. assistant secretary of the treasury for international affairs and now director of the International Institute for International Economics.[128]

The drive toward free trade has come to a crawl as the cost/benefit ratio has lost some of its luster and nationalistic and other political concerns are challenging market fundamentalism. When impersonal market forces are no longer trusted, the scope for public and private sector negotiations about trade and mergers & acquisitions is enlarged. Furthermore, the rhetoric of globalization in the future is more likely to be couched in terms of politics than economics. As veteran public relations counselor John Budd has noted, "globalization is no longer issues of free trade, tariffs and quotes but also about culture, sovereignty and corporate diplomacy."[129]

Planned efforts by business are needed to address opposition to it. The answer is not just some kind of economic education program, but a revision of the policies and practices of MNCs and governments with the aim of creating more symmetrical benefits for host countries, their stakeholders, and citizens. Within the United States, government policies must address the problem of income inequality – not only by the favorite long-term solution of improved education but by enabling the workforce to obtain a greater share of globalization's benefits.

## Revision Questions

1. What are the positive and negative aspects of globalization for both home countries and host countries?
2. What is the evidence of growing resistance to globalization? By whom and for what purposes?
3. What is nationalism and how does it affect the globalization movement?
4. What are some ways the objections to globalization can be overcome?

## Discussion Questions

I. Wal-Mart has found Bangladesh an attractive country in which to have some of its clothing for women manufactured. But it faces opposition from some customers who object to the low wages being paid and fearful of worker safety. What should Wal-Mart do?

II. Caterpillar Corp., a manufacturer of heavy construction equipment, faces demands for a wage increase from unionized workers in Canada, where it has a plant in Windsor, Ontario. It is considering its options, including closing the Canadian plant and transferring work to China. What do you advise? Why?

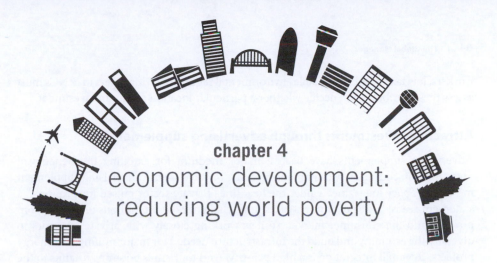

## chapter 4
# economic development: reducing world poverty

Economic development enables economies to increase their gross domestic products (GDPs) and thereby create more jobs, improve standards of living, and, especially in developing countries, help reduce poverty. Economic development is a major goal of cities, regions, and nations. Ongoing international trade and foreign direct investments (FDIs) account for most economic development. This chapter discusses the conscious and deliberate goal to achieve economic development in developing countries with the purpose of reducing world poverty. The eradication of extreme poverty and hunger is one of the eight Millennium Development Goals announced by the United Nations (UN) in 2000. The critical question for multinational companies (MNCs) is how much responsibility they should accept to help achieve that goal.

## Efforts by developing countries to attract foreign investment

Developing nations endeavor to attract direct investments from MNCs by publicizing the benefits of doing business there. Full or multi-page advertisements in newspapers and magazines, as well as distribution of brochures and holding of conferences and expos that extol their comparative advantages. These typically include a desirable climate, low-cost workers, low taxes, and "reasonable environmental regulations." Managers in MNCs must assess these attributes and decide whether a particular location merits an investment.

## Attracting investments through advertising supplements

Advertising supplements have been a major medium for extolling the benefits of investment in countries. Mozambique placed a 14-page special advertising supplement in *Foreign Policy* magazine.[1] Under the headline "Private sector poised for progress," a statement reads: "The government faces huge challenges to lift millions of people from poverty into the consumer market, so it is working closely with private investors to diversity the economy and build the infrastructure needed for major mining and energy projects. Regional integration is a high priority. And tourism is booming, thanks to the safe and stable economy – plus fabulous beaches!"[2] The first section, called "Wide open for business," begins with an honest assessment followed by an encouraging promise of the government's attitude toward business: "Mozambique is a very poor country. But challenges can also spell opportunity, particularly when the government views private involvement and investment as a key part of the solution."

Readers are given a wide array of facts and invited to "explore business opportunities in Mozambique."

Another country, Brazil, extols its advantages as an investment location in a four-page insert in *Bloomberg Businessweek.*[3] Under the headline "A Rainbow of Energy Solutions," the advertisement first praises the strength of its banking and financial services industry and then highlights its energy sector by describing it as "using its vast natural resources and excellent climate to generate up to 90% of its electricity from renewable sources such as hydro-electric, wind and solar power, as well as biofuels." It refers to its "extensive experience of using ethanol produced by sugar cane" and the potential of petroleum subsalt reserves. It claims that "Brazil's Information and Communications Technology (ICT) industry is the continent's best due to major private sector investment in fixed line, mobile, Internet and digital TV networks and systems." It also mentions IESB as "the best and most well-equipped Brazilian culinary school" and MAN as the "undisputed leader in its field" in using "cutting-edge technology" in its truck and bus design and innovation.

## Tourism

Many developing countries depend on tourism to stimulate economic growth for a large part of their GDPs. Tourism is typically the world's first or second largest economic sector and is a major part of some developing countries' GDP. In Malaysia, the tourism industry has been one of the country's success stories in terms of income generation, infrastructure development, and job creation. It ranked as the second highest foreign exchange earner. Through the multiplier effect, it has benefitted such businesses as hospitality, transportation, retail trade, and recreational and leisure facilities. Malaysia attracted 23.65 million tourists in 2009, up from 5.5 million in 1998.[4] As described in Chapter 13, countries engage in extensive marketing efforts to attract tourists.

Even in a highly developed country like Japan, tourism is promoted as a force for economic growth. It hopes to raise its GDP share of tourism-related revenues from 2%

in 2009 to between 3% and 3.9% by 2016. The Japan Tourism Agency set a target of 11 million visitors in 2011. A record 8.61 million foreign tourists came to Japan in 2010, largely from other Asian countries, led by South Korea, Japan aims to increase its "soft power" by heightening the Japanese "brand" in areas like sports, fashion and medicine. It also sees growth in medical tourism.[5]

# Reducing poverty

The United Nations Food and Agriculture Organisation announced in 2008 that the number of hungry people in the world had increased over the past decade. The measurement of poverty was the money income needed to avoid hunger. Using the World Bank's much cited "dollar-a-day" international poverty line, which was revised in 2008 to US$1.25 a day in 2005 prices, 1.4 billion people lived in poverty. Progress had been made since 1981 when the figure was 1.9.[6] However, if China, which accounted for most of this decline, were excluded, there would be at least 100 million more people living in poverty outside China in 2005 than in 1981.[7]

Income inequality is reflected in many ways. At least 80% of humans live on less than $10 a day. The poorest 40% of the world's population accounts for 5% of global income; the richest 20% accounts for three-quarters of world income. According to the United Nations Children's Fund (UNICEF), 25,000 children die each day due to poverty.[8] Using a broader measure, the United Nation's Development Program's Human Poverty Indicator, which measures the extent of deprivation and the proportion of people in the community who are left out of progress, reports that more than a quarter of the 4.5 billion people in developing countries still are deprived of some of the most basic dimensions of human life, namely survival beyond age 40, access to knowledge, and minimum private and public services. "Nearly 1.3 billion people do not have access to clean water. One in seven children of primary school age is out of school, and 840 million are malnourished."[9]

Poverty trends vary among regions. East Asia and South Asia, home to China and India, have seen poverty reduction. Africa, especially sub-Saharan Africa, continues to be a major failure. To some extent, poverty is mitigated when poor people live in rural areas where a subsistence life style includes living on their own produce and bartering to obtain other supplies. .

Beyond poverty other consequences of low income must also be considered. As Michael Hopkins suggests in his book, *Corporate Social Responsibility and International Development: Is Business the Solution?*, that poverty and unequal conditions in many countries lead to instability, corruption, and, therefore much unreliability in negotiating contracts.[10] Moreover, poverty leads to higher costs of doing business and a general reluctance to work and invest in poor countries. Economic development plans are typically the responsibility of national and regional governments. One way for governments to help, as economic historian Walt Rostow noted in 1960, is to create "the preconditions for takeoff." They include the building of "social overhead capital" – railways, ports, and roads – and finding an economic setting in which a shift from agriculture and trade to manufacture is profitable.[11] Such projects require large sums of capital, which governments can best provide. In addition to national governments, the UN can use the development arms of the World Bank and the United Nations Development Programme (whose resources, however, are limited).

## Deciding on business's role in economic development

The UN, which views the elimination of poverty as a human rights goal, has asked the private sector to accept greater responsibility to reduce poverty. As stated by the former UN's secretary general Kofi Annan, "The United Nations once dealt only with governments. By now we know that peace and prosperity cannot be achieved without active partnerships involving governments, international organisations, the business community and civil society. In today's world we depend on each other. The business of the United Nations involves the businesses of the world."[12]

Faced with growing pressure from the UN as well as some nongovernmental organizations (NGOs) to accept greater responsibility for economic development to reduce poverty, MNCs must decide whether deliberately to include economic development as part of their mission. They remind everyone that company operations have already reduced poverty, especially when they are also given credit for the multiplier effect of their activities. In *A Global Solution to Global Poverty*, George Lodge and Craig Wilson urge business to take greater responsibility for economic development. They point out that "poverty-reducing efforts should add considerable value to big companies in the form of lessened political risk, strengthened markets, cheaper or easier finance, and improved corporate reputation."[13] They realized, however, that it would require the help of the leaders of international development institutions and NGOs.[14]

Hopkins concludes that the need for business involvement is important because the problem of world poverty continues to be a serious problem that individual governments and the UN have been unable to solve. He states: "Thus my thesis that the UN and individual governments' efforts must be supplemented by something completely new, that is a major effort by the private sector, in particular by the large MNEs . ..."[15] Business is in the advantageous position of having a presence in developing countries, either through wholly owned subsidiaries, joint ventures or major suppliers.

Hopkins believes that multinational enterprises (MNEs) – his preferred term for MNCs that also includes smaller enterprises – are currently very much involved in development. He predicts that they will be more so over time "in ways that are hard to imagine today."[16] Their involvement is necessary, he says, because nation-states and the UN lack the will and the resources to accomplish the task. MNEs have both economic prominence and growing political power. He urges MNEs to adopt a "development vision," which is a statement on what the corporation thinks it can do in the development arena.[17] Such activities fall under the banner of corporate social responsibility (CSR) and he reviews several actions that MNEs can undertake.

Hopkins dates the shift in thinking about development to around 1969 when economic growth was considered not only a business proposition but also a social phenomenon for "eliminating poverty, unemployment and inequality as well."[18]

Development was also seen in the context of world politics, for it was the time of the Cold War when alternatives to communism were proposed. A strong case was made by Walt Rostow in *The Stages of Economic Growth: A Non-Communist Manifesto*.[19] He connected economic development to the political goal of encouraging poor countries to embrace capitalism and democracy, rather than communism.[20] Rostow conceptualized a five-step scheme of economic growth:

1. The traditional society where modern technology is either unknown or largely unused.
2. Preconditions for industrialization are created, for example, by forming a centralized nation-state.
3. The "take-off" stage in which economic progress becomes the normal condition of society and dominates its development.
4. A society drives for and reaches economic maturity by successfully supplying modern technology over a wide range of its resources, not merely over a few as at the take-off.
5. A society reaches the age of high consumption, as experienced by industrialized nations.[21]

Rostow's solution to the problem of economic development in developing nations is to help them in the "take-off" stage. This view was adopted by Jeffrey Sachs of Columbia University's Earth Institute and well-known economist and author of *The End of Poverty*.[22] He calls for a dramatic increase in aid to developing countries and proposes that nations contribute 0.7% of their GDPs to such aid. His aim is to kick start development in the parts of the world that are stressed.[23]

# Spectrum of business strategies

Global managers can follow three strategies in deciding on their commitment to economic development: (1) follow the free market system, (2) apply CSR, and (3) create social businesses.

## Strategy 1: Follow free market system

Following this strategy, an MNC believes that economic development will be the natural outcome from the process of globalization and the normal operation of the free market system. Accordingly, MNCs aim to maximize profits by seeking the lowest possible wages for workers and finding others ways to reduce costs. It makes the convenient assumption that the public interest, including economic development, is thereby automatically advanced by the operation of the "invisible hand." An MNC creates economic growth directly by providing jobs and indirectly through its suppliers. A "trickle-down" effect occurs from those benefitting from the wealth created.[24] These effects, however, are likely to be marginal, says Hopkins, because poor people in general do not work directly for MNCs and they do not create many jobs because suppliers to MNCs tend to be hi-tech and do not generally employ poor people.[25]

Supply chains, which Hopkins defines as "all stages of the business process from sourcing raw materials to delivering the completed good or service to the customers," are seen as the main contact between a corporation and a developing country.[26] The extent to which buyers are positive enablers of change depends on how far down the supply chain goes, the relative importance of different suppliers, the extent of international standards, and how important CSR is compared with seemingly lower-priced strategies. A report by the UN Conference on Trade and Development (UNCTAD) estimated that for each direct job created at the beginning of the supply chain, to indirect jobs could be provided by the end of the supply chain.[27]

Simply sticking to the free market therefore does not address the issue of poverty directly and efforts to reach the poor though the market system are not generally given serious consideration, following the rationale that the poor do not constitute what economists call "effective demand" – demand not backed up with the ability to pay. Helping the poor with food and other necessities is left to governments and relief organizations.

## Strategy 2: Apply corporate social responsibility

The strategy of applying CSR means that economic development is added to an MNC's mission by deliberately seeking ways to help the poor and other groups that are typically neglected by extreme profit-maximizing enterprises. To accomplish this goal, Hopkins urges MNCs to extend their planning and operations by adding "features" to their operations in developing countries, as illustrated by the following:

### Provide innovative products that meet people's needs

Products are downsized and simplified, prices are accordingly trimmed, and efforts undertaken to reach consumers in their local settings. For example, Danone, Bangladesh produced a very low-cost yogurt that contains all the micronutrients that children are missing.

Another company, Adidas, the German shoe manufacturer, in collaboration with Grameen, produced a pair of shoes for poor people in Bangladesh at a price of less than $1.50. Muhammad Yunus, whose Grameen bank innovated microlending, said, "This will have an enormous impact on health because poor people suffer from diseases like hookworm that come through the skin of their feet."[28]

MNCs can adopt existing products or create new products that might result from local R&D efforts. This feature illustrates how CSR efforts actually promote traditional economic objectives. Most obvious is "reverse innovation" whereby low-cost innovation are incubated in the developing world and then migrated to the up-market world.

### Enrich employee relationships

Instead of following the "subsistence wage" policy associated with the early days of the industrial revolution, an MNC pays at the middle or higher end of the wage scale in the communities where it operates. New employees receive basic training that helps them adjust to modern industrial settings and equips them with marketable skills. As Rostow points out, economic growth starts with the traditional society "based on pre-Newtonian science and technology, and on pre-Newtonian attitudes towards the physical world."[29]

## Develop the supply chain

Companies, such as Unilever, work with producers to certify products and assure future supplies. It enforces its code by conducting risk assessment that determines which suppliers are most likely to contravene any of these standards. It also carries out ethical audits, for example, visiting suppliers' production facilities, and draws up improvement plans and reports and discloses findings.[30]

Another company, Motorola, states in its 2006 social responsibility report, "We are significantly expanding our supply chain corporate responsibility program and participating in the Global e-Sustainability Initiative, in which it co-leads the organizations' supply chain initiatives."[31] In addition to monitoring for conformance with its standards, it helps to train suppliers.

## Provide or supplement infrastructure

Communities in developing nations do not always have the infrastructure to support business operations, a fact especially recognized by companies in the extractive industries. When the Braden Copper Co. in Chile discovered copper deposits in remote and undeveloped regions of the Andes, it constructed a cog rail to the site and built housing facilities for workers at the site. Oil companies have similarly built infrastructure in remote Alaskan sites and on their oil rigs in coastal waters. When MNCs move to developing nations, they must often build or improve roads, which can then also be made available to local communities.

## Develop community relations programs

India's Tata Group illustrates this effort by investing about 30% of after-tax profits in community development programs across India. Its centrally administered agency, the Tata Council for Community Initiatives, helps its companies through specific processes in social development, environment management, biodiversity restoration, and employee volunteering.[32] One of its companies, Tata Steel, caters to over 600 villages and several company towns in the states of Orissa and Jharkhand.

Another illustration is the Gap Foundation. It makes grants to various organizations and community programs around the world, focusing on communities where its factories operate. This is sometimes called "development philanthropy," which is simply giving money to a charitable cause to promote some particular aspect of development that is most commonly targeted at communities in which the company operates.

Although such initiatives are expected to result in future profits, a key motivation is to protect and enhance a company's reputation and to maintain constructive relationships with host countries. In pursuing its antipoverty efforts, an MNC may find it advisable to work with national authorities and international organizations to ensure democratic environment, peace, lack of corruption, reduce bureaucracy and antidiscrimination.

A common argument is that companies that operate abroad have a special moral obligation to be socially responsible and to engage in economic development. From a practical viewpoint, the key, as with philanthropy, is to find the right mix between a company's special strengths and the needs of the programs it selects. Yet, as Hopkins concludes, CSR as currently practiced is unlikely to play a significant role in reducing poverty in developing countries, despite the enthusiasm of many development agencies.[33] Poverty reduction would require a much more positive commitment, for example, to discriminate in favor of the poor in employment, or to provide goods to the poor at discounted prices.

## Strategy 3: Create a social business

A forward-looking strategy for an enterprise is to consider a new kind of business, a social business, that starts with a vision of social good. Making a profit becomes not the primary motive, although social businesses sometimes morph into profitability. The social good focuses on *Creating a World Without Poverty*, which is the title of a book by Muhammad Yunus, the foremost advocate of a social business and recipient of the Nobel Prize in 2006.[34]

Yunus's idea of creating an alternative economy relates to David Bornstein's concept of the social entrepreneur, which examines how business and management skills can be applied to achieve social ends. Bornstein sees them as *transformative forces*: "people with new ideas to address major problems who are relentless in the pursuit of their visions...." [35] Although his interest is mainly in addressing such social problems as inadequate education and health systems and environmental threats, what he says about the qualities of successful social entrepreneurs applies to managers interested in creating social businesses. He says that they must be willing to break free of established structures and to cross disciplinary boundaries, which includes "pulling together people from different spheres, with different kinds of experience and expertise, who can, together, build workable solutions that are qualitatively new."[36]

Yunus demonstrates that the free market can in fact be used to the advantage of the less well off as well as addressing the problem of environmental degradation. Government is not the answer, for "even an excellent government regulatory regime for business is not enough to ensure that serious social problems will be confronted, much less solved."[37] Yunus believes that the capitalist framework should provide not only "money-making machines" (the profit-making model) but also businesses on the basis of selflessness." These social businesses are mission-driven and sustainable companies. "It's all about using your creativity." In his book, *Building Social Business: The New kind of Capitalism That Serves Humanity's Most Pressing Needs*, Yunus calls for the creation of an alternative economy of businesses devoted to helping the underprivileged.[38]

### Microfinance

Microfinance illustrates the social business concept that has proven to be an effective tool for poverty alleviation. It provides funds to poor individuals/groups that cannot access the formal banking/financial system. Without access to financial services, the poor are unable to take advantage of economic opportunities, build assets, and pay for their children's education.[39] Microfinance was innovated by Yunus with the idea of giving small loans to people too poor to be eligible for credit from other banks.

Microcredit is the fuel that enables the poor to start small-scale activities that gradually lead to sustainable business activity. A woman could borrow enough to buy a sewing machine and start a sewing business. He favored women because he considered them to be particularly careful borrowers. He also wanted to raise women's social position in the community. Repayments were required within a short time – weekly, monthly or a few months. This dependence on repetitive financing provided an incentive to the borrower not to default. Peer pressure from others in a borrowing group reinforced this pressure.

Yunus founded the Grameen Bank in 1983. It disbursed almost $10 billion in loans by 2010, benefitting 8.3 million borrowers, mostly women, from 81,000 villages in Bangladesh.[40] The UN estimated that by the end of 2004 more than 92 million families, most of them living on less than a dollar a day, benefitted from microcredit.[41] Microfinancing grew most rapidly in Bangladesh and India, reaching nearly 30 million clients each. For his pioneering work he was awarded the Nobel Peace Prize in 2006 and his model has been exported around the world.

## Commercialization of microfinancing

A social business can become a commercial business. As entrepreneurs recognized the business potential of microfinancing, it became commercialized. For example, SKS Microfinance, an Indian company with rich American backers, planned to raise as much as $350 million in a stock offering. Its message has been that "big profits can be made from small helping-hand loans to poor cowherds and basket weavers."[42] However, a backlash to excessive commercialization ensued and the industry came under attack. In Bangladesh, the government capped the annual interest rate that microfinance institutions may charge at 27%. In 2010, India forbade microlenders from recouping more than LL1 billion of loans amid allegations of exorbitant rates and strong-arm collection tactics. Outstanding microloans totaled $25 billion in 2010 from more than 10,000 institutions.[43]

The motivation for restrictions in both countries was to defend the poor from getting stuck in debt. Commercial entrepreneurs, however, argued that high interest rates were needed to cover the high costs for making and collecting payments on millions of tiny loans, resulting in wafer-thin profit margins, which would make attracting private capital difficult. Furthermore, they argued, the alternative for the poor was to borrow from moneylenders who charge exorbitant rates. The *Economist* advised against attempts to cap interest payments and pointed out commercially oriented microfinance and the millennium development goals were not incompatible, given a supportive environment.[44]

Aware of the entry of commercial banks into microfinance, Yunus hopes that microfinance institutions will remain committed to their mission of helping the poor by charging low interest rates. He also hopes that appropriate laws would be adopted for microfinancing to access local deposits and enable the poor to borrow from them rather than seeking loan funds from commercial investors.[45]

## Other social businesses and investments

Yunus favors the social business model, defining it as a nonloss, nondividend company dedicated to solving social or economic problems. The social business model includes the concept of social investments, which are programs that replenish and strengthen the community's and society's infrastructure. Included are physical resources like roads and other transportation facilities, water and other utilities, a sound educational system that provides a pool of labor, housing, medical facilities, and social services.[46]

The Global Impact Investing Network estimates the size of the global social investment market to be about $1 trillion over the next ten years with potential profits of $667 billion. Opportunities would come primarily from emerging markets in developing countries in such areas as microfinance and green technology. But the financial return would be questionable because such investment must remain "demand-led, needs-based and affordable" and might therefore not yield a laudable financial return.[47]

In the United Kingdom, the government has been designing a Big Society Bank to build the market. The RBS Social Enterprise (SE100) Data Report shows the first year of results of social enterprises from the first index that tracks the growth of social businesses in the United Kingdom.[48] It defines this as businesses trading for social or environmental purposes. Companies voluntarily submit information for the index.[49] The social business idea is spreading and may gradually be integrated in the missions of MNCs.

# Illustrative cases of application of CSR

Strategy 2, applying CSR to economic development, has received the most attention as a means of combating poverty and raising living standards. The strategy is illustrated by Unilever Indonesia, British Tobacco Co., and the Tata Group.

## Unilever Indonesia[50]

Unilever has a strong belief in development. A report by Oxfam on Unilever Indonesia (UI) shows how the addition of a CSR-inspired stakeholder management orientation to its normal business operations can steer the normal operation of free market system toward the alleviation of poverty. At the time (2005), 50% of Indonesia's population lived on less than US$2 a day. An examination of company operations showed that there were both forward linkages through distribution networks and retailers, and backward linkage to suppliers that had the potential to ease poverty.

The company had a workforce of about 5,000, of which 60% were mostly permanent employees and 40% contract workers. Adhering to Unilever's Code of Business Principles, pay and benefits were above those required by law. In addition, the company provided high health and safety standards, good retirement and maternity benefits, sound workplace facilities, and a strong emphasis on training. Employees had a written contract along with clear procedures for negotiations between workers and management. The "job multiplier" was considerable, for when forward and backward linkages were included in the value chain, livelihoods were provided for about 300,000 people. UI also had an influence on other businesses that adopted such UI practices as health and safety standards. A further benefit was that most of its revenues remained in Indonesia, "through its local sourcing, wages, margins, and dividends to local shareholders."[51]

## British America Tobacco

British American Tobacco (BAT) illustrates how a profit-making company can assist economic development by embracing CSR. The highly profitable BAT, condemned by many for selling a dangerous product, seems to have sought redemption by setting the standard for socially responsible actions. BAT's philosophy is reflected in a social report that states, "we believe that companies should be prepared to 'think long,' recognizing that their investments are part of a country's development goal. Indeed we see a fundamental link between acting responsibly and generating sustainable profits."[52]

BAT reports on the following impressive accomplishments:

- Contributes substantially to the economies of over 100 countries; providing employment globally for more than 100 million people, and major revenues for government.
- Has been a leader in the Eliminating Child Labour in Tobacco Growing (ECLT) Foundation. Concomitantly it provides children "with an upbringing that gives them the best chance to succeed in all aspects of life."[53] In Brazil, children under the age of 16 may not work on small land holdings where tobacco is grown until they are first educated. Similarly, in Mexico, the BAT subsidiary Cigarrera La Moderna has eliminated the use of child labor in the tobacco fields, working with government and such civil society organizations as the Mexican Tobacco Growers Association, competitors and suppliers.
- Has tried to institutionalize its development assistance through working with partners in NGOs and the government and, where an institution does not exist, through the ECLT Foundation, which it created.

As summarized in its "International Issues Map," BAT says its values are in creating long-term shareholder value, engaging constructively with our stakeholders, creating inspiring working environments for our people, adding values to the communities in which we operate, providing suppliers and other business partners the opportunity to benefit from their relationship with us.[54]

## The Tata Group

The Tata Group invests about 30% of profits after tax of the group as a whole to invest in community development programs across India. It has a centrally administered agency, the Tata Council for Community Initiatives, that helps its companies through specific processes in social development, environment management, biodiversity restoration and employee volunteering.[55] Tata Steel caters to over 600 villages and several company towns in the states of Orissa and Jharkhand. [56]

Tata is an example of a "diversified global conglomerate," which includes several MNCs in their own right. These large enterprises are more ready to blur the line between public and private spheres. The Boston Consulting Group lists the rise of these diversified global conglomerates as one of the five trends that will shape the future of business. Tata is active in everything from cars to chemicals and from hotels to steel. Tata is so big that several of its companies are important multinationals in their own right. Diversification helps Tata to develop skills across a wide range of businesses. For example, Tata Consultancy Services, Tata Chemicals and Titan Industries cooperated to produce the world's cheapest water purifier. Tata's success is arguably in its ability to recruit talented local staff against stiff Western competition and to assure quality across a wide range of products.

The company's advice to Western companies is to form joint ventures with "old-fashioned" conglomerates in order to win entry to fast-growing emerging markets. Some global companies that are trying to break free of their national moorings include Alfa from Mexico, Koc Holding from Turkey and the Volorantim Group of Brazil. In India about one-third of the companies belong to wider entities. But they face problems. They have thrived because they have close relations with their national governments, but they are held back because they are far too susceptible to scandal and cronyism.[57]

# Role of technology

Technology has been a prime mover of change throughout human history and is a key factor in economic development.

## Some transformative technologies: Mobile phones

Mobile phones – as cellphones are called overseas – have an especially large impact. *The Economist* writes, "Mobile phones have made a bigger difference in the lives of more people, more quickly, than any previous technology.… Mobile phones will have done more than anything else to advance the democratisation of telecoms, and all the advantages that come with it."[58] Sachs calls the mobile phone "the single most transformative tool for development." The rise in home-grown mobile operations in China, India, Africa and the Middle East has been enormous. It started with the "village phone" model but now most households can afford their own handsets.

A producer of mobile phones, Motorola, said the following in its 2006 corporate responsibility report about how it benefits people:

> Wireless communication is transforming lives, especially for millions of people who live in poverty in the developing world.… In 2006, 1.6 billion people in developing countries used mobile phones.… Bringing the first-ever telephone to a village brings possibilities for the people who live there. They can work and earn income in new ways, giving them a path out of poverty.[59]

A *BusinessWeek* special report elaborated on "how basic cell phones are sparking economic hope and growth in emerging – and even nonemerging nations."[60] To illustrate, the report names the Kenyan village of Muruguru where "a mobile phone can dramatically improve living standards by saving wasted trips, providing information about market prices of crops, summoning medical help and even serving as a conduit to banking services."[61] Farmers have benefitted from the following services made possible by mobile phones:

- The Farmer's Friend in Uganda offers information services to help local farmers, for example, providing seasonal weather forecasts for a region to help them choose best planning season avoid droughts or flash floods. Farming tips are also given, for example, "rice farmers who had trouble with aphids texted for advice and received a message telling them how to make a pesticide using soap and paraffin."

- Reuters Market Line, a text-based service available in parts of India, provides local weather and price information four or five times a day.
- Google Trader, a text-based system, matches buyers and sellers of agricultural produce and commodities.
- Tata Consultancy Services, an Indian operator, offers a service that allow farmers to send queries and receive personalized advice.
- Nokia, once the world's largest handset maker, launched an information service, Nokia Life Tools. In addition to education and entertainment, it provides agricultural information such as prices, weather data, and farming tips.
- China Mobile, in conjunction with the agriculture ministry, offers a service called Nong XinTong. It provides news, weather information, and details of farming-related government policies.

Mobile phones have unlocked entrepreneurship. Plumbers and other crafts can advertise their services and pick up messages from clients without returning to the shop. A woman who runs a small business knitting cardigan sweaters can buy yarn or meet customers by phone instead of walking several hours to the nearest town or ride in a communal taxi. The handling of stock and negotiating prices with suppliers becomes more efficient.

Money transfer, also known as mobile banking, has become more popular. Various mobile-payment systems allow real money to be transferred from one user to another by phone, for example, by allowing someone to send money to family members. It has brought financial services within the reach of billions of "unbanked" people across the developing world. Biggest successes have been Gcash and Smart money in the Philippines, Wizzit in South Africa, Celpay in Zambia and, M-PESA in Kenya which is used to send money to family members. M-PESA is also used as a form of savings account.

Another application of mobile phones has been the introduction of prepaid billing systems. It allows people to load up their phones with calling credit and does away with credit checks. It saves operators sending out bills and chasing up debts.

## Technology transfer in Africa

The role of technology transfer in economic development is most recently illustrated by Africa. The continent wants to diversify African exports from coffee, cocoa, copper, tea, diamonds, and petroleum, according to a study by the United Nations Economic Commission for Africa (UNECA). About one-third of Africa's recent growth has been attributed to the commodities boom.[62] Now it wants to join other developing regions in building a sound manufacturing base to support the production of value-added goods and services.

Africa is succeeding in attaining economic growth. Its economies are consistently growing faster than those of almost any other region of the world. Over the past decade six of the world's fastest-growing countries were African. The World Bank's 2011 report said "Africa could be on the brink of an economic take-off, much like China was 30 years ago and India 20 years ago."[63] Africa is developing a genuine middle class. Although most Africans still live on less than $2 a day, 300 million Africans earn more than $700 a year and 60 million households have annual incomes greater than $3,000 (at market exchange rates).[64] The latter qualifies these households as belonging to the consumer class. In addition to stability, Africa's embrace of technology, as discussed in Chapter 11, is credited with enabling it to achieve these economic strides.

# Removing some political risk barriers to economic development

Companies considering economic development ventures engage in formal or informal investment risk analysis to examine both opportunities and risks. A firm-level study of 77 developing countries shows that constraints related to investment climate hampers FDI. The constraints include physical infrastructure problems, financing constraints, and institutional problems.

Exporter foreign firms are more affected by physical infrastructure hurdles and lack of skilled workers compared to firms supplying the domestic market.[65] For example, the issue that faced Park Jeehee, the CEO of the watchband manufacturer Timepiece, was whether to set up shop in Kaesong Industrial Complex (KIC), a South Korean manufacturing zone in North Korea. In the early 2000s, Hyundai Asan, a division of the South Korean Hyundai Group, led efforts to develop the KIC. Supported by both Korean governments, the complex was intended to promote "coexistence and coprosperity." Although haunted by glimpses of the abject poverty of the North, she favored the project because the workforce appeared organized and efficient and the manufacturing facilities were well maintained and up-to-date.[66]

Press freedom is considered an important political factor, said Hong Kong Financial Secretary Donald Tsang during a two-day official visit to Jakarta. It guarantees the free flow of information, which is needed by investors to assess the economic data as well as the political situations both inside and outside the territory of a country concerned. It assures that "There will be no sudden eruptions in a place without it being reported in the press."

Another factor affecting the attraction of foreign investors are profit margins promised by a country and their protection by the legal system. Tsang said a country's laws must protect every business transaction and must not put the government above or beyond the law. A nation's treatment of foreign investors as well as the existence of a clean government or corruption-free public services is important. Interestingly, he said that if corruption exists, its cost level must be predictable for investors. "If business people do not know the amount in bribes they have to pay in order to carry a deal through, they will not be interested in investing their money." Even in the presence of political risks, the real motivating factor is profits.

## Barriers of bureaucracy and corruption

Despite India's stunning growth, foreign businesses and investors have started looking elsewhere because of inefficiency and bureaucracy. Its economy had grown by nearly

9% a year and its rising consumer class bought cellphones, cars and homes. But in 2010 foreign investment fell and investors took over a billion dollars out of Indian stock markets because of questionable government dealings. A highly publicized government corruption scandal over the awarding of wireless communications licenses was one event; another was the corporate tax battle between Indian officials and the British telecommunications company Vodafone that reached the Indian Supreme Court.[67]

Corruption hinders economic development because it distorts the information needed to make a sound investment decision. For example, government tenders to construct a road or building should go to the company with the best record.[68] Corruption places additional costs upon society and helps to explain continuing under-development in many countries.

## Wal-Mart de Mexico bribes help retail growth

The temptation to engage in bribery is evident, however, in certain circumstances. Wal-Mart was eager to expand into Mexico at the turn of the century to beat potential rivals in expanding retail outlets in Mexico. But it encountered bureaucratic officials notorious for their corruption and slowness. By paying bribes, Wal-Mart de Mexico could win permits and approvals in days and weeks with what would otherwise take years to secure. Through its successful growth, Wal-Mart employed over 200,000 people in 2012 and is the country's largest private employer.[69] Mexican consumers benefit from a wider array of goods at attractive prices. Bribery appears to have helped economic growth and raised the standard of living.

The counter arguments are that potential competing retailers did not face an even playing field and that the new stores resulted in significant social costs. These include the loss of livelihoods for mom & pop stores, the violation of zoning regulations intended to preserve neighborhoods, and possible harm to the environment. These concerns are not addressed when government oversight is corrupted. As for Wal-Mart itself, it risked prosecution for violating the U.S. Federal Corrupt Practices Act (FCPA) and, as its own lawyer warned, also violated similar Mexican laws. Investors were clearly worried as reflected in stock price declines of 4.7% one day and 3% the following day after Wal-Mart's actions were reported.[70] Furthermore, Wal-Mart risks years of aggressive regulatory scrutiny, stiff fines and the appointment of an outside monitor to oversee compliance with foreign bribery laws. Its internal investigation may be required to span stores in the world, not just Mexico. Further dangers are that shareholders may sue and competitors who feel harmed may file racketeering suits, seeking triple damages.[71]

The whole bribery episode came to a head on April 22, 2012, when the *New York Times* published an investigative article.[72] It described how Sergio Cicero Zapata, who headed Wal-Mart de Mexico's real estate department before he resigned in 2004, helped organize years of payoff. This practice was continued by Edwuardo Castro-Wright when he became head of the Mexican company in 2002. He dispensed more than $24 million to *gestores* – people who know their way around the intricacies of administrative bureaucracy – to pay off mayors, city council members, obscure urban planners and low-level bureaucrats who issued permits. Expansion in Mexico was so spectacular that he was promoted to vice-chairman of Wal-Mart in 2004, became a member of the executive committee, and was placed in charge of all U.S. stores. Castro-Wright planned to retire in July 2012.

Wal-Mart became aware of the bribery problem in 2005 when it undertook an investigation. Revealing its hesitancy, it assigned primary responsibility to Jose Luis Rodriguezmacedo, the general counsel of Wal-Mart de Mexico. In an email to top Wal-Mart executives, Maritza I. Munich, the general counsel of Wal-Mart International, expressed his reaction in saying, "The wisdom of assigning any investigative role to management of the business unit being investigated escapes me."[73] Rodriguezmacedo promptly exonerated Castro-Wright and other fellow executives. The unwillingness of Wal-Mart's top management to vigorously investigate the bribery accusations was evident when H. Lee Schott, then Wal-Mart's CEO, rebuked internal investigators for being overly aggressive.

The *New York Times's* investigation prompted Wal-Mart to take the investigation seriously by informing the Justice Department that it had started an investigation. Ronald Halter, one of Wal-Mart's new special investigators who had spent 21 years in the F.B.I., was assigned to lead the initial inquiry. Damage control was now in full swing. David W. Tovar, Wal-Mart's spokesperson said, "We do not and will not tolerate noncompliance with FCPA. anywhere or at any level of the company." He added, "If these allegations are true, it is not a reflection of who we are or what we stand for. We are deeply concerned by these allegations and are working aggressively to determine what happened."[74]

As part of its aggressive steps to address the scandal, Wal-Mart created a new position, global compliance officer. It also added new "escalation and review protocols" at its Bentonville, Arkansas, headquarters and hired outside law and auditing firms to help with its reviews.[75]

### Energy company initiatives

The oil and gas industries have made recent strides against corruption. A major initiative of Royal Dutch/Shell is its six-step initiative against it. The company's "Management Primer" spells out exactly what bribery and corruption entail and the various strategies to deal with the problem. To promote its anticorruption culture, Shell appoints "Country Chairs" in each country in which it operates. It signs up to various international agreements and adheres to Transparency International's Business Principles.[76]

Transparency is an important consideration. A major initiative is the Extractive Industries Transparency Initiative (EITI) launched by Tony Blair at the World Summit on Sustainable Development in September 2002. "It seeks to increase the transparency of payments by oil, gas and mining companies to governments, as well as the transparency of revenues received by governments."[77] It aims to ensure that revenues from the extractive industries fulfill their potential as an important engine for economic growth in developing countries. More than 50 countries are dependent on oil and mining, yet are consistently among the poorest and most corrupt countries in the world.[78]

# Conclusions

There is a growing conviction that MNCs should play a larger role in alleviating world poverty. Even companies that restrict themselves to the classical goal of profit maximization can find opportunities in developing countries. Of the three strategies described – sticking with the free market system, accepting CSR, and creating a social enterprise – CSR receives the greatest attention. The advent of microlending has given strong support to the social enterprise model and attracted commercial interests.

Technology transfer has served as a transformative factor in economic development, as illustrated by the introduction of mobile phones in Africa.

Political risk analysis is used to appraise opportunities and dangers in developing nations. The problems of bureaucracy and corruption are especially harmful, as the case of Wal-Mart in Mexico demonstrated. The implications for an MNC's reputation can be especially damaging.

### Revision Questions:

1. Why is the issue of poverty in the nations of the world important for business?
2. What are the different ways an MNC can deal with poverty in a nation?
3. Some say that corporate social responsibility is the way to address poverty. What argument is made and why do you agree or disagree?
4. What are some of the ways that have been used by MNCs and others to stimulate economic development in various countries?
5. What are some of the "political risk factors" that MNCs should examine when doing business in another country?

### Discussion questions

I. Is it fair and reasonable to burden MNCs with the goal of reducing world poverty? Argue for or against MNC involvement.
II. Why is tourism such an attractive industry for many developing countries? How would a country determine what the potential of its tourism trade might be?
III. An MNC is trying to determine whether to invest in the economic development of a country with a low GDP and high unemployment. Which of the three options, if any, would be most suitable? Illustrate your argument with an actual case.
IV. To what extent, if at all, would you justify Wal-Mart's moves to short-circuit laws and regulations that it saw as hampering its goal of opening stores in Mexico? Was it a smart "calculated risk"?

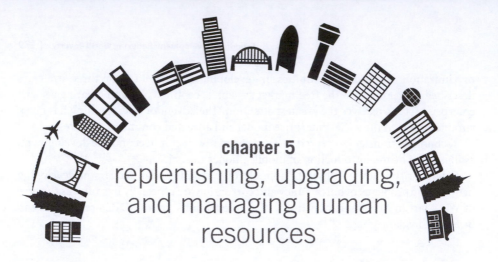

### chapter 5
# replenishing, upgrading, and managing human resources

---

**Objectives**

1. Know the meaning of third-generation globalization and how it affects the human resources function.
2. Recognize how "technonationalism" affects the kinds of workers an organization needs.
3. Understand why global managers extend their concern to the educational systems that train current and future employees and what educational options a company can consider.
4. Know how European Union (EU) countries seek to solve their worker shortage and immigration problems.
5. Recognize the human rights and other problems an organization may encounter when it hires migrant workers.
6. Know what human resources problems McDonald's encountered when it opened its stores in Russia and what it did to solve them.
7. Be able to describe some programs aimed at protecting worker rights.
8. Understand some country differences in human resources practices and how they are influenced by culture.
9. Recognize how human resources practices are becoming more global.

---

A major concern of the global manager is the availability and competency of a labor supply in an era of globalization and high technology. Families in ageing industrialized nations are not producing enough children to meet the needs of employers. They must, therefore, resort to recruitment from other countries. Immigrants, however, present special problems of socialization and assimilation. Advanced technology requires increasingly skilled workers, able engineers, and creative scientists, but educational systems in both developed and developing countries are not keeping up with the changing requirements of the workplace.

What is called the third generation of globalization focuses on the competitive advantage of science and technology (S&T) and the issue of technonationalism – competition for qualified human resources among industrialized and leading developing nations. To gain recognition and competitive advantage, Asian countries, notably China, Japan, and India, have in recent years given high priority to space exploration to the moon to generate pride domestically and demonstrate technological prowess internationally.[1] In Europe, competition between Boeing and Airbus over plans for the next aircraft has been called "the purest expression of European technonationalism."[2] The human resources aspect of these endeavors is an ensuing "war for talent" in recruiting qualified S&T workers.

The United States, which after the Second World War was the preeminent leader in S&T, began to face competition from such developed countries as Germany and Japan as well as the rapidly developing nations such as China and India. A skilled, educated, and trained workforce has become a key component of this competition, with some developing nations upgrading their workforces by hiring students who graduated from Western universities with advanced degrees in engineering and science. Technology transfer has also aided developing nations as sophisticated U.S. products were sold abroad and business alliances were formed. Both of these factors have hastened the decline of the U.S.'s lead in S&T.

For the United States, technonationalism assumes that national boundaries can "contain" innovation and that merely increasing the country's strength in basic science and innovation would lead to a new period of U.S. dominance in the world.[3] The United States would thereby offset the strategies of competing countries such as China and India that are crafting strategies to build up their S&T workforces and capabilities. To maintain its international economic competitiveness, the United States would seek to restore its global "dominance" in S&T.

Global managers face the problem of recruiting, upgrading, and managing human resources. This effort requires them to become more involved in helping guide and improve educational systems. Furthermore, recognizing that domestic labor sources are often inadequate to meet their needs, they must pay more attention to the mobility of labor between nations and continents. They must be aware, however, that immigrant workers are typically discriminated against, or worse, may suffer human rights abuses marked by discriminatory wages, poor working conditions, and servitude. They should cooperate with endeavors by the International Labor Organization (ILO), national governments, and nongovernment organizations (NGOs) to establish international labor standards.

## Improving educational systems

Contributing to a general shortage of labor within industrialized countries is the failure of their educational systems to provide students with the education and skill levels required by today's enterprises. In the United States, the educational system falls short in vocational education as well as providing a sufficient number of college students with majors in engineering. The result is that employers in industries that require workers with trade skills, even as basic as welding, can no longer find them. "There's a tremendous shortage of skilled workers," said Craig Giffi, a vice chairman of the consulting firm Deloitte. It found that "74% of manufacturers said a shortage of skilled production workers had a 'significant negative impact' on either their productivity or expansion plans."[4] A recruiter for Union Pacific Corp. describes how she could not find qualified workers for secure, well-paying jobs with good benefits that do not require a college degree. Similarly, AAR Corp., an aviation-parts manufacturer in the Chicago area, had 600 job openings for welders and mechanics but could not find skilled workers to fill them.[5] The message to employers is that they must examine existing educational systems and when these are inadequate either to cooperate with schools to adjust their programs or provide more company-based training themselves.

## Deficit in technology and science training

There are continual reports that the math and science test scores of 15-year-old students in the United States continue to lag behind to those in such countries as China, Japan, South Korea, and Germany.[6] Jack Jennings, CEO of the Center on Education Policy, a Washington, DC, research organization, confirmed that employers were right to be worried that the United States was falling behind. Some companies have addressed the problem. The National Math and Science Initiative was launched in 2007 – with $163 million of funding commitments from companies such as ExxonMobil as well as foundations and the federal government – to train math and science teachers and give more high-school students a chance to enroll in college-level courses.[7]

## More vocational education needed[8]

Skills must be kept at the cutting edge, but in the United States the educational system falls short on vocational education. Among the reasons for the shortage are an erosion of vocational education at the high-school level and a reduction of in-house training by companies and unions. Disparagement of blue collar occupations contributes to this erosion. A Delotte study found that although a majority of the public thinks it is important for the United States to have a strong manufacturing sector, hardly a third would encourage their children to pursue a manufacturing career.[9] High schools still focus on preparation for college, while vocational education, where it exists, is looked down upon. Vocational education in the United States is considered a "second-class" educational track.

The United States lacks the heralded apprenticeship system of Germany and has only a minuscule apprenticeship system, which is largely the province of unions.[10] Employer-led training, however, helps fill the deficit, for companies invest 10–20 times the amount spent on public-sponsored training. They produce higher rates of return since the skills developed are most closely related to job needs.[11] However, a fundamental restructuring of the educational system is required that would create new high schools that blend a strong education foundation with technical and vocational options that are connected with real occupations.[12]

Community colleges can play a large role in vocational training. Too many employers and job seekers currently view community colleges as providing remedial education rather than being a first choice for high-skill job training. Aware of the problem, the National Association of Manufacturers is leading a drive to establish standardized curricula at community colleges across the United States with the goal of preparing students to qualify for certification in industrial skills ranging from welding to cutting metal and plastics.[13] In Ohio, Lorain County Community College's Nord Advanced Technology Center has provided 41 courses tailored for individual employers in the latest schools year.[14] To improve community colleges in Chicago, its mayor Rahm Emanuel set up a series of partnerships between its community colleges and top employers to draw on their expertise to develop curricula and set industry standards for job training in such high-growth sectors as healthcare, high-tech manufacturing, information technology, and professional services.[15]

## McDonald's recruitment and training program

Some companies have established impressive training programs of their own. When McDonald's started its joint venture in Russia, it applied on-the-job training led by superiors or more experienced colleagues or foreign experts. This practice followed that of German and U.S. companies that spend a large amount of their time and finances on training their employees upon recruitment and throughout their careers. Higher level training was provided by McDonald's Hamburger University, headquartered in Oak Brook, Illinois, with campuses in cities across the world, including Sydney, Munich, London, Hong Kong, Tokyo, and Rio de Janeiro.[16] Its enrollment grew from 14 in 1961 to about 5,000 in 2007. As of January 2008, about 80,000 McDonald's employees from around the globe had graduated from the program. One student tallied up to a full year of college credits.

McDonald's centralized training program was founded in 1961 and grew to become one of the most globally recognized corporate training programs. It was an essential component of the corporation's business model because of the program's emphasis on the quality of training, which made it possible for McDonald's to maintain consistently high standards of service and quality across the globe. The program also reinforced McDonald's culture, which embodies a team approach and diversity.

Employees increasingly took advantage of the program and its upward mobility. Promotion from within is a part of the company's culture. It helps in recruitment and retention of "skilled, dependable, and enthusiastic workers" who are at the heart of the business. McDonald's also points to the larger economic benefit of helping to reduce poverty by providing direct employment of 1.6 million people around the world.

# Labor mobility – the immigration dilemma[17]

Labor mobility within and among nations is needed to fulfill the supply of needed workers. Mobility is high for managerial and professional personnel as reflected in the diversity of backgrounds of multinational corporation (MNC) employees. For other workers, mobility must often be stimulated by government policy or employer programs. MNCs have been able to lobby for reduced restrictions on labor flow to bring highly skilled labor to their home countries. The EU has helped by encouraging mobility among its member countries. Labor migrants contribute to the economies of almost every country in the world. The UN Population Division reported that the estimated overall numbers of international migrants exceeded 190 million people in 2005, constituting about 3% of the world's population.[18]

## Labor mobility in the EU

One of the goals of the EU has been to remove barriers to the free movement of labor. EU citizens have the right to live and work in other EU member states. Russia too recognizes the need to draw labor resources from the outside when the economy expands. Prime Minister Vladmir Putin sees the need for simpler rules of issuing work permits for high-level skilled foreign specialists – engineers, technicians, scientists, and managers. However, he believes that labor migration rules need to be made clearer and more transparent and that Russia "should not be a country where anyone is free to arrive at any time and no matter how."[19] He also believes that the migration service must coordinate with the regions and businesses to have a clear idea of how many people and of what professions are in demand in Russia.

## Germany illustrates the need for immigrants

A decade ago, Germans began to recognize that it was an "immigration country." To encourage immigration, legislation in 2000 opened the way to citizenship for the children of the "Gastarbeiter" (guest workers) and in 2001 the Suessman Commission underlined the need to recruit immigrant workers and do more to integrate those foreigners already in Germany.

Success in integrating immigrants into German society, however, has been increasingly questioned. Chancellor Angela Merkel declared that multiculturalism had "utterly failed" in Germany. Horst Seehofer, prime minister of Bavaria and leader of Christian Social Union CSU), said that Germany did not need any more immigrants from "other" cultures and called for a crackdown on "integration refusers." A public opinion survey showed that 36% felt that Germany was being "overrun by foreigners" and 58% thought the nation's four million Muslims should have their religious practices "significantly curbed."[20]

Germany faces shortages of engineers and skilled workers. Labor Minister Ursula von der Leyen warned, "We all have to be clear on how potentially explosive this labor shortage is."[21] A study by Germany's Association for Electrical, Electronic and Information Technologies estimated that Germany was turning out 3,000 fewer electrical-engineering graduates needed for R&D in technologies such as smart grids and electric cars.[22] Already grappling with one of Europe's fastest aging and shrinking populations, a further problem for Germany is that since 2008 more people emigrated from Germany than were flocking to it. Engineers, scientists, doctors, and other highly skilled workers constitute a disproportionate share of the retreat. Companies from China, Korea, and other Asian countries have heavily recruited in Germany.

Blamed for the exodus are Germany's tough immigration laws, a rigid labor code, and inward-looking hiring practices. The visa process is notoriously cumbersome and recruitment and welcome centers are lacking. Those who succeed in entering face discrimination, as revealed in a study that showed the callback rate was 14% higher for applications sent under the signature Tobia Hartmann than for those sent under Fatih Yildiz. Immigrants feel that they will never be fully accepted and that their social conditions will be inferior. German schools have not worked very well for the descendants of the guest workers; for example, only 9% with Turkish background passed the high-school exit test required to attend university versus 19% of Germany's. Furthermore, the country's entrenched seniority systems make it hard to rise in companies and it is too difficult to penetrate German social and professional networks. Speaking anything other than perfect German still stymies their careers.

In 2005, the German government established a national office of immigration and integration and created several new types of visas for labor immigrants. It started "integration courses," including 600 hours of instruction in German available to all newcomers.[23] Another action was to make entry easier for international students. Among the 60,000 students who arrived each year ,only 6,000 chose to stay. The Association of German Engineers reports 36,000 unfilled engineering positions across Germany. Regarding skilled workers, the IT association says there are 43,000 openings. The German Institute for Economic Research estimates the skilled-worker shortage is costing the country 15 billion euros ($20 billion) a year. No one in Germany or elsewhere understands very much about what attracts high-end knowledge workers.

Recognizing the rising problem of migration in Germany, broadcaster *Deutsche Welle* in December 2011 officially launched "Destination Europe," a project supported by the German Federal Foreign Office and aimed especially at young people in Africa. The multimedia project examines the challenges and opportunities associated with migration and presents a realistic picture of life in Europe. The 15-part series reports on the real lives of African migrants and follows them from the moment they decide to leave their home to their experience in Europe.[24]

## Rising opposition to immigration

Hostility to immigration has become mainstream, said *The Economist's* "A Special Report on Migration" in 2008. In Britain, Prime Minister Gordon Brown called for "British jobs for British workers," and in France a law passed in November 2007 allows DNA testing of immigrants' relatives who apply to come to France under a family reunification program.[25] As economic conditions in Europe worsened in 2012, attitudes toward immigration and the Schengen agreement, which allows mobility within member EU countries, are hardening. A survey by Ipsos MORI showed that a majority of citizens in France (64%), Belgium (62%), Italy (62%), Sweden (59%), Spain (54%), and Germany (51%) favor reintroduction of border controls in the Schengen zone.[26] The main fear of unwanted immigration is not competition for jobs but the perception that immigrants place a burden on public services.

## Problems facing migrant workers

### Posted workers

Employees who have migrated from other nations have faced barriers to equal pay and other rights. One type of barrier is that workers who are "posted" by their employers to work on projects in another country do not have the same rights as workers who migrate as individuals. These posted workers are treated under the "free movement of services" condition, which applies to employees provided by agency labor on a construction site or shipyard.[27] The motive of employers may be to reduce labor costs, but it may also be necessitated by requiring specialized skills not locally available. A result of this system is that posted workers may work alongside local workers but do not have the same rights. This condition caused a wave of wildcat strikes in the United Kingdom in January and February 2009, even though aggrieved workers do not have the right to strike.[28] Trade unions and policy makers have not yet devised a coherent response to the problem.

### Labor "refugees"

Migrant workers may become a new class of the world's "refugees" who are neither in situations of homeland reintegration nor undergoing incorporation into third countries of resettlement. Rather, their own lives and those of their children continue to exist on the margins of societies, outside of schooling, workforce, and other social institutions and with no meaningful sense of belonging, either at home or in a host society. Immigration as a centerpiece of globalization has meant that nation-states have not only become multiethnic, multicultural, multilingual, and multiracial, but also home to a complex mixture of persons with differing degrees of citizenship and status before the law.

In the United States, upward of 12 million undocumented persons, often called "illegals," are estimated to reside in the country in the early 21st century.[29] Those who oppose undocumented persons characterize them as parasitic and a threat to security.

Illegals are falsely connected to acts of crime and terrorism, which symbolically places them outside the scope of legal protection of the role of law and further magnifies their vulnerability. Groups seeking restrictions are increasingly able to mobilize resources and utilize the Internet, social networking, and other media and technologies to portray immigration as a social problem. In response, the 1986 Immigration Reform and Control Act enacted penalties against employers who knowingly hired undocumented workers.

A critical immigration issue is whether aliens or migrant laborers (noncitizens) have the same human rights protections as citizens. Undocumented workers constitute "a new, legally constrained underclass." Immigrants have ill-defined or nonexistent membership, civil status, and legal protection within host societies. This situation threatens the rule of law. The contemporary movement of persons across borders has the effect of commodifying labor under the auspices of global capitalism, which fuels pervasive illegality and invites the unchecked domination and exploitation of migrant labor.

Rights violations are set when governments from sending countries as well as employers from receiving countries fail to see migrant workers as "individuals entitled to full enjoyment of their human rights."[30] Legal scholars have noted that international human rights standards, because they are predicated on one's status as a human being rather than one's affiliation with a particular nation-state, are brought into sharpest relief and most clearly tested by the treatment of foreign nationals.

Supporters of the Global Compact propose that for future anniversaries the compact should be further articulated to make clear that responsibilities for migration patterns are held by the private sector as well as by governments and that governmental policies cannot deal adequately with the issues without collaboration from private institutions. One of the Global Compact's ten principles already contains the following provisions relevant to labor: freedom of association and effective recognition of the right to collective bargaining; the elimination of all forms of forced and compulsory labor; the effective abolition of child labor; and the elimination of discrimination in respect of employment and occupation.[31]

## Consensus growing on immigration

A helpful development is that some NGOs and countries have reached a new consensus on immigration, viewing it as a net positive force for immigrants, origin countries, and host societies alike. They see immigrants, rather than competing with natives and pulling down wages, filling labor-force demands in host societies, especially in the face of steep fertility declines and other socio-demographic trends impacting native labor supply. Immigration is, therefore, seen as exerting a long-term and net positive effect on both originating and destination societies. Nonetheless, in terms of labor market and other outcomes, immigration still often arouses nativism and intragroup conflict in host societies.

In support of its policy, the EU placed a four-page advertisement in the magazine *Foreign Policy* in January/February 2012 on "Immigration and Integration."[32] It stated that EU was home to more than 20 million immigrants, who represent about 4% of the total EU population (which was given as 503 million in 2010). The EU statement said, "To remain competitive and allow it to maintain its social model in a sustainable way, Europe needs to adopt measures to improve the employment rates of EU residents, but must at the same time take concrete steps to meet its projected labor needs via targeted immigration of third country nations."[33] A page, devoted to "Managing Immigration," listed various standards to facilitate immigration of such specific categories as highly skilled workers (who are given an EU Blue Card), researchers (who are invited to a "fast track" procedure), students, intracorporate transfers, seasonal workers, family reunification, and long-term residents.

Another page discusses the "Integration of Immigrants" and lists 11 Common Basic Principles that offer a framework for immigrants' successful integration into society. Also mentioned are the findings of a Eurobarometer public opinion survey conducted in spring of 2011. It stated that EU citizens think the four most important factors that facilitate integration are (1) speaking the language; (2) having a job; (3) respecting local cultures; and (4) enjoying legal status. A statement on religion and integration said: "The EU's Charter of Fundamental Rights guarantees the practices of diverse cultures and religions, which must be safeguarded unless they conflict with inviolable European rights or national law."[34]

## Efforts to protect workers

### Migrant worker protection[35]

Various efforts have been undertaken to protect migrant workers. The ILO realized that globalization had spurred a downgrading of labor regulation set at the national level and that it had to upgrade labor standards through a combination of defining global norms and pursuing local implementation. The ILO illustrated its position by showing how the voluntary implementation approach worked in the Better Factories Cambodia and Factory Improvement Programs.[36] These programs evolved into monitoring and capacity building by government which improved conditions for Cambodia's garment workers.

In 2010, the ILO published a book on *International Labour Migration, A Rights-Based Approach* to further protect migrant workers.[37] The book explains what motivates people to seek work outside their country of origin and how both origin and destination countries are affected. Its main purpose, however, is to expose the often limited access of migrant workers to their fundamental rights at work. The book also describes the international norms that have evolved to protect migrant workers and ensure decent work for all.

Another effort to protect migrant workers is a report by BSR on international labor migration. It refers to the launching of a two-year initiative to ensure the welfare and dignity of migrant workers in global supply chains – particularly those migrating from one emerging economy to another. As outlined by Aron Cramer, president and CEO of BSR, the initiative seeks:

- to increase private sector awareness of the dimensions and impacts of South–South labor migration;
- provide actionable advice for companies on how to integrate greater protections for employees in their supply chains; and
- encourage business to support the development of collaborative solutions to protect international labor migrants through engagement with key stakeholders and participation in international labor migration dialogues.[38]

Unfortunately, industry codes of conduct have failed to incorporate the concrete responsibilities of MNCs to provide fair practices for migrant and immigrant labor, which is a surprising gap in CSR Migrant workers in some of the most labor-intensive industries – such as textile, footwear, agribusiness, tourism, and mining – are denied agency rights. Worsening migrant labor working conditions have been highlighted by extensive media coverage and NGO activist campaigns, which sought to make the term "sweatshop" a household name. Efforts have been launched, however, to improve codes of conduct.

**Protecting recruited workers.** A recent investigative report shows how customers are often unaware of the cruel work conditions and violation of human rights in supply chains that provide them with products. Benjamin Skinner, a senior fellow at the Schuster Institute for Investigative Journalism of Brandeis University, uncovered a story of coerced labor, akin to modern-day slavery in the fishing vessels of South Korean-flagged ships of Melilla, which trawls the waters off New Zealand. [39]

The supply chain begins with the recruiting agency, the East Jakarta offices of Indah Megah Sari (IMS), that hires crews to work on foreign fishing vessels. It promises recruits a salary of $260 a month minus a $225 fee to the agency. Nothing is paid in the first three months and 30% of pay is withheld unless the work is completed. The standard workday is 16 hours. If the vessels owners are not satisfied, they could send a worker home and charge him more than $1,000 for the airfare.

In the middle of the supply chain are fish-processing companies in New Zealand. Although Sanford, the country's second-largest seafood enterprise, promised to improve oversight of foreign-chartered vessels and address allegations of abuse or wage exploitation, another, United Fisheries, the eighth largest, categorically denied mistreatment of crews in foreign charter vessels operating in New Zealand. Furthermore, authorities in New Zealand where the ships unload their catch have ignored evidence of deplorable working conditions on foreign vessels such as the Melilla despite evidence of numerous cases of abuse and coercion among the 2,000 fishermen on New Zealand's 27 foreign charter vessels.

At the end of the supply chain are fish importers, such as Mazzetta of suburban Chicago, who are most vulnerable to reputational damage from its customer. For example, after he read an online version of Skinner's article, Mazzetta's CEO, Tom Mazzetta, sent a letter to Sanford's CEO, Barratt, demanding an investigation of labor practices on its foreign-chartered vessels. Existing safeguards by other retailers, however, have been unenforced. For example, Costco, a major buyer of New Zealand fish products, issues a six-page Supplier Code of Conduct, which specifically prohibits "slave labor, human trafficking – and physical abuse of employees." It also annually audits the processing facilities of its suppliers, but this code and audits have had no effect. Furthermore, vessels escape such audits. Vessel owners and recruiters of labor who are at the core of abuses appear to escaped scrutiny.

## SA8000

Social Accountability 8000 is a global standard designed to make workplaces socially responsible.[40] It is based on conventions of the ILO as well as the Universal Declaration of Human rights and the UN Declaration on the Rights of the Child.[41] It is a voluntary code of conduct that companies choose to enhance their reputations and because they want to do the right thing. It is a verifiable standard for managing, auditing, and certifying compliance with workplace issues. To certify compliance, qualified auditors visit facilities regularly to assess performance on such issues. Matthew J. Hirshland calls it "one of the most widely respected multistakeholder-crafted, voluntary labor standard-setting systems and enforcement organizations."[42]

The list of business benefits to companies implementing the standards includes the following:

- greater employee retention and enhanced performance,
- enhanced product quality and productivity,
- improved management,
- enhanced supply chain management,
- protection of reputation,
- development of new markets and new customers.[43]

SA8000 addresses such issues as discrimination, health and safety, child labor, and compensation. Specifically, SA8000 prohibits child labor, under the age of 15 in most cases; it prohibits forced labor; it requires companies to provide safe drinking water, clean rest-room facilities, applicable safety equipment, and necessary training; respects the rights of workers to form and join trade unions and to bargain collectively; bans discrimination on the basis of race, caste, national origin, religion, disability, gender, sexual orientation, union membership, or political affiliation; it provides for a maximum 48-hour working week, with at least one day off per week; and requires wages that meet all minimum legal standards and provides sufficient income for basic needs, with at least some discretionary income.[44]

Several case studies illustrate the workings of SA8000.[45] One is Dole Food Company, the world's largest producer and marketer of fresh fruit, vegetables, and fresh-cut flowers, which was an early participant in the effort to develop and implement the SA8000 standard. A major issue it faced was its relationships to suppliers, especially small farmers. To help farmers, Dole offers technical, educational, and often financial assistance to help bring them up to the Dole standard of environmental and social responsibility.

Another notable case is Toys "R" Us, the largest toy retailer in the world, which sources all of its products.[46] It obtains products from over 30 different countries, has over 3,000 product suppliers, and employs over 50,000 workers worldwide. It adopted SA8000 in 1999, enabling it to rely on its certification process in lieu of performing in-house compliance reviews of suppliers. However, the company faces the difficulty that many of its product lines have very deep supply chains that produce components difficult to inspect.

### Company codes of conduct – Gap Inc.

Various companies and industries have developed their own codes of conduct to address labor as well as environmental issues. One of them is Gap Inc.[47] It addressed the problem of labor standards in its supply chain when it experienced an inadequacy in compliance and verifications of its codes of conduct. As a result, it collaborated with a variety of organizations – such as other companies, governments, unions, and NGOs – to tackle systemic problems that are beyond the capacity of any one organization to resolve alone. In 1992, Gap's Global Compliance program focused on labor, environmental, and health and safety standards for third-party manufacturers. Many of its employees are vendor compliance officers (VDOs), representing about 25 nationalities, who are responsible for conducting inspections of both prospective and established garment factories that supply Gap.

Gap learned, however, that its "policing model" to factory compliance had serious limitations. Serious problems often came to the company's attention through NGOs. In 1995 in El Salvador, where there were allegations of low pay, excessive overtime, and union busting, Gap collaborated with three NGOs – Business for Social Responsibility, the Center for Reflection, Education and Action, and the Interfaith Center on Corporation Responsibility – to form an independent monitoring working group.

In 2002, Gap established the Global Partnerships function within its Global Compliance Department. Stakeholder engagement became a core component of its social responsibility programs. Accordingly, it developed a stakeholder "mapping, analysis, prioritization, and internal education" system that provided it with insights. In 2003 and 2004, respectively, the company joined two multistakeholder initiatives focused on labor rights in the supply chain: the Ethical Trading Initiative based in the United Kingdom, and Social Accountability International based in New York. In 2003, Gap released its first Social Responsibility Report, focusing on ethical sourcing and labor standards. Gap now publishes CSR reports every two years. They provide details on the steps taken to improve conditions in the garment factories, commitment to communities, its efforts to reduce impact on the environment, and the "ways it is striving to create an inclusive and inspiring place for the employees to work." Social Accountability Initiative and the International Textile, Garment, and Leather Worker's Federation have been participants.[48]

Gap learned the importance of integrating buyers and suppliers into its core business strategies. Thus, production processes were redesigned to avoid deadline problems and last-minute design changes. Gap also worked with suppliers to help them increase their productivity and improve management techniques. It built labor standards directly into their buying decisions by using an "integrated sourcing scorecard." In 2004, Gap stopped doing business with 70 factories for serious noncompliance and rejected 15% of new factories that had not yet been approved for production.

# Country differences in labor relations and hr practices

In the international context, human resources management requires a consideration of different country circumstances and cultures. Managers should examine the possible impact of such factors as leadership styles, current and potential market conditions, the local work environment, competition, and the firm's resources and capabilities.[49] Problems associated with cultural differences have been especially salient for American executives who manage mostly high-technology companies, according to a survey of senior executives of 250 southern California firms.[50] A consideration of national cultures and differences within countries helped managers to improve productivity and the quality of employee relations.

### Cultural entry problems faced by Wal-Mart and Emerson Electric

The contrasting experiences of General Electric (GE) and Wal-Mart illustrate the role of national differences.[51] In the 1990s when Jack Welch, then CEO of GE, spearheaded the acquisition of over 100 companies in such countries as France, Germany, Italy, and Spain, GE had no difficulty in implementing a whole host of American-based management practices, such as the six-sigma program. In contrast, when Wal-Mart entered the German market in 1997, it ran into cultural resistance. Its sales clerks were ordered to smile at customers, but the customers resented the smile and interpreted it as harassment or flirtation. They apparently preferred the cultural pattern of nonaffectivity to that of a display of affectivity. And when management filled the top positions with expatriates, the Germans perceived that as arrogance. A mass exodus of talented German managers ensued. In 2005, Wal-Mart sold its 85 stores to rival Metro at a loss of $1 billion.

In contrast, when Emerson Electric established a new manufacturing facility in Suzhou, near Shanghai, in China, its overall entry was successful despite some cross-cultural conflicts and leadership issues. It learned that although leader competence in the United States is measured by task accomplishment, in China the personal integrity of each manager was critical. Also, the time perspective of U.S. managers was short because they saw their positions as stepping stones to further career advancement, whereas the Chinese managers took a long-term view.[52]

## Wal-Mart and unions[53]

In China, Wal-Mart's well-known resistance toward labor unions has slowly and reluctantly been compromised in the face of compliance with China's 1992 Trade Union Law (modified in 2001) and the 1994 Labor Law, which provide unions with legal means to defend workers' interests. These laws require firms to sign individual contracts with their employees and encourage them to engage in collective bargaining. In addition, several laws were enacted to establish a national labor arbitration system, composed of 3,000 arbitration committees intervening at different levels.

In line with its adamant antiunion policy, Wal-Mart at first refused to recognize the All-China Federation of Trade Unions (ACFTU) union, which was organizing its employees. The ACFTU performs the dual function of a state instrument and a labor organization. Although Wal-Mart used several tactics to resist the union, it was resisted by the ACFTU, which had convinced at least 25 workers at each workplace to sign and join the union. Wal-Mart and ACFTU eventually came to an agreement and by the end of September 2006, all 62 Wal-Mart superstores in China were unionized.

The ACFTU has succeeded in several other situations. It demonstrated its representational role of protecting workers' rights and interests when in 2003 it implemented a directive permitting migrant workers to join a trade union. And by the end of 2006, it succeeded in unionizing Foxconn, the largest Taiwan-owned company in mainland China. It had resisted union organization in its Shanzhen plant where iPods are assembled. The ACFTU has also established a new arbitration system, whereby ACFTU representatives become more involved in mediating disputes at the workplace level.

## Dysfunctional labor relations in South African mines

South African made news on August 16, 2012, when police fired into a crowd of protesting workers of the Lonmin Manikana mine, killing 34 workers.[54] It became known as the "Markiana massacre." The mine is the world's third-largest producer of platinum, a metal used primarily in automobiles and jewelry.[55] South Africa boasts vast reserves of gold, platinum, and diamonds. It is Africa's most advanced economy, with more cell phones, computers, and cars than any other country on the continent. Its gross domestic product is almost twice that of Egypt, Africa's next largest economy.[56]

Conflict arose a week earlier when 3,000 rock drillers from the Lonmin Manikana mine went on strike and security police killed 10 of them. Workers demanded higher wages and better working and living conditions. They were earning less than $2 a day and lived in cement-block houses or shack camps, some no more than tin boxes, which lacked running water and electricity.[57] As commented upon by a visiting sales executive who frequently visits relatives, "Why doesn't the company contribute to the infrastructure of the place? It is basic logic that you would want your workers to sleep well so they can perform well at work. Why don't they improve their life?"[58]

Workers are represented by the National Union of Mineworkers (NUM), which was unable to stop the wave of wildcat strikes. The union also represents striking workers at the gold mines of Gold Fields Ltd. and Gold One International Ltd. The NUM, which was accused of being too cozy with management and with the African National Congress (ANC), faced competition from a rival union, the Association of Mineworkers and Construction Union (AMCU). The protests were in part provoked by the interunion fights between the NAM and AMCU.[59]

Adding to worker frustration was the slow pace of change at mines since the end of apartheid almost two decades ago. The bond between workers and the ANC, the party of Nelson Mandela, was broken as many underlying labor relations issues remained unresolved. The country's leaders "sat back and did nothing as this tragedy sped to its ultimate end.... " As one observer commented, "Where were the unions, where was ... safety and security, where were the community leaders when they were needed most?"[60] It was only after the deadly clash that President Jacob Zuma visited Rustenburg, a town near the mine site. Later he announced that a commission would be formed to investigate the police shooting and consider changes in how wage negotiations are handled. In the meanwhile, management agreed to raise wage by as much as 22%, plus a bonus when workers return to work.[61]

The larger issues of worker equity and economic development were recognized by Susan Shabangu, Minister of Mineral Resources, who said, "We cannot continue to have companies maximize profits while workers don't benefit."[62] At stake was South Africa's reputation as a safe place to invest and operate. The mine companies could no longer ignore labor relations and the related problem of worker housing.

## Differences in HR practices

MNCs face continuing differences in how the human resources function is practiced in different countries. Until a stage is reached when national cultural differences make little difference in the workplace, their impact on country HR practices should be recognized. A contrast between Japan and Britain is illustrative.

### Japan

In Japan, the motivation of workers is especially sensitive to culture in that they rate "social recognition" higher than Americans.[63] For this reason, Japanese bonus systems are usually based on group efforts. The feature of paternalism and collectivism in Japanese culture is also reflected in favoring a system of lifetime employment and seniority. Another indication of cultural influence is that when economic downturns occur, Japanese and American managers tend to handle workforce problems differently. Although the Japanese might reduce labor costs by cutting the pay of managers, Americans are more likely to lay off a great number of manual and some white-collar employees and only cut executive salaries by a paltry 1%. The Japanese cultural norm of collectivism and attitude toward face-saving is reflected in that Japanese employees feel they are part of a workplace in-group that imbues them with a sense of duty and indebtedness to one another. Japanese employees have been found to be more loyal to their companies and more difficult to hire away.[64]

The Japanese style of management reflects a mutual commitment by managers and employees to each other. Managers consider employees an asset rather than a liability. Management therefore takes a long-term view of their relationship and hires someone with broad educational qualifications who can then be trained by the company. Employees reciprocate with a high degree of commitment and loyalty to their work organization. The close relationship between companies and schools allows a company to recruit individuals for a predetermined position.

Japanese managers have been found to perform better abroad in comparison to American managers because they have a higher repertoire of modes of behavior and, hence, greater flexibility. The characteristics they consider essential for overseas success are maturity, emotional stability, breadth of knowledge, a positive outlook, flexibility, cultural empathy, and an affinity for travel.

### Britain

Compared to the Japanese culture of collectivism, the British cultural norm is individualism, which means, for example, that everybody is allowed to work individually and receive individual credit. With another cultural variable, power distance, British workers might express deference and endure inequality because they largely accept disproportionate power, prestige, and wealth among different economic strata and classes. In this regard, the Japanese are similar because social hierarchy is accepted. With the variable of affectivity versus nonaffectivity, the British tend toward the latter; their behavior is formal and they keep personal and family matters apart from organizational ones. They use humor to release the emotions behind the "stiff upper lip." On the time dimension, they engage in sequential planning: "Everything needs to be planned from start to finish."[65] Staying in line and waiting one's turn is part of the culture, as anyone waiting for a bus knows.

British management has a conservative approach toward new technology and places more emphasis on the production rather than the marketing side of their business. One of their main problems is a shortage of skilled workers. In training unskilled workers for specific jobs, the United States does a far better job.

# Globalization of hr practices[66]

Human resources practices still differ among developed and developing countries and among countries with differing cultures. The trend, however, is toward their globalization, which conforms with the spirit of the World Trade Organization. One driver is the desire of some MNCs to centralize HR policies, which is illustrated by the

United States. Another driver is the influence of domestic labor unions and a possible internationalization of the labor movement.

## Centralized policies by U.S. MNCs

U.S. MNCs tend to be relatively centralized in the management of their overseas operations and impose standardized policies on them. The issues are whether to treat a foreign workforce differently from that of the home country and whether responsibility should rest with the HR staff and/or line management. MNCs have found that it is easier to impose home-grown policies on a newly formed subsidiary than one acquired through acquisition.

The policy areas of human resources/employee relations include unionization, pay and performance management, employee involvement and communication, managerial careers, and workforce diversity.[67] With reference to workforce diversity, U.S. firms commonly limit themselves to targeting different groups such as women or ethnic minorities.[68] Regarding unionization, the United States has a strong tradition of nonunion operations, except in specific sectors such as autos and aircraft. This view reflects the dominant management ethos of antagonism to third-party interference in managerial decision making.

In Europe, U.S. MNCs have adjusted to European conditions. In Germany, for example, they must adapt to a strong institutional framework and laws supporting employee representation through company works councils, codetermination – inclusion of labor representatives – in governing boards, and industry-based collective bargaining. The power of works councils makes it difficult for such systems as performance-related pay to be introduced without the councils' approval.[69] American MNCs have learned to rely on local managers to interpret the host environment to them.

Host countries, however, impose real constraints on the ability of U.S. firms to transfer their practices, so they often have to be adapted either overtly or surreptitiously. Facts "on the ground" include not only formal constraints imposed by legislation but also understandings by native managers of MNCs who interpret the host environment for them. For example, several U.S. MNCs that are solidly nonunion in the United States recognize and negotiate with unions in their U.K. operations.

In China, the reshaping of the employee relations system is largely driven by MNCs but their influence is still mainly undetermined.[70] A positive view is that MNCs transfer their best practices to China by, for example, introducing "codes of conduct that urge their subsidiaries and suppliers to put mechanisms in place for voluntary election of worker representatives." A negative view is that MNCs and other foreign firms exploit China's weak and unprotected labor force, particularly migrant rural workers. For example, they violate labor laws and forcefully resist creation of trade unions.[71]

In Russia, McDonald's joint venture illustrates how its standardized policies were applied to overcome certain local practices that were considered undesirable. A Russian practice was to hire personnel based on patronage and personal contacts. When workers were hired from Russian partners, they were found to be deficient in both skills and attitudes and unable or unwilling to work according to international standards. Applying its overall global strategy, McDonald's recruited new workers by placing a single advertisement in Moscow newspapers soliciting applications. The applications became the base for selecting the most energetic, motivated, intelligent, and outgoing young men and women. McDonald's preferred to hire young, inexperienced, "uncontaminated" people and then train them.

## Internationalization of the labor movement

An international labor movement could influence the globalization of HR practices. There is doubt, however, about how much real progress the labor movement has made in becoming more international – either with regard to employers in organizing and bargaining or in relation to governments in setting policy at both the national and international levels. The global labor movement has not yet agreed on its broad political agenda, but it recognizes the pressures it faces. As AFL-CIO Secretary-Treasurer Richard Trumka argues, workers everywhere are boxed in by policies that promote capital mobility, labor flexibility, price stability, and privatization of government. When taken together, those policies, at a global and national level, undermine workers' economic power and social welfare protections. They also make organizing more difficult and limit what unions can do even if they do organize or undertake global campaigns.

A pessimistic view of global union influence is embellished in two new books on labor and globalization: Jeff Faux's *The Global Class War* and Jeffrey A. Frieden's *Global Capitalism: Its Fall and Rise in the Twentieth Century*.[72] Faux, a founder of the Economic Policy Institute, argues "America's bipartisan governing class protects its privileged clients while abandoning the rest of us to an unregulated and therefore brutal and merciless global market."[73] The interests of these privileged clients are articulated by the International Monetary Fund, the World Bank, treaties such as the North America Free Trade Agreement, and organizations such as the EU – all of which remain bound together by an "uncritical commitment to neoliberalism."[74] Frieden, a government professor at Harvard University, sees workers as the losers in global capitalism. While agreeing that economies work best when they are open to the world, he believes open economies work best when their governments address the sources of dissatisfaction with global capitalism.[75]

# Conclusions

Globalization involves the management of human resources and in the current third generation of globalization places greater emphasis on replenishing and upgrading of each company's workforce. This effort requires an examination of two sources of labor: graduates of a country's educational systems and immigrants from other.

Many policy issues and problems arise from immigration. Some relate to corporate responsibility for human rights and to the exercise of global corporate citizenship. Although significant country differences exist in how the human resources function is exercised, the trend is toward globalization. The extent to which the labor movement will be able to internationalize remains uncertain.

Technonationalism has become a major policy issue that United States and Western MNCs are grappling with. Should they continue their competitive strategy of technonationalism or collaborate with other nations in building an S&T "global commons."[76] The United States has the opportunity to take leadership in this commons. A new cadre of managers have multiple affinities and do not view the world as partitioned into competing teams in the same way their predecessor did. They would recognize that the new era of "third-generation globalization" requires different national skill formation policies from past.[77]

Human resources is an essential business function whose execution reflects the goals, values, and culture of an organization. Complicating matters is that activities in an international setting are affected by the local culture of a country and community.

## Revision Questions

1. How do the concepts of "third generation globalization" and "technonationalism" affect human resources management?
2. Discuss the measures that HR managers have taken to assure a sufficient supply of adequately trained workers?
3. What human rights problems must MNCs address in recruiting and managing additions to the workforce?
4. What are some HR problems that companies have encountered in entering other countries and what are some differences in HR practices among them?
5. In what ways are HR practices becoming more global?

## Discussion Questions

I. What needs to be done by various countries to assure that their educational systems can provide employers with adequate numbers of qualified workers? On what does their success depend?
II. Do you think that countries should put restrictions on the entry of immigrant labor? What should those restrictions and conditions be?
III. In the New Zealand fisheries case, what circumstances make it difficult to obtain compliance with the human rights of crew members of South Korean-flag vessels? Do you think codes of conduct are any help? How can vessel owners and operators be persuaded to change their labor practices?
IV. Should MNCs attempt to standardize labor practices in their facilities, or is it better to allow local cultural practices to remain?
V. Do you agree with the Global Compact principle that businesses should uphold the freedom of association and the effective recognition of the right to collective bargaining?

# chapter 6
# religious tensions: understanding islam

**Objectives**

1. *Recognize that religion is a major cultural factor, and become familiar with some of the world's major religions.*
2. *Recognize that religion can affect the sales and operations of an multinational corporation in various countries and be able to discuss cases when that occurred.*
3. *Be able to cite specific grievances by Muslims in various countries.*
4. *Learn how Islamic economics is compatible with capitalism.*
5. *Know in what ways business can accommodate Muslims in their companies and communities.*
6. *Become familiar with sources of information about the Muslim world.*

Globalization is intensifying religious conflict as cultures cross boundaries through international trade, immigration, tourism, entertainment vehicles, missionary work, and the activities of international organizations. Business often encounters diversity in religions without understanding its potential implications. The religion of Islam is emphasized in this chapter because in the past few decades it has been at the center of a major tensions between the Western world and Muslim countries. Business is affected because even isolated religion-based conflicts can flare up into consumer boycotts, employee tensions, and community conflicts. The purpose of this chapter is to sensitize global managers to the challenge of Islam so that they can reconcile their attitudes and practices and undertake appropriate initiatives and responses.

## Religion: a core cultural factor

Business has long been aware that culture is a key variables in many host countries. Marketing people in particular know that cultural preferences by different countries affect what product characteristics are important and who in a family makes decisions. Books such as *Marketing Across Cultures*[1] attest to the importance of this variable. Other activities are also affected by culture, as illustrated by Raymond Cohen's book *Negotiating Across Culture*.[2] Some of the most popular books in communications emphasize culture, for example, Gary R. Weaver's *Culture, Communication and Conflict*.[3]

Religion is at the core of culture, making it important that we understand the major religions of the world.[4] Nearly 75% of the planet's population follows only five of the most influential religions in terms of global impact: Christianity, Islam, Hinduism, Buddhism, and Judaism.[5] Islam is the religion of Muslims, who comprise about one-fifth of the world's population. Although the religion of Islam has received considerable attention in the international relations literature, the management literature makes sparse reference. The key lesson to businesses, and multinational corporations (MNCs) in particular, is that they must consider local religions so as not to cause offense or harm business relationships.

The marketplace and employment offices are major arenas where MNCs have recognized the impact of religion. They know not to sell pork and shellfish in Israel, alcohol in Pakistan, and beef in India. But unintentional errors might be committed. McDonald's learned to heed the religious taboos of its Hindu customers in India when it realized that it unwittingly violated their religious beliefs by frying its French fries in a formulation that included beef talow. Without telling anyone it quickly switched to vegetable oil. But when millions of Hindus became aware of the violation they organized protests and filed a lawsuit.[6] McDonald's also knows that it must pay attention to Muslims because it has three times more customers in the Arab world than in the whole of Europe.[7]

Advertising is also affected by religion because of prohibitions against perceived sexual symbols. For example, sleeveless dresses are considered offensive to Islamic rules; furthermore, Saudi Arabian publications will not accept any advertisement that has a picture of a woman in it. A new law in Qatar as of March 2012 requires that advertising content not be injurious to Islam or any other religion and not contrary to public order, morals, traditions, or customs.[8] To uphold morals, the new government in Egypt is considering regulations that would require shops to close at 10 p.m. and restaurants and cafes at midnight.[9]

In employment relationships, MNCs have also recognized the impact of religion as Muslims migrated to countries in need of labor. Many Muslims who moved to Western European countries complain that their human rights are not recognized. Believing they are discriminated against, they are becoming more vocal and demanding equal rights. Employers are pressured to provide equal employment opportunities, following the example of the recruitment of African-Americans by American companies.

## Meaning of "Islam"

The word "Islam" literally means "surrender" or "resignation" to the will of Allah, the Arabic word for God. Muslims, who are monotheists, believe that Muhammad, a merchant who lived in the 6th and 7th centuries in the Arabian cities of Medina and Mecca, was the last of God's prophets. A visible aspect of the Islamic faith is the Muslim worship five times every day. The Koran, written in Arabic, is the scripture. Muslims also refer to the Hadith, the collected sayings of Muhammad, as authoritative. The *sharia* system of jurisprudence, while not regarded as scripture, contains teachings, proscriptions and rules governing everything from permissible food to marriage and divorce.[10] The Koran mandates flogging for unlawful sex, with the extreme sanction that adulterers should be stoned to death.

Islam's two main branches are Sunni and Shite (also called Shia). Sunnis, making up an estimated 85% of all Muslims, predominate in the United States, Egypt, Saudi Arabia, and most other Arab nations, as well as in Palestine. Shites are a majority in Iran and Iraq and a large part of Lebanon. There is no worldwide leader of Islam, or of its major branches. Nevertheless, Islamosceptics say that "devout Muslims will always, in their hearts, see a global caliphate – a seat of religious-cum-political authority, holding sway over the whole Islamic world – as the ideal form of governance."[11] Imams and other local leaders direct affairs but focus most of their work in interpreting Islamic law. In *Report on Religion: A Primer on Journalism's Best Beat,* journalists are told, "There is no one Muslim leader or even group of leaders who have the responsibility or authority to speak for Islam, or even a branch of Islam, in the United States or worldwide."[12]

The power of Islam is symbolized by Muslim women who choose to "wear the veil." The *hijab or higab* includes a headscarf and a loose-fitting, long-sleeved top and pants or a long skirt. The most conservative form of veil is a *nigab*, a face-covering veil, usually black, that leaves only the eyes uncovered. Muslim women see the veil as a symbol of religious faith and freedom from cosmetics, fashion, and male attention. The Western view is that the veil is a symbol of female oppression and that women should be more interested in the problems of underage marriages, wife beating, and their second-class status in society. The donning of the veil is also interpreted as a rejection of secular public life.

In the Unites States, hiding one's face is considered rude, except on such special occasions as a carnival. Honest people look you straight in the eye! There is a strong feeling that a Muslim woman who wants to cover her face has no right to work in an office or school where face-to-face conversations are part of the job.[13] Jack Straw, Britain's former foreign secretary, called these veils "a barrier to social integration."[14] This view was applied in Yorkshire where a teaching assistant who had refused to remove her veil in the presence of male teachers was fired.[15] Elsewhere too the veil has been controversial. Two hijab-wearing teachers were sacked in Belgium early in 2006 for not complying with "religious neutrality" rules. Risking the wrath of the Islamic world, France in September 2010 banned burqas and other full-body robes.

## Tensions with Islam

The volatile nature of the religious issue of Islam was dramatically illustrated in September 2012 when anti-U.S. protests flared up in Egypt, Libya, Yemen, and other countries after word circulated about a video trailer for a purported film called "Innocence in Muslim." It insulted Muhammad by portraying him as a carouser and dullard. The worst attack was in Benghazi, Libya, where Islamic extremists exploited the situation and stormed the U.S. Consulate and killed Ambassador Christopher Stevens and three other Americans.[16]

The sensitivity to any purported insult to Islam was also evident when American soldiers negligently dumped copies of the Koran (also spelled Quran) in the burn pit at the Bargram air base near Afghanistan's capital, Kabul. When Afghans heard about this they engaged in street protests and violence. At least 40 people were killed and many were wounded in clashes between the police and demonstrators.

The religion of Islam has become an issue in some countries where Muslims have migrated. An extreme reaction is illustrated by the Norwegian gunman who bombed government buildings and then went on a killing rampage at an island youth camp, systematically killing at least 76 members[17] It is Norway's deadliest peacetime atrocity.

The killer, Anders Breivik, who is "ethnic Norwegian and a Christian," wrote a 1,500-page manifesto "2083: A European Declaration of Independence" in which he insisted that he would not "accept an Islamic presence in Europe."[18] In the first half of the manifesto he indicts the European cultural elite for permitting Islam to take root in Europe. He hated what he called the "cultural Marxists" who dominated Norwegian politics. Through his massacre he hoped to create a spectacle that would energize his anti-Islamic cause.

### Findings of public opinion surveys

The Pew Research Center's Global Attitudes Project conducted March 21 to May 15, 2011, confirms that Muslim and Western publics continue to see relations between them as generally bad, although slightly improved compared with 2006.[19] Over half of the French (62%), Germans (61%), Spanish (58%), and British (52%) say relations are poor, and 48% of Americans say so. Many in the West see Muslims as fanatical and violent, with few tolerant or respectful of women. On the other side, Muslims in the Middle East and Asia generally see Westerners as selfish, immoral, arrogant and greedy, as well as violent and fanatical.

The attitudes of Muslims toward the United States is explored in Steven Kull's book, *Feeling Betrayed: The Roots of Muslim Anger at America*.[20] The underlying narrative is that America is seen as oppressing – and at a deeper level, betraying – the Muslim people by coercively dominating the Muslim world and seeking to undermine Islam. Kull states that Muslim anger is fed by an "inner clash of civilizations," between Muslims' desire to connect with America and all it represents and their fear that America seeks to overwhelm and destroy their traditional Islamic culture.

## Muslims in the United States and Europe

In 2010 Muslims comprised 1.6 billion (23.4%) of the 6.9 billion world population, according to the Pew Forum on Religion and Public Life, growing to 2.2 billion by 2030. About 2.6 million Muslims make up 0.8% of the U.S. population and 44 million Muslims constitute about 6% of Europe's population.[21] Countries with the largest percentage of Muslim are France with 8%, the Netherlands with 6%, Germany with 4%, and the United Kingdom with 3%. The Muslim population exceeds 20% in some major European Union (EU) cities such as Marseilles, Malmo, Amsterdam, Stockholm, and Brussels. The Open Society Foundations study, "At Home in Europe," reports on 11 EU cities, including Amsterdam and Rotterdam, Antwerp, Berlin and Hamburg, Copenhagen, Leicester and Waltham Forest–London, Marseille and Paris, and Stockholm.[22]

Muslim populations in the United States and Europe are not homogeneous. According to the Pew Forum, U.S. Muslims are a racially diverse religious group: 38% describe themselves as white, 26% say they are black, 20% say they are Asian, and 16% identify themselves as "other" or "mixed race." In Europe, Britain's Muslims are mainly South Asian (e.g., Pakistanis and Bangladeshi); France's are North African migrants; and Germany's are Turks.[23]

Islam is increasingly important as a symbol of Muslim identity. Young British Muslims, for example, are inclined to see Islam as their true home, rather than the United Kingdom or the city where they live. At a conference titled "Islam and Muslims in the

World Today," held in June 2007, Tony Blair emphasized that Islam is not a "monolithic faith," but one made up of a "rich pattern of diversity." The principal purpose of the conference, he said, was to "let the authentic voices of Islam, in their various schools and manifestations, speak for themselves."[24]

# Huntington's thesis: clash of civilizations

The importance of Muslim sentiments was anticipated and publicized by Samuel P. Huntington in his widely read *Foreign Affairs* article, "Clash of Civilizations." It states: "It is my hypothesis that the fundamental source of conflict in this new world will not be primarily ideological or primarily economic. The great divisions among humankind and the dominating source of conflict will be cultural.... The clash of civilizations will dominate global politics."[25] Huntington sees the world as divided up into seven or eight major civilizations: Western, Confucian, Japanese, Islamic, Hindu, Slavic-Orthodox, Latin American, and possibly African. Western civilization has two major variants, European and North American, and Islam has its Arab, Turkic, and Malay subdivisions.[26] These civilizations represent "the highest cultural grouping of people and the broadest level of cultural identity people have short of that which distinguishes humans from other species."[27]

Huntington defines a civilization as a "cultural entity," saying that "villages, regions, ethnic groups, nationalities, religious groups, all have distinct cultures at different levels of cultural heterogeneity."[28] Civilizations are differentiated from each other by history, language, culture, tradition and, most important, religion.[29] These differences are the products of centuries, but are now accelerating as the world becomes a smaller place and interactions increase, resulting in an intensification as civilizations become aware and conscious of both differences and similarities. People are being separated from long-standing local identities through the processes of economic modernization and social change throughout the world.

The fault line between Western and Islamic civilizations, which has been going on for 1,300 years, is most severe. Efforts by the West, says Huntington, seek "to promote its values of democracy and liberalism as universal values, to maintain its military predominance and to advance its economic interests engender countering responses from other civilizations."[30] One consequence has been a return to the roots phenomenon by non-Western civilizations, resulting in a revival of religion, such as fundamentalist.[31] Huntington states that whereas the West has generated ideologies, the East has generated religions. He explains that religion is now the more menacing force on the international scene. Muslims, however, view Western belief in the universality of Western culture and that it ought to be the culture of the world as a conceit. They use the terms "Coca-colonization" and "McWorld."[32]

## 9/11 and terrorism[33]

Huntington believes that resentment toward globalization, accompanied by anti-Americanism, is partly to blame for 9/11.[34] He characterizes the world in which we live as "a dangerous place, in which large numbers of people resent our wealth, power, and culture, and vigorously oppose our efforts to persuade or coerce them to accept our values of human rights, democracy, and capitalism."[35] Thus he sees 9/11 and the intensification of terrorism in the world in the broader context of "The Clash of Civilizations."

Terrorism is a mainly a problem for governments, but it is also one for MNCs. They are among the targets of terrorists because they serve as highly visible symbols of "exploitative imperialist elements or part of the repressive organization of state."[36] Recognizing this fact, several service-support organizations have been formed: Business Risks International offers counter-training for business; Control Risks, helps insurance companies minimize their exposure to kidnappings of high-profile businessmen and provides political analysis for many corporations, including investigative work linked to investments, security consulting, and crisis management. In 2007, the business group APEC launched an international audit to determine whether corporations delivering essential services could survive a disaster such as a terrorist attack or tsunami.[37] Attacks by extremist Muslim groups are among the concerns of these organizations.

# A boycott in the middle east and a riot in france

Business has faced two major confrontations based on the religion of Islam. The power of Muslim outrage was felt by Arla Foods, the Danish dairy company, when a Danish newspaper printed cartoons caricaturing Mohammed. Another confrontation occurred in the French banilieues (outer suburbs).

## Danish cartoon episode

On September 30, 2005, Flemming Rose, the cultural editor of the Danish newspaper *Jyllands-Posten*, published a series of 12 cartoons satirizing the Prophet Muhammad with the intention of demonstrating Denmark's devotion to freedom of the press. One depicted Muhammad in a turban shaped like a bomb. Another showed a turbaned figure in heaven telling ascending suicide bombers to stop because "we've run out of virgins" (the reward awaiting Islamic martyrs).

The immediate reaction to the cartoons was local. A prominent cleric in Denmark, Ahmed Abu-Laban, felt insulted and wrote a protesting letter to the newspaper and to the Danish culture minister, to which there was no reply. He and others formed the "European Committee for Honoring the Prophet," which claimed to represent 27 organizations across a wide spectrum of the Islamic community.[38] They also sent a petition with 17,000 signatures to Prime Minister Anders Fogh Rasmussen, who did not even show the courtesy of responding. Even when ambassadors from eleven Muslim countries asked for a meeting with Rasmussen, he declined.

Abu-Laban and his colleagues then decided to take their case outside Denmark. They prepared a 30-plus-page dossier to distribute during their travels. This document included a group of other highly offensive pictures never published by the newspaper, including a photograph of a man dressed as a pig, with the caption "this is the real picture of Muhammad."[39] By the end of January 2006, word spread so wide that protesters burned Danish flags and declared boycotts of Danish and other European goods. With the help of cell phone text messages and massive emails, messages reached virtually every area in the Middle East.

People reacted by ransacking Denmark's diplomatic missions in Syria and Lebanon and protesters demanded that the Danish ambassador leave the country. In Lebanon, the Danish and Norwegian embassies were torched. Even as late as June 2008, the Danish embassy in Pakistan was attacked by a car bomb, perhaps incited by an audiotape message in May by Ayman al-Zawahiri, al Qaedia's second-in-command to Osama bin Laden, who stated, "I urge and incite every Muslim who can harm Denmark to do so in support of the prophet."[40]

## Arla foods stricken with boycott

One of the most affected companies of the 2005 Danish cartoons was Arla Foods, a Danish dairy company, the second largest dairy company in Europe, that has plants in Saudi Arabia and sells butter and cheese to Middle Eastern countries. Louis Honore, a spokesman for Aria, declared, "This is a public uprising.... This has spread through the region like wildfire. And the boycott has been practically 100 percent."[41] Other Danish companies, some as large as LEGO, were also affected. Peter Thagesen, a senior advisor from the Confederation of Danish Industries, said, "Danish companies are being taken as hostages in a conflict in which we have no part. In this conflict, as is often the case in a conflict, there have been many misunderstandings on both sides."[42]

Prime Minister Rasmussen and the editor at *Jyllands-Posten* belatedly became aware of the need for diplomacy. On January 2, 2006, Rasmussen apologized on Danish television, saying, "I personally have such respect for people's religious feelings that I personally would not have depicted Muhammad, Jesus or other religious figures in such a manner that would offend other people."[43] He also appeared on *al-Arabiya*, an Arab TV channel, and said he was "deeply distressed that the cartoons were offensive to Muslims," a response the Egyptian ambassador called unsatisfactory.[44] On January 30, Carsten Justen, editor-in-chief of *Jjllands-Posten*, issued a better statement: "In our opinion, the 12 drawings were not intended to be offensive, nor were they at variance with Danish law, but they have indisputably offended many Muslims, for which we apologize." Both seemed to apologize for the offensive perception of the cartoons, however, but not for their publication. European newspapers decried the apologies and added fuel to the fire by republishing the cartoons.

Company responses varied. Nestle, Carrefour, and Kuwaiti Danish Dairy took out advertisements stating they were not Danish companies, or they let people know their stance on the cartoon situation. Arla, hit the hardest, reprinted the text of a news release from the Danish Embassy in Saudi papers on January 27, 2006, which said that Denmark respected all religions, but also that the Danish government has no means of influencing the press.[45] The ads had no impact, however, according to Finn Hansen, head of Arla's international operations.

The company then embarked on diplomatic meetings.[46] In February, representatives attended an industry trade show in Dubai where it displayed posters stating that it was against the publication of the cartoons or anything thing else that causes religious offense.[47] The representatives sat down with Arab businessmen and discussed ways they as a company could become more attuned to the needs of the Arab world. These discussions were effective. This was two-way symmetrical communication intended to illustrate that Arla really cared about people and improving relationships.

Having achieved some acceptance, Arla Foods placed advertisements in 25 Arab newspapers in late March, which won praise from influential Islamic scholars who were meeting in Bahrain.[48] The advertisements outlined the company's 40-year history in the Middle East and reiterated Arla's dissociation from the cartoons, saying that Arla's business in the Middle East had been affected not by its own actions but the actions of others. Consumers were therefore asked to reconsider their attitude toward Arla. Executive Director Finn Hansen of Arla Foods commented, "We hope that the advertisement will get Arab consumers to consider whether it is fair to boycott a dairy company that has had nothing to do with these caricatures."[49]

## Resolution of tension

By the end of March, after a two-month boycott, shops and supermarkets in the Middle East were starting to put butter and cheese from Arla back on their shelves. By April, Arla announced a "Breakthrough for Arla in the Middle East," saying that its products were back in 3,000 shops and supermarkets and that 31 of its largest retail customers in Saudi Arabia confirmed that they would within the week return Arla products to their shelves.[50]

The Danish cartoon crisis demonstrates both the adherence to the principles of a free press and the blindness and stubbornness of Danish editors and government officials to the tensions between European nations and the world of Islam. When an audience member, Natasha Klein from the International Center for Journalists, asked Joergen Ejboel, "Didn't you expect some sort of incendiary reaction? Or were you like somehow oblivious?" he answered: "I can say from my personal point of view I was surprised. Now that I've been working in the Middle East for the last year or almost two years, I think I would still be."[51] Fleming Rose later added:

> This is a highly unique case. It never happened, you know, since the Middle Ages that Muslims were insisting on applying Islamic law to what non-Muslims are doing in non-Muslim countries. It never happened before. So, and in the fall of 2005 after the publication of the cartoons even experts in Denmark on Islam were saying, you know, this is never going to be a big international story. So, yes we were surprised.[52]

To the defenders of the cartoons the core issue is freedom of speech and stubbornness in refusing to be intimidated. Fittingly in a lecture sponsored by the World Press Freedom Committee, Ejboel emphasized the importance of the editorial independence of newspapers and freedom of expression. He criticized the British Parliament for being one vote short of passing a law banning incitements to religious hatred; he also criticized the United Nations Human Rights Council for passing a resolution calling upon governments to pass laws to protect religions against defamation.

Surely the Western world's value of the freedom of expression deserves to be supported, but to ignore the sensitivities of Muslims to desecrations of Prophet Muhammad displays arrogance and social irresponsibility. There seemed to be almost universal agreement that the cartoons were offensive. As *The Nation* stated, "When it comes to freedom of speech, the liberal left should not sacrifice its values one inch to those who seek censorship on religious grounds. But the right to freedom of speech equates to neither an obligation to offend nor a duty to be insensitive. If our commitment to free speech is important, our belief in antiracism should be no less so."[53]

One positive consequence of the cartoon's publication, said Ejboel, is that it resulted "in much better dialogue, at least in Europe, at least in Scandinavia … a lot of people are showing their faces and what they believe." In his speech, quoting Anders Jerichow, a columnist in the newspaper *Politiken* (also owned by Ejboel's group), Ejboel pondered that the cartoon crisis was a "frightening example that make it clear that the world really isn't ready for its own globalization."[54]

## Muslim anger bursts in French banlieues

On Thursday, October 27, 2005, three boys from a Paris *banlieux* – less than an hour's subway ride from the heart of Paris – were coming from a game of pickup soccer when they spotted a police checkpoint where they would be asked for identity papers.[55] One of the boys had left his papers at home, so they ran away and were chased by the police. They scaled a wall and, when they accidentally leapt into power substation cables, two of them, both Muslims, were electrocuted; the third boy, the son of Turkish immigrants, survived.

When news circulated, riots broke out. On Saturday alone, 741 vehicles in Paris and its suburbs were torched; on Sunday 426 vehicles were destroyed. Firebombing and car burning continued for days and spread to a reported 163 cities and towns across France, including Strasbourg, Lille and Nice. Groups of young men attacked postal service vans and a police station, and set fire to trash bins. One man was killed on the second day after being beaten by a gang of rioters. Inflamed by Muslim sites on the Internet, copycat attacks on a few cars were reported as far away as in Brussels and Berlin. It was the worst civil unrest in the country in nearly 40 years.

The French government responded with force. Interior Minister Nicolas Sarkozy (later to become President) said he would deploy more police on the streets and dispatch more undercover agents to penetrate criminal gangs. Even before the riots began, he referred to troublemakers in the poor housing projects of the suburbs as "rabble" that should be cleaned out with a "power hose." After the riots began, he called the perpetrators "scum," and, appearing on television, he called the violence "unacceptable and inexcusable." He characterized the bands of youths, some very young, as "in a state of social, family and educational breakdown. They are in a destructive mind-set." However, a man of Algerian origin said, "It's the attitude of the police; they insult us.... People here don't feel like they're a part of the political system. Their only recourse is to violence."

The far-right's Jean-Marie Le Pen was even more extreme in his views than Sarkozy. The National Front, a far-right party he heads, ran a poster campaign after the riots that read: "Immigration, explosion of the *banlieues* – Le Pen told you so!"[56] He demanded an immediate expulsion of all illegal immigrants and a tightening of the nationality law. In a poll, fully 23% of voters said that they agreed with Le Pen's ideas.

In the United States, *The Washington Post* said the riots "underscored France's failed efforts to stem the growing unrest within a largely Muslim immigrant population that feels disenfranchised and beset by high unemployment and crime. The *Los Angeles Times* reported on the larger problem of fundamentalism in French workplaces. For example, at the Euro Disney resort, Muslim workers were reported setting up ten clandestine prayer rooms. But the spokesperson for Euro Disney said the report was inaccurate. "I thought it was exaggerated to talk about prayer rooms.... During Ramadan, they took a few minutes to pray somewhere. We made it clear that we thought the work floor was not the place to express your personal religion."[57]

Another indication of fundamentalism, according to an executive at a supermarket, was that Muslims pressured co-workers to wear religious garb, defy the authority of female managers, and demand boycotts of products such as alcohol, pork, Israel oranges and American brownies. "For French companies, the rise in power of radical Islam represents a new threat," said Eric Denece in a report by the Center for Intelligence Research, a Paris think tank. "This trend expresses above all a move to take control of behavior and ideas of other workers in order to impose a value system conforming to extremist ideology."[58]

One explanation of the French riots is the high rate of unemployment by Muslim youths. According to a report by Jean-Francois Amadieu, a professor of sociology at the University of Paris, a job candidate with a North African-sounding name has three times less chance than one with a French-sounding name to get an interview after sending out a resume listing the same qualifications.

A hopeful sign, however, is that leading companies in France have begun to scan the country's minority communities for untapped talent because of labor shortages. For example, PSA Peugeot Citroen SA uses local unemployment agencies and community organizations in the *banlieues* that were the locus of unrest to find new hires. Peugeot says that among the 932 engineers and managers it hired in 2005, 61 were not of French nationality, 63 were ethnic minority with French nationality, and 15 came from areas in France classified by the government as "particularly underprivileged." L'Oreal is another high-profile company that has hired "minority" workers. It did so through a job fair organized by France's employers association, MEDEF, and several of the country's blue-chip companies. But the majority of employers still resist affirmative action efforts because it is anathema to the country's deeply rooted egalitarian ideals.[59]

# Media neglect of islam – and the third world

The Western world has had little knowledge of Islam because its media provide little coverage, and what stories do appear deal with disasters and unsolved problems. Since 9/11 and the war in Iraq, the focus has been on conflict. Americans know that Iraq consists of Kurds, Shites, and Sunnis, but know little else. When the tsunami struck, they learned that Indonesia has the largest Muslim population in the world. The Western world learned about Mohammed through the Danish cartoon controversy and Pope Benedict's insensitive remarks that linked Islam with violence.

## The rise of Al Jazeera

A significant advance in the Third World media system was the establishment of *Al Jazeera* in 1996. Based in Qatar, it has become the most important pan-Arab satellite news channel since U.S. military operations started in Afghanistan. Advances in satellite and telecommunication technologies made broadcasts by *Al Jazeera* possible. Previously, news was available on predominantly state-run TV channels, but it was lackluster and consisted largely of "protocol news" heavily laden with government propaganda. The news organization's primary purpose was to improve dissemination of information about the national government and to control access to and formatting of incoming foreign news. "Political news dealing with leadership speeches, official visits, and protocol activities was always topping Arab world TV news agendas."[60]

In contrast, *Al Jazeera* has tried to live up to its tradition as the Arab BBC. It has explored previously taboo subjects such as polygamy and women's rights and was the first to broadcast interviews with top Jewish leaders. During the war it continued to serve as the "middle man" between American news outlets and Osama bin Laden's propaganda efforts. At one point supposed representatives of bin Laden made an offer to CNN through *Al Jazeera* to submit questions to bin Laden. Similarly, *Al Jazeera* served as a mediator by allowing Donald H. Rumsfeld to become the third U.S. government official to be interviewed by them.[61] Al Jazeera claims to be more independent than most of the Middle East TV networks controlled by various area governments. Its viewership was estimated at 35 million.[62]

## Al Jazeera English

Al Jazeera English (AJE), a sister channel of the Arabic Al-Jazeera, was launched on November 15, 2006, with four news centers: Doha, Qatar (its home office); London; Washington; and Kuala Lumpur, Malaysia. Each of the bases is autonomous, directing its own network of bureaus and stringers. Washington, for example, has bureaus in Caracas, Buenos Aires and New York, and stringers in La Paz, Rio de Janeiro, Santiago, Lima, Bogota, Mexico City, and Los Angeles. AJE believes this reporting by people on the ground will give them more authenticity than competing networks that depend on foreign correspondents.[63]

Research showed that 80% of those who tune in, out of a potential audience of 88 million (currently outside North America), speak English as a second language. This audience is believed to have the characteristics of "curiosity, courage, education, a preference for empirical evidence rather than traditional or hierarchical authority, a belief that knowledge and good information matter."[64]

With the closing of many news bureaus and reduction of foreign correspondents by major U.S. publications, AJE's reach may indeed give it a competitive advantage. *Time* and *Newsweek* in 2005 reduced their number of foreign correspondents in bureaus around the world from just under 90 each in 1983 to 86 for *Time* and 85 for *Newsweek*.[65] Between 1977 and 2004, the percentage of stories on newspaper front pages about foreign affairs decreased by 13%.[66] Further exits from foreign reporting by newspapers were announced in early 2009. The Tribune Co., which owns the *Los Angeles Times* and *Chicago Tribune*, held discussions with the Washington Post to pay it for foreign, as well as national, coverage.[67]

*Al Jazeera* has become the preferred station for close to 40% of all Arab TV viewers. A 2004–2005 survey of television viewers in Cairo found that 46% of households watched satellite television, and of these, 88% watched Al Jazeera.[68]

The mobile Internet promises to open new avenues for stories from the Middle East, Africa, and elsewhere. *Al Jazeera* was one of the leaders in launching a service that sent digests of its news programs to cell phone subscribers in both Arabic and English.[69] As the article, "The Power of Media in the Palm of your Hand," states, a Palm Treo smartphone can transmit video to a newsroom. Expanded mobile Internet access and improved mobile Internet connectivity, say Alan D. Abbey and Andrew Friedman, may lead to another media revolution. Media outlets such as *USA Today* are already employing mobile journalists (MOJOs).[70]

To advance its goal to win space with American cable television, AJE on January 2, 2013 acquired Current TV, a left-leaning news network co-founded by Al Gore. He said his network shared Al-Jazeera's mission "to give voice to those who are not typically heard, to speak truth to power, to provide independent and diverse points of view, and to tell the stories that no one else is telling."[71] With this acquisition, Al

Jazeera can reach about 4.7 million homes beyond the few large U.S. metropolitan areas, including New York and Washington, DC However, Time Warner Cable, the nation's second largest cable TV operator, planned to drop Current TV because of the deal. The network was in 60 million homes. The outcome of the acquisition on audience size is still indefinite.


# Fostering co-existence

"Things have gone badly wrong in the Middle East," says Bernard Lewis, a British Arab scholar. Islam has become "poor, weak, and ignorant."[72] "By all the standards that matter in the modern world – economic development and job creation, literacy, educational and scientific achievement, political freedom and respect for human rights – what was once a mighty civilization has indeed fallen low."[73] Lewis reviews several answers to what went wrong: fanaticism; a failure to separate Church and State and "creation of a civil society governed by secular laws"; and "relegation of women to an inferior position in Muslim society, which deprives the Islamic world of the talents and energies of half its people."[74] Although the overwhelming majority of Muslims now live in independent states, the institutional infrastructures of many states are antiquated.

To Western observers the lack of freedom is the root cause of Islam's plight. Lewis describes freedom as: "freedom of the mind from constraint and indoctrination, to question and inquire and speak; freedom of the economy from corrupt and pervasive misman-agement; freedom of women from male oppression; freedom of citizens from tyranny."[75] The Muslim response to this diagnosis is either to embrace fundamentalism or to advocate secular democracy, as proclaimed in 1923 by Kemal Ataturk of the Turkish Republic. Other responses, however, are also possible and there is a basis for guarded optimism.

*The Economist* concludes that in Europe "a process of political assimilation is, hesitantly but visibly, taking place," just as most American Muslims have done.[76] Some facts: in the regional government of Brussels, Belgium Muslims now have about a quarter of the seats; in Amsterdam, coalition-building between Muslims and others is producing some positive results such as the re-election of a Moroccan-born city councilor.

Some public opinion surveys suggest that assimilation is succeeding with the public. German Turks tell pollsters that they are happy with their host country, and with the principle of separation of church and state. This separation explains why assimilation can work even in the face of a survey finding that 85% of Muslims were "rather" or "strictly" religious, and the number of those who think women should cover their head is rising.[77]

That assimilation is possible is found in the teachings of Tariq Ramadan, president of the European Muslim network in Brussels and a former professor of Islamic studies at the University of Fribourg. For the past 20 years he has focused his efforts on ways that Muslims can live their lives in the West and become Western Muslims. This is achievable when Muslims think of themselves as Muslims by religion but American, British, French, German by culture.[78] The city of Marseilles, with more Muslims than any other European city, is seen as a model of assimilation for "its minorities are not geographically ghettoized in suburbs but rather integrated into Marseille's daily life."[79]

## Pragmatism in employment practices

In the private sector, similar forms of assimilation are achievable. MNCs must consider employment policies and practices that over time would encourage the entry of Muslims into the workplace – also eventually to management ranks and the boards of directors. This progression has been succeeding in the United States with African-Americans. Through affirmative action programs they were recruited and through supporting statements from CEOs they were gradually absorbed in the workforce. It is just as easy for Muslims to get a job in America, but not in Europe. In comparison with England, fewer American than British Muslims have turned against their countries. American Muslims tend to be relatively well-off, upwardly mobile types, while many British Muslims are the disaffected, unemployed children of illiterate workers shipped in as cheap industrial labor.[80]

Reflecting the view that diversity is an asset, Ramadan is convinced that the presence of Muslims in the midst of Western countries is a source of strength, saying, "Millions of Western citizens of the Muslim faith have brought a new outlook toward the world and toward Western policy."[81] He strongly believes that Muslims have something to offer Western societies. "By the same token, the presence of Muslims in Western societies is of vital interest for those societies themselves." Furthermore, "People must begin to learn once again that Muslim thought, ever since the Middle Ages, has been an integral part of the construction of Western identity." The reverse is also true. The West, he says, will increasingly have an impact on traditional Muslim societies."[82] It should also be remembered that Islam never discouraged empirical investigation, as the medieval Roman Catholic church fathers did in persecuting Galileo for believing that the earth revolves around the sun, rather than the church view that the earth was the center of the universe.

Ramadan's advice to both Muslims and Westerners is particularly relevant to business's employment practices: "We must turn our backs on a vision that posits 'us' against 'them' and understand that our shared citizenship is the key factor in building the society of the future together. We must move forward from *integration,* simply becoming a member of a society, to *contribution,* being proactive and offering something to the society." "It is crucial that today's Western Muslims – men and women – make their voices heard on such issues [as Danish cartoons and Pope's comments]; they must refuse to withdraw into religious, cultural, or social ghettos. They must no longer see themselves as a 'minority'.... At the grass-roots level, a 'silent revolution' is already taking place in Muslim communities.... "[83]

## Progress in the community

There is no sure-fire answer when it comes to assimilating Europe's Muslims, but there is hope in the younger generation. Regarding France, as observed by Guy Sorman, author of 20 books on French politics and international affairs, "Overall the French tend to ignore how much their national culture implicitly rejects diversity."[84] He says the French suburbs bear more social resemblance to Soweto than Paris and that the French live in a discriminatory society where an invisible line separates the insiders from the outsiders. Not surprisingly, France's prisons hold nine times more young men with North African fathers than ones with French fathers. Women, however, are freeing themselves from the ghetto more than men, largely through marriage. A quarter of young Muslim French women are married to non-Muslim men. Another sign of progress is that in England, Muslims are flocking to British universities.[85]

Many Europeans fear that the rise of immigration in Europe, particularly among Muslims that remain connected to their native languages and cultures, is washing away European cultural identities. The German government has been supporting Islamic studies programs. But in a famous speech in fall 2010 Germany Chancellor Angela Merkel declared that the goal of multiculturalism in Germany had "utterly failed."[86] This view was echoed by French President Nicolas Sarkozy and U.K. Prime Minister David Cameron. In Germany, where about two-thirds of its 4.3 million Muslims have Turkish roots, one of the challenges has been that nearly 90% of the nation's imams come from abroad, mainly Turkey. They have difficulty relating to a new generation of German Muslims.

Believers in the power of economic growth, such as Benjamin Friedman, are tempted to believe that economic growth could create a force to replace patently nondemocratic regimes in the Middle East – with the caveat that this might only happen in the long run.[87]

# Islamic economics[88]

There is no resounding clash between Western and Islamic economics in supporting the market system. Both accept private ownership of property, the legitimacy of markets, the desirability of trade and economic growth, and recognition of self-interest as an economic motivator. The differences lie in judgments of moderation and whether religious values should mediate. A central belief of Muslims is that all human activities must be guided by religion. The guiding rules are derived from the Koran and Sunnah (sayings and practices of Prophet Muhammad).

Muslim writers see a lack of balance and moderation in capitalism, with capitalism placing excessive emphasis on the rights of individual ownership and freedom of enterprise that causes suffering and privation for those who own little. Sayyid Abu al-A'la Mawdudi, who popularized the term *Islamic economics*, thought that "undue emphasis on self-interest and the profit motive resulted in a society devoid of human character, brotherhood, sympathy and co-operation."[89] Capitalism gives little or no weight to personal and social values, which, many Islamic economists say, are inherent in the religion of Islam.

The Western world is no stranger to the role of religion in economic activity, as illustrated by Max Weber's classic book, *The Protestant Ethic and the Spirit of Capitalism*.[90] In the Middle Ages, business activity was subservient to religion, as described by Richard H. Tawney in his classic *Religion and the Rise of Capitalism: A Historical Study*.[91] At that time Christian lenders could not charge interest on money lent because interest was a payment for time, and time belonged to God. The Koran has a similar prohibition of *riba*, which translates into *any level of* interest, or usury. But bankers invented a way banks could advance funds to a client by having the client share in the profits of the enterprises the loan supported.

For example, when bankers from Merrill Lynch in London and Beirut-based Bemo Securitization were wrapping up a $166 million sale of debt-like certificates for a Houston natural gas producer, East Cameron Gas, certificates were so structured that Islamic investors effectively get a fixed rate of return while considering themselves owners of the underlying asset. This was condoned by an official *sharia* adviser who issued a *fatwa*, or declaration, certifying that the instrument "will yield returns, Allah willing, that are lawful and wholesome."[92]

Being a *sharia* scholar has become a lucrative profession, as Hamid Hassan, a 75-year-old Bubai resident and probably the world's biggest figure in *fatwas* for Islamic finance knows. He chairs the *sharia* boards of at least 15 Islamic banks and financial institutions.[93] *The Economist* reports that a critic of these arrangements, Ali A. Allawi, author of *The Crisis of Islamic Civilisation*, concludes that "Islamic economies are corrupt and maladministered, and their supposed ethical principles, such as Islamic banking, are a sham."[94]

A further refinement in Islamic thinking was mark-up trade financing, *murabaha*, whereby a mark-up is agreed in advance between the bank and the trader, and the period until the trader has to repay the bank is also stipulated at the outset. Interest payments, per se, are thereby avoided. Rodney Wilson writes, "*Murabaha* was arguably one of the factors that enabled Islamic banking to take off in the 1970s and prove a viable alternative to conventional banking in many Muslim countries."[95] Islamic banking became a $150 billion industry by the end of the 19th century.[96]

## Values connected with economics

Economics is not value-free, says Muhammad Abdul Mannan, one of the economists of the Islamic Economics Movement in the 1960s. Economics, he said, is "both a positive and normative science, concerned not only with what existed, but rather with what ought to exist."[97] He said the gap must be examined between the Islamic ideal and the secularist structures under which Muslims are forced to live. He considers economics a behavioral science, with the behavior of Muslims shaped by their religious beliefs. In other words, economics was prescriptive, with the rules ultimately determined by the *sharia*. Thus the gap must be examined between the Islamic ideal and the secularist structures under which Muslims were forced to live. Proponents of corporate social responsibility can be said to agree with Muslims by infusing noneconomic values into business activities.

In comparing Islam and Marxism, some economists expressed similar views, saying that capitalists and workers are not just products of a system of production but are also human beings with moral responsibilities.[98] A few employed Marxist arguments to denounce capitalism, saying that exploitation involved in capital accumulation was socially unjust and jeopardized the plight of workers.

## Economic development

Human values are especially important in economic development, states Khurshid Ahmad, a former minister of development and planning in Pakistan in the 1970s. He believes Muslim countries should draw on their Islamic inheritance rather than simply import Western models and concepts, asserting that imitation of the West "has failed to deliver the goods."[99] Western approaches assume "pseudo-value neutrality," believing their analysis is purely objective. Ahmad's core message, however, is that human values are the crucial element in any development process. Thus values should be recognized and enhanced rather than assumed.

But he fuses development with religious objectives by calling the result of development a *falah*, which defines prosperity in both material and spiritual terms and refers to prosperity in this world and the hereafter. "Development is desirable," he says, "and indeed imperative, as it makes believers better equipped to carry out the will of Allah."[100] In contrast to Christian teaching, Islam sees no virtue in poverty, for severe poverty prevents believers from carrying out their religious duties effectively. Thus some Muslims believe economics is divine in nature; it contributes to spiritual enlightenment.[101] The gulf between Western and Islamic notions of development is much wider than pragmatic arrangements with financial institutions.

## Conclusions

Anger in Islam results from Western attitudes of superiority and attempts to convince Muslims to surrender their values about the rights of women, the role of democracy, and the separation of religion from secular life. Some anti-Americanism attitudes in Muslim countries stem from differences in these values. The challenge for Western nations and institutions is to decide how tolerant to be toward Islamic values. Muslims who emigrate to Western nations have for the most part been willing to be assimilated to accommodate workplace needs, community participation, and democratic procedures, while still adhering to the Islamic faith.

The private sector has a large role to play in establishing communications between Muslims and their entities – be these nations, MNCs, or groups in civic society. Western societies should hesitate before misapplying an Islamic label to social problems rather than devising appropriate policies to them, such as increasing diversity in the workplace and other institutions. The West may harbor the belief that the experiences Muslim have in the West will have an impact on their values and behavior. Muslims may hope that narrow economic thinking associated with the free market system will accommodate greater consideration for the larger values of society.

### Revision Questions

1. In what ways must MNCs consider religion as a major cultural factor?
2. Describe the religion of Islam and why an understanding of it has become important in the production and sale of products and services in Muslim countries.
3. Discuss some situations when Muslims reacted against some behavior of Western countries. What lessons did MNCs learn?
4. Explain possible incompatibilities between the Muslim faith and capitalism and the ways "Islamic economics" accommodates differences.

## Discussion Questions

I. Western nations generally espouse a separation of state and religion. Why should not business likewise separate itself from religion?

II. Was Arla wrong in sacrificing the human rights value of "freedom of expression" for commercial reasons? What other options could it have considered? Looking to the future, what policy and action initiatives might Western MNCs consider to prevent future confrontations with Muslim nations?

III. As a bank manager what would you do if a Muslim woman who had worked in the bank for several years suddenly demands that she be allowed to wear a veil and to take time off to pray several times a day?

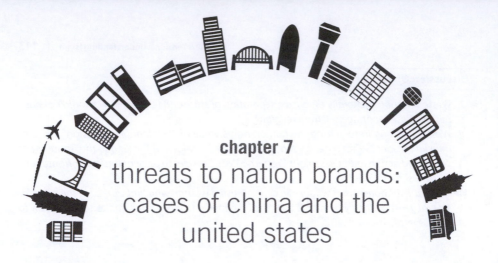

## chapter 7
# threats to nation brands: cases of china and the united states

**Objectives**

1. *Understand the concept of nation brand and be able to illustrate with reference to some countries.*
2. *Understand why the national brand is important in international management.*
3. *Be able to discuss how China's nation brand was hurt by product safety crises by Mattel and Sanlu Milk.*
4. *Know how anti-American attitudes among nations in the world have affected the United States' brand image and harmed American multinational corporations (MNCs)?*
5. *Learn what MNCs can do to counter anti-Americanism?*

Every country should be concerned about the perceptions and attitudes that governments and peoples of other nations have toward it. These views determine a country's reputation and nation brand, which in turn affects attitudes toward multinational corporations (MNCs). The brand affects the prospects for peaceful relationships, a variety of international exchanges, the ability of business to sell goods and services, and willingness of investors to acquire stocks, bonds and property abroad. An atmosphere of soured attitudes impedes the furtherance of globalization, economic development, the easing of tensions with Islam and other goals. The fact that public opinion is a powerful force cannot be ignored, which is demonstrated by the two cases of this chapter: (1) the product safety problems faced by China and (2) the persistence of anti-American attitudes across the world.

## Concept of nation brand

The term *brand* is drawn from marketing where it is used to identify and distinguish one's company and products from competitors. Alternative terms frequently used are the corporate image, corporate reputation, or corporate character. Every company prefers favorable attitudes and positive associations and exercises great care to choose descriptors that benefit it. For example, Exxon Research and Engineering Co. studied whether emphasizing *research* led to more favorable attitudes than *engineering* – and in what contexts.

Just as a brand supports the special qualities of a product or company, it can symbolize a nation to make it become better known and thought of favorably. A nation brand is a lens that colors attitudes toward all aspects of a country, including its government, businesses, social institutions, and people. Based on the psychology of personality and the sociology of impression management, national character is associated with a nation brand. It states that "people of each nation have a distinctive, enduring pattern of behavior and/or personality characteristics."[1] In describing the South Korean national character, for example, the authors of *International Marketing* describe it as passionate, emotional, intense, energetic, fun-loving, and impatient.[2]

## Promotion of nation brands by several countries

A nation brand can help a nation and its businesses and institutions attract tourists, stimulate trade, sell its products, attract investors, and promote its social goals. The nation brand is sometimes expressed as a product's "country of origin," which affects "perceived product quality."[3] Wally Olins, a well-known advertising specialist, is a strong advocate of "making a national brand." He says that "nations have always tried to create and modulate their reputations in order to create domestic loyalties and coherence and promote their own power and influence in neighbouring countries."[4] Certain favorable attributes of a nation that Olin describes are implied in the products they are known for; France is associated with perfume, Switzerland with watches, and Russia with vodka. He reminds us that "For cars, Mercedes, Audi and BMW are Germany and Germany is cars."[5]

### Examples of Finland, Singapore, and Germany

Countries engage in promotional activities to improve their nation brand. For example, Finland undertook a three-year communications program in 2001 to create "the impression of Finland as a modern European country with highly developed industry, breakthrough innovation technologies, and rich traditions."[6] Finland's objective was to broaden trade with other countries, especially Russia, its traditional trading partner.

Marketing techniques were used by Singapore in building a modern nation brand that attracted industry. When it separated from Malaysia in 1965, Singapore had considerable freedom to decide what kind of identity it would form. It decided to adopt all of the benefits Western societies had to offer, such as personal freedoms, mixed with a totally open business environment of "ultimate capitalism." Its core value was to be the ultimate environment for any entrepreneurial company to do business in open markets, a pro-business government, and economic stability.[7]

Singapore also wanted to combine these attributes with ancient Asian values of orderliness, discipline, and adherence to societal rules which benefitted all. In short, it wanted to orient itself to the world yet differentiate itself from neighboring countries. It became a nation brand known as a financial, technological, and manufacturing powerhouse with a diversity of industries. Singapore describes itself as having excellent information and communications technology infrastructure, together with spacious and accessible exhibit centers, good financial systems, and low-risk environment."[8] The "Lion City" has become the number one international expo site in Asia and fifth in the world – after London, Brussels, Paris, and Vienna.

Advanced economies such as Germany also seek to bolster their nation brand, as shown by its promotion of "Germany: The Home of Smart Innovation." The ad asserts: "Germany's reputation for engineering excellence and innovation means that consumers buying German goods are typically looking for that little bit extra – be it cutting edge technology or that special, perfectly designed something that simply can't be found elsewhere." Germany refers to KPMG's *Guide to International Business Location 2010*, which states, "Germany is – alongside the Netherlands and Australia – an international leader in terms of the science and technology industry share of the total work force. Germany, with Japan and the United States, invests the greatest share of gross domestic product (GDP) in research and development internationally."[9] Germany also refers to the World Economic Forum's "Global Competitiveness Report 2010–2010 which ranks Germany eighth out of 139 countries for innovation.

### Special opportunities to promote the nation brand

The World Economic Forum's annual Davos gatherings have become a useful platform to improve national images. The January 2007 meeting comprised 2,400 participants and 500 media people, including 24 heads of state and 800 corporate chieftains. "It's a great platform," says Martin Sorrell, CEO of the marketing firm WPP Group PLC; "you have all the stakeholders you want to influence."[10] In 2006 India used the opportunity to launch a massive campaign to improve its image. When participants arrived at the Zurich airport they were surrounded by posters, and when they boarded buses in the ski resort they faced the slogan: "India – Fastest Growing Free market Democracy."[11]

In similar fashion, the Olympics provide an opportunity for a nation to project its image abroad. In preparing for the 2008 Olympics in Beijing, China completed major building projects and improved Beijing's infrastructure as a way to impress visitors with China's progress. Its message to the world was "We've arrived." For MNCs interested in a top-level international sponsorship, which costs as much as $80 million for one Winter and one Summer Olympics, the value of world attention is enormous. Coca-Cola, McDonald's and Volkswagen expected to reinforce their brands, while Lenovo Group Ltd., whose brand was not yet widely appreciated, had even more to gain.[12]

## Product safety crises threaten China's nation brand

The following two cases illustrate how a crisis threatened the nation brand of China, as well as a company image. Mattel's recall of lead-tainted toys made in China was not only a classic product recall crisis but also involved sensitive diplomacy between the company and the Chinese government. And Sanlu's tainted baby formula scandal involved a Chinese milk producer, a major New Zealand owner, and the governments of both companies.

### Mattel blames China for its unsafe toys

Mattel Inc., the United States' largest seller of toys, faced a major reputational crisis in September 2007 when it withdrew nearly one million lead-tainted toys from the market.[13] The event became part of a wave of product safety issues and actual recalls of Chinese exports of consumer products during the spring and summer that year. Mattel feared that concern about the safety of its toys would jeopardize its sales and brand reputation. The situation warranted the attention of Mattel's chairman and CEO Bob Eckhart. He immediately blamed the media, saying, "the character of Mattel has been maligned."[14] But he went further and blamed China.

China feared that crises like Mattel's toy recall would stigmatize its "Made in China" label and jeopardize other products and seriously disrupt its international commerce. China, which manufactures about 65% of Mattel's toys and nearly 80% of all the toys imported by the United States, was prominently named in news articles.[15] Mattel made matters worse for China because it acted like an innocent victim whose product safety standards were violated by irresponsible Chinese manufacturers. At a Senate subcommittee hearing, Eckhart directly blamed China for the product recall, saying "that certain vendors or their subcontractors violated our well-established rules."

China's nation brand was further severely damaged by media stories suggesting that the fault of safety lapses was attributable to China's culture. The *Wall Street Journal* reporter Emily Parker blamed defects in Chinese products on China's single-minded goal of economic development at the expense of consumer and worker safety and the environment. She described China as "a country without a real rule of law, where everything is subject to Communist Party 'interpretation,' there is no codified set of ethics to guide national behavior."[16]

China's response to safety allegations was one of "defiance and denial." It said U.S. authorities were exaggerating the risks and playing up dangers because of trade disputes. A team of Chinese diplomats in Washington, DC, went to Capitol Hill to present its case and began briefing legislators and reporters. They said China's ability to communicate was "hampered by its overall inexperience at managing public perceptions in a world of instant communications."[17]

Realizing that it was endangering its important economic relationship with China, Mattel belatedly apologized to China.[18] Thomas A. Debrowski, Mattel's executive vice president for worldwide operations flew to Beijing to meet with Mr. Li, the Chinese product-safety chief who heads the General Administration of Quality Supervision, Inspection and Quarantine. In an about-face, Debroski humbly stated:

> Mattel takes full responsibility for these recalls and apologizes personally to you, the Chinese people, and all of our customers who received the toys. It's important for everyone to understand that the vast majority of those products that we recalled were the result of a design flaw in Mattel's design, not through a manufacturing flaw in Chinese manufacturers.[19]

The apology was astonishing, and Mattel knew it because it almost immediately tried to downplay its significance by saying the company "apologized to the Chinese today just as it has wherever its toys are sold."[20] The case demonstrates the growing recognition of diplomacy to a corporation and the need for diplomatic overtures with nation-states. In time, however, China acknowledged the safety problem and took responsible action by arresting and punishing alleged offenders.

## Sanlu's milk scandal further tarnishes China's nation brand

In 2008 a milk scandal further severely damaged China's nation brand. The milk industry was found to cause the death of six infants and injury to 50,000 others who suffered from severe kidney failure.[21] Milk producers in China – farmers, milk traders, and milk manufacturers – had knowingly and secretly contaminated their baby formula with the toxic chemical melamine, which makes protein-deficient or diluted milk appear to contain more protein and thereby pass quality testing.[22] Tainting of milk was an open secret in China.

The crisis focused on the Shijazhuang Sanlu Group, which was China's largest milk producer and a trusted brand. Sanlu started receiving reports of sickened babies in March 2008, but its investigations supposedly revealed no problems. In May a child died of kidney problems, but officials only later connected the death to the tainted formula. In July after a second child died, Sanlu tests revealed melamine contamination.

Had it followed the sound crisis management practice of giving paramount attention to the protection of public health and safety, Sanlu would have made an immediate public announcement and withdrawn the affected products. Instead, Sanlu delayed action. It was not until August 2, just six days before the opening of the 2008 Beijing Olympics, that at a board meeting Sanlu directors were informed of the problem. An important international aspect was that some of the directors were from the Fonterra Co-operative Group Ltd., a New Zealand dairy company which owned 43% of Sanlu. Andrew Ferrier, Fonterra's chief executive urged disclosure: "We encouraged Sanlu, we encouraged the authorities, to go public." It did not, however, insist on disclosure. After some "soul searching," Ferrier decided that Fonterra would not make a public statement on its own and instead let Sanlu exercise "their own judgment."[23]

This was a highly controversial decision that may have taken differences in Chinese and U.S. political systems into account. Some said that the cultural admonition not to let their Chinese partners get offended or "lose face" was a factor in Fonterra's decision.[24] Ferrier defended his decision by saying that to reveal the problem before Chinese officials did would have been "totally irresponsible."[25]

Following the August 2 board meeting, Sanlu limited its actions to informing local health officials. The directors' response was to tell the company not to make a public announcement but to quietly remove tainted product from store shelves.[26] Accordingly, on August 6 Sanlu asked distributors to recall all formula made before that date and removed more than 8,000 tons of products in supermarkets, schools, and Starbucks outlets across China.[27]

It appears that China's nation-building goal of the Olympics prevailed over the health and safety of infants. Local authorities said they were "were not in a position" to make a public announcement," perhaps fearing that the central government would be displeased with such an event days before the opening of the Olympics. In seeking to create an image of a safe and hygienic China, the leadership had suppressed news about the widespread contamination of milk products with melamine, endangering thousands of babies and causing the death of several babies.[28] The crisis damaged China's nation brand as well as the reputation of the Chinese milk industry. Tens of thousands of babies had been affected and several had died. The milk scandal may have destroyed the China brand as much as the Olympics improved it.

## Anti-americanism undermines U.S. brand

World surveys have shown persistent anti-American attitudes by peoples of many nations in the past decade. Business if affected by this public opinion in terms of country entry, the construction of facilities, sales, and government regulatory treatment. American businesspeople must ask themselves whether their behavior may have contributed to anti-Americanism and how it can avoid doing so in the future. They must also decide on the public policy issue of how involved to become in government foreign affairs and in such specifics as whether to comply with government requests to assist their public diplomacy efforts.

## Antagonism toward the U.S. grows

Antagonism toward the United States has been shown by surveys and the statements and attitudes of world leaders. For example, when a relatively minor oil spill 200 miles off the coast of Brazil occurred in November 2011, Chevron was surprised and disappointed in the exaggerated reaction by the Brazilian government and media.[29] The following year, in July 2012, a court barred the company from producing or transporting oil for a month until an investigation into the oil spill was completed.[30]

### What surveys show

Anti-Americanism was dramatically revealed in *What the World Thinks in 2002*, a report of the Pew Global Attitudes Project by the Pew Research Center for People and the Press. Based on a survey with a sample of 38,000 people in 44 countries in Europe, Asia, Africa, the Middle East and Latin America, it found two contrasting global trends: continued strong public support for American ideals and values, and alongside growing criticism of U.S. unilateralism in foreign policy.[31] Furthermore, the report warned that while there was widespread global support of the U.S.-led war on terrorists, there were also large minorities or majorities in some countries who believe that the United States is routinely ignoring the interests of other nations and not doing enough to help solve global problems.[32] Survey reports painted a mostly negative picture of the image of America, its people and policies.[33,34]

The erosion of favorable attitudes toward the United States was confirmed in subsequent surveys conducted in June 2003,[35] 2006 and 2007.[36] Andrew Kohut, director of the Pew Research Center who heads up the Global Attitudes Project, concluded that the main lesson of the surveys is that while there is a reserve of good will toward the United States, it has an increasing number of detractors. Despite the deepening of anti-Americanism, on an optimistic note Kohut said, "it hasn't really widened. It has worsened among America's European allies and is very, very bad in the Muslim world. But there is still a favorable view of the United States in many African countries, as well as in 'New Europe' and the Far East."[37] Freedom of speech, fair elections, and an impartial judiciary are prized goals for people around the world, says Kohut.[38] Majorities in most Western countries associate Americans with the positive adjectives of "inventive" and "hardworking."[39] Furthermore, "Globalization, the free market model and democratic ideals are accepted in all corners of the world."[40]

Anti-Americanism has also vented itself in speeches by some world leaders. The United Nations gathering of 57 nations in September 2006 revealed "a world body awash in grievances over trade, the Iraq War, perceived U.S. unilateralism, Washington's drug policy in Latin America and the 'great powers' structure of the U.N. itself."[41] These voices show "a rising chorus of discontent with the world order envisioned by the U.S." The *Wall Street Journal* wrote that "full-bore anti-Americanism is not only back in fashion, but also much appreciated by many in attendance."[42] A senior U.S. official commented, "There's a new sense of the oppressed versus the oppressor. What they have in common is their hatred of the U.S. and it's created this solidarity across Third World lines."[43]

### Fallen idol

As Andrew Kohut and Bruce Stokes, the international economics columnist for the *National Journal*, found, the worldwide dislike for America had by May 2006 spread: "it's not just our government people their countries can't stand – it's Us."[44] According to the Pew Global Attitudes Study, "Despite near universal admiration for U.S. technology and a strong appetite for its cultural exports in most parts of the world, large proportions in most countries think it is bad that American ideas and customs are spreading to their countries."[45]

University of Toronto Professor of Human Rights Michael Ignatieff explains that American society has become discredited in the eyes of the world. "Once a model to emulate," he said, it "has become the exception to avoid." He cited "the world's judgment of America's lack of health care for the poor; its retention of capital punishment; the curious 'constitutional right' of every citizen to have guns; the religiosity of American conservatives; the arguably unjust outcome of the presidential election of 2000; and the 'the phenomenal influence of money on American elections.'"[46]

The financial crisis of 2007–2008 eroded confidence in the United States and capitalism itself. Support for capitalism is down in nine of the 16 countries surveyed in a 2012 Pew Research Center Global Attitude Project survey.[47] Columnist Schumpeter in *The Economist* states, "America is becoming a less attractive place to business."[48] Debate in Congress over tax and spending reforms and last-minute drama about going over the fiscal cliff reveal that America's political system is dysfunctional and that the country is deeply divided. Although corporate leaders rejoice over having averted a possible recession, they know that another confrontation will occur over fiscal battles in two months' time. As stated by Stephen Wiehe, CEO of software maker SciQuest Inc., "There's huge amounts of uncertainty, and people don't know what will happen with the markets or the economy."[49]

### Explanations of anti-American attitudes

The sources of anti-American attitudes are numerous, ranging from sentiments about the U.S. political and economic policies to cultural traits associated with Americans.

- *Dislike of U.S. policies.* The main reason for rampant anti-Americanism is a strong dislike for government policies, especially the war in Iraq. Business is frustrated with government policy, said a participant of the Global Public Affairs Institute (GPAI) in March 2003 in New York City. (The GPAI was established in 1989 by a group of veteran corporate public affairs officers "to play a role in nurturing the skills and sensitivities of professional communicators whose companies are powerful economic forces in the global economy."[50]) He said, "The thing that affects my business the most, and which limits my ability to do business abroad, is the thing I can't change: the United States' political position."[51] Another member argued however that business could lobby privately in Washington.[52]

- *Arrogance.* It is the manner of conducting foreign policy that irritates many, for America is seen as imperialistic and arrogant. In its first year, the Bush administration withdrew from five international treaties and, as Fareed Zakaria of *Newsweek* said, "did so as brusquely as it could…. It developed a language and diplomatic style that seemed calculated to offend the world."[53] As stated by a GPAI participant, the perception is that "We're arrogant, bullying, and disrespectful of others across all lines."[54]

- *Do not consider problems and interests of others.* At the heart of the decline in world opinion about America is the perception that the United States acts internationally without taking into account the interests of other nations.[55] In 2006, no fewer than 89% of the French, 83% of Canadians, and 74% of the British expressed this opinion.[56] Some participants in the GPAI discussion agreed, saying that the United States is seen as focusing on "self-interest and much less on community impact and needs assessments."[57]

- *Does too little to help solve world problems.* A related complaint by global publics is that the United States does too little to solve world problems and backs policies that increase the poverty gap. The percent saying so is high in every part of the world. In Europe it is highest in France, in Latin America it is Venezuela, in Asia it is Indonesia, in Africa it is Nigeria, and in conflict areas it is Egypt.[58]

- *Uses too much of the world's material goods.* An oft-cited statistic is that countries not included in the developed world represent over 80% of the world's population, but have less than 20% of the GDP. Writing in the *International Journal on World Peace*, Fred Maidment cites these statistics: India has over one billion people, but its GDP is less than $500 billion; Indonesia, the largest Islamic county in the world, has about 300 million people and a GDP of $140 billion, less than that of the State of Connecticut; the entire continent of Africa has a GDP less than that of Texas.[59]

- *American "exceptionalism."* The idea that the United States is superior and that the world should be remodeling according to American ideals is condescending.[60] An example is that in the global War on Terror, the United States acted "as though it had all the right answers, demanding from its 'allies' nothing less than unquestioning loyalty."[61]

- *Resentment of America as a superpower.* Anti-Americanism can be seen as a normal reaction to the United States as the undisputed superpower, mixed with jealousy and envy. Hostility toward power is common, however. Even in small problem-solving groups, the person who is rated as the task leader is generally not liked.[62]

- *America has become an icon for globalization.* The United States is seen as pushing the ideology of free markets, which causes resentment because "American-style business practices are forcing changes in industrial and societal practices – longer work days and the opening of shops on Sunday – and that such accelerations in the pace of modernization threaten to overwhelm traditional ways of life…."[63] The Anglo-American business model is fiercely competitive compared to the Japanese model, the Singapore/Malaysia model, or the European system – countries where competition is tempered.[64] Adherents of communism, relativism, cultural Marxism, and multiculturalism resist the free market ideology and some specifically resent the idea of an impersonal operation of market forces.[65]

- *Cultural differences and political and social divisions.* Deep value differences about political and social policies and values divide Americans and Western Europeans. As Kohut notes, "Americans prize individualism and personal empowerment more than do Western Europeans." For example, there is much more support for an extensive social safety net in Europe than in the United States

Furthermore, more than other issues, religion has come to define the transatlantic values gap. Western Europe is mostly secular whereas the United States is found to be the most religious nation among wealthy nations. A cultural gap exists which is reflected in how entertainment outlets (including American films) are making fun of Americans. At their worst, Americans are regarded as selfish, indulgent, childish, and dangerously righteous. Anything that reinforces those views proves wildly popular in Europe.

- *Ambivalence toward U.S. cultural products.* The Pew Research Center notes that "while most people say they admire American movies, music and TV programs, they dislike the spread of American ideas and customs". More than half (54%) of Canadians say that this diffusion of culture is unfortunate. Europeans feel this more strongly: 71% of the French, 67% of Germans, and 50% of Britons regard the spread of culture negatively. As might be expected, this view is most extreme in conflict areas: 84% in Egypt, 82% in Jordan, 81% in Pakistan, and 78% in Turkey.[66] Also mentioned is that the uniform McDonald's and Starbucks diet threatens other countries' indigenous cultures.[67]

## Implications for U.S. business

The implications of anti-Americanism for U.S. business abroad and the United States' relationship with other nations, says Jeffry Garten, are serious. He worries that the United States could be seeing the rise of a huge counterforce to continued globalization and the potential breakdown in the American-led multilateral system in which U.S. foreign policy and its economic policy were in synch.[68]

In Europe, American foreign policy has hardened the resolve of officials to oppose U.S. wishes in such areas as export tax rebates and the threat by the European Union to impose sanctions to the tune of $4 billion if the United States fails to comply quickly with World Trade Organization rulings. U.S. efforts to achieve relaxation of restrictions on imports of genetically modified foods have run into hardening attitudes. Europeans are also looking critically at competition policy issues affecting Microsoft and others.[69]

MNCs are vulnerable to global forces because they are on the front lines of new markets and operations in many parts of the world. Oil, natural gas, and mining industries are particularly vulnerable because they extract natural resources that citizens, mainly in developing countries, see as exploitation for foreign benefit and spoilation of their natural environments. More generally, MNCs are criticized for being greedy, using excessively aggressive marketing tactics, and being insensitive to foreign cultures.

Back in the 1980s and 1990s, being seen as an "American" company was a distinct advantage. But in a mid-2006 survey by Consultant Simon Anholt of 26,000 consumers in 35 nations of their opinion on national brands, the United States ranked 10th overall, right behind Australia and just ahead of Spain. CEOs of companies such as American Express and American Airlines are not likely to admit that its American roots are hurting sales, but privately they might think otherwise. On an optimistic note, Anholt believes that people are generally adept at separating people and companies of a nation from that nation's government.[70]

A majority of American CEOs now concede that anti-American sentiment is a problem. Consumers seem to be growing angrier and taking it out on American companies by sporadically boycotting American goods, such as Levi's, KFC, and Ford, and buying less from American companies. At the time, several top brands – Marlboro, McDonald's, Wal-Mart, Disney, and Gap – reported weak or falling sales in European markets. One-third of respondents said they would avoid purchasing Mattel's Barbie because of her American origins; indeed, sales fell 13% worldwide in the third quarter of 2004.

Other explanations, however, may account for some of the drop in sales. John Quelch, a Harvard Business School professor and leading skeptic about the link between politics and consumer behavior, says, "It's too simplistic to say [that] what's happened in Europe is just a function of anti-Americanism."[71] Coca-Cola, for example, blames new bottling laws for its 16% sales decline in Germany during 2004's third quarter; and Marlboro attributes its 18.7% drop in sales in Germany and 24.5% drop in France to higher cigarette taxes.[72]

In summing up, a participant in the GPAI discussion worried: "Are we perceived as having gone out and raped the world.... If you're in a country where an American company has come in and done a terrible job, you'll be tarred with the same brush. It doesn't matter how great a job you're doing."[73] Multinationals inevitably serve as change agents, and change is in many cases resisted, especially by vested interests. The key question has become: What can the U.S. government and private sector can do to rebuild confidence in America?

## Protests, boycotts, and loss of sales

Just as Americans took to eating "freedom fries" to punish the French for not endorsing the Iraq war, Europeans have taken to boycotting McDonald's and drinking various clones of Coca-Cola. Jose Bove's attack of a McDonald's in France and fire-bombing of McDonald's, Pizza Huts, and KFC in Lebanon and Saudi Arabia are often cited as examples of citizen outrage against U.S. companies. Furthermore, boycotts have been called in the Middle East against Coca-Cola and other American icons. In 2002, diplomats said that consumers shunning U.S. products could eventually hurt sales, contributing to a projected 10–15% fall in U.S. exports to Saudi Arabia. The spread of a boycott call to the Middle East is being fanned by women's groups, citizen committees, trade unions and other grassroots organizations.[74]

The protest against Pizza Hut in Indonesia illustrates the dynamics of the problem facing American outlets. In rallies to protest the U.S.-led attack on Afghanistan, hundreds of students from various universities in Yogyakarta, Indonesia, burned an effigy of President Bush and planned to "seal" popular American fast-food restaurants. Students from the Indonesian Islamic University carried banners, one reading "Boycott U.S. products." Some students stopped in front of a Pizza Hut restaurant and held a street theater performance depicting hungry Afghans. One protester said, "When you eat here, you help finance the assault on Afghanistan," "Let's boycott this capitalist product from now on." After holding speeches, the protesters symbolically sealed the front door of Pizza Hut with dozens of posters, one which read, "Eating here means killing the poor Afghans." They then went on to McDonald's.[75]

For the most part, however, despite anti-American attitudes American products are still largely immune from consumer boycotts. Only Coca-Cola, McDonald's, and other American icons have sporadically suffered. The products of American popular culture are typically embraced by foreign populations, even though some governments resist it and sometimes complain of cultural imperialism. President Jacques Chirac once urged French TV to set up a 24-hour TV news channel out of fear of the growing influence of American-owned networks such as Murdoch's Fox News and AOL Time Warner's CNN. Even the British government introduced a restrictive measure.

McDonald's suffered sales losses of 30% in the Middle East, and Starbuck's sales also suffered. Citibank in Egypt received a bomb threat and Iran banned all media advertising for U.S.-made goods.[77] Vulnerability to threats varies among different industries, with consumer goods being most vulnerable. Perhaps a larger risk to companies is "a loss of cachet" among younger consumers. Where once Marlboro cigarettes, Big Macs and a can of Coke appeared cool even among French teenagers, a significant percentage may now think twice about the cultural message that U.S. brands project."[78] A 2003 international poll of eleven countries for the BBC shows that the most vulnerable companies are those that are uppermost in people's minds. When asked what the first thing that comes to mind when naming an American product, respondents named (in order of frequency) Coca-Cola, McDonald's, Pepsi, burgers, Nike, computers, Levis, and Ford.[79]

## Country of origin impact on sales

These commercial setbacks illustrate what marketers call the impact of country-of-origin on sales. According to a 2005 Edelman Trust Barometer survey of global elites, 53% of European elites say a company's national identity is "very influential" in their purchasing decisions, as is cultural identity and national government.[80] Another survey – taken by the Seattle-based market-research company GMI of 20,000 international consumers – shows that 80% of European and Canadian consumers distrust the U.S. government. The expected effects are that 41% of Canadian elites were less likely to purchase American products because of Bush Administration policies. Elsewhere, 56% in the United Kingdom, 61% in France, 49% in Germany, and 42% in Brazil.[81]

In Germany, Anabel Houben, a co-founder of the Dusseldorf-based public relations and marketing company C4 Consulting, reports seeing signs everywhere that U.S. brands are learning to fly the flag subtly. "The emphasis on American companies or origins is being de-emphasized. The corporate identity is moving into the background."[82] Starbucks in central Berlin, for example, will not find a U.S. flag or other overt cultural reference to its origins as the Seattle-based coffee chain.

Margaret Scammell, senior lecturer in media and communications at the London School of Economics, goes further in saying, "Our data shows that this is not simply political tension at the root of this, but some underlying discomfort with American culture." Her opinion was supported by Edelman's annual Trust Barometer, which found that 32% of Europeans polled said they were "less likely" to purchase U.S. products because of disagreements with U.S. culture. The Coca-Cola brand, while "trusted" by 69% of U.S. respondents, was trusted by only 45% in Europe and 46% in Canada. The survey also found that Citigroup's banking products were trusted by 56% of Americans but by only 25% of Europeans and 26% of Canadians.

## U.S. government responses to anti-Americanism

The U.S. government's response has been to launch a public diplomacy campaign. The United States Information Agency described its goals as: "to understand, inform, and influence foreign publics in promotion of the U.S. national interest, and to broaden the dialogue between Americans, their institutions, and their counterparts abroad." These goals are reflected in R. F. Delaney's *International Communication and the New Diplomacy*, where he defined public diplomacy as "the way in which both government and private individuals and groups influence directly or indirectly those public attitudes and opinions which bear directly or indirectly on another government's foreign policy decisions."[83]

Business supported the public diplomacy campaign through the formation of Business for Diplomatic Action (BDA). Cari Eggspuehler, executive director of the group, says, "Every single U.S. company operating abroad should be doing its own public diplomacy. Business is a more credible messenger than government."[84] BDA describes itself as "an initiative directed by a task force of preeminent global communications, marketing, political science, research, media, and multinational corporate executives. BDA aims to engage and mobilize American companies and individuals to become better global citizens, and to enlist the U.S. business community in specific actions and initiatives aimed at measurably improving the standing of America in the world."[85]

One way business helped in the public diplomacy effort was to engage in relief efforts. After the devastating Asian tsunami in late December 2004, the United States won a rare surge of goodwill when the navy's warships and aircraft rescued thousands of people. In the private sector, U.S. corporations had pledged more than $80 million in cash and supplies to help disaster victims. Drug makers with offices or plants in the region sent employees out with antibiotics, nutritional supplements, infant formula, baby food, and other supplies. Employees of Coca-Cola, Pepsico, and Marriott International hotels in the region delivered bottled water, food, and other supplies.[86]

A survey taken a week after the tsunami showed that 59% of people in the area were so pleased with American corporations' relief efforts that their impression of these companies improved. Humanitarian efforts seemed to eclipse existing anti-Americanism in the affected regions. A poll of 1,177 Indonesians in late January 2006 found that those with a favorable opinion of the United States jumped from a low of 15% in May 2003 to more than 44%. A June 2005 Pew Research Center survey confirmed that tsunami aid had changed Indonesian opinions of the United States.[87]

These experiences convinced some business leaders that they should become more involved in public diplomacy. One leader who endorsed this engagement was Sanford Weill, chairman of Citigroup Inc., who said, "I think companies are realizing that we all have to be salesmen for America and not just sit back and rely on the government."[88] Weill helped lead the Pakistan relief drive and his company contributed $7 million to an offshoot of the Business Roundtable called the Partnership for Disaster Relief. Altogether nearly 600 U.S. companies contributed around $570 million in recon- struction aid. Along with a U.S. government appropriation of $841 million for relief and reconstruction, including the military airlift and engineering support, the U.S. effort helped boost favorable opinions of the United States in Indonesia to 38% from 15% a year earlier, according to a Pew Research Center survey conducted in the summer of 2005.[89]

A major business initiative in supporting public diplomacy was the formation of Business for Diplomatic Action (BDA). Cari Eggspuehler, executive director of the group, says, "Every single U.S. company operating abroad should be doing its own public diplomacy. Business is a more credible messenger than government."[90] BDA describes itself as "an initiative directed by a task force of preeminent global communications, marketing, political science, research, media, and multinational corporate executives. BDA aims to engage and mobilize American companies and individuals to become better global citizens, and to enlist the US business community in specific actions and initiatives aimed at measurably improving the standing of America in the world."[91]

In a *Foreign Policy* article, "Diplomacy by Other Means," M. Leonard suggests ways the U.S.'s overseas reputation can be improved. He lists four steps: (1) rebuild relationships, (2) develop a strategic communication method which integrates public messages in everyday news, (3) use alternative communication tools, and (4) communicate on a human level to provide relevance to messages."[92] New approaches to public diplomacy recognize the value of business involvement and the absolute necessity to engage in concrete actions. These and other approaches are part of the new diplomatic communication initiatives discussed in Chapter 12.

### Business responds with less arrogance, more sensitivity to needs of others

A simple response by some businesses to prejudice against their national identities in the past was to keep a low profile, for example, by not flying the American flag or brandishing company logos. Another often-used method has been to hire locals rather than expatriates. In the 1950s, as Japanese products and symbols entered southeast Asia, Japanese companies were given similar advice by veteran public relations counselor Roy Leffingwell. He told them not to overwhelm the public with huge neon signs in shopping districts touting Japanese trademarks.[93] These responses, however, are inadequate and have been substituted by more fundamental methods.

The arrogance and insensitivity of U.S. leaders and executives, often mentioned in surveys and anecdotes, requires Americans to become more sensitive to others. While self-confidence is a desirable attribute, it should not lead to an unwillingness to listen to others – nor, after calling for a dialogue, using it to prove you are right and they are wrong.[94] Management should become sensitive to how the behavior of American executives and others is perceived. As one expatriate observed, "Living abroad, you see to a degree that you don't see here how Americans can be heavy-handed and indifferent to or ignorant of the effects of what they do."[95] Much of this insensitivity is caused by failing to understand or adapt to foreign attitudes and cultures.

Another method is to stress the positive attitudes toward the United States that surveys have shown. Thus the safest and likely most effective approach for a company is to serve as a model of U.S. values, standards, and accomplishments. When U.S. entrepreneurs are seen as innovative and efficient that helps to improve attitudes. But the opposite happens when "take charge" attitudes demean others and create an air of superiority. Similarly, although the world craves more goods and services, U.S. consumerism values must stop short of enthroning materialistic values above all others. Profits must not be seen as the sole concern of business.

The following practices can help companies accomplish the above goals:

- *Customize products.* Much can be learned from the marketers' approach. They do not force a standardized product on consumers in other countries; instead they conduct market research to determine their consumers' preferences and desires and modify products accordingly. Since 1997, McDonald's-France has not imported American beef; it also solves the problem of tastes by selling beer in Germany, mango shakes in Hong Kong, and a different hamburger in Japan.[96] In Egypt, McDonald's introduced falafel; and in Saudi Arabia it contributes 30 cents for every Big Mac sold to the Red Crescent or other medical services.[97] Companies have also toned down rampant commercialism and consumerism in countries that resist materialistic values, especially in the Middle East, in accordance with Islamic faith.
- *Use best practices.* To show the benefits of MNCs, their "best practices" are applied abroad, but with sensitivity to local resistance. Personnel policies should exemplify the positive value that pay and promotions should be based on merit and avoid nondiscrimination, including gender.[98] With employees all over the world, MNCs might focus on their own organization's employees and culture, rather than trying to change the world. For example, an American manager in a Japanese drug company saw the need to oppose the traditional Japanese norm of life-time tenure when an employee failed to meet performance criteria.[99] Also, when General Electric purchased a Hungarian bulb manufacturer, it downsized the workforce and replaced the all-too-generous maternity leaves with more limited ones.[100] One suggestion by a participant of the GPAI is to provide employee education and training opportunities and communicate their availability to them.
- *Exercise corporate citizenship.* The following actions associated with corporate citizenship should be exercised: interacting with local communities, creating codes of conduct, conducting social audits, and engaging in social reporting. For example, Fluor Corp., a member of the public works and construction industries, developed anticorruption principles that have been adapted by 25 global engineering and construction firms. The company heads the World Economic Forum's Engineering and Construction sector.[101]

GPAI members believe trust can be restored by demonstrating "the value of U.S. and other business to individual citizens worldwide through contributions to product production and innovation, science and learning, employment, social investments."[102] They also believe that attitudes toward MNCs and the United States can be improved when companies embark on a more active community role – individually or collectively, or by industry or region.[103] They say, "Maybe international organizations should be more active in putting forward cultural, education, and health programs that will have an impact locally, improving people's well being and attitudes toward what the corporation brings to the table."[104]

American MNCs should also consider some of the ways the private sector can help the federal government improve the reputation of the United States around the world through public diplomacy.

- *Participate in public policy issues.* American MNCs are burdened with widespread foreign resentment of U.S. policies, ranging from the war in Iraq to opposition to international efforts to curb global warming. One proposal, therefore, is that U.S. companies apply the same kind of lobbying pressure to change U.S. foreign policy that they do when they influence trade agreements and tariff regulations. As the report by the GPAI indicated, U.S. business should convince the U.S. government to conduct bilateral and multilateral negotiations differently to achieve better results and to minimize anti-Americanism.[105] U.S. business should also encourage participation in such initiatives as the U.N. Global Compact.

Global managers who possess the attributes outlined earlier are more likely to avoid the criticisms of U.S. business and are best equipped to execute the practices outlined above.

## Conclusions

The nation brand is potentially an important consideration for an MNC. As shown in the Mattel and Sanlu cases in China and worldwide anti-American attitudes, reputational damage to a company also damages the nation brand and, therefore, harms other businesses. The reverse is also true: strong company brands, such as Samsung in South Korea and Sony in Japan, helped bolster the national reputations of those countries. Nation brands and company brands tend to be complementary.

MNCs should view their nation brands as intangible assets that can strategically be employed to reinforce their company brands in the international arena. But anti-American attitudes by people in many countries can do the opposite. When translated into behavior, extreme negative attitudes might trigger protests that result in property damage and therefore discourage companies from doing business in some countries. American global managers must be sensitive to negative attitudes and look for constructive remedies, including collaboration with government in public diplomacy efforts. On a personal level, MNC executives should avoid a display of arrogance and a claim of American "exceptionalism." Whenever possible, they should demonstrate the value of such qualities as inventivism and the application of best practices.

### Revision Questions

1. What is a nation brand and how is an MNC affected by it? Cite some cases.
2. Why and in what ways is a nation brand especially important in international management? Describe the incidents that caused a deterioration in China's nation brand regarding product safety?
3. How might MNCs be hurt by anti-American attitudes?

### Discussion Questions

I. "Harm to the U.S. brand is the result of business behavior overseas and the attitudes expressed by business executives" What specific behaviors and attitudes might be at fault? Discuss the extent to which you agree with this assessment and whether changes should be made.
II. Andrew Ferrier, the CEO of the New Zealand company that is a major owner of Sanlu, urged Sanlu's board to disclose the discovery of tainted milk that had already killed two children and sickened others, but after "some soul searching," he did not insist on disclosure and let Sanlu exercise its own judgment. Discuss why his decision is or is not defensible.
III. "Chinese culture is simply inimical to assuring product safety." What features of Chinese culture might this statement be referring to? Does this judgment have merit?
IV. "A nation brand is irrelevant to a company's success as long as its company brand is strong." Argue the pros and cons of this view.

# chapter 8
# corporate responsibility for human rights

**Objectives**

1. *Know what developments and proclamations led human rights to become a significant international issue.*
2. *Know what behaviors are considered human rights violations and which are most likely to affect business.*
3. *Understand how the concept of complicity can implicate business, and know how specific companies have been affected.*
4. *Recognize the specific pressures faced by a multinational corporation (MNC) in its external environment that have persuaded them to conform to human rights standards.*
5. *Know what options an MNC can choose from in conforming with human rights.*

Human rights is a thorny issue for business. It stems from the drive by many businesses to maximize profits by fully exploiting the advantages of globalization through cost savings by hiring low-wage workers with minimal regard for healthy working conditions and avoidance of environmental degradation. Increasingly such behaviors are considered human rights violations, with multinational corporations (MNCs) identified as major violators. MNCs, however, face increasing pressure from the United Nations (UNs) and nongovernment organizations (NGOs) that have announced human rights goals and from consumers who balk at buying products from nations accused of human rights violations.

The focus of human rights traditionally has been on nation-states, particularly in developing countries. Events such the 2012 "Arab Spring" protests revealed abuses by a string of North African nations – Egypt, Tunisia, and Lybia. Incidents have regularly been uncovered by human rights NGOs, such as Amnesty International and Human Rights Watch, and reported by the news media and social media. For example, *The Economist* report on Amnesty International's 2009 "The State of the World's Human Rights" gave an account of "a ghastly tale of torture, state terror, the suppression of free speech and the curtailing of due process, under regimes of every ideological stripe."[1] The article also referred to violations by China, Iran, and other countries. It cited Iran as having carried out at least 346 executions in 2008 and using such punishments as flogging and amputation. Although stoning, a punishment under *sharia* law, was supposedly stopped as of August 2008, Iran's top human rights official, Mohammad-Javad Larijani, defended his country's right to engage in the stoning of criminals, as well as imprisoning lawyers seen as threatening the stability of the Islamic Republic.[2]

In China, authorities were said to have intensified their use of administrative forms of detention that allows police to incarcerate individuals without trial. The blind dissident Chen Guangcheng suffered years of persecution for challenging forced abortions and sterilization. His case garnered international attention after he escaped to the U.S. Embassy from his house arrest a week before Secretary of State Hillary Rodham Clinton's visit to Beijing in May 2012. The conflict was solved when China allowed the dissident and his wife and daughter to apply for a visa and, according to Clinton, "pursue higher education in a safe environment."[3]

In contrast to human rights violations by nation-states, which typically refer to physical harm and suppression of free speech and due process, violations by business pertain mostly to the employment of child labor and poor working conditions. For example, *The Economist's* article, "Ethical Shopping: Human Rights," states that "human rights issues are expected to become more prominent in the future," citing that a growing number of companies in industrialized countries are excluding Third World suppliers that use child labor.[4]

A poll of 30,000 British consumers for CW, Britain's largest co-operative retailer, showed that a third had boycotted stores because of concerns about their ethical standards and 60% said they would be prepared to boycott in the future. Among other well-known companies mentioned by *The Economist* was Levi Strauss, which was cited for purchasing jeans from factories in Saipan, a small U.S.-governed island, where local workers were underpaid, lived in pad-locked barracks, and worked in appalling conditions. Another labor-related human rights issue is the mistreatment of an increasing number of migrant workers in developed countries, as discussed in Chapter 5.

In response to accusations of violating human rights, MNCs typically argue that they conform to the laws of host countries and decline to interfere in domestic matters. Presently very few legal obligations bind MNCs to human rights, but several declarations proclaim that MNCs must not only prevent their own violation of human rights but also prevent others from doing so.

# Legal and other declarations of human rights landmarks

## Alien Tort Claims Act

Dating from 1789, the Alien Tort Claims Act (ATCA) has been prodding business to attend to its own human rights violations. The law permits aliens to sue in a U.S. court for torts committed abroad in violation of the "law of nations" or a treaty of the United States. In her book *International Business Under Adversity*, Gabriele Suder considers the use of the ATCA as a "groundbreaking – and successful – legal strategy" against corporations accused of human rights abuses.[5]

Especially targeted and vigorously litigated has been corporate complicity with paramilitary organizations that use such means as intimidation, abductions, torture, and sometimes murder to discourage union activities or to stop human rights grievances against a corporation. Legal action has been taken against Texaco in Ecuador, Chevron in Nigeria, ExxonMobil in Indonesia, and UNOCAL in Burma.[6] Other implicated corporations mentioned by Suder are Bridgestone-Firestone, Nestle, Archer Daniel Midland, and Cargil. In connection with forced labor, litigation has been pursued against Chiquita Brands, Coca-Cola, Drummond Bompny, DynCorp, and Wal-Mart.[7]

An illustrative case involving ATCA is Chiquita Brands International operations in Colombia. The company was accused of colluding with the paramilitary group, Autodefensas unidas de Colombia (AUC), to suppress labor unrest from 1997 to 2004.[8] A lawsuit was filed by attorneys representing approximately 4,000 people whose family members were killed by the AUC. The suit charges that Chiquita has "secondary liability" for AUC's actions not only for making money payments but also allowing five shipments of 13,000 AK-47 assault rifles and millions of rounds of ammunition to pass through the port facilities of its wholly owned subsidiary Banadex, in Turbo, Colombia. It also claims that when individual banana workers became "security problems," Chiquita notified the AUC, which then typically executed the individual.

The company explains that its rationale for the funding was "motivated by our good-faith concern for the safety of our employees."[9] It accuses the plaintiffs' lawyers of mainly being interested in extorting legal fees from companies, rather than addressing the violence. But a judge in a Florida district court allowed the plaintiffs to go forward against the company for its alleged involvement in "torture, extrajudical killing, war crimes, and crimes against humanity."[10]

As *Business Insurance* magazine noted, after the Battle of Seattle in 1999, "human rights are fast becoming a mainstream business issue, and global corporations are under growing pressure to demonstrate social interest beyond shareholder returns."[11] Writing on "Human Rights, Corporations and the Global Economy," David Kinley and Justine Nolan concluded "Whatever the precise role of corporations in the slow and stilted convergence of human rights and trade goals, it is one that will grow rather than diminish."[12]

## United Nations Declarations

The issue of human rights was given prominence in 1948 by the UN Declaration of Human Rights. Its preamble defines human rights as the "recognition of the inherent dignity and of the equal and inalienable rights of all members of the human family." Such a declaration say W. Michael Hoffman, executive director of Bentley University's Center for Business Ethics, and Robert E. McNulty helps to buttress the resolve of companies. "Even under optimal conditions, good companies sometimes are susceptible to moral lapses, and when companies undertake ventures in authoritarian countries with poor human rights records, even those with the best intentions may find themselves drawn into complicity in human rights abuses."[13]

In 2003, the UN Social and Economic Council declared that human rights has become a significant international issue and, notions of sovereignty aside, human rights violations within countries are now deemed to be included in that community. The UN Norms on the Responsibilities of Transnational Corporations assigned primary responsibility for human rights protection to states, but it included ensuring the compliance of MNCs. It further stated that MNCs have "the obligation to promote, secure the fulfillment of respect, ensure respect of and protect human rights recognized in international as well as national law...." Transnational corporations and other business enterprises, as organs of society, are "increasingly seen as having a positive responsibility or duty for promoting and securing human rights, for using their power and influence to change a given regime's human rights policies and practices." They are also seen as having a responsibility to use their power and influence to change a given regime's human rights policies and practices.

## The Global Compact

Business's responsibility for safeguarding human rights was buttressed by The Global Compact of July 2000, which has special import for MNCs. It was the first time that an international body applied human rights values to multinational corporations. It revised the traditional view that states are the only "subjects of traditional international law" and that private nonstate actors do not have any positive duty to observe human rights, their only duty being to obey the law. At the 1999 World Economic Forum in Davos, Switzerland, UN Secretary General Kofi Annan challenged business leaders to "use these universal values as the cement binding together your global corporations, since they are values people all over the world will recognize as their own." He asked them to "embrace and enact" the Global Compact both in their company practices and by supporting appropriate public policies, including, "Ensure your own organisation is not complicit in human rights abuses."[14]

The Global Compact originally contained nine principles, with a tenth adopted in 2004. Organized into four categories, they are as follows:

- *Broad expectations of the business community:* (1) business should support and respect the protection of internationally proclaimed human rights; and (2) make sure that they are not complicit in human rights.
- *Protecting labor and the exploitation of labor:* (3) businesses should uphold the freedom of association and the effective recognition of the right to collective bargaining; (4) elimination of all forms of forced and compulsory labor; (5) effective abolition of child labor; and (6) elimination of discrimination with respect to employment and occupation.
- *Environmental protection:* (7) businesses should support a precautionary approach to environmental challenges; (8) undertake initiatives to promote greater environmental responsibility; and (9) encourage the development and diffusion of environmentally friendly technologies.
- *Anticorruption:* (10) businesses should work against corruption in all its forms, including extortion and bribery.[15]

By 2007 about 1,700 companies signed the compact. They benefit through association with the UN without being bound to any obligations to do anything. A company participating in the Global Compact is simply expected to publish in its annual report or similar corporate report a description of the ways in which it is supporting the Global Compact and its ten principles. Their activities are summarized in *Communication on Progress* reports.[16] Starting with 50 companies that committed themselves to a set of universal principles related to human rights, labor standards, and the environment, the compact now includes approximately 4,000 participants spread among 100 countries.

But as Surya Deva, who critiqued the Global Compact, points out, this number is still a "drop in the ocean" compared to an estimated 70,000 multinational parent corporations and 900,000 foreign affiliates.[17]

The relationship between the UN and business was underscored in a keynote speech "United Nations Global Compact" by Gavin Power, an advisor to the Global Compact, on January 6, 2006. He noted the "profound sea change" in thinking at the UN and within the international community concerning the role of business and financial markets in meeting development objectives. He noted the "powerful convergence under way between the interests and objectives of the UN and the private sector," arguing that "social and environmental pillars must be part of the globalization process" for markets and communities to thrive and be sustainable.[18]

# Multiple meanings of human rights

The definition of human rights is loose, ubiquitous, and broad. It is embedded in ethics, as demonstrated in Thomas Donaldson's book, *The Ethics of International Business*.[19] He explains that the concept of rights is a fundamental precept, saying, "Rights establish minimum levels of morally acceptable behavior." He quotes the well-known definition of Joel Feinberg that a right is a "justified entitlement *to* something *from* someone."[20] In another book on ethics, Patricia J. Parsons states that a right is "fundamental to our understanding of what individuals can expect in terms of ethical behaviour towards them in a particular society." She explains that "a right is the freedom to act or be treated in a particular way, where this right is protected and endorsed by a higher authority – in the case of human rights, for example, it would be a constitution or declaration of human rights and freedoms."[21]

Specific rights have evolved with specialized issues and stakeholders. For example, President John F. Kennedy told Congress in 1962 that consumers were entitled to four kinds of protection: the right to safety, the right to be informed, the right to choose, and the right to be heard.[22] Similar statements have been made regarding employees, as reviewed by Alan F. Westin and Stephan Salisbury in *Individual Rights in the Corporation*,[23] and by James A. Gross and Lance Compa in *Human Rights in Labor and Employment Relations: International and Domestic Perspectives*.[24]

## Concept of universal rights

In China, a debate questioned linking the issue of human rights to universal values. As *The Economist* states, the philosophical question of whether universal values – such as human rights, freedom, and democracy – exist has become a political fight that has divided scholars, the media, and even Chinese leaders.[25] Beijing newspapers and conservative websites have attacked the idea of universal values as a Western plot to undermine party rule. They sometimes draw a contrast between the "Confucian stress on social harmony and moral rectitude with the West's emphasis on individual rights."[26] Despite these reservations, Prime Minister Wen Jiabao wrote in 2007 that "science, democracy, rule of law, freedom and human rights are not unique to capitalism, but are values commonly pursued by mankind over a long period of history."[27]

Donaldson applies the concept of "universal rights" to the international arena, listing the following "Fundamental International Rights":

- freedom of physical movement
- ownership of property
- freedom from torture
- fair trial
- nondiscriminatory treatment (freedom from discrimination on the basis of such characteristics such as race or sex.)
- physical security
- freedom of speech and association
- minimal education
- political participation
- subsistence.[28]

The list illustrates the generality and ambiguity of the human rights concept. Most people would agree that torture, freedom of movement, and fair trial violate human rights. But some people would consider minimal education as an "entitlement" or "welfare right." Thus, in describing "rights to subsistence," Donaldson includes the right to minimal economic security entailing, in turn, a right to "unpolluted air, unpolluted water, adequate food, adequate clothing, adequate shelter, and minimal preventative public healthcare."[29] These are typical standard benefits of the modern welfare state and include whatever is necessary to satisfy "basic needs" – defined as needs "which must be satisfied in order not to seriously endanger a person's health and sanity."[30] Accordingly, this requirement would include social security insurance, employment, protection against unemployment, healthcare, education, and limits on working hours. These are contentious public policy issues on the agenda of legislative bodies.

## HIV-AIDS as a human rights issue

**Do employers have responsibility?** Whether employers have a responsibility to tend to its workers with HIV-AIDS has become a human rights issue.[31] Some contend that the public responsibilities of MNCs include the global battle against AIDS and that the corporate sector is a natural partner because businesses need healthy employees and consumers.[32] In contrast, a survey of 1,066 businesses drawn from the Zimbabwe National Chamber of Commerce found that 81% shirk what the author calls their moral responsibility toward infected employees and simply lack AIDS policies. The survey also showed that when involved, businesses implement program that are the least costly and mostly involve nonfinancial spending programs. The individual efforts by businesses are less sufficiently complemented by government and societal organizations.[33]

A prominent business initiative is the Global Business Coalition (GBC) on HIV/AIDS, Tuberculosis, and Malaria, which is based in the United States but works mainly in developing countries.[34] In the United States, the focus is on testing and prevention campaigns, with an emphasis on the use of condoms.[35] A campaign is planned to encourage doctors to offer HIV tests as part of routine health checks. With their "Offer the Test" program, the GBC enlists the sales representatives of Pfizer who could take a few minutes during their regular visits to explain the campaign.

## Patent rights of the pharmaceutical industry conflict with human rights

A landmark case highlighted the human rights issue when the patent rights of the pharmaceutical industry were pitted against the needs of HIV-AIDS victims. In 2000, 4.7 million South Africans – one in nine – carried HIV, and AIDS killed a quarter of a million persons. Facing this disaster, the government threatened to ignore drug patents in order to make drugs available. But the pharmaceutical industry adamantly demanded that its patents be protected. Protesters chanted slogans such as "Life Before Profit" and carried posters calling the CEO of GlaxoSmithKline, "deadlier than the virus." The drug industry, said the *Wall Street Journal*, was "reeling from an unprecedented wave of public scorn" that undermined its ability to conduct their business as usual.[36] Its standard practice was to find and patent a few new drugs, price them high, and market them aggressively. As *The Economist* pointed out, "How to increase poor people's access to costly, life-saving drugs is one of the most vexing questions facing governments, drug companies and medical charities."[37]

Thirty-nine drug companies – including Bristol-Myers Squibb, GlaxoSmithKline, Merck, and Eli Lilly – filed a lawsuit aimed at protecting their "constitutional rights" to protect intellectual property rights. But facing criticism from the South African government as well as from the European Community, the World Health Organization, France's National AIDS Council, and many activist and NGO groups, the pharmaceutical companies realized they were losing the public relations battle and that they had to recoup some moral high ground. J.P. Garnier, CEO of GlaxoSmithKlein, declared "We don't exist in a vacuum. We're a very major corporation. We're not insensitive to public opinion. That is a factor in our decision-making." Raymond Gilmartin, Merck's chairman and CEO, said, companies "need to demonstrate that intellectual property is not an obstacle" to access in developing countries." He also warned his fellow CEOs, "If we don't solve the drug access problem, then our intellectual property is at risk."[38]

NGOs also got involved. The nonprofit Oxfam joined with Medecins sans Frontieres (MSF),Treatment Action Campaign, and other partners to cut the cost of the vital portfolio of HIV/Aids medicines. The NGOs' campaigns seek reform of global patent rules and challenge the drugs giant GlaxoSmithKline (GSK) to take the lead within the pharmaceutical industry to promote poor people's access to medicines by lowering their prices.[39] GSK responded to this pressure by releasing a document, "Facing the Challenge," which outlines the company's approach to these issues and represents the industry's first comprehensive attempt to address the issue of drug access in the developing world.[40]

Pharmaceuticals feared that the ripple effect of concessions made in South Africa would embolden other developing countries to demand cheaper drugs. This prospect manifested itself in Brazil where the government decided on a bold plan to manufacture generic versions of patented HIV medications. When the pharmaceutical industry attacked it as violating proprietary property, Brazil responded with an advertisement in the *New York Times* titled "Patent Rights or Human Rights?" The advertisement argued that "AIDS is not a business" and that the local manufacturing of HIV medications is not a "declaration of war against the drug industry."[41]

International organizations also became involved. Writing in *BusinessWeek*, Gary Becker suggested that a better strategy than essentially giving away drugs is "for international organizations such as the World Bank to negotiate with drug companies to buy large quantities of the AIDS cocktails." Kofi Annan joined in by attempting to work out a comprehensive plan financed by rich nations to fight AIDS and other infectious diseases in poor countries. The involvement of supranational organizations and NGOs as well as nation-states in the patent and pricing problems of pharmaceutical companies demonstrates the wide reach and complexity of the human rights issue.

## Environmental harm – cases of Formosa Plastics and Chevron Texaco

Environmental harm has also been considered a human rights violation, implicating both nation-states and businesses. The connection between environmental gradation and human rights was made by Audrey Gaughran, Amnesty's director of global issues, who said the failure to clean up the mess has led to "widespread human rights violations" that included the right to food, clean water, livelihood, and good health.[42]

An illustrative case was discovered by Human Rights Watch when it monitored the Formosa Plastics Group, a Taiwanese company. It shipped and dumped nearly 3,000 tons of Taiwanese toxic waste in the southern port of Sihanoukville, Cambodia in 1998. At the time there was no law against this practice. Thus, when Minister of Environment Mok Mareth objected, he was ignored. After mercury-laden refuse was deposited in an open field, some impoverished villagers who scavenged the poisonous cargo became sick and one quickly died. When angry villagers demonstrated and ransacked buildings, staff members of a local human rights group, the Cambodian League for the Promotion and Defense of Human Rights, were arrested and treated harshly. Ultimately, however, government officials were arrested for permitting the dumping.[43]

Another well-known case of environmental harm is Chevron Texaco in Ecuador. Lawyers for aggrieved indigenous folk filed suit against the company. Legal activists charged Texaco for dumping contaminated water in open ponds in the country's rain forest for a decade, which, they claim, harmed both the environment and people's health.[44] Chevron acquired Texaco in 2001 and in 2003 forty-eight Ecuadoreans sued Texaco in an Ecuadorean court for damaged public lands in the Amazon jungle. For these past activities, an Ecuadorian judge in February 2011 imposed an $18.2 billion contamination judgment on Chevron.[45] The company charges that the case was fraught with fraud by both the plaintiffs lawyers and the Ecuadorean court and has filed a RICO (racketeering) suit against the plaintiffs and the Amazon Defense Coalition (ADC), which is an NGO that advocates on behalf of the lawsuit.[46]

## Inclusion of animal welfare

Animal welfare relates to human rights in that animals are also sentient creatures that experience pain. Although advances have been made in the domestic policies in the United States and Europe, "a regulatory framework for animal welfare has largely been absent on the international level," say Miyun Park, executive director of Global Animal Partnership, and Peter Singer, professor of bioethics at Princeton University.[47] With a sharp increase in demand for animal food, animal welfare has become a global matter. The authors say,

"It is time for a global commitment to reduce animal suffering and to mitigate the many unintended and undesirable consequences of raising animals for food."[48]

In 2009 alone, more than 60 billion land animals were slaughtered for food, including 52 billion chickens, 34 billion pigs, 521 million sheep, 403 million goats, and 298 million cattle. Westerners especially are distressed by the cruel practices in animal living conditions and slaughter employed by farmers and ranchers. This condition has been growing as traditional farming practices were largely replaced by industrial systems with crowded spaces. For example, pigs, one of the more intelligent animals, are confined in large sheds on bare concrete or slatted flooring "without any mental stimulation or basic comforts, causing frustration, boredom, and physical distress."[49] As developing nations, particularly those in Asia and Latin America, increase their food production, they replicate the worst forms of intensive animal farming.

The private sector is implicated because consumers around the world are increasingly demanding that their food be produced humanely and safely. Public opinion in the United States and European Union is supportive of animal welfare legislation. A resounding majority (77%) of those responding to a 2007 European Commission poll wanted further improvements to protect animal.[50] In 2006, the International Finance Corporation of the World Bank published "Creating Business Opportunity Through Improved Animal Welfare." In 2011, the International Organization for Standardization issued its "ISO 26000" guides, which for the first time included references to animal welfare. They require supporters to observe the standard by respecting "the welfare of animals, when affecting their lives and existence, including the provision of decent conditions for keeping, breeding, producing, transporting, and using animals."[51] At its second Global Conference on Animal Welfare in 2008, the World Organization for Animal Health put forth a resolution stating that "ethics is as important as science in the development of animal welfare standards."[52]

## Growing pressure on business to recognize human rights – cases of nike, talisman, and freeport mcmoran

### Nike[53]

One of the most publicized examples of successful action by NGOs against MNCs is the much discussed case of Nike Inc., an American company that sells sports apparel and shoes. All of its goods are obtained from approximately 900 suppliers in 55 countries in Asia, Central American, and Eastern Europe, while Nike itself concentrates on product development and marketing. Since the early 1990s, the company was targeted by student activists and watchdog groups such as Campaign for Labor rights, the National Labor Committee, and Global Exchange for paying low wages, using child labor, and allowing poor working conditions in Asian plants where its goods were produced.

The company received much negative publicity. Articles described the disparity of paying workers about $1.50 a day while selling shoes for $140–180 a pair and paying its management and celebrities such as Michael Jordan and Tiger Woods millions of dollars.[54] Two stories were particularly damaging. One was *Life* magazine's documentation of the use of child labor in Pakistan to produce soccer balls for Nike and other companies. Shown were photographs of small children sitting in a dirty environment stitching together the panels of a soccer ball. The second story was a CBS News *48 Hours* broadcast in October 1996 that focused on low wage rates, extensive overtime, and physical abuse of workers in Vietnam factories that supplied Nike's products.[55]

Nike responded to the initial bad publicity in 1992 by drafting its first Code of Conduct, which applied to subcontractors and suppliers. This effort was reinforced in 1994 by the hiring of the accounting firm of Ernst & Young to monitor alleged worker abuses in its Indonesian factories. In 1996, it took the further step of hiring GoodWorks International, headed by former civil rights leader Andrew Young, to investigate conditions in overseas factories, and in 1998 it formed a Corporate Responsibility Division. But the credibility of these initiatives was questioned and did not prevent further damage to Nike's reputation. The result was loss of sales, revocation of university contracts, and share price decreases.

In May 1998, CEO Philip H. Knight demanded serious improvements of working conditions through stricter controls and prohibition of child labor. Nike revised its code of conduct, including raising the minimum age of employees to 18 years.[56] To gain credibility, Nike in 1999 joined the Global Alliance for Workers and Communities, whose objective was to improve the lives of employees in Asian factories. This membership had a significant impact, at first negative and then positive. When the Global Alliance published a 50-page report in February 2001 that exposed conditions, U.S. sales in Nike shoes fell by 50% compared to the same quarter a year before. Another setback was the drop in share price by 1.5%, representing a market value decline of more than $150 million. These events persuaded Nike for the first time to openly acknowledge the abominable working conditions in Indonesian factories, and when it did so, the share price rose by 2%.[57] Nike learned that reputation matters and that responsibility for human rights violations by suppliers can not be dodged.

## The Talisman case[58]

Calgary-based Talisman Energy Inc. became involved in the Sudan when on August 17, 1997, it acquired the outstanding shares of Arakis Energy, an independent Canadian company, and thus became the holder of that company's 25 percent share of GNPOC in Sudan.[59] It was categorized as a "high-risk-high-return investment" for Talisman.

The risks became apparent shortly after the acquisition. The Canadian Minister of Foreign Affairs expressed reservations about the purchase, and Canadian NGOs immediately approached Talisman, citing the considerable human rights abuses in that country. Among others, Human Rights Watch stated that "forced displacement of the civilian population, and the death and destructions that have accompanied it, are the central human rights issues relating to oil development in Sudan."[60] Also implicating Talisman was the military use of its corporate facilities. While some might argue it was appropriate for Talisman to rely on the government of Sudan to defend its operations against rebel attacks, the use of its airstrip at the Heglig field for "nondefensive" military purposes crossed the line.

There were several signs of Talisman's growing vulnerability. The United States joined Canada in expressing opposition to Talisman's investment. Suits were brought under ATCA, even though alleged actions did not involve American nationals or took place on American territory. However, it was not pressure by the Canadian and U.S. government, nor consumers, but from institutional investors such as CALPERS and TIAA-CREF that convinced Talisman to withdraw from the Sudan. When at least six

American pension funds sold millions of shares of the company's stock, Talisman's market value declined in 1999 and 2000.[61]

## Signs of complicity

Talisman was slow to recognize or admit its complicity. It should have realized that its business operations depended upon, or benefitted from, gross human rights abuses. It should have known that the company would be dependent on the government to protects its concessions and that the concessions were in the mid of a war zone. Any oil firm entering Sudan had to reckon with the fact that it was likely to both benefit from human rights abuses on the part of the government and depend on them for survival.[62]

Talisman violated three recognized acts of complicity: (1) when it knew or should have known that its acts or omissions would provide assistance to a human rights violation; (2) when it knew or ought to have known that its acts or omissions would encourage the perpetrator; and (3) when it enters into a commercial relationship with one or more parties in a conflict zone and anyone of those parties commits acts in violation of the human rights.[63]

Talisman responded to these human rights accusations with the following statements and actions:

- It declared that it "accepted" the need to comply with the International Code of Ethics for Canadian Business and to support the principle of the UN Declaration of Human rights.
- It established a Corporate Social Responsibility Group in early 2000 in which it acknowledged that "In all countries where we operate, we believe that we have a duty to advocate respect for human rights where there are abuses."
- It endeavored to engage in "constructive engagement" with its host country government as an expression of undertaking a positive obligation to influence the policy of the regime and mitigate human rights abuses. During 2001, Talisman reported an attempt to develop an agreement between the Greater Nile Petroleum Operating Company, in which it had partial ownership, and the government of Sudan that contained provisions dealing with respect for human rights, the appropriate use of oilfield infrastructure, and the prohibition of the use of irregular Sudanese military forces for oilfield protection. The government, however, "ultimately rejected the draft security agreement."[64]

These stereotyped responses were totally inadequate and did not assuage critics.

## Canada Mulls over the question of corporate behavior abroad

With free trade under attack by global activists, the fledgling Canadian Democracy and Corporate Accountability Commission explored whether federal laws should ensure that Canadian firms behave responsibly abroad. It considered whether Talisman should be investigated for its controversial oil-production operations in war-ravaged Sudan. Commission co-chairman Ed Broadbent stated, "We want reforms that make human rights and trade compatible, instead of seeing them in opposition."

Supporting the concern was Duff Conacher, coordinator of Ottawa-based Democracy-Watch, saying, "Free trade will be a vicious spiral downward of corporations abusing countries and communities if we do not have legal requirements that corporations act responsibly." Leonard Brooks, executive director of the University of Toronto's Clarkson Centre for Business Ethics, argued, "There ought to be some residual responsibility in Canada when the system is not operating in those other countries."[65] Global activists argue that governments are extending rights "with thoughtless abandon" to corporations without imposing responsibilities in exchange.

The Talisman case reinforces the unavoidable determination that MNCs must take the human rights issue seriously and can no longer rely on legal rights of owners or traditional diplomatic maneuvers such as avoiding responsibility for the actions of host countries. Complicity has become a reality. Pressure from an unexpected stakeholder group, institutional investors, has become a potent force.

## Freeport McMoRan case

Freeport McMoRan, a mid-sized miner of sulfur and other minerals headquartered in Louisiana, became a controversial global multinational when it acquired and developed a gold and copper mine in remote Papua, Indonesia.[66] Because it displaced indigenous people in the Grasberg area where its operations are located, it became the poster child of neo-colonialism. It is also an egregious example of crony capitalism because its growth depended on special arrangements and deals between James R. ("Jim Bob") Moffett, the company's president, and former Indonesian President Soharto. Equitable treatment of native populations, human rights, and environmental concerns were virtually absent in their calculations. When resistance grew, the military and police quelled dissidents and crushed protests, and in the process committed many human rights violations.

The impact on the environment was, at least at the beginning, ignored. Critics say mining operations "brutalized one of the world's most pristine-ecosystems and done little to lift local tribes, just decades removed from Stone Age isolation, out of poverty and primitiveness."[67] Moffett believed in the policy of "no tall trees" – keeping as low a profile as possible – and did everything he could to keep the media out. But as the world eventually learned about these operations in remote Grasberg, public outrage demanded that the company include social and environmental concerns in its thinking. The company responded by making minimal accommodations to indigenous people, environmentalists, the media, and public opinion – a "just noticeable difference" to prevent a crisis.

### History

Freeport acquired the property nearly 50 years ago when the first Americans walked into the wilderness of Papua where primitive people swathed only in penis gourds and armed with bows and arrows lived. Balfour Darnell, a self-described roughneck who built Freeport's first base camps, was able to sooth the suspicion by the tribal leader Tuarek Natkime, who laid claim to much of the land in Papua, by giving him a simple tool that was half hatchet and half hammer. Today, Tuarek's 31-year-old son Titus Natkime is being rewarded. Freeport offered him $250,000 to set up a foundation for his clan, plus $100,000 annually. Freeport had already paid for Natkime's travel across the United States, gave him a house in Jakarta, financed his English language training in New Zealand, and offered him a job in government relations. But he wants more for all Papuans, arguing that they never received a fair portion of the estimated $33 billion in direct and indirect benefits the company claims to have provided Indonesia from 1992 to 2004.[68]

### Use of military and police

Freeport McMoRan had to use force to acquire and maintain control over its operations. At first, it had its own security force but it soon depended on the Indonesian police and military. Indigenous people, mainly the Amungme and Komoro, were forced out of their ancestral lands and some who resisted faced torture and death. Sporadic revolts were squashed. Rioting broke out in March 1996, which resulted in the destruction of $3 million in equipment and ransacking of offices at Grasberg.[69] Another revolt in 1977 was ruthlessly put down by the Indonesian army in a campaign called Operasi Tumpas (Annihilation), a campaign to which Freeport contributed.[70] Between 1975 and 1997 an estimated 160 people were killed by the military in the Grasberg area.[71]

Months of investigation by the *New York Times* into Freeport's support of the military revealed that from 1998 through 2004, the company gave military and police generals, colonels, majors and captains, and military units, nearly $20 million.[72] Several people interviewed by the *Times* believed that payments to individual officers constituted bribes. Direct payments are illegal under Indonesian law. Global Witness, an NGO, released a report "Paying for Protection" in July 2005, which said that while it may be necessary for a company to help governments with security, "they should give the money through the proper channels, in a transparent way."[73]

Defending its actions, Freeport said that it had "taken appropriate steps" in accordance with American and Indonesian laws to provide a secure working environment for its more than 18,000 employees and contract workers.[74] It further argued, "There is no alternative to our reliance on the Indonesian military and policy in this regard.... The need for this security, the support provided for such security, and the procedures governing such support, as well as decisions regarding our relationships with the Indonesian government and its security institutions are ordinary business activities."[75] It also pointed out that these payments are required under its Contract of Work with the Government of Indonesia and that "the Grasberg mine is designated as a vital national asset, resulting in the military playing a significant role in protecting the area."[76]

# Business options in responding to human rights

In response to the human rights issue, businesses can choose one or more of three strategies: reexamining the social contract with its own stakeholders, accepting supply chain responsibility, and avoiding complicity.

## Conforming to the social contract with stakeholders

A sound beginning for a business in addressing the human rights issue is to focus on its primary stakeholder relations, where it has control and influence. By so doing, it supports Principle One of the Global Compact, which says businesses should "support and respect the protection of internationally proclaimed human rights within their sphere of influence."[77] Employee human rights have received the most attention. Of particular relevance are the International Labor Organization (ILO) conventions, as they are directly tackling daily corporate activity and, more specifically, working conditions, job security, and basic human rights in connection with work and employment.

### DelMonte Kenya's employee relations

Consumer pressure will sometimes persuade a company to examine whether it violates human rights in dealing with its employees. It was a boycott in Italy of DelMonte Kenya products that persuaded the company to deal with charges of human rights violations to its employees and community in Kenya. Constitutionally protected fundamental human rights in Kenya include failure to respect employees' privacy, right to assemble, and right to fair labor practices, including striking, clean environment, and consumer rights.

The Kenya Human Rights Commission reported that in 2003 workers in the export processing zones (EPZ) went on strike demanding a wide range of reforms. The report refers to "higher wages, entitlement to leave, including maternity, annual, sick and compassionate leave, and protesting against overwork and compulsory overtime, lack of protective clothing, inaccessibility to emergency exits, sexual harassment, unfair suspension and summary dismissal, unexplained deductions and suppression of their right to organise into trade unions."[78]

The EPZs had noble goals. They were established in 1990 to create jobs, enhance the transfer of technology, diversify export products and markets, and promote industrial investment for export. But companies operating in the EPZs sometimes adopted inhuman policies in order to meet the unrealistic targets set on them by sourcing companies in the United States. It followed the typical pattern of foreign companies of abandoning formerly accepted responsibilities elsewhere when they set up business in Kenya.

Women were especially vulnerable, comprising about 75% of the employees at DelMonte Kenya. They were preferred because they are considered to be "easier to work with, patient, keen and careful … hence less mistakes and rejects, unlike men who are aggressive, easily bored and always looking for trouble."[79]

### Chrysler employee arrested by China

When authorities in China arrested a native employee for participating in a protest against the government, they detained him for three days, knowing that Chrysler had a policy of firing an employee for missing work for three days. Chrysler was about to follow this policy when Chrysler's CEO intervened and allowed the employee to return to work, based on his human rights. Chinese authorities were displeased. But Chrysler followed its company policy of observing human rights in its own operations. This policy was compatible with that of AmCham, Human Rights Watch and the American Chamber of Commerce in Hong Kong (AmCham).

Chrysler's policy adhered to Michael A. Santoro's proposal of a "fair share theory" – one that calls for business to bear some but not all responsibility to undertake the burden of advancing human rights.[80] He believes that an MNC has no duty to address the general human rights situation in China. But he and the Chamber believe in a strong and direct pledge to "refuse to do business with firms which employ forced labor, or treat their workers in inhumane or unsafe ways." They propose that a corporation's responsible is limited to the following:

- Maintain acceptable working conditions in its own operations and uphold the rights of its employees to freedom of expression.
- Take responsibility for the actions of its business partners in such matters as employment practices, wages and benefits, working hours, use of child labor, use of prison labor or forced labor, discrimination, and disciplinary practices.
- Resist pressure from the Chinese government to use the MNC as a vehicle to abuse human rights, for example, by not hiring (or rehiring) employees who are punished by withholding jobs from them.[81]

## Accepting supply chain responsibility

Companies often deny responsibility for human rights and other violations committed by enterprises that perform services for them or produce their products. For example, when Campbell Soup was targeted by the Farm Labor Organizing Committee in Ohio and charged with using child labor, paying low wages, and tolerating poor health and housing conditions, it denied the charges, using the legal argument that growers, not Campbell, were the employers that hired the farm workers.[82]

The same type of argument was used by Nike's CEO Phil Knight when the company was accused of using child labor in the manufacture of its athletic shoes in China. He stated that Nike should not be blamed because it did not own and manage the factories where these conditions occurred. But the media and critics applied the agency principle, namely, that Nike was responsible for the actions of businesses that were contracted to them, that is, that produced and sold the athletic shoes to them. In other words, the supply chain is also a responsibility chain. The dodging of responsibility by blaming suppliers for human rights violation is no longer acceptable.

Some of the biggest names in retailing have been found to receive goods from suppliers that violated human rights. An investigation by the English newspaper *The Observer* found that the Indian suppliers for Gap, Next, and Marks & Spencer's (M&S) paid their workers just 25 p an hour and required them to work overtime. Staff at their Indian suppliers worked up to 16 hours a day. In response, the three companies said they were totally committed to ethical trading and would not tolerate abuses in their supply chain. They said they themselves detected the problem by their own auditing processes and that they took swift action to correct them. In 2009, M&S launched a five-year ethical trading plan under the advertising slogan "Doing the Right Thing."[83]

Many retailers are now going a step further by certifying that their suppliers adhere to labor, environmental, and other standards. IKEA, a Swedish furniture stores, decided not to sell carpets unless they could be certified as made without child labor. A new group, including German rug-importers and a number of charities, launched Rumark, the first "human rights" trademark that indicates that no children are employed in the making of the rug.

The human rights issue is spreading to previously untouched companies, notably Apple, which has been a laggard in policing its code of conduct. It was accused by watchdog organizations of violating workplace safety, requiring unacceptably long work days, and dumping of unsafe hazardous materials. As Ed Bruning, professor of marketing at the University of Manitoba's Asper School of Business, noted, "a number of Apple affiliates weren't abiding by World Health Organization or International Labour Organization conditions." He added, however, that Apple is in the process of making substantial changes in its supply chain network to fix the problems so that it can maintain its image as a good corporate citizen.[84]

These changes were apparently not made resolutely enough to prevent the exposure in 2012 of inhumane working conditions at Foxconn factories in China where many of its products, including the iPhone, are manufactured. Foxconn, the trade name for the Taiwanese company Hon Hai Precision Industry, became notorious for its depressing work conditions and pressure on employees to keep up with the manufacture of time-sensitive consumer electronics. So many employees committed suicide that it put up nets outside the building on some floors of its production facilities. Foxconn was also charged with requiring overtime of 10–15 hours a week. It pledged to bring its overtime policies in line with Chinese law and Apple's code of conduct.[85]

## Avoiding complicity – guilt by association

Complicity binds a company to the actions of governments where they operate. This connection is described in Principle Two of the Global Compact, which states that businesses should make sure that they are not complicit in human rights abuses. Complicity has three meanings: (1) direct complicity whereby a company knowingly assists a state in violating human rights; (2) beneficial complicity whereby a company benefits from the abuse of human rights; and (3) silent complicity when a company fails to raise the question of systematic violations of human rights with authorities. [86]

Accusations have been growing of business complicity of firms that conduct business in an overseas country known for violation of human rights. A lawsuit was filed against Occidental for human rights abuses in Colombia for allegedly providing lethal aid to its armed forces, which the company denied. Even if the charge is unproven, Occidental faced a high-profile trial exposing its relationship with a regime with uneven record on human rights.[87] In another case, plaintiffs alleged that Unocal, a Californian energy company, was working with the Burmese military to conscript forced labor, kill, abuse, and rape citizens while working on the Yadna gas pipeline project.[88] Although the case was settled in 2005, the company later was again accused of benefitting from forced labor deployed by the military government in Myanmar, the new name for Burma.

Retailers are more vulnerable than producer companies to accusation of complicity because of their sensitivity to consumer public opinion. Eddie Bauer, an American retailer and sportswear company, pulled out of Myanmar after demonstrations outside its shops. Liz Claiborne, a designer-clothing company, also left Myanmar. Polaroid faced enormous world pressure, including its own employees, when it sold photo identification equipment to South Africa during Apartheid. To quell discontent, the company sent a delegation to South Africa to report on the situation and make recommendations.

As a result, Polaroid decided to stop selling equipment to the government. But the effort was deceptive because it continued to supply camera equipment to a private outlet, which then surreptitiously sold them to the government.

## Conclusions

The fundamental problem in asking MNCs to accept responsibility for human rights is that the goals of corporate enterprise and those of human rights differ.[89] This view is reflected in Milton Friedman' s classic statement that business's sole obligation was to maximize shareholder value, which also meant that it has no business getting involved with social responsibility and broad human rights issues. However, corporate social responsibility standards are rising. Some developing countries are proposing constitutional changes that explore rising global corporate social responsibility standards, for example, making directors understand their legal obligations toward CSR.[90]

NGOs and supranational organizations such as the ILO provide guidelines and encourage MNCs to aspire to international standards in human rights. However, early attempts to regulate MNCs internally "lacked any form of the robust compulsion, systemic monitoring and effective enforcement mechanism necessary to deal with the magnitude of the global investment area."[91] But that has changed. Friedman's narrow view of business's responsibilities is now outdated. The "rules of the game" are changing and now adherence to human rights standards for corporations is becoming more mainstream and less optional. As David Kinley and Justine Nolan Kinley predict, "Whatever, the precise role of corporations in the slow and stilted convergence of human rights and trade goals, it is one that will grow rather than diminish."[92]

Business is increasingly under pressure to consider three actions to comply with human rights expectations. It conforms to stakeholder rights; it accepts supply chain responsibility, and it avoids complicity with nations that disregard human rights.

### Revision Questions

1. Describe the range of human rights violations and why they have become a significant international issue.
2. What behaviors by MNCs are considered human rights violations and to what extent should they accept responsibility?
3. Explain the concept of complicity and cite examples when it occurred.
4. How might an MNC be harmed when it refuses to accept responsibility for human rights violations?

### Discussion Questions

I. Choose a specific human rights issue – for example, curtailing employee freedom of speech or the discriminatory treatment of women – and discuss how it might affect an MNC. Mention such details as what grievances or problems are associated with the issue, who is accusing the company, what tactics are used against it, and how vulnerable the company is.

II. Foxconn faces a dilemma: An audit by a U.S.-based nonprofit worker-safety group found widespread breaches of Chinese law and Apple policies at three plants. A major violation was excessive overtime, frequently 10–15 overtime hours a week. The company subsequently pledged to bring its overtime policies in line with Chinese law, allowing workers no more than nine hours of overtime a week. But a majority of workers would prefer more overtime to make more money. The company fears many employees may leave. How should Foxconn handle this dilemma?[93]

III. Discuss the wisdom of Talisman's decision to acquire ownership of an oil production facility in the Sudan a wise one? Was this simply a high-risk, high-opportunity situation that justified the investment?

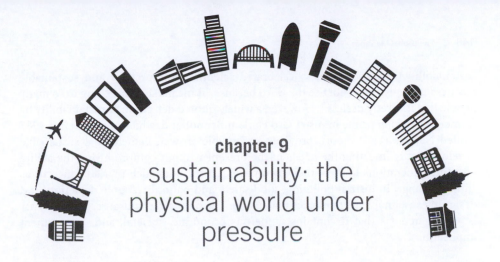

# chapter 9
# sustainability: the physical world under pressure

**Objectives**

1. Be able to name and discuss several urgent areas in which the world is under physical pressure.
2. Be able to discuss the major implications of the sustainability issue for the mission and practices of business.
3. Understand three major strategies available to business to address the problem of sustainability of resources.
4. Know what programs companies have used in specific industries to address sustainability.
5. Be able to propose some themes that can be used in addressing customers.
6. Know the value of preparing sustainability or social reports for a variety of audiences and what guidelines to observe.

As world populations grow and require increasing physical resources of water, food, energy, and raw materials, limits to growth loom and raise the issue of sustainability. The idea of sustainability begins with the realization that humankind lives on only one planet which provides all the available resources. The expression "Spaceship Earth" dramatizes this limit, symbolized by photographs of Earth taken from the moon and outer space. Donnelle H. Meadows, author of *Limits to Growth*, stated at the Future Dialogue conference: "We have now reached an inflexion point. The habits that gave us growth and progress in the past will not give us growth and progress in the future. We will see more change over the next 20 years than in the past 100."[1]

The earth's population is estimated to grow from seven billion in 2012 to nine billion by 2050. A world crowded with so many people simply cannot sustain economic growth at current consumption levels and production methods. Furthermore, the world's resources will further be strained as people everywhere seek the standard of living of developed nations. Sustainability is considered a major "business megatrend." A megatrend presents "inescapable strategic imperatives for corporate leaders" and forces "fundamental and persistent shifts in how companies compete." The concept of megatrends, popularized by John Naisbitt in 1982, refers to "incipient societal and economic shifts such as globalization, the rise of the information society, and the move from hierarchical organizations to networks."[2]

Businesses must face the issue of sustainability, for it will have a material impact on how companies think and act. Yet there is no single established definition for

**147**

sustainability.[3] Amory Lovins, a celebrated scientist, entrepreneur and sustainable business strategist, does not use the word because "it means so many thing to so many people that it's pretty useless."[4] However, a widely quoted definition of sustainability by former Norwegian prime minister Gro Harlem Brundtland, which appeared in a 1987 United Nations (UN) report, provides a workable answer, namely, that sustainable development is "meeting the needs of the present without compromising the ability of future generations to meet their own needs.[5] It includes such myriad concerns as climate change, industrial pollution, food safety and natural resource depletion, and designing sustainable technologies that economize on scarce natural resources. What is agreed upon is that it contains numerous economic, societal, and management implications.

## Some signs of stress

Signs of strain in the earth's ability to supply people with even their basic needs are mounting. The most urgent signs of stress are in food and water supply. Another worrisome shortage is in minerals.

### Food shortages

Food shortages have become common, causing the price of rice, wheat, and other staples to rise. The Asian Development Bank reported that left unchecked, increases in oil and food prices could shave growth across Asia over the next two years. For the planet's' poorest two billion people, who spend 50–70% of their income on food, soaring food prices may mean going from two meals a day to one.[6] Such a food crisis occurred in 2011. It was for real, said Lester R. Brown, president of the Earth Policy Institute and author of *World on the Edge: How to Prevent Environmental and Economic Collapse*. He says it might bring with it more bread riots cum political revolutions.[7] Food prices have doubled since early 2007 and is accounted for by growing demand and shrinking supplies.

Demand has been growing, reflecting the nearly doubling of the world population since 1970. As more families enter the middle class, some three billion people will move up the food chain and consume more meat, milk, and eggs. Supplies, however, are unlikely to keep up with demand for several reasons. The one most blamed is global warming. As temperatures rise, water tables fall as farmers overpump for irrigation. More than half the world's people live in countries where water tables are falling. In India, for example, 175 million people are being fed with grain produced by excessive pumping; and in China the figure is estimated at 130 million. *The Economist* reports that the rate of groundwater extraction is unsustainable. By 2050, when India's population will be a shade under 1.7 billion, India will run short of water.[8]

Soil erosion and mismanagement threaten the productivity of one-third of the world's cropland. A further threat to the world's food supply is that the United States, which historically has served as a global buffer against food shortages, is converting massive quantities of grain into fuel. Of the 400 million tons of grain harvested in 2010, nearly 40 million went to ethanol fuel distilleries. A survey by *Foreign Policy* magazine reported that the highest percentage of respondents say the world will need to increase its food production between 56% and 70%.[9]

## Food nationalism

Access to supplies has emerged as the overriding issue as the world transitions from an era of food surpluses to a new politics of food scarcity, says Brown. Food nationalism is one result.[10] Some governments have reacted to scarcity by seeking to secure their own interests at the expense of the common good. Russia and Argentina, two leading wheat exporters, have restricted exports; and Vietnam, the No. 2 rice exporter, banned exports for several months in early 2008.

Some importing countries have been trying to negotiate long-term grain-supply agreements with exporting countries – and sometimes from the farmers themselves, thus bypassing the large international trading firms. Led by Saudi Arabia, South Korea, and China, they are buying or leasing land in other countries on which to grow grain for themselves. Villagers in theses lands were neither informed or consulted on the new arrangements. Daewoo, a South Korean conglomerate, signed a deal to lease no less than half Madagascar's arable land to grow grain for South Koreans. The island's people in the water-stressed homeland would have received practically nothing.[11] A major benefit of land acquisitions, however, is that farm equipment, fertilizer, pesticides, and seeds that are bought from abroad will increase output. The downside is that foreign companies therefore deprive people of land they have used for centuries and that locals may not find work on these farms.[12] These "land grabs" also affect all downstream countries. For example, water extracted from the upper Nile River basin to irrigate crops in Ethiopia or Sudan will not reach Egypt. Conflicts could easily develop between investors and host countries.

## Water crisis

Water covers more than 70% of the Earth's surface, most of it, however, is seawater. Only 2.6% is potable freshwater, making water one of the world's scarcest natural resources. A Credit Suisse report noted that roughly 80 countries were unable to provide their populations with a sufficient supply of water without great difficulty. The Third World Centre for Water Management estimates that the number of people who did not have access to safe drinking water in 2009 was at least 1.8 billion.[13]

What causes this water crisis? First, there is the boom in China, India, and other emerging markets, which means the world is using far more water than it did five years ago. Add in climate change, environmental degradation, low water tables in Northern China, the United States, and India, and the picture becomes grimmer. Increasingly worrisome is that some world's great rivers – Indus, Rio Grande, Colorado, Murray-Darling, and Yellow – are depleted before reaching the sea. These are arteries of the world's main grain-growing areas.

Water usage varies with crops and foods. Farmers use about three-fourths of the world's water, industry less than a fifth, and domestic and municipal use only a tenth. Different foods require radically different amounts of water, for example, a kilogram of wheat requires about 1,000 liters, a kilo of beef requires 15,000 liters.[14] An ad by

Monsanto, "How Can We Squeeze More Food from a Raindrop?," touts the development of seeds that significantly increase crop yields and can help farmers use one-third less water per unit produced.[15]

Owing to the rapid spread of urbanization and the use of water-intensive agricultural products, the current rate of increase in water usage is double that of the world's population growth, according to the UN's Food and Agriculture Organization (FAO). City people use more water than rural folk, a fact of increasing concern because the prediction is that between now and 2030, there will be two billion additional third-world city dwellers. This strong surge in water usage has not been met by a corresponding growth in water supply.[16]

## Water equity

Rich communities tend of overuse water usage. West Palm Beach, Florida, had only 22 days worth of fresh water in June 2011, which prompted new rules restricting residents to once-a-week watering schedules for lawns and plants. The community uses more than one million gallons of water a month to keep their properties green. The largest water consumption was in a single property that consumed more than 13 million gallons of water from June 2010 to May 2011.[17]

Conflicts over water use are becoming more common. In Australia scuffles over water occurred when official called for a cut of nearly 40% in the volume of water taken for irrigation from the 1,350 mile Murrumbidgee River. Australia is the world's second-driest continent after Antarctica and no crops would grow in the dry plains of south-western New South Wales without irrigation.[18] In India, a project to develop 160 million tons of steel capacity was questioned because it would consume 640 billion gallons of water a year, enough to provide adequate water for drinking and cooking for 133 million people in India over the same period.[19]

## Nestle overreaches in California

Conflicts within communities have occurred over the sale of water to outsiders. A highly publicized case, as reported in "Town Torn Apart by Nestles," is the resort town of McCloud in Northern California,"[20] Nestle made a deal with elected board members to open one of the largest water bottling plants in the United States at a defunct lumber mill. It would be five times the size of Wal-Mart stores and could pack 300 semi-trailers of bottled water a week. The benefits to the town would be an annual payment of $350,000 and the creation of 240 jobs. Residents were uninformed about the plan until a town meeting at which a video was presented extolling the company's environmental credentials. No public discussion followed and only board members were allowed to vote because you "can't have 50 different opinions."

Opposition quickly grew as ground water levels fell. Residents argued "Water is for life, not profit." They formed the McCloud WaterShed Council, which conducted research financed by a wealthy San Francisco family. Nasty rumors circulated that Nestle gave board members bank accounts in Switzerland and bought condos for them. The council undertook legal action based on depleting lakes, wetlands, and streams. Research showed that social costs were not considered, that Nestle was paying less than elsewhere, that jobs and revenues never materialized, and that waste water, traffic, and air pollution problems were ignored. In short, the costs outweighed the benefits.

The long-term solution to the water shortage is to change the way water is used, which requires a fundamental change in corporate and personal behavior, says Koichiro Maytuura, the head of UNESCO, the main UN agency dealing with water.

## Shortages of other natural resources

Natural resources are becoming increasingly scarce and expensive. An article, titled "Mining the Scarcity Boom," advised investors to "devote a bigger chunk of their portfolio to commodities that pass the one crucial test, namely, scarcity."[21] It featured four commodities: metals, primarily demand for copper, which is expected to grow 45% in 2011 and for which the expected surge in global demand is expected to increase by 53%; energy, which is getting more expensive as the cost of finding new stores of oil has tripled since 2001; and agriculture, where some crops, such as soybeans and cotton, are fundamentally in short supply. Economic repercussions are evident. Minerals such as copper have already risen sharply in price. Oil is increasingly sought in deep seabeds and in the Arctic. Some even suggest a scheme to mine asteroids for nickel, platinum, and other key ingredients for metals. Taking an optimistic view, Andrew McKenzie, a geologist and BHP Billton PLC's chief executive for nonferrous metals, says, "We think there are 10,000 more years of minerals left for civilization."[22] Such statements, however, confound the question of what "the long term" really means.

The severe scarcity of rare-earth elements has received recent attention. Access to these materials is essential for 21st-century technology like smart phones – and smart bombs. China is the dominant producer and user of rare-earth elements, and has imposed quotas on its exports.[23] Alarmed by China's action, Japan was scrambling to find alternative suppliers, particularly by developing new mines abroad.[24] The U.S. military has also taken action. It started a new plan, dubbed the Strategic Materials Security Program by the Pentagon, that would give it greater power to decide what it stockpiles and how it goes about buying the materials. [25]

# Approaches to attainment of sustainability

Sustainability extends environmental concerns over a greater geographical area and the health of the Earth as a whole. Reducing environmental harm is therefore a continuing approach to the attainment of sustainability. The second approach seeks sustainable development by safeguarding specific resources from depletion, such as water, needed for long-term sustainable development. The third approach urges the building of alliances with others, especially environmental groups.

## Reducing environmental harm

Much of the sustainability issue is rooted in the environmental movement and sometimes confused with it. Like the concern for depletion of resources, the basic idea is to stop degradation of the environment by reducing air and water pollution and maintaining the health of rivers, forests, and land. More specifically, environmental references are made to greenhouse gas emissions, the ozone hole, acid rain, species extinction, destruction of rainforests, dying coral reefs, energy use, waste management, global warming, and the like. Reference to the environment serves as a "catch-all" for preserving the Earth and the space surrounding it. The related subject of climate change will be heating up over the years and drastically affect our survivability.

The earth's stratospheric ozone layer has received particular attention. Not to be confused with global climate change, ozone protects life on Earth by absorbing most of the highest energy ultraviolet (UV) radiation in sunlight.[26] Ozone near the ground is a health hazard and a component of smog. This "bad ozone" is different from the "good ozone" up there. Scientists realized beginning in the 1970s that a group of man-made chemicals, mainly the chloroflouorocarbons (CFCs), could destroy stratospheric ozone, which could allow more intense UV radiation to reach the surface. It would bring increased skin cancer, cataracts, and other harms to human health and ecosystems. In the late 1980s and 1990s nations adopted strict regulations that have nearly eliminated most ozone-depleting chemicals in industrialized countries.

An outstanding spokesperson against environmental degradation and poverty, which are often linked in developing nations, is Wangaie Maathai, a Nobel Peace Prize Laureate. She founded the Greatbelt movement in 1977, whose mission is to plant trees across Kenya to fight erosion and to create firewood and jobs for women. Land used by natives for firewood and streams used for water were taken over by large land owners to grow coffee and tea. The movement has planted more than 30 million trees and has helped nearly 900,000 women. She was known for taking a holistic approach to sustainable development that embraces democracy, human rights and women's rights in particular.[27]

Not surprisingly, more than half of corporate marketers and communicators believe that their organizations will increase their involvement in environmental sustainability initiatives during the next two to three years, according to a survey conducted by the Chicago-based American Marketing Association. Fleishman-Hillard, a communications firm, says that half of those surveyed believe that economic realities will encourage the adoption of such practices. A book by Dalcacio Reis Taschew, *Product Design in the Sustainable Era,* reports on a worldwide survey of companies and products that are pushing the boundaries of technology and product design to engage in changes necessary for a new environmental friendly world.[28]

## Sustainable development

Economic development is a key driving force for countries and businesses in this century. Along with it is a search for natural resources to feed that growth. As the most accessible resources are exploited, more remote regions are explored, including the world's oceans and, some would include, outer space. Technological barriers, for example in deep sea drilling, must however be overcome. The objectives of sustainable development therefore are to protect natural resources and prevent depletion; encourage moderation and prudence in not wasting natural resources; and optimize the use of natural resources. These are some of the concepts in Amory Lovin's book *Natural Capitalism,*[29] which could dramatically improve the productivity of natural resources by redesigning production around biological models, rethinking business as a service and reinvesting in natural capital.[30] At the World Summit on Sustainable Development, which took place in Johannesburg from August 26 to September 4, 2002, world leaders agreed that eliminating unsustainable production and consumption is an overriding objective of sustainable development.[31]

Economic systems become more efficient with reliable infrastructure. Examples abound. Water is saved when leakage in distribution system is minimized and in agriculture by irrigating the roots of plants rather than their surfaces where water evaporates. A modern electricity grid allows power produced from several sources in many locations, including wind power, solar power, and tidal changes, to be collected and distributed to where it is needed. Efficient rail and public transportation systems reduce vehicle usage and energy consumption. The Internet reduces the need for transportation of people and documents.

Jeffrey D. Sachs is a strong proponent for building infrastructure suitable for the 21st century. He says, "This includes an efficient electricity grid fed by renewable energy; fiber and wireless networks that carry telephony and broadband internet; water, irrigation, and sewerage systems that efficiently use and recycle fresh water; urban and intercity public transit systems; safer highways; and networks of protecting natural areas that conserve biodiversity and the habitats of threatened species."[32] He recognizes that many of these infrastructure investments require public sector leadership to forge partnerships with the private sector. He also believes that developed countries have to do far more to help poor countries by the transition to sustainability, saying the rich world somehow expects poor countries to restrict their use of fossil fuels without any significant help in financing new and sustainable sources of energy.

## Building new alliances

As Lovins states, "it's the hidden connections between your business and other opportunities that you think are well outside your boundaries that create extraordinary opportunities, depending on the way you handle them."[33] The advantages of working with environmentalists have become evident since Earth Day in 1970, sometimes helping both the bottom line and the public image. When a private equity firm planned to take over the Texas utility TXU Corp., it sought environmentalists' support. As *Business Week* wrote, "The TXU takeover is a sign of a remarkable evolution in the dynamic between corporate executives and activists. Once fractious and antagonistic, it has moved toward accommodation and even mutual dependence."[34]

The mere threat of bad publicity can force business to change. On the eve of the 2000 Sydney Olympics, where Coca-Cola was a sponsor, Greenpeace launched an email campaign against the soft-drink giant for using a potent greenhouse gas in its nine to ten million coolers and vending machines. Jeff Seabright, Coca-Cola's vice-president for environment and water resources, responded by asking what it could do. As a result, Coke along with PepsiCo, Unilever and McDonald's have spent $30 million developing a less damaging system.

On the issue of water conservation, working with WWF's U.S. president Carter Roberts, Coca-Cola will give $20 million to the WWF over several years to help it run water-conservation efforts in seven major river basins around the world, including the Yangtze in China, the Mekong in Southeast Asia, the Danube in Europe, and the Rio Grand and Rio Bravo in the United States and Mexico.[35]

# Implications for management mission and practices

The challenge of the sustainability crisis for business requires a reconsideration of existing ways of doing business. Referring to "today's turbulent world," Darcy Hitchcock and Marsha Willard in their book *The Business Guide to Sustainability: Practical Strategies and Tools for Organizations* examine "our world as a whole system, revealing threats and opportunities. It forces you to see relationships between social, economic and environmental trends."[36] The authors say the impact is so enormous that it must eventually infiltrate all aspects of a business organization. The authors apply sustainability to the industry sectors of services and general office practices, manufacturing and product design, and government agencies. They also explain what different organizational functions – senior management, facilities, human resources, environmental affairs, marketing/public relations, and accounting and finance – can do to implement sustainability efforts in their organizations.

Recognition of the impact of sustainability pressures was documented in the third annual Sustainability & Innovation Global Executive Study, jointly produced by a collaboration between the *MIT Sloan Management Review* and the Boston Consulting Group. Based on the responses from 2,874 managers and executives from 113 countries, 70% say they have placed sustainability on their management agenda within the past six years, and 20% have done so in just the past two years. Two-thirds said that sustainability was critically important to being competitive in today's marketplace.[37]

Many organizations now view sustainability as a profit opportunity, with 31% of respondents saying their companies are currently profiting from sustainability business practices. Impetus is provided by several external factors: regulations, green score cards and other sustainability metrics, media and NGOs, climate change science, resource scarcity and consumer demand. Important internal drivers are also stated by respondents. They name benefits related to operating costs, revenue growth, brand integrity, and employee engagement.

The survey differentiates between "embracers" and "cautious adopters." The former believe that sustainability is critical to being competitive and placed the issue on their management agenda. They are three times as likely to have a business case for sustainability. They are also twice as likely to say that sustainability has increased their collaboration with competitors and that they are likely to be collaborating more with customers, suppliers, government, local communities, and NGOs. The survey also refers to "harvesters" of sustainability who link sustainability, performance, and profits. They have strong organization support, have a separate business unit that focuses on sustainability, have a chief sustainability officer, and issue a separate sustainability report.[38]

Another study shows that executives do not have to choose between the largely social benefits of developing sustainable products or processes and the financial costs of doing so. After studying the sustainability initiatives of 30 large corporations, Ram Nidumolu, C.K. Prahalad and M.R. Rangaswami found that sustainability is "a mother lode of organizational and technological innovation that yield both bottom- and top-line returns."[39] They outline the five stages that most companies go through on the path to becoming sustainable: (1) viewing compliance as opportunity, (2) making value chains sustainable, (3) designing sustainable products and services, (4) developing new business models, and (5) creating next-practice platforms. Illustrations from several companies following this path are:

- Hewlett-Packard began experimenting with alternatives to lead solders.
- Cargill and Unilever worked with farmers in their supply chain to develop sustainable practices in the cultivation of palm oil, soybeans, cacao, and other agricultural commodities.
- Clorox became the first mainstream consumer products company to launch a line of nonsynthetic cleaning products after learning that its Clorox was people's second biggest environmental concern.
- Waste management set up a unit, Green Squad, to generate value from waste, estimated to be $9 billion of its $14 billion market.
- The "smart grid," an intersection of the Internet and energy management, is used by Cisco, HP, Dell, and IBM to manage the energy needs of cities, companies, buildings, and households.[40]

In his book, *Strategy for Sustainability: A Business Manifesto,* Adam Werbach foresees nine fundamental changes needed by business.[41] Among the most important four are, first, that every organization's operating environment will change as dramatically in the next three to five years as it has changed in the last five. A second is that management can no longer follow the sequence of discover, define, plan, execute, and measure. The time horizon for strategic development is getting shorter. A third change is that a chaotic external world requires internal cohesion and flexibility, and a fourth that only the truly transparent will survive. "You must have pertinent, accessible, and engaging information readily available inside and outside the organization."[42]

In sum, today's corporation must go beyond the conventional practices of pollution prevention and product stewardship toward a holistic and proactive model of management in a network of mutually beneficial relationships with the Earth and communities.[43]

To cope with these challenges, companies have created new positions for chief sustainability officers who report to the CEO and are responsible for the company's saving of energy and environmental matters. United Parcel Service Inc. appointed such an officer in March 2011, and Coca-Cola in May 2011 created an office of sustainability that would look into such areas as recycling, water management, and climate protection. In the previous two years, online job posting showed the keyword "sustainability" more than quadrupled to 8,245.[44]

## Creating a vision for value creation

Companies that seek to gain advantage in sustainability are benefitted by formulating a vision for value creation and executing on it.[45] To achieve this vision they update their traditional business tools and engage in trend spotting and scenario planning They must be convinced that their companies will survive and thrive by following emerging trends in society, technology, and natural resources. Based on this thinking, Wal-Mart launched its Sustainability 360 program in 2006 to establish explicit goals to purchase 100% renewable energy, create zero waste, slash greenhouse gas emissions, and sell "products that sustain our resources and the environment."[46] Another company, Fujitsu, employs "a performance assessment scorecard – its 'cost green index' – that assesses the potential cost, productivity, and environmental impacts of eco-efficiency initiatives across the firm."[47]

Recognizing the need for new thinking, M.I.T. has tackled the issue of water shortages. Philip S. Khoury, M.I.T.'s associate provost and Ford International Professor History, stated, "The problems associated with this crisis will require, at the most fundamental level, new thinking about science and technology." More than 50 faculty from each of the Institute's five schools are now tackling what he considers one of the greatest global challenges of the 21st century.[48] One researcher, Sanjay Sarma, who grew up in India where water is a scarce resource, concentrates on the world's water distribution systems, which are notoriously inefficient. In the United States, nearly 30% of the water never reaches its destination and in developing counties as much as 50%. He is building a robot that "listens" for the sound of small leaks and then reports their location.[49]

## Applying CSR's social investment initiative

By embracing social investment, corporate social responsibility moves further up the CSR pyramid – beyond providing mutual benefits for its stakeholders, reducing such social costs as environmental degradation, and helping to solve social problems, as discussed in Chapter 15. This elevation of CSR leads some to say, "CSR will become the key driving force for business in this century towards achieving sustainable development."[50] Corporate social investment (CSI) embraces both the mission of sustainable development and corporate sustainability. As stated by the Association of Development Financing Institutions in Asia and the Pacific (ADFIAP), which comprises 108 financial institutions in 41 countries, sustainability has come to mean "advancing and institutionalizing environment, social and governance principles and practices."[51] One sign of this development is that venture capital investment totaled $9 billion in 2008.[52]

Working with the right NGO partners is an important factor. But all parties must develop a common language and metric, such as return on their CSI investment, and plan for a cumulative, longer-term impact. Its member institutions have promoted and adopted the means in which to put "sustainability into practice such as reducing travel-related carbon emissions, finding innovative solutions to cutting electricity, water and paper use, and striving to become a socially involved organization."[53] Coca-Cola cooperated with the WWF , among other NGOs, to attain "water neutrality" by replenishing watersheds to the full extent of the water it extracts.

## Recognizing business opportunities and benefits

The price system in economics serves as the classical mechanism for equilibrating supply and demand. When a product becomes scarce relative to demand, its price rises and demand falls. People are motivated to find ways to reduce their consumption and find substitute products. But there is no substitute for water, and people consider it a human right to obtain a necessary amount. In rural areas, people get water from wells; in town and cities, water is supplied by the community, charging households either a flat fee or one based on consumption. A new solution is proposed: to provide some water free or at low cost and then charge for it. In other words, to treat water as a commodity.

Ger Bergkamp, director-general of the World Water Council, the organization that coordinates the World Water Forum, says, "One of the challenges is to get the right procurement in place to allow the private sector to enter the market." He sees no difference in the water sector from any other sector, disagreeing with those who see water as a basic human need that could benefit by being treated as a public utility. The basic argument is that: "For universal access to clean water, there is simply no other choice but to price water at a reasonable rate." But a good framework and legal certainties would be necessary, otherwise "there is no chance that any private sector company would enter a contract."

Among possible arrangements are that the poor would be subsidized, for example,, South Africa provides 20 liters of free water a day. At present there is unequal pricing. Poor people from Manila to Mexico City pay 10–15 times more than the rich to buy water of indifferent quality from private vendors. In the city of Phnom Penh, Cambodia, the management of water was improved through equitable pricing. Income is used to make public utilities more efficient and to improve water distribution systems to reduce leakage.

## Water entrepreneurship[54]

Legendary Texan billionaire investor T Boone Pickens, who made his money from oil, is one person who now sees the increasing shortage of water as a market opportunity. His firm, Mesa Water, recently acquired water rights for 200,000 acres in Texas and is busy buying water rights across the United States. When a business tycoon acquires something, it is only natural for the rest of the world to assume that something will go up in price and that there will be buyers willing to purchase it. Observers believe that Pickens will end up selling his water rights to nearby cities in Texas, such as Houston. Pickens said that oil and water are the two big commodities he is bullish about for the long term[55] General Electric's CEO Jeff Immelt also sees water as the one sector that the world's biggest conglomerate was looking to increase its exposure in.[56] Pickens, Immelt, and others can not be wrong. Water's time has come!

According to consulting firm Beverage Marketing Corp., Americans drank 8.7 billion gallons of bottled water in 2008. It was America's third most popular drink, after soda and milk. Between 2003 and 2008 sales of bottled water swelled 59% to $5.1 billion. About 70% of consumers said they drink bottled water.[57] In South Korea, imported bottled water sales have rising in recent years and was selling at higher prices than Dubai crude.[58] Sometimes people rebel against bottled water. Its sale was banned in Bundanoon, a small Australian town 90 minutes from its capital Canberra[59] Some regions see themselves as suppliers of fresh water, with Quebec, for example, calling itself the Saudi Arabia of roaring water.

Bottled water, however, is creating an environmental waste problem. The beverage industry's ravenous appetite for plastic has added piles of it to dumps.[60] The industry is responding by seeking to reduce the amount of plastic used.[61] For example, the new half-liter bottle for Aquafina, the largest U.S. bottled-water brand, weighs about 20% less than the one it is replacing.

# Some company initiatives

Company initiatives in addressing the sustainability are growing.[62] The case study of Unilever reviews its lengthy and slow management process of investigating the sustainability issue and undertaking some initiatives. Other companies can use it as a guide. This case is followed by a sampling of actions by other companies.

## Case study: how unilever addressed the sustainability issue[63]

The issue of sustainability was introduced in1994 by Dr. Jan-Kees Vis, former Unilever Foods Executive Quality Assurance Group, when he told his new boss, Jan Peelen, the Chairman of the Foods Executive, that Unilever was not doing enough work with sustainable development. Unilever Foods was a major unit, supplying nearly half of Unilever's 1995 turnover of $50 billion. Vis's responsibility was to enable the Foods operating companies to implement environmental management policies, such as BS7750 and other precursors to ISO 14000-type environmental management systems. Environmental strategic goals, however, were the responsibility of the Unilever Environmental Group, an independent, internal consulting group. Vis wanted to set management guidance on how to deploy program to meet environmental goals. In the spirit of ISO 9000 quality management systems, he wanted to (1) train people to implement environmental management systems; (2) develop and implement environmental auditing programs; and (3) work to improve eco-efficiency.

Unilever was already committed to sustainability with a broadly worded policy statement, "Unilever wishes to be part of a sustainable future, in which economic growth combines with sound environmental management to meet the needs and aspirations of people through the world."[64] Vis improved the specificity of this policy statement in 1995 by saying, "We will aim for sustainable development. In the years to come, we will work towards a definition of sustainability that is meaningful to our business and acceptable to relevant stakeholders." [65]

Vis recognized the difficulty in linking the statement to business operations. He brought in external consultants to provide outside perspectives. One was SustainAbility, a U.K. environmental consulting company, which sought the opinions of different stakeholders around the world to construct a definition of sustainable development that was appropriate for Unilever's Foods businesses. Reorganization ensued, replacing the Foods Executive with the Foods Category, a new management body with strategic responsibility for Unilever's Foods business worldwide. This new organization did not want to support and maintain the environmental and quality assurance function, so the function was moved to the Safety and Environmental Assurance Center.

To translate the concept of sustainability into a set of operational indicators for use in Unilever practice, the top management executives group decided on 15 measurable sustainability indicators and added a further step of describing how sustainable development contributed to Unilever's business performance. TME prepared a proposal that each issue should be addressed from three different perspectives: to (1) clean up product and process emissions, introduce management systems; (2) design and implement clean processes and much cleaner and less resource-intensive products, on the basis of rational environmental product strategies; and (3) radically redesign systems and services, so as to deliver outstanding consumer benefits within the limits of global carrying capacity.

They agreed to organize workshops and pilot projects in 1998 to investigate the feasibility of measuring environmentally sustainable initiatives. Agriculture was selected as the major source of dependency and environmental impact for Unilever Foods. A study by Jules Pretty, an author of several books on sustainable agriculture, provided descriptions of the popular opinions on the future of agriculture. They were divided into two categories: (1) environmental pessimists, and (2) business-as-usual optimists who, in turn, were divided into industrialized-world-to-the rescue, the new modernists, and sustainable intensifiers.

A report identified two major issues: (1) intensive, chemical-based farming, and (2) preservation of farming and rural communities. Regional differences resulted in further sub-division of issues, for example, on the issue of genetically modified organisms, North America was concerned about whether there was support for labeling of foodstuffs containing GMOs while in Europe such foodstuffs were labeled to give consumers a choice. In the developing world the issue was the ownership of generic resources and equitable distribution of profit derived from the commercial use of genes from these countries.

Adopting new agriculture practices would require Unilever to have some influence over agricultural operations, which is connected with the issue of ownership of supply chains. It owned only roughly 25% of its agricultural supply chain. With fish, it had no ownership and purchased 100% of its fish from independent fisheries. With soya, there was a problem in being able to guarantee to consumes that its products were GMO free because of the quantities required for its products.

Paul Polman, CEO of Uniliver outlined the company's Sustainable Living Plan, with 2020 as a target, in an interview by the *Harvard Business Review*. It included:

- *Health and hygiene*: helping more than a billion people improve their hygiene habits and providing safe drinking water to 500 million people.
- *Nutrition*: double the proportion of portfolio that meets the highest nutritional standards.
- *Greenhouse gases*: halve the greenhouse gas impacts of its products across the life cycle.
- *Water*: halve the water associated with the consumer use of its products, focusing on countries that are populous and water-scarce.
- *Waste*: halve waste associated with disposal of its products.
- *Sustainable sourcing*: source 50% by 2026 and 100% by 2020.
- *Better livelihoods*: link more than 500,000 smallholder farmers and small-scale distributors into its supply chain.[66]

In recognition of Unilever's leadership, Polman was named the most effective corporate communicator among FTSE 100 CEOs in Britain. The study looked at which CEOs best used communications to influence how they and their companies were perceived, and how they can influence other businesses, consumes, or government policy.[67]

## Initiatives by other companies

The actions taken by various companies illustrate the variety of approached used to address the sustainability issue.

- *Recycling:* C&A Floorcoverings recycles old carpet into new carpet.[68] Concentrating on the concept of "flow of services" rather than product, Ray Anderson, chairman of Interface, placed sustainability at the core of its business model, "reinventing and recycling carpet rather than creating it to be destroyed."[69] He vowed to never take another drop of oil from the Earth.[70] In Europe, some firms require safe disposal of packaging materials and the product itself

- *Reducing energy consumption:* To help lower companies' energy consumption, Xerox provides document services instead of copiers and it refurbishes discarded copier. "The result is higher customer satisfaction, lower energy usage, and a 91% rate of recycling of printers."[71] Procter & Gamble introduced a new *Tide* that achieves the same laundry results with cold water. SunChips introduced a resource-conservation program by powering its Modesto plant with solar power. It also worked on reducing the environmental impact of its packaging and getting involved with reputable sustainability initiatives.

- *Reducing water consumption:* When ice cream giant Ben & Jerry's discovered that it wasted up to one million liters of water a day because its staff worldwide were told to run taps nonstop to wash scoops, it discontinued the practice. At Coca-Cola, which uses 73 billion gallons of water a year, the CEO wants to build Coke's reputation as a local benefactor and global diplomat. It created "Global Water Challenge" – a coalition of corporations and other organizations. It initiated 70 clean water projects in 40 countries. It bought water purification systems in Kenya and built rainwater-harvesting structures in India.

- *Reducing packaging:* Many companies are using fewer materials in their packaging. For example, Coca-Cola has worked intensively with its bottling partners to "light weight" its packaging and cut greenhouse gas emission, thereby generating savings in the tens of millions of dollars.

- *Use resources more efficiently:* Frito-Lay, one of world's largest snack-food makers, uses limited resources to make a better Frito-Lay product. It recognized society's changing expectations about making healthier snacks that use more wholesome manufacturing processes. It launched new brands like SunChips, a whole-grain snack.

- *Design innovative products:* Hewlett-Packard brought technology to villages around the world by developing a solar powered printer to make photo ID cards in rural India. Toyota and Honda developed hybrid cars and General Motors created the Volt all-electric vehicle. 3M allows its engineers to spend up to 20% of their time working on innovation projects. GE's Healthcare unit developed a portable electrocardiogram device in Bangalore, India, for the local market.[72]

# Communicating about sustainability

The task of communicating about sustainability is enormous because so many audiences are involved. Many organizations concerned about their image and their brand have found that attention to sustainability can enhance both. Audiences include customers whose cooperation is needed, the partners with whom a company collaborates, and various advocacy groups that monitor corporate behavior. Marketing communications have been used to reach consumers and social reports to reach multiple audiences.

## Reaching consumers

As with the environmental issue, companies that produce green products hope to be rewarded in the marketplace as the sustainability appeal resonates with more customers. They are exploring ways the appeal can be used in marketing communications. Hitchcock and Willard devote an entire chapter to the role of public relations and marketing, saying that professionals in these fields have critical skills to support a sustainability initiative.[73]

Governments and NGOs have carried out various programs and activities to educate the public on the importance of practicing sustainable consumption. They have launched awareness campaigns and distributed pamphlets and articles on sustainable consumption. Their public education programs promote recycling and encourage the practice of the 3Rs – reduce, reuse, and recycle. Under the banner of social marketing, companies have encouraged employees to check tire pressure to improve fuel economy or to set printers for double-sided printing.[74]

## Sustainable consumption

An article, "Can advertising Save the World?," describes how an industry that stands accused of being responsible for much of the planet's environmental and social problems might now be in a position to help solve them.[75] It states, "Because social and environmental effects are not properly accounted for, the market tends to oversupply goods that may have a significantly negative environmental or social impact – such as cheap consumer goods and complex financial products." Rory Sutherland, the president of IPA consultancy and vice-chairman of the Ogilvy Group, thinks that over-consumption can occur because "people often seriously overestimate the joy brought by a new car or bigger house. And conspicuous consumption is not always economically valuable because your new BMW can make other people feel worse about themselves."[76]

The issue now is how best to change people's behavior to mitigate the worst effects of our over-consumption. In the words of Futerra, a "sustainable communications" agency which opened in 2001, this means "climate change is no longer a scientist's problem, it's a salesman's problem." The communication industry seems aware of this. Sir Martin Sorrell, CEO of the marketing firm WPP Group PLC, has spoken many times of it being "our job to make fashion unfashionable." Havas sees it as a huge business opportunity. "Clients across every sector are now either highly engaged or under mounting pressure to instigate significant changes in the name of sustainability. We believe sustainability represents the single largest opportunity for forward thinking businesses today," said its chief executive Fernando Rodes Vila.

A few consultancy networks are leading the way. Aegis has a sustainability practice called Clownfish. Ogilvy set up Ogilvy Earth, which aims to give its clients a more positive take on sustainability. Last year, Saatchi & Saatchi bought the environmental consultancy Act Now, rebranded it SaatchiS, and built it into a global network with 20 offices. "We see the power of brands to drive social change."

Companies must increasingly explain the realities of sustainable consumption in consumers' daily lives. The British industry magazine *Marketing Week* claims that the financial crisis comes at a moment in history when we are shifting away from consumerism anyway. It describes the future as a "premodern age" when "we're seeing a new emphasis on social rather than individual production and we're buying things less for instant gratification, and with social goals in mind. We're thinking of the environmental impact of our purchases and the ethical questions they raise, and so on."[77]

An Australian newspaper reports on a thousand community centers across Australia where people are changing how they live their lives. They cook at home instead of eating out, restaurants replace gourmet with "home-inspired" meals, and friends share clothes. Op shops are in fashion, a claim shown by talking to the fashion designer who picked up a pair of leather pants for (just!) $120 from Salvos. It rebranded its stores as "Fashion with a Conscience," making the leap from evangelical Christians with a focus on charity, to "urban recyclers" with celebrity endorsements describing the shops as a "new shopping hot spot".[78]

In the long run, consumers must be prepared for price increases because that is the market's method of reducing consumption to meet the realities of smaller supplies in the face of increasing demand. They must also be prepared for rationing for when the price mechanism fails. Governments may impose it and expect businesses to cooperate.

## Publishing sustainability reports

A sustainability report is a specialized type of social responsibility report, although increasingly used as an alternative name for it. A program called the Global Reporting Initiative institutes international guidelines for sustainability reporting, and today over 1,000 organizations, including many corporations, use the GRI guidelines to assess their sustainability practices.[79] Most social reports are now increasingly available on company websites.

The annual Ernst & Young Excellence in Sustainability Reporting awards provide a sampling of corporate sustainability objectives and performance. Joanne Jones, of AngloGold Ashanti, says that "in addition to being key to interaction with stakeholder, it serves as a process for developing the company's strategies internally, including ensuring that approaches to sustainability and operational issues are integrated."[80] Timberland's report provides metrics on pollution and use of natural resources. Clorox' refers to Greenworks for its eco-friendly cleaning products.

Most ambitiously, GE mentions its financial services business for "its ecomagination product line has generated tens of billions of dollars in revenues and positioned that company as a leader in rapidly growing market segments such as energy infrastructure and high-efficiency appliances, jet engines, and locomotives."[81] In May 2005, CEO Immelt publicly announced that the company was betting its future on clean technology with the aim of aggressively commercializing the new technologies such as wind power, solar energy, fuel cells, high-efficiency gas turbines, hybrid locomotive, lower-emission aircraft engines, lighter and stronger materials, energy-efficient lighting, and water purification technologies.

**Guidelines for sustainability communication.**

Among the guidelines for sustainable communication are these:

- be careful and avoid greenwashing;
- use labels that show source of food, so that people can "buy locally" if they choose;
- appeal to "green" consumers (The Roper Green Gauge lists five market segments: true blue greens, greenbacks, sprouts, grousers, basic browns);
- sometimes go beyond what customers expect, for example, Toyota and Honda built hybrids and Home Depot adopted sustainability after being targeted by a Rainforest Action Network;
- decide whether to attach the green or sustainable label to one product or all (as IKEA does);
- decide how to frame the message, for example, price benefits for Basic Brown customers or the emblem of a smile on the side of every approved can of dolphin-safe tuna.[82]

# Conclusions

The issue of sustainability recognizes that the physical world is undergoing stress from enormous economic growth since the industrial revolution. Scarcity of food and fresh water are most obvious in parts of the world. Was economist Thomas Malthus right when he predicted that food production could not keep up with population growth? The Green Revolution with its use of hybrid seeds and fertilizers seems to disprove him, but that cornucopia is becoming overburdened. Genetic engineering now seems like the most technological development for food today, but it has faced resistance from some environmentalists and consumers.

Whatever technological progress might be made, businesses that comprise the economic system must confront the problem of sustainability. The sole pursuit of maximizing profits is increasingly unable to provide the motivation to solve the problem. Management must experiment with eco-friendly and socially responsible practices to achieve corporate survivability.[83] As Stuart L. Hart concludes in *Capitalism at the Crossroads*, "… we have reached the tipping point for the change and transformation required to move us toward a more sustainable world."[84] His book appropriately carries the sub-title: "Next-Generation Business Strategies for a Post-Crisis World."

## Appendix: Sustainability by industry sectors

Different industries face unique sustainability problems and develop their own responses. Some of the industries and their initiatives mentioned in the sustainability literature are listed below.

**Construction.** Heavy emphasis is currently being placed on new green buildings and refurbishment. One example is Gerding/Edlen a small Portland, Oregon, a property development firm, which was recognized for its "green building" practices.[85] Another example is Ty Mawr, a traditional and ecological building company in Wales, that has experienced rapid growth on the basis of its sustainable products. After concerns about the amount of sand extracted and dredged in the United Kingdom, it pioneered in the development of "glaster and limecrete," which are natural alternatives to plaster and concrete, made from glass and lime respectively.[86] Fueled largely by the LEED (Leadership in Energy and Environmental Design), a "system of checklists has made it easy for architects, developers and facilities managers to make more sustainable choices."[87]

**Agriculture – Certifying products.** Kraft is switching its entire Kenco brand to Rainforest Alliance-certified coffee; a move it hopes will win over more ethical shoppers and give it a point of difference over market leader Nescafé. Kenco's Really Rich, Really Smooth and Decaffeinated jars will be the first to switch, with 75% of the beans for the freeze-dried range sourced from farms certified by the Rainforest Alliance by the end of this year. Kraft director of corporate affairs Jonathan Harrell says, "There's a consumer trend for people looking for sustainability in what they buy. Even better if they get that through a trusted brand."[88]

**Fishing.** The fisheries sector of any given country has huge potential for promoting sustainable livelihoods of the people, says an article about Gambia. Because livelihoods in Africa are so closely linked to natural resources, local people are the most logical entry point into sustainable management. In Gambia, fishing centers are handed to the local people themselves to manage. "People will only be able to consider the long-term perspective required for sustainable management of the fisheries sector when their immediate needs for health and well-being are met."[89]

**Tourism.** Although tourism is a major contributor to many country's economic development, it can fundamentally disrupt their local socio-economic systems and lead to a self-reinforcing cycle of ecosystem degradation. The sustainable development of tourism at destination areas has become an important issue. One example is Scandic Hotels in Sweden, which used "the natural step framework to transform their practices and their image.[90]

**Timber and logging.** The boreal forests of northern Quebec and Ontario may be at stake as Greenpeace and the nation's largest logging company arm wrestle over how to protect the land and its endangered species.[91] In the Amazon, Greenpeace in 1992 opened an office in the rainforest to track illegal logging, cattle ranching and soy harvesting. It was noted that deforestation accounts for 20% of climate change. Home Depot adopted sustainability after being targeted by a Rainforest Action Network campaign. Customer do not get a choice. No fuss is made about some products having a Stewardship Council certification label. IKEA has "greened" its entire line.[92]

**Chemical industry.** The United Nations Environment Program (UNEP) is urging chemical companies to become active participants in international chemical safety and sustainability programs. The aim is for industry to provide a greater level of financing and to be more proactive in handling hazardous chemicals. Recently BPA (bisphenol), a carcinogen, has been found in dental sealants, baby bottles, the liners of food cans, CDs and DVDs, eyeglasses and hundreds of household goods. More than six million pounds are produced in the United States each year. One bottle maker, Nalgene, whose bottles are popular with hikers and other outdoor enthusiasts, will phase out BPA. And some retailers, such as Wal-Mart, plan to phase out baby bottles with BPA.[93]

**Financial.** Although most major commercial and investment banks have long not considered environment and social concerns to be of particular relevance to their operations, they have now become aware of "sustainable finance." On the international level, decisions by the World Bank and IMF to finance such projects as building roads in the Amazon have been questioned by NGOs.

---

### Revision Questions

1. What if the significance of sustainability for business? Why has it become such an important issue? Name some industries that are most affected and explain why.
2. What are the major strategies and programs businesses use to address the issue?
3. What themes are relevant for consumer relations? Give some examples.
4. Why is it a good idea to prepare sustainability reports? What information should they contain and for whom are they intended?

---

### Discussion Questions

I. You work for a food processing company that has just created the position of "chief sustainability officer" who has asked you to list the kinds of matters she should explore. Name five areas and discuss why you included them.

II. A car-rental company is wondering what it can do to convert to more sustainable operations and yet maintain its profitability. What ideas should it consider? Would these be more attractive to select consumer segments?

III. Is the sustainability issue overstated? Can't we expect modern technology, as with genetically modified organisms, to solve the problem of shortages?

IV. The subject of nationalism should be revisited. Discuss the reasonableness of national policies to restrict the sale of foods or scarce minerals when there are shortages in a country. Should not this be a limit to the globalization movement?

# chapter 10
# debate over climate change

**Objectives**

1. Recognize to what extent the issue of climate change is relevant to a specific industry or multinational corporation (MNC).
2. Realize how the welfare of an MNC might be damaged if it ignores the consensus of the scientific community that global warming is a reality?
3. Recognize the dangers in publicly debunking global warming.
4. Help a global manager identify possible marketing or other advantages in undertaking projects to ameliorate global warming.
5. Know the existing public policies by business about climate change exist and be able to determine which to support.
6. Become familiar with global efforts and treaties to control climate change and why past efforts have largely failed.

Climate change is the ultimate long-term sustainability issue with widespread and diverse effects. It affects all aspects of our lives: food production and water shortages, occurrence of natural disasters, destruction of land and glaciers, and the threat to human and animal species. Even small climate changes have had substantial impact on agriculture, trade routes, and the types of products and commodities for sale. Business is broadly affected by climate change's impact on the availability of natural resources, location of its facilities, and the demand for its products and services. Furthermore, there could be broad-based disruptions of the global economy unparalleled by any event since World War II and an existential threat to human security, said Jeffrey Mazo of the International Institute for Strategic Studies.[1]

Climate change increases the frequency and intensity of weather-related natural disasters and may put people at risk by restricting access to water, causing coastal flooding, menacing disease and hunger, and leaving people with more degraded environments. In the near future there may be more devastating effects of these weather events as a result of population growth and unsustainable economic growth. These trends put ever larger numbers of people and their assets at risk while reducing environmental buffering capacities, such as those associated with appropriate vegetation cover on steep slopes, intact wetlands in coastal zones, or coral reefs. In his article, "Don't Provoke the Planet" in the *New Scientist,* Richard Fisher investigates how climate change affects the planet's delicate balance and unleashes a host of geological disasters.[2]

# Global warming

Climate change has resulted in global warming, a connection that is denied by some skeptics because it implies that recent climate change has been abrupt and caused by human activity.[3] They believe climate change is a natural phenomena with the Earth's temperature rising and falling in cycles. There is a growing consensus among scientists, however, that the concentration of greenhouse gases (GHGs) has increased significantly since the industrial revolution. GHGs in the Earth's atmosphere include such gases as water vapor, carbon dioxide, methane, and nitrous oxide that trap some of the sun's heat.[4]

## Evidence

Support for the global warming effect of climate change has been mounting. A 1995 report by scientists of the Intergovernmental Panel on Climate change (IPCC), a United Nations group, stated that there was "a discernible human influence on global climate."[5] This report is backed by hundreds of scientists and more than 100 governments.[6] In 2006, a 579-page report by Sir Nicholas Stern concluded that climate change is fundamentally altering the planet, that the risks of inaction are high, and that time is running out.[7] Although the report was criticized by some as being a "pseudo-scientific and pseudo-economic document," it served to review the status of climate change.[8]

Several researchers have strongly argued that global warming exists and constitutes a threat. After describing the problem of global warming to a Congressional committee, James Hansen, a well-known climatologist and director of NASA's Goodard Space Institute, told reporters, "The evidence is pretty strong that the greenhouse effect is here."[9] Andrew Dressler and Edward A. Parson, who analyzed information about trends in the Earth's temperature, concluded: "We have documented the extensive scientific evidence that the Earth is arming, that human beings are very likely responsible for most of the rapid recent warming, and that climate change will continue with impacts that may be severe within this century."[10] Their corroborating evidence refers to "decreased Northern Hemisphere snow cover, thawing of Arctic permafrost, strengthening of mid-latitude westerly winds, fewer extreme cold events and more extreme hot events, increased extreme precipitation events, shorter winter ice season on lakes, and thousands of observed biological and ecological changes consistent with warming (e.g., poleward expansion of species ranges, earlier spring flowering and insect emergence, etc.)."[11]

Human activities contribute to the greenhouse effect. Major ones are the heating of buildings, driving of vehicles, and the production and use of electricity. Another cause is inefficient or incomplete combustion, which occurs in two-stroke engines and in low-temperature cooking fires burning traditional fuels such as dung or crop residues. Changes in land use are another cause, including cutting down forests and cultivating farmland, which replaces a dark vegetation surface with a lighter one, thus reflecting more sunlight and cooling the climate.

The German-based insurer Munich Re unequivocally states that climate change is a fact and is almost entirely made by man. It refers to the number of major weather-related natural catastrophes, such as floods, that have tripled since 1980. Wind storms have more than doubled in number as well.[12] It claims to have been analyzing natural hazards and natural hazard losses for more than 40 years and that its findings are based on a comprehensive natural catastrophe database which currently comprises more than 30,000 events.

Al Gore's documentary *An Inconvenient Truth* authoritatively summarizes some of the major findings that explicitly link human activity to global warming.[13] It reflects the level of concern felt at all levels of global civil society for the imminence of the threat to our sea, air, and earth posed by un-managed economic and industrial growth. The report is backed by hundreds of scientists and more than 100 governments.[14] Gore was awarded the Nobel Peace Prize in October 2007.[15] To influence public attitudes, Gore advocated an "Create-An-Ad Contest." He believed the best way to reach public hearts and minds is through the time-tested medium of advertising.[16]

An extreme view of climate change is taken by Kevin Trenberth of the U.S. National Center for Atmospheric Research. He is so convinced of its scientific evidence that he feels the burden of proof should be on those who deny it. He said that all unusual events should be assumed to be due to human emissions, unless shown otherwise.[17]

## Public attitudes

The Pew Research Center for the People and the Press reports that two-thirds of Americans (63%) are convinced that the Earth is really heating up. The percentage is down, however, from the 2007 peak of 77%.[18] A 2009 Pew poll showed that Americans support the idea of controlling emissions: 55% of those who had an opinion supported limits and 39% were opposed.

Changes in opinion are not wholly determined by scientific developments. The economy plays a large role, so when people get poorer they are less willing to support policies that will cost them money. By professing skepticism they are absolved of selfishness.[19] In Europe, a poll by the European Commission found that the number of EU citizens who thought climate change was the world's gravest problem dropped from 62% in spring 2008 to 50% in July 2009. Those citing the recession as their major concern rose from 24% to 52% during the same period.[20] In contrast, many developing nations viewed climate change as "a very serious problem." A 2010 Pew survey showed that more than 70% of people in China, India, and South Korea were willing to pay more for energy in order to address climate change; only 38% of Americans were willing.

In the United States, the passion for doing something about climate change has dropped. According to the Pew Research Group, the number of Americans who believe the earth is warming dropped to 59% in 2011 from 79% in 2006. Climate change has become a partisan issue. A spring 2010 poll showed that 7% of staunch conservatives, 63% of libertarian and 55% of Main Street Republicans said there was no solid evidence of global warming.[21]

### The tactic of uncertainty

Sowing uncertainty has been a standard tactic used by opponents to undermine research findings. Well-financed advertising and other campaigns by companies associated with fossil fuels who do not want to recognize the scientific evidence of climate change have deliberately created the impression that scientists do not agree about global warming.

Explaining how uncertainty influences public opinion is a study published in the journal *Nature Climate Change* by researchers at George Mason, San Diego State, and Yale Universities. They found that people who believe there is a lot of disagreement among scientists about global warming tend to be less certain that global warming is happening and less supportive of climate policy. Upholding this contention is a June 2010 national survey which found that two-thirds of respondents said they either believed there is a lot of disagreement among scientists about whether or not global warming is happening (45%), that most think it is not happening (5%), or that they did not know enough to say (16%).[22] It is believed that such widespread public misperception about scientific agreement on global warming undermines climate policy support.

The extent of media coverage also accounts for some of the changes in public attitudes because fewer stories dampen public concern. As reported in 2011 by the Virginia-based news aggregator DailyClimate.org, coverage of climate change dropped by 20% from 2010 and by more than 40% from 2009. In 2010, at least 7,140 journalists and opinion writers published about 19,000 stories on climate change and in 2009 more than 11,100 reporters filed 24,000 stories. The number of editorials also dropped from 1,229 in 2009 to 580 in 2010. Burgeoning online coverage, however, may have offset some of the drop. Maxwell Boykoff, author of *Who Speaks for the Climate?*, reports that hits in DailyClimate.org in 2011 were double that of 2010, rising to 4 million from 2 million.[23]

Extreme weather-related catastrophes may be influencing public attitudes more than scientific evidence. Hurricane Sandy, which struck the East Coast of the United States on October 29, 2012, razed waterfront areas in New Jersey, Long Island, and Staten Island and flooded the lower part of Manhattan, including some of its subways and tunnels. Seawater crippled utility systems in many basements. As Mayor Michael Bloomberg of New York City declared, "Our climate is changing."[24]

## Urgency of issue

Consensus is growing that doing something about climate change is urgent. Andrew Simms and his colleagues at the New Economics Foundation say the time-frame for action is 100 months. [25] Most say that a maximum temperature change that human societies might be able to tolerate is 2°C above pre-industrial temperature.[26] At 4°C or higher, sea levels would inundate the majority of the world's largest cities. Peter Newell and Matthew Paterson warn, "The continued existence of large-scale, organised human societies becomes far from secure."[27]

The consequences of global warming would be horrific for several regions. The Maldives and Bangladesh have most to fear. A 3-foot rise would sink the Maldives and flood much of Bangladesh. It would also threaten the national survival of the Netherlands, Shanghai and Hong Kong, which sit right on the water. Parts of eastern United States are also threatened. A 4-foot rise in ocean water levels would imperil parts of coastal Florida and the Carolinas. As regions of the earth become submerged, the result may be a loss of possibly 10% of the land mass. On the other hand, the growing season in Alaska, Canada, and Greenland has already been extended two weeks longer than in 1970s. Russia and Scandinavia also stand to gain.[28]

To dramatize the urgency of the climate change problem, those seeking urgent attention to the problem have conceived the "doomsday clock." They say that doomsday has moved one minute closer to midnight. Inaction on international tensions, as well as climate change, motivates the movement of the clock. The publication *Genetics & Environmental Business Week* says one of the major challenges "at the heart of humanity's survival in the 21st century?" is how to meet the energy needs for economic growth in developing and industrial countries without further damaging the climate.[29]

# Business switches strategies

The typical reaction to an unwanted problem or crisis is denial. A prominent example was Exxon Corp. president Lee R. Raymond who was quoted in *BusinessWeek* in 1997 as stubbornly rejecting the very existence of global warming.[30] His remarks led to dozens of demonstrations around the world, such as the "Stop Esso" campaign in the United Kingdom and "Expose-Exxon" campaign in the United States. The coalitions that organized the demonstrations claimed a membership of 10,000 in the United Kingdom and 500,000 in the United States.[31] In explaining Raymond's remark, Exxon's vice president of public affairs Ken Cohen said, "Honesty and directness are virtues.… But they can also lead to scrutiny and attack."[32]

## Early industry resistance

As international efforts such as UN's Intergovernmental Panel on Climate Change conference in Rio in 1992 gained momentum, industries whose interests were threatened began to organize resistance. The industries included oil extraction, car and steel manufacturing, electricity generation, and other industries associated with the National Association of Manufacturers and the National Mining Association. Two organizations (now abandoned), were notable players: the Global Climate Coalition (GCC) and the Climate Council.

The GCC, formed in 1989, was a high-powered lobby created by the oil, gas, coal, automobile and chemical companies to counter fears of global warming. Their basic arguments were that climate change was not happening; that if it was it had nothing to do with human activity (such as the burning of fossil fuels); and that any steps to limit emissions would cripple U.S. industry. Their major strategy was to "shoot the messenger" by questioning the science behind climate change and by creating confusion. They focused on schools, local media and "middle America." with the aim of creating the appearance of public opposition to action on climate change.[33] ExxonMobil, together with the American Petroleum Institute, followed the tactic once used by the tobacco companies, which for decades insisted that the science linking cigarette smoking to lung cancer was uncertain.

An important issue for business is whether it harms itself by ignoring scientific evidence. The GCC is accused of having done so. A document filed in a federal lawsuit revealed that in a backgrounder provided for the GCC the scientific and technical experts belatedly advised, "The scientific basis for the Greenhouse Effect and the potential impact of human emissions of greenhouse gases such as $CO_2$ on climate is well established and cannot be denied."[34] In defending earlier denials, William O'Keefe, the leader of the GCC claimed that he had not been aware of a gap between the public campaign and the advisers' views.

## Profound shift

Soon, however, a "profound shift" by industry occurring on global warming," as some companies formerly opposed to global warming claims changed position. One of the first was DuPont.[35] It switched sides soon after the first meeting of the UN's Intergovernmental Panel on Climate Change and GCC's losing of the PR battle. It decided to abandon its membership in the GCC and began to lobby government to stop global warming.[36]

Trade associations in the energy industries, representing the traditional targets of environmental groups, followed DuPont's action. These included the three industry groups – the Edison Electric Institute (EEI), the American Gas Association, and the Electric Power Supply Association – who had strongly opposed controls on carbon dioxide emissions. One of their motivations is the fear that in the absence of federal government action, state governments would impose an array of mandatory caps, which would increase the uncertainty faced by them.[37] They now supported mandatory curbs on GHGs.[38] So did the industrial titans of Alcoa, Caterpillar, General Electric, BP America, Dow Chemical, Du Pont and Shell.[39] ConocoPhillips became the first oil company to call for carbon caps. Jim Rogers, CEO of Duke Energy Corp has called for mandatory GHG reductions from power plants and other sources. He advocates a cap-and-trade system and supports a surcharge on electricity to fund R&D on low-carbon technologies.

A major sign of accommodation occurred when in a joint statement the World Business Council for Sustainable Development and its longtime critic Greenpeace issued a joint statement calling for an "international framework" to counter global warming. They said, "We call upon governments to be responsible and to build an international framework to tackle climate change on the basis of the UN convention on climate change and its Kyoto Protocol." General Motors, however, lagged, saying "We would not support any kind of Kyoto-like framework that would put limitations on developed economies."[40]

Even ExxonMobil, which in the past stubbornly denied the existence of global warming, changed its strategy by stopping to fund research of several groups that questioned the validity of global warming, saying that climate science had grown more robust.[41] In response to public reaction and pressure from stockholders, including the Rockefeller family which held a major number of share, the company announced on November 10, 2002, that it would give $100 million over ten years to a groundbreaking Stanford University project dedicated to researching new energy options.[42] At the 2008 annual meeting, John D. Rockefeller's great-granddaughter, Neva Rockefeller Goodwin, who was co-director of the Global Development and Environmental Institute at Tufts University, planned to offer several shareholder resolutions concerning global warming. The company's new CEO Rex Tillerson, who succeeded Lee Raymond, subsequently pursued a more conciliatory line. After the 2008 annual meeting, he stated:

> My view is that climate change policy is so important to the world that to not have a debate on it is irresponsible. We don't know everything about it. Nobody has this figured out. Anybody who tells you they have this all figured out is not telling you the truth. We have to understand that climate change policy, whatever it turns out to be, is going to hurt some people. But let's at least have an open debate about it, so everybody knows what the facts are.[43]

But speaking before an industry group on the issue of climate and energy fears, Tillerson did not create a conducive atmosphere for an open debate. He blamed a public that is "illiterate" in science and math, a "lazy" press, and advocacy groups that "manufacture fear" for energy misconceptions. Nevertheless, he acknowledged that the burning of fossil fuels is warming the planet. He believed however that society would be able to adapt, saying "It's an engineering problem and there will be an engineering solution."[44]

Most members of the Rockefeller family felt that "their" company should be doing more to help the world move to alternative sources of energy. Rival company, BP, had already departed from opposition to vocal support for alternative energy sources, as publicized through its "Beyond Petroleum" campaign (which, however, was more fluff than reality as shown in its alternative energy budget which was reduced from $1.4 billion to between $500 million and $1 billion in 2009).[45]

In Britain, the government encouraged the setting up of a task force to explore how Britain's companies can turn themselves green. Ian Cheshire, CEO of Kingfisher , Europe's largest home improvement retailer, heads the Ecosystem Markets Task Force which helps politicians know what the corporate world thinks about climate change. His starting point is the realization that "There's the need to understand the context any business operates in because we've all seen the environment changing and becoming much more volatile." Businesses must ask "What am I dependent on?" Utility companies will think about water, Unilever will think about palm oil, but "very few people have thought about the broader idea of the ecosystem they rely on."[46]

## New strategy of risk management

Most businesses now accept the reality of climate change and are rethinking how to respond to it. They figure that the costs of responding might not be too bad. It would make more sense, they reasoned, to present themselves in a green light and to adapt to and shape the policies that governments would implement.[47]

**Insurance industry becomes a powerful force.** Led by the insurance industry, industry trade groups began to think of climate change in terms of risk management rather than a threat by incorporating climate change into business strategies.[48] In the United States, the goal was to preempt regulation by arguing that in the absence of federal government action, state governments would impose an array of mandatory caps, thereby increasing the uncertainty faced by industry.[49] Among the uncertainties were the cost of regulation, risks to their reputation, risks of legal liabilities, and risks of losing out on new market opportunities.[50]

Contrary to conventional wisdom, fear of climate change by business has been the biggest boon in insurance industry history, states Lawrence Solomon of the *Financial Post*. The potential market for insurance industry products grows the more that risks exist. It must be sure, however, to set the level of premium that are commensurate with the risk.[51] Adaptation to climate change is a critical issue to the commercial success of the private insurance industry. It realizes that successful response to the issue can benefit the industry by giving rise to commercial opportunities and reputational reward. The sustainability of the industry is also at stake.[52]

In the short term, climate change was expected to affect underwriting practices by necessitating risk quantification approaches, including a forward-looking view of risk that is not purely grounded in historical experience. The industry reasoned that in the longer term, insufficient adaptation in areas of rising risk could threaten the concept of insurability itself, by limiting the availability and affordability of private insurance coverage.

Insurer Munich Re believes that insurers can play a vital role in the development of renewable energy by producing risk-transfer programs and making corporate investments themselves. "Innovative solutions" are widespread, including a performance guarantee that covers photovoltaic modules and geothermal drilling projects. Torsten Jeworrek, CEO of Munich Re's reinsurance operations, urges nations that have adopted climate goals to take the lead and "concentrate all their efforts on promoting renewable energy."[53] He urges insurers to help facilitate the introduction of innovative technology by making specific investments and giving investors greater security. His company plans to invest 2.5 billion euros ($3.33 billion) directly into renewable-energy projects over the next couple of years.

Influential insurance companies are also developing principles that could discourage large projects worldwide, like hydroelectric dams and fossil fuel plants that increase emissions and destroys natural habitat.[54] Tony Kuczinski, CEO of Munich Reinsurance America Inc., said at a UN conference in Washington, "Because if climate change is real – regardless of your view – if it's real and it has an impact on the atmosphere, it means things like hurricanes and tornadoes, and any weather event you can think [of] having a different outcome in years to come." [55]

# Business approaches: profit-making and reputation-building

Companies have been discovering that support of environmental safeguards is compatible with profitmaking. HSBC estimates that $10 trillion in capital expenditure will be required from 2010 to 2020 for low-carbon energy alone[56] In the United Kingdom, twice the number of investors than three years ago are now urging governments and international policymakers to take new and meaningful steps in the fight against climate change. Wolgang Engshuber, chair at the Advisory Council of the Principles for Responsible Investment (PRI), said, "Climate change will transform economies throughout the world, creating new opportunities for investors."[57] But that would require governments to play their part in laying down well-designed and effective climate change policies.

## Green investments

MNCs have been discovering that support of environmental safeguards is compatible with profitmaking and has accordingly sharply increased green investments.

## GE and China

General electric (GE) has been a leader in the burgeoning area of green investments, reasoning that "greenery can be handsomely profitable, as well as socially responsible."[58] In two-day "dreaming sessions," GE bosses took away a clear message that rising fuel costs, ever tighter environmental regulations and growing consumer expectations will translate into demand for cleaner technologies, especially in the energy industry. It will hold corporate bosses "accountable for helping to save the planet."[59] In 2005, GE announced its initiative of doubling investment in research for cleaner technologies to $1.5 billion a year by 2010, doubling sales of environmentally friendly products to at least $20 billion by 2010, and cutting its overall GHG emissions by 2012 to 1% below their level in 2006.[60]

GE's CEO Immelt is convinced that clean technologies will be the future of the company. When he assumed office in 2001 he argued that GE was operating in a rapidly changing environment which included diminishing domestic oil and natural gas supplies, consumer demands for efficient products, and the need to deal with climate change.[61] He calls the new strategy "Ecomagination," hoping to convince Wall Street "that clean energy can be a lucrative business." Goldman Sachs endorses Immelt's judgment: "Every one of the Ecomagination initiatives looks commercially viable, even without the green angle."[62] Seeing a potential for dramatic growth for infrastructure technologies in developing markets such as China and India, GE expects 60% of its overall revenue growth to come from such markets over the next decade.

Some critics question whether this rhetoric is "greenwash" – "little more than a public relations ploy to confuse the public about the true nature of its business."[63] But GE's Immelt continues to publicly proclaim that global warming is real, convincing several companies to take a new position on climate change. Three dozen big firms, including DuPont, United Technologies and Whirlpool, have been united by the Pew Centre on Global Climate, a non-partisan charity, to lobby for action by government.[64]

Governments as well as companies have recognized the opportunities in green investments. Having overtaken the United States to become the world's biggest carbon emitter, China has now sped ahead of the world in green technology investment. In 2010 it invested $54 billion in low-carbon energy technology, compared to the U.S.'s $34 billion.[65] China's vision is outlined in The China Greentech Report, a 2,500-page study sponsored by the China Greentech Initiative, a commercial collaboration of clean technology companies. The report, which was planned to be unveiled at the 2009 Summer Davos in Dalian, was the result of collaboration between 80 foreign and domestic companies involved in China's green-tech industry.[66] The report detailed market, financial, technological, and regulatory challenges in the industry. For example, one of the problems is that "investments are often complicated by intellectual property rights with technology transfers from abroad and unevenly enforced government policies."[67]

A growing number of investors, particularly from the United States see opportunities in this exploding clean-energy sector in China, especially because Beijing allocated more than $220 billion of its $586 billion stimulus package to green projects. Randall Hancock, co-founder of the China Greentech Initiative, says, "Business must play a key role in developing and providing green technology solutions that are affordable to help China and the rest of the world solve environmental issues."[68]

## Innovative alternative energy projects

In the effort to reduce GHGs, major attention has been given to alternative energy sources to the use of fossil fuels. The long-term hope is that science will provide the miracle source of breaking up hydrogen. But until that time comes, reliance will continue to be coal-burning power plants, greater use of growing supplies of natural gas, and nuclear power plants. The nuclear alternative, however, looks bleak since the March

2011 Japanese Fukushima disaster. In May 2012 all of Japan's nuclear power plants were shut. Germany is planning to eliminate all nuclear plants by 2050 and France, which receives 75% of its electric energy from this source, is reviewing its energy policy.

In the search for alternative energy, several ambitious projects are being contemplated:

- Two international consortiums led by German and French industrial giants are investigating projects to capture solar and wind energy across Arab deserts to power homes in Europe, the Middle East, and Africa. Solar panels and wind turbines would be deployed in arid regions, and cables would be sunk across the Mediterranean. It is estimated that these projects would meet 15% of Europe's electricity demand by 2050, said EU Energy Commissioner Guenther Oettinger.[69]
- For the frigid Yukon region of Canada where ice shelves are rapidly melting, Leona Aglukkaq, the minister responsible for the Canadian Northern Economic Development Agency (CanNor), announced ideas for geothermal, wind, hydro, and solar alternative energy projects.[70]
- In the United Kingdom, granite found between three and six miles underground could be the source of heat for a geothermal energy plant and possibly trigger to a second industrial boom in the north-east. Business leaders are investigating whether such a plant could be build between Aberdeen and Peterhead.[71]

## Biotechnology solutions

The biotechnology industry eyes a window of opportunity for adapting food crops to climate change.[72] An international team of the world's leading climate and agricultural researchers are providing adaptation strategies for more than a dozen crops, such as potatoes, beans, bananas and cassava on which billions of people depend worldwide.[73] One avenue is the development of drought-resistant genetically modified crops. Another is the development of trees that increase the absorption of CO2 and can thus serve as carbon sinks. The "agro-fix" of biofuels for depleting oil supplies, heavily promoted by Brazil, is already well under way.

"Sunrise industries" – those involved in renewable energy, energy efficiency and conservation – have emerged. For example, new engineering sciences are figuring out ways of offsetting global warming by sucking up CO2s and pumping it underground. Companies in the lead see "first mover" competitive advantages.[74]

## Improving corporate images – the CSR approach

If businesses find no investment opportunities, they can alternatively view the climate change as an issue that allows them to be seen as socially responsible environmental leaders. Wal-Mart became an outstanding example. It made climate change a flagship issue, putting pressure on suppliers to reduce their carbon footprint. It powered its facilities and fleet of vehicles with renewable energy, cut back on waste, and sold green products.[75]

Adoption of a CSR approach to climate change allows companies to engage their critics and, ideally, form partnerships with them. An example is HSBC's climate partnership with the Climate Group, WWF, and EarthWatch on projects to raise the awareness of employers about climate change. Another is Tesco, a U.K.-based super-market, that promises to label all its products according to their carbon footprint. A global example is Coca-Cola which has worked intensively with its bottling partners to "light weight" its packaging, thereby cutting GHG emission and generating savings in the tens of millions of dollars. It has also reduced GHG emission in its new vending machines and coolers by 99%, and these machines would be HFC-free by 2015.[76]

The CSR approach has stimulated efforts to get companies to measure and report on their GHG emissions, based on the premise that what matters is what can be counted. One result is the Greenhouse Gas Protocol, which was jointly created by the World Resources Institute and the World Business Council for Sustainable Development in 1998. It claims to be "the most widely used international accounting tool for government and business leaders to understand, quantify, and manage CHG emissions. Another is the Carbon Disclosure Project, which attempts to get companies to actually report their emissions.[77]

In sum, CSR efforts have led to greater collaboration with NGOs such as The Climate Group, Rising Tide, Climate Justice, and Plane Stupid![78] These NGOs had changed away from confrontation to finding long-term solutions. The activist movement became more middle class, seeking a more integrated and coherent approach and the need for a mass awakening

## Public policy options

The efforts of private businesses – whether motivated by profit or safeguarding reputations – can help mitigate some of the causes of climate change. But climate change basically is a deeply political and moral issue that requires collective action through public policy initiatives.[79] The UN launched an early effort to tackle global warming through the Convention on Climate Change (UNFCCC), which was adopted at the Earth summit in Rio de Janeiro in 1982.[80] Its aims were expected to be realized through the UN Framework Convention on Climate Change and the 1997 Kyoto Protocol.[81]

### Market-based regulatory mechanisms

Before market mechanisms were established, emissions were controlled through conventional regulation that set a performance target for each emitter, which could be a factory, a location of a firm, or a product. The aim was to reduce or ban the use of fossil fuels. In the past 10 to 20 years, however, this rigid regulatory system has been predominantly replaced by market-based regulatory mechanisms. Their underlying principle is to make pollution sufficiently costly that industry would have an incentive to reduce emissions. These mechanisms are attractive because they allow emitters the flexibility to decide how to respond as long as they pay the tax or hold permits.

### Carbon tax

Two types of market-based regulatory mechanisms prevail. One is a carbon tax, which is an emission fee or tax, determined by the government, whereby a source must pay a specified charge for each ton of pollution emitted. The tax would be charged on fossil fuels in proportion to their carbon content. A tax on carbon emissions is generally favored by academics and includes prominent Democratic economists such as former Treasury Secretary Lawrence Summers and Nobel laureate Joseph Stiglitz and Republican economists such as N. Gregory Mankiw, a former Bush adviser.[82] The EU emissions trading scheme (ETS) is the largest multinational emissions trading scheme in the world and obliges large emitters to produce no more than their particular "European unit allowance."[83]

An example is the EU-imposed carbon tax on airlines flying in and out of Europe beginning January 2012. The airline industry is estimated to be responsible for 650 million tons of carbon emissions, or 2% of the global total. Airlines are required to purchase permits to cover the carbon emissions of the whole length of the flight, not just the portion over Europe. China announced, however, that its airlines will not pay the tax, and airlines in other countries, including the United States, said they strongly opposed the tax. The International Air Transport Association (Iata) also strongly opposes the tax.[84]

Australia passed a law that is the most ambitious carbon tax scheme outside Europe. The legislation would force about 500 of the biggest polluters to pay for each ton of carbon dioxide they emit. Australia is the biggest per capita GHG emitter in the developed world, and also the world's largest coal exporter.[85] Quantas plans to charge passengers for the carbon tax, by planning to raise fares by up to $13 on a return ticket.[86]

## Cap-and-trade system

Despite the simplicity of the carbon tax, most current public policy proposals are cap-and-trade systems. They are also called tradable emission-permit systems whereby each source must hold a permit for each ton of GHGs it emits. These permits are initially distributed by government, which decides on the total quantity of emissions to be allowed, and distributes them either by auction or free distribution. Emitters may thereafter buy and sell them among themselves, with the price determined by the permit market, not by the government.[87] Emitters with high marginal costs would be motivated to pay for a permit rather than make more costly reductions. The term carbon market was coined to describe the totality of these sorts of approaches to climate change – markets for emissions, of new or expanding markets for renewable energy technologies, and of new investment opportunities.[88] Most business and environmental groups, as well as labor unions, generally back cap and trade.[89]

In their book, *Climate Capitalism,* Peter Newell and Matthew Paterson state the significance of market-based regulatory mechanisms and, despite misgivings, support it. They say, "In response to climate change, we have the first instance of societies collectively seeking a dramatic transformation of the entire global economy."[90] The challenge, they say, is to decarbonize the economy by taking the carbon out of the energy we use to run the economy. Their book describes "a model which squares capitalism's need for continual economic growth with substantial shifts away from carbon-based industrial development."[91]

Newell and Paterson recognize that the creation of markets allows money to be made for trading carbon allowances within limits set by government. Even though financial institutions are non-emitters, they, along with large transnational corporations, have been empowered to turn climate change into an opportunity for trading and investment. Financial institutions entered the emissions markets because they are a source of significant business.[92] The authors, however, recognize the dilemma that the buying and selling of units of carbon may become little more than a scam, "where business people and financiers get to make money without delivering real cuts on greenhouse gas emission."[93] They recognize the danger of climate politics manipulated by financiers for short-term profit. Furthermore, they are highly skeptical that capitalism can deliver either a socially just or sustainable future.

Putting these doubts aside, however, they conclude that these new markets might represent the start of the greening of the global economy, recognizing that urgent action is needed within a short time-frame. Thus their book presents the case for the construction of markets in carbon emissions as the most viable solution to climate change.[94] They turn to government to use their power to shape how carbon markets operate so as to limit speculation in emissions trading markets to ensure that prices reflect the scarcity in the allocation of permits rather than the short-term strategies of finance houses. For example, to prevent "climate fraud" – defined as "a range of strategies for claiming greenhouse gas emission reductions that are either exaggerated or non-existent"[95] – they envision a certification system as the Gold Standard that might become essential for project operators.

Also called the Voluntary Carbon Standard, the Gold Standard consists of business-led voluntary codes of conduct and certification schemes. They are intended to allay consumer fears and lessen NGO pressure about increasingly mobile companies taking advantage of poor working conditions and lower environmental standards in a globalized economy.[96] Newell and Paterson hope that at least some benefits will accrue to the majority of the world's poor and prevent the kind of "carbon colonialism," defined as an insidious attempt to regain control of developing countries' resources.[97]

The cap-and-trade scheme should also not become a means by which rich consumers in the West displace their high-carbon consuming practices by buying carbon offsets for their emissions cheaply in the South. The system has become a North–South issue, for while countries in the North would be short on permits, those in the South would have a surplus and thus earn income from selling permits to the North. [98]

Some countries and companies have benefitted from the carbon market. China accounts for 60% of the seller primary market. Its buyers are United Kingdom 45%, the rest of Europe 41%, Japan 8%, and United States 1%. Companies can bankroll emission-cutting projects in the developing world, where projects are cheaper; and in return receive carbon credits. Two Chinese companies will receive about $1 billion through 2012 from a private sector consortium. The Chinese government benefits because it sets a minimum price for carbon credits and taxes the profits from the sale of the credits.[99] Companies are also beneficiaries as illustrated by British Airways (BA) which saw emissions trading as a way to avoid such less "business-friendly solutions" as a fuel tax. By engaging early with emissions trading it allowed BA to help share its rules and operations while minimizing the financial costs of regulation.[100]

According to *The Economist*, "the charms of economy-wide cap-and-trade have faded badly, largely because of the financial crisis. In the United States, the EPA in December 2009 declared GHGs a danger to public health, opening the way to new emissions regulations. This has angered businesses and created a great deal of uncertainty. The preference now seems to be to favor legislation.[101]

# Keystone XLTrans-Canada pipeline

The plan by TransCanada Corp. to construct an oil pipeline from Alberta, Canada, to Houston, Texas, has become an international issue because it crosses the boundary between the two countries. It has also become a symbolic climate change issue because environmentalists say it would only heighten U.S. dependence on hydrocarbons and further contribute to global warming. "It doesn't make sense for Americans to be building infrastructure for dirty oil for the next five decades," said Susan Casey-Lefkowitz, a director with the Natural Resources Defense Council.[102] Supporters of the pipeline argue that it would bolster America's energy security and create jobs. Moreover, Canadian oil industry executives have threatened to go elsewhere, for example, China, to sell their oil. The Obama administration decided to postpone a decision until after the 2012 election. It said the delay, ordered by the state Department, was needed to ensure that environmental concerns were adequately addressed.

A particular concern by farmers in Nebraska was that the pipeline would cross the sensitive Sandhills area that sits atop an aquifer supplying fresh water to Nebraska and other states. This concern was heighten by recent accidents. In 2010, a pipeline owned by Calgary-based Enbridge dumped 19,500 barrels of oil into Michigan's Kalamazoo River, much of which was still there a year later.[103] Then July 1, 2011, an ExxonMobil pipeline in Montana, dumped an estimated 1,000 barrels of oil into the Yellowstone National Park.[104]

TransCanada has engaged in intense lobbying to influence the U.S. government position and is accused of threatening landowners along the proposed route with eminent domain (which a foreign company cannot do) and taking them to court, even before it had a permit. Keystone XL was turned into "a symbol of ecological plunder, corporate arrogance, and political cronyism."[105] It is, however, open to an alternative route that would avoid Sandhills area. By the end of 2012 the issue was not yet resolved.

# Steps toward global agreements

Because climate change is truly a global issue, agreement is needed by all emitters of GHGs everywhere on Earth. Agreement has been slow in coming. In addition to nation-states, international organizations are involved. The World Bank, for example, was criticized when its private sector arm, the International Finance Corporation, made a $90 million loan to the Bertin group, Brazil's leading beef exporter. Cattle farming was widely regarded by NGOs and others as the biggest threat to the Amazon's trees.[106] The World Bank later pulled out of the project. It has also in recent years helped by abandoning finance for fossil fuels and instead greatly expanding investment in renewables and energy efficiency in developing countries.[107] In 2008, it lent $7.5 billion for energy projects, with $2.7 billion going to efforts aimed at saving energy or boosting renewable power.

## Kyoto protocol

As nations in the world realized that significant emission reductions would be required to prevent global warming, a plan was adopted in 1995 to negotiate binding national greenhouse-based emission limits for a group of industrialized countries. These negotiations concluded in December 1997 with the signing of the Kyoto Protocol. Specific emission targets were imposed for each industrialized country over a five-year "commitment period" from 2008 to 2012. These targets pertained to the total emissions of a basket of $CO_2$ and five other GHGs. The emission targets were set at 8% below 1990 levels for the EU and a few other European nations; 7% for the United States, 6% for Japan and Canada, and zero for Russia and Ukraine. If all nations met these targets, the emissions would be 5.2% below 1990 levels over the commitment period. [108]

Members of the EU ratified the Kyoto agreement, but the United States never did, arguing it would severely crimp the U.S. economy. A further objection was that developing nations were not required to meet the targets. Within two months after taking office in 2001 the Bush administration announced that it would not ratify the protocol, saying that there was too much scientific uncertainty about climate change and because the limits would harm the U.S. economy.

Significant changes in business attitudes occurred by the time climate negotiations were renewed in Bali in December 2007. In the run-up to negotiations, 150 of some of the world's best-known companies signed the "Bali Communique on Climate Change," which called for a comprehensive, legally binding UN agreement to tackle the problem. A statement by the Corporate Leaders Group on Climate Change says, "As business leaders, it is our belief that the benefits of strong, early action on climate change outweigh the costs of not acting." It also stated, "In summary, we believe that tackling climate change is the pro-growth strategy, ignoring it will ultimately undermine economic growth." Among the signatories were such notable companies as Volkswagen, Shell, Nokia, Kodak, Philips, HSBC, General Electric, Nestle, Adidas, Nike, Rolls Royce, DuPont, Johnson & Johnson, and Tetra Pak.[109]

## Copenhagen Climate Change Conference in 2009

Support for a global climate change waned, however, when the next meeting of international representatives convened in Copenhagen in December 2009. When the Earth Day Network began planning events nearly two years before the Copenhagen meeting, organizers thought they would be celebrating the signing of a global climate agreement at the end of the meeting. But while the "Copenhagen Accord" led to many national statements of increased commitments, including several significant advances on any prior agreement, no accord was reached.

In the United States, Gene Karpinski, president of The League of Conservation Voters hoped that the occasion [of the Copenhagen meeting] "will be the catalyst to pass the climate bill. That's our goal, and that's the challenge we face."[110] But efforts to pass a climate-change bill were mired in the Senate. More progress was made by the EU. It made the most serious efforts to reduce emissions by setting 2020 levels 20% below 1990 levels, to be tightened to a 30% cut if other industrial countries agreed to make similar efforts.[111]

In Copenhagen, objections from five of the 28 nations blocked the accord from formal adoption. Commenting on the meeting, Dressler and Parsons concluded: "In sum, despite modest favorable signs before and at Copenhagen, and current high attention to climate change, it remains unclear whether leaders of major nations are willing to act strongly enough to address the problem, or whether the current international negotiation process is able to motivate and coordinate such action."[112] They arrived at the disappointing conclusion that society has not yet been able to solve the global warming danger, noting that present actions were utterly inadequate relative to the gravity of the issue.

The main action must occur on the international level, but negotiations and debate remain largely deadlocked along familiar lines of conflict. Developing nations do not want to be burdened, arguing that developed nations have caused the problem and that they need to catch up. Dressler and Parsons conclude, "the most urgent priority is enactment of policies by major nations, coordinated and linked through international negotiations, to limit GHG emissions through market-based measures that put an appropriate price on emissions, supplemented by support for research and development in climate-safe energy technologies and other sectoral regulations."[113] Giving up on international action, they advocate "a major unilateral initiative by the United States, followed immediately by negotiation of a package deal of linked climate and energy commitments among a small group of major industrialized and developing nations."

The subsequent 2010 United Nations Climate Change Conference held in Cancun, Mexico, helped mend the negotiation process but left open the question of a successor treaty to Kyoto.[114]

## UN Climate Summit in Durban, South Africa, in 2011

Representatives of the 291 UN countries plus the EU gathered in Durban, South Africa, from November 28 to December 9, 2011, to seek an agreement on "what to do after the first stage of the Kyoto Protocol expires in 2012."[115] But the meeting was almost universally judged as being a disastrous failure. One voice, Friends of the Earth International, said the world took a significant step back by further undermining an already flawed, inadequate multilateral system that is supposed to address the climate crisis.[116] It said that instead of implementing the existing, ambitious, and equitable negotiating roadmap that was agreed in Bali four years ago, the new "Durban Platform" would delay climate action for a decade. However, a deal was reached to extend the Kyoto Protocol, which expires in 2012, for another five years. It was essentially an act to start again.

Two achievements were nevertheless made. A Green Climate Fund was agreed upon to channel billions of dollars to poorer nations to green their economies and help protect them against the effects of climate change. $100 billion in pledges were received.[117] This fund would provide money to help poor countries invest in renewable energy rather than in coal and oil. This was a boon to China because, as previously stated, it is the main producer of renewable-energy technology.[118] MNCs would also have direct access to the fund, and financial interests could push through further possibilities for speculation via the carbon market. [119]

The other accomplishment was that it forced major developing nations such as China, Brazil and South Africa to accept the principle of future binding targets on their GHG emissions for the first time.[120] China, in a major shift, said, "We accept a legally binding arrangement," but only after 2020.[121] Showing sensitivity to air quality, China in January 2012 announced that Beijing will publicize hourly air quality data, yielding to public pressure exerted mainly over the Internet via microblogs.[122]

After the Durban meeting, a new business survey found that global warming has fallen to the bottom of European company concerns. As a result global warming will have a smaller impact on strategy and investment decisions than any of the seven other key events, such as the recession or the Arab Spring.[123] The view of David Cameron,

Britain's prime minister, seemed to prevail: "We're not going to save the planet by putting our country out of business."[124]

## The argument for adaptive approaches

Concluding that there is a growing realization that the effort to avert serious climate change has run out of steam, more voices are recommending that mankind should simply do what it has always done, namely, adapting to changes in our environment in a variety of ways – to "adapt to whatever changes in temperature may be in the future."[125] We must find ways to live with scarcer water, higher peak temperatures, higher sea levels, and erratic weather patterns. Such an approach is more cost-effective than anything discussed at Copenhagen argued David G. Victor, Charles F. Kennel, and Veerabhadran Ramanathan in their article "The Climate Threat We Can Beat."[126]

A precedent for this approach is the 1987 Montreal Protocol whereby CFCs were fazed out. The same piecemeal approach could be used to reduce or eliminate HFC-134a, a gas used in industry that delivers more than 1,000 times more warming than carbon dioxide. With respect to higher ocean levels, the Dutch has taken the infrastructure approach of planning to add to their dike structures. Similarly, other areas facing flooding must adapt by building flood barriers. The Marina Barrage in Singapore offers some protection, as does London's Thames Barrier. With respect to agriculture, the technique of mitigation can be used to develop better farming techniques to help store moisture. If climate change converts land into deserts, the solution may be mass migration or abandoning the farm for the city, where already half the world's people live. The proposed $100 billion a year fund which transfers funds from the north to the south can be seen as effort in mitigation and adaptation.

Following this thinking about adaptation, the journal *Science* reviewed ways in which global warming could be slowed, other than mandating the reduction of fossil fuel. An international team of researchers in climate modeling, atmospheric chemistry, economics, agriculture, and public health wanted to overcome what Roger Pielke Jr. in his book *The Climate Fix* calls the iron law of climate policy: "When there's a conflict between policies promoting economic growth and policies restricting carbon dioxide, economic growth wins every time."[127] Besides, only half of man-made global warming comes from CO2, with the rest coming from a variety of other sources.[128]

The team therefore looked for ways of reducing the soot and smog that are damaging agriculture and health. One estimate is that at least 40% of current global warming comes from four types of pollutants: dark soot particles called black carbon, ethane, lower atmospheric ozone, and industrial gases such as chlorofluorocarbons (CFCs) and hydrofluorocarbons (HFSX), which are used as coolants in refrigerators.[129] Black carbon from the soot spewed from diesel engines and traditional cookstoves and kilns covers snow in the Arctic and absorbs the sun's rays rather than reflecting it. Methane, released from farms, landfills, coal mines, and petroleum operations contributes to ground level ozone which lowers crop yields and is a GHG more powerful than carbon dioxide at trapping the sun's heat. But implementation would be difficult. Villages would have to be encouraged to use diesel engine filters and drain their rice paddies.

If these strategies were used, the team estimates that the amount of global warming in 2050 would be reduced by about one degree Fahrenheit, or roughly a third of the warming project if nothing is done. Ted Nordhaus, a founder of the Breakthrough Institute, states, "This what the post-Kyoto world will look like. We'll increasingly be managing ecological problems like global warming, not solving them."[130]

## Conclusions

Climate change is by nature a global issue that requires the cooperation of all nations and people. Such cooperation is flagging because it threatens national interests, business interests, and individual consumption. The result is procrastination. It is easier to postpone doing anything drastic than to resolve to take action that in the short run impedes economic growth and prosperity. When coastal areas become flooded, food and water shortages occur, and people develop skin cancer, the tide may turn to favor climate change action. In the interim, the best hope lies with incremental progress through "green" business opportunities and occasional bursts of corporate social responsibility.

The realities of global warming challenge everyone's way of thinking and doing things. The existence of capitalism as we know it is implicated because its emphasis on short-term profit maximization and promotion of consumption aggravate global warming. Climate change is related to other issues, such as social and the human rights of the world's poor and marginalized.

### Revision Questions

1. What is the scientific evidence that climate change exists and that human activity is a major cause?
2. How does climate change affect an MNC and in what industries is it especially relevant?
3. Why is it important for an MNC to acknowledge climate change and determine how best to adjust to it?
4. Are there business advantages in addressing the climate change issue? Give some examples of changes in company policies and operations.
5. What efforts have countries made to control climate change? Should an MNC support such efforts and, if so, how?

### Discussion Questions

I. In Beijing in October 1997, CEO of Exxon Corp. Lee R. Raymond told the 15th World Petroleum Congress three things: (1) the world is not warming, (2) even if it were, oil and gas would not be the cause, and (3) no one can predict the likely future temperature rise. To what extent do you think Raymond is right? Should the public impact of expressing such views openly be considered by him?
II. Regardless of the outcome of the Keystone pipeline from Canada to the United States, argue for or against it.
III. Sentiment for a carbon tax appears to be growing. Should it be opposed by business? What are the pro and con arguments?
IV. Aren't the advocates of the "adaptive" approach to climate change right: Recognize that it's too difficult for the entire world to agree on climate controls, so why not attempt what's doable?

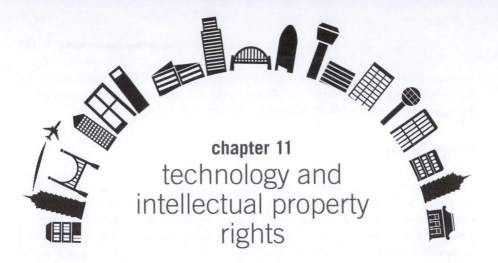

# chapter 11
# technology and intellectual property rights

**Objectives**

1. *Understand why technological innovations are important for continuing profitability and growth.*
2. *Realize that innovations incur both opportunities and risks. Be able to use genetically modified foods and nanotechnology to illustrate that resistance to innovation can occur.*
3. *Recognize the role of patents in the protection of intellectual property (IP) rights.*
4. *Learn from the Prometheus and Apple versus Samsung cases what kinds of ideas are patentable.*
5. *Recognize the dangers of industrial espionage and theft of intellectual property and the methods used by countries such as China and India to acquire IP.*
6. *Learn what measures a multinational corporation can take to minimize the dangers of IP loss.*

Technology has been a prime mover of change throughout human history. Technology and science are the keys to understanding our physical surroundings and enabling us to transform resources into energy and products. Technology has also revolutionized the way people and organizations communicate. Some epoch events have been the harnessing of steam for railroad engines and pumps to remove water from coal mines, the generation of electricity, the invention of the internal combustion engine, the development of rockets and nuclear power, and innovations in information technology.

In what *The Economist* calls a third industrial revolution, manufacturing goes digital, which "allows things to be made economically in much smaller numbers, more flexibly and with a much lower input of labour, thanks to new materials, completely new processes such as 3D printing, easy-to-use robots and new collaborative manufacturing services available on line."[1] Each technology hastens economic development but sometimes with unwanted side-effects of degrading the environment, worsening some workplaces, and creating a host of human rights problems as people confront new technologies.

Most of today's companies are linked to specific technologies. General electric (GE) was based on the discovery of electrical devices, General Motors on the combustion engine, and GlaxoSmithKline (GSK) on the chemistry and biology of drugs. The development of the Internet and digitalization of communications has developed new industries and new companies. Microsoft, Google, and Apple have become giant companies. The phenomenal rise of Google as a search engine and Facebook as a social medium has skyrocketed the value of their respective companies to join the ranks of the largest nonfinancial companies, along with the three largest, GE, ExxonMobil, and Apple.[2]

# Keeping up with technology

Managers are aware that keeping up with technology and surpassing one's competitors determines how well the management goals of profitability, growth, and survival are achieved. Multinational corporations (MNCs), in particular, have been technology creators, says John Cantwell in "Innovation and Information Technology in MNEs."[3] The United States was the preeminent leader in science and technology immediately after World War II, so their MNCs became an efficient mechanism for transferring knowledge across national borders. At first, MNCs could squeeze out extra profits by transferring obsolescent technologies to less demanding markets and using less skilled workforces. Now, however, advanced technologies are transferred as the price for being allowed to do business in some countries, and new technologies are originated in host countries.

## Procter & Gsamble's "connect and develop" innovation model

Procter & Gamble illustrates the innovation model. It knows that product innovation is necessary to maintain growth. In the past, it did so exclusively by building centralized global research facilities and hiring and holding on to the best talent in the world. They increasingly fortified their R&D departments with acquisitions, alliances, licensing, and selective innovation outsourcing. By 2000, however, it realized that such efforts were not capable of sustaining high levels of top-line growth. Important innovations were generated at small- and midsized entrepreneurial companies and the Internet had opened up access to talent markets throughout the world. P&G knew that while its best innovations had come from connecting ideas across internal businesses, highly profitable innovations were also created through external connections. The then-president A.G. Laffely decided that in the future 50% of its innovations would be made outside the company. He called it the "connect and develop" innovation model.[4]

By 2006, 35% of P&G's new products in the marketplace had elements that originated outside the company, up from about 15% in 2000. Furthermore, 45% of the initiatives in its product development portfolio had key elements that were discovered externally, including other countries. Its innovation success rate more than doubled, while its R&D investment as a percentage of sales dropped from 4.8% in 2000 to 3.4%. Learning how to print pop culture images on Pringles, which was an idea to make snacks more novel and fun, illustrates the value of external sources of innovation. After defining the problem and disseminating it throughout its global network, it learned through its European network that a small bakery in Bologna, Italy, had invented an ink-jet method for printing edible images on cakes and cookies. P&G quickly adapted this method and within two years the Pringles business achieved double-digit growth.

## Future technological developments

The pace of growth of technology is speeding up and making it difficult for managers and people to assess its impact and determine which technologies to adopt or reject. Ray Kurzweil, an inventor and futurist, has shown how the adoption rates of communication technologies over the past century have accelerated. He states, "the time to adopt new paradigms is going down by half each decade. At this rate, technological progress in the twenty-first century will be equivalent (in the linear view) to two hundred centuries of progress at the rate of progress in 2000."[5] He predicts that by 2020 artificial intelligence will match the capability of the brain. Expressed another way, he says, "we won't experience one hundred years of technological advance in the 21st century; we will witness on the order of 20,000 years of progress ... or about 1,000 times greater than what was achieved in the 20th century."[6] Because technology grows rapidly at an exponential rate, we must expect that society's absorption of change will not be smooth and crises are likely to occur with increasing frequency. For example, the explosion of BP's Deepwater Horizon rig in the Gulf of Mexico, causing a massive oil spill, attests not only to mismanagement but also the limited knowledge of deep-well drilling.[7]

Kurzweil's prediction of future technological developments is illustrated by the City of Edenvale, California. It "shows how Silicon Valley's start-up economy has quietly broadened beyond information technology." It now includes a growing cadre of bioscience and "clean technology" firms, which provide a more diversified economic base.[8] A sample of new companies include the clean-tech outfits of Bloom Energy Corp and Nanosolar, the U.K. bioscience company Oxford BioTherapeutics, the electric car maker Tesla Motors, the biofuels start-up Codexis Inc., and several app makers and networking companies. The number of clean tech and related jobs in the San Francisco Bay Area rose from 585 to around 44,000 positions between 1995 and 2008, according to Collaborative Economics.

A new technology that is making splashes is electronics printing of solid objects out of material, one layer at a time. Three-dimensional printers make it possible to print an entire product in a single machine.[9]

# The challenge of new technologies: case of biotechnology

Innovation leads to new technologies that improve the profitability and competitiveness of businesses. Biotechnology is a prime example of an industry that has been coping with rapid innovation. It has produced successful genetically modified (GM) crops and foods that represent the "second green revolution." Despite its promise and the absence of serious side-effects, however, this development is still being challenged because its long-term consequences remain unknown.

GM foods and crops are the major outcomes of the science of biotechnology. The industry proclaims, "The mission of the biotechnology industry is to heat, fuel, and feed the world."[10] In the health arena alone, there are new treatments, preventions, and, ultimately, cures for some of the world's most deadly and debilitating diseases. In fuels, work is done on advanced biofuels and biochemicals that will reduce reliance on fossil resources. The industry believes that it is vitally important to ensure that our public policies value innovation and encourage investors to support biotech research. Maintaining its intellectual property (IP) rights is important, says Monsanto, to maintain its research budget of nearly $1 billion a year. It costs a lot of money to bring a new GM seed to market, so its IP must be protected if there is to be innovation.

Monsanto, therefore, requires the purchase of seeds anew each season. "When farmers purchase a patented seeds variety, they sign an agreement that they will not save and replant seeds produced from the seed they buy from us," states Monsanto.[11] Critics say that Monsanto's restrictions rob consumers and farmers of the most basic right to choose what they will eat and grow. They argue that the poor in underdeveloped countries would not be helped. Proponents of this arrangement, however, argue that these seeds help lift them out of poverty and Monsanto declares that only through the use of GM crops can the growing population of the world be fed. Argentina and Brazil are both growing GM corn (maize) and soybeans. Monsanto is also attempting to create a "green revolution in Africa." It has created a public–private partnership, Water Efficient Maize for Africa (WEMA), to develop drought-tolerant genes that are expected to help Kenya, Mazambique, South Africa, Tanzania, and Uganda.[12]

Much attention is now focused on Africa because sporadic droughts have led to widespread starvation. GM foods are aggressively being promoted by the agri-industrial complex as the solution to the global food security challenge.[13] Africa resisted early attempts to introduce GM foods, and Zimbabwe has thus far refused outright. But as drought menaced the Horn of Africa in 2011, Kenya, a country also affected by drought, announced that it would open its borders to GM crops for the first time. African leaders are moving to eliminate the ban after seeing that more than a billion hectares of the world's agricultural land is now given over to GM crops.[14]

But unease persists. Looking at Ghana that has accepted GM crops, Public Agenda fears that its peasant farmers will be impoverished while enriching the foreign companies that specialize in the production of GM seedlings and seeds. In Ghana, agriculture is largely for subsistence, which includes about 60% of the population. Growers would eventually become more dependent on MNC seed companies and possibly subject food prices to the dictates of the seed companies.

Europe keeps U.S. companies such as Monsanto and DuPont out of the European Union's (EU) $7 billion-a-year seed market. Until recently, the EU banned the planting of all GM crops, except one kind of corn, Monsanto's pest-resistant GM maize, approved in 1998. The European Commission also proposed a ban on cloning farm animals and a prohibition of imports of cloned livestock and their meat and milk.[15] In 2010, however, the EU approved a GM potato, developed by German chemical company BASF. The potato, Amflora, is designed to optimize starch yields and will be cultivated for industrial uses, such as paper-making, with the by-products used for animal feed.[16]

## Opposition to GM foods still alive

Greenpeace has consistently attempted to dissuade Monsanto from genetic engineering. Besides arguing that the interests of agribusiness rather than farers and consumers were served, Greenpeace and other anti-GMO (genetically modified organism) activists contend that the safety of genetically engineered crops has not been proven beyond reasonable doubt. They can point to a recent setback for GM crops in northern China, where millions of hectares of farmland were struck by infestations of bugs following the widespread adoption of Bt cotton, an engineered variety made by the U.S. biotech giant, Monsanto.[17]

This finding marked the first confirmed report of mass infestations arising as an unintended consequence when farmers used less pesticide, which is a feature of Bt cotton that was supposed to save money and lessen the crops' environmental impact. Critics used this evidence to argue that better ecological assessments are needed, for example, monitoring at the landscape level to better understand the impacts of GM crop adoption. A further setback for the GM food industry is that recently traces of a maize type that was approved only for feed use appeared in maize products for human consumption in the United States.[18]

When farms first experimented with GM crops, activists frequently destroyed them. While the number of such attacks has declined, occasional incidents still occur. Critics criticize GM seeds for being undemocratic and that large biotech agribusinesses, such as Monsanto, control too much of the global seed market with GM crops. "This centralization of GM seeds threatens food safety, food security, bio-diversity, and democratic ideals."[19] Furthermore, critics object to the knee-jerk faith in the free market that has led to the overwhelming centralized control of nearly all our food stuffs from farm to fork.[20]

The GM food industry has made some accommodations. The first GM crops promised farmers in the developing world higher yields and lower costs because the crops were engineered to resist herbicide spray and insect attack. Now a new "golden rice" promises to help improve the health of the world's poorest. Growers of this rice would not be charged a "technology fee" because the rice and attendant IP right would be given free by national research centers operating under the aegis of the International Rice Research institute.[21]

## Public confidence in science and technology[22]

The issue of GM crops and foods is itself highly complex because it represents advances in technology that three major groups – opposing farmers, environmentalists, and consumers – perceive to be risky. Some farmers, especially organic farmers, fear that genetically engineered crops would spontaneously breed with their wild relatives, creating hybrid "superweeds." Credence was given to this fear when the optimistic initial assumption by scientists that genes were unlikely to flow from transgenic crops to weeds – because hybrids are often sterile – had not materialized. Furthermore, pollen can often travel far afield; for example, a pollen from oilseed rape fields traveled as much as two kilometers.

Environmentalists are concerned about the long-term effects of GM crops on nature. As Susan George said of the scientists who created GMOs, they "proceed as if Darwin had never existed. They ignore the obvious fact that weeds and insects will develop resistance and require larger and larger doses of chemicals for effective control."[23] Some environmentalists have turned to drastic measures. In 1998, activists in France ruined five metric tons of transgenic seeds – seeds that have been genetically engineered – trashed genetically altered crops in German fields, and persuaded seven European supermarket chains to stop selling store-brand goods containing bi-engineered products. Environmentalists are concerned about the risky aspects of allowing the food chain to be controlled by a few giant corporations.

Consumers, especially in Britain, have been resisting foods grown from Monsanto's gene-modified seeds. Lack of knowledge about the technology, sometimes combined with antiscience attitudes, added to public resistance. Such attitudes were reflected in the United States where a 1993 Harris poll showed that most people think genetic engineering (as distinct from genetic testing) is likely to lead to more harm (65%) than good (26%) in the future.[24] Monsanto consequently became known as arrogant and a "bully" – attributes that contribute to anti-Americanism. Especially in Britain, which was still mindful of the "mad cow" disease, a growing number of consumers became leery of the new GM foods. At minimum, they demanded and got product labels indicating whether foods contained GM ingredients. The biotech industry opposes such labeling because, as stated by Carl Feldbaum, president of the Biotechnology Industry Organization, "the label would be seen as a stigma, like a skull and crossbones."[25]

The lessons of the science of biotechnology are that business must (1) consider public attitudes toward science; (2) gauge the reaction of environmental groups such as Greenpeace; (3) engage in rigorous testing to obtain scientific evidence that harm is not caused; and (4) inform those potentially affected and seek to collaborate with them, which may take a long time.

Collaboration – often defined as "partnership" by industry – is the defining strategy for business development, says Carola Schropp, president of EBD Group. She says "collaboration is the most direct path to innovations, and ultimately to the patients who need." In the last BIO-Europe conference in Vienna, more that 12,500 meetings were held among 2,500 industry executives. As a result, 158 life-science companies announced new collaborative agreements in 2009. The obvious lesson, said Schropp, is that to succeed in our industry, you will need to make partnering a priority.[26]

## Intellectual property rights

IP consists of copyrights, patents, trade secrets and know-how, and confidential information. IP is often more valuable than physical structures and equipment and may account for nearly 80% of the value of many *Fortune* 500 companies.[27]

Tech patents in particular have soared in value. In April 2012, Microsoft agreed to pay nearly $2.2 billion buying and licensing about 1,100 patents from AOL, Inc., covering such areas as e-mail, Web-search rankings, Web browsers, instant messaging, and video conferencing. Microsoft agreed to spend nearly $1.1 billion to buy and license about 1,100 patents, covering some of the Internet's basic software form AOL Inc., motivated in part by keeping the patents away from rivals.[28] Telecom equipment company Nortel Networks sold some of its patents to a consortium including Apple and Microsoft for $4.5 billion.[29] Further demonstrating the value of patents, Eastman Kodak Co. has put 1,100 patents on the block as part of its bankruptcy proceedings.

Recognizing the value of patents, EU research ministers have undertaken efforts to boost national programs for innovation, including transforming their predominantly public-financed research and innovations systems to ones where investments are provided by the private sector.[30] MNCs have been major investors in technology. The money spent on R&D and the number of patents acquired are measures of this IP. Because it is a major competitive asset, the protection of IP rights is a critical issue that involves an understanding of the patent system and the dangers of theft and counterfeiting.

## Patent laws

Patent laws protect the IP rights of inventors and authors. In the United States, authority for patent laws is provided by the Constitution, which gives Congress the power "to promote the progress of science and useful arts, by securing for limited times to authors and inventors the exclusive right to their respective writings and discoveries." The first patent act was passed in 1790. It was replaced by a slightly longer act in 1793, which defined as patentable "any new and useful art, machine, manufacture or composition of matter and any new and useful improvements on any art, machine, manufacture or composition of matter."[31] Under the current law, the term of a patent is 20 years from the earliest claimed filing date (and for applications filed before June 8, 1995, 17 years from the issue date).

Patents are treated as property rights, so they can be sold, licensed, and otherwise treated by the inventors. Some companies, known as "patent trolls," buy lots of obscure patents and then sue alleged infringers with lawsuits.[32] Patents are associated with innovation. The United States leads insofar as Americans file four times as many patent applications per person as Europeans.[33]

The America Invents Act, passed into law on September 16, 2011, changes how patents are processed and reviewed. The act states that "first to file" patents will be assigned to the first person or entity to file an application rather than to the first person or entity to invent a product or idea.[34] One of the bill's goals was to relieve the patent office's backlog of applications, which have increased as a result of the Internet age. Many large corporations – such as GE, Caterpillar, and IBM – supported the bill, leading some to believe it to be at the expense of the small inventor.[35] These inventors are less likely to have an in-house legal department or patent lawyers on retainer to file for a patent as soon as they discover something useful and nonobvious. The first-to-file system brings the United States in line with Europe and Japan.[36] The new law has increased the flow of patents and a growing demand for patent lawyers. Out of about 1.2 million lawyers licensed in the United States, according to the American Bar Association, 40,000 are registered patent lawyers.[37]

## What can be patented?

A major question about patents is just what constitutes an innovation that can be patented. A specific issue facing the drug and biotechnology industries is whether diagnostic-test makers can claim that their new products are patent eligible. Myriad Genetics Inc. contended that its discovery of two genes that can signal if a woman faces greater risk of developing breast cancer or ovarian cancer was eligible for a patent. In August 2012, a U.S. Court of Appeals decided that a patent was justified.[38] The pro and con arguments were similar to the Prometheus case, which received much attention. Another question is what constitutes a patent infringement, which is explored by the Prometheus case and the Apple v Samsung case.

### The Prometheus case

In the Prometheus Laboratories case, the patents held by the company to determine the proper dosage of drugs that treat gastrointestinal and other autoimmune diseases were challenged by the Mayo Clinic on the grounds that its procedures do not sound like much of a discovery.[39] It said that Prometheus improperly sought to claim a patent monopoly on the right to observe a natural phenomenon, namely, how the human body reacts to ingesting certain drugs.[40]

In March 2012, a unanimous ruling by the U.S. Supreme Court threw out two medical-testing patents. Defending the ruling, Justice Breyer wrote that the controversial patents "consist of well-understood, routine, conventional activity already engaged in by the scientific community."[41] The decision reinforced the long-standing rule that inventors cannot patent laws of nature.

Following similar reasoning, the European court said that stem cells obtained through the destruction of human embryos were unpatentable on the grounds that the destruction of embryos fails to respect human dignity.[42] It said that the use of a human embryo at the blastocyst stage entailing the destruction of that embryo cannot be patented, but that the use of human embryos for therapeutic or diagnostic purposes that are applied to the human embryo and are useful to it is patentable. This ruling reversed the "mission creep" in patent law, which may have started in 1972 when the Supreme Court first considered software patents. In general, "fuzzy and overly broad concepts like thought processes" are not protected.[43]

## Apple sues Samsung

One of the most contentious patent battles is Apple's suit against Samsung, which claims the Korean manufacturer "slavishly copied" Apple designs. The suit also attempted to prevent Samsung from selling three types of phones and a tablet, claiming that without judicial order it would suffer "irreparable harm.[44] Based on four of its patents, Apple argued that its phones are "earthshakingly new, completely novel." It claimed that Samsung aped "Apple's innovative technology, distinctive user interfaces, and elegant and distinctive product and packaging design."[45] The suit raises the question of what kinds of ideas, including business processes, are patentable.

Samsung retorts, "just how amazingly innovative are rounded corners on a rectangular communication device?" Basic patent law states that if an idea is "obvious" to an "ordinary observer" at the time of its invention, it does not deserve patent protection. A judge in the case, Lucy Koh, ruled that while a product design is patentable, aspects "dictated by functionality" are not. For example, Apple's patent "does not give it ownership of the idea of making smartphones small enough to hold conveniently." A more fundamental problem, says Willy Shi, an IP scholar and professor of management practice at Harvard Business School, is that most modern technology exists at the top of "a pyramid of innovation, so that new products often have components that build on earlier inventions."[46]

On August 24, 2012, a Jose, California, jury awarded Apple $1.05 billion in damages, finding that Samsung infringed all but one of the seven patents at issue in the case. It decided that basic design elements incorporated in electronic devices that affect the way gadgets look and feel are patent protected.[47] In a European case, in August 2011, the regional court of Dusseldorf issued a preliminary injunction, requested by Apple, barring Samsung from distributing its Galaxy Tab 10.1 touchscreen tablet across Europe.[48] This suit shows the danger of aggressively suing supposed patent infringers, namely, that it spreads the patent war worldwide – to Britain, France, Germany, Holland, Italy, and Australia.

# How IP rights are compromised

When U.S. firms open operations in other countries, they bring along their technological property. Technology transfer is a common practice of MNCs when they make direct foreign investments in a host country. An illustration is the upsurge in economic development in Africa. A study titled "A Technological Resurgence: Africa in the Global Flow of Technology" shows that there has been a rapid growth rate in Africa's industrial technology acquisition. Inflows of foreign direct investment soared by over 800% between 2000 and 2008, and some of which has gone into the production of drugs, steel, automobiles, and electronics.[49] These investments have been the main channel for technology transfer, accomplished through royalties and licensing fees, capital goods, business, professional and technical services, research and development, and IP rights. Some technology development and transfer has been achieved through university–industry–government partnership.

## Lawful business and military deals with China

A big question with technology transfer is whether too much is given away when business deals are made. When an MNC forms an alliance with another entity in the host country, the technology can easily be copied and potentially used to compete against the United States. In Germany, a best-selling book, *The China Trap*, warned businesses investing in China that their IP would be stolen.[50] IP risks are among the top three operating issues currently facing MNCs operating in China, according to a survey by a committee of the Beijing-based China Association of Enterprises With Foreign Investment, a coalition of multinational companies that have invested more than $60 billion China. About 10% of the members surveyed estimated revenue losses from IP violations amounted to more than 20%.[51] Foreign companies expanding into China face a boundless and potentially costly risk of theft of their IP.[52] Recent ventures by GE in China and Chinese companies in Europe illustrate that danger.

## GE shares advanced technology with Chinese partner

Doing business in China often requires MNCs to share technology and trade secrets that might eventually enable Chinese companies to compete against them. GE, one of aviation industry's biggest suppliers of jet engines and airplane technology, has been aggressively helping China acquire technology. During President Hu Jintao's visit to the United States in January 2011, GE planned to sign a joint venture agreement in commercial aviation by which GE would be sharing its most sophisticated airplane electronics with the Chinese joint venture partner, Aviation Industry Corp of China, which is a state-owned company. Included would be some of the same technology used in Boeing's 787 Dreamliner.[53] The technology involves "avionics," which constitutes the "brains" that guide navigation, communication, and other operations on an airplane.

The first customer for the GE joint venture would be the Chinese company building a new airliner, the C1919, that is scheduled for completion in 2016 and meant to be China's first entry in competition with Boeing. Dismissing this danger, most Western aviation executives said that the Chinese are simply too far behind in civilian and military airplane technology to cause any real danger in the near future. The opportunity for GE is that the commercial aircraft market in China is expected to generate sales of more than $400 billion over the next two decades. John G. Rice, vice chairman of GE, said "We can participate in that or sit on the sidelines. We're not about sitting on the sidelines."[54]

As a *Wall Street Journal's* headline questioned, "China Venture Is Good for GE but Is It Good for U.S.?"[55] Furthermore, according to Clyde Prestowitz, a former U.S. trade negotiator, China is violating World Trade Organization rules that prohibit making technology transfer a condition of market access. GE, however, said it had briefed the U.S. Commerce, Defense, and State Department on details of the deal.

To critics, GE's claim that it has built protections into the venture is not credible in a business shared 50–50 by the U.S. and Chinese firm. The venture's first big customer, Commercial Aircraft Corp. of China, is already developing a passenger jet to compete with Airbus and Boeing. It will also sell its avionics to aircraft manufacturers globally. China is known for its "indigenous innovation" industrial strategy, which incorporates foreign technology and makes it its own.[56] It is a set of practices that American officials say result in discrimination against foreign products and technology. On a related practice, Timothy F. Geithner, the U.S. treasury secretary, criticized a proposal by China to require that certain products be accredited before being sold to its government, a requirement that might violate standards of the WTO.[57]

## United Technology and Siemens transfer technology

In another transfer of military technology, United Technologies took the "calculated risk" of illegally providing China with engine-control software that enables it to build its first military attack helicopter. To skirt U.S. arms control laws, UTC sold the equipment through Pratt Canada. When Canada hesitated, China used the subterfuge that the technology would be used for a parallel civilian helicopter program and Canada approved the export. UTC was lured by the promise of a $2 billion opportunity to become the exclusive engine supplier to China's civilian helicopter program. But China decided to open the program to other bidders. UTC pleaded guilty and will pay $20.7 million to the Department of Justice and another $55 million to the State Department for this and hundreds of previous arms export law violations.[58]

Siemens is another company that experienced the results of technology transfer. In 2005, the China National Railway Signal and Communication Corporation (CNR) invited Siemens to join in building trains for the Beijing–Tianjin high-speed railway, with most of the technology coming from Siemens. It trained 1,000 CNR technicians in Germany, but most of the trains were built in China. For the next project, the Beijing–Shanghai high-speed rail, the Ministry of Transportation decided on domestic technology, and CNR bumped Siemens. DSR Corporation, another Chinese trainbuilder, did the same with Kawasaki Heavy Industries of Japan.[59]

Business expressed concern to China about required transfer of IP in business deals. In July 2010, Peter Loscher, CEO of Siemens, and Jurgen Hambrecht, then chairman of BASF, personally complained to Wen Jiabao, the Chinese prime minister, about the way Western companies were being forced to hand over intellectual capital in order to gain access to China's markets.[60]

## Technology transfer problems in India

Other countries have also created technology transfer problems. India explicitly demanded technology transfer as a condition of investing in the country or receiving a government contract. Foreign direct investment is limited to 26% for overseas companies that are unwilling to part with technology without gaining voting rights in a joint venture company. This condition is a deterrent because international companies consider market size and profit in determining whether technology can be transferred.

The French shipbuilder DCNS, which is constructing six diesel-electric Scorpene submarines in Mumbai, has been involved in one of the biggest technology transfer programs. Patrick Boissier, chairman and CEO defended the decision, saying that while its goal was to give all necessary competencies, it did not include surrendering its IP rights. Similarly, William Blair, president of Raytheon India said, "We are looking at ways to work with the defense ministry and private sector on this issue. It can be a win-win situation – we bring our technology and adapt it to the Indian market while retaining intellectual rights."

## Spying and theft by China

China obtains IP rights not only through technology transfer but also through spying and theft, which it is suspected of fostering.[61] Alberto R. Gonzales, former Attorney General, warns, "IP theft is a serious problem that threatens our nation's economic security. America is the global leader in creativity and innovation; it is our competitive advantage in the world. Indeed, America's greatest export and the strength of our robust economy is the creative output of Americans – the labor of our imaginations. But the creative community – those who devote their energy and imagination to creating products that enrich our society – is besieged by IP theft."[62] A senior U.S. intelligence official estimated losses of $50 billion in 2009 due to lost IP and counterfeiting.[63]

China and Russia are identified as the most aggressive collectors of U.S. economic information and technology. Economic espionage is part of each country's national economic development policy, said a senior U.S. intelligence official. Most of this theft of U.S. corporate and economic secrets occurs in cyberspace. The leading areas of theft are in information technology, military technology, and clean-energy and medical technology.[64]

Dow Chemical experienced a new kind of spy. Huang Kexue, born in China and a legal U.S. resident, faced a rare criminal charge that he engaged in economic espionage on China's behalf. For five years, he was a scientist at a Dow Chemical laboratory in Indiana studying ways to improve insecticides. Before being fired in 2008, he began "sharing Dow's secrets with Chinese researchers, then obtained grants from a state-run foundation in China with the goal of starting a rival business there."[65] Motorola faced a similar situation. Jin Hanjuan, a software engineer for Motorola and a naturalized U.S. citizen, was charged with economic espionage. She was arrested with a laptop full of company documents while boarding a plane for China. She had downloaded company documents during two sick leaves and tapped into the company's computers from China where, prosecutors say, she met with a company linked to the Chinese military.[66]

In the new global economy, our businesses are increasingly targets for theft," said Lanny A. Breuer, the assistant attorney general in charge of the Justice Dept's criminal division. "In order to stay a leader in innovation, we've got to protect these trade secrets."[67] A key article in *Bloomberg Businessweek* describes how American Superconductor Corp. (AMSC), a maker of computer systems that serve as the electronic brains of wind, found that its major Chinese purchaser, Sinovel, suddenly stopped purchasing its turbine technology. It did not need AMSC any more because it had stolen AMSC's proprietary source code. It obtained this information from Dejan Karabasevice, a Serbian software engineer who worked at AMSC's research facility in Klagenfurt, Austria, and who admitted he stole the company's software, modified it and secretly sold it to Sinovel.[68] Investigators found a consulting contract with Sinovel and a related company signed by Han Junliang, the head of Sinovel. When AMSC announced the loss of Sinovel's business in April 2011, its market value dropped 40% on one day and 84% by September.[69]

The *Bloomberg Businessweek* article contains a "compendium of intellectual thievery," which briefly describes 12 cases, including such well-known ones as Apple, Boeing/Rockwell Intl., Dow Chemical, DuPont, Ford Motor, General Motors, Motorola, Sanofi-Aventis, and Northrup Grumman.[70] The Motorola case cites Jin, a software engineer who is a native Chinese naturalized U.S. citizen, who was stopped at O'Hare with 1,000 Motorola documents, $30,000, and one-way ticket to China. Among the papers were confidential documents relating to Motorola's "Push-to-Talk" mobile-phone technology.[71]

In the case of Sanofi-Aventis, Yuan Li, a Chinese citizen who was the company's research scientist, was charged with stealing trade secrets and making them available to a rival, Abby Pharma Tech. She was a partner in this U.S. subsidiary of a Chinese chemical company and made the compounds available for sale on Abby's website.[72] DuPont was awarded $919.9 million in damages after it sued South Korea's Kolon Industries for stealing trade secrets and confidential information related to Kevlar, a high-strength fiber used in its Kevlar body armor. The fiber generated $1.4 billion in sales in 2010.[73]

With these cases as a background, it is not surprising that the United States blocked the Chinese telecommunications giant Huawei Technologies Inc. from expanding in the United States on the grounds that it poses a cyberespionage threat to U.S. defense systems and companies. The House Intelligence committee recommended that the Committee on Foreign Investments block acquisitions or mergers by Huawei and another firm, ZTE. Both are partly owned by the Chinese government and their organizations contain Communist "party committees." The fear is that both companies may be required to comply with Chinese government requests for access to their systems. Although both companies deny this possibility, they have failed to provide sufficient information to allay these concerns and are considered a security risk.[74]

## Counterfeiting and patent infringements

Consumers too engage in theft by blatantly buying pirated software and equipment or cheaper counterfeit items manufactured abroad – batteries, auto parts, electrical cords, lamps, and fire extinguishers – as well as counterfeit drugs that can threaten the public's health and safety. The case of Avastin, a cancer drug, illustrates the problem. Investigation of the business dealings of two Canadian businessmen engaged in the

Internet pharmacy trade showed that they shipped fake vials of Roche Holding AG's Avastin to U.S. citizens. The motivation was the price differential, for Roche charges $2,400 for a 400-milligram vial of Avastin, whereas the Canadian seller charges $1,995. A major health danger is that counterfeit products may truly be fake and adulterated. In one examination by Roche, the fake Avastin contained starch, salt, cleaning solvents, and other chemicals, and none of the drug's active ingredient, bevacizumab. The sellers of counterfeit drugs routinely deny knowledge that they were selling counterfeit products, even though they should know when the supply chain involves several countries.[75]

Among U.S. trading partners, China was the No.1 source of counterfeit products seized at U.S. borders, accounting for 81% of the total value of such products, according to the U.S. Customs & Border Protection agency. In 2005, the value of copyrighted material alone that was pirated in China exceeded $23 billion, according to testimony by Chris Israel, U.S. coordinator for international IP enforcement.[76]

Patent infringements are another source of IP loss. India's patent laws allows authorities to require patent holders to license their products if they are priced beyond the reach of patients and do not have access to the medicines. Bayer was forced to grant a compulsory license to a local generic manufacturer to produce its branded drug Nexavar, an expensive new cancer drug. Bayer's drug sells for $5,698 for a monthly supply. The generics competitor Natco sells a month's supply for $178. It only has to pay Bayer a royalty of about 6% of net sales.[77]

## Business responses to IP infringements

### Diplomatic, administrative, and regulatory efforts

Government and business leaders have routinely complained to Chinese officials about theft and counterfeiting, receiving the repeated promise that protection of IP rights would be enforced. To appease owners of IP rights and satisfy a condition to enter into the WTO, the Chinese government revised its patent, copyright, and trademark laws to comply with an agreement among WTO member countries known as the Trade-Related Aspects of IP Rights. It requires WTO members to take certain steps to protect the IP of foreign companies. On other occasions too, Chinese official have repeatedly promised to improve their protection of IP.[78] In December 2010 at the Joint Commission on Commerce and Trade in Washington, Chinese officials promised better protection for foreign software.

But such promises are at odds with its development strategy, warn skeptics.[79] "Foreign companies operating in China complain that Beijing views the appropriation of foreign innovations as part of a policy mix aimed at developing domestic technology."[80] As stated earlier, foreigners are sometimes forced to disclose their technology in order to gain contracts, or IP is acquired deviously. For example, in 2009 the U.S. International Trade Commission banned imports of cast steel railway wheels made by the Chinese group Tianrui because it had hired nine employees from the Chinese licensee of Amsted industries of Chicago, a maker of railway parts.

Tian Lipu, the commissioner of China's State Intellectual Property Office, wrote an Op-Ed article in *Wall Street Journal* in which he counters charges that China lacks protection for IP. He claims that since 2003 the Chinese government has published action plans every year to enforce the protect IP. He agreed with a statement by John Morton, director of U.S. Immigration and Customs Enforcement made at the Quality Brands Protection Committee, an industry-based coalition, in Beijing in 2010 where he said that IP enforcement was no longer the problem of the United States, nor a problem of China; it was now a global problem.[81]

Administrative proceedings are the most common method of stopping patent infringements. The limitation, however, is that punishment is usually limited to confiscation of the counterfeit products or a monetary fine. An alternative option is to file civil lawsuits against infringers, but it is a time-consuming procedure and the awards generally do not adequately compensate for the infringement. Many brand owners are pressing for criminal prosecutions as the only way to get serious impact on the problem. The penalties awarded, however, are typically negligible; for example, a court awarded five brand owners about $2,500 each in damages for IP infringement. A better option is to seek insurance options, but insurance is very expensive in Asia.[82]

Frustrated with their individual efforts to combat theft of IP rights, MNCs seek the third option of regulatory protection. As stated by Ravi Ramamurti, "Convergence of regulations allows MNCs to adopt globally standardized methods of operation, which can lower costs and reduce policy uncertainty."[83] To accomplish this, MNCs engage in government relations at different levels – home country, at regional level, in host countries, and occasionally in a coordinated fashion at the global level. The latter, says the author, is the ultimate challenge in business–government relations.

The World IP Organization (WIPO) is the principal global agency for managing relations between countries on matters relating to IP. It was created in 1967 "to administer international treaties relating to copyrights ... and industrial property or patents."[84] It required national treatment but left signatory countries free to frame IP as they deemed fit. The WIPO reached a major understanding with the TRIPS agreement as part of the Uruguay Round trade talks and went into effect in January 1995. To date it is the most comprehensive multilateral agreement on IP.

But poor countries tend to have weak IP laws and still weaker enforcement. They and those that produce little IP may prefer weak laws so they can "steal" it. One rationale is that by copycating generic drugs, they could make health care more affordable. Rich countries have stronger IP laws, but they still vary greatly among themselves. The advantage of homogeneity and regulatory convergence is that it allows MNCs to comply with global regulations at lower cost. Another advantage that it enables interconnections with foreign firms or suppliers, for example, on technical standards for telecommunications. On the other hand, "Regulatory heterogeneity also allows countries to use national standards and rules to protect home markets from competing imports ...."[85]

## Improved security

A key lesson about IP protection is that companies must take theft of IP more seriously and improve security. According to a survey with senior members of the management teams of 127 U.K. companies in the information technology, life sciences, and telecoms sectors, they "fail to investigate, monitor and protect their IP assets as diligently as they should, possibly jeopardising the millions of pounds that investors put into research and development programmes annually." The report said it is vital that companies in these industries "have programmes in place to protect ownership and to ensure that all IP elements of a product are protected as fully as possible before a product is brought to market."[86]

## Conclusions

Technology is an important contributor to corporate success and economic development. MNCs are among the chief investors in R&D efforts and have benefitted from diversity of its workforce and outside contacts. As the growth in technology accelerates, it introduces more risks, as reflected in controversy over GMOs, and uncertainties about the future of nanotechnology. Public understanding of science has become more important than ever.[87]

The value of technology is reflected in IP rights and the patent system. When an MNC makes direct foreign investments it must decide how much technology to transfer and how willing it is to share its technology with its partners. The value of technology is so great that industrial espionage, theft, and counterfeiting by countries have continually undermined IP rights. The responses by MNCs are limited to administrative and diplomatic efforts and attempts at regulation. At a minimum, an effort should be made to strengthen security measures.

### Revision Questions

1. Why are technological innovations important for a business? What are the benefits and dangers of new technologies?
2. What lessons have been learned from the introduction of GM crops and foods?
3. How are company IP rights protected?
4. In what ways have MNCs knowingly given up IP assets to countries such as China and India or lost them through various forms of industrial espionage?

### Discussion Questions

I. Are the British and Europeans right by requiring that GM foods be labeled so that consumers have a choice?
II. Some critics argue that GE sacrificed U.S. national interests when it signed a joint venture agreement with a Chinese joint partner whereby it would be sharing its most sophisticated airplane electronics technology. Should such transfers be allowed?
III. Was Apple pushing IP rights too far when it considered product design, such as round corners on an iPad, to be patentable?
IV. Should MNCs take an ethnocentric approach to its research activities and attempt to keep all or most of it in the United States?

# part 3
# corporate responses

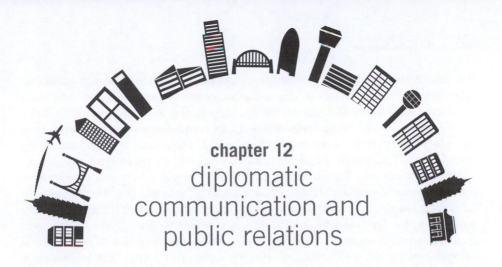

## chapter 12
# diplomatic communication and public relations

**Objectives**

1. *Understand the nature of diplomatic communications.*
2. *Recognize how the "field of experience" of people and their cultures affect their perception of a message.*
3. *Recognize the importance of public opinion and the role of publicity in influencing it.*
4. *Know the key characteristics of diplomatic language and how to apply them.*
5. *Recognize the wide use of English in international discourse.*

International communications by multinational corporations (MNCs) and other private sector organizations are modeled after the art of diplomacy. Like diplomats, all communicators should always have objectives in mind and consider the effect their words will have on the attitudes of international players and their willingness to cooperate. Diplomatic communicators should also consider the backgrounds and cultural habits of receivers to achieve maximum understanding and agreement.

The attributes of diplomatic communication are summarized in the following description of diplomacy: "Diplomacy means communicating your needs, wants, feelings, beliefs and opinions to others in a manner that does not hurt anyone's feelings. Characteristics include but are not limited to using clear, open inoffensive communication, flexibility, specific wording, a positive approach, being nonjudgmental and demonstrating a relaxed manner both verbally and nonverbally. It is connected with the concept of tact, being tactful."[1]

Business executives, in many walks of life, have recognized the value of diplomacy. Rick King, an executive vice president and CEO at Thomson North American Legal, characterized a "diplomat" as someone on the staff who can sit down with anyone anywhere and break down issues to arrive at a solution that the technical people can execute and the business people are happy with. Another executive, Ken Lehman, a group director of shared services operations at Northrop Grumman Corp in Los Angeles, states, "I strongly believe diplomacy is all about people. It's really about learning and gaining their trust, putting yourself in their shoes and understanding their perspective."[2]

## Role of Communications in Modern Diplomacy

The essential role of communication is widely recognized in the field of diplomacy and has historical roots. In *The Essence of Diplomacy*, Christer Jonsson and Martin

Hall describe diplomacy as a regulated process of the international society's communication system, with diplomats serving as its messengers.[3] Reference is sometime made to ancient Greece where Hermes was the divine messenger and most prominent diplomatic emissary.[4] In current societies, diplomats are seen as messengers between nations and any of the players in the international arena. Diplomatic communications by nations have set the pattern for communications by MNCs in the international arena.

In the division of communication into mass communication and interpersonal communication, diplomacy is chiefly associated with the latter. As news commentator Edward R. Murrow observed, person-to-person contact – "the last three feet" – is the most important element in the communication process.[5] Modern diplomacy, however, requires communications in a wider variety of settings than face-to-face conversations between two people, with gatherings ranging from small groups and assemblies of people to large-scale conferences.

Along with an enlargement of diplomatic settings, "diplomatic culture" has also changed, becoming less universal and containing greater varieties of national and regional differences. As personal diplomacy has grown at the head of state or government level, "there has been a corresponding rise in regional diplomacy, through meetings, conferences and less formal gatherings of political, diplomatic and technical experts."[6] In international institutions, the characteristic procedures for negotiation and problem-solving have seen the introduction of such features as the general use of inner, limited membership specialist working groups, correspondence groups, and a variety of preparatory meetings.

## Field of experience and cultural context

The modern world of international relations has placed new burdens on the process of communication. Communication theory posits that the success of communication between a sender and a receiver is largely determined by each one's *field of experience*. As described by Bryant Wedge of the Institute for the Study of National Behavior, "Every person carries in his mind a picture of the world – sets of assumptions and expectations by which he acts." We are able to deal with one another "because we share certain conventions which we have learned by experience – conventions such as language, gesture, and habits of belief and value."[7]

In other words, the field of experience is the sum total of each person's knowledge, attitudes, and feelings. It is not identical between any two individuals. Diagrammatically, by drawing a circle representing the field of experience for the sender and a similar circle for the receiver, one can see how close or different these individuals are by the degree of overlap of these circles. With persons similar to ourselves, the circles overlap substantially; with those different from ourselves, the circles may not overlap at all or barely overlap. To convey a meaning and have it actually understood in the same manner by the receiver, a sender of a message must bridge the gap between the different fields experience, typically by providing more background information.

Communication is more difficult in the international arena because the overlap between the fields of experience of the sender and the audience is likely to be small, reflecting differences in educational backgrounds, organizational cultures, and national and regional cultures. What is readily understood by members of a small group must slowly and carefully be explained to outsiders. Through an understanding of the receiver's background and culture, a sender must guess what additional information to add to a message to make it understood. This calculation is based on the realization that all understandings and perceptions formulated by a receiver are the sum of the message and the stored knowledge related to that message.

In psychological experiments with "figure and ground," the stored information is represented by the "ground"; the "figure," representing the message, is interpreted in the context of the ground. The meanings of the sender and receiver are easily conveyed when the ground, representing the field of experience, is the same. When they are different, a sender must attempt to provide more of the information contained in "background."

## High-context cultures

The larger cultures to which a sender and receiver belong also affect the understanding of a message and further complicates international communications. It is another layer beyond the field of experience. The concept of high- and low-context cultures, popularized by Edward T. Hall, is applicable. In a high-context culture, people interpret a message through the lens of the shared culture, which can be either in the physical context or in the behavior of a person through nonverbal communication or body language, in silences and pauses, and in relationships and empathy.[8]

In the language of figure and ground, there is much overlap in the "ground" between high-context senders and receivers. In contrast, in low-context societies, most information is contained in explicit codes, such as words; the bonds between people are often fragile and involvement of people with each other is low; fewer distinctions are made between insiders and outsiders; and change is easy and rapid.[9] Brief messages can consequently carry larger meanings. "Cultural interpreters" who understand the cultures of interacting groups, therefore, possess an important qualification for diplomacy.

When Hall was asked how Arabs were different from North Americans, he explained that the basic difference is that Arabs are highly "contexted." Arabs examine the entire circumstance in which events are happening in order to understand them. Hall gives the example of banking in the Middle East. Reflecting a low-context approach, an American banker has to send a financial statement to his home office in the United States to obtain approval for a loan above a certain amount. But a Middle East banker could simply agree on a loan on the strength of a personal recommendation by a mutual friend. As Hall stated, "if you know the man and you know his business and he knows you and you're part of the same social group, he cannot afford not to pay back that loan."[10] High-context societies require much less legal paperwork than in the United States; a persons' word is his or her bond and you need not spell out the details to make him behave.

Related to high- and low-context cultures is the communal ethos, the roots of which lie in the primacy of the extended family, clan, or caste – also in rigid, stratified forms of social and religious organization. The guiding theme of the collectivist ethic is the welfare of the group and the desirability of cooperative endeavor; individual wishes and desires are subordinate to the group. Maintaining group harmony and face is important in communal societies, as evidenced in the importance of "saving face" in Japanese and other Asian cultures. There is no more powerful sanction than disapproval. Loss of face – humiliation before the group – is an excruciating penalty to be avoided at all costs.[11]

Speakers in high-context cultures must weigh their words carefully because they know that whatever they say will be scrutinized and taken to heart. Consequently, "Truth is not an imperative when a lie avoids unpleasantness." Furthermore, "the concern with social effect and not just the transmission of information results in a propensity for rhetoric and verbal posture. Public discourse may be rich in invective, but nothing personal is meant or perceived in the hyperbole."[12]

Before a frank exchange is possible with a stranger in a high-context culture, a personal relationship must be established. Americans, however, are known for wanting immediately to delve into business matters. They view a relationship instrumentally because the United States has a low-context culture. Therefore, language "performs an informational rather than socially lubricative function," with accuracy (the "truth ethic") as the highest virtue. What has to be said is stated explicitly. Indirection is much disliked, while "straight-from-the shoulder" talk is admired. "'Get to the point' is the heartfelt reaction to small talk and evasive formulations."[13]

## Information is power

One reason why familiarity with diplomatic communication is important in management is that all leaders know the adage that "information is power" – not only the power to make wise decisions but also the power to dominate. Those executives who possess high-quality information are accorded organizational and societal status. A leader is someone who possesses resources that others need, and information is a key resource. A person cannot constructively participate in decision making in our complex age without commanding appropriate information. Nor can an activity be evaluated without a kind of information called feedback – information about actual results that can then be compared with objectives.

Too often, no provision is made in speeches and communication campaigns to measure feedback. Feedback is particularly important when there is little familiarity with distant audiences. As Wedge notes, "The great acceleration in the flow of information across national boundaries during the last half-century, together with radical changes in the organization of international life, confront diplomacy with unprecedented challenges. The world has never been like this before; new thinking is demanded by new conditions of the human venture."[14]

## Power of Public Opinion and Public Relations

In extending communication channels beyond the personal to the realm of mass communication, diplomats consider the power of public opinion and the influence of the press. They have learned that the general public can be reached directly through the mass media or, in what is known as the two-step flow, through opinion leaders. They must also consider what such social media as Facebook and Twitter say about them and other players. International communicators must become concerned with their public image because they know it influences their nation's standing and the credibility of their messages. Diplomats representing nations or the private sector increasingly recognize that they must reach opinion leaders in civil society as well as the general public.

## Ascendency of Publicity

Ascendency of publicity refers to the trend by international players to seek public attention and support for their causes, viewpoints, and missions. MNCs are familiar with planned efforts to attract positive news coverage to build public understanding and a favorable image. Their business objectives include the ability to make direct invest-ments abroad, to acquire other companies, to sell goods and services, and to obtain favorable government treatment. When they are attacked by the news media or social media for alleged harmful behavior, such as engaging in human rights violations or endangering the environment, MNCs make public statement to defend their policies and actions or to apologize for them. They may also wish to garner public support for their business position on issues, as Monsanto has done with the GM food and crop issue and Microsoft with its antitrust dispute with the EU.

Supranational organizations have also engaged in mass communications and public information activities to gain public support for their causes. One of them is UNESCO that has publicized itself and its programs of mass education. To this end, it crafted extensive message themes: world heritage, education for all, ethics of science and technology, environmental protection, prevention of natural disasters, and conflict resolution. It uses an array of media: monthly journals, documentary films, and a variety of cultural events.[15] Other supranational organizations are also engaged in campaigns. The EU seeks support from member nations for a new constitution; an NGO, Environmental Defense, seeks public support for stopping construction of more coal-fired power plants. Nation-states also use publicity to improve their national images for political and economic purposes. The United States engages in public diplomacy to combat anti-Americanism, and China publicized its 2008 Olympics to build its "nation-brand."

The annual World Economic Forum held in Davos portrays itself as an intimate brainstorming session for business and political leaders and provides many publicity opportunities for corporations and nations to promote their images.[16] It is as much about marketing and networking as it is about an exchange of ideas. As stated by Tom Mattia, Coca-Cola's senior vice president in charge of world-wide public affairs and communication, "For us, it really is a platform to get our voice heard, far more than it is about trying to respond to something."[17] For example, to offset criticism that it is draining water from poor communities, it planned to use speaker panels and other events to highlight projects to improve community water supplies and reduce emissions of global-warming refrigerants. The company also used the occasion to unveil new "eKOfreshment" beverage coolers, an initiative with Greenpeace and Unilever PLC, to reduce emissions of global-warming gases.

Because public relations efforts often ask communicators to "put the best foot forward" and call a glass "half full" rather than "half empty," public relations is viewed as a promotional activity that engages in "puffery" – exaggerated, perhaps unjustified, praise.[18] It aggressively seeks to get its message across to selected audiences to influence their attitudes and persuade them to take some action. In the marketer's concept of promotion mix, publicity is one of the components, along with advertising, sales promotion, personal selling, and the Internet.

Publicity is associated with public relations, which is stereotypically perceived as the sending of press releases and arranging media events. The social media have been added to the communications mix. Sabrina Horn, founder and CEO of the Horn Group and a pioneer in the use of social media, warns, "Gone are the archaic days of using the press release as the single tool to get the word out. Gone are the days of the lone publicist in the department cranking out media alerts and the spray-and-pray distri-bution of news to reporters that don't care."[19] She tells communication professionals that today communications are "digital," which she explains as the delicate combination of PR with interactive web capabilities and social media.

## Beyond publicity

The visible activities of publicity and other communications, however, are supported by research and planning, and, more broadly, by the social sciences. This extended view of publicity is exemplified by Edward L. Bernays, one of the founders of public relations. *Time* magazine called him U.S.'s publicist No. 1. But he disliked being called a "publicity man" or "press agent, preferring instead to be associated with the "profession of the public relations counsel." In his classic, *Crystallizing Public Opinion*, published in 1923, he described the counselor as follows:

> He interprets the client to the public, which he is enabled to do in part because he interprets the public to the client. His advice is given on all occasions on which his client appears before the public, whether it be in concrete form or as an idea. His advice is given not only on actions which take place, but also on the use of mediums which bring these actions to the public it is desired to reach, no matter whether these mediums be the printed, the spoken or the visualized word – that is, advertising, lecture, the stage, the pulpit, the newspapers, the photograph, the wireless, the mail, or any other form of thought communication.[20]

Although his examples of media exposure are now dated, he was a major advocate of public relations and, in actual practice, a leader in the use of publicity to promote many causes. What distinguishes him from other practitioners is that he made extensive use of the social sciences and often referred to public relations as an applied social science. He considered ideas more important than words, as the title of his autobiography: *Biography of an Idea*[21] reflects. Among his famous statements are "I find it easier to change the viewpoint of millions than one man's," and "Age-old customs, I learned, could be broken down by a dramatic appeal, disseminated by the network of media."

James E. Grunig, a leading scholar in public relations, defined public relations as the "management of communication between an organization and its publics."[22] In doing so, he distinguished between the extremes of one-way asymmetrical communications and two-way symmetrical communications. Too many people associate public relations with the former, seeing it as a way for communicators to get their messages out to achieve organization gains. Two-way symmetrical communication, however, is most appropriate in international communications where both parties listen to each other and seek mutual benefit. If communications were asymmetrical, the sender would listen to the other only to obtain feedback to improve upon the message and not to be influenced by his or her arguments.

The Public Relations Society of America's Official Statement on Public Relations favors the two-way symmetrical model, saying, "Public relations is a strategic communication process that builds mutually beneficial relationships between organizations and their publics."[23] Although PRSA avoids referring to public relations as a "management function," fearing that the latter "can evoke ideas of control and top-down, one-way communication," it nonetheless explains that public relations encompasses three management functions:

- Anticipating, analyzing, and interpreting public opinion, attitudes, and issues that might impact the operations and plans of the organization.
- Counseling management at all levels in the organization with regard to policy decisions, courses of action, and communication, taking into account their public ramifications and the organization's social or citizenship responsibilities.
- Researching, conducting, and evaluating, on a continuing basis, programs of action and communicating to achieve the informed public understanding necessary to the success of an organization's aims. These may include marketing, financial, fund-raising, employee, community or government relations, and other programs.[24]

Mutuality requires that both parties acknowledge respect for each other. Much can be learned from customer service people who have been trained not to talk to a customer in a manner that belittles him or her. They learn to develop an "I'm OK, You're OK" attitude. Instead of sounding critical of another person and blaming him or her for some difficulty, the matter of blame is avoided and the problem itself is tackled. As the book *Getting to Yes* recommends, communicators should focus on the problem, not the personalities.[25] Similarly, communicators are taught to apply transactional analysis to their messages.[26] This approach views a person as playing the role of a parent, adult, or child. The advice is not to sound like a parent or adult talking to a child. An adult-to-adult mode is usually the appropriate one, and certainly the one compatible with diplomatic communication.

One diplomat who rejected the whole idea of "You're OK" is John Bolton. While serving as the U.S. ambassador to the United Nation, another Western ambassador complained, "He has succeeded in putting almost everyone's back up, even among America's closest allies."[27] His inability, or unwillingness, to make friends and build alliances was out of tune in an organization where networking, compromise, and consensus are the norm. He brushed away diplomatic niceties, preferring an "abrasive, my-way-or-the highway style."[28] Especially in international affairs, the regard that each party has for the other is an essential factor. The Bolton approach is anathema to diplomacy and reinforces the lesson that arrogance leads to anti-Americanism.

## Openness is favored

Public relations favors openness and operates best in the context of transparency. Openness is propelled by two forces. One is that the dangers of secrecy are recognized as the public demands greater transparency. The other is the practical fact that in an age of omnipresent smart phones with cameras and the posting of blogs it is hard to keep secrets, as evidenced by a steady flow of news media reports of corruption and wrongdoing. Furthermore, there is greater awareness that secrecy can impede the equitable and efficient functioning of society. It is well known that individuals in positions of power use secrecy to cover up real or imagined mistakes, thus hoping to prevent punishment and demands for restitution. Other dangers of secrecy are that it can be used by holders of privileged information to benefit economically and politically; harm the decision-making process; and erode trust within an organization and society.

The value of privileged information is particularly obvious in financial markets and the reason why in the United States the Securities & Exchange Acts of 1935 and 1936 sought to prevent "insider trading." The Securities and Exchange Commission (SEC) enforces "full & timely disclosure" laws that require public corporations to communicate "material facts" – facts that could influence the stock market price – to all investors. The SEC's belief is that all investors, both current and potential, need adequate and accurate information to make prudent decisions about whether to buy or sell a security. The SEC's full and timely disclosure laws have become a model of *transparency*.

A feature of openness is the willingness to speak out. One of the lessons learned by all organizations and nations that have suffered from negative publicity is that it is usually unwise to maintain a low profile. The strategy of not sending out news releases or holding news conferences, and only warily responding to journalists' telephone calls, can be risked only if there is little public interest in an organization, which is often the case with manufacturers of producer goods, but not with manufacturers of consumer goods. The mining company Freeport McMoRan is known for having shunning the press by following a "No tall trees" policy."[29] The problem with such a low-profile approach is that should a crisis occur an organization suffers from lack of public good will and possible hostility by the media. A greater loss may be that by maintaining a low profile, an organization losses the opportunity to advance its views on public issues.

Ideally, public relations identifies the source of its messages and uses honest, straightforward means of conveying information. On a technical level, information theorists define information as symbols used in the transmission of messages, using the term *bits* to measure the amount of information.[30] On a practical level, we know that our messages should contain information that allows the sender to produce the meaning intended by the sender. Good writers know that a message should not contain "empty" words devoid of information. They also know the value of applying readability tests, such as the Flesch formula that is based on average sentence lengths and average number of syllables per word.[31] The purpose of information is to reduce uncertainty and disorder (technically called entropy) and to clarify meaning.

## Diplomatic language

Diplomatic language has its own peculiarities. Raymond Cohen says it might broadly be viewed as semiotics – as the production and interpretation of signs, which serve as a code shared by other members of the diplomatic community.[32] He cites the American writer Caskie Stinnett who humorously characterized a diplomat as "a person who can tell you to go to hell in such a way that you actually look forward to the trip." Another ironic characterization is a person who "thinks twice before saying nothing."[33] Charles Maurice de Talleyrand is known for saying "Speech was given to man to disguise his thoughts."[34] He also said, "A diplomat who says yes means maybe, a diplomat who says maybe means no, and a diplomat who says no is no diplomat."

English literature provides pithy examples of the significance of language and words. Alice in Lewis Carroll's *Through the Looking-Glass* said, "The question is, whether you can make words mean so many different things." John Locke in his *Essay on Human Understanding* said, "We should have a great many fewer disputes in the world if words were taken for what they are, the signs of our ideas only, and not for things themselves."[35]

## English as the new lingua franca

Diplomacy has had a tendency to develop a *lingua franca*, which in the eighteenth century up to World War I was French. Now it is English, which has achieved global status. Some 380 million people speak English as their first language and perhaps two-thirds as many again as their second.[36] After the United States, the highest populations of English speakers are in the United Kingdom, Nigeria, and India. It is not, however, the most-spoken language in the world; because of China's large population, Chinese (mostly Mandarin) is. About 1,113 million people speak Chinese as their mother tongue, whereas about 372 million speak English.[37]

English is the chief language of international business, as noted by the *Harvard Business Review*.[38] It is widely used by many MNCs. In Japan, it includes Sony Corp, Nissan Motor Co, Fast Retailing Co., Nippon Sheet Glass Co., and Sumida Corp.[39] English has official status in 87 countries and territories. Of the world's roughly 12,500 international organizations, 85% make use of English, with one-third using English exclusively.[40] English is also the official language in several professional spheres: (1) the European Central Bank (which is located in Frankfurt); (2) ships and aircraft, for example, "Seaspeak," or the new "Standard Marine Communications Phrases (SMCP)," is used by ships' pilots around the word, and (3) "Airspeak" is used by airplane pilots and air-traffic controllers.[41] English is also the de facto working language of 98% of German research physicists and 83% of German research chemists.[42] Specialized fields must consider the language used in their professional communities.

English has become the EU's dominant working language. French, however, is spoken in the EU's corridors and meeting rooms because EU institutions are located in the francophone cities of Brussels, Luxembourg, and Strasbourg. Considering the implications of the Whorfian hypothesis – that the language and words we use shape our thoughts – the French worry aloud whether "it is possible to speak English without thinking American."[43] They feel that France's own distinct intellectual tradition in economics, philosophy, and law has been eclipsed. Humorously, however, the French subdue the trauma with the thought, "Our only revenge is that the English language is being killed by all these foreigners speaking it so badly."[44]

As well as having become the unofficial language of global trade in the last century, English is also the official language of the Internet. A survey of 600 million Web pages in 1999 by Excite AtHome Corp. found that 78% were written in English.[45] Nevertheless, communicators should not fixate on English for all uses. A study by Euro Marketing Associates estimates nearly 44% of the world's online population now speak a language other than English at home. Even though satellites can deliver programming and advertising instantaneously and simultaneously across the more than two dozen language spoken in Western Europe, viewers want their television delivered in local tongues.[46] Diplomats with a knowledge of local languages of the people with whom they deal have a distinct advantage.

Translations from English to other languages must be carefully scrutinized. Many examples appear in advertising where funny, but serious blunders have been made. Some examples are as follows:

- When American fast food giant Kentucky Fried Chicken opened their first restaurant in Beijing in 1987, they accidentally translated KFC's famous slogan, "Finger-lickin 'good' to "We'll Eat Your Fingers Off."

- In 2006, hair care company Clairol introduced a curling iron called the Mist Stick, which did very well in U.S. markets. When the company marketed the product in Germany, however, they failed to realize that "mist" means "manure" in German.
- The Ford Motor Company introduced the subcompact Pinto in 1971. The company could not understand why they were not selling more cars in Brazil, until they learned that "Pinto" is Brazilian slang for "male genitals."
- When Parker Pen's famous slogan "It won't leak in your pocket and embarrass you" was translated into Spanish, it confused many Mexican consumers who read it as, "It won't leak in your pocket and make you pregnant."[47]

Some of these mistranslations are so basic that one wonders why companies did not use the simple procedure of checking with native speaking people among their employees or friends.

## Key characteristics of diplomatic communication

Just as writers and TV and film producers have manipulated the meaning of their books and shows for their audiences, professional diplomats are adept in choosing forms of communicating that suit their aims. Among these are misdirection, the use of ambiguity, synchronizing messages themes with selected audiences, and maintaining secrecy.

## Misdirection and ambiguity

Magicians are associated with *misdirection* – directing the viewers' attention with one hand while performing some magic with the other. This deceptive device is used in detective fiction, where the identity of the murderer is concealed by deliberately focusing on a red herring. Diplomats engage in similar practice by drawing attention to a particular action in order to conceal the intended action.

Diplomats prefer ambiguity to making one's meaning clear, which defies the principles of journalism. Communication books stress the importance of clear writing and speaking. One rule is to use simple words that are understandable by one's audiences, rather than ornate language to show off education. Often cited as an example of clear, powerful language is Winston Churchill's tribute to the RAF and the RCAF after the Battle for Britain: "Never in the field of human conflict was so much owed by so many to so few."[48] Another often quoted phrase is Patrick Henry's speech before the Virginia House of Burgesses which helped bring on the Revolutionary War: "I care not what course others may take but as for me, give me liberty or give me death."[49]

Traditional diplomatic language, however, often favors the opposite by deliberately using ambiguity to conceal vital information, maintain flexibility, and make signals disclaimable. The sender can then always argue, "I never said that," "this is not what I meant."[50] Furthermore, ambiguity allows a message to be received by multiple audiences, each of which can interpret ambiguous messages to their liking. As Peggy Noonan states in her review of Alan Greenspan's book, *The Age of Turbulence: Adventures in a New World*, he artfully and deliberately obscured his public statements with "stylings marked by barely penetrable syntax, passive voice and oblique phraseology," which "allowed partisans to twist his words into whatever shape they wanted."[51] This illustrates the figure versus ground concept mentioned earlier. Thus, in traditional diplomacy, truth often suffers, for often it must be camouflaged – hidden from the receiver. There is a further danger that ambiguity may be accompanied by duplicity and deception, including disinformation.

Nonverbal cues and body language can contribute to ambiguity. Complicating factors might be the status of those representing an entity, the selection of envoys, and the shape of a table for meetings. For example, an hexagonal table was used at six-party talks with North Korea in order to avoid any connotation of precedence or unequal status. Communicating through visual cues is another device. When Henry Kissinger visited Beijing during one of his trips, Prime Minister Zhou Enalid took him to an ostentatious public appearance at the Summer Palace in plain view of spectators, among whom was a North Vietnamese journalist taking photographs. This was a way for China to signal it would not permit North Vietnam's problems to stand in the way of a *rapprochement* with the United States. The exchange of gifts was another.[52]

The use of positive declarative language and power words is advisable when the intention is to avoid ambiguity. Saying that negative words tend to be destructive, James E. Lukaszewski, a veteran public relations counselor and expert on crisis management, gives these examples of converting negative approaches into positive declarations:

- Instead of "I don't believe it … or you," say, "Here's what I believe," or "Here's what we believe."
- Instead of "It won't work; it never worked," say, "Here's how it might work." or "Here are some suggestions to make it work."
- Instead of "That's a lie" or "You're wrong," say, "Check the facts more carefully and you'll find" or "Let's look at the facts."
- Instead of "That's not our style," say, "We're known, even respected for.… "
- Instead of "We don't do that" or "We've never done that," say, "Here's what we actually do" or " Here, specifically, is what we do.…"[53]

The use of "power words" is also important as a way to confront words that are emotionally negative in nature, for example, such words as ashamed, afraid, worried, frightened, and embarrassed. Some power responses are given as follows:

- When a reporter asks, "Was it a bad or stupid choice?," the response might be "In their place, I would have made different choices."
- When asked, "It sounds like they hate your plan," say "As we emphasize solutions, they'll be more positive about what we're doing."
- When asked, "Will this problem destroy your reputation?," say "These matters are certainly urgent, and we will do our best to deal with them."
- When asked, "Shouldn't your company be ashamed of its performance?," say "We're surprised at the public interest, but intend to respond powerfully and aggressively to the public's concerns."[54]

## Awareness of nonverbal language

The language of nonverbal communication is highly important in diplomatic communication. Cohen recognized this in his *Theatre of Power: The Art of Diplomatic Signalling*, saying "Not even costume and gesture can be left to chance when the length of a handshake or the warmth of an embrace may be carefully noted."[55] This reality was evident during the 1954 Geneva conference when Chou En-Lai offered his hand to John Foster Dulles but was cuttingly ignored. Cohen recognized the "need for greater sensitivity to this form of communication 'gesture' on the part of the sometimes too literal-minded West. Talleyrand's famous piece of advice: 'Above all avoid an excess of enthusiasm.'"[56]

In the world of mass media, the diplomat and the national leader are required to be TV performers. As Cohen states, the theatrical metaphor fits the reality of the age of television as "the separate requirements of public politics, peacetime diplomacy and media technology have converged to reinforce the role of nonverbal communication between states."[57] Furthermore, "states have also become adept at using extra-linguistic forms of communication." "Posture, gesture, facial expression, body movement, dress and so on equally pass on important clues about such things as status, role, identity and feeling." When President Clinton pausing a little too long in front of intern Monica Lewinsky when she was in a crowd, much meaning was attached to it.

Michael Deaver, communications adviser to President Reagan, recognized the importance of backdrops in visual communication. During Reagan's visit to China, the press was tightly controlled and access to him and other principals limited or prevented. TV cameras were set up on platforms and the speeches and ceremonies were written and choreographed in advance. Pictures were always taken in scenic and dramatic settings with Reagan prominently in the foreground as "high profile presidential visuals."[58] As sociologist Erving Goffman, the author of *Presentation of Self in Everyday Life*, pointed out, "When an envoy makes a personal gesture in public he is, or should be, acting under instructions or at last in conformity with a predetermined policy."[59]

Goffman recognized the importance of impression management and used the metaphor of a stage to portray the way people interact in everyday life. He said that people try to make a good impression as a way of establishing the "terms of trade" in their relationship with another. Thus, well-dressed people who create an upper-class impression are accorded more attention and receive more benefits than "two-bit" characters.

## Synchronizing message themes with selected audiences

Identification and analysis of one's audiences, as well as selecting effective messages for each, has always been a major element of communications. This step is part of the communication process model of "who says what to whom through what channels with what effects." Being vague about an audience, for example, simply referring to "the public," prevents a communicator from sharpening his or her message. Diplomatic communication must especially synchronize message themes with selected audiences. Charlotte Beer paid too little attention to this process in her public diplomacy efforts for the United States.

In a Rand Corporation occasional paper, Charles Wolf, Jr., and Brian Rosen apply the so-called constituency/adversary hypothesis to this audience analysis process, saying:

> The effectiveness of public diplomacy efforts and messages – and, more generally, effective marketing of public goods – depends on (a) appealing to the identified *constituency* by focusing on the goods [public benefits] and goals to be achieved, (b) explicitly or implicitly recognizing the *adversary* or adversaries standing in the way of the constituency's interests in the delivery of those goods, and (c) capitalizing on

the tensions between public diplomat's appeal to the constituency and the adversary's resistance to it.[60]

Diplomatic communications are carefully planned and structured, so that application of known principles of effective communication becomes routine. As receivers of messages, an MNC or other international player must be aware of the strategies others use to influence their perceptions and understandings. In turn, a diplomatic communicator must learn how to use these strategies effectively and to be mindful that the objective is to establish and maintain relationships for the achievement of organizational goals. Such communications are always instrumental and purposive.

## Use of the Apology

Making apologies has become not only acceptable but also routine, says Barbara Kellerman in her *Harvard Business Review* article, "When Should a Leader Apologize and When Not?"[61] It is no longer seen as an act of weakness but a sign of respect for the rights and sensitives of others. The Japanese, who have made an art of the apology and apologize far more frequently than Westerners, consider it a virtue by showing that a person takes responsibility and avoids blaming others.[62] In international affairs, Jennifer M. Lind's book *Sorry States: Apologies in International Politics* shows how governments increasingly offer or demand apologies for past human rights abuses.[63] She mentions how after World War II West Germany leaders issued apologies and paid extensive reparations. She also criticizes the Japanese for having repeatedly denied past atrocities, which continues to poison relations with South Korea, China, and Australia more than 60 years after the war. Lind believes that international reconciliation requires apologies and other contrite gestures.

Corporations increasingly apologize for behavior considered unacceptable by the public. Recent ones include Apple's CEO Tim Cook's apology to Apple customers, fans, and critics on the issue of inferior maps in its new operating system, BP's former CEO Tony Hayward's apology on the company's Gulf of Mexico oil spill, and News Corp.'s CEO Rupert Murdoch's apology for its subsidiary's invasion of people's privacy. These apologies should be judged on the extent to which the rules of a sincere apology are followed. Kellerman says they are as follows: acknowledging the offenses; accepting full responsibility, expressing regret, providing assurance that the offenses will not be repeated, and immediacy.[64] The apology signed by Marcus Agus, Group chairman of Barclays, in connection with the Libor scandal demonstrates the application of these rules:

> To all Barclays customers and clients,

> We are truly sorry for what has happened and that you have been let down. It is our actions now and over the coming months and years that will make the difference. You are the lifeblood of our business, and we will not allow ourselves to be distracted from what really matters – delivering for you, day in and day out. My colleagues work tirelessly to do just that. The Board and I thank them for their commitment and for their determination to ensure that customers and clients are at the heart of everything we do. I also thank you for your business. It is our responsibility to earn the right to retain it.[65]

Apologies have become a standard part of image restoration strategies in crisis communications.[66] They have become part of the lexicon of diplomatic communications.

## Conclusions

This chapter opens the broad topic of communication strategies and tools used in diplomatic communication. These extend the toolkit of the traditional diplomat and introduce the techniques of modern communication, which is the overall goal of Part III.

Diplomacy is dependent on carefully crafted communications. Accordingly this chapter draws on communication theory. The relevant elements in communication – sender, message, media, audience, receiver, and effects – are explored. A form of risk analysis also always occurs that examines the best way to deal with specific senders and receivers. Knowing the differences in their fields of experience helps each party in communications to gauge the difficulties they will encounter. Communicators also learn to factor in differences in language and how to adjust to the habits of various audiences. Some of the characteristics of diplomatic communication, such as misdirection and ambiguity, must be expected and taken into account.

### Appendix: Public Diplomacy

The U.S. government's public diplomacy campaign in response to anti-Americanism illustrates the importance of public opinion and the application of principles of public relations and communications. When the Eisenhower administration created the U.S. Information Agency (USIA) in 1953, the modern era of public diplomacy was inaugurated.[67] Its programs included the Voice of America, Radio Free Europe/Radio Liberty, Radio Free Asia, and Worldnet TV, which reached millions of people in dozens of countries.[68] The stated purpose of these programs was "to submit evidence to peoples of other nations by means of communication techniques that the objectives and policies of the United States are in harmony with and will advance their own legitimate aspirations for freedom, progress, and peace."[69]

President Ronald Reagan furthered public diplomacy during the 1980s by creating an Office of Public Diplomacy dedicated to "managing" foreign media to encourage popular support at home and abroad for America's arms race with the Soviet Union and its aggressive military interventions in Central America. After the collapse of the Soviet Union in 1989 and the spread of the ideology of the market economy, the U.S. government saw no need for public diplomacy and withdrew funds from the USIA, which was closed down in 1999.[70]

Public diplomacy regained importance after 9/11 in the mid of a rising tide of anti-Americanism. The U.S. State Department seized upon public diplomacy as a way of explaining government policies abroad and "of explaining and advocating American values to the world."[71]

In 2004, the State Department spent $685 million on public diplomacy efforts aimed at capturing foreigners' hearts and minds – promoting American values of democracy, tolerance, and pluralism abroad while combating negative images. The effort was not just governmental. As Wilson P. Dizard, Jr., who worked in the U.S. State Department and the USIA from 1951 to 1980, explains, these government operations were eclipsed by the massive global activities of private groups, which "emerged as the largest force influencing America's ideological impact abroad in the past half-century."[72] He includes in this group the mass media, the advertising industry, and cultural and educational institutions, along with multinational corporations and other organizations concerned with overseas public opinion.

## Charlotte Beer's nation-branding campaign

When the problem of anti-Americanism was recognized and confirmed by public opinion polls, the U.S. State Department employed public diplomacy, applying Madison Avenue advertising and public relations tools. Reflecting the business orientation of the Bush White House, advertising star Charlotte Beers was appointed undersecretary of state for public diplomacy and public affairs. Fittingly, she said, "I consider the marketing capacity of the United States to be our greatest unlisted asset."[73] She said she did not find the notion of selling Uncle Sam like Uncle Ben's rice was all that different from product branding, saying, "The whole idea of building a brand is to create relationships between the product and its user."[74] Supporting her, secretary of State Colin Powell declared, "There is nothing wrong with getting someone who knows how to sell something. We are selling a product. We need someone who can rebrand U.S. foreign policy, rebrand diplomacy.... Besides, she got me to buy Uncle Ben's rice."[75]

Beers created an advertising drive known as "shared values" based on her belief that the way to win over Muslims was to present television snippets in Muslim countries that showed successful and satisfied Muslims in the United States.[76] Accordingly, McCann-Erickson Worldgroup, a unit of Interpublic Group, created a series of television spots featuring five Muslims who live in the United States: a baker, a journalism student, a schoolteacher, a paramedic, and a public official. The schoolteacher spot, for example, depicted three scenes: working with children in the classroom, watching a softball game, and hanging out in her Toledo, Ohio, kitchen. (The baker owner said he was paid for his role in the campaign.) The spots went on the air in most countries starting October 28, 2002, and ran through December 10. In early January 2003, however, the State Department announced that it was abandoning the TV campaign.

The 15-million dollar video ad campaign was universally derided as wrong-headed and counterproductive.[77] One criticism was that Beers failed to conduct audience analysis and to study the specific interests and concerns of the Arab-Muslims who were stirring up anti-American sentiment. By representing freedom and democracy as American values, ignoring that these ideals can be found in almost all cultures at different times, her efforts could easily be branded as neo-colonization. Steger says that the videos portrayed the United States (and West) as an attempt by a "superior" culture to "civilize" an "inferior" one.[78] This perception helped to intensify anti-American sentiments. A further criticism is that one-way communication programs are known to be highly ineffective in changing people's perceptions and attitudes. The perception that these public diplomacy efforts amount to no more than propaganda undermines their effectiveness.

Beers resigned unexpectedly in March 2003, stating health reasons, and after a brief time in office by Margaret Tutwiler, a former U.S. Ambassador to Morocco, was succeeded by Karen Hughes.[79]

## Improvements by Karen Hughes

When Karen Hughes assumed office in July 2005, she promised to listen to the people she wanted to reach.[80] Accordingly, in September 2005, she embarked on a five-day "listening tour" of the Middle East to showcase her four strategic pillars of engagement, exchanges, education, and empowerment. But the trip received mixed reviews and repeated some of the mistakes of Beers. She came under fire for using the listening tour as a "photo opportunity" and platform for reiterating U.S. policies with "handpicked audiences." The rhetoric of promising to listen was not fulfilled. The Arab media gave her negative reviews and she received catcalls from domestic critics.[81] As described by Thomas L. Harris, author of *Marketing Public Relations*:

> Too bad that Karen took an entourage of 16 reporters along to listen in on what had been billed as a "listening tour" of three Middle Eastern countries. Karen did her best to try to present herself as 'mom' who loves her kids. She told an audience of 500 Saudi university women that driving a car was 'an important part of my free-dom' and expressed the hope that Saudi women would soon be able to drive and "fully participate in society."[82]

This was another one-sided exercise in which America was speaking to the world. The government, not the broader American public, was again the main messenger to a world that is mightily suspicious of it. As Michael Holzman of *The New York Times* described it, "United States public diplomacy is neither public nor diplomatic."[83] Furthermore, such a marketing view must be distinguished from a relationship view that "sets a broader objective of cultivating better diplomatic relations through methods of listening, understanding and engagement."[84]

Karen Hughes soon realized that government efforts needed reinforcement from the private sector, mainly business. She appeared to agree with author Jan Melissen that involving nongovernmental agents was one of the most effective ways of promoting and developing public diplomacy.[85] People's experience with a nation, it appeared, was the critical determinant of their attitudes toward it and that business could play a role. As Nancy Snow, a former USIA official, forcefully said, "Public diplomacy cannot come primarily from the U.S. government because it is our President and our government officials whose images predominate in explaining U.S. public policy. Official spin has its place, but it is always is under suspicion or parsed for clues and secret codes. The primary source for America's image campaign must be drawn from the American people."[86] As expanded in the Rand Corporation report on *Public Diplomacy: How to Think About and Improve It*, responsible business, academic, research, and other nongovernmental organizations could be enlisted and motivated through a competitive bidding process.[87]

Public diplomacy efforts illustrate two communication principles: the need for a two-way symmetrical approach and support from a behavioral approach. Charlotte Beer's approach basically applied the one-way asymmetrical approach of Madison Avenue advertising. Karen Hughes's approach was another one-sided exercise in which America was speaking to the world. The government, not the broader American public, was again the main messenger to a world that is mightily suspicious of it. As Michael Holzman of *The New York Times* described it, "United States public diplomacy is neither public nor diplomatic."[88] Furthermore, such a marketing view must be distinguished from a relationship view that "sets a broader objective of cultivating better diplomatic relations through methods of listening, understanding and engagement."[89]

People's experience with the economic system is the final arbiter of whether a communication program works. As the experience with economic education programs demonstrated, the actual experience Americans have with the economic system has greater impact than the "let's give them the facts" approach of business.[90] As explained by public relations counselor Philip Lesly, formal economic education programs are doomed to failure because of the following faulty assumptions and practices: (a) the assumption that education will *take* if facts alone are exposed to the public, (b) continued insistence of business on formulating a gospel and projecting it at the audience to be swallowed whole, (c) failure to recognize the drastic change in the way influence is disseminated, (d) the assumption that the audience has the same interests and aspirations as the company, (e) use of the wrong semantics, such as the reference to "the free enterprise system," and (f) lack of clear objectives."[91] More dialogue and participation – the essence of diplomacy – are needed.

## Why communication programs fail – or succeed

Communication campaigns, such as public diplomacy to counter anti-Americanism, are typically based on the convenient assumption that negative attitudes are the result of ignorance or misunderstandings. This assumption allows communicators – typically advertising and public relations professionals – to engage in a one-way communication campaign. American business engaged in economic education programs after the Second World War to influence employee attitudes against socialism and communism. The same faith in the "let's give them the facts" approach basically underlies the U.S.'s public diplomacy campaign. The likely ineffectiveness of such programs is explained by communication theory.

In "*Some Reasons Why Information Campaigns Fail*," Herbert H. Hyman and Paul B. Sheatsley identify some of the psychological barriers that impede the free flow of ideas. Their main conclusion is that "it is naive to suppose that information always affects attitudes, or that it affects all attitudes equally."[92] Among the specific reasons are the following: (a) the problem of chronic "know-nothings" in every population who are not familiar with any particular event; (b) overlooking the importance of motivation, that audiences must be interested in our messages; (c) realizing that the facts that are presented may or may not be congenial with the attitudes of any given individual; (d) that, in accordance with the principle of selective exposure, people seek information congenial to prior attitudes; and (e) the same information is interpreted differently by different audiences. Simply increasing the flow of information, therefore, is not likely to be effective; the theory of the communications "hypodermic needle" is faulty.[93]

In answer to these obstacles, Harold Mendelson in "*Some Reasons Why Information Campaigns Can Succeed*" counsels that campaigns must carefully determine appropriate targets, themes, appeals, and media vehicles.[94] Even though the mass media may be used in a campaign, the monolithic mass must be broken down into a continuum ranging from those whose initial interest in a given subject area may be extremely high to those who literally have no interest in what may be communicated.[95]

In a campaign to reduce highway traffic accidents in which bad drivers are involved, Mendelsohn decided that his first task was to identify the audience of "bad drivers." With the cooperation of CBS, he publicized and aired "The National Drivers Test." Prior public apathy and overconfidence in their ability to operate motor vehicles correctly was overcome because drivers could judge for themselves. Attitude change could be converted into behavior by those who discovered themselves to be less well accomplished because another part of the program directed and enabled them to enroll in driver improvements programs, which were already available in their respective communities. Some 35,000 drivers actually enrolled in driver improvement programs throughout the nation following the initial telecast of the "test"; an additional 600,000 individuals were made to realize their own driving deficiencies and presumably the need to correct them in some way. An important feature of this successful program is that it represented "middle-range objectives" that can reasonably be achieved through a campaign. The use of existing support systems, for example, driving schools, adds to a campaign's effectiveness.

## Revision Questions

1. *How are diplomatic communications different from ordinary communications? What have been some key characteristics of diplomatic language?*
2. *How do people's "field of experience" and cultures affect their perception of messages?*
3. *What are the narrow and extended applications of public relations in diplomatic communications?*
4. *What are some of the best practices in the application of public relations?*

## Discussion Questions

I. *In the aftermath of the BP oil spill in the Gulf of Mexico, BP's CEO Tony Hayward made several public statements. Comment on how appropriate each of the following statement was: (1) Before a U.S. congressional committee, he said: "The explosion and fire aboard the Deepwater Horizon and the resulting oil spill in the Gulf of Mexico never should have happened, and I am deeply sorry that it did." (2) When he meet with the families of the 11 men who died, he apologized for the massive disruption and said: "There's no one who wants this over more than I do. You know, I'd like my life back." (3) "The Gulf of Mexico is a very big ocean. The amount of volume of oil and dispersant we are putting into it is tiny in relation to the total water volume." What principles of communication were applied or misapplied?*

II. *Four years after the financial crisis, the banking industry was still seeking to restore its reputation. Speaking to about 600 bankers, financial executives, lobbyists and other industry members, Irene Dorner, CEO of HSBC North America, said, "The trust in the whole of our industry has plummeted. Trust is to be earned, and it takes years to create, and a matter of seconds to destroy."[96] Do you agree with her? To what extent can the banking industry use public relations and communication tools to restore trust?*

III. *In response to media stories about deplorable working conditions and a rash of worker suicides at the Chinese factory Foxconn where Apple's iPhones are made, CEO Steve Jobs made the following public statement at a gathering at the All Things Digital conference: "Foxconn is not a sweatshop.... You go in this place and it's a factory but, my gosh, they've got restaurants and movie theatres and hospital and swimming pools. For a factory, it's pretty nice," Jobs said. How would you judge his comment?[97]*

IV. *With respect to the U.S.'s public diplomacy campaign's use of advertising techniques (see Appendix), Secretary of State Colin Powell said, "There is nothing wrong with getting someone who knows how to sell something. We are selling a product. We need someone who can rebrand U.S. foreign policy, rebrand diplomacy... Besides, she got me to buy Uncle Ben's rice."[98] Discuss whether you agree or disagree.*

# chapter 13
# global marketing communication

**Objectives**

1. Show how marketing provides insights for developing corporate responses to a variety of contemporary issues.
2. Understand how marketing's concept of standardization versus customization has relevance to an MNC's global activities.
3. Learn how the "marketing mix" can enlarge a communicator's choice of marketing appeals and media in a communication campaign.
4. Appreciate the full meaning of "brand" and how it applies not only to products and services but also to a company or nation.
5. Recognize how a company can benefit by collaborating with other players to achieve certain goals.
6. Learn how to measure the effectiveness of establishing sound relationships.

The strategies and tactics used in marketing communications are applicable to the "marketplace of ideas" as well as conventional markets where products and services are sold. Because marketing is a vital management activity that creates revenue for an organization, probably more research has been done to discover the most effective means of achieving customer sales than in any other area of communications. Marketing strategies and skills are comprehensive and include some associated with public relations and diplomatic communication. The frontiers of marketing have been expanded to include not only the marketplace of goods and services but also the arena of people's attitudes and behavior toward social issues, to which the designation of social marketing has been applied.

This chapter shows how marketing can be applied to the issues of economic development, the strengthening of nation-brands, gaining support for human rights, encouraging sustainable use of resources, and persuading people to take action to slow down global warming. Furthermore, viewing marketing as relationship building with customers provides further insight into the goal in international affairs to create long-term relationships with players.

Marketing communication applies communications to the operation of a market, which can be a physical place or a communications address where sellers and buyers set the terms for the sale of goods and services. In a competitive economy there are many sellers and buyers so that no single trader can set the price and other terms. What makes the market a powerful concept is that it is impersonal and universal. Politicians, for example, don't determine the outcomes. The market recognizes the symmetry between the buyer and seller, with each pursuing his or her own interests. As Adam Gopnik states in his review of Nicholas Phillipson's biography, *Adam Smith: An Enlightened Life*, the market allows anonymous individuals to work together.[1] Furthermore, even though each is not motivated by the will to cooperate, Adam Smith's "invisible hand" translates selfish behaviors into a socially desirable outcome. This feature is amenable to the international arena.

The dynamics of the market draws on the idea of David Hume, a contemporary of Adam Smith, that a player in the market not only "sees the self as shifty and uncertain," but also recognizes that people "find it very difficult to follow their own reasons or inclination, in opposition to that of their friends and daily companions." As Gopnik comments, "Where can you find a sympathetic community, people working in uncanny harmony, each aware of the desires of the other and responding to them with grace and reciprocal charm? The market recognizes the idea that people live in groups, and that a shared sense of well-being is essential to an individual's sense of himself."[2] The market becomes a mechanism to achieve social integration and potentially helps develop a global community. It can overcome national and regional rivalries and jealousies.

# Foundations of marketing

Although persons engaged in diplomatic communications or public relations efforts know that it is helpful to understand their audiences, the field of market research digs deeper and farther. Marketers engage in massive research to learn about consumer needs, wants, desires and concerns. In this pursuit they conduct focus group interviews, opinion surveys, motivation research, and study the mountain of details about consumer searches on the Internet and their purchases. Marketers are leaders in behavioral economics research and the use of MRIs and other instruments to understand the behavior of the brain.

## Defining marketing

Peter Drucker, the management guru, defines marketing as a "system of integrating wants, needs, and purchasing power of the consumer with the capacity and resources of production."[3] Philip Kotler, the author of the best-selling textbook in marketing, *Marketing Management: Analysis, Planning, Implementation and Control*, says, "the objective of marketing is to attract customers and satisfy their needs and wants at a profit." This purpose is reflected in Coca Cola's mission statement: "we must recognize that we and our franchisees are fundamentally in the business of servicing our customers and meeting the needs, real or perceived, of our consumers."[4] When this is done well, loyalty is created and consumers become "customers for life."[5]

Customer relations are of unquestioned strategic importance because sales are the source of revenue. The function is assigned to a company's marketing or consumer affairs department that is imbued with a corporate culture that recognizes the central importance of consumers. Everyone in a company, not only those in specialized departments, must take responsibility for customer relations in their own sphere. Marketing also applies to transactions between organizations, such as in business-to-business marketing. These transactions are not restricted to tangible products but may include concepts and services. Especially as applied to the international sphere, marketers not only sell existing products but also modify them or create new ones to meet different consumer needs or restrictions.

The international application of marketing is achieved in Sak Onvisit and John Shaw's book, *International Marketing: Analysis and Strategy*. They define international marketing as "the multinational process of planning and executing the conception, pricing, promotion, and distribution of ideas, goods, and services to create exchanges that satisfy individual and organizational objectives."[6] Their reference to the "multinational process" states that marketing strategies used abroad are not simply a repetition of identical domestic strategies. As later described, the four P's of marketing – product, price, place and promotion – must be integrated and coordinated across countries to achieve the most effective marketing mix.[7]

## Standardization versus customization of products and advertising[8]

An important indication that corporations are evolving into global organizations is their recognition of local needs and preferences in geographically dispersed markets. This advance is most evident in the marketing activities of MNCs where the strategic question of whether existing products can be standardized for every country or whether they must be customized to meet local needs and preferences.

A convenient view of consumer needs is that "buying habits are becoming increasingly homogeneous throughout the world" because everyone in the world has the same needs and desires.[9] This belief was popularized in 1983 by Theodore Levitt in his *Harvard Business Review* article "The Globalization of Markets."[10] One of his arguments is that a firm could achieve substantial economies of scale in production and marketing by supplying global markets. Another voice, Joyce Wouters, an international public relations professional, said the trick in international marketing is to find the right combination of product standardization – propelled by improvement in modern, worldwide communications – and customization, which takes into account different customer preferences and local resources and environment. Among these are differences in consumers' lifestyles, variations in worldwide market infrastructure, language diversity, and government regulation of advertising media.[11]

European experience in selling corn flakes, which we tend to consider a standard product, demonstrates the complications of standardization. Marta Baffigo, Kellogg's regulatory and public affairs manager for Europe, failed to persuade regulators to allow the American cereal maker to sell the same vitamin-fortified cereals throughout Europe. For example, Denmark did not want vitamins because it feared that cereal eaters who already take multivitamins might exceed recommended daily doses, which some experts say can damage internal organs. Netherlands officials do not believe either Vitamin D or folic acid is beneficial. Finland, however, likes more Vitamin D than other countries to help Finns compensate for sun deprivation.[12]

Other products and industries faced similar problems of standardization. Caterpillar Inc. was required to install a louder backup horn on its tractors and locate lights in different places. "The yield signs and license-plate holders on the backs of vehicles must be different, sometimes by just centimeters, from country to country."[13]

Although customer wants and needs may be converging around the globe, the means by which consumers evaluate products continues to differ substantially.[14] This was evidenced in a study comparing French and Malaysian consumers which showed that product attributes were valued differently in developed and emerging countries. Malaysians focused more on practical, tangible aspects of a product. For example, with groceries, Malaysians focused on direct quality, so they advised, "make product attractive to look at, emphasize characteristics of ingredients (e.g., nutritional content), and ease by which product can be obtained." With clothing, image appeals were less important than their functional, practical aspects.[15] Of 16 product characteristics studied, only two were deemed universal, and the others, which showed that preferences were influenced by the level of economic development.[16] Malaysian consumers had a low level of purchasing power and lower product familiarity, experience and knowledge.

Studies in other countries also demonstrate how adaptations were made to local needs and preferences. A study of consumerism in Singapore, India, Nigeria, and Kenya shows that some degree of consumer discontent exists and grows with increasing levels of development. Singaporeans rated business greed and lack of concern for customers the highest, and they desired the greatest amount of government control and intervention in the marketplace. Consumer protection, education, and information programs are recommended actions that governments can take to "emancipate their citizens."[17] The issue of GM foods has been a major obstacle. Big European grocery-store chains like France's Carrefour SA and England's J Sainsbury PLC have declared themselves "GM free" and say they will not sell the products either.[18]

In general, companies should not expect that a product sold in the home country can be marketed in similar fashion elsewhere. Poor countries may want to buy soap in smaller sizes and lower prices. Some products may not be suitable because the necessary infrastructure is absent. Nestles infant formula sold in developing countries is a notorious example: income levels were so low that women often diluted the powder with impure water. Refrigeration and adequate cooking facilities were also lacking. In another example, that of affordable washing machines, people wanted smaller and simpler ones at lower prices. Housewives in some countries wanted them on pedestals so they could wash the floor under the appliance. In Japan where many houses have thin wall, refrigerators should be as noiseless as possible.[19]

It is common for food companies to adapt to local tastes, for example, Frito-Lay experimented with the use of *tom yam*, or prawn, in its potato chip, but natives thought the flavor was inappropriate.[20] McDonald's-France added items such as a hot ham-and-cheese sandwich dubbed the Croque McDo.[21] Procter & Gamble learned to modify its household cleaners in Italy to accommodate women's habits because on the average they spend 21 hours a week on household chores other than cooking – compared with just four hours for Americans. Labor-saving convenience, therefore, is a big turnoff. A spray cleaner had to be strong enough, especially on kitchen grease, and they felt they needed different cleaners for different tasks, for example, for removing lime scale from bathroom fixtures. P&G made bottles 50% bigger because Italians clean so frequently.[22] In China, P&G marketed diapers in pink packaging associated with female babies. But many Chinese consumers shunned the product because under their country's one-child-per-family rule the preference in many families is for a son.[23]

Companies have also learned to avoid certain products and packaging. In France, Chase & Sanborn's attempt to introduce instant coffee failed because brewing real coffee is a cherished culinary delight for most French people. Instant coffee was considered a somewhat vulgar substitute."[24] In Japan, Snapple learned to avoid marketing its bottled drinks through vending machines because cans load more easily and are less fragile than glass."[25] Optional package modifications have been made in several countries; for example, mayonnaise, cheese, and mustard come in tubes in Europe; six-packs are not wanted overseas; smaller packages at lower prices are preferred; green dot packages indicating environmental standards are popular in Germany.[26]

Another aspect of international marketing is the consideration of reactions by consumers and society to the social implications of what is being sold, who is doing the selling, and the social effects of products. The inclusion of these factors is traditionally the concern of public relations, which is one of the reasons why the approach of integrated marketing communication (IMC) has been welcomed.

## Integrated marketing communication

Integrated marketing communication is a bold concept that seeks to coordinate and consolidate all of forms of communication.[27] One definition is "IMC is the concept and process of strategically managing audience-focused, channel-centered, and results-driven brand communication programs over time."[28] IMC examines the relation to the field of public relations, and how IMC and PR can be integrated in actual practice.[29]

In the extreme, advocates of IMC believe that it encompasses public relations and the evolving social media. In terms of aptitudes and skills, both marketing and public relations are part of the vocational field of promotion – findings ways to attract attention to something and persuading people to support it, be it a product, person, idea or cause. IMC's often-stated purposes are to win customers to products and services, win advocates for ideas and causes, and build an organization's brand. These purposes are shared with public relations. Public relations, however, is concerned with more than consumers. It deals with a wide range of other stakeholders such as investors, employees, community citizens, advocacy groups and government. Communications and relations with these stakeholders require a knowledge of the various fields associated with them, such as finance in investor relations, organizational behavior with employees, sociology with the community, and political science with advocacy groups and government.

What the fields of marketing and public relations have in common is an interest in media integration and synergy, media planning, and measurement. This is especially important in an era of greater technological innovation and changing audience media behavioral patterns. Nontraditional media and marketing communication channels have been proliferating, coupled with changing media consumption patterns of today's audiences. Consumers now determine which media they want to get exposed to and the amount of time they wish to devote to each medium. The view is growing that consumers now control the marketplace.

IMC involves more than communications. It is considered as a "business process" that strives for greater accountability and business success. An aspect of this orientation stems from an important feature of IMC, namely, media synergy – the realization that the combined impact of a variety of media is much greater than the sum total of their individual efforts. IMC is an audience-driven business process. Reflecting the purpose of marketing, its aim is to "strategically manage the total customer experience by under-standing customer needs, wants, desires and behaviour in the marketplace, and align the entire organisation to meet those customer requirements."[30]

## The marketing mix

One of the most useful concepts of IMC is the "marketing mix." It consists of four components: (1) product, (2) price, (3) place, and (4) promotion. The decision of what product to sell, its price, and its distribution, including the place where it is sold, are typically associated with marketing rather than public relations. Promotion, however, directly recruits public relations as one of several ways to reach audiences, for example, through publicity and emphasis on the corporate image. In addition to public relations, promotion includes advertising, direct sales, and salesmanship. IMC can therefore be viewed as integrating the functions of advertising, public relations, and other forms of communication.[31] In recent years, the social media, such as Facebook and Twitter have increasingly become a larger part of the marketing mix, endangering the past dominance of television and print advertising.

Although most advertising is product advertising, it also includes institutional (or image) advertising as well as advocacy advertising. The former focuses on the reputation of the seller. Advocacy advertising, sometimes called issues advertising, seeks to influence government policies of concern to an organization. Public relations are especially associated with image and advocacy advertising.

## Concept of product and company brand

A brand associates a particular seller with a product and attaches the attributes of the seller's "personality" with it. It may be a name, term, sign, or symbol design. The ideal brand reflects an entity's mission (essence) and how it differentiates itself from its competitors. A company brand is likened to the "corporate image," which refers to three aspects: (1) recognition – letting others become "familiar" with you; (2) favorability (assuming attitudes toward the brand are positive); and (3) association with key attributes, for example, friendliness, credibility, having historical roots, and supporting key values such as sustainability. A brand makes product differentiation possible. By distinguishing its own product from those of competitors, a company's brand attracts certain kinds of consumers and, if the impression is positive, commands a higher price.

A seller's reputation is also called the "company brand," which is an umbrella that covers all of its individual products. But as the title of an *MIT Sloan Management Review* article cautions, "Don't Confuse Reputation with Brand."[32] What the two concepts have in common is that both are intangible assets and rely on strategic communica-tions to shape people's perception. Where they differ is that a brand is *customer centric* while reputation is *company centric*. The brand focuses on what a product, service, or company has promised to its customers and what that commitment means to them. A company's reputation focuses on the "credibility and respect that an organization has among a broad set of constituencies, including employees, investors, regulators, journalists, and local communities – as well as customers."[33] It is based on more than the product it sells and includes such factors as a company's ethics, management strength, financial performance, ability to innovate, its treatment of employees, and the handling of a variety of issues, such as the environment. In short, reputation is a broader concept than brand.

The brand concept has also been applied to nations, as discussed in Chapter 7. They too are affected by the perceptions and attitudes that governments and peoples of other nations have toward them.

# Marketing as relationship building

Relationship building, which is a central concept in international relations, applies marketing to consumers. Known as consumer relationship management (CRM), its basic idea is to extend the relationship with consumers beyond simple exchanges and isolated transactions to more durable engagements.[34] In the extreme, a purely economic transaction is one in which a seller offers a product or service for sale at a given price, and the buyer either accepts or rejects the offer. If accepted, both seller and buyer are assumed to be satisfied. The law asserts that a contract has been consummated and economists proudly proclaim that the market miracle of mutual benefit has been achieved. The encounter is often anonymous and characterized by *caveat emptor* – let the buyer beware. But a relationship requires more than that.

## Aspects of relationships

The concept of a relationship has many components. The basic ones are that a long-term time perspective is taken and there is an understanding that an inherent "social contract" exists between the players wherein mutual benefit is achieved. Both undertake to understand and accept each other. This requires a willingness to disclose information about oneself and to work together. Each seeks participation by the other.

### Pre- and post-sale phases

The CRM approach requires a long-term time perspective. This extended time perspective is consistent with the economists' view that a product is not only a physical object, but represents a stream of services over time. The relationship with consumers is extended both backward to the pre-sale phase and forward to the post-sale phase. In the pre-sale phase, the seller attempts to understand consumer needs and wants through market research. This understanding is consequently used in several ways: (1) designing products and services to meet consumer needs and expectations, (2) exercising quality control, and (3) providing full and timely information for rational consumer decision making.

In the post-sale phase, the seller takes responsibility for consumer satisfaction and stands behind the product and service. The post-sale phase includes such programs as: (1) product stewardship, (2) consumer education on use of product or service, (3) a consumer complaint system, and (4) announcing product recalls when necessary. As with all relationships, all parties subscribe to a mutual understanding of the social contract between them. Basic to this implied contract is what has become a Consumer Bill of Rights. In the United States, these were pronounced by President Kennedy in1962 to include the right to safety, the right to be informed, the right to choose, and the right to be heard. Added to these are the right to redress/warranty and the expectation that a company will exercise social responsibility, such as avoiding environmental harm.

## Value-added and collaborative types[35]

Many types of relationships between sellers and buyers exist. In one model, two types of exchanges are described. One is the value-added exchange, which consists of developing a better understanding of customer needs and changing requirements. For example, Hertz has a dedicated line for preferred customers and presents them with the waiting rental car with the customer's name in lights. Another type consists of collaborative exchanges that "feature very close information, social, and process linkages, and mutual commitments made in expectation of long-run benefits."[36] For example, Pioneer HiBred created a database that contains details about each farm and its crops, what seeds were used in the past, and such background information as growing conditions that could influence subsequent decisions. The ability to know a customer is enhanced by the use of databases that show types of products they purchase, frequency of purchases, potential to purchase more products, and special requirements.

## Disclosure policies

CRM requires a company to provide consumers with adequate information to make an informed decision. Kotler refers to "informing the marketplace." A useful frame of reference is the Security & Exchange Commission's rule that sellers of securities must engage in "full & timely disclosure." Another guide is the model of two-way, symmetrical communications which would include a willingness to make adjustments to one's "product" to make it more acceptable and attractive to consumers.

Judging when information is "truthful" or "accurate" is a thorny subject and includes such considerations as the legitimate use of "puffery," deceptive advertising, and warning labels. Puffery simply means that the positive aspects of a product are emphasized or exaggerated.

Bayer is legally free to say, "the world's best aspirin" and Hush Puppies can claim, "The earth's most comfortable shoes," because it is assumed that nobody would believe some of the "puffs" anyway. But if the puffs become too specific and can be measured, an advertiser may be in trouble. For example, a federal court ruled in 2000 that Papa John could not claim "Better Ingredients, Better Pizza," after Pizza Hut, which uses the slogan "Best Pizza Under One Roof" sued the competitor. It would have been legal if Papa John had broadly claimed it was "better overall."[37]

Advertising is legally not classified as "free speech," which would allow anything to be claimed. Instead, it is considered commercial speech, which contains many restrictions. Another kind of information is the warning label, which may be relevant for drugs, tobacco, alcohol and some foods. How much information a label should provide is always a problem. For example, should a proposed label for transfats simply state the amount of transfats in a product or, in addition, recommend "daily value," or "minimum intake"?[38]

## Benefits of CRM illustrated by banks[39]

A company expects that by establishing a relationship it will gain several benefits: (1) attract sales and increase repeat sales, (2) obtain cross-over sales, for example, taking out a loan in addition to holding a deposit account, (3) encourage customers to recommend products to others, (4) have customers become less price sensitive, (5) have customers serve as ambassadors for the seller, and certainly not bad-mouth it, (6) encourage customers to support its public affairs objectives. Some of these benefits are illustrated by the application of CRM by banks.

In the early 1980s, banks began to realize the benefits of "corporate banking relationships" as a supplement to the prevailing "transaction banking." The relationship concept seeks to increase earnings by "maximizing the profitability of the total customer relationship over time rather than by seeking to extract the most profit from any individual product or transaction." As banking products proliferated, banks sought greater customer penetration to reap the benefits of "economies of scope." Customers benefit because their needs are better understood by the bank and they are assured preferred access to credit.

For the relationship strategy to work, a bank must relate it to such other elements as market segmentation and product development. To begin with, the unmet needs of the target segment must be identified. A position of relationship manager may then be created. Such a manager must possess special abilities, such as product knowledge, so cross-selling of credit, noncredit, and deposit services can be maximized. Other abilities are knowledge of the client's financial needs and the ability to help design business plans. Finally, the sales efforts must be coordinated with the delivery of services.

Relationship banking takes several years to develop and is only appropriate when a bank has a sufficient number of products to offer. Some banks therefore prefer other approaches. They may develop a limited number of advanced or low-cost products for sale to transaction-oriented customers. Or they may use a dual-marketing strategy of seeking only a limited number of banking relationships with larger customers. The relationship model is suitable for other businesses which meet such criteria as the existence of a wide scope of products and the desirability of understanding the needs of customers in depth.

As previously discussed, in all relationships a healthy relationship is measured by four results: (1) mutual satisfaction: customers are pleased with the variety, quality and price of products and services purchased; (2) trust: confidence in each others' reliability, integrity, and competence; (3) loyalty: both the seller and the customer are committed to each other and want the relationship to continue; (4) harmony: both parties are willing to face problems and conflicts in their relationship and seek to find agreement.

# Marketing applied to contemporary issues: social marketing

Traditionally, marketing is what producers do to persuade consumers to buy their products and services. Their ability to influence consumer behavior is so exceptional and highly regarded that their capability is also applied to gaining acceptance for an idea or cause. International managers see potential in using the strategies and tools of marketing to tackle issues of concern to them. Those particularly amenable to marketing are the alleviation of poverty, stimulation of economic development, debating of climate change, and promotion of sustainability. More broadly, marketing can help build relationships with stakeholders and other players whose cooperation is needed. The principles and techniques of social marketing are particularly relevant.

Social marketing – not to be confused with the use of social media in marketing – is particularly helpful in applying marketing to contemporary issues. In a sense it applies marketing principles and techniques to the "marketplace of ideas" because it is defined as advancing a social cause, idea, or behavior.[40] It began as a formal discipline in 1971 with the publication of "Social Marketing: An Approach to Planned Social Change" in the *Journal of Marketing* by marketing experts Philip Kotler and Gerald Zaltman.[41] Philip Kotler defines social marketing as "the design, implementation, and control of programs seeking to increase the acceptability of a social idea or practice in a target group(s)."[42] Simply stated, social marketing seeks to achieve specific behavioral goals for a social good. Social marketing has gained academic recognition, as illustrated by the establishment of the Stirling University and the Open University Institute for Social Marketing, directed by Professor Gerard Hastings.[43]

In contrast with "commercial marketing" where the aim is primarily "financial," the primary aim of social marketing is to promote the "social good" – encouraging people to do something that will be beneficial to others besides just themselves. Social marketing is often described as the application of standard commercial marketing practices to achieve noncommercial goals. However, another important aspect is that it has become an integrated and inclusive discipline that draws on the full range of social sciences and social policy approaches. It is useful to think of social marketing as having "two parents": a "marketing parent" involving commercial and public sector marketing approaches, and a "social parent" involving the social sciences and social policy.

Another feature of social marketing is that it crosses institutional boundaries. Although associated with social institutions, such nonprofits, it is also used by government and by business. Government may sponsor "no smoking" and "anti-litter" campaigns. One program in Australia focused on reducing suicides, which is a major killer of Australians in the prime of life, from adolescence to middle age. Forty percent more people die from suicide each year than die on roads. Although suicides are one of the greatest preventable public health and social challenges, the media has been reluctant to report on them. One suggestion was to ask the Victorian Transport Accident Commission to engage in an advertising campaign.[44]

Cause-related marketing is sometimes confused with social marketing. What the two have in common is that they may refer to nonprofit organizations. In cause-related marketing a company supports a particular program of a nonprofit for the purposes of increasing a company's sales or improving its position in the marketplace through actions. One of the more frequently used practices is the transaction-based promotion whereby a company donates a specific amount of cash or something else of value to the charity in direct proportion to sales revenue.[45]

## Improving public health and safety

Craig Lefebvre and June Flora introduced social marketing to the public health community in 1988, where it has been most widely used and explored. It has been found relevant to virtually any social change effort, social problem solving, or the marketing of social behaviors.[46] This may include asking people not to smoke in public areas, asking them to use seat belts or engage in a breast self-examination, and prompting drivers to observe speed limits. An example of such an application is the Harvard School of Public Health's national media campaign against drunk driving, spearheaded by an alliance of Harvard, Hollywood, Madison Avenue and the broadcast networks. Its goals were to change American social norms regarding drinking and driving and thereby reduce alcohol-related traffic deaths. Widespread adoption of the designated driver concept was one of the immediate objectives.

Among the business applications of social marketing are sponsorship of HIV/AIDS education programs aimed at a company's employees. Another application was by the drinks industry in Scotland which approached the Institute of Social Marketing at Stirling University to explore the suggestion that the best way to reduce the harm caused by heavy drinking was by introducing minimum pricing.[47]

## Safe drinking water

In 1995, P&G began researching methods of water treatment for use in communities facing water crises. It reasoned that many of the deaths attributed to contaminated water were preventable if a product that sanitized water was paired with effective systems of education and distribution. Although other companies were already in the water-purification business by mid-1990s, P&G decided it could address the safe drinking water crisis as a way to contribute to the UN's Millennium Development Goals, which included the goal to cut by half by 2015 the world population that currently did not have access to safe drinking water. It said the company's mission had always been "to solve the world's drinking water problems."[48]

In 1999, P&G acquired PUR Water Filtration System, a point-of-use system, from Recovery Engineering Co. (The PUR water filtration system used a combination of the floccvulant iron sulfate, an agent that causes articles suspended in water to bind and form sediment, and calcium hypochloreite, a disinfectant.) It began experimenting with a small point-of-use purifier: small sachets of flocculent-disinfectant. In 2001 a strategic partnership was created when its new Procter & Gamble Health Sciences Institute (PGHSI) partnered with the nonprofit International Council of Nurses (ICN) and CDC to improve the technology for use in developing nations. When it tested the product in Guatemala and Haiti, it found that the use of PUR sachets resulted in a 25% decline in instances of diarrhea among children younger than two.

P&G called it a social marketing breakthrough rather than a commercial initiative. Between 2003 and 2007, 85 million sachets of PUR were sold, treating 850 million liters of water. It sold the sachets at no cost, made no profit on PUR sales, and donated programmatic funding to some of the projects. With the help of various partners, PGHSI made the product available in 23 countries and with the help of its various NPO partners began purchasing and shipping it all over the globe.

Nevertheless, it was difficult to persuade people in target water crisis areas to use it, so P&G teamed up with Population Services International (PSI) and the Aquaya Institute that were both experienced in the methods of social marketing and disaster relief planning. PSI had experience in family planning and reproductive health. Its approach to social marketing was to engage private sector resources and techniques to encourage healthy behavior and make markets work for the poor.

In June 2004, P&G's PUR Purifer of Water won the International Chamber of Commerce World Business Award in support of the Millennium Development Goal. It was one of the first annual worldwide business awards to "recognize the significant role business can play in the implementation of the UN's targets for reducing poverty around the world by 2015."

## Addressing the climate change issue

When Kofi Annan, former head of the United Nation, asked Havas Worldwide to work pro bono for his campaign for Climate Justice, it did not hesitate. It felt that global warming was clearly the biggest issue facing the planet, and that Annan was engaged in the plight of those who have contributed least to the problem but who are suffering the most. Havas's CEO David Jones developed the 'tck tck tck' campaign for Climate Change.[49] The British government officially supported the campaign and asked the country's top 100 businesses and media personalities to give it their backing. Peter Mandelson said it was an excellent catalyst for galvanizing support from the business sector and leading the way toward a low-carbon economy. The combined total of 'tck tck tck' actions – measured by using the official website as an online petition – has reached more than one million, and the movement has been taken up around the world, from Oxfam's stunts in Central Park to Young & Rubicam in Brazil producing a great TV ad. Moreover, the international TV and press coverage has been remarkable.

In support of the campaign, the U.K.'s Department of Energy and Climate Change commissioned two advertisements to raise awareness of climate change. The adverts were based on the nursery rhymes Jack and Jill and Rub-ADub-Dub. One of the posters juxtaposed extracts from the nursery rhymes with prose warnings about global warning began: "Jack and Jill went up the hill to fetch a pail of water. There was none as extreme weather due to climate change had caused a drought." Beneath was written: "Extreme weather conditions such as flooding, heat waves and storms will become more frequent and intense."[50]

The ads were banned, however. The ASA – the U.K.'s independent regulator of advertising across all media – ruled that the adverts made exaggerated claims about the threat to Britain from global warming. In asserting that climate change would definitely cause flooding and drought, the adverts went beyond mainstream scientific consensus, the watchdog said. ASA noted that predictions about the impact of global warming made by the Intergovernmental Panel on Climate Change "involved uncertainties" that the adverts failed to reflect.

Friends of Science, a Calgary-based nonprofit group, ran a national radio advertising campaign which mocked the whole idea of climate change. It had mainstream environmental groups miffed. The green groups claim funding for the antiglobal-warming effort came from the oil and gas industry. One of the group's leaders, James Hoggan, chairman of the David Suzuki Foundation, lashed out at Friends of Science in a speech in Toronto, calling it one of several "industry front groups" in North America trying to create uncertainty about the existence of climate change to undermine next month's UN climate-change talks.[51]

Social marketing becomes more effective when it is supplemented by "social mechanisms." In Cambridge, Massachusetts, the Cambridge Energy Alliance performed this function with some concrete applications, such as visiting sites and encouraging the use of a new clay plaster.[52]

## Green marketing

Some companies have expressed their concern about climate change through green marketing programs. Sometimes these served as an extension of sustainability efforts. An early example of green marketing was when McDonald's announced its decision to replace its polystyrene foam packing with paper. It was the result of negotiations between Ed Rensi, president of McDonald's USA, and the Environmental Defense Fund, a public interest group. They had formed a joint task force to study the solid waste problem.[53]

Some of U.K.'s biggest retailers are addressing the huge issues around sustainability, including downstream in their supply chains and upstream into their customers' homes. Marks & Spencer's innovative plan encompasses several aspects: trials of eco-friendly factories, signing up 10,000 farms to a sustainable farming program, and reducing energy usage 35% per square foot by 2015. The British retailer expects that while a small percentage of consumers will be prepared to pay a premium for sustainable products, mainstream consumers will eventually come to expect it as standard.[54]

A poll conducted by professors at George Mason, Yale, and American University showed that respondents who were most alarmed about climate change were more than eight times more likely to express their concern through shopping for "green" products than by contacting an elected official multiple times about it.[55] The opportunity for green marketing has spawned the rise of green megabrands – such as Seventh Generation, Method and Burt's Bees in mass retail in the past decade – produced three nine-figure brands that certainly got the attention and spurred changes by their bigger competitors. Clorox Co., for example, responded by buying Burt's Bees and launching its own line of cleaning products based on natural ingredients, such as Clorox Green Works.

*Advertising Age* described some of the milestones in green marketing over the years:

- Although it was more about a wide range of environmental problems and decidedly vague on its call to action, no environmental commercial is so widely remembered as the 1971 "Keep America Beautiful" ad from the Ad Council. It is best remembered for a close-up of Iron Eyes Cody with a single tear running down his face.
- Energy Star's certification program for energy-efficient electronics from the U.S.

Environmental Protection Agency, launched in 1997, has eliminated greenhouse gases equivalent to those produced by 30 million automobiles, by the EPA's account. That is about equal to 3% of annual net emissions in the United States.

- "An Inconvenient Truth," the 2006 documentary about former Vice President Al Gore's efforts to raise awareness about global warming, was key in making climate change and greenhouse gases the focal point of environmental activity in the United States.
- Rise of the Toyota Prius may not have saved the world, but at 1 million cumulative vehicle sales the Prius became the predominant fuel-efficient hybrid vehicle since its 1997 launch and the unofficial status symbol of eco-consciousness.[56]
- The versatility of marketing is demonstrated by its wide application to both commercial and social purposes. Its concepts and tactics draw from and contribute to the larger field of communications when its aims are to convince people to take certain actions.

## Conclusions

Marketing is a major strategy that provides both general and specific solutions to a wide range of management and communications issues. Two aspects are particularly important. One is the concept of IMC which embraces such allied fields as public relations and the social media. Another is CRM which serves as a paradigm for a wide range of relationships required in international management and communications. It emphasizes the importance of moving beyond "transactions" to long-lasting and stable relationships. Among its dimensions, disclosure is a basic consideration and expresses the desirability of maximum openness by organizations.

Another kind of marketing, known as social marketing, reaches out to the applied social sciences as a means of influencing important behaviors regarding health and safety issues, economic development, safeguarding the environment, and other major global issues. Marketing should not be confined to consumer relations alone. It represents a creative, proactive attitude in dealing with a wide range of management and communication issues.

---

**Revision Questions**

1. *How can marketing contribute to effective responses to contemporary issues?*
2. *How are the concepts of "standardization vs. customization" and "marketing mix" applied to an MNC's strategies and tactics in response to contemporary issues? How might the cultural pattern of universalism versus particularism affect an MNC's choice of standardization versus customization of its products?*
3. *What is the meaning of "brand" and why is it important in company communications with other players in the international arena?*
4. *Why is the value of collaborating with others and establishing sound relationships? What are some of the dimensions of a relationship?*

## Discussion Questions

I. *Procter & Gamble wants to sell toothpaste to poor people in India. What questions should it ask itself to determine whether the plan is feasible? If P&G decides to go ahead, how would it market its toothpaste?*

II. *Starbucks faces the problem of protests that have erupted in some regions of Ethiopia where the world's best coffee is grown. Local populations are upset that Starbucks has "expropriated" their regional names by using them as trademarks for their premier Ethiopian coffees. How should Starbucks respond to these protests?*

III. *A food company wants to expand its sales of infant formula in the relatively poor country of Botswanna. What advice would you give the company?*

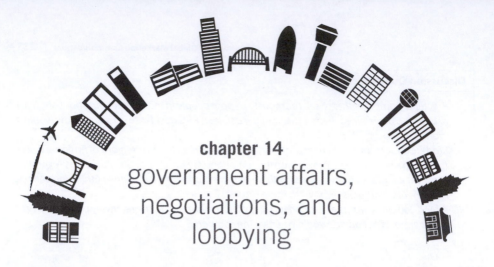

## chapter 14
# government affairs, negotiations, and lobbying

**Objectives**

1. *Understand how each of the functions of government affairs, negotiations, and lobbying can help advance your position on an issue.*
2. *Recognize the typical problems and tensions that can arise between a multinational corporation and host country governments.*
3. *Understand how government affairs in China are influenced by its political structure and cultural features.*
4. *Recognize how negotiations work and what the differences are in various countries with differing cultures.*
5. *Learn the basics of lobbying as well as what variations occur in different countries.*
6. *Recognize the special problem when lobbying in the European Union.*
7. *Learn why foreign countries lobby in the United States and what strategies they use.*

Government affairs, negotiations, and lobbying are essential tools to help global managers resolve disagreements and conflicts, enter new relationships, and advocate desired policies and decisions. The first of these tools, government affairs, is often needed when establishing business in a foreign country where many regulatory requirements must be met. The "license to operate" that companies in the United States often speak of symbolically has literal meaning in such countries as China and India.

The second tool, negotiations, is commonly seen as the core of diplomacy and often called "the ultimate form of diplomatic communication."[1] Negotiations are helpful in a variety of situations; for example, as a means of resolving crises of confrontation or smoothening relationships when new agreements are made. Lobbying, the third tool, typically a part of public affairs in the United States, pertains to planned efforts, mainly by corporations and public interest groups, to influence the policies and decisions of government, rather than the fine-tuning associated with government affairs. Lobbying is becoming more prevalent internationally, largely because extra layers of legislative and regulatory bodies, such as the EU, affect what an organization or country can do. It is a form of advocacy used by global managers to promote their employer's or client's policies and views.

## Government affairs

Government affairs deal with an organization's relations with any level of government to reach agreement on the terms of its political engagement. The term is loosely used. It may refer to all kinds of corporate political activity that mixes business with politics, and specifically include the functions of lobbying and negotiations. When broadly used, the term "public affairs" is more appropriate because it refers to an organization's broader concern for its sociopolitical environment. A survey by the Foundation for Public Affairs formally defines it as "the management function responsible for interpreting the corporation's non-commercial environment and managing the corporation's responses to that environment."[2] This definition includes interaction with advocacy groups, such as NGOs, as well as government officials and legislators.

On an international level, the term "government affairs" tends to be used. It is at the forefront when a multinational corporation (MNC) enters a host country and inevitable tensions arise as each seeks to promote its own interests. Questions about where facilities are allowed to be located, what natural resources might be used, and what taxes have to be paid are typical. In the early days of globalization, relations with host country governments were often marked by confrontations. A notable one was Chilean expropriations in 1971 of foreign companies, including International Telephone and Telegraph Co. (ITT). Another was the war-related engagements between OPEC and major foreign oil companies in 1973. By that time, however, confrontation was on the way out.[3]

Host country governments came to recognize that their national interests had to include a recognition of the benefits of internationalism and their instruments, the MNCs. Some early writers on international trade, Jack Behrman, Franklin Root, Richard D. Robinson, John Fayerweather; Raymond Vernon and Charles Kindleberger, most of whom were economists, began to add new terms to our lexicon and analytical tools. Among them were "national interests," "investment climate," "the obsolescing bargain," "political exposure and risk," "legitimacy," and "sovereignty at bay."[4]

## Differing perspectives of MNCs and host countries

From an MNC's viewpoint, the purpose of globalization is to expand markets and increase the profitability of the firm. In deciding where to invest, political risk assessments are made by a variety of consulting firms such as Business International (BI), Control risks Group, and Kroll. BI analyzes political risk in terms of whether they center on ownership or operations, whether firm-specific political risks are more relevant than general ones that apply either to the entire economy or exclusively to foreign direct investment (FDI), and what indices of political instability are most useful.[5]

The concept of the "the obsolescing bargain" became important as MNCs recognized that once they made direct investments in a country, they could not easily leave without jeopardizing their investment. As stated by Raymond Vernon, "from the moment an investment is made, the foreign investor's bargaining position begins to deteriorate on account of his investment's sunk costs which cannot be readily recovered."[6] The implications of this reversal of bargaining power were enormous:

- foreign investors would have to expect frequent renegotiations, even with friendly governments;
- their control of foreign subsidiaries would be impeded by requirements for joint ventures, management contracts, import and export quotas, and co-production agreements;
- these firms could retain ownership control and large profits only if they could renew

their competitive advantages (e.g., with new technologies and products, access to larger markets, and the value of their brands).[7]

Differences in bargaining largely depended on whether the business activity in question was extractive, market-seeking, offshore assembly, or aimed at obtaining strategic assets such as technology. For example, the bargaining power of the extractive industries is weak because resources are locked in a host country.

From a country's viewpoint, the broad thrust was to obtain the maximum benefit from company activities. Countries often complained that MNC projects did not take national interests sufficiently into consideration. In extreme cases, this perception made an MNC vulnerable to nationalization and expropriation in less-developed countries and to severe restrictions on the operations in developed ones.

Considering the different perspectives of an MNC and a host country, the difficulty of building trust is considerable. An MNC knows that a host country government has the sovereign right to raise taxes, impose other constraints on the company, or offer incentives. On the other hand, it is difficult for a government to trust a foreign company when it knows that company may shift its production and employment overseas, transfer funds abroad and thus cause problems for the balance of payments.

In the love-hate relationship between MNCs and countries, more than economics is involved. Referring to "sentiments, "Charles Kindleberger in his 1969 book, *American Business Abroad* said, "political issues of power, prestige, independence, neocolonial status, domination, and the like" played a large role.[8] In the war between the participants, bargaining strategy, which later became game theory, was an important competency. It required adaptations by NMCs to foreign cultures and their systems of social relations.

The social sciences thereby contribute to government affairs. Robert Grosse explains that a wide range of social science disciplines has turned their analytical efforts to explaining company behavior, which was previously a focus mainly of economists and management theorists.[9] Agreement grew that the distinctive aspects of international business as distinguished from a domestic one involved an interconnection between "relations with host societies" and "resource transmission."[10]

Government affairs by an MNC translate into advocacy on behalf of the firm. It pertains to relations with all levels of government – national, provincial, and local – and includes both the functions of influencing its policies and decisions pertaining to a company and monitoring what government decides. The importance and scope of government relations is determined by a country's political system and the degree of regulation of a particular industry. In a free enterprise system, government regulation is at a minimum, but industries such as the chemical and pharmaceutical face the greatest degree of regulation. In a socialistic system, government plays a larger role.

The main lesson learned from past studies of international business-government relationships is that the broader concern of multinational firms is the quest for legitimacy in international, national, and local environments. As reflected in one of the major themes of this book, an MNC must learn to relate to the interests of a wider group of stakeholders than investors. It must also consider concomitant social costs, such as diseases, human rights violations, and cultural imperialism.[11]

## Practices in China

Government affairs in China is particularly instructive because the country has the "intriguing environment" of a socialist market economy, an authoritarian political system, and a complex structure of governing, says Yi-Ru Regina Chen, who studied 25 MNCs in China.[12] Furthermore, because China has a weak legal infrastructure, people are allowed "to play a more significant role in shaping commercial activities."[13] She suggests that government affairs officials not use lawyers and avoid the term "lobbying" because it suggests their companies are losing power in their interaction with the government.

Chen states that the government is a company's most important public because an MNC must conform to government requirements about what "markets" it may enter and under what rules it must operate. Licensing – "entry" – is needed, not only nationally but for each city in which the MNC operates. An external affairs manager for an express-shipping firm, for example "assisted the MNC in expanding its business by obtaining governmental approvals to launch shops in new locations."[14] Furthermore, government is involved in separate industry sectors, such as hi-tech. Inspections by government may be a regulatory requirement. The need for government affairs was the greatest in highly regulated industries, for example, energy and oil, express-shipping, aerospace, automotive and telecommunication.[15]

### Communications advice

Chen found that 16 of the 25 MNCs she studied included government affairs managers in strategic management. The main objective of government affairs was to obtain "smoothened" relations. Such relations are particularly important in China because of its "high context" culture. By continually talking to government officials, *guanxi* – the building of interpersonal relationships – is achieved. Government officials do not mind being asked why a certain policy exists. Although they hold public meetings to explain policies, a government affairs official should not hesitate to go beyond such conferences to ask for more information. Yet, some management officials do not even understand such basics as how to make an appointment.

In meeting with a government official, a government affairs representative must understand the culture of these officials because they have their own ways of thinking and doing things. It is wise to respect them and not to be confrontational; otherwise expect to be challenged. An official's "personal situation" – the status associated with his or her office – as distinguished from a private location must also be considered. In turn, the government official will want to know more about the MNC representative. For example, is he a Japanese-Chinese person? Chen provides additional advice on how to manage such meeting. She says that "appearance is very important," for example, giving credit to the official by saying "What a smart idea," even if the idea was yours.[16]

Establishing personal relations is a delicate matter because it can lead to corruption. Both sides must know "rules of game," for example, whether an "appropriate payment" is needed. In this connection, the anti-corruption policies of MNCs are a useful impediment and the situation is improving.

## Environmental scanning

The input aspect of government affairs, environmental scanning, is a major strategic management tool, writes Chen.[17] As described above, interaction with government officials is a major source of direct information. But to keep up with policy changes, a government affairs specialist may use some of the following additional sources of information:

- Print and electronic media are an indirect information source. Some newspapers, such as the *People's Daily*, are the mouthpiece of the Communist Party of China and the central government and provide indications of emerging trends in policies and regulations. Chen warns, however, that the "media usually do not reveal potential policy changes until it is finalized."[18]
- "The Internet has increasingly become an important medium for environmental scanning because of rapid electronic-government (e-government) development and the growth of Internet users in China," states Chen. "Almost every government department or institution has official websites containing important notices, as well as information about the latest issues, policies, or regulations in development." The high rise of Internet users in China makes the "Internet the most powerful medium forming issues or public attitudes in a relatively short amount of time," as happened in the SARS crisis.[19]
- Third-party reports from consulting firms, research institutions, commercial organizations, and think tanks are another source. Reports from these sources provided useful insights of potential policy changes and directions of China's development and, in general, the ongoing trial-and-error process of political and legal reforms. A government affairs manager in an oil and gas MNC reported that third-party analyzes can let her better understand the policy or regulation from the angle of the Chinese government.[20]

Chen found that the government affairs practices of the sampled companies were professional and sophisticated, helping to empower an organization's strategic management process.[21]

# Negotiations

Among nations, "the purpose of diplomatic negotiation is to obtain the acquiescence of another state (or states) in adjustments in relations that advance national interests and address national concerns," states Charles W. Freeman, Jr. in *Arts of Power*.[22] The private sector is also concerned with relationship building. As Raymond Cohen observed, today "mediating roles are assumed not only by diplomats and other representatives of governments, but also by representatives of intergovernmental and nongovernmental organizations as well as private individuals, such as businessman Armand Hammer."[23] The desirability of negotiations is recognized when both sides in a disagreement recognize that their common interests are of greater importance than the disputes that divide them. Confrontation crises are often resolved through negotiations. They are also relevant when opportunities appear that require collaboration with others.

## The negotiating process

A precondition for negotiations is that the parties involved recognize their interdependence, that is, that each needs something that the other has or controls. The Baker-Hamilton Report recommending that the United States meet and possibly negotiate with Iran and Syria makes sense if these two countries have something to lose or gain in what happens in Iraq.[24] As long as they recognize their mutual legitimacy and right to survive, negotiators do not have to like each other; they must, however, be aware of the power each possesses. They must recognize that more can be gained through accommodation than confrontation and conflict. Often the need for negotiations is realized after a period of conflict. Negotiations, however, do not resolve basic differences that cause a conflict. Dealing with zealots and extremists that are intent on destroying you is rarely advisable.[25]

In international negotiations, the titles of the negotiators are important because each must perceive their power as equal. Based on the ascription versus achievement cultural variable, the assessment of power may be based on education and titles, or it may be based on membership in a particular social class, as in England, or caste in India. The cultural variable of *power distance*, as described in Geert Hofstede's scheme, is also in play. He defines it as the extent to which power, prestige, and wealth are distributed disproportionately among people of different social strata or classes.[26] In Japan, for example, there is a marked degree of social hierarchy, as reflected in language and the appreciation of accommodating others.[27] Where power distance is large, real power will be more centralized and perhaps concentrated in one individual. Such an individual may be frustrated in a situation when he or she faces Americans who have several negotiators in charge of specific issues.[28] Americans may unwittingly make people from countries like Japan feel uncomfortable by acting informally and playing down status distinctions. Each Japanese is very aware of his or her own position relative to others with whom he or she deals.[29]

## The communication dilemma

For negotiations to work, both parties must have information about each other's aims, expectations, and acceptable solutions. Ideally, each party seeks to uncover three kinds in information about the other: resistance point, beyond which no bargaining will take place; status quo point, which leaves conditions unchanged; and a level of aspiration, which is the agreement each prefers. Each party faces a communications dilemma about how much to reveal. The whole process is based on how much one party can find out about the other's position to assess his strength. How bad is he hurting? If he is hurting badly enough, you are going to drive a harder bargain. These information strategies vary among nations. The American strategy essentially is to find out what percentage of the asking price to offer at the start of negotiations. Arabs, on the other hand, have many asking prices. They have what they consider the "insult price," the "go-away price," the "don't-bother-me price," and "I-don't-want-to-sell price."[30]

## Pervasiveness of negotiations

Negotiation is a very common process, not only in settling disputes but also in handling all kinds of exchanges between different persons and organizations when neither has formal power or authority over the other. Its use is spreading in dealings with nations, supranational organizations, and private sector entities. Referring to nations, John S. Odell in his *Negotiating the World Economy* says, "Considering the depth and speed with which their policies penetrate each other's societies, government negotiations may cover more aspects of world society today than at any previous time."[31] News media reports range from agreements to cease hostilities, e.g, between Israel and the Palestinians or the Tamil Tigers and Sri Lanka, to agreements among nations after a World Trade Organization meeting, or between nations or world bodies like the International Monetary Fund and World Bank.

With the rising attention to global warming by nations and businesses, more agreements about exchanging carbon dioxide emissions rights will occur, and the Kyoto Accord will get renewed attention. As Odell summarizes, "Concretely, the process of international economic negotiation refers to what finance and trade ministers and diplomats as a group, joined sometimes by others, do with one another."[32]

Among private sector parties, corporations have learned the value of negotiations in dealing with interest groups. The continuing popularity of seminars for executives offered by the Program on Negotiation at the Harvard Law School attests to the importance of negotiation and negotiating skills for managers. For example, a 2007 brochure on "Dealing With an Angry Public" tells senior executives "how to restore your relationships and your image with dissatisfied customers, potential litigants and concerned stakeholder groups."[33] Previous brochures announced that negotiation techniques could also be used to defuse threatening international crises, repair intra- and intergovernmental conflicts, and address critical labor management issues.

In the commercial world, negotiations are needed for all kinds of agreements. In international marketing, for example, sales contracts, licensing agreements, joint ventures and various kinds of partnerships, agency and distribution agreements, turnkey contracts, and so forth. In *Marketing Across Cultures*, Jean-Claude Usunier and Julie Anne Lee analyze the strategies used by negotiators to get maximum payoffs. Although the focus is on specific agreements, the broader goal of negotiations is to build relationships and alliances for future cooperation.[34]

### Negotiations in China, Ethiopia, and India

Negotiations are important between a nation and MNCs. In negotiations to open an outlet at China's Great Wall, Starbucks showed the need to deal with China and to consider the value of going beyond the specifics of a particular issue. Howard Schultz, the architect of Starbucks' brand image, recognized the value of public relations when he extolled the company's role in building "the harmonious society that China is heading towards" – a reference to a Communist Party slogan coined when former president Jiang Zemin was in power. Although many locals in the Forbidden City were outraged when Starbucks opened an outlet there, nobody seemed to object when the outlet was opened at the Great Wall. Schultz makes sure that in China as elsewhere, "We have been a very forward-thinking company and very sensitive to all the environmental issues you might bring up."[35] Starbucks was also negotiating the resolution of a dispute with Ethiopian coffee producers over rights to use certain trademarks for coffee.

Pepsi Cola and Coca-Cola are involved in negotiations with both NGOs and India over the accusation that they consume excessive groundwater and allow pesticide residue from groundwater to get into locally made soda.[36] Coca-Cola asked for a meeting with an Indian environmentalist, Sunita Narain, to discuss the findings of the Centre for Science and Environment (CSE), Narain's a research and lobbying group, that soft drinks made by Coca-Cola and PepsiCo contained pesticide residues far above limits.[37] The meeting did not go well.

## International variations in negotiating styles

"Global leadership demands global skills," stated Harvard's John F. Kennedy School of Government when in 2007 it advertised a one-week program called "Mastering Negotiation: Building Sustainable Agreements."[38] The ad says, "The program addresses the challenge of negotiating across cultures, organizations, and sectors." It is important to study the different negotiating styles among countries and to recognize that negotiations among people from different cultures are more difficult than those conducted within a culture.

### The language of negotiations

For true communication to occur in negotiations, "the parties engaged must be able to draw upon matching semantic assumptions," which occurs optimally within the boundaries of a common culture or language.[39] Cultural strangers, however, cannot rely on shared experience of family, church, schooling, community, and country.[40] In discussing communication problems that arise in negotiations, Fisher and Ury recognize that misunderstandings can arise when the parties speak different languages. In Persian language, for example, the word "compromise" does not have the same positive meaning it has in English as "a midway solution both sides can live with." Persians attribute negative meanings to such statements as "her virtue was compromised" or "our integrity was compromised." Furthermore, a mediator is seen as a "meddler," someone who is barging in uninvited.[41] In such dangers of misunderstanding, Fisher and Ury suggest asking the other party to spell out carefully and clearly exactly what they mean.[42]

Language is recognized as having "particular importance as the repository of that shared common sense directing a culture's conduct of negotiation. It is the link between culturally embedded meaning and practice," says Cohen.[43] Negotiations can be considered a special case of communications because, as proposed by Lorand Szalay, communicatory interaction – the exchange of messages, or proposals – lies at the heart of negotiation.[44]

### American-style negotiations

In the widely read book, *Getting to Yes,* Roger Fisher and William Ury describe negotiations as "back-and-forth communication designed to reach an agreement when you and the other side have some interests that are shared and others that are opposed."[45] They developed a method of "principled negotiation" in their Harvard Negotiation Project, which is a method of negotiation explicitly designed to produce wise outcomes efficiently and amicably.

The Fisher-Ury approach reflects the American style of negotiations, which combines rationality and pragmatism. As noted by Stanley Hoffman, Americans believe "political issues tend, first to be fragmented into components each of which will be susceptible to expert techniques and, second, to be reduced to a set of technical problems that will be handled by instruments which are equipped to deal with material obstacles but much less so to cope with social ones."[46] Furthermore, in choosing between results and relationships, results take priority over relationships.[47] Accordingly, Fisher & Ury apply the four basic elements in their method of principled negotiation: separate the people from the problem; focus on interests, not positions; generate a variety of possibilities before deciding what to do; and insist that the results be based on some objective standard.[48] Also, develop your BATNA – the best alternative to negotiated agreement.

The problem-solving approach is easier with a partner from the same culture, say Jean-Claude Usunier and Julie Anne Lee in their *Marketing Across Cultures*.[49] Among the reasons is that the negotiators are more inclined to engage in honest communication and exchange of information. Furthermore, an integrative rather than a distributive orientation prevails and *fair play*, as used in English, is exercised. This approach assumes that the size of the "cake" can be increased if the parties adopt a cooperative attitude, whereas those with a distributive orientation assume a "zero sum game," in which a gain by one results in a loss for the other.

The management of time is another feature of negotiations. Americans prefer an efficient sequential style rather than the synchronic one practiced by Latin American cultures and to a lesser extent by those of the Japanese, Chinese, South Korean, and Singaporean. The sequential pattern places the past, present, and future in a straight line whereas the synchronic pattern tend to telescope them – overlapping the three time periods to some degree.[50] Synchronic cultures see a continuity with the past and give a higher priority to establishing durable relationships. They tend to regard appointments as modifiable.

## Japanese style: focus on relationships

In contrast to the Fisher-Ury goal of achieving a result, the Japanese emphasize the building of relationships and harmonious cooperation. Frank R. Pfetsch in his *Negotiating Political Conflicts* adds an historical dimension by referring to the dynamic tension between harmonious cooperation and a classical "warrior ethic."[51] A related cultural factor is the emphasis on group orientation rather than individualism.

In contrast to the Japanese focus on relationships, Americans are task oriented. The Japanese concept of *Ningensei* favors smooth interactions and the underplaying of conflict to the benefit of social harmony. The concept is based on Confucian philosophy, which contains these four interrelated principles:

- *jen:* a form of humanism based on active listening that translates into "empathetic interaction and caring for the feelings of negotiating associates, and seeking out the other's views, sentiments and true intentions."
- *Shu:* "emphasizes the importance of reciprocity in establishing human relationships and the cultivation of 'like-heartedness.'"
- *i:* "concerned with the welfare of the collectivity, directing human relationships to the betterment of the common good."
- *Li:* refers to the codes that lead to precise and formal manners; for example, the Japanese *meishi* ritual of exchanging business cards.[52]

Developing a relationship takes time. One study found that negotiations between Americans and Japanese take six times as long and are three times as difficult as those purely between Americans.[53] But for the Japanese, "negotiation is not an end in itself, to be treated in isolation, but simply one episode in an ongoing relationship. The implication is that short-term wisdom may be long-term folly."[54] Consequently, negotiations should be seen as continuous and not merely ad hoc endeavors, especially in the context of diplomacy. A long-term time perspective is necessary in which the quality of the relationship is of central concern.[55] Thus, written agreements that result from negotiations are simply one point in an ongoing relationship.[56] The larger concern is to establish trust that can serve as a foundation for future dealings.

Some of the attributes of a relationship can be discerned in the concept of consumer relationship management (CRM) used in marketing. As defined by Philip Kitchen and Patrick De Pelsmacker, it "stresses the importance of developing long-term win-win relationships with prospects and customers."[57] It is aimed at establishing profitable relationships with loyal customers. In CRM the seller makes a conscious effort to satisfy consumer rights and expectations, and to "know" the customers. The seller establishes collaborative exchanges that "feature very close information, social, and process linkages, and mutual commitments made in expectation of long-run benefits."[58]

The American approach to negotiations reflects the view that humans can control their environments. "Americans saw every problem, material and social alike, as amenable to an engineering or technological solution," observed Cohen.[59] In contrast, a noted Japanese political scientist, Mushakoji Kinhide, said the difference between American and Japanese negotiators derives "from a fundamental philosophical difference in views about the relationship between humans and their environment." The American *erabi* (roughly, "manipulative," can-do, or choosing) style, he argues, is grounded in the belief that "man can freely manipulate his environment for his own purposes."[60] Little attention, he says, is paid to the negotiator, that is, the need to cultivate personal ties or to special circumstances. The Japanese *awase* (roughly, "adaptive") style instead assumes that man adjusts himself to the environment.

## Study of other cultures

A study of "cultural tendencies in negotiation" paid attention to the orientations and behaviors of negotiators, as well as the effect of contextual factors. It listed ten factors:

- task orientation (high or low),
- attitudes (win-lose or win-win),
- personal styles (informal or formal),
- communications (direct or indirect),
- time sensitivity (high or low),
- emotionalism (high or low),
- agreement form (specific or general),
- agreement building (bottom up or top down),
- team organization (one leader or consensus), and
- risk-taking (high or low).[61]

The study covers five countries: Finland, India, Mexico, Turkey, and the United States. Because the Turks are highly task-oriented, their goal preference is a contract. In contrast, the Finns, like the Japanese, prefer relationship-building. In this study the United States is not depicted as extremely task-oriented; negotiators fall between the two extremes. They want to establish rapport quickly and then move to negotiating where they seek results in the form of a contract. U.S. negotiators, while usually centering their responses between the two poles, showed a greater preference for win-win results, direct communication, and consensus decision making.[62]

In India, negotiators are characterized as having the following preferences:

- formality in personal style, for example, in dress and use of titles,
- direct communication rather than indirect, more complex style,
- high time sensitivity in negotiating quickly and making a deal,
- mixed display of emotions,
- strong preference for a specific agreement with detailed clauses that attempt to provide specifically for as many future events and risk as possible,
- preference for a bottom-up approach by negotiating specifics – such as product characteristics, price, and terms of delivery – rather than starting from general principles and then proceeding to specific items, which the Finns prefer,
- split on whether the negotiating team is led by one individual possessing complete authority to decide matters or whether consensus should be sought, which is preferred by Turks,
- strongly favor a risk-taking approach, as do all other countries with the exception of the Finns.[63]

The attitude toward risk-taking is further explained by another cultural variable, uncertainty avoidance, which Hofstede defines as the extent to which people in a given society feel threatened by uncertain, ambiguous, risky or undefined situations.[64] One study shows that Americans tend to be risk takers, in contrast to the Thai, who are highly risk averse. Risk aversion tends to be greater for people who work in bureaucratic structures because negotiators must obtain top level approval for positions taken.

Time perspectives differ among cultures. Americans think of time in economic terms, as a resource not to be wasted. Thus they do not want to spend much time on "getting to know each other" and establishing rapport, as favored by Asian and Latin American cultures. These cultures are also likely to use time in a polychronic fashion, so they view with suspicion the monochronic view of time as shown in the setting of an agenda and scheduling of negotiations. The French, for example, almost never assign a finishing time for meetings and are very likely to arrive late.[65]

### Case: Nu Skin in Malaysia

The importance of developing a relationship and establishing trust was critical when Nu Skin, a U.S. company headquartered in Utah, entered the market in Malaysia. The company had been successful in negotiating market openings in more than 25 countries, but it learned bitterly that what is successful in one culture does not necessarily translate to other cultures. Malaysia's Direct Sales Act of 1993 stipulates that no sales or recruiting activity could be undertaken in Malaysia before a company's marketing plan is officially approved by the government.

Despite company policies and Malaysian laws, distributors – who were granted high independence by Nu Skin – began doing business in the country several months before the intended opening date. One local newspaper estimated that hundreds of distributors violated the rules. Despite numerous attempts to negotiate with the government, Nu Skin was denied a license to operate in the country. One reason is that the government saw the company as failing to control its distributors and, after violations were discovered, to discipline them.

Another problem later recognized by Nu Skin was its use of a local legal firm to accompany Nu Skin executives in meetings with government ministries. A public relations practitioner used by the company later suggested that using a legal firm for negotiation in Malaysia is a cultural problem in itself. "Like people in many Asian cultures, Malaysians rely on unwritten – sometimes even unspoken – agreements based on growing relationships of trust."[66] The presence of lawyers in the early stages of the relationship was perceived by the government as a sign that the company did not trust the government. Nu Skin's company representative was an inexperienced expatriate, which probably added to the problem, because, as learned in this case, it is important that a company's representative be perceived as credible by individuals in the culture. Among the lessons learned by Nu Skin, is that a company should not assume that advice from one local source is good; several sources should be consulted.[67]

# Lobbying

Lobbying is part of the larger function of advocacy. In traditional diplomacy among nations, the term advocacy describes the major task of diplomats when they argue in favor of their government's policies and views. Following the practice of lawyers, diplomats are charged with advancing the interests and viewpoints of their client, which is the government, regardless of their own opinion or evaluation of it. They urge relevant authorities of other nations either to do something or not do something that the diplomat's government wishes. They "have a professional duty to advise their government how best to advance its interests while keeping both its internal deliberations and their counsel to it in utmost confidence."[68] To succeed in advocacy, diplomats seek to persuade those with an influential interest in an issue as well as opinion leaders and the news media.

Advocacy is also a task of private sector players, but the relevant advocates and audiences and channels of reaching them are more varied and numerous. The advocates may be lawyers, public affairs and public relations professionals, marketers, and management consultants, among others, and the audiences may include all private sector entities: supranational organizations such as the UN or EU, nation-states, MNCs, NGOs, and others. The methods of persuasion include one-on-one conversations, meetings, dialogues, media relations, and lobbying.

Lobbying is a form of advocacy that seeks to influence government public policy and decisions. Interested organizations and citizens urge legislators to vote for or against laws and other matters and pressure the executive branch and its agencies and other bodies to favor certain decisions. In the United States, lobbying is specifically allowed under the First Amendment of the Constitution, which states, "Congress shall make no law... abridging the freedom of speech or of the press; or the right of the people peaceably to assemble and to petition the government for redress of grievances."

Lobbying can be direct or indirect. Direct lobbying is most prevalent, involving one-on-one contact with lawmakers or governmental officials. Suspicion of direct lobbying persists in many countries, including the United States, based on the belief that interest group representation is unequal and that public officials might be corrupted. Indirect or grassroots lobbying is pressure from the bottom up, with "folks back home" telling a legislature what they have on their minds. It is associated with activities of ordinary citizens, even though it is more often organized by powerful interest groups. It is strong in some countries, such as the United States and United Kingdom, but weak in other countries, like France. When a foreign entity employ grassroots lobbying in a country, it faces the danger of backlash by government and citizens that may resent foreign interference with domestic affairs. As stated by Charles Freeman,

> the open engagement of diplomats in the rough and tumble of their hosts' internal deliberations and policy process is likely to be counterproductive, even in societies where decision making is relatively transparent. It may evoke rebuke or xenophobic resentment as foreign interference in domestic affairs. It risks focusing attention on the interests of the diplomats' nation rather than those of the host nation. This is more likely to raise suspicion than to persuade.[69]

Indirect lobbying, often called grassroots lobbying, involves building up back-home pressure by activating natural constituencies and state/provincial or local political networks. The goal is to build on a politician's motivation to get reelected by creating public opinion favorable to one's interests and motivating the "folks back home" to communicate with their legislators and other government officials. Organizing political action committees for PAC funds and hosting political fundraisers helps. As Justin Dart, CEO of Dart Industries once quipped, "With a little money they hear you just a little better."[70]

Lobbying is not restricted to private sector players, a country's diplomats also engage in it. Beijing engaged in diplomacy in defending its "Made in China" brand, as described earlier in the Mattel and Sanlu cases. In recent years China has made strides on the lobbying front, although it avoids big lobbying and public relations firms. Its main contact is with the Washington law firm of Patton Boogs LLC.[71]

Japan's Toshiba Corp., on the other hand, conducted intensive lobbying when for almost a year in 1988, it faced the threat of a total ban of its $2.6 billion exports to the United States in retaliation for the illegal sale by one of its subsidiaries, Toshiba Machine Company, of sophisticated equipment to the Soviets which enable them to make ultra-quiet submarine propellers difficult for detection by the United States. When it discovered that congressional members were ready to follow through on a trade ban, Toshiba hired big Washington guns and launched a massive lobbying campaign, which included meetings with congressional members and letters to them by Toshiba's president, advocacy advertisements, and mobilization of grassroots efforts by its U.S. employees, suppliers, distributors, and customers.[72]

## Country variations in lobbying

### Europe

The prevalence and tolerance for lobbying by interest groups varies among countries. The Netherlands, for example, is considered a "highly organized nation," with thousands of foundations and associations representing different interests. There are also many "public law industrial organizations" and advisory councils.[73] All of these organizations are expected to express their viewpoints and engage in lobbying. In Germany pressure groups enjoy a semi-official status in that the executive branch is obligated by law to consult the various big "interest organizations" before drafting legislation.[74] Countries with an "open government culture" have a greater tolerance for lobbying.

Lobbying in Norway, compared to the United States, is very open and informal. CEOs lead company lobbying, with the public relations manager playing a crucial role.[75] The CEO speaks only to the cabinet minister, whereas the public relations manager seeks to influence the deputy minister.[76] One study found that 14 of 24 companies met regularly and informally with politicians or civil servants, "usually in the form of more or less regular dinner parties."[77] Such arrangements are fruitful for both sides: company managers can present their views and become acquainted with politicians and civil servants; politicians and civil servants get to know the companies on which their decisions have an impact and open the possibility to discuss future decisions in an informal atmosphere. These regular meetings are not seen as courting corruption because the government expects and openly encourages them.

## Japan and China

In Japan powerful pressure groups have turned large areas of public policy into virtual no-go areas. Zenchu, the Central Union of Agricultural Co-operatives farmers, with more than 9 million members, can usually obstruct any policy that damages their interests. It benefits from an electoral system that gives farming communities up to three times the voting weight of urban voters. Another group, the teachers union, has had the power to block all attempts at educational reform. The tolerance for lobbying is reflected in the existence of so-called *Zoku giin* (political tribes), which consist of Diet members who have made themselves knowledgeable about one industry or another. The industry pays for their services and provides campaign funds.[78]

In China, lobbying is a tricky affair because its political system lacks democracy. Lobbyists often do not hear about new legislation until it has already been enacted, and if they do hear, they don't know whom to lobby. For example, a law was passed in 2000 that would severely restrict the use of encryption technology affected Motorola's cellular telephones, Intel's microprocessors, and Microsoft's Outlook e-mail program. Although the law had originated with China's public-security ministry, seemingly making it a logical place to lobby, the European and Japanese companies decided to "bypass the spooks" and instead lobby the ministries of trade and economics that would be more concerned about loss of foreign business. "The Chinese weighed things up, did some sums, took account of trade talks pending in the United States, and eventually relaxed the law."[79]

Lobbying in China follows the model of a high-context culture; starting with building contacts and influence. As stated by a Chinese-born representative of British American Tobacco, "it is expected that you get to know officials and their families, have dinner at each other's homes, and remember their birthdays." Another lobbyist talked about taking the wives and children of Chinese officials to private swimming clubs. Some lobbyists also say that just being a "good corporate citizen" helps, for example, contributing to an educational foundation or flood relief. Sometimes the hiring of a government researcher makes it easier to meet with officials. As in the United States, hiring former government officials can help.

China's culture, like the Japanese, is characterized as high on power distance, reflecting Confucianism in its social structure. This doctrine holds that stability of society is based on unequal relations in which low-level people owe their superiors respect and obedience in exchange for protection and consideration. One implication for lobbying is the importance of protocol. An American business lobbyist would be considered senior enough to meet a deputy minister, but a minister would expect to see a chief executive.

## Lobbying in the European Union

The EU is a very significant player in the global arena and the target of lobbying efforts by nations, international bodies such as the WTO and special interest groups, including MNCs. Sonia Mazey reports a sharp increase in the number of interests represented in Brussels. They include various Euro-groups such as federations officially recognized by the Commission, for example, the Union of Industrial & Employees Confederation of Europe (UNICE).[80] She reports that national associations also lobby independently at the European level.

Business groups are the most important category of interests. The weaker ones are organized labor, for example, European Trade Union Confederation, (ETUC); environmental groups, for example, European Environmental Bureau (EEB); and consumer groups. Non-ETUC groups and governments have also become more active, especially Japanese and American groups, such as AMCHAM and the Economic Committee of the American Chamber of Commerce, which are among the most effective.[81] The dynamic role of the private sector and nation states can be observed as they seek to influence the outcome of decisions by the various bodies of the EU.

The key bodies of the EU that lobbyists target are the Parliament, the Commission, and, increasingly, the Council of Ministers and its President. Although the Commission, which is the executive arm of the EU, has formally lost some power, it remains the motor of the system and the priority for effective lobbyists.[82] Commercial interests – MNCs and trade associations – are the most successful lobbyists; organized labor, environmental and consumer groups are among the weaker groups. Nevertheless, NGOs have gained influence in the policy-making process. They are often part of alliances, which are recognized as a way to gain maximum influence. They have the benefit of presenting a global front or combining the influence of commercial and civil society. The Council, says Robin Pedler, remains the most opaque of the EU institutions. Despite the uncertainty as to their effectiveness, lobbyists do exert their energies on the council level and have achieved measurable results, especially when they obtained support from the council's president.[83]

### How the EU works

As in lobbying within nations and provinces, knowing how the system works is basic to all campaigns. The Commission is typically the initiator of policies, in addition to being a key player in developing and implementing them. For example, it initiated public policy on the issue of electricity liberalization. However, the electricity supply industry, through EURELECTRIC, engaged in a regulator dialogue with the Commission and managed to tone down some of the more radical ambitions of the Commission.[84]

The key time to influence policy, it is generally agreed, is during the agenda-setting stage. New forums in the EU make it easier for all players to influence agendas and, even earlier to contribute during the idea stage. The WWF, a leading NGO, was particularly successful not only in influencing the agenda for the development of the EU's environment policy but also writing the agenda for it.[85] In the "Lafarge and Global Warming" case, Lafarge entered a formal partnership with WWF, stating the importance in its objectives that the "agreement with WWF in a way that satisfies their environmental objectives as well as our business objectives."[86] A leading association, the European Round Table of Industrialists (ERT), was an important source of support for Lafarge.[87]

The balance of power among the EU institutions has shifted in recent years, resulting in a *defacto* change in the decision-making process. The power of the European Parliament (EP), for example, has increased as it engages in co-decisions with the Council of Ministers at the final stage of conciliation. One illustration is CASTER, which represents regional and local authorities concerned with the future of the steel industry. It engaged in continuous lobbying with the EP over a five-year period, which helped it to put across its case.[88] Member states are also active participants in the decisions by the Council of Ministers and, eventually, as implementers.[89]

A review of real-life cases in Pedler's *European Union Lobbying* shows the role played by various players and what factors lead to success. One highly successful case was Slovenia's campaign to avoid imposition of anti-dumping duties. The key role was played by the government of Slovenia itself, which made effective use of the media. In a second successful case, called "Safe Harbor: An Alternative Regulatory Model," the objective of several involved companies was to avoid a EU Directive on Data Protection. They formed a coalition that developed an imaginative *modus vivendi* that enabled them to transfer data freely across the Atlantic.[90] In this connection, the American Chamber of Commerce EU Committee (AmCham) helped to organize U.S. business interests in Europe. A third well-publicized case is the trans-Atlantic trade dispute by Chiquita, which joined forces with its rival, Fyffes. Frustrated by its efforts to protect its market-share by lobbying within the EU, it succeeded by using U.S. law to make the American government launch, pursue, and win a WTO dispute.[91]

## Regulation remains the key concern

Fear of regulation remains the most common stimulant to lobbying, as shown by continuing conflicts between EU and several companies.[92] For example, EU's antitrust officials suspected the British-Swedish company AstraZeneca of "misuses of governmental systems and procedures" during a recent patent-extension process. These efforts were seen as thwarting the aim of EU's antitrust officials, notably antitrust chief Mario Monti, to hold down drug prices. The EU challenged AstraZeneca's decision which asked national medical authorities to stop authorizing the marketing of an older capsule form of Losec in favor of exclusive marketing of a tablet form.[93]

Lobbying is so rampant in the EU that a battle over disclosures of government spending and lobbying is developing. Estonia and other Northern European countries, as well as the Dutch, are urging Brussel's burgeoning lobbying industry to voluntarily register and disclose their contacts with government officials and their clients.[94]

## Lobbying in NATO

Another player engaged in lobbying is the North Atlantic Treaty Organization (NATO), which has increased it lobbying since it expanded to Eastern Europe. Former Soviet republics and client states eagerly seek out influential middlemen with the necessary contacts and know-how to obtain favors and conduct events. The *Wall Street Journal* carried a profile of Sally Painter, a former official in the Clinton Commerce Department who has become one of the most prominent lobbyists specializing in NATO. She organizes conferences at NATO's annual summits and she helped in obtaining $100,000-plus donations for a gala dinner and foreign-policy conference at one of the summits, and lobbies for some clients. For example, after Latvia joined NATO in 2004, she engaged in the following activities:

- lobbied for Latvia's successful bid to host a 2006 NATO summit;
- lobbied on banking issues in the United States for the Parex Bank in Riga;
- advised AQMI Strategy Corp., a Florida company, which was looking for investment opportunities in Latvia and elsewhere;
- monitored trade issues for a Latvian steel maker; and
- lobbied Congress to allow Latvian citizens to visit the United States without visas.[95]

The range of lobbying appears to expand with the growth of supranational organizations and the problems and opportunities they represent.

Lobbying, along with government affairs are part of the broader function of corporate political activity – the mixing of business with politics. A study by three authors on this subject finds conflicting results about whether such activities lead to increased business performance. The encouraging finding is that businesses active in political activity generally receive handsome returns. But they hazard risks that can hurt performance and the methods used might offend some company stakeholders. Political activity is "transparent" and can lead to retaliation. For example, Starbucks' image and reputation and, ultimately, it sales were hurt when customers learned that it lobbied to have coffee bean roasting regarded by tax code as a form of manufacturing to obtain tax breaks. Similarly, endorsing a candidate can lead to public outcry. Overall, however, they conclude that mixing business with politics is beneficial if activities are pursued with a hint of caution.[96]

## Lobbying in the United States by Foreign Entities

American political influence is a commodity for sale to foreigners – not unlike assets in real estate, factories, and equipment – that is increasingly being sold to West European, Japanese, Indian, and other interests. As stated by *U.S. News & World Report*, "Advocates for foreign interests are shaping U.S. policy as rarely before in a high-stakes campaign of persuasion that rivals American groups' own efforts to sway their government."[97]

Traditionally, the embassies of foreign countries represented their countries' interests by tactfully meeting with U.S. administrative officials. Lobbying Congress directly was viewed as too bold and meddling in internal U.S. affairs. And even when direct lobbying was employed, grassroots lobbying was considered not only inadvisable but not feasible because of the lack of a significant U.S. constituency.

Today, embassies and foreign companies use more than diplomats to influence Congress. The expanded arsenal includes a slew of U.S. lawyers, public relations people, political and economic analysts, and management consultants. Many of these individuals are former congressmen, White House officials, cabinet members, and other government officials. They are as willing to sell their services to foreign countries and companies as to American clients. Ability to pay appears to be the only requirement for American lobbyists to accept a foreign client. If one lobbyist turns down a client for political or even personal reasons, there is always another one available and willing to oblige.

News reports about public relations, legal and other firms representing foreign nations started to appear in the late 1970s with such articles as "More Nations Seek a P-R Polish on Their U.S. Image," with PR firms representing about 50 countries around the globe.[98] The public relations objectives were several. One was foreign aid, for these countries received a total of $4.5 billion in economic, military, and credit assistance the previous year. Two other objectives were to counter President Carter's emphasis on human rights issues abroad and to affect businessmen's decisions about foreign investment.

### Criticism of public relations firms

Referring to the attitude of public relations firms that worked for governments that violate human rights, Michael McIntyre, Washington representative of the church-sponsored North American Coalition for Human rights in Korea said, "It's troubling that these U.S. companies aren't making ethical judgments about what countries they should represent."[99] In defense, public relations firms typically compare themselves with the legal profession where all sides have the right to be represented by their advocates.

For example, when Burson-Marsteller was picketed in 1978 by Amnesty International for working for Argentina's former junta, Harold Burson defended the action by saying, "Law firms handle the same clients with no moral judgments being made about them, while we [in public relations] become part of the issue."[100] An anonymous PR person is quoted as saying, "Whom you work for is a business decision, not a moral one."[101] Nevertheless, a PR firm's image can be blemished by representing the wrong clients. Carl Byoir & Associates is to this day mentioned in textbooks for having represented the Nazi regime. Because the firm promoted the German government-owned railway in the 1980s, it was accused of being a Nazi propagandist.[102] The Carl Byoir firm no longer exists.

# Conclusions

Negotiations, government affairs, and lobbying are forms of focused communications aimed at arriving at agreements and decisions. The greater formality of negotiations sharpens the nuances in language and the dangers of diplomatic communication characteristics as ambiguity. Negotiations involve an increasingly wide variety of players as the composition of the private sector grows. Because many negotiations are across cultures, knowing how they affect the negotiating styles employed in specific countries becomes critical.

As more supranational organizations, such as the EU, are given the right to make decisions that affect nations, MNCs, and other players, the need for lobbying has grown.

The inner workings of various national and supranational governments vary and must be studied to improve advocacy programs and lobbying. Opportunities also exist to apply the type of government affairs practiced in China.

This chapter complements others in Part III. Diplomatic communications is expressed in specific settings and with targeted objectives. Knowing where to draw boundary between secrecy and openness becomes part of negotiating strategy. Applying the techniques of publicity and promotion to negotiations and lobbying opens further opportunities for exerting influence. Crisis diplomacy uses negotiations and lobbying as tools to resolve disputes. Apologies can themselves become agenda items in negotiations. Those involved in diplomacy must view all the tools available to them and how they can be combined for maximum effectiveness. But they must never lose sight of the ultimate goal of diplomacy: the formation and strengthening of relationships among players.

## Revision Questions

1. Explain the similarities and differences in the functions of government affairs, negotiations, and lobbying and how they are used by an MNC to advance its position on an issue.
2. How does a country's political structure and culture affect the way these functions are exercised? Apply to specific countries.
3. What are the special problems of lobbying in the EU?
4. Why do foreign countries lobby in the United States and what strategies and tactics have they used?

## Discussion Questions

I. Under what circumstances, if any, should a foreign company engage in lobbying in the United States. Should a distinction be made between direct lobbying and grassroots lobbying?
II. A large American telecommunications company sought to introduce a new technically superior product in Latin America. It initially targeted Mexico, where a carefully scheduled day was planned. It would start with a video presentation describing the company's growth potential. Then the vice president of the group would personally give a presentation to the Mexican minister of communications. The afternoon session after a two-hour lunch was set aside for questions and answers. The team expected to conclude the deal after discussions and was scheduled to leave Mexico City in the company jet at the end of the day. Would this tight efficient plan impress the Mexican team? A French team was also competing for the contract. How would you expect it to handle its visit? Which team was likely to win the contract? Why?[103]

# part 4
# corporate governance: direction and guiding values

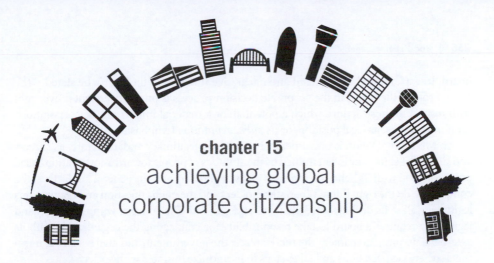

# chapter 15
# achieving global corporate citizenship

## Objectives

1. Understand the meaning and importance of corporate governance and the connection with global corporate citizenship.
2. Recognize the difference between the classical and managerial business creeds and how the latter supports the doctrine of corporate social responsibility (CSR).
3. Recognize that proclamations from supranational organizations and pressure from NGOs makes a consideration of corporate citizenship unavoidable.
4. Be able to describe the five levels of the CSR pyramid and what might be expected from multinational corporations (MNCs).
5. Understand how implied social contracts with stakeholders and other players spell out the mutual expectations between an MNC and its stakeholders.
6. Recognize the importance of social reports as a means of communicating and detailing MNC policies and actions that support corporate citizenship.

Part IV begins with the concept of global corporate citizenship. It serves as a foundation for corporate governance, which is basically a system of government required by any organization or institution.[1] It deals with such questions as what direction the organization should take, what values should guide its activities, and who its leaders should be.

Corporate governance is exercised by a corporation's board of directors, which is a corporation's highest decision-making body with ultimate power of direction and control. It is the members of the board who determine a corporation's organizational structure, appoint the chief executive officer, decide on the corporate mission, determine major policies, and establish control systems to assure that goals are achieved. In his book *Global Dimensions of Corporate Governance*, Yadong Luo says that corporate governance "specifies the rights and responsibilities among the various corporate participants" starting with board members and other top level officers.[2]

The rights of board members are explained by Peter Drucker who outlines three functions exercised by the board: (1) It is a review organ whose members counsel, advise, and deliberate with top management; (2) it has the power to remove a top management that fails to perform, and (3) it fulfills an enterprise's need for "public and community relations."[3] The latter function is especially important for the purposes of Part IV because it acknowledges that corporate governance also deals with the relationship of a multinational corporation (MNC) to the external environment – the larger society. In describing this association, General Electric's Ian H. Wilson included external relations as a concern of the board. In explaining the command and integrative function of the board, he stated, "The crucial role of the board in the corporate decision process is one of oversight – oversight with respect to those actions which a potential for a material impact on the corporation's economic results, its legal position, or its *public reputation* (emphasis added)."[4]

An MNC's reputation is instrumental in achieving legitimacy and, therefore, its success and survival. Legitimacy is determined by the attitudes of people toward a corporation based on satisfaction with its behavior. It means that stakeholders and the general public trust the company to do the right thing. When stakeholders and the public question an organization's legitimacy all of its dealings with them are undermined. The concern with reputation and legitimacy requires a board to take responsibility for connecting the organization with its external environment, namely, the marketplace, the government, and civil society. It interprets society's expectations and takes steps to harmonize business with society.

Corporate governance therefore must play a prescriptive, action-guiding, or 'normative function,'" says Thomas Donaldson, a professor at the University of Pennsylvania's Wharton School who teaches business ethics.[5] This means that corporate governance should aim to influence organizational behavior as well as understand it. It views rules, policies, and other elements of governance as instruments to guide a firm. These are ways of doing business that in essence constitute a corporation's culture. This culture reflects its values and sets the moral tone for an organization's decisions and behavior. Its culture strongly determines the "wholeness of the organization" and its reputation.

## Corporate governance embodies global corporate citizenship

Corporate governance embodies CSR in that it "refers to a broad range of principles and mechanism assuring due control of power in order to 'protect the interests of stakeholders of business entities.'"[6] Because MNCs operate globally their board of directors should accordingly aspire to global corporate citizenship.[7] The acceptance of corporate citizenship by MNCs is especially important in host countries because it helps to compensate for the inadequacies of government regulation in many developing countries that have not kept up with the growth and expansion of global markets.[8] When NGOs and other advocacy groups expose poor labor conditions, abuse of human rights, and poor environmental conditions, company reputations are undermined and made vulnerable to consumer reaction. Companies are then motivated to embrace corporate social responsibility (CSR) to enhance their acceptance by society.

In the European marketplace, companies are particularly sensitive to even a slight consumer backlash because they face a wider range of players, including national and supranational policy makers, NGOs, and media. Many of the goals of CSR in Europe, however, are incorporated in social programs that displace some of the need for CSR. Thus, as stated by Christina Keinert, "Where unions and social partnerships between employers' and employees' representatives are strong, and regulation of corporate behaviour is also tight, the question about an existence of ethical and social obligations exceeding laws and regulations is not so necessary."[9]

## Evolution of CSR to corporate citizenship

Corporate social responsibility is the most widely used term to describe how a business redefines its role and obligations to its stakeholders, surrounding communities, and the larger society. CSR starts with the recognition that the narrow view of a corporation as an economic institution whose sole obligation is to earn profits for its owners is increasingly outmoded and occasionally dysfunctional. The singular bottom line orientation on an earnings statement has been supplemented by a double or triple bottom line. The second bottom line acknowledges a responsibility to all corporate stakeholders; the third bottom line specifically recognizes responsibility for the physical environment, both locally and globally, as the issue of climate change illustrates.

Just what the obligations of CSR are, however, remains "elusive," says Keinert, and an organization's response is purely voluntary.[10] For this reason, the term "social responsiveness" is sometimes used to describe how a company deals with external demands or threats from stakeholders and activist groups. It also implies that a firm will exhibit a generally responsive posture and conceive of appropriate "response mechanisms."[11] Generally, the aim of social responsibility, as explained by Michael Hopkins in discussing economic development, is "to create higher and higher standards of living, for its stakeholders both within and outside the corporations."[12]

The broad view of business's responsibilities implied by CSR has been so deeply incorporated in corporate governance that recruitment managers are "seeking M.B.A.s who have taken courses and gained practical experience related to social and environmental responsibility."[13] One source is the Haas School of Business at Berkeley which offers courses in "Social Entrepreneurship" and "Business Strategies for Emerging Markets," and "Strategic Corporate Responsibility" which have made it attractive to incoming students.

In the international arena, the concept of global corporate citizenship (GCC) is more appropriate than CSR because it implies that an MNC recognizes its responsibilities as a member of all societies of which it is a part. As a major player, it must act in accordance with society's values and demonstrate a concern for the public interest beyond its own interest. An MNC recognizes the importance of other cultures, economic circumstances, and sociopolitical systems, as well as the kinds of global issues discussed in this book Keinert even suggests that "Corporations may thus ask themselves in the future what they could do for their country"[14] – and, we should add, for other countries where they operate.

A landmark event was the joint statement on "Global Corporate Citizenship – The Leadership Challenge for CEOs and Boards" that was signed during the World Economic Forum in New York in January 2002, by CEOs from 34 of the world's largest MNCs.[15] A statement that describes the meaning of GCC is that of ExxonMobil Corp., one of the companies that committed itself to corporate citizenship:

> We pledge to be a good corporate citizen in all the places we operate worldwide. We will maintain the highest ethical standards, comply with all applicable laws and regulations, and respect local and national cultures. We are dedicated to running safe and environmentally responsible operations.[16]

Such proclamations set a standard that MNCs must endeavor to meet, but they must support rhetoric with concrete actions.

## Reaching beyond the bottom line

The extension of CSR to global dimensions has not greatly altered its meaning. In his *Corporate Responsibility and the Shaping of Global Public Policy,* Matthew J. Hirschland embellishes CSR by saying it refers to "some basic notion of a business role in providing some 'good' to society in the forms of jobs, growth, philanthropy, law abidance, environmental stewardship, rights protections, and other expectations."[17] He also refers to "the expectations of businesses by nonstate stakeholder groups, and the strategic management of these demands by businesses that help to assure profits and enterprise sustainability."[18]

### Classical versus Managerial Business Creed

CSR is an ideological concept, as reflected in a book on *The American Business Creed* which contrasts the "classical creed" with the "managerial creed." The former is a legalistic construct, described as follows by the authors: "It is expected, and it is deemed entirely proper, that the owners of business property will see fit to employ it to their own maximum profit. Employees, customers, suppliers, and the general public are outsiders, and, in dealing with them, the firm has no responsibilities other than to seek lawful contracts and bargain most advantageous to the owners."[19] In contrast, the managerial creed states, "businesses possess very real and binding responsibilities to a wider set of stakeholders that their operations impact and are impacted by, and are not necessarily codified in law."

The managerial creed is therefore supportive of the stakeholder management approach to business.[20] Accordingly, management's mindset is that the "private office is a public trust" and requires management to mediate among the various stakeholder groups. Management believes that "the actions of individual enterprises are and should be dominated by considerations of the public interest...."

This view is compatible with GCC and Hirschland's description of CSR as the "strategic, high-quality, and comprehensive business management of stakeholder expectations."[21] He states: "Smart business leaders know that CSR is a strategic business tool for running a strong enterprise. At its core, CSR is about operating in demanding business environments. It means having in place the infrastructure and expertise for engaging and understanding a wide variety of stakeholder expectations of the company and delivering on these in ways that make sense for the business and the communities it touches. Successfully executing on this, like on other business strategic tools, will help to secure profits and assure the very sustainability of the business."[22]

Critical comments about the managerial creed come from both the right and left of the ideological spectrum. On one side, shareholders are given priority over other stakeholders in recognition that without capital a corporation would not exist. As Procter & Gamble's CEO A. G. Lafley put it, the company's first responsibility is to make money.[23] But he also acknowledged the managerial creed and the practice of stakeholder management when in 2006 he told *Wall Street Journal* columnist Alan Murray that his obligation is to P&G stakeholders, not just shareholders. "Like it or not, we are in a global economy and a global political world; honest to god, the responsibility is huge ...."[24] P&G demonstrated its global citizenship when it was one of the first companies to respond to Hurricane Katrina in the United States. It also helped victims of the tsunami that struck Asia by providing water-filtration systems to ravished area.

A corporation's version of the business creed is sometimes reflected in its mission statement. McKinsey & Company's worldwide managing director Ian Davis believes that the purpose of business should be articulated publicly in less dry terms than shareholder value by describing "business's ultimate purpose as the efficient provisions of goods and services that society wants." Profits, he says, "should not be seen as an end in themselves, but rather as a signal from society that their company is succeeding in its mission of providing something people want – and doing it in a way that uses resources efficiently relative to other possible uses." Although Davis omits mention of any obligation to stakeholders other than consumers, he does recognize they might become relevant. He does this by saying that business should endeavor to shape the debate on social issues much more consciously by "becoming much more actively involved in external debates and in the media on social issues that shape their business context."[25] The issues discussed in this book, which were selected because of their relevance to business, would therefore be considered by Davis.

## The widening endorsement of Global Corporate Citizenship

In his *Foreign Affairs* article, "Global Corporate Citizenship" (GCC)," Klaus Schwab, executive chair of the World Economic Forum, strongly endorsed this concept. He sees it as a new imperative for business that "expresses the conviction that companies not only must be engaged with their stakeholders but are themselves stakeholders alongside governments and civil society."[26] He says, "Global corporate citizenship refers to a company's role in addressing issues that have a dramatic impact on the future of the globe, such as climate change, water shortages, infectious diseases, and terrorism."[27]

GCC entails focusing on "the global space," says Schwab, "which is increasingly shaped by forces beyond the control of nation-states."[28] He sees the sphere of influence of business as having widened as state power has shrunk. Schwab's view drastically changes the role and obligations of MNCs on the global stage. Their relationship to civil society, the third pillar of society, becomes more critical. Fortunately, instead of the past pattern of targeting business, NGOs are now working with business.[29]

Another staunch proponent of GCC was the Global Public Affairs Institute (GPAI), a group of veteran corporate public affairs officers.[30] With reference to anti-American attitudes abroad, it says they can be countered when companies individually or collectively, by industry or region, supplement their business activities with CSR. Its report states, "Maybe international organizations should be more active in putting forward cultural, education, and health programs that will have an impact locally, improving people's well-being and attitudes toward what the corporation brings to the table."[31]

GCC is expressed in the foreign operations of MNCs when as guests in host countries they must convince foreign governments that their presence benefits their countries and is acceptable to their citizens. MNCs that seek only to promote their private interests without considering the impact of their activities on society are bound to jeopardize their welcome. Furthermore, CSR reflects the communal values of Chinese, Japanese, and other South Asian cultures. Communal values consider the interests of others and not only self-interest and profit-making associated with "exchange relationships."

## Integrating citizenship into decision making

GCC is an essential ingredient in business decision making. It should not just be used to plan programs to address specific social problems and opportunities. Its larger application is as a business strategy, says Boston College's Center for Corporate Citizenship, "that shapes the values underpinning a company's mission and the choices made each day by its executives, managers and employees as they engage with society."[32]

Illustrating how a routine decision can be a corporate citizenship issue is the example of frogs exported from India and Bangladesh. Sounds like ordinary commerce until one considers that "frogs eat their body weight in insects every day." This simple scientific fact means that their depletion has several undesirable consequences, such as increasing the threat of malaria and encephalitis, causing damage to food stocks, and creating the need to import or manufacture thousands of tons of insecticides annually.[33] An exporting company might want to discuss its decision with health authorities and relevant NGOs.

Another example reflecting the wide variety of decision dilemmas involved in GCC is P&G's laundry detergent plant in Barquisimeto, Venezuela. It was criticized by a Roman Catholic missionary for refusing to help supply water to a cluster of impoverished Venezuelans living in a shantytown, or barrio, less than 100 yards from the plant. The plant is surrounded by trees and shrubs, which led the missionary to say, "They have water for trees but not for people."[34] P&G director of international public government Bill Dobson explained that, although the company would like to help, it could not because the government view was that it is not an appropriate place to encourage continued development of housing on government-owned land zoned for industrial use. This explanation, however, does not serve to enhance P&G's reputation, nor does it show concern for the increasing issue of water shortages in many regions of the world.

## Widening collaboration with NGOs

Support for GCC is widening and strengthening with increasing collaboration and partnering between MNCs and NGOs, who have been major promoters of corporate citizenship. For example, effective lobbying by the World Wildlife Fund and Greenpeace, among others, led to the addition of the goal of "sustainable growth" to the EU Treaty of Amsterdam. Lobbying discussions went beyond green issues to a reiteration of the concept of CSR. NGOS and MNCs have been gradually changing their stance toward each other, as explained by Mike Kramer and John Kania in an article on "Changing the Game":

> Businesses and nonprofits must reject their old stereotypical roles. Business must abandon its defensive and cosmetic approach to social issues. After all, it is hard to win a game when the team is playing only defense. Companies must also be willing to exploit their full capabilities to find and implement solutions to social problems, even if the company had nothing to do with creating the problem. And nonprofits must be willing to share their halo by accepting business as an ally rather than as an opponent, and by welcoming its enormous capacity to solve social problems.[35]

Kramer and Kania view companies such as BP, General Electric (GE), and Nike as the new agents of CSR. Rather than simply reacting to critics who charge them with pollution or unfair labor practices, these firms proactively seek to solve some social problems.[36] In his speech at Stanford University in May 1997, Lord John Browne, BP's former CEO, raised the issue of global warming and said that BP would not wait for definitive scientific proof, but would take action merely because "the possibility cannot be discounted and is [being] taken seriously."[37] With a similar proactive attitude, GE undertook a healthcare initiative in Africa, even though it was not a primary market for the company's products. "CEO Jeffrey Immelt recognized the relevance of GE's capabilities to the problem. He knew that the local healthcare infrastructure depended not only on medicines and doctors, but on clean water, reliable energy, and state-of-the-art medical technology – all businesses in which GE had substantial expertise."[38]

In a seminar held in late June 2001 at the London Chamber of Commerce, Balfour Beatty, Cargill, DuPont, Monsanto, Nirex, and Syngenta, among others, listened to the benefits of "Getting Engaged," the first conference of its kind in the U.K. Facilitated by the Environment Council, the objective was to bring people together in constructive dialogue to implement long-term environment solutions.

Suspicion about corporate motives still lingered, however. When Denise Deegan, author of *Managing Activism*, suggested the strategy of "two-way symmetrical communications," Andy Rowell derogatorily depicted it as PR jargon for "learning as much as possible about activists and seeking to initiate two-way dialogue with them with a view to working together on an ongoing basis to reach a situation that benefits both parties."[39] In his book *Green Backlash: Global Subversion of the Environmental Movement*, Rowell advised against too much engagement.[40] He described a previous round of Shell stakeholder dialogue sessions, held in Lima, London, and Washington, as an "ineffective attempt to undermine opposition to the company's controversial plans to drill for gas in Peru's ecologically and culturally sensitive Amazon rainforest."

As WWF Program Director Francis Sullivan, who chaired the conference admitted, there "could be a future where a number of NGOs get too close to business and could be seen to be out of touch with the public." Simon Heap of Intrac, the International NGO Training and Research Center, cautioned, "That NGOs will have to interact with companies is not in doubt, how they will interact is the question."

# Developing a global CSR pyramid

GCC strategies and programs build on the categories of the CSR pyramid.[41] It consists of five levels: (1) performing the basic economic functions of providing society with goods and services and creating jobs; (2) minimizing social costs, such as pollution; (3) helping to solve social problems; (4) making social investments to strengthen society's infrastructure; and (5) improving the quality of life. Starting at its base, each step upward represents an advance in a company's acceptance of social responsibility. Corporations are urged to climb the CSR pyramid to ever higher levels.

Although the pyramid was designed for developed nations, the categories apply to developing nations. The deficits and deficiencies in their economic base, social institutions, and living conditions burden all levels of the pyramid, especially the economic functions. The needs confronting MNCs are very heavy and therefore must be carefully analyzed and judiciously selected. A fortunate development is that major opportunities exist to work collaboratively with NGOs and governments

## Performing the basic economic functions

The basic function of business is to provide consumers with the goods and services they want and to provide employment for people. This category therefore focuses on the economic relationships with consumers and employees. One of the successes of MNCs has been in customizing their products and marketing activities to the needs and preferences of consumers in different countries and regions. A problem, however, is that the established norms of business in a developed nation are not yet matched in developing nations. In the former, consumers are provided with essential product information, receive judicial handling of complaints, and benefit from other consumer-friendly policies. But in developing nations, economic transactions are more likely conducted on a very elementary basis where *caveat emptor* prevails and consumers are given little protection.

In worst case situations, developed countries have sometimes sold products deemed unsafe in their own countries to developing countries. Examples are baby pajamas treated with dangerous fire retardant and food oils containing motor oil. An MNC can gain favor by maintaining product standards and applying the norms of the host country to countries deficient in them.

With regard to jobs, an MNC fulfills this function on the most basic level by creating jobs through the globalization process. It may outsource jobs, make direct investments, and develop supply chains. An example is Motorola which located its manufacturing plants for mobile phones in developing countries. As stated in one of its social report, "We are significantly expanding our supply chain corporate responsibility program and participating in the Global e-Sustainability Initiative, in which it co-leads the organizations' supply chain initiatives."[42] Motorola established standards and helped train the employees of its suppliers.

The major problem facing job creators has been the treatment of workers in often abysmally unhealthy and unsafe workplaces. As discussed with reference to replenishing and upgrading human resources, MNCs have often been negligent and despite codes of conduct much progress remains to be made. The UN's Global Compact and conventions by the International Labor Organization are helping by directly tackling daily corporate activity and, more specifically, working conditions, job security, and basic human rights in connection with work and employment.

An encouraging sign is that an increasing number of MNCs have realized that applying CSR to developing nations is necessary to maintain a favorable reputation and moreover that it's good business. For example, Microsoft's citizenship report begins with a statement by chairman Bill Gates and CEO Steven A. Ballmer about the company's Global Citizenship Initiative. It refers to its "innovative technology, partnerships, and programs to create economic, educational, and social opportunities in local communities worldwide, and to help foster a more secure computing experience for people everywhere."[43]

Microsoft's unique contribution is said to bring the benefits of technology to millions of people in the world. Recognizing that they cannot do it alone, Gates and Ballmer mention two flagship digital inclusion programs developed by the company: Partners in Learning and Unlimited Potential – Community Technology Skills Program. In both programs, Microsoft works with governments, schools, NGOs, and community organizations. The *Financial Times* reports that Microsoft has more than 1,000 partnerships with NGOs, governments, and international organizations, such as the UN, to give skills training to disadvantages people.[44]

## Reducing social costs

The second level of CSR, the reduction of social costs, focuses on the burdens a business places on others and thereby reduces its own costs. Considering only the bottom line is no longer acceptable, as governments and NGOs demand that businesses reduce their social costs. Harm is inflicted in a variety of ways on both people and the environment.

The burden placed on workers has already been mentioned in connection with job creation, but should also include the wider range of harm to employee health and morale that affect their private lives, families, and communities.

Environmental degradation has been the main social cost of doing business. It is especially evident in the extractive industries that must search for resources in remote regions of the world or deeper into the earth and seas. The operations of Freeport McMoran in Indonesia serve as an example. After discovering some of the world's richest deposits of gold and other minerals, the company dumped almost a billion tons of mine waste directly into a jungle river of what had been "one of the world's last untouched landscapes."[45] Before it is through, it will have generated an estimated six billion tons of waste – more than twice as much earth as was excavated for the Panama Canal. The streams and the wetland inundated with waste became "unsuitable for aquatic life." At risk is the Lorentz National Park, a pristine rain forest that has been granted special status by the United Nations.

Proclamations by the UN and statements by NGOs are intended to discourage such environmental degradation which continues to erode life-sustaining eco-systems. The UN's Global Compact recognizes the need for environmental protection and urges business to undertake initiatives to promote greater environmental responsibility and encourage the development and diffusion of environmentally friendly technologies.

An encouraging sign is that MNCs and NGOs are collaborating to achieve environmental goals.[46] Too often, as noted by Salvatore Gabola, director of European public affairs at Coca-Cola, NGOs "were very much on the attack with us and other companies." Coca-Cola, along with such companies as Unilever, are working with Greenpeace to develop alternative refrigeration technology and persuade suppliers to make the switch. Coca-Cola acknowledges that Greenpeace has environmental and technical expertise that the company could use. Coca-Cola is also partnering with the World Wildlife Fund on a water conservation program to protect seven of the world's most crucial freshwater river basins.[47]

## Social problem-solving

Social problems abound in developing nations as a consequence of depressed economies and insufficient community resources. The problems center on the well-being of employees, their families, neighborhoods, and communities. Individuals may be afflicted with alcoholism and drug abuse and other health issues. Families may face problems of inadequate housing and need for child- and elder-care. Neighborhoods and communities face problems of crime, adequate transportation, adequate education.

Social problems have traditionally been the responsibility of government. In former socialistic and communist countries or countries that use taxes to finance welfare programs, governments assume major responsibility. Citizens in these countries often prefer a large government role because every citizen, in theory, has some form of control over it. One of the main functions of charitable and other nonprofit organizations in developed nations is to assume a major role in social problem-solving.

In all nations, governments are increasingly unable adequately to address rising social problems while nonprofit organizations are too few and lack funds. As the number and kinds of social problems grow with increasing economic development and urbanization, all three institutions comprising the triangle of society realize that joint efforts are required. As recognized by Alan R. Andreasen, professor of marketing at Georgetown University, "in order to survive, nonprofit organizations must develop explicit ties with for-profit corporations" and not just hope to become the lucky beneficiaries of a company's independent cause-related marketing campaign.[48] The division of labor among them is determined by deciding what aspect of a problem each is best equipped to handle and competent to do. Public/private partnership has become more common.

An example of a partnership is Anglo American's partnership with loveLife in South Africa to combat HIV/AIDS. About 30,000 of the company's workers in South Africa are HIV positive, representing more than a quarter of the workforce in some business units. Anglo-American became one of the first companies to recognize the potential threat of HIV/AIDS both to their business and to society. Anglo-American provided three years of funding to loveLife because of its focus upon youths, of whom those under 20 account for about 50% of HIV infections. LoveLife was able to set up adolescent-friendly clinics in the six provinces where Anglo-American has business units. Together with further financial support from the Kaiser and Mandela Foundations, a broader, comprehensive approach was devised, including identification of the delivery infrastructure required to support the rollout of Anti-Retroviral Treatment and help to their partners for improving the standard of care provided in clinics throughout the national public health system.[49]

## Strategic philanthropy

Philanthropy is a traditional way MNCs have contributed to social problem-solving. For example, the Bill and Melinda Gates Foundation chose malaria, which kills an estimated one million people a year, as a priority. It gave $40 million in July 2000 to the London School of Hygiene and Tropical Medicine whose objectives include the training of malaria fighters in Africa, where malaria is especially deadly and malaria experts are in short supply. It will also craft an interdisciplinary program aimed at a better understanding of "cultural barriers" to treatments and preventative actions against malaria so that the new vaccines aren't scotched by social resistance arising from local beliefs.[50] Microsoft benefits from these philanthropic acts by enhancing its reputation, as shown in the eighth-annual Harris Interactive/*The Wall Street Journal* survey. It ranked Microsoft as the world's best corporation, beating Johnson & Johnson which was in first place for seven consecutive years, but fell to 18th in the *Forbes* list of the world's most reputable companies.[51] The first place was held by BMW, followed by Sony.

Several other companies have been active in philanthropic activities. In 1987 Merck started to donate Mactizan, a drug used to treat 30 million people every year for river blindness across sub-Saharan Africa.[52] The company also donated $100 million worth of vaccines against such scourges as hepatitis to the Global alliance for Vaccines and Immunisation, and it committed $50 million to Botswana, working with the Bill and Melinda Gates Foundation, to build a better healthcare delivery system to combat AIDS. The reduction of prices for antii-retroviral drugs for treating HIV/AIDS can also be regarded as an example of pro-poor corporate responsibility. Rhys Jenkins, however, believes this action has been driven "not by CSR but by the growth of competition from generic products, increased funds made available by donors, and the companies' loss of public support in the face of pressure from NGOs."[53]

Another example of corporate philanthropy is ExxonMobil's distribution of mosquito nets in Tanzania, an activity that is unrelated to its core business activities.[54]

Some companies' existing infrastructures can contribute to philanthropic pursuits. For example, "Condoms on Coke trucks" is an idea that uses Coca-Cola's massive distribution system and marketing muscle to fight AIDS. Working in partnership with UNAIDS, the UN agency that coordinates the global AIDS battle, Coke trucks could deliver AIDS-prevention fliers and possibly condoms.[55]

In choosing which social problems to tackle, Michael Porter argues that a company should contribute to those causes that also advance its own interests by improving its competitive position.[56] When "doing good," a company should consider its core business, competencies, and strategies. He restates this belief as follows: "Corporate philanthropy – or CSR – is becoming an ever more important field for business. Today's companies ought to invest in corporate social responsibility, as part of their business strategy to become more competitive."[57] By itself, however, "Philanthropy does little or nothing to help companies make profits, while all CSR activities are linked to improving a company's bottom line."[58] CSR, he states, is sustainable while philanthropy is not, for "CSR actions become part and parcel of the way in which a company carries out its business."[59] He sees philanthropy as having an inclination to be whimsical, often depending on the whims of the company directors at a particular time.

In a rare application of philanthropy, Mohammed Ibrahim, a telecom billionaire, made honest government a goal of his philanthropy. He was concerned about the lack of good governance in Africa, recognizing that it has impeded investment and economic development. He backed up his concern through the Mo Abrahim Foundation, begun in 2006, rather than through his cell phone company, Celtel.

The foundation administers the Ibrahim Prize for Achievement in African Leadership, which offers $5 million over 10 years and then $200,000 annually for life. "Heads of state or government become eligible for the prize if they were democratically elected, served within their constitutional term limits, demonstrated 'excellence' in office and peacefully transferred power within the past three years."[60] The foundation created the Abrahim Index of African Governance to choose candidates. The index ranks each of Africa's 54 nations by 86 indicators by their "effectiveness in delivering safety, rule of law, civil rights, economic opportunity and human development." In 2011 Mauritius topped the list, but he hopes Sudan, where he was born, will be influenced.

## Making social investments

Social investments refer mainly to infrastructure projects such as roads, ports, parks, civic centers, and other major public facilities. Infrastructure projects are capital intensive and developing nations have been unable to find funds for them. MNCs that enter countries with weak infrastructure must therefore expect to be burdened with infrastructure development. For example, firms wanting to set up in Nigeria sometimes faced a problem known locally as "BYOI" – Bring Your Own Infrastructure. Because of an absence of reliable power or water suppliers, Cadbury Nigeria had to generate eight megawatts of its own electricity and drill 2,500 feet down to obtain the 70,000 gallons of water an hour it needs for its Lagos food-processing plant.[61]

Companies in extractive industries are familiar with the need to build infrastructure to enable them to operate in remote and undeveloped areas. Infrastructure may include housing, educational and health facilities as well as recreational activities. In addition to physical structures social investments may be made in human capital through training and education programs. Ernst & Young, a leader in social accounting, includes these and other programs in its Corporate Social Investment strategy statement.[62]

An MNC should look for opportunities to provide added benefits to people in countries where it does business. For example, beverage companies and other industries dependent on large supplies of water can concentrate on helping to preserve and improve the water supply in water-deprived areas. Some companies, such as Unilever, provide enriched training programs and scholarships for children of employees.

In a speech "Who Cares Wins – The Convergence of Global Corporate Citizenship and Financial Markets" at the Investment Management Institute Conference, Gavin Power noted that financial institutions were launching scores of CSR initiatives relating to climate change, conflict situations, labor standards, disease, or general poverty. He specifically referred to a July 2004 initiative called "Who Cares Wins" which was signed by CEOs of 20 mainstream global investment houses, including Goldman Sachs, Credit Suisse, UBS, ABN Amro, and Morgan Stanley. The initiative calls on endorsers to actively integrate environmental, social, and governance criteria into research and investment processes. Power also mentions the launching of the Principles for Responsible Investment project which is intended to integrate environmental, social, and governance criteria into research and investment processes.[63]

## Quality of life

The ultimate social goal of economic activity and of globalization is improvement in people's quality of life. In developing countries, this is done by achieving the goals of economic growth, reducing social costs, solving social problems, and making social investments. The attainment of human rights such as freedom of expression and privacy would also enhance the quality of life. In developed nations, this apex in the CSR pyramid has the higher purpose of helping employees fulfill their aspirations as human beings.

Enriching the lives of employees, however, is a utopian goal that has largely been abandoned by companies since the heyday of the human relations movement in industry in the late 1920s. At the time it was postulated that a business had two goals: to earn a profit and to provide job satisfaction for its employees. The two goals were related because a causal relationship was assumed between high job satisfaction and high productivity – and, therefore, profits. Furthermore, when employee retention is desired, job satisfaction helps. Whether in developing or developed nations, the goal of improving the quality of life of people is a philosophical one. As discussed in the next chapter, the fulfillment of this goal relates to how a better balance is achieved between the economy and society.

# Drafting a global social contract

In addressing the relationship of the citizen to the state, Thomas Hobbes, John Locke, and Henri Rousseau applied the idea of a social contract. In his book, *Leviathan*, Hobbes describes life at some distant past when human beings living in a "state of nature" had no government and no laws. To escape their "solitary, nasty, poor, brutish and short" lives, people voluntarily gave up authority to a ruler by forming a social contract.[64]

This idea sounded appealing to some advocates of CSR because they saw a parallel in the relationship between business and groups in society. One of them is Ian Davis, who sees the relationship between big business and society as implying a "social contract."[65] Business, he said, must acknowledge "that in return for the ability to function it is subject to rules and constraints."[66] Specifically, business should recognize that an implicit "contract" exists with various stakeholders and actively seek to manage these relationships. Business should do so through: "more transparent reporting; shifts in R&D or asset reorganisation to capture expected future opportunities or to shed perceived liabilities; changes in regulatory approach; and, at an industry level, development and deployment of voluntary standards of behaviour."[67] Davis cites the example of GE's announcement that it is doubling its research spending on environmentally friendlier technologies.

A social contract is implied in an MNC's relationship to a host country. The basic agreement would specify both what a country and an MNC might expect. For example a country might expect an MNC to sell products and services suitable to the needs, infrastructure, and other conditions of a country.[68] In return an MNC might expect permission to make direct investments and to sell its products and services.[69]

Along similar lines George Stiglitz applies the social contract to his discussion of how to make globalization work. He stated that a new global social contract must be agreed upon between developed and less developed countries and listed ten ingredients which include the following:

- a commitment by developed countries to a fairer trade regime that would actually promote development;
- a new approach to intellectual property and promoting of research that would recognize the importance of developing countries' access to knowledge, the necessity of the availability of lifesaving medicines at affordable prices, and the rights of developing counties to have their traditional knowledge protected;
- an agreement by the developed countries to compensate developing countries for preserving biodiversity and contributing to global warming through carbon sequestration;
- a recognition by both developed and developing countries that global warming represents a real threat to the planet;
- a commitment by the developed countries to pay the developing countries fairly for their natural resources and avoiding environmental degradation.[70]

These terms, and others, such as the extension of the agreement for debt forgiveness, are frequently brought up and discussed at trade and other international meetings. The last two ingredients were the subject of the 2007 Bali conference on climate change.[71]

## Social contracts with stakeholders

Organizational theorists have applied the social contract to the relationship of an MNC with specific stakeholders. James E. Post, Lee E. Preston, and Sybille Sachs view stakeholders as members of a company's "extended organization."[72] Although not under the authority of a company's management as employees are, all stakeholders can affect an organization because they are in a position to help or hurt it. Thomas Kochan, a labor specialist, says that the social contract can be applied to separate stakeholder groups that have "voluntary relationships, with their companies, one mutually agreed upon and that over time has processes and procedures that ensure continued 'consent of the governed.'"[73]

Companies can draft social contracts for all of their stakeholders, with public relations and public affairs departments exercising oversight over them. For example, Edmund M. Burke, founder of the Boston College Center for Corporate Citizenship, applied the social contract concept to community relations. Preferring to call it the "psychological contract," he defines it as "the implicit expectations that companies and communities have for each other."[74] He sees people in communities, including companies, jointly engaged in building and supporting institutions that define a "good" community.[75] BP's John Browne expressed a clear philosophy and strategy about community relations, saying that for BP to thrive so must the communities in which it does business. "Browne has insisted that the economic and social health of the villages, towns, and cities in which BP does business be a matter of central concern to the company's board of directors."[76] The fortnightly *Business & Public Affairs* newsletter reported in 1990 that a small, but growing number of U.S. companies were developing international community relations programs. Among the companies were IBM, Digital Equipment, Exxon Chemical, Ford, GTE, Merck, and Polaroid.[77]

Social contracts with employees, whether formal or implied, are commonplace. A corporation would likely expect productivity and cooperation from them, and in return employees would expect good pay, reasonable working hours, and a safe work environment. Companies in most developed nations have dropped lifetime employment as an employee expectation, but sometimes offer the alternative of guaranteeing employability through company training programs. These companies really seem to be saying, "We'll use you as long as we need you."[78] At least, many companies are viewing employees as an asset to be developed, rather than a cost to be cut. This view is expressed by Cliff Hakim, author of *We Are All Self-Employed*, who states, "The bottom line is that individual development and organizational growth are no longer separable, if we want organizational renewal."[79]

## Suspicion lingers

Despite concrete accomplishments in global corporate citizenship, many critics remain critical. Some say CSR efforts are not the answer because they are too limited and too defensive sounding. Company references to the triple bottom line are seen "as a means to avoid NGO and reputational flak, and to mitigate the rougher edges and consequences of capitalism."[80] For example, a member of the GPAI suspects that constructive CSR programs by the pharmaceutical industry to reduce drug prices in developing nations, provide drug access programs and build an infrastructure for physician training are still viewed cynically. Corporate philanthropy has helped in addressing health problems, but some "wonder whether we use philanthropy to advance our competitive edge."[81]

Development NGOs have for the most part been extremely critical of corporate efforts, including both normal operations and CSR efforts. They say that it became evident by the late 1990s that the market alone was not sufficient to bring about development because firms may not "make the long-term investments necessary to promote human development or benefit the poor." With regard to job creation, these development experts say that companies do not invest in enough training which would help develop employee capabilities because the returns are not immediate.... "[82] They say that to tackle global poverty would require a much more positive commitment, for example, to discriminate in favor of the poor in employment, or to provide goods to the poor at discounted prices.[83] One study by a development expert concluded that CSR as currently practiced is unlikely to play a significant role in reducing poverty in developing countries, despite the enthusiasm of many development agencies.

GCC is the dominant response by MNCs to the growing expectation of society that they take responsibility for the negative consequences of their activities on stakeholders and the environment. The question has been raised, however, whether this accepted responsibility and the often accompanying political activities by business is compatible with the idea of democratic accountability. In the absence of legal governance, the legitimacy gap for MNCs widens.

In their chapter on "The Future of Global Corporate Citizenship; Toward a New Theory of the Firm as a Political Actor," Gluido Palazzo and Andreas Georg Scherer say that the debate on corporate citizenship "has to develop effective and legitimate concepts for the 'non-electoral democratic accountability' and the 'public control over public decision-making.'"[84] It helps when there is more promised engagement and collaboration by corporations with civil society actors and transnational or national political bodies. But the challenge to the democratic ideal of civic sovereignty and representativeness remains. For this reason, they see the need for a thorough evaluation of emerging global problems, fresh answers, and new theoretical concepts.


## Conclusions

MNCs extend the widely recognized concept of CSR to global corporate citizenship. Managers have been integrating CSR into everyday global decision-making because other international players expect them to do so. A positive development is that NGOs are often willing to cooperate with MNCs to achieve social goals.

The five levels in the "pyramid of social responsibility" have relevance in the international arena, as the various illustrations prove. For example, the first level of performing the basic economic function shows how MNCs are contributing to the economies of developing nations; the second function, reducing social costs, is applied to the emerging issue of climate change; and the third function, helping to solve social problems, discusses how corporate philanthropy helps solve problems of malaria. To check on these and other areas of performance, social reporting is increasingly used, along with more stringent compliance requirements.

The concept of stakeholder management has been applied globally, as illustrated by Wal-Mart, the world's largest company by revenue, which was $421,8 billion in 2011. It created a new post of "senior director of stakeholder engagement." Said a spokesperson, "We're trying to centralize our [social responsibility] efforts."[85]

# Appendix: social reporting and compliance efforts

## Social reporting

Social contracts provide a reference point for evaluating how well a corporation exercises its CSR. Many corporations publish periodic (usually annual) social reports that summarize their performance – mostly accomplishments, but sometimes also shortcomings – in various areas of CSR. A social report – also variously called a public report, sustainability report, or corporate citizenship report – is to inform stakeholders and the general public about a company's social performance in selected areas, such as its handling of environmental issues, health and safety, community investment and philanthropy, governance, workplace issues, and ethics.

A comparison of such reports with a corporation's various social contracts can determine how well objectives are met. Because the "gap between what companies do and what they say remains wide," the opportunity can be seized for corporations "to be open and honest with themselves, their employees, their customers, and the community about what they are doing."[86] Hirschland reported that in 2006 over 700 organizations employed formal global reporting initiative (GRI) disclosure guidelines.[87]

Social reports are often a part of financial annual reports. An example is the Annual Report 2006 of Teijin Limited which includes a four-page section on Corporate Social Responsibility. It begins with the statement:

> The Teijin Group recognizes that fulfilling its responsibilities as a global corporate citizen is essential to ensuring sustainable growth. In line with our conviction that corporate growth and expansion depends on social development, we have established extensive programs for addressing environmental problems and contributing to the communities in which we operate.[88]

Its environmental preservation programs states two goals: lowering emissions of waste, carbon dioxide ($CO_2$), and other substances that negatively impact the environment, and developing new technologies and products to improve the environment. Among its community activities, it mentions running a children's soccer school led by veterans of the company's Tokuyama factory soccer club.

Social reports can be sent to important audiences to demonstrate the value of U.S. businesses to individual citizens worldwide and thereby help build trust. The reports describe company contributions such as product production and innovation, science and learning, employment, social investments.[89] A social report can be a valuable document for use in diplomacy with nation-states, NGOs, and stakeholders. They can also be used in various dialogue sessions, such as those convened by the UN Global Compact. The more than 3,000 companies in about 120 countries that have signed on to the compact are required to report their progress in ten core principles to guide business behavior in areas such as human rights, the environment, labor practices, and corruption.[90]

The Coalition for Environmentally Responsible Economies (CERES) provides one of the most thorough and well-respected environmental disclosure programs in the United States. CERES is a ten-year partnership between large investors and public pension trustees, environmental groups, labor unions, and corporations.[91] It has formulated the CERES principles, which include such goals as protection of the biosphere, sustainable use of natural resources, reduction of disposal of wastes and energy conservation. By endorsing the CERES Principles, companies "actively commit to an ongoing process of continuous improvement, dialogue and comprehensive, systematic public reporting."[92]

Another guideline for social reporting is Social Accountability International's (SAI) Social Accountability 8000 (SA8000) workplace labor standard and verification system.[93] SAI is an offshoot of the now defunct NGO, the Council on Economic Priorities, which is one of the true pioneers of CSR. Its reputation was built on assessing company performance on a range of social and environmental issues and producing the best-selling book *Shopping for a Better World*. Hirshland calls it "one of the most widely respected multistakeholder-crafted, voluntary labor standard-setting systems and enforcement organizations."[94] The SA8000 system accomplishes its task by obtaining participation by all key sectors, including workers and trade unions, companies, socially responsible investors, nongovernmental organizations and government."[95] Each individual manufacturing facility is required to undergo certification.

## Compliance

Compliance with implicit social contracts or explicit codes of conduct can be monitored and violations identified so that corrective action can be taken. The auditing of labor conditions, especially in low labor cost nations like China, has received the most attention and consequently mushroomed into a multimillion-dollar industry. Various global auditing agencies such as Cal Safety Compliance, SGS of Switzerland, and Bureau Veritas of France check on a variety of corporate codes of conduct.

Sometimes widespread deceptive practices, such as hiding noncompliance, are found, as when conditions at Chinese suppliers were audited. The good-sounding firm Shanghai Corporate Responsibility Management & Consulting Co helped in the deception by advising companies facing an audit how to fool the auditors by, for example, creating fake but authentic-looking records and coaching managers and employees. A fabric factory in Guangzhou, Duangdong, was given the following advice in the event of an outside audit of conditions: "First notify underage trainees, underage full-time workers, and workers without identification to leave the manufacturing workshop through the back door. Order them not to loiter near the dormitory area."[96]

The need for compliance with codes of conduct is increasingly recognized by companies. Nike uses compliance reports to help reform its suppliers, says Hannah Jones, Nike's Inc's vice-president for corporate responsibility. But the success of compliance is doubted by some. Auret van Heerden, chief executive of the Fair Labor Association, a coalition of 20 apparel and sporting goods makers and retailers, questions whether goals can be met in a nation that lacks real unions and a meaningful rule of law. The association released its own study in November 2005 based on unannounced audits of 88 of its members' supplier factories in 18 countries; it found an average of 18 violations per factory, including excessive hours, underpayment of wages, health and safety problems, and worker harassment.[97]

Monitoring efforts go beyond concern for the workforce. Wal-Mart, for example, started environmental audits of its factories in China after several of its suppliers turned out to be using carcinogens in their clothing dyes. Companies are learning to adopt industry standards, which can be pointed to when things go wrong. After China's State Environmental Protection Administration (SEPA) released a study listing 2,700 companies that violated water regulations, the 33 MNCs on the list were sure to examine their environmental record. Because of China's attention to pollution, company programs that address the issue are likely to earn a lot of publicity and goodwill.[98]

### Revision Questions

1. What is the meaning and significance of corporate governance in an MNC?
2. What is the underlying managerial ideology of corporate citizenship and what is its connection with corporate governance?
3. How do proclamations of supranational organizations and pressure from NGOs influence the acceptance of global corporate citizenship? What are some of these proclamations?
4. Name and describe the five levels of the CSR pyramid and explain what responsibilities an MNC should subscribe to.
5. Explain how social contracts with various stakeholders can describe the nature of an MNC's relationship with specific stakeholders.
6. What benefits can an MNC expect when it engages in social reporting?

### Discussion Questions

I. Discuss whether CSR is a realistic goal for MNCs facing the pressures of a world economy dominated by the free market system? Are the expectations for an MNC different from those of a domestic corporation? How far up the global CSR pyramid should an MNC strive to reach?

II. Reflecting on the key issues facing MNCs, choose one which most invites the application of CSR? How does an MNC benefit by including considerations of CSR in its decision making?

III. Isn't it unrealistic to expect an MNC to embrace the managerial creed? Isn't a corporation legally bound to maximize profits for its stockholders?

IV. Discuss whether P&G made the right decision at its Barquisimeto, Venezuela, plant when it refused to supply water to squatters in an adjacent shantytown, even though water was used for landscaping?

V. Do you agree with the view that McDonald's should climb beyond the second level of the global CSR pyramid, namely, minimizing social costs. How would you argue that it should go further?

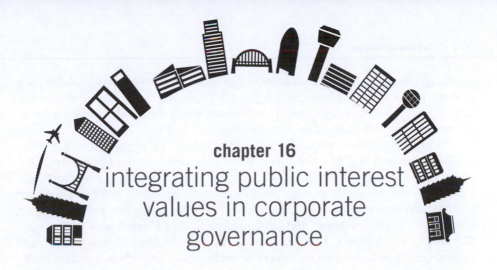

## chapter 16
# integrating public interest values in corporate governance

**Objectives**

1. Be able to argue that the public interest should be a concern of a corporation's board of directors.
2. Be able to defend the argument that the economy should be a subset of society, and not the other way around.
3. Understand the arguments by Frederick Hayek and Milton Friedman, two conservative economists, to accept restraints on the "free market system."
4. Recognize the pressures multinational corporations face to reform corporate governance, even if they are not inclined to do so.
5. Know the arguments for encouraging CEOs to become more involved in public policy issues.
6. Become familiar with some of the ways CEOs can play a larger role as "corporate statesmen."

Pressure from stakeholders, international players, and public opinion is steadily convincing multinational corporations (MNCs) that they must integrate public interest values in their corporate governance. Much of it is done through the normal operation of the free market system. The elegance of the model of marketplace is that when the supply curve intersects the demand curve an equilibrium price is established that reflects mutual satisfaction by both sellers and buyers. Similarly, when management and labor meet over a table in the process of collective bargaining, the final agreement represents mutual satisfaction between the two parties. We cannot, however, claim that the public interest is equally served. In labor negotiations, union members may be satisfied with higher wages and managements in monopolistic industries may not worry about higher labor costs when they can easily raise prices; it is the consumers who suffer.

## Grappling with the public interest

The *public interest* is often invoked in political discourse and used by politicians to cloak more parochial and self-seeking interests. Most advocacy groups claim that their particular solutions to problems of the environment, women's rights, and economic development serve the public interest. Businesspeople and their lobbyists likewise take positions on policy issues that they claim to be in the public interest. The media will often judge the position of debaters on controversial political or social issues on the basis of their criteria of the public interest. A journal, called *The Public Interest,* specialized in publishing lively views on contemporary issues, which their authors defended with reference to various social and political theories.

It is in the legal arena where the *public interest* has been applied to disputes that explicitly define the rights and responsibilities of business. In the United States, the 1876 case of Munn v. State of Illinois, the Supreme Court ruled that because a particular privately owned grain warehouse was in the nature of a monopoly and the community had no choice but to use the service, the business had become akin to a "public franchise" clothed with a "public interest" and subject to "public duties" regulatable by the State.[1] The 1934 case of Nebbia v. New York created the doctrine that the government could regulate prices or control terms of service if businesses are "affected with a public interest."[2] Because of its pervasive impact, the banking industry was often described as being clothed with the public interest. All businesses, however, are expected to incorporate public interest values into their decision making regarding day-to-day operations as well as long-term growth and survival.

The public interest theme is reflected in a book co-authored by John Mackey, the co-CEO of Whole Foods. Called *Conscious Capitalism,* Mackey and Raj Sisodia, a marketing professor at Bentley College, say that "The heroic story of free-enterprise capitalism is one of entrepreneurs using their dreams and passion as fuel to create extraordinary value for customers, team members, suppliers, society, and investor."[3] They proclaim that conscious businesses have conscious leaders who are "primarily motivated by service to the purpose of the business and its stakeholders, and not by the pursuit of power and personal enrichment." They warn that "When any profession becomes primarily about making money, it starts to lose its true identity and its interests." The money motive makes them start to "diverge from what is good for society as a whole."

## The public policy process

This book deals with contemporary issues of concern to MNCs that arise in the conduct of business and interaction with other players. Global managers must decide which issues to place on their "public agenda" and how to respond to them. To do so they apply the process of issues management. Specialized books such as *Strategic Issues Management: How Organizations Influence and Respond to Public Interests and Policies* by R.L. Heath and Associates describe the process.[4] Other books, such as *Management Response to Public Issues* by Rogene A. Bucholz, William D. Evans and Robert A. Wagley, more specifically describe what is known as the "public policy process" – all the various ways public policy is made in our society and which implicitly advance the public interest.[5]

An important contribution to corporate thinking about the public policy process is a seminal book, *Private Management and Public Policy* by Lee E. Preston and James E. Post.[6] Instead of talking about the public interest, they use the framework of stakeholder relations and propose the principle of public responsibility. It states that a company should consider the impact it has on its primary and secondary stakeholders and the natural environment for which society wishes to hold them accountable. They place limits, however, on the scope of responsibility. Although the stakeholders of a company's foreign subsidiaries would be covered, other players in the international arena might not.

Preston and Post did not apply the principle of public responsibility to the racial policies in South Africa and the forms of government adopted by Chile (which were socialistic in 1973 when I.T.T. meddled in internal affairs). These were considered "matters clearly outside the scope of U.S. parent companies."[7] The broader public interest principle, however, would consider these matters because they violate human rights.

The public interest principle would also exceed Preston and Post's public responsibility principle in other ways. They dismissed "individual moral judgments and personal concepts of 'what's good for people.'" They also rejected demands from "the specific goals and interests of narrowly defined interest groups and special publics."[8] Firms, they say, should confine themselves to those problems that corporations themselves create or those that affect them. They should therefore limit secondary involvements, such as responsibility by the auto industry for the educational system. On the other hand, the issue of expanding employment opportunities for minorities would enter the public policy agenda. In summary, their public responsibility principle extends as far as the limits of secondary involvement, but no further.[9]

Judgments will vary as to what should be included in secondary involvements and the passage of time and new circumstances will affect those opinions. Preston and Post do recognize that ultimately the guidelines for managerial performance are to be found in the "larger society."[10] Furthermore, in the closing paragraph of their book, they invoke the public interest by saying, "However, there seems to be a wide-spread feeling in our society that, without any major social upheaval, a great deal of managerial activity could and *should* be carried out in a manner that contributes somewhat more to the public interest."[11]

In this book, the public interest criterion is incorporated in the concept of global corporate citizenship. For example, when MNCs help solve social problems and make social investments (levels 3 and 4 of the CSR pyramid) that are commensurate with their own abilities and capacities, they exercise social responsibility, which is an expression of the public interest. Business's larger responsibility was recognized by The Committee on Economic Development (CED), which developed the CSR pyramid. It said, "Business functions by public consent, and its basic purpose is to serve constructively the needs of society – to the satisfaction of society."[12]

Although the concepts of the public policy process and global corporate citizenship in various ways suggest ways in which the public interest can be integrated into corporate governance, a more fundamental approach is to examine the relationship between the economy and society. If the needs of society are satisfied, many would agree that the "common good" is served, which is a frequent definition of the public interest.

## Relationship between the economy and society

Sociology provides the broadest framework for an understanding of the relationship between the economy and society. From the sociologist's viewpoint, the economy is a sub-system of society and must thereby be subordinate to society and not the other way around as the free market system seems to imply. Using the analogy of astronomy, the free market system positions the economy at the center of the universe with society revolving around it, similar to Ptolmey's claim that the sun revolved around the earth.

We should adopt the modern Copernicus theory that the sun, standing for society, is at the center of the universe and the earth with the economy revolves around it. This positioning implies that the purpose of the economy is to serve the needs of society. In other words, the economy should be seen as a means to an end and not focus on itself as the purpose of human activity.

This isolation of business from society and its expectations largely accounts for the periodic outburst of public indignation against business. Starting approximately in 1776, when Adam Smith's *Wealth of Nations* was published, business moved in the direction of separating itself from the rest of society. It rebelled against the kind of government regulation and guidance associated with mercantilism and against such theological notions as *just price* – a price that produces revenue commensurate with a merchant's status in society. The new law for business became the law of supply and demand, and the connection with society was almost exclusively focused on the marketplace.

The result of this separation of business from society is that business has become too myopic in attending to its own needs and paying too little attention to undesirable side-effects or social costs. In the early days of industrialization, Social Darwinians like Andrew Carnegie imposed an 84-hour week on steelworkers in Pittsburgh, not seeing it as a human rights issue. To his credit, however, late in life he righted matters by becoming a generous philanthropist who established several universities and built many community libraries.

Sociologists have examined the separation of their discipline from economics and some have sought to find rapprochement. A theoretical approach to the subject was undertaken by Talcott Parsons, former head of the Social Relations Department at Harvard University, and Neil J. Smelser in *Economy and Society: A Study in the Integration of Economic and Social Theory*. The authors felt it "necessary for the future of both disciplines to reestablish interest in the borderline relations."[13] Their major contribution is the assertion that the economy is a sub-system of society – which they call the "adaptive" system.[14] The goal of the economy therefore is to produce goods and services that satisfy "consumers' wants" (described by the authors as "maximizing utility or the economic value of the total available means to want satisfaction").[15] In short, economics should be seen as dealing with only one major aspect of social life.

Basically, Parsons and Smelser sought to dispel the belief that economics is "a science sufficient unto itself" and to "demonstrate that economics must lean on the other social sciences, both on the theoretical and empirical levels …."[16] In examining the subject of consumer behavior, for example, they point to the contribution of psychology as explaining consumers' tastes and the forces that influence their "marginal propensity to consume." John Maynard Keynes, known for his ideas about macroeconomics, also analyzed this propensity as well as such concepts as the "stickiness of money wages" and instabilities in employment and income.[17] Another economist, Joseph Schumpeter, centered on how society contributed to entrepreneurial innovation.[18] This Austrian economist became famous when he referred to technology as a force of "creative destruction."

In summary, sociological theory supports the view that business should not be viewed in isolation from society nor superior to it. The many business and management books bearing the title "Business & Society" support this contention. Each needs the other. Society provides business with needed factors of production – land, capital, labor – and in return receives rents, interest, profits from business, and wages and salaries. Society's reward is that business provided it with goods and services and with jobs. The concept of stakeholder relations, sometimes called "stakeholder capitalism," is associated with global citizenship and reflects the sociological view.[19] Sociology, however, should not be confused with socialism

## Free market system revisited

Although the free market system is the antithesis of socialism, it is not devoid of concern for the public interest. Several free market economists explain the connection.

### Hayek attacks socialism

F.A. Hayek's *The Road to Serfdom* sharply attacked socialism and promoted the free market system. He recognized that socialism seems attractive because "the ideals of social justice, greater equality and security … are the ultimate aims of socialism."[20] Praiseworthy as these aims are, the methods by which most socialists hope to attain these ends, he says, are through "the abolition of private enterprises, of private ownership of the means of production, and the creation of a system of 'planned economy' in which the entrepreneur working for profit is replaced by a central planning body."[21] The dispute about socialism is about these means, he said, not the ends.

In his chapter "Individualism and Collectivism," Hayek gets at the core of the socialist argument: "whether the holder of coercive power should confine himself in general to creating conditions under which the knowledge and initiative of individuals is given the best scope so that they can plan most successfully; or whether a rational utilisation of our resources requires central direction and organisation of all our activities according to some consciously constructed 'blueprint.'"[22]

Hayek alludes to the well-known cultural pattern of individualism versus collectivism. Individualistic cultures, as described by author Raymond Cohen, "hold freedom, the development of the individual personality, self-expression, and personal enterprise and achievement as supreme values."[23] In such cultures, status is acquired and only rarely inherited. Rights and duties are defined by law, not ascription. Contract, not custom, prescribes the individual's legal obligation to a given transaction, role, or course of action. Similarly, conflict is resolved through the courts rather than by group opinion or informal methods of conciliation. This emphasis on individualism is in accord with American values, but it is an exceptional rather than a universally accepted ethic.

The public interest is served by the mechanism of competition. Hayek sees it as the means of coordinating human efforts, based on a conviction "that where effective competition can be created, it is a better way of guiding individual efforts than any other."[24] Put even more strongly, "one of the main arguments in favour of competition is that it dispenses with the need for 'conscious social control'…." For example, "Any attempt to control prices or quantities of particular commodities deprives competition of its power of bringing about an effective co-ordination of individual efforts, because price changes then cease to register all the relevant changes in circumstances and no longer provide a reliable guide for the individual's actions."[25] Hayek recognizes a central concept in economics that the single piece of information called price elegantly summarizes many market forces and largely displaces the need for much government decision making and planning.

Hayek, however, did not propose a "dogmatic *laissez-faire* attitude." He recognized that competition requires a "carefully thought-out legal framework." He accepted some government regulations, such as the use of certain dangerous substances, limitations on working hours, and safety requirements. He went further and said that an "extensive system of social services" is not incompatible with competition. Where Hayek draws a line is between social regulations and planning, saying, "Although competition can bear some admixture of regulation, it cannot be combined with planning to any extent we like without ceasing to operate as an effective guide to production."[26] Furthermore, he was also open to finding "some method other than competition" to supply services in instances where "there is a divergence between the items which enter into private calculation and those which affect social welfare."[27] In other words, competition by itself is not a guarantee that the public interest is served.

## Milton Friedman advocates free markets

In many ways, Milton Friedman is Hayek's ideological successor. Upon his death in November 2006, obituaries named Friedman one of the greatest economists of the 20th century, known for advocating free markets over government intervention. He was the recipient of the Nobel Prize in 1976. Two of his most-cited books are *Capitalism and Freedom* and *Free to Choose*.[28] He conveyed to millions "an understanding of the economic benefits of free, competitive markets, as well as the close connection that economic freedoms bear to other types of liberty."[29] Like Hayek, he espoused the "idea that the government should stay out of individuals' affairs whenever possible, and that markets can solve economic problems much more efficiently than government officials can." He had a low regard for government policy-making. One of his best barbs on the size of government was, "Given our monstrous, overgrown government structure, any three letters chosen at random would probably designate an agency or part of a department that could be profitably abolished."[30]

Friedman provided the intellectual foundations for "the anti-inflation, tax-cutting and anti-government policies of President Ronald Reagan and British Prime Minister Margaret Thatcher."[31] He believed that the free market system could solve most social problems. He thought social security should be privatized and the problems of failing public schools could be solved through educational vouchers. He will always be known for his view that "there is no such thing as a free lunch." His idea of the role of the public intellectual, like himself, was: "We do not influence the course of events by persuading people that we are right when we make what they regard as radical proposals. Rather, we exert influence by keeping options available when something has to be done at a time of crisis."[32]

Friedman is often cited as saying that the sole objective of business was to make as much money for their stockholders as possible. But he agreed with Hayek in the meaning of "free" in the free market system. His full statement is, "There is one and only one social responsibility of business – to use its resources and engage in activities designed to increase its profits so long as it stays within the rules of the game, which is to say, engages in open and free competition, without deception of fraud."[33] In short, he, like Hayek, was not in favor of unbridled capitalism.

## Challenges to the free market system

### Alternative futures

A growing number of authors foresee, and sometimes advocate, alternatives to the free market system. The literature on alternative futures presents "some of the best new thinking and action for creating a new global trade and finance system," say Sarah Anderson and John Cavanagh.[34] One source of new ideas mentioned by them is the International Forum on Globalization (IFG) which formed a task force in 1999. Its ideas about alternative futures contain both widely known and relatively new goals. Two well-known goals are the reduction of the growing gap between rich and poor nations and support of human rights. The IFG supports the United Nations Universal Declaration on Human Rights, which calls for a standard of living adequate for people's health and well-being, including "food, clothing, housing, and medical care, and necessary social services, and the right to security in the event of unemployment."[35]

To promote its policies, the IFG proposes the principle of "new democracy." As stated by Anderson and Cavanagh, "Democracy flourishes when people organize to protect their communities and rights and hold their elected officials accountable."[36] Some new forms of active democracy would focus on winning community control over natural resources; another way would be through "subsidiarity" – preserving local control over economic activity, which represents well over half of the people on earth. On the surface such demands conflict with globalization, but as Starbucks has shown in its dealings with coffee growers in Ethiopia, negotiations can sometimes help.

Other goals aimed at correcting "market fundamentalism" – that the market can solve all economic problems – are stronger checks on corporate power at the local, national, and global levels; a belief that certain goods and services, such as water and other parts of the global commons, should not be subject to global market forces or agreements; and that speculative capital flows should be slowed down.[37] Joseph Stiglitz supports this sentiment and condemns the IMF for pushing countries throughout the developing world to liberalize their capital and financial markets prematurely.[38] Proponents of "an alternative future" recommend new international institutions: an international insolvency court and an international finance organization under the mandate and direction of the UN.[39]

## Social capitalism and state capitalism

In contrast to the United States, Europe maintains much better social regulation to protect workers. Its cushion of a strong welfare state coupled with public investment seems to be the political price the electorate demands in exchange for tolerating the vagaries of the open economy, where jobs are always at risk. Instead of a free-enterprise system, a "mixed economy" and a brand of social capitalism prevail.

Social capitalism is exemplified by the Nordic countries – Sweden, Finland, and Denmark (Norway is omitted because of its oil riches), which have the world's most generous welfare benefits and the world's highest taxes. Yet they have delivered strong growth and low unemployment and rank among the world's most competitive economies. From 1994 to 2004, after the severe international recession, Finland and Sweden's GDP growth exceeded that of all other industrialized countries in Europe except Ireland and Spain. Denmark, Norway, and Sweden have the highest employment rates of any of the industrialized countries, employing between 70% and 72% of the working-age population.[40]

The belief is growing, however, that welfare in the Nordic countries has gone too far, as the strain on taxes shows. A high percentage of the workforce has been receiving sick and disability pay. Compared to 15.2% of the total population aged 15–64 in 2004 in the United States, 21.6% in Sweden were receiving social benefits. Furthermore, 14.7% of these received sickness and incapacity benefits, even though the World Health Organization says Swedes are among the healthiest people in the world. Sweden has now decided it can no longer support such a costly system. Sweden's prime minister, Fredrik Reinfeld, however, prefers to say, "I'm reshaping part of Sweden, I'm not tearing it down."[41]

State capitalism is an even greater concern. A special report in *The Economist* concluded that "state capitalism is the most formidable foe that liberal capitalism has faced so far."[42] State companies accounted for one-third of the emerging world's foreign direct investment between 2003 and 2010. They make up 80% of the value of the stock market in China, 62% in Russia, and 38% in Brazil. As the report states, "The Chinese have a phrase for it: The state advances while the private sector retreats."[43]

Dealings by MNCs with China and Russia have demonstrated to global managers that they will have to pay more attention to dealings with business heads and politicians in countries with state capitalism. Commercial criteria may therefore enter political decisions and political decisions into commercial ones. The pressure to transfer intellectual property in combination with investments is one area of consideration. Another concern is that competition with state-owned enterprises (SOES) may encourage trade wars from free market economies that attack subsidies and retaliation from state-capitalism countries.[44]

## Harmonizing the market system with society

The excesses of market fundamentalism have led to demands for reforms in the free market system. Reformers of the free market system range from those who seek marginal improvements to those who seek fundamental changes. Among the major proposals are recognition by MNCs that government must be involved and that partnerships should be formed with it.

### Involve government

Among the central choices facing all societies is the role of government. The economic system requires societal rule setting and guidance in which the government's fundamental role is twofold: to establish the "rule of law" that provides a reliable legal framework for business transactions, and, secondly, to enforce regulations within which markets can function efficiently. Included in such regulations would be the establishment and enforcement of product and pricing standards, antitrust laws to preserve competition and discourage restrictive business practices, securities and exchange laws to protect financial markets and the right of access to credit and capital, oversight of bank operations, and guidelines for viable contracts and adjudication of disputes. Even conservative economist Milton Friedman saw this need, but warned that government involvement in the economy should be kept at a minimum.

At a minimum, government should assure that competition prevails. As Hayek noted, competition is supposed to insure that economic activities are compatible with the public interest. Sellers cannot charge a higher price than their competitors and buyers must be willing to pay the price as determined by the market. But such a setting of a market price for a product depends on the existence of a "pure and perfect" market, which requires that there be enough sellers and buyers and that they possess sufficient information about a market to make the system work. In a global economy, competition is more likely because it potentially includes all market participants in the world, which in the auto industry would include Mercedes Benz, Toyota Acuras, and Fiats.

Maintaining a system of competition is not the same as laissez faire whereby anything goes, including the destruction of competition. Nor is competition preserved when governments condone mergers and acquisitions that increase the concentration of business so that at best only monopolistic competition – competition among the few – remains. Such limited competition lessens the possibility that the public interest is served. Perhaps the word "free" should be tempered as a qualifier for the market system. Government, along with civil society institutions such as professional associations, should play a role in economic affairs.

As expressed by Joseph Stiglitz, "Economic success requires getting the balance right between the government and the market."[45] Globalization, as it has been pushed, has often made it more difficult to obtain this balance. The real question is what the right thing is for government to do to make the market work better. Another liberal economist, Robert Reich, favors tighter, rather than looser, social and economic regulation.

### Consider partnerships

To compensate for market inadequacies, business partnerships with government can play a role.[46] For example, world health could be improved with government involvement in the production of drugs to fight the world's biggest killers, such as malaria. Drug companies do not find enough profit potential in such drugs, because they are mostly needed by poor nations. This market deficiency, says Stiglitz, could be overcome by government grants to produce them. By taking advantage of competition, the market could be used to get the price as low as possible. Furthermore, because drugs companies have often attempted to reduce access to generic drugs for poor countries of the world, a better balance has to be sought to obtain the gains of innovation resulting from protection of intellectual property rights and the costs of giving drug companies a monopoly on products they create.

## The arbiter role of corporate governance

It falls upon corporate boards to decide how to address the problems of excesses and deficiencies of the free market system and resolve the tensions between economy and society. One of their roles is external relations – to relate their corporations to the larger sociopolitical environment. These problems and tensions are magnified for MNCs and other large companies because they are confronted by growing criticism and demand for enlightened governance.

### Pressure for change

In the United States, the 2009 Edelman Trust Barometer showed that Americans' trust in businesses dropped to its lowest point in a decade. It found that only 38% of 35- to 64-year-old Americans trust businesses, a 20% drop from the years before, and the lowest in the 10-year history of the survey.[47] The plummet in trust levels has a severe impact on communications, with 60% of respondents saying they need to hear information three to five times before believing it. CEOs face a credibility crisis, with only 17% of Americans trusting information from them. The 2009 Gallup Poll confirmed business's loss of public trust. When people were asked, "Which of the following will be the biggest threat to the country in the future – big business, big labor, or big government?," the answer was business. It was the only category to see a significant increase from 2006 to 2009, from 25% to 32%.

## Accusations of greed

Companies have been criticized for exorbitant profits and greedy CEOs. CEOs have unashamedly increased their incomes to what many call "obscene" levels. In 2011, the total direct compensation for 248 CEOs at public companies was a median of $10.3 million, according to an analysis by the *Wall Street Journal* and Hay Group. In what is called internal pay equity, the average CEO in a broad sample of S&P 500 firms earned 380 times more than the typical U.S. worker, according to an AFL-CIO analysis.[48] In comparison, the ratio in Japan is 11; in France 15, in Canada 20, and in Britain 22.[49] In his final book, *The Economics of Innocent Fraud*, the late John Kenneth Galbraith lambasted the "unrestrained power of self-enrichment ... of executives backslapped and enriched by sheepish boards." He commented that perks, options, salaries, and severance deals often result in "rewards that can verge on larceny."[50] Critics suspect that CEOs are less concerned about the welfare of their stockholders than about themselves.

## Banks fail the "clothing with the public interest" test

During the financial crisis of 2008, bankers were blamed for reckless behavior in the pursuit of ever greater profits. Theoretically, banks are supposed to temper their zest for profits because they are "clothed with the public interest." But their attitude, as some charged, was "privatize profits and socialize risks."

The excessive drive to maximize profits was displayed in the United Kingdom during the summer of 2012 with the Libor scandal. Barclays PLC, Britain's 322-year-old bank, was exposed for trying to rig the benchmark interest rate known as Libor, which is the overnight rate that a bank pays to borrow from another bank and used by banks generally to set the interest rate for a variety of loans, including mortgage rates. By understating Libor, Barclay and other banks that set the rate, were able to borrow at lower rates and benefit at the expense of lending investors and institutions who were cheated out of higher returns. Many of the latter plan to sue Barclay's and other involved banks for a potential legal liability of about $1.76 billion.[51]

Other U.K. banks were exposed for other kinds of wrong-doing. HSBC Holdings PLC was accused of allegedly handling money for drug gangs and terrorist groups and Standard Chartered PLC, the U.K.'s fifth largest bank, for money-laundering violations involving Iran.

In the case of J.P. Morgan, with a reputation for prudent risk management, the bank apparently reverted to making risky investments in its London investment office. Because of the large amounts involved, the trader involved was called "the whale." Trading losses were at first estimated at $2 billion, then 5.4 billion, and then 7 billion or more.[52]

In the United States, the alleged cultural deficit of some top bank managements was exemplified by Goldman Sachs when it was brought into the limelight in a resignation letter by Greg Smith, a Goldman Sachs executive director, and head of its equity derivatives business in Europe, the Middle East, and Africa. The letter, published by *The New York Times,* said, "I knew it was time to leave when I realized I could no longer look students [who were being recruited] in the eye and tell them what a great place this was to work."[53] He gave Goldman Sachs's culture a quotient of exactly zero percent, describing the company's heads-I-win, tails-you-lose approach to its dealings with clients. "It's purely about how we can make the most possible money off of them. If you were an alien from Mars and sat in on one of these {derivatives sales] meetings, you would believe that a client's success or progress was not part of the thought process at all." Goldman was stung by the whistle-blower. It came under pressure as its shares fell 3.4%.

Goldman immediately launched a public relations counteroffensive, saying it would examine the claims made by Greg Smith. It also sought to denigrate the status of Smith, saying he was one "of nearly 12,000 vice presidents" among more than 30,000 employees at the company. Chairman Lloyd Blankfein and chief executive Gary Cohn asserted that Smith's allegations did "not reflect our values, our culture and how the vast majority of people at Goldman Sachs think about the firm and the work it does on behalf of our clients."[54] Nevertheless, Smith's resignation letter prompted *Bloomberg Businessweek* to print an article saying, "There is a massive leadership vacuum at the top of Wall Street today, and it's quite possible that only continued, relentless public shaming will force the leaders of these firms to make the kinds of cultural changes necessary to bring their actions in line with normative behavior." [55]

## Two reform experiments in corporate governance

Some companies have undertaken efforts to improve their corporate governance, as illustrated by the two following cases. Royal Dutch Shell illustrates a major effort at transformation and ExxonMobil illustrates an attempt to change the relationship with a nation-state in oil production.

### Shell undertakes to transform itself

Royal Dutch Shell, perhaps more than other oil companies, has felt the pressure to behave as a global corporation. One study describes the company's transition from acting like a colonial power to recognizing that a different social contract was necessary.[56] Shell's reputation was sullied because it was seen as harming the land and people of Ogoniland, the location of its major oil fields in Nigeria.

The effort began when Shell commissioned a report, titled *Society's Changing Expectations*, based on extensive roundtable discussion with Shell executives, stakeholders, academics, and journalists. Also included in the study were young person focus groups and consultations with public relations professional in all regions of the world. The report's central finding: "Shell's reputation had suffered because the company's behavior had not kept pace with society's changing expectations." The consultants concluded, "economic, society, and technological changes have created a more cynical, questioning, indeed challenging attitude toward institutions, not the least, MNCs."[57]

Shell realized it had to become more open and transparent: "We realized that we were a company of head but not heart. Brand values are about treating people with respect. No company is squeaky-clean and always right, but companies can change and I'm proud of Shell," said Mark Wade, Shell's leading thinker on sustainable development.[58] Shell now has incorporated human rights into its business principles, publishes annual reports on its ethics, and runs a website that allows virulent criticism. Its new values are "honesty, integrity, respect for people, as well as professionalism, pride and openness, sustainable development and human rights." In its website section on "Living by Our Values," Shell declares, "Our commitments are to the communities and the nations in which we operate, not just to the government of the day."[59]

### ExxonMobil's Chad Cameroon Pipeline[60]

In an attempt to avoid the errors and problems of Shell in Nigeria, an enlightened approach was used in the planning and operation of the Chad Cameroon Petroleum Development and Pipeline Project. ExxonMobil constructed a 663-mile pipeline from Chad through a tropical rain forest to the coast of Cameroon. Major environmental and human rights problems plagued the project. The Cameroon's pristine Cameroon's Atlantic Littoral Forest – which is home to a myriad of plant and animal species, such as chimpanzees, elephants, gorillas, and black rhinos – was endangered. Cameroon's indigenous Pygmies were a special problem and linked to environmental concerns because "They see the forest as a personal god, fruitful and kind, and enact their relationships with it and with the spirits of the forest in ritual and song."[61] The companies addressed these environmental and cultural sensitivities through consultation with the indigenous population and by rerouting of the pipeline.

In a first-of-its-kind agreement, Chad relinquished part of its sovereignty over how the revenues would be spent. ExxonMobil thereby hoped to avoid the "natural resources curse," which so often doomed African countries endowed with oil or other resources to deepening corruption and violent conflict. ExxonMobil persuaded the World Bank to become involved in this model of how oil firms can function in unstable parts of Africa. The bank became the main lender and established conditions of how oil revenues were to be spent. Chad would have to submit to the World Bank's stern demands for transparency and accountability, which would placate environmental and human rights lobbyists who had been loudly critical of the project. The money was to be sent to an escrow account in a Western bank in London, then the money would be transferred to two commercial banks in Chad, where an oversight committee would apportion payments for development projects.

Unfortunately, Chad did not adhere to the terms of the agreement. It spent money to buy arms and diverted money intended for education and health care to less worthy causes. The situation turned worse in late August 2006 when President Idriss Deby ordered the expulsion of two big oil firms in the consortium, Petroliam Nasional (Petronas) of Malaysia, and Chevron of America, saying they had not paid enough tax.[62] These tax disputes and threats of expulsions "smack of 'resource nationalism' as practiced in Venezuela and Bolivia," stated *The Economist* , adding, "Chad's status as a model of natural-resource management has suffered."[63] In his book, *Private Empire: ExxonMobil and American Power*, Steve Coll concluded, "Chad today is a poster child for the resource curse." The expectations of Exxon-Mobil in forging a new relationship with oil-rich countries were not met. The project was a set-back for innovations in corporate governance. "We're not the Red Cross," said an ExxonMobil executive about the Chad arrangement.[64]

# Preparing corporate statesmen

The essence of reform in corporate governance lies with the attitudes and skills of a company's top management, especially the position of chief executive officer. As global managers they must learn to become corporate statesmen who head relationships with the myriad of domestic and international players. They necessarily perform the function of relating the organization to the external environment and becoming involved with public issues.

Today's CEOs who serve as global managers must have the sensitivities of a diplomat in the everyday running of a company abroad – to make sure that various publics are not offended and, even more, that public expectations are recognized. The reality that a firm's environment consists of more than markets is painfully clear. Depending on the industry, the pressures of the sociopolitical environment in various locations throughout the world are mounting, and thereby create a need for a response. The top executives in parent and subsidiary companies need to be statesmen who command diplomatic skills.

## Lack of involvement

For most of the past decade, the CEOs of major corporations have unfortunately been absent from the public forum. In 2004, David Wessel, *Wall Street Journal*'s economics columnist, asked, Where have all the corporate statesmen gone? when he interviewed Peter G. Peterson, former secretary of commerce under President Richard Nixon and chairman of the Blackstone Group, a New York investment company.[65] Peterson answer was that they seem to have disappeared.

Peterson particularly noted the silence of the Business Roundtable, established in 1972, on such major issues as the ever-widening deficits in government spending and U.S. trade, deficits that in his opinion are unsustainable. Since its early days, the Business Roundtable has confined itself to immediate legislation of narrow interests of its members. In first half of 2000, its major public announcements centered on applauding Congress's passage of normal trade relations with China, opposing the patients' bill of rights in Congress, complying with SEC's request for views on international accounting standards, and opposing class-action lawsuits. The Business Roundtable, said Jeffrey E. Garten in 2001, makes no effort in "identifying what the government ought to be addressing but isn't."[66] It is not sufficiently involved in public agenda-setting.

Agreeing with Peterson is public relations counselor Robert L. Dilenschneider. Writing in 2004, he thought CEOs needed to go public at a time when America seemed adrift with a lack of vision or direction on matters of grave importance to America's future major issues. Among them were "our shrinking industrial base, the skyrocketing cost of health care and pensions, inequitable trade policies, record federal budget and international trade deficit, global warming, lack of a forward-looking energy policy and mounting anti-American sentiment worldwide."[67] These are broader issues than those immediately and directly affecting business. Yet, said Dillenschneider, the CEOs of powerful MNCs "remain silent and are virtually unknown to the vast bulk of the American people." What they hear about are the extraordinarily high salaries paid to CEOs of large companies.[68]

When stepping down as dean of the Yale School of Management in 2005, Garten reminisced on his career with William J. Holstein, editor in chief of *Chief Executive* magazine, and said: "Ten years ago, the role of business in society was on an upward trajectory. There was a sense that business leaders would be the champions of globalization and would in fact fill in where governments had left a huge vacuum in terms of the rules of the world economy."[69] But in the post 9/11 and post Enron era, he said, that now seemed a very fanciful notion as the role of business leaders was enormously diminished. When asked whether chief executives were doing enough, he pessimistically answered.

> What C.E.O.'s are not doing is presuming to play a broader role than just ensuring that their companies are profitable. There was a time when leaders of big multinational companies were thinking about supplying some governance of the global economy. The idea was that there was no such thing as world government and that national governments were much too focused on their own jurisdictions to create the rules of trade or finance or environmental protection or labor. Companies were going to move into this vacuum, gingerly, but the world would be run more according to business and market principles. Over this past decade, most C.E.O.'s decided this is not for them. They have created a vacuum into which governments are moving, for better or worse.[70]

An explanation for CEO silence is that a bunker mentality may have set in because by the end of 2005, 561 CEOs from companies large and small were replaced. A 2003 study showed that CEO turnover had increased by 53% between 1995 and 2001 and CEO tenures in 2003 were averaging four years.[71] CEOs were seeking a lower profile as corporate scandals exploded into headlines. "Many CEOs are reluctant to speak for fear their words might come back to haunt them in the form of shareholder lawsuits, if results disappoint and share prices sink," said Hollis Rafkin-Sax, head of the New York corporate practice at Edelman Public Relations Worldwide.[72]

Consistent with Holstein, a 2007 study conducted by McKinsey & Company found that fewer than half of the senior executives surveyed in the United States believed that they or their peers should take the lead in shaping the debate on major issues such as education, healthcare, and foreign policy.[73] Of the one-seventh of respondents who believed they were playing that role, the majority did so for personal, not business reasons. As observed by Holstein, CEOs are unfortunately staying quiet these days, many unwilling to participate in open analysis of the issues of the day, including corporate governance.[74] When asked whether the business community created the problem of executive overcompensation, Nell Minow, editor and co-founder of The Corporate Library, said: "they don't care how bad it gets. I will tell you that the biggest disappointment I've had in this mess has been the absolute vacuum of leadership on the part of the business community."[75]

But inertia can be overcome when conditions get bad enough. The willingness of CEOs to speak out changed in 2012, as suggested in a front page headline in the *Wall Street Journal*, "CEOs Call for Deficit Action."[76] Executives from more than 80 big-name U.S. corporations banded together in a Fix the Debt campaign to pressure Congress to reduce the federal deficit with both tax-revenue increases and spending cuts. They did not rely on traditional Washington groups, such as the Business Roundtable or National Association of Manufacturers, to speak for them because reaching consensus was too difficult. Among the CEOs who signed the statement are GE's Jeffrey Immelt, J.P. Morgan's James Dimon, Honeywell's Dave Cole, Deere & Co's Samuel Allen, and Motorola Solutions' Gregory Brown.

A few CEOs were very specific in their views. Randall Stephenson, CEO of AT&T said, "When you talk about a $16 trillion debt, I don't see how you can avoid addressing both sides," spending cuts and tax increases. Executives were motivated to act by the recent inaction and "political theatrics" of Congress. After the "fiscal cliff" was averted at the last day of 2012 several CEOs saw the event as a further indication of the "dysfunction in the legislation process."[77] Commenting on the event, David Cole, CEO of Honeywell International and leader of a business coalition pushing for deficit reduction, said, "All it did was address the fiscal-cliff problem and set us up for a debt-ceiling debacle."[78] The likelihood, however, is that in the future CEOS will continue to speak out on broad government fiscal policies.

In England, business was finding another way to influence government. Former BP CEO John Browne was given a Whitehall role to find efficiencies across government. The Cabinet Office minister said, "His experience will be a real benefit in our drive to make Whitehall work in a more businesslike manner."[79]

## Some supportive solutions

Although remedies for CEO fears about jobs security and lawsuits are not easily found, some solutions do exist to encourage and enable CEOs to speak out more. New supporting positions can be created and better preparation made available.

### New supporting positions

Too large a burden is often placed on the modern CEO who is already occupied with running ever larger enterprises. The process of delegation must be applied to a CEO's statesman role. The existing approach is to establish a public affairs position whose manager has responsibility not only to communicate to external audiences but to influence corporate governance policies and decisions on issues involving the inter-relationship of business interests with large public interests. To help in this task, the Public Affairs Council in Washington, DC urges public affairs professionals to apply the following ethical guidelines:

- Endeavors to ensure that responsible and diverse external interests and views concerning the need(s) of society are considered within the corporate decision-making process.
- Bears the responsibility for management review of public policies which may bring corporate interests into conflict with other interests.

- Acknowledges dual obligations – to advocate the interests of his or her employer, and to preserve the openness and integrity of the democratic process
- Present to his or her employer an accurate assessment of the political and social realities that may affect corporate operations.[80]

A more radical organizational arrangement was proposed by W. Howard Chase, often credited for originating the field of issues management. He considered the sociopolitical environment so important that he thought it deserved a position on the organizational chart comparable to operations. Accordingly, he proposed the position of executive vice president-public policy to parallel that of the executive vice president-operations.[81] This new office would have two subdivisions: law and issue management and its major functions would be external constituencies (including federal and state government relations and advocacy groups relations), contributions management, internal constituencies, and communications and media relations.[82]

Chase's proposal can be enlarged to include new international relations positions. As mentioned in Chapter 1, Clyde Prestowitz believes that CEOs should at least have "real secretaries of state" in their organizations. Similarly John Budd, a public relations professional, suggests creating an Office of Diplomacy or expanding the purview of public affairs and public relations departments to include the international arena.

A frequent recommendation is that large companies split the positions of CEO and chairman of the board. Following this model, Garten suggests giving the chairman major responsibility for handling global issues and relationships.[83] He describes the FedEx model of "an office of the chairman." and a five-person executive committee that not only oversees the operations of its companies but has responsibility for the complexities of the global environment. Its members include, the CFO, the chief information office, the head of marketing and communications, the general counsel, and Jeffrey Garten.[84]

## Better preparation

University programs should help prepare executives for their new role as statesmen. Referring to the larger problem in the United States, Michael L. Eskew, chairman and CEO of UPS, asks whether enough well-qualified global professionals are being educated in a variety of areas: "Are we, as a nation, producing enough global trade specialists, engineers, materials researchers and other professions that are in demand in a global economy?"[85] Are we producing enough executives who can serve as statesmen? Are our schools sufficiently global in outlook?

Courses in schools of management and schools of communications prepare executives to relate with people and organizations in the external environment. Managers become skilled in identifying and analyzing issues that are likely to affect their organizations and in lobbying governments' legislative and executive branches to make decisions favorable to their organizations. They accept the basic precept that public policy is very much the business of business as well as government. They learn to deal with activist groups and NGOs who pressure corporations to cease certain actions, like pollution, and undertake others, such as affirmative action. They learn to include noneconomic variables in their decision making, such as a concern for corporate social responsibility and the value of a favorable reputation and image. They address many of the deficiencies of the free market system and learn to civilize "economic man" and rejoin the economy with society.

## Developing a public service culture

An encouraging development is that a public service culture in business is slowly evolving and finding expression at universities. One sign was the Harvard Business School's Global Leadership Forum in Washington, DC in June 2006 which featured the title "The Private Sector and the Public Interest." At it, Dean Light remarked that the founders conceived the Harvard Business School as "a school of public service and business" intended to train students "with an intellectual respect for business as a profession, with the social implications and heightened sense of responsibility that goes with that."[86]

Another participant, Richard Haass, a former State Department official, urged the business community to get involved in public issues. He said, "Traditionally the business community in America has been the most powerful consistent voice in favor of openness toward the world, including openness on trade and investment," but, he asked, "Where are the CEOs and others who used to lead public opinion on these issues?"[87] Former Treasury Secretary Robert Rubin, although finding comfort in the U.S.'s enormous resilience in the face of difficult challenges, added, "However, I think we should all be deeply troubled about the way our political system is functioning."[88]

The trend is clear: business executives must add a public service culture to their training in finance, production, marketing, human resources, and other traditional business knowledge and skills. Such a public service culture helps to balance economics with the requirements of society. It also helps prepare executives to take positions in government, as the late Sol Linowitz did as troubleshooter for past presidents. As a young lawyer and businessman he achieved acclaim as a principal developer of the Xerox Corporation and later its chairman. His first call from the White House seeking advice came from President John F. Kennedy. Over the years, Linowitz also became a trusted counsel to Presidents Lyndon B. Johnson and Jimmy Carter. Among the complex jobs he filled were negotiator for the Panama Canal treaties and special presidential envoy for the Middle East.[89] The idea of a position as "CEO-emeritus" deserves attention.

# Conclusions

Acting in the public interest is increasingly important for MNCs as the model of stakeholder relations gains acceptance. This requirement is suggested by the sociological perspective which views the economy as serving the needs of society. Both the economy and society, however, need each other. Even conservative economists realize that the model of the free market system recognizes the goal of serving the public interest must be attained beyond total reliance on competition and operation of the invisible hand.

Capitalism faces competition from rival systems, mainly alternative futures, social capitalism, and state capitalism. Their purpose is to reign in the excesses of the free market system and to serve the needs of the larger society. This is why the means of harmonizing society and the economy becomes important and the role of government in doing so is recognized. Companies such as Shell have undertaken studies to help transform their corporate governance. And ExxonMobil, which upholds the classical business creed, experiments with new models of dealing with stakeholders.

An implication of accepting a broader purpose of corporations is that its leaders must recognize their role as statesmen, become more involved in the public arena, and develop a public service culture. To help them do so various organizational remedies are proposed, such as splitting the roles of chairman and CEO and creating new positions in international public affairs that perform a diplomatic function.

## Revisions Questions

1. How does the concept of the public interest relate to corporate governance?
2. What do sociologists say about the relationship between the economy (including MNCs) and society?
3. What restraints have the conservative economists Frederick Hayek and Milton Friedman placed on the operation of the "free market system"?
4. What are some reforms in corporate governance that MNCs should consider?
5. What are some of the ways in which CEOs can play a larger role as "corporate statesmen."

## Discussion Questions

I. The concept of the "public interest" is simply too vague to serve as a criterion for business decisions. Discuss whether you agree or disagree with that view?

II. Jeffrey Garten proposes that the leaders of big multinational companies should fill a vacuum created by government leaders and provide more leadership in the governance of the global economy? (See Garten's quote.) If so, what are the dangers? Is that a proper function of business?

III. On what public issues should CEOs of MNCs speak out? What urgency would you assign to the following: (a) personal taxation items in the federal budget, (b) corporate taxation, (c) corporate subsidies, (d) reform of a country's public education system, (e) rising cost of college education, (f) the role of the federal government in providing healthcare, (g) the cost of healthcare, (h) immigration, (i) possibly going to war with Iran over the nuclear weapons issue? Any other issues?

IV. What degree of involvement should CEOs consider – only speaking out or becoming politically active? When should the resources of the MNC be used?

# afterword

The aim of this book has been to fill a perceived void in business education and management practice in the area of international affairs. With the continuing growth in globalization, it became clear that managers who had significant responsibilities in dealing with new players in the international arena would need to identify contemporary issues under discussion and how to deal with them.

The purpose of this book therefore became to describe the key features and issues of the international arena and to review what management responses were available. Because globalization is symbolized by modern multinational corporations (MNCs), attention was focused on them. Within MNCs, the construct of "the global manager" was used to describe the characteristics of persons responsible for interacting with the new players. Such a manager did not primarily represent a new position but possessed a new layer of competencies and responsibilities over existing ones. These competencies were summarized in a list of attributes or qualities, such as believing in diversity and understanding different cultures.

The focus of a global manager's responsibilities was not on internal, everyday operations but on the understandings and misunderstandings with outside entities over their interests and responsibilities *vis-à-vis* each other. In this sense, global managers were the private sector's equivalent of diplomats in foreign embassies. Their function was to establish and smooth relationships, to explain their organization's aims and activities, and to resolve problems that arose. In a domestic setting, this function is performed by a corporation's public affairs officer who is familiar with its socio-political environment and knows how to deal with it. In an international setting, this function is performed by the global manager, who has become familiar with the environments and problems of a multitude of countries. These managers understand a country's socio-political structure and the cultures that guide the behavior of their players.

## Issues

In examining what it is that international players discuss among one another, the simple answer was "issues" – the topics or problems that reflect the goals players want to achieve and the difficulties that arise from them. Issues have become an increasingly important factor in corporate decision making because they summarize some key concerns in a firm's external environment.

The media are full of references to issues. They are a way of capsulizing and categorizing the myriad daily events reported by journalists. As shown in the book's contents, the issues of the greatest relevance to global managers are summarized in nine broad categories, which draw on the classical references to economic, socio-political, cultural, physical, and technological factors. Any one issue, however, covers several sub-issues, so that globalization also refers to the resurgence of nationalism; threats to national brands refer to safety issues as well as anti-American sentiments; and sustainability refers to the ability of business to satisfy the health and physical needs of people. Problems in any one industry, however, like those faced by the extractive industries or agro-businesses, could themselves serve as separate issues.

Alternative ways of categorizing the issues might have been used, such as the five levels of the pyramid of global corporate responsibility. The first level, which deals with the economics of producing goods and services, as well as jobs, could refer to the issues of globalization, economic development, human resources, and technology. Similarly, the second level's concern about social costs could include the issue of sustainability and climate change. The highest level, human betterment, could include human rights and investment in human capital. For certain purposes this approach might yield insights and should be applied.

But the most important aspects of the issues covered by this book are to examine why a particular issue is relevant and important for a specific company and what its options are in responding to it. Does the issue represent a risk or an opportunity? Is the issue one that is normally the responsibility of government or a civil society organization? Or would collaboration with one or both lead to better results?

Global managers must constantly engage in issue management to gauge the importance of particular issues to their specific company. In so doing, trends regarding an issue must also be considered. For example, some believe that human rights is moving up on the agenda and fast becoming a mainstream issue. Others say that global warming is an ever-present, simmering danger and needs attention now. They point to steady occurrences of natural catastrophes, such as fires in Australia, droughts in the United States' Southwest, and superstorms like Hurricane Sandy that devastated low-lying areas in New Jersey and New York City. Events with a low probability of occurring often result in the most serious consequences.

## Developments to watch

1. Globalization continues to generate an interconnected global economy with complex results. Powerful new economies, notably China and India, have emerged, and new areas, such as Africa, are moving beyond the status of resource suppliers only. While the GDP of nations rises, so do problems of increasing inequality of income and concentrations of wealth. At risk is the stability of nations and the human development of their people. Challenges to globalization appear sporadically in the form of protests and the resurgence of nationalistic interests and sentiments. As worldwide communications proliferate, however, some cultural differences and barriers may dissolve and make standardized products and procedures more common. At

the same time, some nations may assert their distinction from other cultures, as China and Russia have with respect to human rights.

2. The boundaries of the three major institutions of society – business, government, and civil society – are shifting and overlapping. Business is asked by international organizations, especially the UN and NGOs, to assume burdens that were previously government's. Included are the achievement of human rights and the elimination of poverty. From business's viewpoint it benefits from privatization opportunities. It has ventured into traditional government activities, such as the construction and operation of airports, prisons, bridges, and roads. Its contributions to military operations include the provision of special security forces for high-ranking visitors and managing highly technical hardware.

3. Civil society's NGOs have become a potent force in monitoring whether corporations develop enforce codes of conduct in their operations and supply chains. In doing so, NGOs perform a function that some governments have neglected. Rather than confront corporations, NGOs increasingly work with them to achieve environmental goals and other standards of behavior. Some issues are so complex and difficult that joint efforts by all three institutions are needed.

4. Technology has produced both stupendous benefits and problems for the world. Advances in the life sciences hold the promise of improving and lengthening human life and exploring the intricacies of human brains. Biotechnology continues to be the main answer to providing food for the world population surge. Chemistry and physics may unravel the mysteries of hydrogen and produce the ultimate energy source that lessens global warming. Engineering advances in the development of robotics will help solve labor shortage problems, especially among developed nations that are experiencing declines in their native populations.

5. The digital revolution has led to the explosive growth of the Internet and the proliferation of mobile phones in the developing countries. They bring large bodies of information to virtually everyone and stimulate the formation of social communities. But digital technology has also increased the vulnerability of business to cyberattacks that threaten their operations and intellectual property. Cybersecurity concerns are therefore mounting. Another danger is that governments are attempting to control the Internet because they fear its open, uncontrolled nature. Recently, some of the U.N.'s 193 member states sought to persuade the International Telecommunications Union (ITU) to take over the Internet's rules and workings. Iran, along with Russia, wants an ITU rule that lets them monitor Internet traffic routed through or to their countries, allowing them to eavesdrop or block access. Business must help guard the freedom of the Internet.

6. Business must reckon with growing outside sources of pressure that will compel it to respond to contemporary issues. Traditional advocacy groups will continue to confront business on issues of concern to them, sometimes by threatening to seek more government regulation. Consumer pressure will continue to mount on those companies who have to protect their strong brands and reputations. Other stakeholders, such as large investors, will also exert pressure for changes. An unknown factor is whether professional societies, such as public accountants, engineers, and lawyers, will become more active as a countervailing source of power. So far they have not exerted much influence, because they are beholden to their clients or employers.

Independent groups, notably labor unions, may gather strength depending on economic and political events.

7.  Business, especially retailers, must prepare contingency plans for the possibility of rationing, as periodic shortages of basic foods, fuel, medicines, and other essentials occur. They can no longer rely on the price mechanism to handle rationing by pricing some users out of the market, because that is not politically feasible or ethical. During the United States' oil crises in 1973 and 1979, the government imposed price controls and rationing, which businesses had to implement. Various plans were discussed, one being that motorists could buy a certain amount of fuel at a low price but that larger amounts would be priced higher. Another plan, used in India, was to open public shops that distributed rations at a subsidized price to the poor.

8.  Corporate recognition of contemporary issues is reflected in the creation of new positions, such as vice president for environmental sustainability or corporate social responsibility and sustainability. Further recognition is found in the publication of social reports, which increasingly are called sustainability reports. More companies are using the guidelines of the Global Reporting Initiative. MNCs also recognize international operations more by creating such titles as vice president of international relations, vice president of world-wide operations, or vice president for world-wide public affairs and communication.

9.  Risk management is becoming more important, not only in deciding what countries and areas to invest in, but also how long a supply chain should be, what technologies to pursue, and what products to sell. Decisions include building nuclear power plants in certain locations and the continuing debate about the extension of new GM crops. Organizations like the Global Organization of Risk Professionals will likely become more important.

## Corporate responses

When a global manager concentrates on any one issue, he or she must decide on its relevance to a particular company, whether action should be taken, and, if so, what its response should be. The responses are of two types: one deals with techniques, and the other with corporate governance. The main trend in techniques is the continuing application and reach of the social media. They create awareness of issues and can exert pressure on business to respond to them. Developments in corporate governance may have far wider effects on how issues are treated. Proxy statements continue to call for reforms by splitting the roles of chief executive and chairman of the board, requiring more independent directors, and reviewing the pay of high-level executives and board members. More important, however, is whether corporate governance boards will go beyond traditional profit maximizing and concentration on short-term results. Public expectations are changing and requiring boards to heed the public interest. The idea of altering the composition of the board to include environmental, consumer, labor, and other interests may take hold.

A consequence of studying how business responds to contemporary issues is that the free market system itself is being judged. Ultimately, business must satisfy the needs of the society. To what extent this can be achieved through the market system is the big question. That is why this book ends with an examination of challenges to the free enterprise system by alternative approaches. The common denominator of these alternatives is that corporations are seen as more than working in the interests of stockholders; they must also care about the larger purpose of the corporation. That purpose includes paying attention to other stakeholders of the corporation and, gradually, to the larger requirement of serving the public interest.

Consideration of the public interest is reflected by the willingness to recognize the issues outlined in this book. Corporations should first be expected to ask themselves whether attention to some issues would enhance their profit-making ability, in keeping with the legal definition of a corporation. But secondarily, in light of the urgency of many of the world's problems, corporations must also ask themselves what issue(s) most affect them. Further questions are what issues a corporation is morally obligated to help solve and what issues it is in the best position to help do so.

This book places the burden of answering these questions on the global manager. He or she must be among society's leading thinkers to help corporations keep pace with interlocking global changes. To succeed, the global manager must keep abreast of developments with the issues discussed in this book and remain alert for the emergence of new ones.

The global manager is aligned with those management practices that encourage the sharing of information and decision making among all relevant members of an organization. This mindset is extended to outside individuals and organizations that can contribute to the solution of environmental and societal problems. These problems are becoming so momentous and intractable that they require long-term, joint efforts to solve. Collaboration will be the only way to do business in the future. And in keeping with Alcoa's slogan, global managers must remember that "The Future is Now."

# Notes

## 1 Globalization creates need for global managers

1  The term "multinational corporation" (MNC) is used in this book. Other authors prefer the term "transnational corporation" (TNC), or "multinational enterprise," which includes private corporations and other kinds of businesses. The reference to MNCs also includes SME's – small and medium sized enterprises.

2  Thomas L. Friedman, *The World Is Flat; A Brief History of the Twenty-first Century* (New York: Farrar, Straus and Giroux, 2005), p. 48.

3  Ibid. The ten forces are discussed in Chapter 2, pp. 48–172.

4  Ibid., p. 49.

5  Ibid.

6  Ibid., p. 132.

7  Ibid., p. 469.

8  Thomas L. Friedman, *Hot, Flat, and Crowded: Why We Need a Green Revolution – and How It Can Renew America* (New York: Farrar, Straus and Giroux, 2008), p. 26.

9  Ibid., p. 181.

10  Ibid., pp. 23–24.

11  Hill, Charles W. L., *International Business*, 7th edn (New York and London: McGraw-Hill International Edition, 2005).

12  Robin Kramar, *Human Resource Management in a Global Context: A Critical Approach* (New York: Palgrave Macmillan, 2012); Ronald P. Babin and Brian Nicholson, *Sustainable Global Outsourcing: Achieving Social and Environmental Responsibility in Global IT and Business Process Outsourcing* (New York: Palgrave Macmillan, 2012); T.C. Melewar and Suraksha Gupta, eds., *Strategic International Marketing: An Advanced Perspective* (New York: Palgrave Macmillan, 2012).

13  Alan M. Rugman and Thomas L. Brewer, eds., *The Oxford Handbook of International Business* (Oxford: Oxford University Press, 2001).

14  Jean J. Boddewyn, "The Domain of International Management," *Journal of International Management*, Vol. 5, 1999, pp. 3–14.

15  Ibid., pp. 9, 13.

16  Rajib N. Sanyal *International Management: A Strategic Perspective* (Upper Saddle River, NJ: Prentice Hall: 2001), p. 2.

17  For more on this theme, see Talcott Parsons, *The Social System* (Glencoe, IL: The Free Press, 1951).

18  George Lodge and Richard Walton, "The American Corporation and Its New Relationships," *California Management Review*, Vol. 31, Spring, 1989, pp. 10–24.

19 Samuel B. Graves and Sandra A. Waddock, "Beyond Built to Last ... Stakeholder Relations in 'Built-to-Last' Companies," *Business and Society Review*, Vol. 105, No. 4, 2001, pp. 393–418.

20 Robert D. Putnam, *Bowling Alone: The Collapse and Revival of American Community* (New York: Simon & Schuster: 2000), p. 19.

21 "Bring Back the Quilting Bee," review of Robert D. Putnam, Bowling Alone: The Collapse and Revival of American Community, *BusinessWeek*, June 26, 2000.

22 Paul S. Adler and Seok-Woo Kwon, "Social Capital: Prospects for a New Concept," *Academy of Management Review*, Vol. 27, No. 1, pp. 17–40.

23 Geoff Gloeckler, "Here Come the Millennials," *BusinessWeek*, November 24, 2008, p. 47. Reference is to a study of Generation Y students entering MBA programs.

24 Gary Bonvillian and William A. Nowlin, "Cultural Awareness: An Essential Element of Doing Business Abroad," *Business Horizons*, Vol. 37, No. 6, November–December 1994, p. 44.

25 Edward B. Tylor, *Primitive Culture* (London: John Murray: 1871), p. 1. Mentioned in Thomas Neil Gladwin and Vern Terpstra, "Introduction," in Vern Terpstra, ed., *The Cultural Environment of International Business* (Dallas, TX: South-Western Publishing, 1978), p. xii.

26 Mentioned in Richard C. Lewis, *When Cultures Collide: Managing Successfully Across Cultures* (London: Nicholas Brealey Publishing, 1996). p. 25.

27 Fons Trompenaars and Charles Hampden-Turner, *Riding the Waves of Culture: Understanding Cultural Diversity in Global Business*, 2nd edn (New York: McGraw-Hill: 1998).

28 Ibid, p. 8.

29 Ibid., p. 11.

30 Thomas L. Friedman, *The World Is Flat; A Brief History of the Twenty-first Century* (New York: Farrar, Straus and Giroux, 2005), p. 324.

31 Ibid., p. 326. Reference is to David S. Landes, *The Wealth and Poverty of Nations: Why Some Are So Rich and Some So Poor* (New York: Norton, 1998).

32 Ibid., p. 328.

33 R. Edward Freeman, *Strategic Management: A Stakeholder Approach* (New York: Basic Books, 1984). The stakeholder relationship management concept is summarized in Sandra Waddock, *Leading Corporate Citizens: Vision, Values, Value Added*, 2nd edn (New York: McGraw-Hill Irwin, 2006), pp. 9–10.

34 Lee Preston and James E. Post state that they don't consider the environment a stakeholder but an essential underpining for human civilization to survive. See their *Private Management and Public Policy: the Principle of Public Responsibility* (Englewood Cliffs, NJ: Prentice hall, 1975).

35 James R. Emshoff and R. Edward Freeman, "Who's Butting Into Your Business?," *The Wharton Magazine*, Vol. 4, Fall 1979, pp. 44–59.

36 James E. Post, Lee E. Preston, and Sybil Sachs, "Managing the Extended Enterprise: The New Stakeholder View," *California Management Review*, No. 45, No. 1 (2002), pp. 6–29.

37 Ibid., p. 8.

38 Theodore Levitt, *The Third Sector: New Tactics for a Responsive Society* (New York: AMACOM, 1973), p. 73.

39  "Vision Statement: What Keeps Global Leaders Up at Night," *Harvard Business Review*, Vol. 90, April 2012, pp. 32–33.

40  Bob Davis, "Economic Forum Focuses on Conflict," *Wall Street Journal*, January 29, 2002, p. A13.

41  Geffrey E. Garten, *The Mind of the CEO* (New York: Basic Books, 2001), p. 192.

42  These are major topics in Otto Lerbinger, *Corporate Public Affairs: Interacting with Interest Groups, Media, and Government* (Mayway, NJ: Lawrence Erlbaum Associates, 2006), pp. 18–23.

43  For an overview of issues management see R.L. Heath and Associates, *Strategic Issues Management: How Organizations Influence and Respond to Public Interests and Policies* (San Francisco, CA: Jossey-Bass, 1988).

44  For a discussion of these topics, see Otto Lerbinger, *Corporate Public Affairs: Interacting With Interest Groups, Media, and Government* (Mahway, NJ: Lawrence Erlbaum Associates, 2006).

45  Christopher A. Bartlett and S. Ghoshal, "What Is a Global Manager?," *Harvard Business Review*, Vol. 70, No. 5, September–October 1992, pp. 124–132.

46  Cynthia Macdonald, "A Global Affairs: The Munk School Takes on the World," *U of T Magazine*, Autumn 2010, p. 34.

47  Fons Trompenaars and Charles Hampden-Turner, *Riding the Waves of Cultures: Understanding Cultural Diversity in Global Business*, 2nd edn (New York and London: McGraw-Hill, 1998), p. 9.

48  Stephen Green et al., "In Search of Global Leaders," *Harvard Business Review*, Vol. 81, August 2003, pp. 38–45.

49  Macdonald, op. cit., p. 35.

50  Trompenaars and Hampden-Turner, op. cit., pp. 8–11.

51  Charles M. Hampden-Turnerand Fons Trompenaars, "A Mirror-Image World: Doing Business in Asia," in Malcom Warner and Pat Joynt, eds., *Managing Across Cultures: Issues and Perspectives* (London: Thomson Learning, 2002), pp. 144–145.

52  See Christopher A. Bartlett and Sumantra Ghosphal, *Managing Across Borders: The Transnational Solution*, 2nd edn (Boston: Harvard Business School Press, 1998), chapter 8, "Legitimizing Diversity: Balancing Multiple Perspectives."

53  Barlett, op. cit.

54  Ibid.

55  Bartlett op. cit., "What Is a Global Manager?"

56  Interview by Cynthia Churchwell of Christopher A. Bartlett, "Research & Ideas," December 15, 2003. http://hbswk.hbs.edu/item/3827.html

57  Daniel Goleman, *Emotional Intelligence* (New York: Bantam Books, 1995).

58  Ibid., p. 42.

59  Ibid., pp. 43–44.

60  Joseph S. Nye, Jr., *Soft Power: The Means to Success in World Politics* (New York: Public Affairs, 2004), p. x.

61  Boris Holzer, "Corporate Power and Transnational Civil Society," in Ingo K. Richter, Sabine Berking and Ralf Müller-Schmid, eds., *Building a Transnational Civil Society: Global Issues and Global Actors* (New York: Palgrave Macmillan, 2006), p. 41.

62  Ibid., p. 43.

63  Otto Lerbinger and Nathaniel H. Sperber, *Key to the Executive Head* (Reading, MA: Addison-Wesley Publishing Company, 1975), p. 44.

64  Nathaniel H. Sperber and Otto Lerbinger, *Manager's Public Relations Handbook* (Reading, MA: Addison-Wesley Publishing Company, Inc., 1982).

65  Mentioned by Jerry Useem, "From Heroes to Goats and Back Again? How Corporate Leaders Lost Our Trust," *Fortune*, November 18, 2002, p. 48.

66  Ibid.

67  Leslie-Gaines-Ross, *CEO Capital: A Guide to Building CEO Reputation and Company Success* (New York: John Wiley & Sons, Inc., 2003), p. 13.

68  Burson-Marsteller, "Building CEO Capital," 2001. Leslie Gaines-Ross, "CEOs Stranded in Wonderland," *Journal of Business Strategy*, March/April 2002, p. 19 .

69  Often quoted, e.g., in John Coyle, "Business & Media: Media: Flattery Will Get You Everywhere: But It Shouldn't," *The Observer*, April 18, 2004, p. 6.

70  Burson-Marsteller news release, "97% of Business Leaders Believe Damaged Corporate Reputations Can Be Restored – Though It May Take Up to Four Years," September 16, 2003.

71  R. P. Barston, *Modern Diplomacy*, 2nd edn (London and New York: Longman, 1997), p. 5.

72  Barston, op. cit., p. 303.

73  Christer Jonsson and Martin Hall, *The Essence of Diplomacy* (New York: Palgrave Macmillan, 2005), p. 134.

74  Raymond Cohen, *Negotiating Across Cultures: International Communication in an Interdependent World* (revised edition, Washington, DC: United States Institute of Peace Press, 1997), p. 23.

75  Sir Ernest Satow, *A Guide to Diplomatic Practice* (London: Longmans, Green, 1917), p. 25.

76  "Diplomacy," *Encyclopedia Britannica*, 1973, p. 472.

77  Satow, op. cit., p. 25.

78  Ibid., p. 26.

79  Ibid., p. 28.

80  Robert Trice, Miyako Hasegawa, and Michael Kearns, eds., *Corporate Diplomacy: Principled Leadership for the Global Community* (Washington, DC: Center for Strategic & International Studies, 1995).

81  Kristi Heim, "Forging Ties with China Suits Locke," *Seattle Times*, September 8, 2006, p. A1.

82  Melissen, op. cit., p. xx.

83  Elizaeth Dwoskin, with Indira A.R. Kakshmanan, "Politics & Policy: Secretary of Commerce," *Bloomberg BusinessWeek*, January 14–20, 2013, pp. 22–25.

84  Ulrich Steger, *Corporate Diplomacy: The Strategy for a Volatile, Fragmented Business Environment* (New York: Wiley, 2003).

85  Examples of such literature are James E. Post, et al. *Business and Society: Corporate Strategy, Public Policy, Ethics* (Irwin/McGraw Hill, 1999) and Otto Lerbinger, *The Crisis Manager: Facing Risk and Responsibility* (Mahway, NJ: Lawrence Erlbaum Associates, 1997).

86  Steger, op. cit., pp. 6–7.

87  Ibid., p. x.

88  Prestowitz, op. cit. However, Prestowitz dismisses the idea of the vice president of public affairs as a secretary of state because few are to be found talking to the National Security Council or the foreign and defense ministers of the major countries about foreign and national security policy. A public affairs person, he says, is almost invariably a lobbyist focused rather narrowly on tax, trade and regulatory issues. He or she is typically a former member of Congress, congressional staffer or executive branch official with a legal background; a person who spends a lot of time working on legislative matters and meeting with officials from the trade, commerce and agriculture departments of the United States and other key countries.

89  Nicholas Kralev, "Diplomatic Reorientation; Foreign Service Experiences Recruitment Changes," *The Washington Times*, April 12, 2004, p. A15.

90  Tatyana Yegorova, "Boeing's Ambassador Sees Supersonic future," *The Moscow Times*, May 30, 2001.

91  Caroline Daniel, "Boeing Turns to the Benefits of Diplomacy...." *Financial Times (London)*, October 15, 2003, USA Edition 1, p. 8.

92  Within a year after his appointment, Pickering hired 10–12 country and regional vice-presidents in key markets. Murdo Morrison, "Heavyweight Pickering Moves to Transform Boeing's Global Profiles," *Flight International*, August 13, 2002, p. 35.

93  Asked whether he is now a businessman or a diplomat, Pickering's answer was "I don't see myself as either. I see myself as somewhere in between, learning about business and bringing a background in skilled diplomacy to that effort .... Many of the CEOs I have come to know have an awful lot of skills and knowledge of a good diplomat.... It's just that the measures of effectiveness are different."

94  Caroline Daniel, "Boeing Turns to the Benefits of Diplomacy: Aerospace," *Financial Times (USA Education)*, October 15, 2003, p. 8.

95  www.chinaconcept.com/index2.asp.

# 2  Building sound relationships with global players

1  Sarah Anderson and John Cavanagh, "Top 200: The Rise of Corporate Global Power," CorpWatch, http:://www.coorpwatch.org/article/php?id=377.

2  Stuart Hart, *Capitalism at the Crossroads: Next Generation Business Strategies for a Post-Crisis World,* 3rd edn (Upper Saddle River, NJ: Pearson Education, publishing as Wharton School Publishing, 2010), p. 13.

3  "Fortune 500: Our Annual Ranking of America's Largest Corporations," CNNMoney, 2011.

4  Ibid., p. 100.

5  Antonia Juhasz, *The Bush Agenda: Invading the World, One Economy at a Time* (New York: Regan Books, 2006), p. 100.

6  A classification proposed in an early article on MNCs by Howard V. Perlmutter, "The Tortuous Evolution of the Multinational Corporation," *Colombia Journal of World Business,* January–February 1969.

7  Ibid., p. 16.

8  As outlined in the first article of the Charter, the UN's primary purpose is the

maintenance of international peace and security. The organization is also dedicated to the development of friendly relations among nations, based on the principle of equal rights and self-determination of peoples; to the achievement of international cooperation in solving international economic, social, cultural, or humanitarian problems; and to serving as a centre for harmonizing the actions of nations in the attainment of these ends.

9   "Caribbean Calls for End to Sexual Exploitation," BBC Monitoring Latin America – Political Supplied by BBC Worldwide Monitoring, November 26, 2008.

10  "Global Targets, Local Ingenuity," *The Economist*, September 25, 2010, pp. 34–35. Also, "The Eight Commandments," *The Economist*, July 17, 2007, p. 25. For more information see UN Millennium Development Goals Report (New York: United Nations, 2006).

11  Ibid.

12  Ibid., p. 26.

13  Ibid., p. 28.

14  Richard Boundreaux, "The World; Leaders See World Closing in on Malaria; New Pledges Totaling $3 Billion Could Help Wipe Out Deaths From the Mosquito-Borne Disease by 2015," *Los Angeles Times*, September 28, 2008, p. A13.

15  www.worldbank.org

16  "World Bank Disgrace" editorial, *Wall Street Journal*, January 14, 2008, p. A12. Also see "The World Bank: Dirty Linen," *The Economist*, March 22, 2008, p. 68.

17  Matt Moffett and Bob Davis, "Insufficient Fund: Booming Economy Leaves the IMF Groping for Mission," *Wall Street Journal*, April 21, 2006, p. A12.

18  "Face value: Globalisation's New Cheerleader," *The Economist*, September 7, 2002, p. 60.

19  "China and the WTO: Let Me Entertain You," *The Economist*, August 15, 2009, p. 36.

20  "EU Focus: Understanding the European Union," *FP: Foreign Policy*, May/June 2011, Special Advertising Section, EU Focus, p. 1.

21  Ibid.

22  "Charlemagne: The Puny Economic Powerhouse," *The Economist*, December 10, 2005, p. 60.

23  Charles Forelle, "EU to Propose Energy Overhaul," *Wall Street Journal*, September 17, 2007, p. A5.

24  "Europe's Mid-Life Crisis," *The Economist*, March 17, 2007, p. 13.

25  Grainne Hehir, "GE Tries to Prepare EU for Honeywell Deal," *Wall Street Journal*, January 30, 2001, p. A17.

26  Kathryn Kranhold, "Europe Tentatively Backs GE Deal," *Wall Street Journal*, July 29, 2003, p. A6.

27  See Dan Carney, with Amy Borrus and Jay Greene, "Microsoft's All-Out Counter-attack," *BusinessWeek*, May 15, 2000, pp. 103–106; also see Otto Lerbinger, *Corporate Public Affairs: Interacting With Interest Groups, Media, and Government* (Mahway, NJ, Lawrence Erlbaum, 2006), p. 12.

28  Adam Cohen, "Microsoft Faces Threat of More Fines in Europe," *Wall Street Journal*, February 15, 2006, p. B2. For more background, see Brandon Mitchener, "Focus on Microsoft Now Turns to EU," *Wall Street Journal*, November 5, 2002, p. B5.

29  Charles Forelle, "Neelie Kroes, Antitrust Chief, European Union," *Wall Street Journal*, November 19, 2007, p. R3.

30  Charles Forelle, "Europe's Antitrust Chief Defies Critics, and Microsoft," *Wall Street Journal*, February 25, 2008, p. A1, A12.

31  Charles Forelle, "Microsoft Loss in Europe Raises American Fears," *Wall Street Journal*, September 18, 2007, p. A1.

32  Charles Forelle, "EU Fines Microsoft $1.35 Billion," *Wall Street Journal*, February 28, 2008, p. B2.

33  Charles Forelle, "Microsoft Yields to EU on Browsers," *Wall Street Journal*, July 25–26, 2009, p. B1.

34  Mary Jacoby, "Microsoft Talks of Breakthrough in European Antitrust Hearings, *Wall Street Journal*, April 1/2–2006, p. A4.

35  Charles Forelle and Nick Wingfield, "EU Hits Microsoft With New Antitrust Charges," *Wall Street Journal*, January 17–28, 2009, p. B5.

36  Peppi Kiviniemi, "Intel to Get EU Antitrust Fine," *Wall Street Journal*, May 11, 2009, p. B2.

37  Charles Forelle, "EU Draw Rebuke in Intel Case Lapse," *Wall Street Journal*, August 8–9, 2009, p. A7.

38  "The Luddites Make Ground; GM Foods and Trade," *The Economist*, July 2, 2005. Also see Neil King Jr., "U.S. to Challenge EU Moratorium on Genetically Modified Foods," *Wall Street Journal*, May 12, 2003, p. A4.

39  Anthony Browne, "Protests After Europe Ends GM Food Freeze," *The Times* (London), May 20, 2004, p. 18.

40  Alex Scott, "WTO Rules Against EU on GM Crop Bans; Greens Claim Victory," *Chemical Week*, May 24, 2006, p. 15.

41  "EU Set to Approve GM Potato, *Chemical Week*, July 25, 2007, p. 35.

42  "Chaebol Trouble," *The Economist*, March 15, 2003, p. 62.

43  Dejan Vercic, "Public Relations in a Corporativist Country: The Case of Slovenia," in Krishnamurthy Sriramesh and Dejan Vercic, eds., *The Global Public Relations Handbook: Theory, Research, and Practice* (Mahway, NJ, Lawrence Erlbaum Associates, 2003), p. 288.

44  "Special Report: State Capitalism – The Visible Hand," *The Economist*, January 21, 2012, p. 6.

45  Ibid., pp. 8–9.

46  Ibid., p. 9.

47  "Chinese Industry and the State: The Myth of China Inc.," *The Economist*, September 3, 2005, p. 53.

48  "China Eases Overseas-Investment Approvals," *Wall Street Journal*, December 25, 2003, p. A6.

49  See Keisuke Nakano, "More Companies Look to NPOs for Support in Corporate Social Responsibility Activities," *The Nikkei Weekly* (Japan), April 16, 2012.

50  "Facts and Figures about Charitable Organizations," Independent Sector, www.independentsector.org. Last updated January 4, 2007.

51  Leonora Angeles and Penny Gurstein, "Introduction: Learning Civil Societies for Democratic Planning and Governance," in Penny Gurstein and Leonora Angeles, eds., *Learning Civil Societies: Shifting Contexts for Democratic Planning and Governance* (Toronto: University of Toronto Press, 2007), p. 5.

52    John G. Ruggie, "Taking Embedded Liberalism Global," in David Held and Mathias Koenig-Archibugi, eds., *Taming Globalization: Frontiers of Governance* (Cambridge, UK: Polity Press, 2003). Mentioned in George Lodge and Craig Wilson, *A Corporate Solution to Global Poverty: How Multinationals Can Help the Poor and Invigorate Their Own Legitimacy* (Princeton, NJ: Princeton University Press, 2006), p. 48.

53    Nancy Folbre and Jennifer Robock Morse, *The Invisible Heart: Economics and Family Values* (New York: New Press, 2001).

54    Mark Lehrer and Christian Delaunay, "Multinational Enterprise and the Promotion of Civil Society: The Challenge to 21st Century Capitalism," *California Management Review*, Vol 51, No. 4, Summer 20 09, p. 127.

55    Christopher Gunn, *Third Sector Development* (Ithaca, NY: Cornell University Press, 2004) (mentioned in Hart, p. 36).

56    "The World's View of Multinationals," *The Economist*, January 29, 2000, p. 21.

57    Lodge and Wilson, op. cit. pp. 47–59.

58    Comments by Michael McDermott and Jonathan Wootliff at a session on "Building Relationships with Non-government Organizations" held at the Public Relations Society of America International Conference, October 27–30, 2001.

59    Rob Van Tulden, with Alex van der Zwart, *International Business-Society Management* (London and New York: Routledge, 2006), p. 291.

60    Boris Holzer, "Corporate Power and Transnational Civil Society," in Ingo K. Richter, Sabine Berking and Ralf Müller-Schmid, eds., *Building a Transnational Civil Society: Global Issues and Global Actors* (New York: Palgrave Macmillan, 2006) p. 45.

61    Van Tulden, op.cit., p. 195.

62    Ragnar E. Lofstedt and Ortwin Renn, "The Brent Spar Controversy: An Example of Risk Communication Gone Wrong," *Risk Analysis*, Vol. 17, No. 1, 1997, pp. 131–136.

63    Ibid., p. 133.

64    Van Tulden, op. cit., pp. 297, 343

65    This situation is further described in *purview No. 390,* a supplement of *pr reporter,* August 7, 1995.

66    Linda Hon, "Negotiating Relationships With Activist Publics," in Kathy Fitzpatrick and Carolyln Bronstein, eds., *Ethics in Public Relations: Responsible Advocacy* (Thousand Oaks, CA: Sage Publications, 2006), p. 62.

67    Ibid., p. 54.

68    Edelman TrustBarometer, January 19, 2012.

69    Shai Oster, "Pact May Ease Impact of Three Gorges Dam," *Wall Street Journal*, January 29, 2008,.p. A7.

70    "Dual responsibilities of NGOs: market and institutional responsibilities and ethics," *Journal of Corporate Citizenship*, No. 17, March 2005, p. 26.

71    Wootliff, op. cit Wootliff also worked as Managing Director of Edelman Public Relations Global Stakeholder Priace and for the PR firm of Hill & Knowlton.

72    Reviewed in "Better Nonprofit-Government Partnerships Exist Abroad," *Nonprofit World*, Mar/Apr 2000, Madison, NJ.

73    Michael Kunczik, *Images of Nations and International Public Relations* (Mahway, NJ: Lawrence Erlbaum Associates, 1997), pp. 91–92. After consulting experts, Greenpeace concluded that the risk of being in a Siberian prison were low.

74    Ibid.

75   David Moberg, "Solidarity Without Borders," *In These Times*, Institute for Public Affairs, 2007, p. 48.

76   Glenn Burkins, "Labor Reaches Out to Global Economy," *Wall Street Journal*, April 11, 2000, p. A2.

77   See http://www.global-unions.org?IMG/pdf/MakingWorldDifference 4.pdf

78   See Hal Weitzman, "Foreign Investors Agree to Bolivia's Gas Plans," *Financial Times* (London), October 30, 2006, p. 10.

79   "Both countervailing power and power-sharing relate to what the relationship literature calls control mutuality, defined as: "the degree to which parties agree on who has the rightful power to influence one another." Although it is recognized that symmetry is not natural in an organizational setting, "stable relationships require that organizations and publics each have some control over the other." L.C. Hon and J.E. Grunig, *Guidelines for Measuring Relationships in Public Relations* (Gainesville, FL: Institution for Public Relations, 1999), p. 1.

80   James E. Grunig and Yi-Hui Huang, "From Organizational Effectiveness to Relationship Indicators: Antecedents of Relationships, Public Relations Strategies, and Relationship Outcomes," in John A. Ledingham, and Stephen D. Bruning, eds., *Public Relations as Relationship Management: A Relational Approach to the Study and Practice of Public Relations* (Mahwah, NJ: Lawrence Erlbaum Associates, Publishers, 2000), pp. 42–49.

81   Webster's 7th New Collegiate Dictionary (Springfield, MA: G&C Merriam Company: 1963), p. 952.

82   Grunig and Huang, op. cit., p. 44.

83   Ibid., pp. 42–43.

84   Hon and Grunig, op. cit.

85   Grunig and Huang, op. cit., pp. 43–46.

86   Roger Fisher and Scott Brown in *Getting Together: Building Relationships As We Negotiate* (New York: Penguin Books, 1988).

87   From Howard V. Perlmutter, "The Tortuous Evolution of the Multinational Corporation," *Colombia Journal of World Business*, January–February 1969.

# 3   Resistance to globalization and resurgent nationalism

1   Jane Sasseen, "Economists Rethink Free Trade," *BusinessWeek*, February 11, 2008, p. 32.

2   Ibid.

3   Bob Davis, "Surge in Protectionism Threatens to Deepened World-Wide Crisis," *Wall Street Journal*, January 12, 2009, p. A2.

4   John W. Miller, "Nations Rush To Established New Barriers to Trade," *Wall Street Journal*, February 6, 2009, p. A1.

5   Mark A. Hofmann, "Interest in Enterprise Risk Management Is Growing," *Business Insurance*, May 4, 2009. Also see the special advertising section "Risk Management, in the *Wall Street Journal*, May 11, 2011, p. C10.

6   Shivan S. Subramaniam, "Management Trends ... Keep It Simple: Getting Your

Arms Around Enterprise Risk Management," Executive Action Series, No. 165 (New York: The Conference Board, October 2005), p. 1.

7   Randy Myers, "The Risk of Globalization," a special advertising section on risk management, *Wall Street Journal*, May 11, 2011, p. C10.

8   Douglas W. Hubbard, *The Failure of Risk Management: Why It's Broken and How to Fix It* (Hoboken, NJ: John Wiley & Sons, Inc. 2009), p. 10.

9   David Wessel and Bob Davis, "Job Prospects: Pain From Free Trade Spurs Second Thoughts," *Wall Street Journal*, March 28, 2007, p. A1.

10  "The World View of Multinationals," *The Economist*, January 29, 2000, p. 21.

11  "Globalization and Freedom: The Prosperity League," *The Economist*, June 22, 2002, p. 68.

12  "Economics Focus/Trade Disputes: Nagging Doubts About the Benefits of Globalisation, and a Look at the Evidence," *The Economist*, September 18, 2004, p. 80.

13  Justin Lahart, "Paul Krugman Is Awarded Nobel in Economics," *Wall Street Journal*, October 14, 2008, p. A6.

14  Benjamin M. Friedman, *The Moral Consequences of Economic Growth* (New York: Knopf, 2005), p. ix.

15  Ibid., p. 5–6.

16  Conor Dougherty, "Income Slides to 1996 Levels," *Wall Street Journal*, September 14, 2011, p. A1.

17  Ibid., p. 8.

18  Ibid., p. 242.

19  Ibid., p. 263.

20  Ibid., p. 294.

21  Ibid., p. 436.

22  "Hot Topic: Will the New Congress Shift Gears on Free Trade?" *Wall Street Journal*, November 18–19, 2006, p. A7.

23  Michael Mandel, "Multinationals: Are They Good for America," *BusinessWeek*, March 10, 2008, p. 42.

24  *The Economist*, September 18, 2004, op. cit., p. 80.

25  Wessel and Davis, op. cit., p. A1.

26  Ibid., p. A14.

27  Paulo Prada and Niraj Sheth, "Delta Air Ends Use of India Call Centers," *Wall Street Journal*, April 18–19, 2009, p. B1.

28  Kris Maher and Bob Tita, "Caterpillar Joins 'Onshoring' Trend," *Wall Street Journal*, March 12, 2010, p. B1.

29  Charles Fishman, "The Insourcing Boom," *The Atlantic*, Vol. 310, No. 5, December 2012, p. 45. Also see such headlines "China Begins to Lose Edge As World's Factory Floor," by Yajun Zhang et al., *Wall Street Journal*, January 17, 2013, p. A1.

30  Ashley Seager, "Globalisation: Gap Between Rich and Poor Widens: Unskilled Workers Suffer in World Economy: Governments Urged to Improve Social Safety Nets, *The Guardian (London)*, June 20, 2007, p. 29.

31  Phil Izzo, "Bleak News or Americans' Income," *Wall Street Journal*, October 14, 2011, p. A6.

32  Conor Dougherty, "Income Slides to 1996 Levels," *Wall Street Journal*, September 14, 2011, p. A1

33  Fran Hawthorne, "Color the 1 Percent 99 Percent Conflicted," New York Times; Special Section, February 9, 2012," p. F1.

34  Don Peck, "Can the Middle Class Be Saved?" *The Atlantic*, Vol. 308, No. 2, September 2011, pp. 60–61.

35  Daisy Maxey, "Ranks of Rich in U.S. Grow at Faster Pace," *Wall Street Journal*, June 28, 2007, p. D6.

36  James Edgar, "Sharp Increase in Income Inequality," in OECD study, *Divided We Stand: Why Inequality Keeps Rising*, December 5, 2011.

37  Amelia Gentleman and Helene Mulholland, "Unequal Britain: Richest 10% Are Now 100 Times Better Off Than the Poorest" *The Guardian (London)*, January 27, 2010.

38  "Poverty: The Bottom 1.4 Billion," *The Economist*, August 30, 2008, p. 70.

39  Joseph Stiglitz, Globalization and Its Discontents (New York: W.W. Norton, 2002). Stiglitz was chairman of the president's Council of Economic Advisers under Bill Clinton, chief economist of the World Bank, winner of the Nobel Prize in Economics in 2001, and is now a professor at Columbia University.

40  Bob Davis, John Lyons, and Andrew Batson, "Wealth of Nations: Globalization's Gains Come With a Price," *Wall Street Journal*, May 24, 2007, p. A1. Quote appears in the spring 2007 issue of the *Journal of Economic Literature*.

41  Joseph Stiglitz, *Making Globalization Work* (New York and London: W. W. Norton, 2006), p. xiii.

42  Alan Murray, "Voters' Doubts About Sharing in Prosperity Send a Danger Signal, *Wall Street Journal*, October 25, 2006, p. A2.

43  Michael J. Mandel, "Where Global Markets Are Going Wrong," *BusinessWeek*, June 17, 2002, p. 17.

44  Stiglitz, op. cit., p. 9.

45  Marcus Walker, "Free-Trade Group Warns of a Popular Backlash," *Wall Street Journal*, June 20, 2007, p. A2.

46  "Sharp Drop in American Enthusiasm for Free Market, Poll Shows," World Public Opinion Org, news release, April 6, 2011.

47  Ibid., p. 72.

48  Ibid., p. 80.

49  David Wessel, "Why Job Market Is Sagging in the Middle," *Wall Street Journal*, October 11, 2007, p. A2.

50  For a discussion of crises of confrontation, see Otto Lerbinger, *The Crisis Manager: facing Disasters, Conflicts, and Failures*, 2nd Edn (New York and London: Routledge: 2012, pp. 159–183.

51  "Storm Over Globalisation," *The Economist*, November 27, 1999, p. 15.

52  Paul Magnusson, "Meet Free Traders' Worst Nightmare," *BusinessWeek*, March 20, 2000, pp. 113–118.

53  "Perspective 2000: The Year of Global Protest Against Globalization," *Business World (Philippines)*, December 26, 2000.

54  After Seattle: A Global Disaster," *The Economist*, December 11, 1999, p. 19.

55  Citizens Groups: The Non-Governmental Order," *The Economist*, December 11, 1999, pp. 20–21.

56   James W. Thomson, "Globalization: Obsession or Necessity?" *Business and Society Review*, Vol. 104, Winter 1999, pp. 405.

57   Michael M. Phillips, "IMF, Weary of Criticism, Braces for Protests at Its Annual Meeting," *Wall Street Journal*, September 22, 2000, p. A2.

58   Michael M. Phillips, "Sitting Out: An Environmentalist Group Decides not to Take Protest to the Streets," *Wall Street Journal*, September 22, 2000, p. A2.

59   Marcus Walker and Paul Hofheinz, "Prague's Subdued Protest Score Points," *Wall Street Journal*, September 25, 2000, p. A27.

60   Ibid.

61   Walker and Hofheinz, op. cit.

62   Ibid., p. 30.

63   Floyd Norris, "Corporate Chiefs Take a Dim View of Politicians, Davos Survey Shows," *New York Times*, January 28, 2006, p. C-3.

64   G. Pascal Zachary, "Movers and Shakers Shake Up Their Forum," *Wall Street Journal*, January 17, 2001, p. A23.

65   Del Jones, "CEOs Around the World Want to Speak From This Podium," *USA Today*, January 20, 2006, p. 1B.

66   Bob Davis, "Economic Forum Focuses on Conflict," *Wall Street Journal*, January 29, 2002, p. A13.

67   Marc Champion, "World Economic Forum: Davos Grows, As Do Worries of Elite Crowd," *Wall Street Journal*, January 19–20, 2008, p. A2.

68   Jim Carlton, "Protests May Be Toned Down at WTO's Meeting in Cancun," *Wall Street Journal*, September 9, 2003, p. A10.

69   Neil King Jr. and Scott Miller, "U.S. Races to Break WTO Impasse," *Wall Street Journal*, September 12, 2003, p. A2.

70   Neil King Jr. and Scott Miller, "Trade Talks Fail Amid Big Divide Over Farm Issues," *Wall Street Journal*, September 15, 2003, p. A1.

71   Neil King Jr. and Scott Miller, "Cancun: Victory for Whom?," *Wall Street Journal*, September 16, 2003, p. A4.

72   Stiglitz, *Making Globalization Work*, op.cit. p. 96.

73   John Fayerweather, John, *International Business Management* (New York: McGraw-Hill, 1969), p. 88. See Chapter 4, "Conflicts with Nationalism and National Interests," pp. 87–132. He credits the definition of nationalism to Louis L. Snyder (ed.) *The Dynamics of Nationalism* (Princeton, NJ: D. Van Nostrand, 1964), p. 2.

74   "Obituary: Raymond Vernon," *The Economist*, September 11, 1999, p. 93.

75   Raymond Vernon, *Sovereignty at Bay: The Multinational Spread of U.S. Enterprise* (New York: Basic Books, 1971), p. 265; also *Storm Over the Multinationals: The Real Issues* (Cambridge, MA: Harvard University Press, 1977), p. 27.

76   Paul M. Barrett and Peter Millard, "Over a Barrel," *Bloomberg BusinessWeek*, May 14–20, 2012, p. 66.

77   Ibid., pp. 66–67.

78   "America's Ports and Dubai: Trouble on the Waterfront," *The Economist*, February 25, 2006, p. 33.

79   Bill Spindle, Neil King Jr., and Glenn R. Simpson, "Political Gulf: In Ports Furor, a Clash Over Dubai," *Wall Street Journal*, February 23, 2006, p. A1.

80  Benton Ives-Halperin, "Senate Passes Bill on Foreign Deals," *Wall Street Journal,* June 30/July 31, 2007, p. A3.

81  "French Protectionism: Fearful Fortress France," *The Economist,* October 29, 2005, p. 49.

82  "The Invasion of the Sovereign-Wealth Funds," *The Economist,* January 19, 2008, p. 11.

83  "Asset-Backed Insecurity," *The Economist,* January 19, 2008, p. 78.

84  Niels C. Sorrells, "Germany Aims to Block Takeovers by Foreign-Government Investors," *Wall Street Journal,* July 17, 2007, p. A2.

85  Gregory L. White, Bob Davis and Marcus Walker, "Russian Wealth Fund Rattles West," *Wall Street Journal,* May 7, 2008, p. A15.

86  Ibid. Fred Bergston says these investments represent a major power shift and create a concern over fear of manipulation.

87  "Asset-Backed Insecurity," op. cit., p. 80.

88  Bob Davis, "Americans See Little to Like in Sovereign-Wealth Funds," *Wall Street Journal,* February 21, 2008, p. A9.

89  "Briefing Sovereign-wealth Funds: Asset-Backed Insecurity," *The Economist,* January 19, 2008, pp. 78–79.

90  David Luhnow, Jose de Cordoba and Raul Gallegos, "Chavez Moves New Socialism to Faster Track," *Wall Street Journal,* January 9, 2006, p. A1.

91  Jose de Cordoba, "Venezuela's Revenue Push Comes With Big Risks," *Wall Street Journal,* January 22, 2007, p. A3.

92  Russell Gold, "Exxon, Conoco Exit Venezuela Under Pressure," *Wall Street Journal,* June 27, 2007, p. A1.

93  *The Lehrer News Hour,* December 31, 2003.

94  David Luhnow and Jose de Cordoba and Marc Lifsher, "Latin America's Season of Discontent," *Wall Street Journal,* October 16, 2003, p. A21.

95  "Latin America: The Return of Populism," *The Economist,* April 15, 2006, p. 39.

96  "The Latinobarometro Poll: A Warning for Reformers," *The Economist,* November 17, 2007, p. 45.

97  Ibid., p. 46.

98  Stiglitz, op. cit., p. xv.

99  Said on John Ashbrook's NPR program, September 21, 2006; www.thenation.com.

100  Franz Fischler, "Why Can't America Be More Like Us?" *Wall Street Journal,* February 19, 2004, p. A2.

101  Matthew Slaughter and Kenneth Scheve, "A New Deal for Globalization," *Foreign Affairs,* Vol. 86, No. 4, July/August 2007, p. 37.

102  Scott Miller, "Trade Negotiations Fail in Advance," *Wall Street Journal,* November 9, 2005, p. A3.

103  John W. Miller, "U.S. Offers Farm-subsidies Cap to Spur Global Trade Talks," *Wall Street Journal,* July 23, 2008, p. A9.

104  John W. Miller and Greg Hitt, "Tariff Disputes Make Breakthrough Unlikely in Doha Trade Talks," *Wall Street Journal,* July 18, 2008, p. A5.

105  Stiglitz, op. cit., p. 62.

106  Ibid., p. 270.

107  Ibid., p. 85.

108  "A Plague of Finance," *The Economist*, September 29, 2001, p. 21.

109  Ibid.

110  Stiglitz, op. cit. p. 277.

111  Paul Blustein, *The Chastening: Inside the Crisis That Rocked the Global Financial System and Humbled the IMF* (Public Affairs, 2003).

112  Vijay Joshi and Robert Skidelsky, "One World?" *The New York Review*, March 25, 2004, p. 21.

113  Robin Broad, *Global Backlash: Citizen Initiatives for a Just World Economy* (New York: Rowman & Littlefield Publishers, Inc. 2002), p. 251. Also see Manuel Montes, *The Currency Crisis in Southeast Asia* (Singapore: Institute of Southeast Asian Studies, 1998).

114  William Greider, "Born-Again Rubinomics," *The Nation*, July 31/August 7, 2006, p. 23.

115  Howard Rosen, "Assisting American "Workers and Their Families Adversely Affected by Globalization," *Perspectives on Work*, Vol. 11, No. 2, Winter 2008, p. 28.

116  Deborah Solomon, "Off the Job: Federal Aid Does Little for Free Trade's Losers," *Wall Street Journal*, March 1, 2007, p. A1, A10.

117  David Wessel, "Fed Chief Warns of Widening Inequality," *Wall Street Journal*, February 7, 2007, p. A6.

118  Deborah Solomon, "Seeking to Soften Blows of Globalization," *Wall Street Journal*, June 26, 2007, p. A8.

119  Nick Timiraos, "Democrats Seek New Trade Safeguards," *Wall Street Journal*, March 31–April 1, 2007, p. A9.

120  Ibid.

121  The case for doing this was summarized by David Wessel, "Capital: The Case for Taxing Globalization's Big Winners," *Wall Street Journal*, June 14, 2007, p. A2.

122  Jonathan Weisman, "House Passes Bill to Ease Alternative Minimum Tax," *Washington Post*, November 10, 2007, p. A01.

123  Slaughter and Scheve, op. cit., p. 45.

124  Ibid, p. 43.

125  Ibid., p. 45. Also see Sasseen, op. cit., p. 34.

126  Stephanie Banchero, "SAT Reading, Writing Scores hit Low," *Wall Street Journal*, September 15, 2011, p. A2.

127  Craig R. Barrett, "A Corporate Science Project," *BusinessWeek*, December 19, 2005, p. 108.

128.  Fareed, Zakaria, "Globalization Grows Up and Gets Political," *New York Times*, December 31, 2000, Section 4, p. 9.

129.  John Budd, *Observations*, a policy impact paper, Vol. 6, No. 8, December 9, 1999.

# 4 Economic development: reducing world poverty

1  *Foreign Policy*, March–April 2011, pp. 35–48.

2  Ibid., p. 35.

3   "Brazil: A Rainbowo of Energy Solutions" Special Advertising Section. www.businessfocus.org.uk.

4   "Tourism Sector Continues to Drive Growth," *South China Morning Post*, August 31, 2010, p. 4.

5   "Promoting Tourism," *The Japan Times*, March 21, 2011, Np.

6   "Poverty: The Bottom 1.4 Billion," *The Economist*, August 30, 2008, p. 70.

7   Jomo Kwame Sundaram, "My Say: Rethinking Poverty Reduction," *The Edge Malaysia*, January 25, 2010, p. 48.

8   Global Issues, 2009. www.globalissues.org/.

9   Amal El Tigani Ali, "Islamic Finance Solutions: The Role of Islamic Finance in Poverty Alleviation," *The Journal of American Academy of Business*, Cambridge, Vol. 16, No. 2, March 2011, p. 307. See http://www.globalissues.org/poverty, September 5, 2009.

10  Michael Hopkins, *Corporate Social Responsibility and International Development: Is Business the Solution?* (London, Sterling, VA: Earthscan, 2007), p. 131.

11  W. W. Rostow, *The Stages of Economic Growth: A Non-Communist Manifesto* (Cambridge: Cambridge University Press, 1960), p. 6.

12  Richard Lambert, "Money Makes the World Go Around," *The Times* (London), April 16, 2003, Features 2, 14.

13  George Lodge and Craig Wilson, *A Corporate Solution to Global Poverty: How Multinationals Can Help the Poor and Invigorate Their Own Legitimacy* (Princeton, NJ: Princeton University Press, 2006), pp. 148, 149.

14  Ibid., pp. 2–3.

15  Hopkins, op. cit., pp. 110, 112.

16  Ibid., p. 235.

17  Ibid., p. 145.

18  Ibid., p. 2.

19  Rostow, op. cit., pp. 1–3. President Kennedy had declared the 1960s the "decade of development." See "Obituary: Walt Rostow," *The Economist*, February 22, 2003, p. 83.

20  *The Economist*, op. cit., p. 83.

21  As summarized by Harry Schwartz, "Nations Have Their Phases," *New York Times Book Review*, May 8, 1960, p. 6.

22  Jeffrey D. Sachs, *The End of Poverty: Economic Possibilities for Our Time* (New York: Penguin Press, 2005).

23  Tony Keller, "Apostle of Aid," *National Post* (Canada), June 30, 2005, p. A22.

24  Ibid., p. 132.

25  Ibid., p. 144.

26  Ibid., p. 147.

27  Ibid., p. 153.

28  "Record 128 Million of World's Poorest Received a Microloan in 2009," *PR Newswire*, March 7, 2011.

29  Rostow, op. cit., p. 4.

30  Ibid., p. 155.

31  Zander, op. cit., www.motorola.com/citizenship/supplierexpectations.

32  Hopkins, op. cit., p. 83.

33 Ibid., p. 214.

34 Muhammad Yunus, *Creating a World Without Poverty: Social Business and the Future of Capitalism* (New York: Public Affairs, 2007). Also see his talk titled "Social Business and Poverty Reduction."

35 David Bornstein, *How to Change the World: Social Entrepreneurs and the Power of New Ideas* (New York: Oxford University Press, 2004), p. 1.

36 Ibid., p. 237.

37 Ibid., pp. 6–7.

38 Mohammed Yunus, "Building Social Business: The New kind of Capitalism That Serves Humanity's Most Pressing needs," *Public Affairs*, 2007, sequel to his 2007 book *Creating a World Without Poverty: Social Business and the Future of Capitalism.*

39 Hopkins, op. cit., p. 223.

40 Adeline Pau Raj, "A Passion for Promoting Social Business," *New Straits Times (Malaysia)*, December 2, 2010, p. 5.

41 Hopkins, op. cit., p. 222.

42 Stephanie Strom and Vikas Bajaj, "Who Benefits as Microlender Prepares Initial Public Offering?, *The International Herald Tribute*, June 31, 2010, p. 9.

43 Peter Stiff, "How $27 Became $25 Bn," *The Times* (London), April 7, 2011, Edition 1, Ireland, Business, p. 35.

44 "Leave Well Alone: Microfinance," *The Economist*, November 20, 2010 (Online). Also see Heather Montgomery and John Weiss, "Can Commercially-Oriented Microfinance Help Meet the Millennium Development goals? Evidence from Pakistan," *World Development*, January 2011, Vol. 39, No. 1, pp. 87–109. For full report go to http://www.microcreditsummit.org/news

45 Microcredit Summit Campaign, "A Project of Results Educational Fund; Record 128 Million of World's Poorest Received a Microloan in 2009," *Investment Weekly News*, March 26, 2011, p. 764.

46 Social investments are the 4th level in the CSR pyramid. See Otto Lerbinger, *Corporate Public Affairs: Interacting With Interest Groups, Media, and Government* (Mahway, NJ: Lawrence Erlbaum, 2006), p. 406.

47 John Kingston, "Finance & IT – Social Finance – Is Social Investment About Financial or Social Returns?," *Third Sector*, January 11, 2011, At Work, p. 19.

48 Hopkins, op. cit., p. 350.

49 "Low Growth for Social Enterprises," *Daily Post* (Liverpool), June 10, 2010, p. 25.

50 Hopkins, op. cit., p. 53.

51 Ibid., pp. 55–56.

52 Ibid., p. 65.

53 Ibid.

54 Ibid., pp. 63–64.

55 "Tata Sauce: Emerging-Market Giants," *The Economist*, March 5, 2011, p. 83.

56 Ibid.

57 Some examples are furor in India over the sale of mobile-phone licenses to favored group and incapability of managing their diverse portfolios.

58 "Mobile Marvels: A Special Report on Telecoms in Emerging Markets," *The Economist*, September 26, 2009, p. 19.

59 Edward J. Zander, Motorola Social Report, www.motorola.com/citizenship.

60 Jack Ewing, "Upwardly Mobile in Africa," *BusinessWeek*, September 24, 2007, pp. 64–71.
61 Ibid., p. 64.
62 "Briefing Africa's Hopeful Economies: The Sun Shines Bright," *The Economist*, December 3, 2011, p. 83.
63 Ibid., p. 82.
64 Ibid.
65 Tidiane Kinda, "Investment Climate and FDI in Developing Countries: Firm-Level Evidence," *World Development*, April 2010, Vol. 38, No. 4, p. 498.
66 John Coleman and Nabil El-Hage, "Setting Up Shop in a Political Hot Spot," *Harvard Business Review*, October 2010, Vol. 88.
67 Vikas Bajaj, "India's Economy Starts to Lose Its Allure," *International Herald Tribune*, February 25, 2011, Finance, p. 23.
68 Hopkins, op. cit., p. 92.
69 "Walmart's Mexican Morass," *The Economist*, April 28, 2012, p. 71.
70 Miguel Bustillo and David Luhnow, "Wal-Mart Ups Defenses," *Wall Street Journal*, April 25, 2012, p. B3.
71 "Walmart's Mexican Morass," op. cit.
72 David Barstow, "Vast Mexico Bribery Case Hushed Up by Wal-Mart After Top-Level Struggle," *New York Times*, April 22, 2012, pp. 1, 12ff.
73 Ibid., p. 12.
74 Ibid., p.12.
75 Bustill and Luhnow, op. cit.
76 Ibid., p. 81. See also www.earthscan.co.uk.
77 Ibid., p. 92.
78 Ibid., p. 93.

# 5 Replenishing, upgrading, and managing human resources

1 Peter Ford, "What's Behind Asia's Moon Race?" *Christian Science Monitor*, October 25, 2007, p. 6.
2 Tony Emerson, Scott Johnson and Barbara Koh, "Coff, Tea … or Tennis,? *Newseek*, June 5, 2000, p. 50.
3 Leonard Lynn and Hal Salzman, "The Globalization of Technology Development: Implications for U.S. Skills Policy," in James A. Gross and Lance Compa, eds., *Human Rights in Labor and Employment Relations: International and Domestic Perspectives*, Labor and Employment Relations Association Series, p. 59.
4 Ben Casselman, "Help Wanted: In Unexpected Twist, Some Skilled Jobs Go Begging," *Wall Street Journal*, November 26–27, 2011, p. A1.
5 Rahm Emanuel, "Chicago's Plan to Match Education With Jobs," *Wall Street Journal*, December 19, 2011, p. A19.
6 James R. Hagerty, "Industry Puts Heat on Schools To Teach Skills Employers Need," *Wall Street Journal*, June 6, 2011, p. A6.

7    Ibid.

8    See Mary Gatta and David Finegold, "Introduction: Meeting America's Skills Challenge," in David Finegold, Mary Gatta, Hal Salzman, and Susan J. Schurman, eds., *Transforming the U.S. Workforce Development System: Lessons from Research and Practice* (Urbana-Champaign: Labor and Employment Relations Association, 2010).

9    Casselman, op. cit., p. A12.

10   Leonard Lynn and Hal Salzman, "The Globalization of Technology Development: Implications for U.S. Skills Policy," in Finegold et al., op. cit., p. 57.

11   Gatta and Finegold, op. cit., p. 14.

12   Ibid., p. 6.

13   Hagerty, op. cit.

14   Ibid.

15   Emanuel, op. cit.

16   Laura P. Hartman and Patricia H. Werhane, eds., *The Global Corporation: Sustainable, Effective and Ethical Practices: A Case Book* (New York and London: Routledge, 2009), p. 247. See "Started as Crew: McDonald's Strategy for Corporate Success and Poverty Reduction," pp. 224–247.

17   Kim Korinek and Thoms N. Maloney, "Immigration in the Early 21st Century: Lessons from a Multidisciplinary Perspective," in Thomas N. Maloney and Kim Korinek, eds., *Migration in the 21st Century* (London and New York: Routledge, 2010), Chapter 14, pp. 269ff.

18   Bernardette S. Sto. Domingo, "UN Says Social Costs of migration Worrisome," *BusinessWorld*, September 2006, p. S1/12.

19   "Putin Urges Clear Rules of Labor migration," ITAR-TASS, January 26, 2012.

20   Kate Connollly, "Multiculturalism Is a Failure Says Merkel: German Chancellor's RemarksReflect Heated Debate and Suggest Shift in Attitude Towards Immigration," *The Guardian*, October 18, 2010, p. 16.

21   Vanessa Fuhrman, "Exodus of Skilled Labor Saps Germany," *Wall Street Journal*, March 11, 2011, p. A12.

22   Ibid.

23   "Draft of New German Immigration Act," *BusinessWorld*, January 22, 2002, p. 22.

24   "German Broadcaster Targets Africa with Project on Migration," BBC Monitoring World Media, December 8, 2011.

25   "Open Up: A Special Report on Migration," *The Economist*, January 5, 2008, p. 7.

26   Bobby Duffy, "Europe's Anti-Immigrant Voters," *Wall Street Journal*, May 22, 2012, p. A15.

27   Nathan Lillie, "International Worker Posting an National Industrial Relations; The End of 'Social Europe'?" *Perspectives on Work*, Vol. 14, Summer 2010/Winter 2011, p. 9.

28   Ibid., p. 11.

29   In March 2002 there were 9.3 million. undocumented immigrants in the United States. See March 2002 Current Population Survey U.S. – Urban Institute, www.urban.org/publcations/10000587.html.

30   Ibid., p. 275.

31   Hirshland, p. 166.

32 "Eufocus," Special Advertising Section, *Foreign Policy*, Vol. 191, January/February 2012, pp. 19–22.

33 Ibid.

34 Ibid.

35 Erin Ortiz et al., op. cit., p. 54.

36 Dana L. Brown, "Global Labor Standards – What the ILO Is Doing Building Capacity-Changing Worker-Management Relations Through Targeted Training," *Perspectives on Work*, Vol. 13, No. 1, Summer 2009, p. 7.

37 International Labour Organization, *International Labour Migration. A Rights-Based Approach*, April 2010.

38 From preface to the above book.

39 Case is based on E. Benjamin Skinner, "The Cruelest Catch," *Bloomberg Businessweek*, March 4, 2012, pp. 70–76.

40 Deborah Leipziger, *SA8000: The Definitive Guide to the New Social Standard* (New York: Financial Times/Prentice Hall, an imprint of Pearson Education, 2001), p. xxi.

41 Ibid., p. 1.

42 Matthew J.Hirschland, *Corporate Social Responsibility and the Shaping of Global Public Policy* (New York: Palgrave Macmillan, 2006 ), p. 115.

43 Ibid., p. 2.

44 Ibid., pp. 10–11.

45 Ibid., pp. 25–26.

46 Ibid., pp. 34–36.

47 Based on Sean Ansett, "Labor Standards in the Supply chain: The Steep Climb to Sustainability," *Perspectives on Work*, Vol. 9, No. 2, Winter 2006, pp. 11–.

48 Erin Ortiz, Esther Agyeman-Budu, and George Cheney, "How Should Corporate Social Responsibility Address Labor Migration in Light of Market Globalization?," in Korinek and Maloney, op. cit., pp. 54ff.

49 John L. Graham, "Culture and Human Resources Management," in Alan M. Rugman and Thomas L. Brewer, eds., *The Oxford Handbook of International Business* (Oxford University Press, 2001), p. 523?

50 Ibid., pp. 503–504.

51 Discussed in Vas Taras, Piers Stell, Bradley L. Kirkman, "Three Decades of Research on National Culture in the Workplace. Do the Differences Still Make a Difference?" *Organizational Dynamics*, Vol. 40, 2011, pp. 189–198.

52 Carlos Sanchez-Runde, Lucrara Nardon, Richard M. Steers, "Looking Beyond Western Leadership Models; Implications for Global Managers, *Organizational Dynamics*, Vol. 40 (2011), p. 211.

53 This section is based on Christian Levesque and Hao Hu, "Multinationals and Employment Relations in China," *Perspectives on Work*, Vol. 11, No. 1, Summer 2007, pp. 13–15.

54 Devon Maylie, "Mine Strikes Spread in South Africa," *Wall Street Journal*, September 11, 2012, p. B3.

55 Maylie, "Lethal Clashes Shut Platinum Mines," *Wall Street Journal*, August 15, 2012, p. B3.

56 Weld Royal, "Back to South Africa," *Industry Week*, October 19, 1998, p. 82.

57 Maylie, "Tensions Persist as South Africa Strike Ends," *Wall Street Journal*, September 20, 2012, p. A13.

58    David Smith, "Special Report: Marikana Massacre" *The Guardian,* September 8, 2012, p. 27.

59    Maylie, "Lethal Clashes Shut Platinum Mines," op. cit.

60    Maylie, "Shootings Weigh On South Africa's Leaders," *Wall Street Journal,* August 18–19, 2012, p. A6.

61    Maylie, "Tensions Persist as South Africa Strike Ends," op. cit.

62    Maylie, "South Africa to Probe mine Shootings," *Wall Street Journal,* August 20, 2012, p. A5.

63    See "Human Resource Management," in Monir H. Tayeb, ed., *The Management of International Enterprises: A Socio-Political View* (New York: St. Martin's Press, 2000), p. 132.

64    John L. Graham, "Culture and Human Resources Management," in Rugman and Brewer, p. 503–524.

65    Many of the examples are from various sections in Fons Trompenaars and Charles Hampden-Turner, *Riding the Waves of Cultures: Understanding Cultural Diversity in Global business,* 2nd edn (New York and London: McGraw-Hill, 1998).

66    Leonard and Hal Salzman, "The Globalization of Technology Development: Implications for U.S. Skills Policy," in Finegold, Gatta, Salzman and Schurman, op. cit., p. 57.

67    Anthony Ferner and Phil Almond, "Managing People in U.S.-Based Multinationals: the Case of Europe." *Perspectives on Work,* Vol. 11, No. 1, Summer 2007, p. 4.

68    Ibid., pp. 4, 5.

69    Ibid., p. 5.

70    Christian Levesque and Had Hu, "Multinationals and Employment Relations in China," *Perspectives on Work,* Vol. 11, No. 1, Summer 2007, p. 15.

71    Ibid., pp. 13–15.

72    See a review of these books in Robert Taylor, "Labor and Globalization: A Review Commentary," *Perspectives on Work,* Vol. 10, No. 2, Winter 2007, pp. 56–59.

73    Ibid., p. 57.

74    Ibid.

75    Ibid.

76    Lynn and Salzman, op. cit., p. 77.

77    Ibid., p. 59.

# 6  Religious tensions: understanding islam

1    Sak Onkvisit, Sak and John J. Shaw, *International* Marketing: *Analysis and Strategy,* 4th edn (New York and London: Routledge, 2004).

2    Raymond Cohen, *Negotiating Across Cultures: International Communication in an Interdependent World,* revised edition (Washington, DC: United States Institute of Peace Press, 1997).

3    Gary R. Weaver, ed. *Culture, Communication and Conflict: Readings in Intercultural Relations,* 2nd edn (New York: Simon & Schuster Publishing, 1998).

4    Akbar Ahmed, *Journey Into Islam: The Crisis of Globalization* (Washington, DC: Brookings Institution Press, 2007), p. 26.

5   Thoms R. McFaul, "Religion and the Future Global Civilization," *The Futurist*, Vol. 40, No. 5, September–October 2006, pp. 30–31.

6   Timothy L. Fort, "Instruments of Peace? How Businesses Might Foster Religious Harmony," in Gabriele G. S. Suder, eds., *International Business under Adversity: A Role in Corporate Responsibility, Conflict Prevention and Peace* (Cheltenham, UK, Northampton, MA: Edward Elgar, 2008), p. 51. Event is covered in "McDonald's Fries: Not Done Yet," *Hinduism Today*, October/November/December, 2003.

7   Tun Musa Hitam, "Firms Stand to Lose by Ignoring the Muslim World," *The Straits Times* (Singapore), October 10, 2012, Opinion Section.

8.  David Salt and Michael Earley, "Qatar: Qatar's New Advertising Law," *Mondaq Business Briefing*, July 12, 2012.

9   "Egypt's Government Tries to End Cairo's Reputation As a City That Never Sleeps," *The Telegraph*, November 1, 2012.

10  Liberal paraphrasing from Diane Connolly, *Report on Religion: A Primer on Journalisms' Best Beat*. Westerville, OH: Religion Newswriters Association, 2006, p. 65. Online version available from www.RNA.org.

11  "Islam's Philosophical Divide: Dreaming of a Caliphate," *The Economist*, August 6, 2011, p. 22.

12  Ibid., p. 66.

13  Ibid.

14  Brian Whitaker, "The Veil Controversy: The Muslim World," *The Guardian*, October 21, 2006, p. 13.

15  Anne Applebaum, "Veiled Insult," *Washington Post*, October 24, 2006, p. A19.

16  Farnaz Fassihi, "Amid Chaos, Extremists Spur Violence," *Wall Street Journal*, September 15–16, 2012, p. A6.

17  Vanessa Fuhrmans and John W. Miller, "Norway Mourns Fallen Young Leaders," *Wall Street Journal*, July 26, 2011, p. A10.

18  Bret Stephens, "What Is Anders Breivik?," *Wall Street Journal*, July 26, 2011, p. A15.

19  Pew Research Center, "Muslim-Western Tensions Persist: Common Concerns About Islamic Extremism," http://pewresearch.org/pubs/2066/muslims-western-ers-christians-jews-islamtic-extremism-2…2/28/2012.

20  Steven Kull's, *Feeling Betrayed: The Roots of Muslim Anger at America* (Washington, DC: The Brookings Institution Press, 2011).

21  "The Future of the Global Muslim Population," Pew Forum on Religion and Public Life, January 27, 2011. Also see "Islam and Demography: A Waxing Crescent," *The Economist*, January 29, 2011, p. 59.

22  *Muslims in Europe: A Report on 11 EU Cities*, Open Society Foundations, December 2009.

23  "Tales from Eurabia," and "Look Out, Europe, They Say." *The Economist*, June 24, 2006, p. 11.

24  R. James Woolsey and Nina Shea, "What About Muslim Moderates?" *Wall Street Journal*, July 10, 2007, p. A21.

25  Samuel P. Huntington, "The Clash of Civilizations," *Foreign Affairs*, Vol. 72, No. 3, 1993. It is reprinted in Patrick O'Meara, Howard D. Mehlinger, and Matthew Krain, eds. *Globalization and the Challenges of a New Century; A Reader* (Bloomington and Indianapolis: Indiana University Press, 2000), p. 3. Also see Robert D.

Kaplan, "Looking the World in the Eye," *Atlantic Monthly*, Vol. 288, December 2001, pp. 68–82.

26 Huntington, op. cit., p. 5.

27 Ibid., p. 4.

28 Ibid., p. 4.

29 Ibid., p. 5.

30 Ibid., p. 8.

31 Ibid., p. 6.

32 Samuel P. Huntington, "The West Unique, Not Universal," *Foreign Affairs*, November/December 1996, p. 28.

33 The material loss caused by 9/11 was enormous. L. Mammen estimates that physical assets damage at $10 billion and that about $11 billion were spent in cleaning destroyed urban sites. In addition, the Manhattan area lost about 25% of its corporate space, several small businesses stopped their activities, and some 200,000 job positions were damaged or relocated.

34 Kaplan, op. cit, p. 82.

35 Ibid.

36 Charles A. Russell, Leon J. Banker, J., and Bowman H. Miller, "Out-Inventing the Terrorist," in Yonah Alexander, David Carlton, and Paul Wilkinson, eds., *Terrorism: Theory and Practice* (Boulder, CO: Westview Press, 1979), p. 12.

37 Www.busrisk.com.au/about/news/Training) Ben Harrington and Josephine Moulds, "Support Services Control Risks in Talks with Rival to Form 'Strategic Partnership,'" *The Daily Telegraph* (London), December 11, 2007, p. 1; Katharine Murphy and Brendan Nicholson, "Business to Audit Disasser Plans," *The Age* (Melbourne, Australia), August 29, 2007, p. 4.

38 Andrew Higgins, "How Muslim Clerics Stirred Arab World Against Denmark," *Wall Street Journal*, February 2, 2006, p. A1.

39 Ibid.

40 Zahid Hussain and John W. Miller, "Pakistan Bomb Targets Danes, May Prolong Rift," *Wall Street Journal*, June 3, 2008, June 3, 2008, p. A9.

41 Adam Jones and William Wallis, "Middle East Boycott of Danish Goods Hits Hard; Commercial Impact," *Financial Times*, February 4, 2006, London ed. 2, p. A6.

42 Raphael Minder and Annukka Oksannen, "Denmark Warns on Saudi Arabia Trips," *Financial Times*, January 31, 2006, London ed., sec A-9.

43 Anthony Shadid and Kevin Sullivan, "Anatomy of the Cartoon Protest Movement; Opposing Certainties Widen Gap Between West and Muslim World," *Washington Post*, February 16, 2006, Final ed., sec. A-1.

44 Lauren Etter, "The Cartoons That Shook the World," *Wall Street Journal*, February 11–12, 2006, p. A7.

45 Eric Pfanner, "Danish Companies Endure Snub by Muslim Consumers," *New York Times*, February 27, 2006, p. C2.

46 Andrew Higgins, "Danish Businesses Struggle With Big Dilemma," *Wall Street Journal*, February 10, 2006, p. A4.

47 Pfanner, op. cit.

48 Ibid. Also see excellent case study by John G. Knight, Bradley S. Mitchell and Hongzhi Gao, "Riding out the Muhammad Cartoons Crisis: Contrasting Strategies and Outcomes," *Long Range Planning*, Vol. 42, 2009, pp. 6–22.

49 Ibid.

50 "Arla Attempts a Comeback in the Middle East," March 20, 2006; "The Middle Eastern Boycott Is Slowly Lifting," March 29, 2006; and "Breakthrough for Arla in the Middle East," April 6, 2006, www.arlafoods.com, downloaded April 29, 2006.

51 Joergen Ejboel, "At the Center of the Storm," The 19th Annual Andersen-Ottaway Lecture, A Lecture Series on Global Communications Issues, April 11, 2007, World Press Freedom Committee, Reston, Virginia.

52 Ibid.

53 Gary Younge, "The Right to Be Offended," The Nation, February 27, 2006, p. 5.

54 Ejboel, op. cit., p. 23.

55 For background see Sebastian Rotella, "Riots Put a Fear in the French," Los Angeles Times, November 4, 2005, p. A1; Molly Moore, "Anger Erupts in Paris Suburb After Deaths of Muslim Boys," Washington Post, November 2, 2005, p. A15.

56 "The Wily Old Trooper Won't Go Away, The Economist, August 12, 2006, p. 41.

57 Sebastian Rotella, "The World; Fundamentalism in French Workplace; Private Employers Wrestle with Expressions of Islam, While Study Alleges Criminal Links," Los Angeles Times, November 26, 2005, p. A3.

58 Ibid.

59 Marie Valla, "France Seeks Path or Workplace Diversity," Wall Street Journal, January 3, 2007, p. A2.

60 Philip J. Auter, "Developing and Maintaining the Aljazeera Websites," in Michael G. Parkinson and Daradirek Ekachai, eds., International and Intercultural Public Relations: A Campaign Case Approach (New York: Pearson, 2006), p. 240.

61 "Media War and Security: The Right to Know vs. USA's Best Interests Can Lead to Conflicts," USA Today, October 17, 2001, p. 6A.

62 Anne-Marie Crawford, "The Middle East Gets Its Own BBC," Ad Age Global, November 1, 2001, p. 20)

63 David Marash, "Al Jazeera English: News With a New Perspective," Global Journalist, Vol. 12, December 2006, pp. 17–19.

64 Ibid., p. 17.

65 Reena Vadehra, "The End of an Era?," Global Journalist, Vol. 12, December 2006, p. 38.

66 Ibid., p. 37.

67 Russell Adams and Shira Ovide, "Newspapers Move to Outsource Foreign Coverage," Wall Street Journal, January 15, 2009, p. B4.

68 Philip Seib, "Building the New International Media," Global Journalist, Summer 2007, p. 22.

69 "Cellphone News from Al-Jazeera," Financial Times (London), April 3, 2003, p. 5.

70 Alan D. Abbey and Andrew Friedman, "The Power of Media in the Palm of Your Hand," Global Journalist, Vol. 12, No. 2, Summer 20007, pp. 3–4.

71 "Al Jazeera Buys Al Gore's Current TV," USA Today, January 3, 2013.

72 Bernard Lewis, "What Went Wrong," The Atlantic Monthly, Vol. 289, No. 1, p. 43. Also see his "The Roots of Muslim Rage," Foreign Policy, Vol. 17, No. 4, Summer 2001/2002.

73 Ibid.

74  Ibid., p. 45.

75  Ibid.

76  "Look Out, Europe, They say," *The Economist*, June 24, 2006, p. 34.

77  Ibid.

78  Tariq Ramadan, "What the West Can Learn From Islam," *The Chronicle Review*, February 16, 2007, pp. B6–B8.

79  Karl Meyer, "Who Gets to Be French," *New York Times*, April 12, 2012, Op-Ed Section.

80  "After the Terror Plot: British Exceptionalism" *The Economist*, August 19, 2006, p. 10.

81  Ibid., p. B7. It may interest some readers that Ramadan was not allowed entry to the U.S. because he contributed to a Swiss Palestinian-support group that is on the American blacklist. He says, the lesson he learned is: "A 'moderate' Muslim, in particular, should never discuss the Middle East, the suffering of the Palestinians, or the arrogance of longstanding Israeli policy." He feels his freedom of speech has been threatened.

82  Ibid.

83  Ibid.

84  Guy Sorman, "Apartheid a la Francaise," *Wall Street Journal*, December 4, 2007, p. A21.

85  "Tales from Eurabia," *The Economist*, June 24, 2006, p. 11.

86  Jamaes Angelos, "Germany Tries to Forge European Brand of Islam," *Wall Street Journal*, August 3, 2011, p. A9.

87  Benjamin M. Friedman, *The Moral Consequences of Economic Growth* (New York: Knopf, 2005), p. 320.

88  This section is based mainly on Rodney Wilson, "The Development of Islamic Economics: Theory and Practice," in Suha Taji-Farouki and Basheer M. Nafi, eds., *Islamic Thought in the Twentieth Century* (London and New York: I.B. Tauris, 2004), pp. 195–222. Another source of information is Karen Hung Ahmed, "Islamic Banking and Finance: Moral Beliefs and Business Practices at Work," in Laura P. Hartman and Patricia H. Werhane, eds., *The Global Corporation: Sustainable, Effective and Ethical Practices: A Case Book* (New York and London: Routledge, 2009), pp. 168–181.

89  Hibba Abugideiri, "On Gender and the Family," in Wilson, op. cit., p. 203.

90  Max Weber, *The Protestant Ethic and the Spirit of Capitalism*, translated by Talcott Parsons (New York: C. Scribner & Sons, 1930).

91  Richard H. Tawney, *Religion and the Rise of Capitalism: A Historical Study* Tawney (Harcourt Brace, 1926).

92  David Henry, "Islamic Law; Returns Muslims Can Live With," *BusinessWeek*, July 17, 2006, p. 9. The Sharia-compliant financial arrangements of the first Sharia-compliant real-estate investments in the United States is being tested in a foreclosure process involving a Connecticut developer backed by a Kuwaiti equity investor. See Alex Frangos, "How Islamic Finance Handles Foreclosures," *Wall Street Journal*, December 12, 2007, p. B6.

93  "United Arab Emirates; How to Be Islamic in Business," *The Economist*, June 9, 2007, p. 56.

94   "Islam: The Choice Facing Muslims," *The Economist*, April 18, 2009, p. 89.
95   Wilson, op. cit., p. 212.
96   Ibid., p. 213.
97   Ibid., p. 198.
98   Ibid., p. 202.
99   Ibid., p. 207.
100  Ibid., p. 208.
101  Ibid., pp. 209–210.

# 7  Threats to nation brands: cases of china and the United States

1   Terry Clark, "International Marketing and National Character: A Review and Proposal for an Integrative Theory," *Journal of Marketing*, Vol. 54, October 1990, p. 66.
2   Sak Onkvisit and John J. Shaw, *International Marketing: Analysis and Strategy*, 4th edn (New York and London: Routledge, 2004), p. 193.
3   Ibid., pp. 199–201.
4   Wally Olins, "Making a National Brand," in Jan Melissen, ed., *The New Public Diplomacy: Soft Power in International Relations* (New York: Palgrave Macmillan, 2005), p. 170.
5   Ibid., p. 172.
6   Katerina Tsetsura, "Image Building in the International Media: A Case Study of the Finlandia Communications Program in Russia," in Michael G. Parkinson and Daradirek Ekachai, eds., *International and Intercultural Public Relations: A Campaign Case Approach* (New York: Pearson, 2006), p. 273.
7   S.P. Jaworski and D. Fosher, "National Brand Identity and Its Effect on Corporate Brands: The Nation Brand Effect (NBE)," *The Multinational Business Review*, Vol. 11, No. 2, 2003, pp. 99–108. Also see Christopher Lingle, *Singapore's Authoritarian Capitalism: Asian Values, Free Market Illusions, and Political Dependency* (Fairfax, VA: Locke Institute, 1996).
8   Constance Chay-Nemeth, "Becoming Professionals: A Portrait of Public Relations in Singapore," in Krishnamurthy Siramesh and Dejan Vercic, eds., The Global Public Relations Handbook: Theory, Research, and Practice (Mahwah, NJ: Lawrence Erlbaum Associates, 2003).
9   As stated in a *Wall Street Journal* advertisement, October 4, 2010, p. A16.
10  Marc Champion and Betsy McKay, "Gathering Gives Chance to Burnish Images," *Wall Street Journal*, January 24, 2007, p. A7.
11  Fareed Zakaria, "The New Indian Powerhouse: India Rising," *Newsweek*, March 6, 2006, p. 34.
12  Mei Fong, "Brand Strategies," *Wall Street Journal*, April 12–13, 2008, p. R3.
13  For a summary of this case see Patricia A. Curtain, "Negotiating Global Citizenship – Mattel's 2007 Recall Crisis," in W.T. Coombs and Sherry Holladay, eds., *The Handbook of Crisis Communication* (Chichester, U.K. and Malden, MA: Blackwell, 2010), pp. 467ff.

14  Nicholas Zamiska, Jason Leow, and Shai Oster, "China Confronts Crisis Over Food Safety," *Wall Street Journal*, May 30, 2007, p. A3.

15  Jane Spencer and Nicholas Casey, "Toy Recall Shows Challenge China Poses to Partners," *Wall Street Journal*, August 3, 2007, p. A1.

16  Ibid.

17  Neil King Jr. and Rebecca Blumenstein, "On message: China Launches Public Response to Safety Outcry," *Wall Street Journal*, June 30/July 1, 2007, p. A1. Also see Chapter 10 on lobbying by China.

18  Nicholas Casey, Nicholas Zamiska, and Andy Pasztor, "Mattel Seeks to Placate China with Apology," *Wall Street Journal*, September 22–23, 2007, p. A1. Also see "Chinese Manufacturing: Plenty of Blame to Go Around," *Economist*, September 29, 2007, p. 68.

19  Ibid.

20  Ibid.

21  Gordon Fairclough, "Tainting of Milk is Open Secret in China," *Wall Street Journal*, November 3, 2008, p. A1. Also Loretta Chao, "Ex-Executive Pleads Guilty in China's Tainted-Milk Case," *Wall Street Journal*, January 2, 2009, p. A4.

22  Gordon Fairclough and Loretta Chao, "Chinese Formula Maker hid Toxic Danger for Weeks," *Wall Street Journal*, September 18, 2008, p. A15.

23  Gordon Fairclough and Loretta Chao, "Chinese Formula Maker hid Toxic Danger for Weeks," op. cit.

24  "China: Saving Face Goes Sour," *Newsweek*, October 6, 2008, p. 7.

25  Shai Oster and Loretta Chao, "China Arrests 2 in Milk Scandal as Number of sick Infants Rises," *Wall Street Journal*, September 16, 2008, p. A16.

26  Chao, op. cit., January 2, 2009, p. A4.

27  Sky Canaves and Juliet Ye, "Chinese Parents File Milk Lawsuit," *Wall Street Journal*, October 1, 2008, p. A21; also Loretta Chao and Jason Leow, "Chinese Tainting Scandal Pulls milk off Shelves," *Wall Street Journal*, September 20–21, 2008, p. A10.

28  "Food Safety in China: In the Gutter," *The Economist*, October 29, 2011, p. 49.

29  "Chevron and Brazil's Oil Industry: Oil, Water and Trouble," *The Economist*, December 31, 2011, p. 23.

30  Jeff Fick, "Chevron, Transocean Halted in Brazil for Month," *Wall Street Journal*, August 2, 2012, p. B3.

31  The Pew Global Attitudes Project, *Views of a Changing World How Global Publics View: War in Iraq, Democracy, Islam and Governance, Globalization* (Washington, DC: The Pew Research Center for The People & The Press, June 2003), p. v.

32  Richard Morin, "World Image of U.S. Declines; Poll Says Countries Suspicious of Iraq Motives, Global Role," *Washington Post*, December 5, 2002, p. A26.

33  The Pew Global Attitudes Project, op. cit., p. 1.

34  A BBC World Service Poll conducted between November 2008 and February 2009 confirms that most countries continue to have predominantly negative views of the United States. Negative attitudes are highest in Germany (65%), Spain (56%), and France (53%). President Barack Obama was aware of anti-American sentiments and his speeches during in speeches during his visits to European countries and Turkey, he has proclaimed his intention to change American policies that have in part caused the problem. Richard Wilke, associate director of the Pew

Global Attitudes Project concluded in 2011, "Once the fearsome colossus, many now see the financially strapped U.S. as a great power in decline."

35 The Pew Global Attitudes Project, op. cit.

36 78% of Germans who said they had a favorable view of the United States fell from 78% in 2000 to 61% in 2002, and 45% in 2003. Similar drops occurred in France (from 62% to 63% to 43%); Britain (83% to 75% to 70%); Italy (76% to 70% to 60%); Russia (37% to 61% to 36%); and drops elsewhere in the world, such as Brazil and South Korea. People in predominantly Muslim countries showed the lowest favorability ratings: Morocco and Lebanon 27%, Indonesia and Turkey 15%, and Pakistan 13%.

37 Meg Bortin, "U.S. Faces More Distrust From World, Poll Shows," *New York Times*, June 28, 2007.

38 Andrew Kohut, "Anti-Americanism: Causes and Characteristics," press release from The Pew Research Center, December 10, 2003, p. 4.

39 "U.S. Image Up Slightly, But Still Negative; American Character Gets Mixed Reviews," report of Pew Global Attitudes Survey released June 23, 2005. See http://pewglobal.org/reports/display.php?ReportID=247.

40 Ibid.

41 Neil King, Jr., "Anti-Americanism Is a Big Hit at U.N.," *Wall Street Journal*, September 21, 2006, p. A4.

42 Ibid.

43 Paul Richter, "Anti-Americanism Is Providing a Glue; The Rhetoric from the Leaders of Iran, Sudan and Venezuela at the U.N. Shared a Theme of Outrage at the U.S., despite their differences," *Los Angeles Times*, September 22, 2006, p. A6.

44 Andrew Kohut and Bruce Stokes, "Pushing Back at the U.S.; Surveys Show That Worldwide Dislike for America Has Grown in Recent Years. And now, It's Not Just Our Government They Can't Stand – It's Us," *Baltimore Sun*, May 14, 2006, p. 1F.

45 Pew Global Attitudes Project, op. cit.

46 Ibid.

47 Lynn Forester de Rothschild and Adam S. Posen, "How Capitalism Can Repair Its Bruised Image," *Wall Street Journal*, January 2, 1013, p. A17.

48 "This Time It's Serious," *The Economist*, February 18, 2012, p. 71.

49 Damian Paletta, James R. Hagerty, and Sudeep Reddy, "Some Executives Hoped for Broader Reach," *Wall Street Journal*, January 2, 2013, p. A6.

50 "Global Public Affairs Institute Names New Executive Director," news release downloaded October 26, 2007. Unfortunately, the group disbanded in 2008.

51 Global Public Affairs Institute, "Report on "Anti-Americanism and Global Business," op. cit., p. 28. Members of GPAI consisted of its two facilitators and eleven participants – all senior government relations advisors at counseling firms or MNCs.

52 Ibid., p. 6.

53 Fareed Zakaria, "The Arrogant Empire," *Newsweek*, March 24, 2003.

54 "Report on Anti-Americanism and Global Business," op. cit., p. 9.

55 Global Opinion: "The Spread of Anti-Americanism, Trends," 2005, p. 108.

56 "Global Unease with Major World Powers; Rising Environmental Concern in 47-Nation Survey," news release by Pew Research Center, June 27, 2007.

57 "Report on Anti-Americanism and Global Business," op. cit., p. 9.

58  Pew Research Center, "Global Opinion: "The Spread of Anti-Americanism," p. 113.

59  Fred H. Maidmen, "Who's Big? The Top 100," *International Journal on World Peace*, Vol. 19, No. 1, March 1, 2002, p. 67.

60  Charles M. Blow, "Decline of American Exceptionalism," *New York Times*, November 19, 2011, p. 21. Also see Andrew J. Bacevich, *The Limits of Power: The End of American Exceptionalism* (New York: Metropolitan Books, 2009).

61  Manfred B. Steger, "American Globalism 'Madison Avenue-Style': "A Critique of US Public Diplomacy after 9/11," in Patrick Hayden and Chamsy el-Ojeli, eds., *Confronting Globalization: Humanity, Justice and the Renewal of Politics* (New York: Palgrave Macmillan, 2005), p. 227.

62  See Robert F. Bales, *Interaction Process Analysis: A Method for the Study of Small Groups* (Reading, MA: Addison-Wesley, Inc., 1950).

63  Kohut and Stokes, op. cit.

64  Ibid., pp. 21, 30.

65  Ibid., p. 9.

66  Global Opinion: "The Spread of Anti-Americanism, Trends," op. cit., p. 115.

67  Kohut and Stokes, op. cit.

68  Jeffrey E. Garten, "Anti-Americanism May Harm U.S. Firms," *International Herald Tribune*, April 16, 2003, p. 9; also "It's Getting Serious," *Newsweek*, April 7, 2003, p. 54.

69  Clyde Prestowitz "CEOs and Foreign Policy; CEO Agenda 2004," *Chief Executive (U.S.)*, No. 194, December 1, 2003, p. 36.

70  James M. Pethokoukis, "America's Image Problem," *U.S. News & World Report*, September 25, 2006, Money & Business section.

71  Dan Roberts and Gary Silverman, "Tarnished Image: Is the World Falling Out of Love with US Brands?" *Financial Times* (London), December 30, 2004, p. 9.

72  Ibid.

73  Report on Anti-Americanism and Global Business, op. cit., p. 16.

74  Hugh Pope, "Arabs Fuel a Boycott of U.S. Goods," *Wall Street Journal*, January 19, 2002, p. A11.

75  "Protesters 'Seal' American Fast-Food Chains," *The Jakarta Post*, October 11, 2001; obtained from FT Asia Africa Intelligence Wire.

76  "Anti-Americanism and Television: The One Where Pooh Goes to Sweden," *The Economist*, April 5, 2003, p. 59.

77  Report on Anti-Americanism and Global Business, op. cit., p. 25.

78  Dan Roberts, "US Icons Lose Their Cool in Europe," *Financial Times (London)*, October 25, 2004, p. 23.

79  Burson-Marsteller, *What the World Thinks of America*, June 18, 2003, p. 16.

80  Karen Krebsbach, "Business Gets on Diplomacy's Fast Track," *US Banker*, Vol. 115, No. 8, August 2005, p. 20.

81  Ibid.

82  Kevin J. Obrien, "U.S. Brands Learning to Fly the Flag Subtly," *The International Herald Tribune*, February 14, 2005, p. 13.

83  R. F. Delaney, "Introduction" in A. S. Hoffman, ed., *International Communication and the New Diplomacy* (Bloomington: Indiana University Press, 1968), p. 3.

84  Krebsbach, op. cit.

85   See Business Wire article; also www.businessfordiplomaticaction.org

86   Guy Taylor, "U.S. Firms Contribute $80 Million," *Washington Times*, December 31, 2004, p. A1.

87   Tom McCawley, "US Tsunami Aid Still Reaps Goodwill," *Christian Science Monitor*, February 28, 2006, p. 12.

88   Neil King Jr., "Goodwill Hunting, Trying to Turn Its Image Around, U.S. Puts Top CEOs Out Front," February 27, 2006, p. A1. See www.businessfordiplomaticaction.org/news/articles/goodwillhunting doc

89   Ibid.

90   Krebsbach, op. cit.

91   See Business Wire article; also www.businessfordiplomaticaction.org

92   M. Leonard, "Diplomacy by Other Means," *Foreign Policy*, Vol. 132, September–October 2002, pp. 48–56.

93   Based on personal conversation with Roy Leffingwell in Honolulu in 1989.

94   Ibid., p. 33.

95   Ibid., p. 12.

96   Joyce Wouters, *International Public Relations: How to Establish Your Company's Product, Service, and Image in Foreign Markets* (New York: Amacom, 1991), pp. 165–166.

97   Global Public Affairs Institute, op. cit., p. 30.

98   Ibid., p. 16.

99   See case of "John Higgins: An American Goes Native in Japan," in Tom L. Beauchamp, *Case Studies in Business, Society, and Ethics* (Englewood Cliffs, NJ: Prentice-Hall, 1983), pp. 209–214.

100  "General Electric in Hungary," James E. Post, Anne T. Lawrence, and James Weber, *Business and Society: Corporate Strategy, Public Policy, Ethics,* 9th edn (New York: Irwin/McGraw Hill, 1999), pp. 166–168.

101  "Global Heavyweights Vow 'Zero' Tolerance for Bribes," *Wall Street Journal*, January 27, 2005, p. A2.

102  Global Public Affairs Institute, op. cit., pp. 2, 11.

103  Ibid., p. 35.

104  Ibid., p. 15.

105  *Anti-Americanism and Global Business*, a report by The Global Public Affairs Institute (New York: 2003). See section on Perceptions of the Relationship Between U.S. Business and the U.S. Government.

# 8 Corporate responsibility for human rights

1   "Amnesty International: Taking on the Sins of the World," *The Economist*, May 30, 2009, p. 61.

2   Jay Solomon and Farnaz Fassihi, "Iran Rights Envoy Assails U.N. Censure," *Wall Street Journal*, November 19, 2010, p. A13.

3   Peter Coy, Dexter Roberts, and Bruce Einhorn, "The Great Fall of China," *Bloomberg BusinessWeek*, May 7–May 12, 2012, p. 6.

4  "Ethical Shopping: Human Rights," *The Economist*, June 3, 1995, pp. 58–59.

5  Gabriele G.S Suder., ed. *International Business Under Adversity*. Northampton, MA: Edward Elgar, 2008, p. 18.

6  Ibid., p. 194.

7  Ibid.

8  See Kirk Nielsen, "Chiquita in the Dock," *The Progressive*, October 2011, pp. 22–25.

9  Ibid., p. 24.

10  Ibid., p. 23.

11  Carolyn Aldred, "Human Rights Seen as Business Issue," *Business Insurance*. Chicago, April 17, 2000, vol. 34, No. 16, pp. 29–31.

12  David Kinley and Justine Nolan, "Human Rights, Corporations and the Global Economy: An International Law Perspective," in Andreas Scherer and Guido Palazzo, eds., *Handbook of Research on Global Corporate Citizenship.* (Northampton, MA: Edward Elgar, 2008), p. 358.

13  W. Michael Hoffman and Robert E. McNulty, "International Business, Human Rights, and Moral Complicity: A Call for a Declaration on the Universal Rights and Duties of Business," *Business and Society Review.*, Vol. 114, No. 4, Winter 2009, p. 541.

14  Tim Wallace, "Melbourne Embraces UN Business Charter; Triple Bottom Line," *Australian Financial Review*, February 27, 2002, Supplement, p. 23.

15  David Atkinson and Richard Pierre Claude, "Human Rights and Multinational Corporations: The Global Compact and Continuing Evolution," in Gabriele G.S. Suder, ed., *International Business Under Adversity* (Northampton, MA: Edward Elgar, 2008), p. 12.

16  Suder, op. cit., p. 13.

17  Ibid., p. 21.

18  Gavin Power, "Keynote Speech on United Nations Global Compact," at the Investment Management Institute Conference, January 6, 2006.

19  Thomas Donaldson, *The Ethics of International Business* (New York, Oxford: Oxford University Press, 1989). This book is discussed by George G. Brenkert, "Can We Afford International Human Rights?," *Journal of Business Ethics*, Vol. 11, July 1992, pp. 515–521.

20  Joel Feinberg, "Duties, Rights and Claims," *American Philosophical Quarterly*, 1966, pp. 137–144. Mentioned by Donaldson on pp. 65–66.

21  Patricia J. Parson, *Ethics in Public Relations: A Guide to Best Practice* (London and Philadelphia: Kogan Page, 2008), p. 32.

22  James E. Post, Anne T. Lawrence and James Weber, *Business and Society: Corporate Strategy, Public Policy, Ethics*, 10th edn (New York: McGraw-Hill Irwin, 2002), p. 354.

23  Alan F. Westin and Stephan Salisbury, *Individual Rights in the Corporation: A Reader on Employee Rights* (New York: Pantheon Books, 1980).

24  James A. Gross and Lance Compa, eds., *Human rights in Labor and Employment Relations: International and Domestic Perspectives*, Labor and Employment Relations Series (Labor and Employment Relations Association, 2009).

25  "China: The Debate Over Universal Values," *The Economist*, October 2, 2010, p. 43.

26 Ibid.
27 Ibid., p. 44.
28 Donaldson, op. cit., p. 81. Additional human rights violations could be added: summary execution, slavery or forced labor, genocide and cruel, inhuman or degrading treatment, p. 194.
29 Ibid., p. 70.
30 Ibid., p. 69.
31 A good argument can be presented that it is in the self-interest of an employer to accept responsibility because it preserves the workforce.
32 Robert Grosse, ed., *International Business and Government Relations in the 21st Century* (Cambridge: Cambridge University Press, 2005), p. 99.
33 George Tichaona Dzimiri, *Business Ethics, Social Responsibility and AIDS in Workplaces in Zimbabwe.* Doctoral Dissertation, Loma Linda University, 2007.
34 "HIV/AIDS: Altogether Now," *The Economist*, June 5, 2010, pp. 37–38.
35 The mayor of Oakland, California, which has a high population of high risk groups such as Latinos, African-Americans and gay men, launched campaign to include the business community. Chevron, Walgreens, the Levi Strauss Foundation, Young & Rubicam and the city's basketball team will work with the city's team. "Companies are smart about marketing, campaigns, advertising, technical assistance," said the mayor. Ibid.
36 Reference to *Wall Street Journal* article is April 23, 2001 and is mentioned in "Pharmaceutical Face Uphill Communications Challenge," *pr reporter*, Vol. 44, June 11, 2001, p. 1.
37 Ibid. Reference to *The Economist* is in March 10, 2001 issue.
38 Ibid.
39 Rob van Tulder, with Alex van der Zwart, *International Business-Society Management: Linking Corporate Responsibility and Globalization* (New York: Routledge, 2006), p. 304.
40 Ian W. Jones, Michael G. Pollitt and David Bek, *Multinationals in Their Communities: A Social Capital Approach to Corporate Citizenship Projects* (New York: Palgrave Macmillan, 2007), p. 263. The document is available at: http://www.gsk.com/community/downloads/facing the challenge.pdf.
41 Ibid., p. 307.
42 "Nigeria; Dutch Lawmakers Grill Shell Over Operations in the Country," *Africa News*, January 27, 2011.
43 Suder, op. cit., pp. 16–17.
44 "Business: Big Oil's Dirty Secrets, Corporate Ethics," *The Economist*, May 10, 2003, Vol. 367, p. 62. Also see Ben Casselman, Isabel Ordonez, and Angel Gonzalez, "Chevon Hit With Record Judgment," *Wall Street Journal*, February 6, 2011, p. A1.
45 Paul M. Barrett and Peter Millard, "Over a Barrel," *Bloomberg Businessweek*, May 14–May 20, 2012, p. 67. Also see Paul M. Barrett, "Amzaon Crusader. Corporate Pest. Fraud?" *Bloomberg Businessweek*, March 14–March 20, 2011, pp. 57–64.
46 Mary Anastasia O'Grady, "Chevron's Ecuador Morass," *Wall Street Journal*, May 14, 2012, p. A13.
47 Miyun Park and Peter Singer, "The Globalization of Animal Welfare," *Foreign Affairs*, Vol. 92, No. 2 March/April 2012, pp. 122–133.

48   Ibid., p. 133.

49   Ibid., p. 127.

50   Ibid., p. 129.

51   Ibid., p. 132.

52   Ibid., p. 131.

53   See Case 8–1, Debora I. Spar and Jennifer I. Burns, "Hitting the Wall: Nike and international Labor Practices," in Christopher A. Bartlett, *Transnational Management: Text, Cases, and Readings in Cross-Border Management*, 6th edn (New York: McGraw-Hill Irwin, 2011), pp. 679–697.

54   Rob van Tulder, with Alex van der Zwart,, op. cit., p. 283.

55   Post et al., op. cit., p. 575.

56   See case study: "Nike's Dispute With the University of Oregon," in Post et al., op. cit., pp. 570–580. Also see Van Tulder and Zwart, op. cit., pp, 279–288.

57   Van Tulder with van der Zwart, op. cit., pp. 283–284.

58   The case appears in Stephen J. Kobrin, "Multinational Enterprise, Public Authority, and Public Responsibility: The Case of Talisman Energy and Human Rights in Sudan," in Robert Grosse, ed., *International Business and Government Relations in the 21st Century* (Cambridge: Cambridge University Press, 2005).

59   Ibid., pp. 203–2–203. Arakis Energy (a Canadian independent) gained control of a large part of the concession Chevron was granted in 1974. It owned 25% of GN-POC, the Greater Nile Petroleum Operating Company. Others shares of GNPOC were 40% by Chinese National Petroleum Company, 30% by Petronas of Malaysia, and 5% by the Sudanese national firm.

60   Ibid., p. 207.

61   Ibid., pp. 204–205.

62   Ibid., pp. 209, 212.

63   Ibid., p. 209.

64   Ibid., pp. 212–214.

65   Mary Janigan, "Special Report: Wake Up, Corporate Canada," *Maclean's*, April 16, 2001, p. 26. The Commission went too far, however, said Mary Janigan, when it mailed 1,000 letters to large Canadian firms, asking six tough questions about how Canada should control corporate behavior at home and abroad. Not a single corporations replied, perhaps because they dismissed the Commission's approach as naive.

66   Two articles especially provide summaries of this case: Michael Shari and Sheri Prasso, "A Pit of Trouble," *BusinessWeek*, August 7, 2000, pp. 60–63; and Jane Perlez and Raymond Bonner, "Below a Mountain of Wealth, a River of Waste," *New York Times*, December 27, 2005, p. A1.

67   Peter Waldman, "Hand in Glove: How Suharto's Circle and a Mining Firm Did So Well Together," *Wall Street Journal*, September 29, 1998, p. A1.

68   Jane Perlez, "The Papuans Say, This Land and Its Ores Are Ours, *New York Times*, April 5, 2006, p. A4.

69   Dorothy Kosich, "Sustainable Mining; N.Y. Times Takes on Freeport McMoRan, Www.mineweb.net/sections/sustainable, posted December 28, 2005.

70   John P. Clark, "Freeport McMoRan: Giving Something Back (And It's Toxic)." www.greens.org/s-r/11/11–22.html.

71  Kosich, op. cit.
72  Perlez and Bonner, op. cit.
73  Ibid.
74  Ibid.
75  Ibid.
76  Kosich, op. cit.
77  David Atkinson and Richard Pierre Claude, "Human Rights and multinational Corporations: The Global Compact and Continuing Evolution," in Suder, op. cit., p. 209.
78  Kenya Human Rights Commission 2004.
79  Ibid., p. 144.
80  Michael A. Santoro, "Engagement With Integrity: What We Should Expect Multinational Firms to Do About Human Rights in China," *Business & the Contemporary World*, Vol. 10, No. 1, 1998, pp. 25–54.
81  Michael A. Santoro, "Engagement With Integrity: What We Should Expect Multinational Firms to Do About Human Rights in China," *Business & the Contemporary World*, Vol. 10, No. 1, 1998, pp. 25–54. (???FIND – pp. 34–45.)
82  The case is described in Otto Lerbinger, *The Crisis Manager: Facing Risk and Responsibility* (Mahway, NJ: Lawrence Erlbaum, 1997), p. 131ff.
83  Gethin Chamberlain, "Revealed: Gap, Next and M&S in New Sweatshop Scandal," *The Observer*, August 8, 2010, p. 8.
84  Rebecca Walberg "Multinational Strategies Are Changing. Debt and Demographics Major Problems Looming for Global Business," *National Post* (The Financial Post) (Canada), August 10, 2010, p. FP14.
85  Paul Mozur, "Foxconn Workers: Keep Our Overtime," *Wall Street Journal*, December 18, 2012, p. B1.
86  Atkinson and Pierre Claude, op. cit., p. 209.
87  "Business: Big Oil's Dirty Secrets," op. cit.
88  Kinley and Nolan, op. cit., p. 350.
89  David Kinley and Justine Nolan, "Human Rights, Corporations and the Global Economy: An International Law Perspective," in Scherer, op. cit., p. 351.
90  Doc. Kiarie Mwaura, "Corporate Citizenship and Human Rights: Reality and Prospects of the Proposed Constitutional Changes in Kenya," in Mahad Huniche and Esben Rahbek Pedersen, eds., *Corporate Citizenship in Developing Countries: New Partnership Perspectives* (Copenhagen Business School Press: 2006). A classic example is A.P. Smith Manufacturing Co. v. Barlow et al. involving donations to Princeton university that were considered proper even though the corporate charter did not expressly grant the power to make charitable contributions. The courts said that such power existed "even though there might not be express statutory privilege granted under the laws of the state." Morton J. Simon, *Public Relations Law* (New York: Appleton-Century-Crofts, 1969), p. 470
91  Emily F. Carasco and Jang B. Singh, "Towards Holding Transnational Corporations Responsible for Human Rights," *European Business Review*. Bradford: 2010, Vol. 22, No, 4, p. 432.
92  Kinley and Nolan, op. cit., p. 358.
93  Based on article by Mozur, op. cit.

# 9 Sustainability: the physical world under pressure

1  Donnella H. Meadows, *Limits to Growth* (New York: Universal Books, 1972). See "Towards a Sustainable Future: The changing Role of Science, Business and Politics in the 21st Century," advertising feature in Future Dialogue.

2  David A. Lubin and Daniel C. Esty, "The Sustainability Imperative," *Harvard Business Review*, May 2010, p. 44. Among other megatrends are environmental issues; globalized workforces and supply chains; rise of new world powers, notably China and India – all of which have intensified the competition for natural resources.

3  Maurice Berns et al., "The Business of Sustainability: What It Means to Managers Now," *MIT Sloan Management Review*, Vol. 51, No. 1, Fall 2009, p. 21.

4  Interview by Michael S. Hopkins of Amory Lovins, "What Executives Don't Get About Sustainability," *MIT Sloan Management Review*, Fall 2009, p. 36.

5  Adam Werbach, *Strategy for Sustainability: A Business Manifesto* (Boston, MA: Harvard Business Press, 2009), p. 8.

6  Lester R. Brown, "The New Geopolitics of Food," *Foreign Policy*, Vol. 186, May/June 2011, p. 55.

7  Ibid., p. 57.

8  "When the Rains Fail," *The Economist*, September 12, 2009, p. 28.

9  Brown, op. cit., p. 64.

10  Ibid., pp. 58–61.

11  "Water: Sin Aqua Non," *The Economist*, April 11, 2009, pp. 58–61.

12  Ibid., pp. 57–61.

13  Peter Brabeck-Letmathe (chairman of Nestle), Asit K. Biswas (president of the Third World Centre for Water Management) and Lee Kuan, "Putting a Price on Clean Water," *Wall Street Journal*, March 21, 2011, p. A15.

14  "Water: Sin Aqua Non," op. cit., p. 61.

15  From Monsanto Imagine, www.ProduceMoreConserveMore.com

16  Assif Shameen, "Big Money: Money in Looming Global Water Crisis," *The Edge* (Singapore), March 3, 2008.

17  Aarian Campo-Flores, "Big Water Users Get Flak in Drought," *Wall Street Journal*, July 11, 2011, p. A5.

18  "Australia's Water War: Refilling the Basin," *The Economist*, December 11, 2010, p. 54.

19  Steel: India's Bitter Choice: Water for Steel or Food," *Bloomberg BusinessWeek*, October 11, October 17, 2010, pp. 20–21.

20  Michelle Conin, "Town Torn Apart by Nestles," *BusinessWeek*, April 14, 2008, pp. 42–47.

21  Ben Levisohn and Jessica Silver Greenberg," *Wall Street Journal*, April 16–17, 2011, pp. B7, B10.

22  John W. Miller, 'Under Earth: Rocks or a Hard Place?," *Wall Street Journal*, June 5, 2012, p. B1.

23  Nathan Hodge and James T. Areddy, "China Hold on Metals Worries Washington," *Wall Street Journal*, September 24, 2010, p. A19.

24  Yuka Hayashi and James T. Areddy, "Japan Scrambles for Rare Earth, *Wall Street Journal*, October 16–17, 2010, p. A10.

25 Liam Pleven, "Pentagon in Race for Raw Materials," *Wall Street Journal*, May 3, 2010, p. A3.

26 A formal definition is "A region of the atmosphere with elevated concentration of ozone, lying roughly between altitude of 15 and 25 kilometers. The ozone layer protects life on Earth's surface by absorbing most of the high-energy ultraviolet (UV) radiation in sunlight." Dressler, p. 202.

27 "Wangaie Maathai, Nobel Peace Prize Laureat, Dies at 71," *New York Times*, September 26, 2011. Also BBC "On Being" October 1, 2011.

28 *Product Design in the Sustainable Era*, edited by Julius Wiedermann. Available in London's Museum of Science bookstore.

29 Paul Hawken, Amory Lovins, and L. Hunter Lovins, *Natural Capitalism – Creating the Next industrial Revolution* (Boston: Little Brown, 1999). Free at

30 As summarized by Darcy Hitchcock and Marsha Willard, *The Business Guide to Sustainability: Practical Strategies and Tools for Organizations* (London & Sterling, VA: Earthscan, 2006).

31 info.html – cached – similar.

32 The U.S. military has also taken action. It started a new plan, dubbed the Strategic Materials Security Program by the Pentagon, would give it greater power to decide what it stockpiles and how it goes about buying the materials.

33 Interview by Michael S. Hopkins of Amory Lovins, "What Executives Don't Get About Sustainability," *MIT Sloan Management Review*, Fall 2009, p. 40.

34 John Carey, "Hugging the Tree-Huggers," *BusinessWeek*, March 12, 2007, pp. 66, 67.

35 Andrew Batson, "Coke Aims to Improve Water Recycling," *Wall Street Journal*, June 6, 2007, p. A10.

36 Hitchcock and Willard, op. cit., p. 23.

37 David Kiron, Nina Kruschwitz, Knut Haanaes and Ingrid Von Streng Velken, "Sustainability Nears a Tipping Point," *MIT Sloan Management Review*, Vol. 53, No. 2, Winter 2012, p. 70.

38 Ibid., pp. 72–73.

39 Ram Nidumolu, C.K. Prahalad, and M.R. Rangaswami, "Why Sustainability Is Now the Key Driver of Innovation," *Harvard Business Review*, Vol. 87, No. 9, September 2009, p. 57.

40 Ibid., pp. 58–64.

41 Adam Werbach, *Strategy for Sustainability: A Business Manifesto* (Boston, MA: Harvard Business Press, 2009).

42 Ibid., pp. 28–32.

43 Dilip John Ikerd Mirchandani, *Organization Management Journal*, New York: Spring, 2008. Vol. 5, No. 1, p. 40.

44 Joe Light, "Sustainability Jobs Get Green Light at Large Firms," *Wall Street Journal*, July 11, 2011, p. B5. In addition, Clorox appointed Bill Morrissey as vice president for environmental sustainability, and Campbell Soup appointed Dave Swtangis as vice president of corporation social responsibility and sustainability. Nidumolu et al., op. cit.

45 See Sandra Waddock, *Leading Corporate Citizens: Vision, Values, Value Added*, 2nd edn (New York: McGraw-Hill Irwin, 2006).

46 Ibid., p. 48.

47  Ibid.

48  Philip S. Khoury, "Water: An Urgent Challenge for the 21st Century," *Spectrum*, an MIT newsletter. Spectrvm.mit.edu.

49  Ibid., p. 11.

50  Gloria L. Krisana Gallezo, "Popular Economics; Sustainable Finance, *Business-World*, November 27, 2009.

51  Ibid. See ADFIAP's 2008 Integrated Annual and Sustainability Report.

52  Erica Webster, "A Common Language of Engagement Is Needed," *Business Day* (South Africa), April 30, 2009. Some business schools offer postgraduate diplomas in CSI management practice. Hitchcock and Willard, op. cit., p. 44.

53  Ibid., p. 48.

54  For background, see Jeneen Interlandi, "The New Oil; Should Private Companies Control Our Most Precious Natural Resource?" *Newsweek*, Vol. 156, October 18, 2010, p. 40ff cover story.

55  Shameen, op. cit.

56  Kate Linebaugh, "GE's Immelt on Delivering for Investors," *Wall Street Journal*, September 6, 2011. Interview conducted August 30.

57  Ylan Q. Mui, "Bottled Water Boom Appears Tapped Out; Environmental Concerns, Recession Put Crimp in Sales, *Washington Post*, August 13, 2009, p. A10.

58  Yoon Ja-young, "Imported Water More Expensive than Crude Oil," *Korea Times*, January 11, 2010,

59  Claire Low, "Town Pulls the Plug on Bottled Water Sales," *Canberra Times* (Australia), July 9, 2009, p. A3.

60  "Branded-Water Craze Adds to Piles Of Plastic, Spurring Innovation at Coke, Pepsi. (Subtitle of Betsy McKay, "Message in the Drink Bottle; Recycle.." ) *Wall Street Journal*, August 30, 2007, p. B1.

61  Also see: "Pepsi to Pare Plastic for Bottled Water," by Valerie Bauerlein, *Wall Street Journal*, March 25, 2009, p. B6.

62  Most of the illustrations can be found in the books by Werbach and Hitchcock, op. cit.

63  The case is presented in Laura P. Hartman and Patricia H. Werhane, eds., *The Global Corporation: Sustainable, Effective and Ethical Practices: A Case Book*. New York and London: Routledge, 2009, pp. 317 ff.

64  Laura P. Hartman and Patricia H. Wehane, *The Global Corporation: Sustainable, Effective and Ethical Practices: A Case Book* (New York: Routledge, 2009), p. 318.

65  Ibid., p. 319.

66  "The HBR Interview: Unilever CEO Paul Polman," *Harvard Business Review*, Vol. 90, June 2012, p. 112.

67  Alec Mattinson, "Unilever's Polman Tops FTSE 100 Survey," *PR Week*, November 30, 2012, p. 12.

68  Hitchcock and Willard, op. cit., p. 15.

69  Anderson's personal and organization vision is described in "Case 3.1 Interface, Inc. Green Carpets for a Sustainable World," Sandra Waddock, *Leading Corporate Citizens: Vision, Values, Value Added,* 2nd edn (New York: McGraw-Hill Irwin, 2006), pp. 98–100.

70   Stuart H. Hart, *Capitalism at the Crossroads: Next Generation Business Strategies for a Post-Crisis World*, 3rd edn (Upper Saddle River, NJ: Pearson Education, publishing as Wharton School Publishing, 2010), p. 294.

71   Werbach, op. cit., p. 25.

72   Megha Bahree, "GE Remodels Businesses in India," *Wall Street Journal*, April 26, 2011, p. B8.

73   Hitchcock and Willard, op. cit., pp. 199–212.

74   "Sustainable Consumption Benefits All," *New Straits Times* (Malaysia), July 26, 2008, p. 4.

75   Alex Benady, "Can Advertising Save the World?, *Campaign*?," January 15, 2010.

76   Ibid.

77   Chris Berg, "Crisis? What Crisis?" *Sunday Age* (Melbourne, Australia), June 28, 2009, p. 15.

78   Ibid.

79   Ibid.

80   Alf James, "Face to Face: Companies Answer Some Crucial Questions," *Business Day* (South Africa), October 23, 2009.

81   Hart, op. cit., p. 122.

82   Hitchcock and Willard, op. cit., pp. 203–205.

83   Pete Engardio in his article "Beyond the Green Corporation" asks the read to "Imagine a world in which eco-friendly and socially responsible practices actually help a company's bottom line." Special Report, *BusinessWeek*, January 29, 2007, p. 50.

84   Hart, op. cit., p. 314.

85   Ibid., p. 200.

86   "Meeting the Demand for Sustainable Materials," *The Western Mail*, May 17, 2008, p. 17.

87   Hitchcock and Willard, op. cit., p. ix.

88   Rachel Barnes, "Kraft to Swtich Kenco Brand to 100% Rainforest Alliance," *The Grocer*, May 3, 2008, p. 66. Also see "Brazil's Agriculture Miracle: How to Feed the World," *The Economist*, August 28, 2010, pp. 10–11. The article states that the key to its success are agricultural research, capital-intensive large farms, openness to trade and to new farming techniques, p. 11.

89   "Gambia: Promoting Sustainable Livelihood," *Africa News*, July 21, 2009.

90   Hitchcock and Willard, op. cit., p. 199.

91   See "Seeing the Wood: A Special Report on Forests, *The Economist*, September 25, 2010. Also see "Special Report – The Logging Trade, Down in the Woods," *The Economist*, March 25, 2006, pp. 73–75.

92   Hitchcock and Willard, op. cit., pp. 202–203.

93   "Companies Move to Curb Risk from Chemical BPA," *Wall Street Journal*, April 21, 2008, p. B2.

# 10  Debate over climate change

1   Scientists preparing the fifth report of the Intergovernmental Panel on Climate Change (IPCC), due in 2013, have broadened the threats to include human security.

2    Richard Fisher, "Don't Provoke the Planet," *New Scientist*, September 26–October 2, 2009, Vol. 203, p. 8.

3    Gregg Easterbrook, "Global Warming: Who Loses – and Who Wins?," *The Atlantic*, April 2007, pp. 52–62. The author transitions from climate change to global warming and warns that it could be enormously disruptive.

4    Andrew Dressler and Edward A. Parson, *The Science and Politics of Global Climate Change: A Guide to the Debate*, 2nd edn (New York: Cambridge University Press, 2010). Page 201 provides a fuller definition of greenhouse effect: "The process by which trace gases in the atmosphere absorb and re-emit infrared radiation, thereby impeding the release of infrared radiation from the Earth's surface to space and warming the surface. The greenhouse effect is a natural process that warms the Earth's surface to its present comfortable state. Human-caused climate change is driven by the increases in atmospheric greenhouse gases to increasing the strength of the greenhouse effect."

5    "Getting Warmer," A Special Report on the Carbon Economy, *The Economist*, December 5, 2009, p. 3. Also, "Bush Reiterates Global Warming Should Be Studied," *Wall Street Journal*, February 6, 1990, p. A20.

6    Gautam Naik and Jeffrey Ball, "U.N. Report Adds Pressure to Global-Warming Fight," *Wall Street Journal*, February 2, 2007, p. A4.

7    David Adam and Larry Elliott, "Stern Report: Simple Verdict After a Complex Inquiry: Time Is Running Out," *The Guardian*, October 31, 2006, p. 4.

8    Nigel Lawson, "Time for a Climate Change Plan B," *Wall Street Journal*, December 22, 2009, p. A23.

9    Ibid. See his book *An Appeal to Reason: A Cool Look at Global Warming* (London: Gerald Duckworth & Co., 2008).

10   Dressler and Parson, op. cit., p. 194.

11   Ibid., p. 81.

12   Caroline McDonald, "Munich Re Initiates Climate Change Debate As Global Summit Begins, National Underwriter Property & Casualty/Risk & Benefits Management, December 1, 2010, News No. 12.

13   Peter Newell and Matthew Paterson, *Climate Capitalism: Global Warming and the Transformation of the Global Economy* (Cambridge University Press, 2010), p. 4.

14   Gautam Naik and Jeffrey Ball, "U.N. Report Adds Pressure to Global-Warming Fight," *Wall Street Journal*, February 2, 2007, p. A4.

15   Ibsen Ketata and John R. McIntyre, "Corporate Social Responsibility as a New orientation in Response to Crisis Management of Sea Changes and Navigational Dead Reckoning," in Gabrile G.S. Suder, ed., *International Business Under Adversity* (Northampton, MA: Edward Elgar, 2008), p. 154.

16   John M. Broder, "Create-an-Ad Contest Aims to Push Climate Message," *New York Times*, July 13, 2007, p. C5.

17   Fred Pearch, "The Climate Blame Game," *New Scientist*, No. 904, November 12, 2011.

18   "Climate Coverage Cools as Planet Heats Up; Traditional Media' Interest in Global Warming Wanes as Online Mentions Soar," *The Toronto Star*, January 15, 2012, Insight Section, p. IN1.

19   "Who Cares? Don't Count on Public Opinion to Support Mitigation," *The Economist*, December 5, 2009, A Special Report on the Carbon Economy, p. 15.

20  Ibid.
21  Elisabeth Rosenthal, "Global Warming Faces from U.S. Spotlight; As Other Nations Act, Americans Become More Skeptical About Urgency," *International Herald Tribune*, October 17, 2011, p. 8.
22  Ding Ding, Edward W. Maibach, Siaoquan Zhao, Connie Roser-Renouf and Anthony Leiserowitz, "Support for Climate Policy and Societal Action Are Linked to Perceptions About Scientific Agreement," *Nature Climate Change*, November 2011.
23  Ibid.
24  Nikhil Kulmar, "Barack Obama: Climate Change We Can Believe in? Michael Bloomberg Backs 'Green' President," *The Independent*, November 3, 2012.
25  Newell and Paterson, op. cit., p. 184.
26  Ibid., p. 5.
27  Ibid., p. 183.
28  Easterbrook, op. cit.
29  "Climate Change; Doomsday Clock Moves 1 Minute Closer to Midnight," *Genetics & Environmental Business Week*, January 26, 2012, Editor's Choice, p. 2.
30  Paul Raeburn, "Global Warming: Is There Still room for Doubt?," *Business Week*, November 3, 1997, pp. 157–160.
31  Newell and Paterson, op. cit., p. 50. Thaddeus Herrick, "CEO's Controversial Views Lead to Tough Summer for Exxon Mobile," *Wall Street Journal*, August 29, 2001, p. B1.
32  Thaddeus, "Exxon Proxy Vote Shows Advances for Edgy Policies," *Wall Street Journal*, May 30, 2002, p. A8.
33  Ibid., pp. 37–38.
34  Andrew C. Revkin, "On Climate Issue, Industry Ignored Its Scientists," *New York Times*, April 24, 2009, p. A1.
35  The new refrigerant produced by DuPont and Honeywell was, however, probed by EU Anatitrust officials. Ian Young, "EU Antitrust Probe Targets Honeywell-DuPont Refrigerant," *Chemical Week*, January 2–9, 2012, p. 13.
36  Lawrence Solomon, *National Post (ak/a The Financial Post)* (Canada), June 27, 2009, p. FP23.
37  "Hot Topic: Businesses Rethink Carbon Curbs," *Wall Street Journal*, March 3–4, 2007, p. A7.
38  Naik and Ball, op. cit. p. A4.
39  Sharon Begley, "Jim Rogers: The CEO of Duke Energy Could Make Dreams of Renewable Power a Reality," *Newsweek*, December 29, 2008/January 5, 2009, p. 78.
40  Jeffrey Ball, "Kyoto Discord Leads Firms to Call for Unified Rules," *Wall Street Journal*, August 29, 2002, p. A10.
41  Naik and Ball, op. cit., p. A4.
42  Newell and Paterson, op. cit., p. 50.
43  Joe Nocera, "At Exxon's Can't-Miss Meeting," *New York Times*, May 31, 2008, p. C1.
44  Bulldog Reporter's Daily Dog, July 6, 2012.
45  Ibid., p. 44.
46  Oliver Shah, "Tell Us How Companies Can Become more Green…." *The Sunday Times* (London), January 1, 2012, p. 9.
47  Newell and Paterson, op. cit., p. 42.

48  Ibid., p. 43.

49  "Hot Topic: Businesses Rethink Carbon Curbs," *Wall Street Journal*, March 3–4, 2007, p. A7.

50  Newell and Paterson, op. cit., p. 44.

51  Lawrence Solomon, "Fear of Climate Change Has Been the Biggest Boon in Insurance Industry History," *National Post* (Canada), June 6, 2009, p. FP23.

52  Celine Herweijer, Nicola Ranger, Robert E. T. Ward, "Adaptation to Climate Change: Threats and Opportunities for the Insurance Industry," Geneva Papers on Risk & Insurance. Basingstoke: July 2009, Vol. 34, No. 3, p. 360. Also see Easterbrook, op. cit., p. 64.

53  Mark E. Ruquet, "Insurers Can Facilitate Renewable Energy Development," *Property and Casualty 360*, November 28, 2011.

54  Evan Lehmann (E&E reporter), "Risk: 'Sustainable Insurance' Plan May turn Some Companies Away from Profit If It Harms Climate," *ClimateWire*, Spotlight, Vol. 10, No. 9, October 27, 2011.

55  Ibid.

56  Nine Chetney, "What Does Durban Deal Mean for Green Investment?

57  Ibid

58  "A Lean, Clean Electric Machine," *The Economist*, December 10, 2006, p. 78.

59  Ibid., p. 77.

60  Newell and Paterson, p. 45.

61  Ibid., p. 46.

62  Ibid., p. 78.

63  Ibid., p. 77.

64  "Beyond the Green Corporation, *BusinessWeek*, January 29, 2007, pp. 77–78.

65  Barbara Lewis, "Technology vs. Diplomacy: Who's Winning the Climate Race?, *Climate Spectator*, December 14, 2011.

66  "Green Initiatives Attracting Investments, Chinadaily.com.cn, September 10, 2009. Statement attributed to the U.S. Pew Environment Group.

67  Ibid.

68  Www.china.org.cn/business/summerdavos2009

69  "EU Takes Crucial Step in Solar Energy Project in Arab Deserts," *Oil & Gas News*, December 26, 2011.

70  Adam Chamberlain (National Chair, Climate Change Group), "Canada: Sustainable Strategies in Canada's North," Mondaq Business Briefing, December 21, 2011.

71  Ryan Crighton, "Granite 'hot rocks' Set to Ignite Energy Boom," *Aberdeen Press and Journal*, November 10, 2011, New; Business; Energy/Utilities, p. 3.

72  "Climate Change: Scientists Eye 'Windows of Opportunity' for Adapting Food Crops to Climate Change," *Biotech Week*, October 19, 2011, p. 254.

73  Their efforts appear in Shyam S. Yadav et al., *Crop Adaptation to Climate Change* (Chichester, West Sussex and Ames, IA: Wiley-Blackwell, 2011).

74  Ibid., p. 43. The "first-mover advantage" was also mentioned by Darcy Hitchcock and Marsha Willard. *The Business Guide to Sustainability: Practical Strategies and Tools for Organizations* (London & Sterling, VA: Earthscan, 2006), p. 200.

75  Newell and Paterson, op. cit., pp. 52–53.

76  Examples are from Adam Werbach, *Strategy for Sustainability: A Business Manifesto* (Boston, MA: Harvard Business Press, 2009), pp. 48, 53, 56.

77   Newell and Paterson, op. cit., p. 54.
78   Ibid., p. 31.
79   *BusinessWeek*, April 23, 2007, pp. 90–92; John J. Fialka, "Carbon Curbs Gain Backers," *Wall Street Journal*, February 27, 2007, p. A8.
80   "Getting Warmer," op. cit., p. 3.
81   David G. Victor, Charles F. Kennel, and Veerabhadran Ramanathan, "The Climate Threat We Can Beat," *Foreign Affairs*, Vol. 93, No. 1, May–June 2012, p. 112.
82   Deborah Solomon, "Climate Change's Great Divide," *Wall Street Journal*, September 12, 2007, p. A4.
83   "How They Compare: China Praised as US Fiddles, *The Guardian* (London), July 11, 2011, p. 14.
84   Stafford Thomas, "Carbon Tax. Too Heavy a Load," *Financial Mail* (South Africa), January 23, 2012, Economy, Business & Finance Section.
85   Bonnie Malkin Sydney, "Australian Parliament Passes Historic Carbon Tax Law..." *The Telegraph* (UK), October 12, 2011."
86   Neil Wilson, "Qantas the First to Pass on Gillard Slug to Passengers; Carbon Tax Gets Wings," *Herald Sun* (Australia), February 3, 2012, p. 3.
87   Dessler and Parson, op. cit., pp. 134, 198.
88   Newell and Paterson, op. cit., p. 34.
89   Solomon, op. cit.
90   Newell and Paterson, op. cit., p. 1.
91   Ibid.
92   Ibid., pp. 10, 28. To facilitate the operation of the emissions markets, the new associations of the International Emissions Trading Association and the Emissions Marketing Association have been formed. Annual carbon finance and carbon market conferences were also started. In 2005 alone emission reduction purchase agreements for more than 100 projects were signed or reached advanced negotiations at the Carbon Expo.
93   Ibid., p. 2.
94   Ibid., pp. ix, 2.
95   Ibid., p. 192.
96   Ibid., p. 33.
97   Ibid., p. x.
98   Ibid., pp. 26, 32.
99   Jeffrey Ball, John D. McKinnon, and Shai Oster, "China Cashes in on Global Warming," *Wall Street Journal*, January 8, 2007, p. A11.
100  Newell and Paterson, op. cit., p. 48.
101  Rebecca Smith and Timothy Aeppel, "EPA's Carbon Proposal Riles Industries," *Wall Street Journal*, December 8, 2009, p. B1; Ian Talley, "EPA Declares Greenhouse Gases a Danger," *Wall Street Journal*, December 8, 2009, p. B4.
102  Deborah Solomon, "U.S. Puts Oil Pipeline on Hold," *Wall Street Journal*, November 11, 2011, p. A3.
103  "Pipe Dreams," *Bloomberg Businessweek*, November 20, 2011, p. 90.
104  Jeffrey Ball and Edward Welsch, "Montana Spill Clouds Pipeline Plan," *Wall Street Journal*, July 25, 2011, p. A4.

105 "Pipe Dreams," op. cit., p. 87.
106 "The World Bank and the Environment: When the Learning Curve is Long," *The Economist*, June 27, 2009, p. 68.
107 Ibid., p. 173.
108 Dressler, op. cit., pp. 25–26.
109 Newell and Paterson, op. cit., p. 47.
110 David A. Fahrenthold and Juliet Eilperin, "Born in 1970, Event Has Cause for Celebration – and a Midlife Crisis", *Washington Post*, April 22, 2010, p. C01.
111 Ibid., p. 28.
112 Dressler and Parson, op cit., p. 29.
113 Ibid., p. 195.
114 Michael McCarthy, "Another Climate Summit, Another Chance Goes Up in Smoke; A New Deal on Limiting Carbon Emissions Is Looking Increasingly Unlikely, with Leading Players Remaining Intransigent," *The Independent* (London), December 9, 2011.
115 Alistser Doyle and David Fogarty and David Cutler, "How the World Discovered Global Warming: a Timeline," *Climate Spectator*, December 2, 2011.
116 Friends of the Earth (London), "Climate; Disastrous 'Durban Package' Accelerates Onset of Climate Catastrophe," *Africa News*, December 13, 2011.
117 Devon Maylie, "Climate Summit In Africa Looks at Farmers' Woes," *Wall Street Journal*, November 29, 2011, p. A11.
118 "Climate Change: An Agreement to Make an Agreement," *This Week*, December 23, 2011, p. 18.
119 Friends of the Earth, op. cit.
120 Fred Pearce, "Our Climate's Dangerous Decade," *New Scientist*, No. 909, December 17, 2011.
121 Patrick McGroarty, "Chinese Overture Jolts Climate Talks, *Wall Street Journal*, December 6, 2011, p. A10.
122 Jeremy Page, "Beijing Bows to U.S. on Air Quality Report," *Wall Street Journal*, January 7–8, 2012, p. A11.
123 Tom Bawden, "Company Bosses Grow Cooler Over Global Warming Concerns; Survey Shows Climate Change Is at the Very Bottom in the List of Firms' Worries," *The Independent*, December 13, 2011.
124 "Leading Article: Climate Change: Brownfield Thinking," *The Guardian* (London), November 29, 2011, Guardian Leader Pages, p. 32.
125 "How to Live with Climate Change," *The Economist*, November 27, 2010, p. 15; Lawson, op. cit.
126 Victor, et al., pp. 112–121.
127 As paraphrased by John Tierney, "Climate Proposal Puts Practicality Ahead of Sacrifice," *New York Times*, January 17, 2012, p. D2.
128 "Unpacking the Problem," *The Economist*, December 5, 2009, A Special Report on the Carbon Economy, p. 21.
129 Victor et al., op. cit., p. 113.
130 Ibid. Nordhaus endorsed similar measures in a report called "Climate Pragmatism."

# 11 Technology and intellectual property rights

1 "Special Report: Manufacturing and Innovation," *The Economist*, April 21, 2012, p. 4.

2 "Largest Non-Financial Companies," *The Economist*, August 20, 2011, p. 86.

3 John Cantwell, "Innovation and Information Technology in MNE," in Alan M. Rugman and Thomas L. Brewer, eds., *The Oxford Handbook of International Business* (New York: Oxford University Press: 2001), p. 434.

4 P&G's model is described in a case study by Larry Huston and Navil Sakkab (vp for innovation and knowledge and senior vice president for corporate research and development respectively at P&G) "Connect and Develop: Inside Procter & Gamble's New model for Innovation," in Christopher A. Bartlett and Paul W. Beamish, eds., *Managing Across Borders: The Transnational Solution* (Boston, MA: Harvard Business School Press, 2011), pp. 487–495.

5 Ray Kurzweil, *The Singularity Is Near: When Humans Transcend Biology* (New York: Viking, 2005), p. 50.

6 "Questions and Answers on the Singularity," distributed by Viking Press, p. 3. Kurzweil's book identifies three great overlapping revolutions: genetics, nanotechnology, and robotics – using the acronym GNR. Technology has always been a mixed blessing. Despite its dangers, it will extend life and free us from physical and mental drudgery. The technology of gene engineering "has the potential to bypass evolutionary protections by suddenly introducing new pathogens for which we have no protection, natural or technological." For this reason, some scientists believe that it is better not to carry out certain technologies to avoid possible disastrous outcomes. Opposition to genetically modified organisms (GMOs) – often resulting in crises of confrontation and, sometimes, malevolence – is one consequence of this attitude. Furthermore, GNR can be employed by a bioterrorist "to create a bioengineered biological virus that combines ease of transmission, deadliness, and stealthiness...."

7 For a discussion of this case, see Otto Lerbinger, *The Crisis Manager: Facing Disasters, Conflicts, and Failures*, 2nd edn (New York and London: Routledge, 2012), pp. 134–139.

8 Pui-Wing Tam and Cari Tuna, "Silicon Valley 3.0: Tech's New Wave," *Wall Street Journal*, October 22, 2010, pp. A1, A16.

9 "3D Manufacturing: Print Me a Phone," *The Economist*, July 28, 2012, p. 71.

10 From an independent supplement from MediaPlanet called "Biotechnology: Emerging Innovations; How Pioneering Concepts Are Breaking Into the Marketplace," *Wall Street Journal*, September 17, 2010, p. B4A.

11 Christopher D. Cook, "Control Over Your Food: Why Monsanto's GM Seeds are Undemocratic...." *Christian Science Monitor*, February 23, 2011.

12 Ibid.

13 "Ghana Must Tread Cautiously on GM Foods (editorial)," *Public Agenda* (Accra), April 2011.

14 "Kenya; To Abolish Hunger and Malnutrition, Africa Must Embrace GM Technology," *Africa News*, July 14, 2011.

15 John W. Miller, "EU Extends 'Frankenfood' Fight, Nears Ban on Farm-Animal Clones," *Wall Street Journal*, October 20, 2010, p. A15.

16   Alistair Driver and William Surman, "EU Approves First GM Crop in 12 Years," *Farmers Guardian*, March 5, 2010.

17   "GM Crops Suffer Setback After Explosion in Numbers of Pests on Neighbouring Farms; Surge in Bug Infestations Found on Modified Plants. Scientists Say Long-Term Risks Should be Reassessed," *The Guardian (London)*, May 14, 2010.

18   "Control Your Food," *The Christian Science Monitor*, February 23, 2011.

19   Ibid.

20   See Christopher D. Cook, *Diet for a Dead Planet: Big Business and the Coming Food Crisis* (New York: W.W. Norton & Co., 2004).

21   Michela Wrong, "Comment & Analysis: Field of Dreams: Golden Rice is a Genetically Modified Grain That Could Improve the Health of the World's Poorest," *Financial Times (London)*, February 25, 2000, p. 18.

22   Background of the GMO controversy is based on Charles C. Mann, "Biotech Goes Wild," *Technology Review*, Vol. 102, July–August 1999, pp. 36–43. Explanation of bioengineering appears in Richard A. Melcher and Amy Barrett et al., "Fields of Genes," *Business Week*, April 12, 1999, pp. 62–74. Current situation is described in Paul Jacobs, "Protest May Mow Down Trend to Alter Crops; Biotech: Public Outcry Over Genetically modified Foods Has the U.S. Agricultural Industry Back-pedaling," *Los Angeles Times*, October 5, 1999, p. A1.

23   Susan George, "Transnational risks: A New Challenge for Global Civil Society," in Ingo K. Richter, Sabine Berking and Ralf Müller-Schmid, eds., *Building a Transnational Civil Society: Global Issues and Global Actors* (New York: Palgrave Macmillan, 2006), p. 33.

24   Eleanor Singer, Amy Corning, and Mark Lamias, "The Polls-Trends: Genetic Testing, Engineering, and Therapy," *Public Opinion Quarterly*, Vol. 62, Winter 1998, pp. 633–664.

25   Rick Weiss, "Next Food Fight Is Over Listing Genes on Labels; Processors, Retailers Resisting Demand of Some Consumer Groups," *Washington Post*, August 15, 1999, p. A17.

26   Carola Schropp, "Partnering – the Key to Innovation," *Wall Street Journal*, September 17, 2010, p. 4B4.

27   The estimate is made by Bob Felber who leads the IP Practice Group at Waller Lansden in Nashville, Tenn. "De-mystifying IP," *Tactics*, January 2012, p. 7.

28   Shira Ovide and John Letzing, "Tech Patents Soar in Value," *Wall Street Journal*, April 10, 2012, p. B1.

29   Asby Jones, Dana Mattioli, and Mike Spector, "Apple, Google Line Up for Kodak's Patents," *Wall Street Journal*, July 28–29, 2012, p. B3.

30   Tamaas Kugyelo, "Competitiveness Council: EU in Need of More Entrepreneurial Scientists," *Europolitics*, February 22, 2012, No. 4369.

31   Ladas and Parry, "A Brief History of the Patent Law of the United States." www.ladas,com/Patents/USPatentHistory.html

32   Ibid.

33   "Patent Reform: The Spluttering Invention Machine," *The Economist*, March 19, 2011, p. 69.

34   Mike McLean, "America Invents Act Navigating the Shifts in U.S. Patent Law," *Electronic Engineering Times*, September 26, 2011, p. 54.

35   Edward Wyatt, "Fighting Backlog in Patents, Senate Approves Overhaul," *New York Times*, September 9, 2011, p. B4; Edward Wyatt, "Legislation to Change U.S. Pat-

ent System Called Threat to Small Inventor," *International Herald Tribune*, March 1, 2011, p. 18; Amy Schatz, "Patent Overhaul Bill Passes in Senate," *Wall Street Journal*, September 9, 2011, p. B7.

36  Amy Schatz and Don Clark, "Patent Overhaul Nears," *Wall Street Journal*, September 7, 2011, p. B1.

37  Bloomberg News, "New Law Creates a Demand for Patent Specialists," *New York Times*, October 10, 2011, p. B4.

38  Brend Kendall, "Court Rules Biotech Firm Can Patent Human Genes," *Wall Street Journal*, August 27, 2012, p. B3.

39  Robert Barnes, "High Court Hears Case on Medical Patents," *Washington Post*, December 8, 2011, p. A02.

40  Brent Kendall, "Medical-Testing Industry Heads to the Supreme Court," *Wall Street Journal*, December 5, 2011, p. B5.

41  Brent Kendall, Jonathan D. Rockoff, and Christopher Weaver, "Top Court Decision Alarms Biotechs," *Wall Street Journal*, March 21, 2012, p. A1.

42  "Twitter Spreads Disease," *New Scientist*," October 22, 2011, News No. 900. "Court Bans Patents on Stem-Cell Research That Destroys Embryos," *The Guardian*, October 19, 2011, p. 16. "European Court Says Stem Cell Technique Cannot Be Patented," *The Irish Times*, October 31, 2011, p. 20.

43  Reynolds Holdings and Robert Cole, "Making Sense of Patent Law," *New York Times*, November 18, 2011, p. 2.

44  Paul M. Barrett, "Apple's Jihad," *Bloomberg Businessweek*, April 2–8, 2012, p. 60.

45  Ibid., p. 61.

46  Ibid.

47  Jessica E. Vascellaro, "Apple Wins Big in Patent Case," *Wall Street Journal*, August 25–26, 2012, p. A1, and Jessica E. Vascellaro and Don Clark, "Apple Victory Shifts Power Balance," *Wall Street Journal*, August 27, 2012, p. B1.

48  Philipp Grontzki, "Samsung to Appeal ban on Galaxy Tablet Sales," *Wall Street Journal*, August 15, 2011, p. B3.

49  "Africa; Continent Builds New Manufacturing Base," *Africa News*, January 21, 2011.

50  Tian Lipu, op. cit.

51  Gloria Gonzalez, "IP Theft Is Top Risk for Firms with Operations in China; International Pressure Placed on China to Effectively Enforce Laws," *Business Insurance*, March 26, 2007, p. 16.

52  Ibid.

53  David Barboza and Steve Lohr, "Worth Billions, G.E. jet Engine Deal Puts Secrets at Risk," *The International Herald Tribune*, January 18, 2011, p. 1.

54  Ibid.

55  John Bussey, "China Venture Is Good for GE but Is It Good for U.S.?" *Wall Street Journal*, September 30, 2011, p. B1.

56  "Sewell," U.S. Steps Up Criticism of China's Practices, *New York Times*, September 17, 2010, p. B1.

57  Ibid.

58  Kate Linebaugh, "UTC Helped Build China's First Military Attack Copter," *Wall Street Journal*, June 29, 2012, p. B1.

59  "China and IP," editorial, *New York Times*, December 24, 2010.

60  "Special Report: State Capitalism," *The Economist*, January 21, 2012, p. 16.

61  Christopher Drew, "New Spy Game: Firms' Secrets Sold Overseas," *New York Times*, October 18, 2010, p. A1.

62  Alberto R. Gonzales, "IP Theft Is a Scourge on the U.S. Economy," *COMMWEB*, June 22, 2006, Op-Ed.

63  Siobhan Gorman, "China Singled out for Cyberspying," *Wall Street Journal*, November 4, 2011, p. A8.

64  Ibid.

65  Ibid.

66  Ibid.

67  Christopher Drew, "New Spy Game: Firms' Secrets Sold Overseas," *New York Times*, October 18, 2010, p. A1.

68  Rebecca Smith, "Chinese Turbine Firm Tied to Software Theft," *Wall Street Journal*, September 24–25, 2011, p. B3.

69  Michael Riley and Ashlee Vance, "It's Not Paranoia If They're Stealing Your Secrets," *Bloomberg Businessweek*, March 19–25, 2012, p. 78.

70  Ann Wooiner et al., "The Great Brain Robbery: A Compendium of Intellectual Thievery," *Bloomberg Businessweek*, March 19–25, 2012, pp. 78–84.

71  Ibid., p. 81.

72  Ibid., p. 84.

73  Doug Cameron, "DuPont Wins Nearly $1 Billion in Secrets Case," *Wall Street Journal*, September 15, 2011, p. B3.

74  Siobhan Gorman, "China Tech Giant Under Fire," *Wall Street Journal*, October 8, 2012, p. 1.

75  Christopher Weaver, Jeanne Whalen, and Benolt Faucon, "Drug Distributor Is Tied to Imports of Fake Avastin," *Wall Street Journal*, March 7, 2012, p. A1.

76  Alberto Gonzales, op. cit.

77  Geeta Anand and Rumman Ahmed, "Bayer Gets Setback in India," *Wall Street Journal*, March 13, 2012, p. B2.

78  "China and IP," *New York Times*, December 24, 2010, editorial, p. 22.

79  Ibid.

80  Ibid.

81  Tian Lipu, "China Is Serious About IP," *Wall Street Journal*, December 15, 2010, editorial, p. A19.

82  Gonzalez, op. cit.

83  Ravi Ramamurti, "Global Regulatory Convergence: The Case of IP Rights," in Robert Grosse, ed., *International Business and Government Relations in the 21st Century* (Cambridge: Cambridge University Press, 2005), p. 359.

84  Ibid., p. 357.

85  Ibid., pp. 344–346.

86  Kiran Sandford and Simon Walker, "Technology Companies – Are Investors Making the Most of Their Investments?" *UK Venture Capital Journal*, February 1, 1999.

87  See an editorial "Communicating with the Publics," in *Science*, Vol. 194, November 1976.

## 12 Diplomatic communication and public relations

1 "Diplomatic Communication," Http://www.softpanorama.org/Social/Toxic_man-agers/Communication/diplomatic_communication shtml
2 Ibid.
3 Christer Jonsson and Martin Hall, *The Essence of Diplomacy* (New York: Palgrave Macmillan, 2005), p. 67.
4 Ibid., p. 68.
5 Hans N. Tuch, *Communicating With the World* (New York: St. Martin's Press, 1990), p. 82.
6 R. P. Barston, *Modern Diplomacy*, 2nd edn (London and New York: Longman, 1997), p. 103.
7 Bryant Wedge, "Communication Analysis and Comprehensive Diplomacy," in Hoffman, Arthur S., ed., *International Communication and the New Diplomacy* (Bloomington and London: Indiana University Press, 1968), p. 25.
8 Philip R. Harris and Robert T. Moran, *Managing Cultural Differences*, 2nd edn (Houston, TX: Gulf Publishing, 1979), p. 36.
9 Thomas Neil Gladwin and Vern Terpstra, "Introduction," in Vern Terpstra, ed., *The Cultural Environment of International Business* (Cincinnati: South-Western Publishing Co., 1978), p. xix.
10 Edward T. Hall and Elizabeth Hall, "How Cultures Collide," in Gary R. Weaver, ed. *Culture, Communication, and Conflict: Readings in Intercultural Relations*, 2nd edn (New York: "Simon & Schuster, 1998), p. 18.
11 Cohen, op. cit., pp. 28–32.
12 Ibid., p. 32.
13 Ibid., pp. 32–33.
14 Wedge, op. cit., p. 24.
15 Vincent Defourny, "Public Information in the UNESC: Toward a Strategic Role," in Krishnamurthy Sriramesh and Dejan Vercic, eds., *The Global Public Relations Handbook: Theory, Research, and Practice* (Mahway, NJ: Lawrence Erlbaum Associates, 2003), p. 434.
16 Marc Champion and Betsy McKay, "Gathering Gives Chance to Burnish Images," *Wall Street Journal*, January 24, 2007, p. A7.
17 Ibid.
18 As defined by Richard Weiner, *Webster's New World Dictionary of Media and Communications* (New York: Simon & Schuster, 1990), p. 382.
19 Sabrina Horn, "The Evolution of PR to Digital Communications," *PR Week*, May 11, 2012, Op-Ed.
20 Edward L. Bernays, *Crystallizing Public Opinion* (New York: Boni and Liveright, 1923), p. 14.
21 Edward L. Bernays, *Biography of an Idea: Memoirs of Public Relations Counsel Edward L. Bernays* (New York: Simon and Schuster, 1965).
22 James E. Grunig, ed., *Excellence in Public Relations and Communication Management* (Hillsdale, NJ: Lawrence Erlbaum Associates, 1992), p. 4.
23 See PRSA website on "What is Public Relations."
24 This third aspects accommodates the definition of public relations in Philip Lesly, ed., *Lesly's Handbook of Public Relations and Communications*, 4th edn (Chicago, IL:

Probus Publishing Company, 1991, pp. 5–7. He defines public relations as the overall term for the specialized areas covered in his book, which include publicity, communication, public affairs, issues management, government relations, investor public relations, employee relations, community relations, industry relations, minority relations, advertising, press agentry, promotion, media relations, and propaganda.

25  Roger Fisher and William Ury, *Getting to Yes: Negotiating Agreement Without Giving In* (Boston, MA: Houghton Mifflin Company, 1981).

26  See Dorothy Jongeward, *Everybody Wins: Transactional Analysis Applied to Organizations* (Reading, MA: Addison-Wesley Publishing Company, 1973).

27  "Bolton Resigns: His Undoing," *The Economist*, December 9, 2006, pp. 32–33.

28  "Bolton's Power Plays Are Never Polite," *Toronto Star*, October 29, 2006, p. A14.

29  See Chapter 11.

30  For more on this subject, see Claude E. Shannon and Warren Weaver, *The Mathematical Theory of Communication* (Urbana: University of Illinois Press, 1949).

31  See Doug Newsom and Bob Carrell, *Public Relations Writing: Form & Style*, 4th edn (New York: Wadsworth Publishing Company, 1995), pp. 483–384.

32  Raymond Cohen, *Negotiating Across Cultures: International Communication in an Interdependent World*, revised edition (Washington, DC: United States Institute of Peace Press, 1997), p. 72.

33  Ibid., pp. 72–73.

34  www.softpanoramoa.org/Social/Toxic_managers/Communication/diplomatic_communication_.shtml.

35  John Locke, *An Essay Concerning Human Understanding*, available on website of Institute for Learning Technologies. See Locke's Book III, "Of Words," especially Chapter 2, "Of the Signification of Works."

36  "A World Empire by Other Means," *The Economist* December 22, 2001, p. 65.

37  Barbara Wallraff, "What Global Language," *Atlantic Monthly*, November 2000, pp. 55–56.

38  Tsedal Neeley, "Global Business Speaks English: Why You Need a Language Strategy Now," *Harvard Business Review*, Vol. 90, May 2012, pp. 116–124.

39  Daisuke Wakabayashi, "English Gets the Last Word in Japan," *Wall Street Journal*, August 6, 2010, p. B1.

40  Howard Richler, "The Language of Globalization is English," *The Gazette (Montreal)*, December 12, 2000, p. H2.

41  Ibid., p. 58.

42  Ibid., p. 52.

43  "Charlemane: The Galling Rise of English," *The Economist*, March 1, 2003, p. 50.

44  Ibid.

45  Thomas York, "Internet Age Web Cements English As Global Commerce Language," *Investor's Business Daily*, January 10, 2001, p. 6.

46  Ibid., p. 61.

47  "10 Funniest Badly-Translated Ads," May 12, 2011 under Funny Signs by Beverly Jenkins, www.oddee.com/item_97732.aspx. Also see David A. Ricks, *Blunders in International Business*, 3rd edn (Malden, MA and Oxford, U.K.: Blackwell Business, 1999).

48  Arthur Secord, *How to Tell What You Know: A Handbook for Management Men* (New York: The American Press, 1956), p. 19.

49  Ibid., p. 20.

50  Cohen, op. cit., p. 76.

51  Peggy Noonan, "Now He Tells Us," *Wall Street Journal*, September 22, 2007, p. W10.

52  Ibid., pp. 78, 85, 89.

53  James E. Lukaszewski, "The Power of Positive Language: Avoiding Negative Slant and Defensiveness with Declarative Language and Power Words," *Tactics*, August 2006, p. 10.

54  Ibid.

55  Raymond Cohen, *Theatre of Power: The Art of Diplomatic Signalling* (London and New York: Longman, 1987), p. 2.

56  Ibid., pp. 7, 11, 16.

57  Ibid., pp. 1–3.

58  Jack Hilton, *How to Meet the Press: A Survival Guide* (New York: Dodd, Mead & Company, 1987).

59  Cohen, *Theatre of Power*, op. cit., p. 3. Also see Erving Goffman, *The Presentation of Self in Everyday Life* (Garden City, New York: Doubleday, 1959) and Robert A. Giacalone and Paul Rosenfeld, eds., *Impression Management: How Image-Making Affects Managerial Decisions* (Newbury Park, CA: Sage Publications, 1991).

60  Charles Wolf, Jr. and Brian Rosen, *Public Diplomacy: How to Think About and Improve It* (Santa Monica, CA: Rand Corporation. Occasional Paper, 2004), p. 9.

61  Barbara Kellerman, "When Should a Leader Apologize and When Not?" *Harvard Business Review*, Vol. 84, April 2006, pp. 73–81.

62  The Japanese language uses many expressions to apologize, ranging from apologizing for something that has been done to casual expressions similar to "excuse me." More formal expressions are used with superiors. Namiko Abe, "Expressing Apologies: How to Say I Am Sorry in Japanese." See specific Japanese words in www.About.com.

63  Jennifer M. Lind, *Sorry States: Apologies in International Politics* (Ithaca, NY: Cornell University Press Studies in Security Affairs, 2008).

64  Kellerman, op. cit.

65  "'We Are Truly Sorry' The 10 Most Famous Corporate Apologies." www.huffingtonpost.com. The Apology appeared in its Facebook page and in *The Telegraph*.

66  See Keith Michael Hearitt, *Crisis Management by Apology* (Mahway, NJ: Erlbaum, 2006). Also Otto Lerbinger, *The Crisis Manager: Facing Disasters, Conflicts, and Failures*, 2nd edn (New York and London: Routledge, 2012), Chapter 4, "Image Restoration Strategies," pp. 61–75.

67  An earlier version of public diplomacy is described in an historical review by Manfred B. Steger. He describes how after the U.S. entered First World War, the Woodrow Wilson administration created the Committee on Public Information. It had the twin objectives of strengthening the "war will" among an ethnically diverse home population and to convince foreign publics that a reliable and invincible America would defeat the German war machine and "make the world safe for democracy." Most scholars describe these programs as propaganda. See Manfred B. Steger, "American Globalism 'Madison Avenue-Style': "A Critique of US Public Dipiomacy after 9/11," in Patrick Hayden and Chamsy el-Ojeli, eds., *Confronting Globalization: Humanity, Justice and the Renewal of Politics* (New York: Palgrave Macmillan, 2005), p. 229.

68  Ibid., pp. 229–230. Also see Wilson P. Dizard, *Inventing Public Diplomacy: The Story of the U.S. Information Agency* (Boulder, CO: Lynne Rienner Publishers, 2004), p. 4.

69  As quoted by Martha Bayles in "The Art of Global Public Relations," WSJ, July 24, 2008, p. A13.

70  Ibid., p. 231.

71  Benno H. Signitzer and Timothy Coombs, "Public Relations and Public Diplomacy: Conceptual Divergences," *Public Relations Review*, Vol. 18, No. 2, Summer 1992, pp. 139–140.

72  Dizard, op. cit., p. 5.

73  Ibid., p. 220.

74  Alexandra Starr, "The War on Terror: Charlotte Beers' Toughest Sell," *Business-Week*, December 17, 2001, p. 56.

75  "Brand USA," *Los Angeles Times*, March 10, 2002, p. 1.

76  Vanessa O'Connell, "U.S. Suspends TV Ad Campaign Aimed ate Winning Over Muslims," *Wall Street Journal*, January 16, 2003, p. A1.

77  Douglas Quenqua, "US Diplomacy Efforts – Can the Private Sector Lead Public Diplomacy Efforts?" *PR Week* (US), November 3, 2003, p. 7.

78  Ibid., pp. 234–235.

79  Further aspects of the program are discussed by Cynthia P. Schneider, "Culture Communicates: US Diplomacy That Works," in Jan Melissen, ed., *The New Diplomacy: Soft Power in International Relations.* New York: Palgrave Macmillan, 2005), p. 161.

80  Krebsbach, op. cit.

81  Glenn Kessler, "Hughes Tries Fine-Tuning to Improve Diplomatic Picture," *Washington Post*, April 19, 2006, p. A15.

82  Thomas L. Harris ViewsLetter, November 2005, p. 1. Also see Karen Hughes, "Remarks to the 2005 Forum on the Future of Public Diplomacy," transcript, Washington, D.C., October 14, 2005.

83  Michael Holzman, "Washington's Sour Sales Pitch," *New York Times,* October 4, 2003 (online).

84  Abbie Lin, "Addressing America's Image problem: A Public Relations-Centered Approach to Public Diplomacy," a class paper for Dr. Edward Downes, Boston University, College of Communication, November 8, 2005, p. 4.

85  Jan Melissen, *The New Diplomacy: Soft Power in International Relations* (New York: Palgrave Macmillan, 2005), p. xxiii.

86  Nancy Snow, "How to Build an Effective U.S. Public Diplomacy: Ten Steps for Change," Address delivered to the World Affairs Council, Palm Desert, CA, December 14, 2003, in *Vital Speeches of the Day*, Vol. 70, No. 12, April 1, 2004, pp. 369–374. Mentioned in Charles Wolf, Jr., and Brian Rosen, op. cit., p. 22.

87  Wolf and Rosen, op. cit., p. 22.

88  Michael Holzman, "Washington's Sour Sales Pitch," *New York Times*, October 4, 2003 (online).

89  Abbie Lin, "Addressing America's Image problem: A Public Relations-Centered Approach to Public Diplomacy," a class paper for Dr. Edward Downes, Boston University, College of Communication, November 8, 2005, p. 4.

90  Otto Lerbinger, *An Evaluation of Company Economic Education Programs.* A Ph.D. thesis at the Massachusetts Institute of Technology, June 1954.

91   Philip Lesly, "Why Economic Education Is Failing," *Management Review*, Vol. 65, October 1976, pp. 17–23.

92   Herbert H. Hyman and Paul B. Sheatsley, *Public Opinion Quarterly*, Vol. 11, Fall 1947, p. 529.

93   Ibid., pp. 412–423; also in Katz, Daniel, Dorwin Cartwright, Samuel Eldersveld, and Alfred McClung Lee, *Public Opinion and Propaganda* (New York: The Dryden Press, 1954), pp. 522–531.

94   Harold Mendelsohn, "Some Reasons Why Information Campaigns Can Succeed," *Public Opinion Quarterly*, Vol. 37, pp. 50–61.

95   Ibid., p. 51.

96   Maria Aspan, "Banks Must Do 'A Lot More' to Repair Image; HSBC's Dorner," *American Banker,* October 18, 2012.

97   From the *Bulldog Reporter's Daily Dog*, June 2, 2010.

98   "Brand USA," *Los Angeles Times*, March 10, 2002, p. 1.

# 13  Global marketing communication

1   Adam Gopnik, "Market Man: What Did Adam Smith Really Believe?," *The New Yorker*, October 18, 2010, p. 84.

2   Ibid., p. 83.

3   Peter Drucker, "Marketing and Economic Development," *Journal of Marketing*, Vol. 22, No. 3, 1958, p. 256.

4   Roberto C. Goizueta, Coca-Cola, A Business System Toward 2000: Our Mission in the 1990s, The Coca-Cola Company, p. 3.

5   Diana L. Deadrick, R. Bruce McAfee and Mytron Glassman, "'Customers for Life': Does It Fit Your Culture?, *Business Horizons*, Vol. 40, July–August 1997, pp. 11–16. Philip Kotler's book is *Marketing Management: Analysis, Planning, Implementation and Control*, 7th edn (Englewood, NJ: Prentice Hall, 1991).

6   Sak Onkvisit and John J. Shaw, *International* Marketing: *Analysis and Strategy*, 4th edn (New York and London: Routledge, 2004), p. 3.

7   Ibid., pp. 3, 4.

8   Scholars use various terms to reflect the issue of standardization vs. customization: ethnocentrism, polycentrism, and geocentrism. Ethnocentrism is defined as "plans for overseas markets are developed in the home office, using policies and procedures identical to those employed domestically"; polycentricism as allowing each over seas subsidiary operates independently of the others, establishing its own marketing objectives and plans; and geocentric (and regiocentric): company "developed politices and organizes activities on a regional or worldwide basis" – to "project a uniform image of the company and its products." Ali Kanso, "Standardization Versus Localization: Public Relations Implications of Advertising Practices in Finland," in Hugh M. Culbertson and Ni Chen, eds., *International Public Relations: A Comparative Analysis* (Mahway, NJ: Lawrence Erlbaum Associates, 1996), p. 301.

9   Ibid., p. 299.

10   Theodore Levitt, "The Globalization of Markets," *Harvard Business Review,* Vol. 61, May–June, 1983, pp. 92–102.

11   Wouters, op. cit. pp. 165–167.

12   G. Thomas Sims, "Uncommon Market: Corn Flakes Clash Shows the Glitches in European Union," *Wall Street Journal,* November 1, 2005, p. A1.

13   Ibid.

14   G. Tomas M. Hult, Bruce D. Keillor, and Roscoe Hightower, "Valued Product Attributes in an Emerging Market: A Comparison Between French and Malaysian Consumers," *Journal of World Business,* Vol. 35, No. 2, 2000, p. 217.

15   Ibid., p. 216.

16   These product attributes were product quality, product appearance, product composition, service availability, packaging appearance, product availability, warranty/ guarantee, product price, product features, recyclability/environmentally friendly, package functionality, product safety, brand image, store image/retailer image, financing/credit availability, product country-of-origin. Ibid., pp. 211, 216–217.

17   William Darley and Denise Johnson, "Cross-National Comparison of Consumer Attitudes Toward Consumerism in Four Developing Countries," *Journal of Consumer Affairs,* Vol. 27, Summer 1993, pp. 37–54.

18   Vikram Dodd, "Sainsbury's Bans GM Food in Own Labels," *The Guardian (London),* March 17, 1999, p. 9.

19   "GMO Update: Supermarket Revolt Underway," *The Grocer,* March 20, 1999, p. 11.

20   Pascal Zachary, "U.S. Companies Target Consumers Abroad Emerging Nations Are Viewed Not Just As Sources of Cheap Labour But As Fertile Sales Territories, *Globe and Mail (Canada),* June 13, 1996.

21   Carol Matlack and Pallavi Gogoi, "What's This? The French Love McDonald's? *BusinessWeek,* January 13, 2003, p. 50.

22   "Women in Italy Like to Clean but Shun the Quick and Easy," *Wall Street Journal,* April 25, 2006, p. A1.

23   Tim R.V. Davis and Robert B. Young, "International Marketing Research: A Management Briefing," *Business Horizons,* Vol. 45, March–April 2002, p. 31.

24   Ibid., p. 31.

25   Ibid.

26   Sak Onkvisit and John J. Shaw, *International Marketing: Analysis and Strategy,* 4th edn (New York and London: Routledge, 2004), pp. 337–338.

27   Early references are D.E. Schultz, S.I. Tannenbaum, and R. F. Lauterborn, *Integrated Marketing Communications* (Chicago: NTC Publishing Group, 1992), and T.A. Shimp, *Advertising, Promotion, and Supplemental Aspects of Integrated Marketing Communication,* 4th edn (Florida: The Dryden Press, 1997).

28   Jerry Kliatchko, "Revisiting the IMC Construct: A Revised Definition and Four Pillars," *International Journal of Advertising,* Vol. 27, No. 1, 2008, p. 140.

29   Ibid., p. 135.

30   Ibid., p. 143.

31   For a discussion of consumer advocacy see Glen L. Urban, "The Emerging Era of Customer Advocacy," *MIT Sloan Management Review,* Vol. 45, No. 2, Winter 2004, p. 77.

32   Richard Ettenson and Jonathan Knowles, "Don't Confuse Reputation with Brand,"
     *MIT Sloan Management Review*, Vol. 49, No. 2, Winter 2008, pp. 19–21.
33   Ibid., p. 19.
34   For an introduction to relationship marketing, see Philip J. Kitchen and Patrick
     DePelsmacker, *Integrated Marketing Communications: A Primer* (New York and
     London: Routledge, 2004).
35   George S. Day, "Managing Market Relationships," *Journal of Academy of Marketing
     Science*, Vol. 28, No. 1, 2000, pp. 24–30.
36   Ibid.
37   Noel C. Paul, "Supersize It!," *Boston Globe*, August 8, 2004, p. D5.
38   Lleila Abboud and Patricia Callahan, "Food Industry Gags at Proposed Label Rule
     for Trans Fats," *Wall Street Journal*, December 27, 2002, p. B1.
39   Based on Rowland T. Moriarty, Ralph C. Kimball, and John Gay, "The Manage-
     ment of Corporate Bahnking Relationships," *Slocan Management Review*, Vol. 24,
     Spring 1983, pp. 3–15.
40   Philip Kotler and Eduardo Roberto, *Social Marketing and Strategies for Changing
     Public Behavior* (New York: Free Press, 1989), p. 3.
41   Philip Kotler and Gerald Zaltman, "Social Marketing: An Approach to Planned
     Social Change," *Journal of Marketing*, Vol. 35, July 1971, pp. 3–12.
42   Philip Kotler, *Marketing for Nonprofit Organizations* (Englewood Cliffs, NJ: Pren-
     tice Hall, 1975), p. 283.
43   *The Herald* (Glasgow), July 26, 2005, http://www.stir.ac.uk
44   Patrick McGorry, "The Next Government Must Take Real Action to Reduce Sui-
     cide," *Sunday Mail* (South Australia), August 29, 2010, p. 26.
45   Described in Alan R. Andreasen, "Profits for Nonprofits: Find a Corporate Part-
     ner," *Harvard Business Review*, November–December 1996, p. 47. Also see his
     *Marketing Social Change: Changing Behavior to Promote Health, Social Develop-
     ment, and the Environment* (San Francisco, CA: Jossey-Bass, 1995).
46   R.C. Lefebvre and J.A. Flora, *Social Marketing and Public Health Intervention*, 1988.
     Some major references for social marketing are: Philip Kotler and Gerald Zaltman,
     "Social Marketing: An Approach to Planned Social Change," *Journal of Marketing*,
     Vol. 35, 1971, pp. 3–12; Andreasen, op. cit.,
47   Brian Currie, "Alcohol Industry Under Fire," *The Herald (Glasgow)*, February 18,
     2011, p. 6.
48   Case is from Laura P. Hartman, Justin Sheehan and Jenny Mead, in Hartman,
     "Procter & Gamble: Children's Safe Drinking Water," in Laura P. Hartman and Pa-
     tricia H. Werhane, eds., *The Global Corporation: Sustainable, Effective and Ethical
     Practices: A Case Book* (New York and London: Routledge, 2009), pp. 159–167.
49.  "Giving the UN's Climate Justice a Sense of Time, *Campaign*, October 9, 2009,
     Closeup, p. 10.
50   Matthew Moore, Global warming ads 'overstated the risk', *The Daily Telegraph*
     (London), March 15, 2010, p. 8.
51   Martine Mittelstaedt, "Skeptical Ads Anger Green Groups," *The Globe and Mail
     (Canada)*, November 18, 2009, p. A12.
52   Mentioned in Moyers show on CBS, March 25, 2008.
53   Thomas Harris, *Tips & Tactics*, newsletter by the weekly newsletter, *pr reporter,* Vol.
     29, No. 15, November 18, 1991, p. 2.

54  Joanna Perry, "Analysis – Sustainability – the Green Team," *Retail Week*, April 23, 2010.

55  David A. Fahrenthold and Juliet Eilperin, "Born in 1970, Event Has Cause for Celebration – and a Midlife Crisis," *The Washington Post*, April 22, 2010, p. C01. See Chapter 10 for a further discussion of the survey.

56  Jack Neff, "10 Green Marketing Milestones," *Advertising Age*, April 19, 2010, p. 0094.

# 14 Government affairs, negotiations, and lobbying

1   Raymond Cohen, *Negotiating Across Cultures: International Communication in an Interdependent World*, revised edition (Washington, DC: United States Institute of Peace Press, 1997), p. 82.

2   Foundation for Public Affairs, *Corporate Public Affairs: The State of Corporate Public Affairs Survey Final Report 1999–2000* (Washington, DC: Public Affairs Council, 1999), p. 3.

3   Stated by John Fayerweather in Robert Grosse, ed., *International Business and Government Relations in the 21st Century* (Cambridge: Cambridge University Press, 2005), p. 46.

4   Ibid., pp. 27–28, 46.

5   Ibid, p. 36.

6   Ibid.

7   Ibid.

8   Ibid., pp. vi and 39.

9   Ibid, p. 465.

10  Ibid., p. 42.

11  Ibid., pp. 472–473.

12  Yi-Ru Regina Chen, "The Strategic Management of Government Affairs in China: How Multinational Corporations in China Interact With the Chinese Government," *Journal of Pubic Relations Research*, Vol. 19, No. 3, 2007, p. 284. Chen is faculty member at the University of Macau. Also see her book, *The Business of Corporate Government Affairs in China – Corporate Competitive Advantage in China's Marketization* VDM Veerlag Dr. Muller: 2009. The author interviewed her in 2007.

13  Ibid., p. 287.

14  Ibid., p. 290.

15  Ibid., p. 296.

16  Such advice is also given by Dale Carnegie, *How to Win Friends and Influence People* (New York: Pocket Books, Inc., 1936; originally published by Simon and Schuster).

17  Chen, op. cit., p. 286.

18  Ibid, p. 287.

19  Ibid., p. 298.

20  Ibid., p. 299.

21  Ibid., p. 304.

22  Charles. W. Freeman, Jr., *Arts of Power: Statecraft and Diplomacy* (Washington, DC: United States Institute of Peace Press, 1997), p. 88.

23  Cohen, op. cit., p. 83.
24  Baker-Hamilton Report is formally known as *The Iraq Study Group Report. The Way Forward – A New Approach.*
25  Iraq, for example, who vowed to wipe Israel off the map, was not invited to the Annapolis Conference. Raymond McCaffrey and Robin Wright, "Annapolis To Host Mideast Summit," *Washington Post*, September 29, 2007, p. B01.
26  Dejan Vercic, Larissa A. Grunig, and Jame E. Grunig, "Global and Specific Principles of Public Relations: Evidence From Slovenia," in Hugh M. Culbertson and Ni Chen, eds., *International Public Relations: A Comparative Analysis* (Mahway, NJ: Lawrence Erlbaum Associates: 1996), p. 48.
27  Noted by Frank R. Pfetsch, *Negotiating Political Conflicts* (New York: Palgrave Macmillan, 2007), p. 51.
28. Jean-Claude Usunier and Julie Anne Lee, *Marketing Across Cultures*, 4th edn (New York: Prentice Hall, 2005), p. 503.
29  Ibid., p. 508.
30  A reference to Edward T. Hall in Weaver, Gary R., ed. *Culture, Communication, and Conflict: Readings in Intercultural Relations*, 2nd edn (New York: "Simon & Schuster, 1998), p. 19.
31  John S. Odell, *Negotiating the World Economy* (Ithaca & London: Cornell University Press, 2000), p. 2.
32  Ibid., p. 4.
33  From an announcement of a two-day program on November 8–9, 2007 and May 1–2, 2008. See www.pon.harvard.edu.
34  Jean-Claude Usunier and Julie Anne Lee, *Marketing Across Cultures*, 4th edn (New York: Prentice Hall, 2005), p. 507
35  Jamil Anderlini, "Have a Coffee, and Think Public Relations," *South China Morning Post*, March 6, 2006, p. 2.
36  Diane Brady, "Pepsi Repairing a Poisoned Reputation in India," *BusinessWeek*, June 11, 2007, pp. 46–54.
37  "Face Value: The Real Thing," *The Economist*, August 26, 2006, p. 51.
38  *The Economist,* January 13, 2007, p. 80.
39  Cohen, op. cit., p. 26.
40  Ibid., p. 27.
41  Roger Fisher and William Ury, *Getting to Yes*: *Negotiating Agreement Without Giving In* (Boston, MA: Houghton Mifflin Company, 1981), p. 34.
42  Ibid., p. 35.
43  Cohen, op. cit., p. 13.
44  Ibid., p. 25. The reference to Larand B. Szalay is "Intercultural Communication: A Process Model," *International Journal of Intercultural Relations*, Vol. 5, 1981, pp. 133–146.
45  Fisher, op. cit., p. x.
46  Stanley Hoffman, *Gulliver's Troubles, Or the Setting of American Foreign Policy* (New York: McGraw-Hill, 1968, p. 148.
47  Cohen, op. cit., pp. 36ff.
48  Fisher, op. cit., pp 10–11.
49  Usunier and Lee, op. cit., p. 505–507.

50  See Fons Trompenaars and Charles Hampden-Turner, *Riding the Waves of Cultures: Understanding Cultural Diversity in Global business*, 2nd edn (New York and London: McGraw-Hill, 1998), pp. 136–139, and Malcom Warner and Pat Joynt, *Managing Across Cultures: Issues and Perespectives* (London: Thomson Learning: 2002), pp. 158–161.

51  Frank R. Pfetsch, *Negotiating Political Conflicts* (New York: Palgrave Macmillan, 2007), p. 51.

52  Ibid., p. 502.

53  Ibid., p. 506.

54  Ibid., p. 37

55  Ibid., p. 83.

56  Usunier and Lee, op. cit., p. 520.

57  Philip Kitchen and Patrick De Pelsmacker, *Integrated Marketing Communications: A Primer* (New York and London: Routledge, Taylor & Francis Group, 2004), p. 125.

58  George S. Day, "Managing Market Relationships," *Journal of the Academy of Marketing Science*, Vol. 28, Winter 2000, pp. 24–30.

59  Cohen, op. cit., p. 37.

60  Ibid., pp. 36, 37.

61  Lynn E. Metcalf et al., "Cultural Tendencies in Negotiation: A Comparison of ," *Journal of World Business*, Vol. 41, 2006, pp. 382–394.

62  Ibid.

63  Ibid., p. 383.

64  Usunier and Lee, op. cit., p. 504.

65  Ibid., p. 511.

66  Robert I. Wakefield, "Public Relations in New Market Development: The Influence of Converging Multi-cultural Factors," in Judy VanSlyke Turk and Linda H. Scanlan, eds., *Fifteen Cases Studies in International Public Relations; The Evolution of Public Relations: Case Studies From Countries in Transition* (Gainesville, FL: The Institute for Public Relations, 1999), p. 110.

67  Ibid.

68  Freeman, op. cit., pp. 107, 118.

69  Charles W. Freeman, Jr., *Arts of Power: Statecraft and Diplomacy* (Washington, DC: United States Institute of Peace Press, 1997), p. 120.

70  David Cohen, "PAC Power: An Abuse of Power," in *Political Action for Business: The PAC Handbook*, ed. Ken Clair (Washington, DC: Fraser/Associates, 1981), p. 313.

71  Neil King Jr., and Rebecca Blumenstein, "On Message: China Launches public Response to Safety Outcry," *Wall Street Journal*, June 30/July 1, 2007, p. A1.

72  Damon Darlin, "The Toshiba Case: Japanese Firms' Push to Sell to Soviets Led to Security Breaches, *Wall Street Journal,* August 4, 1987, pp. 1ff.

73  Ben Pauw, "Lobbying in the Netherlands: Public Affairs in a European Context," in Eric Denigard and Anita Weisink, *State of the Art and Future Trends. International Public Relations Association Gold Paper No. 13,* October 2000.

74  "Politics Brief: 'Ex Uno, Plures," *The Economist,* August 21, 1999, p. 44.

75  Magne Haug and Haavard Koppang, "Lobbying and Public Relations in a European Context," *Public Relations Review*, Vol. 23, No. 3, 1997, p. 233.

76  Ibid., p. 239.

77  Ibid., p. 242.

78  "Ex uno, Plures," The *Economist*, August 21, 1999.

79  "The Gentle Art of Lobbying in China," *The Economist*, February 17, 2001, p. 43.

80  Sonia Mazey in Irina Michalowitz, *EU Lobbying – Principals, Agents and Targets: Strategic Interest Intermediation in EU Policy-Making* (London and New Brunswick: Rutgers University, Transaction Publishers, 2004).

81  Ibid., see pp. 7, 41, 42, and 44.

82  R. H. Pedler, ed., *European Union Lobbying: Changes in the Arena* (Basingstoke: Palgrave Macmillan, 2002), p. 323.

83  Ibid., p. 319.

84  Ibid., p. 315.

85  Ibid., p. 314.

86  Ibid., p. 319.

87  Ibid., p. 321.

88  Ibid., p. 317.

89  Ibid., p. 3.

90  Ibid.

91  Ibid., p. 313.

92  Ibid., 322.

93  James Kanter, "EU Alleges AstraZeneca Misled Regulators to Stymie Generics," *Wall Street Journal*, August 1, 2003, p. A2.

94  "Rules for Lobbyists Pressure Grows for Greater Transparency in Brussels," *Financial Times (London)*, October 11, 2007, p. 10.

95  Mary Jacoby, "Lobbyists' NATO Goldmine," *Wall Street Journal*, June 2–3, 2007, p. A4.

96  Sean Lux, T. Russell Crook and Terry Leap, "Corporate Political Activity: The Good, the Bad, and the Ugly," *Business Horizons*, Vol. 55, 2012, pp. 307–312.

97  Kathryn Johnson, "How Foreign Powers Play for Status in Washington," *U.S. News & World Report*, June 17, 1985, p. 35.

98  David M. Cloan, "More Nations Seek a P-R Polish on Their U.S. Image," *New York Times*, August 6, 1978, p. F3.

99  Cooney, op. cit.

100  Ibid.

101  Ibid.

102  Ibid.

103  The case appears in Trompenars and Hampden-Turner, op. cit., pp. 137–138.

# 15 Achieving global corporate citizenship

1   Viewing corporate governance as a system of government in democracies is presented in John L. Colley, Jr., Jacqueline L. Doyle, George W. Logan, and Wallace Stettinus, *Corporate Governance*, the McGraw-Hill Executive MBA Series (New York: McGraw-Hill, 2003), pp. 1–5.

2   Yadong Luo, *Global Dimensions of Corporate Governance* (Oxford: Blackwell Publishers, 2007).

3   Peter F. Drucker, *Management: Tasks, Responsibilities, Practices* (New York: Harper & Row Publishers, 1975), pp. 631–632.

4   Ian Wilson, "One Company's Experience with Restructuring the Governing Board," *Journal of Contemporary Business*, Vol. 8, No. 1, 1979, p. 73.

5   Thomas Donaldson, "The Epistemic Fault line in Corporate Governance," *Academy of Management Review*, Vol. 37, No. 2, 2012, p. 257.

6   Ibid., p. 46.

7   Barbara W. Altman, a former research fellow at Boston College's Center for Corporate Community Relations, characterized this blend as a new business model. The name of the center was subsequently changed to The Center for Corporate Citizenship. See her "Transformed Corporate Community Relations: A Management Tool for Achieving Corporate Citizenship," *Business and Society Review*, Vol. 102, No. 1, pp. 43–51.

8   This argument is used by David Vogel in an unpublished article "Global Corporate Citizenship: The Scope and Limits of Corporate Social Responsibility" available on the Internet.

9   Christina Keinert, *Corporate Social Responsibility as an International Strategy* (Physica-Verlag: A Springer Company, 2008), p. 5.

10  Ibid., pp. 38–39.

11  Ibid., pp. 43–44.

12  Michael Hopkins, *Corporate Social Responsibility and International Development: Is Business the Solution?* (London, Sterling, VA: Earthscan, 2007), p. 9.

13  Ronald Alsop, "B.B.A. Track/ Focus on Academic, Careers and Other B-School Trends," *Wall Street Journal*, December 13, 2005, p. B6.

14  Keinert, op. cit., p. 50.

15  Dirk Matten and Andrew Crane, "Corporate Citizenship: Toward an Extended Theoretical Conceptualization," *Academy of Management Review*, Vol. 30, No. 1, 2005, p. 166.

16  Ibid., p. 167. Also see http://www.exxonmobil.com.

17  Matthew J. Hirschland, *Corporate Social Responsibility and the Shaping of Global Public Policy* (New York: Palgrave Macmillan, 2006), p. 5.

18  Ibid., p. 7.

19  Francis X. Sutton, Seymour E. Harris, Carl Kaysen, and James Tobin, *The American Business Creed* (Cambridge, MA: Harvard University Press, 1956).

20  For a modern view of stakeholders, see James E. Post, Lee E. Preston, and Sybille Sachs, "Managing the Extended Enterprise," *California Management Review*, Vol. 45, Fall 2002, pp. 6–27.

21  Hirschland, op. cit., p. 7.

22  Ibid., p. 156.

23  Alan Murray, "Business: The CEO as Global Corporate Ambassador," *Wall Street Journal*, March 29, 2006, p. A2.

24  Murray, op. cit. Also see Alan Murray, "After the Revolt, Creating a New CEO," *Wall Street Journal*, May 5/6 2007, pp. 1–2.

25  Ian Davis, "The Biggest Contract," *The Economist*, May 28, 2005, p. 71.

26  Klaus Schwab, "Global Corporate Citizenship," *Foreign Affairs*, Vol. 87, No. 1, January–February 2008, p. 108.

27  Ibid., p. 114.

28  Ibid.

29  Ibid., p. 109.

30  See Chapter 7 for reference to the GPAI. "Global Public Affairs Institute Names New Executive Director," news release downloaded October 26, 2007. Unfortunately, the group disbanded in 2008.

31  Global Public Affairs Institute, pp. C15, 35.

32  www.bc.edu/corporatecitizenship

33  Jay L. Laughlin and Mohammad Badrul Ahsan, "A Strategic Model for Multinational Corporation Social Responsibility, *Journal of International Marketing*, Vol. 2, No. 3, April 1994, pp. 101–115.

34  Jeff Harrington, "How Well Do U.S. Firms Overseas Address Social Responsibility? Gannett News Service, September 19, 1994, Nexis.

35  Mark Kramer and John Kania, "Changing the Game," *Stanford Social Innovation Review*, Vol. 4, No. 1, Spring 2006, pp. 20ff.

36  An observation of Wes Pedersen, "CSR: It's Morphing From Corporate Community Service Into a 'Social Contract,'" *impact* (newsletter of the Public Affairs Council), May 2006, pp. 1 and 2.

37  Kramer and Kania, op. cit.

38  Ibid.

39  Andy Rowell, "Corporations 'Get Engaged' to the Environmental Movement," PR Watch, Third Quartet 2001, Vol. 8, No. 3.

40  Andy Rowell, *Green Backlash: Global Subversion of the Environmental Movement* (London and New York: Routledge, 1996).

41  One of the earliest references to the CSR pyramid is by Archie B. Carroll, "The Pyramid of Corporate Social Responsibility: Toward the Moral Management of Organizational Stakeholders," *Business Horizons*, Vol. 34, July–August 1991, pp. 39–48.

42  Zander, op. cit., www.motorola.com/citizenship/supplierexpectations.

43  "Global Citizenship at Microsoft," published April 25, 2007, www.microsoft.com/about/corporatecitizenship/citizenship/default.mspx.

44  "More Than the Sum of the Parts: Corporate Citizenship," *Financial Times (London)*, July 5, 2007, p. 10.

45  Jane Perlez and Raymond Bonner, "The Cost of Gold/The Hidden Payroll: Below a Mountain of Wealth, a River of Waste, *New York Times*, December 27, 2005.

46  The change in thinking is reflected in Amy Cortese, "Business; The New Accountability: Tracking the Social Costs," *New York Times*, March 24, 2002.

47  "More Than the Sum of the Parts: Corporate Citizenship," *Financial Times* (London), July 5, 2007.

48  As recognized by Alan R. Andreasen, professor of marketing at Georgetown University, nonprofit organizations must deliberately develop ties with for-profit corporations rather than hope to become the lucky beneficiaries of company cause-related marketing campaigns. Alan R. Andreasen, "Profits for NonProfits: Find a Corporate Partner," *Harvard Business Review*, Vol. 76, No. 6, November 1996, pp. 47–59.

49 Ian W. Jones, Michael G. Pollitt, and David Bek, *Multinationals in Their Communities: A Social Capital Approach to Corporate Citizenship Projects* (New York: Palgrave Macmillan, 2007), pp. 248–250.

50 G. Pascal Zachary, "Gates Puts His Money Where Malaria Is," *Wall Street Journal*, July 10, 2001, p. A12.

51 Ronald Alsop, "How Boss's Deeds Buff a Firm's Reputation," *Wall Street Journal*, January 31, 2007, p. B1. The 2012 ranking is from Jacquellyn Smith, "The World's Most Reputable Companies," *Forbes*, June 7, 2012.

52 "Face Value: The Acceptable Face of Capitalism? *The Economist*, December 14, 2002, p. 61. In 1978, the WHO estimated that some 340,000 people were blind because of onchocerciasis, the disease that causes blindness. See Laura P. Hartman and Patricia H. Werhane, *The Global Corporation: Sustainable, Effective and Ethical Practices: A Case Book*. New York and London: Routledge, 2009, pp. 25–26.

53 Rhys Jenkins, "Globalization, Corporate Social Responsibility and Poverty," *International Affairs*, Vol. 81, No. 3, 2005, p. 538.

54 Brugmann and Prahalad, op. cit., p. 85.

55 Betsy McKay, "Coca-Cola, Gates Help Step Up Assault on AIDS," *Wall Street Journal*, June 20, 2001, p. B1.

56 Michael Porter, *The Competitive Advantage of Business* (New York: Free Press, 1997); also see Keinert, pp. 72–73.

57 Described in Hopkins, op. cit., p. 113.

58 Ibid., p. 114.

59 Ibid., p. 115.

60 Anne Jolis, "The Weekend Interview with Mohammed Abrahim – The Philanthropist of Honest Government," *Wall Street Journal*, September 8–9, 2012, p. A13.

61 "A Survey of Nigeria", special supplement, *The Economist*, January 15, 2000, p. 10.

62 Ernst & Young, "An Integrated Approach for Ernst & Young," www.ey.com/GLOBAL/content.nsf/South_Africa/Corporate Social_Investment.

63 Power, op. cit.

64 See reference in Hobbes, Thomas in *Encyclopaedia Britannica*, Vol. 11 (London: Encyclopaedia Britannica, Inc., 1973), p. 566.

65 Davis, op. cit., p. 69. Also see Wes Pedersen, "CSR: It's Morphing From Corporate Community Service Into a 'Social Contract'," *Impact*, a publication of the Public Affairs Council, Washington, DC, May 2006, p. 1.

66 Ibid., p. 71.

67 Ibid., p. 71.

68 Other aspects might be: fair prices and other terms; adherence to international standards of conduct regarding employees: fair wages, good working conditions, recognition of human rights, etc.; avoidance of environmental harm; helping a community or nation help solve social problems; and willingness to engage in community improvements and economic development.

69 In addition, an MNC might expect recognition of its property rights, including intellectual ones; and acceptance of organizational values to operate efficiently; and minimum government interference in business's right to operate under the principles of a free market system.

70    Stiglitz, *Making Globalization Work*, op. cit., pp. 285–286.

71    Carol Sarler, "Kyoto? Balil? Heck, They're Miles from the Bit of America, *Times (London)*, December 19, 2007, p. 17.

72    James E. Post, Lee E Preston, and Sybille Sachs, "Managing the Extended Enterprise: The New Stakeholder View," *California Management Review*, Vol. 45, No. 1, Fall 2002, pp. 6–28.

73    Thomas A. Kochan, "Building a new Social Contract at Work: A Call to Action," *Perspectives on Work*, Vol. 4, No. 1, 2000, p. 4.

74    Edmund M. Burke, *Corporate Community Relations: the Principle of the Neighbor of Choice* (Westport, CN: Quorum Books, 1999), pp. 3, 5–10.

75    Ibid, p. 103.

76    Jeffrey E. Garten, "Globalism Doesn't Have to Be Cruel," *BusinessWeek*, February 9, 1998, p. 26.

77    "Corporate/Trade Association Public Affairs," *Business & Public Affairs*, Vol. 11, No. 21, January 1, 1990, p. 1.

78    Barbara Ettorre, "Empty Promises," *Management Review*, Vol. 85, July 1996, pp. 16–23.

79    Ibid., p.23. Reference to Cliff Hakim, *We Are All Self-Employed: How to Take Control of Your Career* (San Francisco, CA: Berrett-Koehler Publishers, 1994).

80    "The Biggest Contract – Business and Society, Special Report (2)," *The Economist*, May 28, 2005, p. 70.

81    Global Public Affairs Council, op. cit., p. 32.

82    Ibid., p. 539.

83    Ibid., p. 540.

84    Ibid., p. 583. This argument is made by Gluido Palazzo and Andreas Georg Scherer, "The Future of Global Corporate Citizenship; Toward a New Theory of the Firm as a Political Actor," in Andreas Georg Scherer and Guido Palazzo, eds., *Handbook of Research on Global Corporate Citizenship* (Northampton, MA: Edward Elgar, 2008), pp. 577–587.

85    "A Social Strategist for Wal-Mart," *BusinessWeek*, February 6, 2006, p. 11.

86    Alastair Ray, "CSR: Altruistic Policy or Cover for Corporate Gaffes? Join the Debate," *Impact*, January 2004, p. 1.

87    Hirschland, op. cit., p. 9.

88    Annual Report 2006 of Teijin Limited.

89    Global Public Affairs Council, op. cit., p. 2.

90    Schwab, op. cit., p. 112.

91    Hirschland, op. cit., p. 158.

92    Ibid., pp. 159–160.

93    Ibid., p. 115.

94    Ibid.

95    Ibid., p. 116.

96    Dexter Roberts and Pete Engardio, "Secrets, Lies, and Sweatshops," *BusinessWeek*, November 27, 2006, p. 55.

97    Ibid., pp. 53–54.

98    "China: How Multinationals Address Pollution Woes," *Wall Street Journal*, May 30, 2007, p. B11.

# 16 Integrating public interest values in corporate governance

1   Munn v. State of Illinois, 94 U.S. 113.
2   Nebbia v. New York, 291 U.S. 502; 78 L. Ed. 940; 54 Sup. Ct. 505, 1934.
3   John Mackey and Raj Sisodia, *Conscious Capitalism: Liberating the Heroic Spirit of Business* (Boston, MA: Harvard Business Review Press, 2012). From a book review by Alan Murray, "Chicken Soup for a Davos Soul," *Wall Street Journal*, January 17, 2013, p. A15.
4   R.L. Health and Associates, *Strategic Issues Management: How Organizations Influence and Respond to Public Interests and Policies* (San Francisco, CA: Jossey-Bass, 1988).
5   Rogene A. Bucholz, William D. Evans, and Robert A. Wagley, *Management Response to Public Issues*, 2nd edn (Englewood Cliffs, NJ: Prentice Hall, 1989).
6   Lee E. Preston and James E. Post, *Private Management and Public Policy: The Principle of Public Responsibility* (Englewood Cliffs, NJ: Prentice-Hall, Inc., 1975), pp. 9–10. Also stated by Sandra Waddock, *Leading Corporate Citizens: Vision, Values, Value Added*, 2nd edn (New York: McGraw-Hill Irwin, 2006), p. 9.
7   Ibid., p. 149.
8   Ibid. p. 100.
9   Ibid., p. 97.
10  Ibid., p. 102.
11  Ibid., p. 152.
12  Committee for Economic Development, *Social Responsibilities of Business Corporations* (New York: Committee for Economic Development, 1971), p. 11.
13  Talcott Parsons and Neil J. Smelser, in *Economy and Society: A Study in the Integration of Economic and Social Theory* (New York: The Free Press, 1956), p. xviii.
14  Ibid., pp. 15, 19.
15  Ibid., p. 20.
16  Ibid., p. 1.
17  Ibid., p. 3.
18  See ibid., p. 3, for a review of these ideas.
19  Waddock, op. cit., p. 8.
20  F.A. Hayek's *The Road to Serfdom* (London: George Routledge & Sons Ltd, 1944), p. 24.
21  Ibid.
22  Ibid., p. 26.
23  Raymond Cohen, *Negotiating Across Cultures: International Communication in an Interdependent World,* revised edition (Washington, DC: United States Institute of Peace Press, 1997), p. 29.
24  Hayek, op. cit., p. 27.
25  Ibid.
26  Ibid., p. 31.
27  Ibid., p. 29.
28  Milton Friedman and Rose Friedman, *Free To Choose: A Personal Statement* (New York and London: Harcourt Brace Jovanovich, 1980). Milton Friedman, *Capitalism and Freedom* (New York: Harcourt Brace Jovanovich, 1962).

29  Greg Ip and Mark Whitehouse, "How Milton Friedman Changed Economics, Policy and Markets," *Wall Street Journal*, November 17, 2006, p. A8.

30  "Capitalism and Friedman," editorial, *Wall Street Journal*, November 17, 2006, p. A20.

31  Ip and Whitehouse, op. cit., p. A1.

32  Editorial "Capitalism and Friedman," *Wall Street Journal*, November 17, 2006, p. A20.

33  "Business Ethics: Doing Well by Doing Good," *The Economist*, April 22, 2000, p. 65.

34  Sarah Anderson and John Cavanagh, "Another World Is Possible: New Rules for the Global Economy," in Schor and Taylor, ibid., p. 155.

35  Ibid., pp. 165, 168.

36  Ibid., p. l66.

37  Stiglitz, pp. 161–162.

38  Ibid., p. 156.

39  Herman E. Daly, "Five Policy Recommendations for a Sustainable Economy," in Juliet B. Schor and Betsy Taylor, eds., *Sustainable Planet: Solutions for the Twenty-first Century* (Boston, MA: Beacon Press, 2002), p. 171.

40  Jonas Pontusson, "Whither Social Europe," *Challenge*, Vol. 49, No. 6, November–December 2006, pp. 45–46.

41  Marcus Walker, "RX for Change: Sweden Clamps Down on Sick and Disability Pay," *Wall Street Journal*, May 9, 2007, pp. A1, A15.

42  "Special Report: State Capitalism – The Visible Hand," *The Economist*, January 21, 2012, p. 8.

43  Ibid., p. 4.

44  Ibid., p. 18.

45  Walden Bello and Marylou Malig, "Commentary; A Shot in the Arm for Global Civil Society, *BusinessWorld*, February 9, 2006, p. xv.

46  Fritjof Capra, author of *The Web of Life* (New York: Anchor Doubleday, 1995) consider partnership one of the hallmarks of life.… "As a partnership proceeds, each partner better understands the needs of the other. In a true, committed partnership both partners learn and change – they coevolve." Mentioned by Waddoch, ibid., p. 265.

47  Tonya Garcia, "Trust in Business at 10-Yr. Low," *PR Week (U.S.)*, February 2, 2009, p. 3. "Occupy Wall Street Highlights Perils of Corporate Complacency," *PR Week (U.S.)*, November 1, 2011. Gina Chon and Anupreeta Das, "Goldman Reviewing Policies on Its Deal Makers' Conflicts," *Wall Street Journal*, March 17–18, 2012, p. B1.

48  Leslie Kwoh, "Firms Resist New Pay-Equity Rules," *Wall Street Journal*, June 27, 2012, p. B8. In 2006, the average annual CEO pay was $10.5 million, 369 times average worker pay of $28,310, compared to a multiple of 28:1 in 1970 David Henry, "The Big Picture," *BusinessWeek*, October 30, 2006, p. 13.

49  Lauren Etter, "Hot Topic: Are CEOs Worth Their Weight in Gold?" *Wall Street Journal*, January 21–22, 2006, p. A7.

50  John F. Wasik, "Influential U.S. Economist Detailed "Innocent Fraud"; John Kenneth Galbraith – Execs, Boards Put Self-Interest Ahead of Investors," *Seattle Times*, May 14, 2006, p. E5.

51 Jean Eaglesham, "Suits Mount in Rate Scandal," *Wall Street Journal*, August 27, 2012, p. A1.

52 David Enrich, Max Colchester and Sard Schaefer Mufioz, "U.K. Banks in the Eye of the Storm," *Wall Street Journal*, August 8, 2012, p. C1.

53 Greg Smith, "Why I Am Leaving Goldman, " *New York Times*, March 14, 2012, p. A27. Also see his book *Why I Left Goldman Sachs: A Wall Street Story* (New York: Grand Central Publishing, 2012).

54 Liz Rappaport, "Goldman's New 'Lead'Man," *Wall Street Journal*, April 5, 2012, p. C1.

55 William D. Cohan, "Guess Who Wins," *Bloomberg Businessweek*, March 19–March 25, 2012, pp.16–17.

56 "Shell Oil in Nigeria" and "The Transformation of Shell," in James E. Post, Anne T. Lawrence and James Weber, *Business and Society: Corporate Strategy, Public Policy, Ethics*, 10th edn (New York: McGraw-Hill Irwin, 2002), pp. 581–603.

57 "Petroleum and Principles," *Brand Strategy*, July 26, 2002, p. 18.

58 Anne T. Lawrence and James Weber, *Business and Society: Corporate Strategy, Public Policy, Ethics*, 10th edn (New York: McGraw-Hill Irwin, 2002), p. 597.

59 See www.shell.com – Living by our values.

60 For background information, see the case study "ExxonMobil and the Chad/Cameroon Pipeline," in Laura Hartman and Patricia H. Werhane, *The Global Corporation: Sustainable, Effective and Ethical Practices: A Case Book* (New York and London: Routledge, 2009), pp. 89–103. Also see Roger Thurow and Susan Warren, "Pump Priming: In War on Poverty, Chad's Pipeline Plays Unusual Role," *Wall Street Journal*, June 24, 2003, p. A1.

61 Hartman, op. cit., pp. 98–99.

62 Chip Cummins, "Exxon Oil-Fund Model Unravels in Chad," *Wall Street Journal*, February 28, 2006, p. A4.

63 "Oil in Chad; Useful Stuff, Maybe for Once," *The Economist*, September 14, 2002, p. 49.

64 Steve Koll, *Private Empire: ExxonMobil and American Power* (New York: Penguin, 2012).

65 Peter G. Peterson, "Where Are the Business Patriots?; CEOs Need to Be Statesmen Again," *Washington Post*, July 18, 2004, p. B01.

66 Garten, pp. 242–243.

67 Robert L. Dilenschneider, "CEOs Need To Go Public," *Chief Executive*, October 2005, Issue 212, p. 14.

68 Ibid.

69 William J. Holstein, " Are Business Schools Failing the World?" *New York Times*, June 19, 2005, Section 3, p. 13.

70 Ibid.

71 News release on B-M 2003 Building CEO Capital survey.

72 *The Holmes Report*, Vol. 2, No. 41, October 21, 2002, p. 3.

73 Klaus Schwab, "Global Corporate Citizenship," *Foreign Affairs*, Vol. 87, No. 1, January/February 2008, p. 116.

74 William J. Holstein, "Diplomat Without Portfolio in Davos," *New York Times*, February 12, 2006, Section 3, p. 9.

75  Maria Bartiromo, "FACETIME: Nell Minow on Outrageous CEO Pay – and Who's to Blame," *BusinessWeek*, March 2, 2009, p. 16.

76  David Wessel, "CEOs Call for Deficit Action," *Wall Street Journal*, October 25, 2012, p. 1.

77  Damian Paletta, James R. Hagerty, and Sudeep Reddy, "Some Executives Hope for Broader Reach," *Wall Street Journal*, January 2, 2013, p. A6.

78  Damian Paletta, "Fresh Budget Fights Brewing," *Wall Street Journal*, January 3, 2013, pp. 1, 4.

79  "Former BP CEO John Browne Gets Whitehall Role," *The Guardian*, June 30, 2010.

80  *Public Affairs Council 45! Sapphire Anniversary Report* (Washington, DC: Public Affairs Council, 1999), p. 31.

81  W. Howard Chase, *Issue Management: Origins of the Future* (Stamford, CN: Issue Action Publications, 1984), pp. 140–143.

82  Ibid., p. 146.

83  Jeffrey Garten, *The Mind of the CEO* (New York: Basic Books, 2001), p. 239.

84  Ibid., p. 240.

85  Asked in his talk on "The Ethics of Globalization: Oxymoron or Path to Peace and Prosperity," The Raytheon Lectureship in Business Ethics at Bentley College, October 6, 2005. Also see *Chief Executive*, Issue 207, April 2005, p. 14.

86  "In Brief," *HBS Alumni Bulletin*, September 2006, p. 3.

87  Ibid., p. 4.

88  Ibid.

89  Neil A. Lewis, "Sol M. Linowitz Dies at 91; Businessman and Diplomat," *New York Times*, March 19, 2005, p. A13.

# Index

Printed in China